THE ASTROTW
2020
HOROSCOPE

CREDITS

Contributing Editors: Suzanne Gerber, Elizabeth DeCleyre
Copy Editors: Amy Anthony, Lisa M. Sundry

Cover illustration © 2019 by Bodil Jane. www.bodiljane.com
Interior Illustrations: Rosie Dienhart, The Grande Dame, Gabriel Stromberg

ASTROSTYLE

2020 CONTENTS

Dear Astro-Friend,

Does it feel like nothing is the same anymore—but your go-to strategies and solutions no longer do the trick? It's not a "system error." It's the current astrological reality.

If you find yourself stumbling around in a surreal state, you're not alone. The new decade—momentous enough on its own—begins with great galactic intensity.

Change is unavoidable in 2020. Our power lies in how we greet it.

Year one of the new decade delivers a mandate to tear down shaky structures and rebuild on a new foundation. With an unusual party of planets in Capricorn's cosmic construction zone—bolstered by a bootstrapping 4 Universal Year in numerology—change-making will require time and patience. When the industrious Metal Rat takes rulership of the Chinese lunar calendar in late January, we'll need to think strategically before we act.

While uncertainty looms around every "climate"—from the economic to the electoral to the ecological—our noblest mission in 2020 could be leaning into human spirit, taking care of ourselves and each other. Can we access compassion, even when we feel judged or defeated? Carve out moments of comfort and connection when there's so much to "do"?

By the end of 2020, the planets begin shifting to a communal and idealistic Aquarian sensibility. Sacrifices and hard work show signs of paying off. How will we share the fruits of our 2020 labor? And how can we lift each other as we ascend? Keep this big-picture vision in mind all year. And plan the celebration you'll throw at the summit!

There's never been a more useful time to "plan it by the planets" and allow the stars to make sense of what's happening. We're in this together—and we're cheering you on each step of your journey.

Ophira & Tali
The AstroTwins

2020 FORECAST

What's in the Stars for All of Us?

Welcome to 2020! A new decade is upon us, and this one begins on a highly industrious note. Have one more sip of that bubbly beverage, then roll up your sleeves. Since December 2, 2019, maximizer Jupiter has joined purpose-driven Saturn and transformational Pluto in Capricorn. The zodiac's Sea Goat is among the most ambitious signs, and we're betting your New Year's resolutions are loftier than ever. This is a year to build a legacy!

At the same time, any structural "flaws" will demand attention—personally and globally. Until May 5, the lunar South Node is also winding through

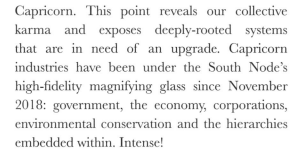

Capricorn. This point reveals our collective karma and exposes deeply-rooted systems that are in need of an upgrade. Capricorn industries have been under the South Node's high-fidelity magnifying glass since November 2018: government, the economy, corporations, environmental conservation and the hierarchies embedded within. Intense!

On January 12, Saturn and Pluto will make a precise connection in the skies, an event that only happens every 33 to 38 years. This watershed moment may call for a total teardown and rebuild of some major institutions. Jupiter and Pluto will make three rare connections in Capricorn in April, June and November. As Jupiter shines its klieg light into Pluto's underground cellar, we might discover some not-so-pretty secrets that shake up business as usual. Ignorance is no longer bliss, and we'll need to get to work on those repairs.

From January through July, three final eclipses activate the Capricorn/Cancer axis, rounding out a series that began in July 2018.

4

While Capricorn is the "father sign" associated with all things patriarchal, Cancer is the galactic governess of home, family and the matriarchal realm. The divine feminine continues to rise this year, both as a matter of historical timing and in an "equal but opposite" reaction to the trenchant Capricorn influence. It's an uncomfortable but necessary contrast we'll keep learning to navigate. Does it feel like we've co-starred in this "movie" before? Maybe so. But as we enter the next decade, we have to be prepared to greet the foreboding trends being forecast—from recessions to climate events to reproductive rights rollbacks—with a new set of power tools.

> "Structured Saturn syncs with no-limits Jupiter, a precise mashup called The Great Conjunction that only happens every 20 years."

Good news: Out-of-the-box innovations can spark solutions between March 21 and July 1, when builder Saturn zooms into progressive Aquarius for the first time since its 1991-94 visit. With Saturn in this high-tech sign, artificial intelligence (AI) and machine learning will continue to boom. Will the robots inherit the earth...or at least, become a bigger part of our daily lives?

Aquarius is also the sign of society and humanitarian issues. This "power to the people" Saturn cycle arrives every 29.5 years and has historically dovetailed with social justice initiatives, often in response to Saturn's law-and-order approach gone too far. Although Saturn doesn't elicit rapid change, the ringed disciplinarian helps us make the kinds of cultural shifts that can resonate for decades.

With the cosmic Capricorn confluence adding a materialist urge to the year, 2020 could have a tinge of "gotta get mine!" As we continue pushing toward individual gain, certain resources may stretch to a snapping point. There's more than enough to go around, if only we'd share. Can we share? There's hope! The year will end with the spirit of collectivism in the air. On December 17, Saturn returns to Aquarius until March 7, 2023, joined by expansive Jupiter two days later until late 2021.

Then, on December 21, structured Saturn makes its second epic connection of the year, syncing up with no-limits Jupiter at 0°29' Aquarius. This precise mashup only happens every 20 years, a paradoxical planetary pairing that astrologers have dubbed The Great Conjunction.

Since 1802, Great Conjunctions have all been in earth signs (with the exception of a trio in Libra in 1981), putting their push-pull focus on material world concerns: land ownership, wealth accumulation and the commodifying of the planet's natural resources. As oceans fill with plastic and carbon emissions heat the air and melt the ice caps, we are getting clear signs that our planet can no longer sustain the systematic expansion that has occurred under the last 200 years of earth-sign Saturn-Jupiter conjunctions.

Now, the trend is shifting. For the next 150 years, all Great Conjunctions will occur in air signs: Aquarius, Gemini and Libra. While we may never cease the human compulsion to create, expand and build, this new wave of energy could blow open the doors of invention. (Fun fact: The New Wave movement in fashion and art began near the 1981 Great Conjunction in Libra, the first to hit an air sign since the 1400s!)

In the year ahead, land grabs could evolve into bids for airspace. From upzoned building regulations that allow high-rise developments to ascend further into the sky, to satellite and WiFi signals buzzing through the ether, the atmosphere will be the next hot commodity.

> "Love planets Venus and Mars both turn retrograde in 2020, eliciting a deep review of the way we 'do' relationships."

The animated space age series, *The Jetsons*, aired when Saturn toured Aquarius in the early 1960s. Could Elroy's jetpack replace the Hoverboard? It might not be long before we're taking our kids to school in pod-sized rockets. Regardless, we're certain that companies will continue to utilize VR technology to create "experience marketing," giving consumers a multisensory way to interact with products. And that's just the tip of the Aquarian iceberg—which, we pray this scientific trend will help us figure out how to "re-polarize" before the ominous ten-year climate warning expires.

Worldwide border policies could take an unprecedented turn after May 5, when the lunar nodes shift to the Gemini/Sagittarius axis, bringing with them a new 18-month eclipse series. Globalism or nationalism? Sagittarius is the cross-cultural connector and also rules religion, the media and the laws that govern us. Can presidents, royals and prime ministers all align around trade regulations, humanitarian aid, missile treaties and the climate? With the karmic South node roosting here, they may have no choice but to form new accords. As the North Node shifts into cooperative Gemini until December 3, 2021, the negotiating table could be a lively (and intense!) space.

Gemini/Sagittarius is the axis of communication, ruling over publishing and the media. Will journalistic ethics tighten up or will regulations lead to censorship or more so-called fake news? As Instagram travelers popularize every hidden niche of the planet—and "developers" hack through miles of pristine jungle and beach to build boho-chic hotels—this nodal cycle will force us to reckon (once again) with the impact that modernization has on indigenous cultures. Simultaneously, we can expect further adoption of sacred healing modalities, like plant medicine ceremonies, that originate from the very populations that are being crowded out by #ResortLife.

Love planets Venus and Mars both turn retrograde in 2020, eliciting a deep review of the way we "do" relationships. Venus will hover in gender-fluid Gemini for an extended period, from April 3 to August 7, lending creativity and seduction to our romantic trends. The retrograde cycle wages from May 13 to June 25, which could bring a few blasts from the past. If an old flame heats up again, explore with cautious optimism.

Couples may revisit a conflict you never fully put to bed. Diplomatic Venus helps you deal and heal, and in Gemini, communication is key! If you're marrying under this cycle, fret not. Since Venus only turns retro every 18 months, plan to renew your vows on your first anniversary in 2021 as an added astrological insurance policy.

Lusty, feisty Mars will host an extended homecoming celebration, landing in its native sign of Aries from June 27, 2020 to January 6, 2021. As the warrior planet doubles its strength—and turns retrograde from September 9 to November 13—the United States presidential elections could be one of many catalysts that churn up everyone's fighting spirit. Aries rules independence and reinvention, but it can also be connected with authoritarianism. Will the forthcoming revolution be a peaceful one? That could take legions of self-control.

Some cooling influences are afoot, however, as 2020 is a 4 Universal Year in numerology. Like the quartet of pillars that hold up a room, this energy is a grounding and stable force. The risk? We could become so serious and staunch that we lose our senses of humor. It will take concerted effort not to become further divided into "us" and "them" camps under the influence of a judgmental 4 Year.

In Chinese astrology, the Year of the Metal Rat begins with the Lunar New Year on January 25. The Rat is known for being sensitive, strategic and communal. A pack of these creatures are called a "mischief," which we could certainly get ourselves into plenty of this year. The metal element brings rigidity, but also conducts electricity, allowing for a powerful energetic exchange to ripple through us all. Our hard work will not be in vain with the industrious Metal Rat bringing scraps of unwanted material back to the nest and transforming them into something totally new and useful. Waste not, want not! *

         The AstroTwins' 2020 Horoscope

2020–2030

IN THE STARS FROM

FORECASTS FOR THE NEW DECADE

THE (EXTRA)TERRESTRIAL ERA

The new decade begins with major planets in earth signs, putting our focus on money, natural resources and the environment. Tech-savvy Uranus brings innovation and progress while shadowy Pluto transforms at the core level.

pluto in capricorn
2008-2024

Border and land disputes

Government and church shakeups

Recession looms, 2008 crash comes home to roost

Oil and fossil fuels replaced by new energy sources, uranium sought by energy-challenged countries

Gun control

Social Security under scrutiny

uranus in taurus
2018-2026

New forms of money

Cryptocurrency regulated by the government

3D printing goes "mass market"

AI and machine learning boom

Farming and food supply reform

New climate science innovations

THE AGE OF AIR

Going up? As we proceed into the decade, outer planets shift from earth to air signs, turning our attention from land to sky—and space.

pluto in aquarius 2024-2044

Air quality & airspace rights are the new "real estate"

Wind power gains traction

Communal living rises

Virtual schools & universities

More political uprisings, protests against oppressive social policies and government

Reform to voting system

With Saturn here until 2023, tension between "big government" and "power to the people"/decentralizing

uranus in gemini 2026-2033

Commercial space travel

UFOs & extraterrestrials found?

New forms of dispersing media and information, beyond the screen

Regulation of algorithms

Prior Uranus in Gemini transits brought the first airplane flight and the printing press

Uranus-Pluto Trine
Nov-Dec 2026

A rare catalyzing connection between changemaker Uranus and transformer Pluto could bring major revolution or a breakthrough tech innovation. The second half of the '20s, could be the "Decade of Disruption"!

2020-2030

PEAK SPIRITUALITY

Namaste the stress away? Spiritual and artistic Neptune spends the first half of the decade in its home sign of Pisces, then it won't return for more than 150 years. Will it soothe our stress...or drive the world deeper into denial?

neptune in pisces | 2012-2025

Spirituality becomes its own form of "religion"

The "search for the soul" through plant medicine ceremonies and a rising interest in past lives and life after death

Healing high: Crystals, chakras, all things esoteric become even more mainstream

Gender nonconformity, fluid identities

Art, music and poetry against the machines

Saving oceans & the water supply, clean drinking water

Alternative healing modalities, naturopathic medicine

WATER MEETS FIRE

Receptive, watery Neptune enters aggressive fire-sign Aries for the first time since 1861-75, setting off the dynamic tension of these opposite forces.

neptune in aries | 2025-2039

Warming oceans and rising global temperatures creates uprisings and metamorphic lifestyle shifts

Desalinization of ocean into drinking water and new hydroelectric energy sources pioneered

Water found on Mars or other planets?

Rise of independent governments and nation-states; possible civil wars

Saturn–Neptune 2025+26 conjunctions

As structured Saturn melds with nebulous Neptune, there could be tension between authority and "the people" or new legislation could regulate "water rights." Suppressed populations may rise up—Neptune's last visit to Aries brought the U.S. Civil War.

NEW & FULL MOONS

Learn when to plan and produce by the monthly lunar phases.

Following moon cycles is a great way to set goals and reap their benefits. Energy awakens at the new moon, then peaks two weeks later at the full moon. In many cultures, farmers have planted by the new moon and harvested by the full moon. Why not get a little lunar boost for your own life?

Every month, the new moon begins a two-week initiating phase that builds up to a full moon, when we reap what we've planted. There is a six-month buildup between new and full moons. Each new moon falls in a specific zodiac sign. Six months later, a full moon occurs in that same zodiac sign.

New moons mark beginnings and are the perfect time to kick off any new projects or idea. Lay the groundwork for what you want to manifest in the coming six months. Set intentions or initiate plans and tend to them for a half year.

Full moons are ideal times for completions, emotional outpourings, and reaping results. They're also your cue to cash in on anything you started at the corresponding new moon six months earlier. What have you been building toward? Full moons act as cosmic spotlights, illuminating what's been hidden. Take stock of your efforts and change course at the full moon. ✳

2020 New Moons

1/24	Aquarius 4:42pm
2/23	Pisces 10:32am
3/24	Aries 5:28am
4/22	Taurus 10:25pm
5/22	Gemini 1:38pm
6/21	Cancer 2:41am (solar eclipse)
7/20	Cancer 1:32pm
8/18	Leo 10:41pm
9/17	Virgo 7:00am
10/16	Libra 3:31pm
11/15	Scorpio 12:07am
12/14	Sagittarius 11:16am (total solar eclipse)

Based on Eastern Time (ET) in New York, NY.

2020 Full Moons

1/10	Cancer (lunar eclipse) 2:21pm
2/9	Leo 2:33am
3/9	Virgo 1:47pm
4/7	Libra 10:35pm
5/7	Scorpio 6:45am
6/5	Sagittarius (lunar eclipse) 3:12pm
7/5	Capricorn (lunar eclipse) 12:44am
8/3	Aquarius 11:48am
9/2	Pisces 1:22am
10/1	Aries 5:05pm
10/31	Taurus 10:49am
11/30	Gemini (lunar eclipse) 4:29am
12/29	Cancer 10:28pm

ECLIPSES IN 2020

At solar and lunar eclipses, we can expect the unexpected.

Eclipses happen four to six times a year, bringing sudden changes and turning points to our lives. If you've been stuck in indecision about an issue, an eclipse forces you to act. Unexpected circumstances can arise and demand a radical change of plans.

Truths and secrets explode into the open. Things that aren't "meant to be" are swept away without notice. Shocking as their delivery can be, eclipses help open up space for the new.

The ancients used to hide from eclipses and viewed them as omens or bearers of disruptive change. And who could blame them? They planted, hunted, fished and moved by the cycles of nature and the stars. While the modern astrological approach is not fear-based, we must still respect the eclipses' power.

Solar vs. Lunar Eclipses

There are two types of eclipses—solar and lunar. Lunar eclipses fall at full moons. The earth passes directly between the Sun and the moon, cutting off their communication and casting a shadow on the earth, which often appears in dramatic red and brown shades. A solar eclipse takes place when the new moon passes between the Sun and the earth, shadowing the Sun. The effect is like a spiritual power outage—a solar eclipse either makes you feel wildly off-center, or your mind becomes crystal-clear.

The effects of an eclipse can usually be felt for three to five days before and after the event (some astrologers say eclipses can announce themselves a month before or after, too). Expect the unexpected, and wait for the dust to settle before you act on any eclipse-fueled impulses. ✳

2020 Eclipses

January 10: Cancer (lunar eclipse)

June 5: Sagittarius (lunar eclipse)

June 21: Cancer (annular solar eclipse)

July 5: Capricorn (lunar eclipse)

November 30: Gemini (lunar eclipse)

December 14: Sagittarius (total solar eclipse)

RETROGRADES IN 2020

When planets reverse their course, delays and chaos can ensue.

You've heard the hype about retrogrades—but what are they, really? When a planet passes the Earth in its journey around the Sun, it's said to be going retrograde. From our vantage point on Earth, it is almost as if the planet is moving in reverse. This is an illusion, but it's a bit like two trains passing at different speeds—one appears to be going backward. When a planet goes retrograde (for a few weeks, or sometimes even months), everything that falls under its jurisdiction can go a bit haywire.

The most commonly discussed retrograde is Mercury retrograde, which happens 3-4 times a year. Mercury rules communication, travel and technology, and these transits are notorious for crashing computers, causing misunderstandings, delaying flights and even souring deals. Astrologers typically warn against traveling, buying new electronic gadgets or signing legally binding contracts during Mercury retrograde. However, all planets go retrograde at a certain point. Venus reverses course every 18 months; Mars, every two years. The outer planets—Jupiter, Saturn, Uranus, Neptune and Pluto—spend four to five months retrograde every year.

Survival tip: Think of the prefix "re-" when planning the best use of a retrograde. Review, reunite, reconnect, research. Retrogrades aren't the best times to begin something new, but they can be stellar phases for tying up loose ends or giving a stalled mission a second chance. ✳

2020 Retrograde Planets & Dates

MERCURY
Feb 16–Mar 9 (Pisces/Aquarius)
June 18–July 12 (Cancer)
Oct 13–Nov 3 (Scorpio/Libra)

VENUS
May 14–June 25 (Gemini)

MARS
Sep 10–Nov 13 (Aries)

JUPITER
May 14–Sep 12 (Capricorn)

SATURN
May 11–July 1 (Aquarius)
July 1–Sep 29 (Capricorn)

URANUS
January 1–10; Aug 15, 2020–
Jan 14, 2021 (Taurus)

NEPTUNE
June 23–Nov 28 (Pisces)

PLUTO
April 25–Oct 4 (Capricorn)

CHIRON
July 11–December 15 (Aries)

14

Tools from The AstroTwins
for your 2020 PLANNING

Visit all year long for
new updates & additions!

www.astrostyle.com/2020tools

JUPITER IN CAPRICORN

Calculated risks and growth within a structured plan? We'll navigate this paradox as daring Jupiter visits cautious Capricorn from December 2, 2019, until December 19, 2020.

Ask, believe...achieve! On December 2, 2019, jovial Jupiter soared to the top of the zodiac wheel, joining stalwart Saturn and power-driven Pluto in Capricorn here until December 2020. Clarify goals and map out those milestones! The groundswell of ambition that's been percolating since Jupiter's counterpart, Saturn, entered Capricorn in late 2017 could reach a fever pitch during this 12-month cycle. With Jupiter's foot on the accelerator, stalled missions will forge ahead. Competition could get fierce as we all find ourselves on a quest to become our best. And we're sure to see some unprecedented developments in government, economy and corporate policies—all realms over which Capricorn presides.

There *is* a catch here, though. Jupiter is in "fall" in Capricorn, its most challenging position on the zodiac wheel. Many of the red-spotted planet's free-flowing and adventurous traits are constrained in the sign of the Sea Goat. By nature, Jupiter wants to swing out and take a risk, while Capricorn can be sober and discerning. Jupiter says, "All are welcome!" while Capricorn wants to curate an elite crew. There will be moments throughout this

yearlong cycle where we feel as if we are pumping the gas and riding the brake at the same time! Our gambling instincts could miss the mark—or even lead to corrupt choices if we leap before we look. Conversely, we may become so risk averse that we get stuck in archaic traditions that stall progress.

The perfectionist tendencies of Capricorn can be amplified by Jupiter's beams. Even if you are sitting on a million-dollar idea, you may be hesitant to move forward after December 2. One of the key lessons of Jupiter in Capricorn? Learning how to fail faster and bounce back quicker. After all, "mistakes" are part of the process. At the same time, don't overdo it on the trial and error. Not only can that be expensive, you might waste precious time reinventing a pre-existing wheel.

Jupiter in masterful Capricorn is a prime time to work with pro-level mentors and experts who can help you map out sound strategies for long-term growth. Capricorn is the zodiac's structure junkie and architect; it doesn't create legends, it creates legacies, baby!

Expansion and growth are the holy grails of the modern age. Normally, "can't stop, won't stop" Jupiter feels right at home in this wildly excessive mindset. But under earth-guardian Capricorn's watch, progress must be harnessed and directed. More isn't necessarily more during this transit. Jupiter in clean, green Capricorn wants us to evaluate our footprints and then assess the impact that our empires have on the environment.

In financially savvy Capricorn, Jupiter can act as an abundance agent—or a giant magnifier of our economic state of affairs. Whatever Jupiter touches, it expands. If you've been manifesting consciously, it may soon feel like someone poured Miracle-Gro on your balance sheet. This is a golden era for business-savvy types. Is it time to step into being the CEO of your own company or to rise to greater leadership at your day job? Jupiter in Capricorn will spur you on.

On the downside, the galactic gambler's tour of success-obsessed Capricorn can make some folks susceptible to get-rich-quick schemes. People who have taken shortcuts to the top could also be exposed—and forced to move way back on the game board. Jupiter in Capricorn may reveal corrupt corporate practices, asking us to "vote with our dollars" by aligning with ethical companies. Executives may be forced to step down over scandals (most likely in the form of mismanagement of finances or HR violations), carving out a space for rising stars to settle on those thrones.

> **"In financially-savvy Capricorn, Jupiter can act as an abundance agent."**

Jupiter's last visit to Capricorn—from December 18, 2007, to January 5, 2009—serves as a cautionary tale of what *not* to do in 2019-20. This marked a major moment for the global economy, and not in a good way. Like a stadium klieg light, Jupiter exposed the fault lines in our banking system as the Federal Reserve and U.S. government were forced to bail out financial institutions. The stock market crashed and Wall Street Goliaths, including Goldman Sachs and Bear Stearns, fell to their knees. Taxpayers had to bail out U.S. mortgage companies Fannie Mae and Freddie Mac. The real estate market took a major hit; homes plunged in value and record numbers foreclosed—while others discovered, in late 2008, that their life savings had been stolen by Bernie Madoff's firm. The toll was *major*!

In 2008, while Jupiter was in Capricorn, the United States elected the first ever African American President. One of Barack Obama's first tasks? To put an "economic stimulus plan" in place to repair the shattered financial state of the nation.

As alliances shift and trade wars erupt, stabilizing the world economy will become mission critical in 2020—which might mean embracing Jupiter's global mindset and working closely with other nations to fortify the collective good.

Will we learn from the past round of Jupiter in Capricorn and take a different approach? It remains to be seen. We have most of the year 2020 to work out this complex equation. ✳

SATURN *meets* PLUTO

On January 12, a rare conjunction of inspector Saturn and secretive Pluto shakes up the norm, exposing what's been hidden.

Tear it down and build it back up again! On January 12, 2020, karmic Saturn and alchemical Pluto meet for a rare celestial summit. This formidable planetary pair only unites in the skies every 33 to 38 years, and when they do, antiquated structures must be brought up to code. This conjunction, their first since 1982, takes place in Capricorn (at 22°46'), the sign that rules governments, corporations and the economy. As we march into the brand-new decade, major global institutions get a seismic shakeup!

Secretive, power-hungry Pluto has been on a slow roll through Capricorn since late 2008 and lingers in the Sea Goat's realm until 2024. Sober taskmaster Saturn joined up on December 19, 2017, and they've been inching closer to each other ever since. Since December 6, 2019, the two have been in ultra-close proximity. We've already felt the metamorphic demand for transformation, from global trade wars to shifting national alliances, along with steely grabs for power. Meanwhile, large-scale resistances are surging, like the 1.7 million "umbrella protesters" who took to Hong Kong's streets and demonstrated against mainland China's inexorable and far-reaching legal extradition mandates during the summer of 2019. Last year in Puerto Rico, hundreds of thousands of protesters forced then-Governor Ricardo Rossello's resignation after a series of scandalous texts deriding women, the LGBTQ community and Hurricane Maria victims were exposed.

The "rip it down to the studs" renovations that a Saturn-Pluto conjunction demands is rarely gentle. Pluto, the galactic Grim Reaper, has no problem destroying anything that comes into its path. The dwarf planet demands total transformation, and that means getting rid of whatever is keeping us stuck in an old groove. Saturn is like an uncompromising inspector and architect rolled into one. After peering in every corner, this planet will help us map a master blueprint for the new structures we need to put into place.

18

Saturn's largely forgotten, pre-modern dual archetype is as the god of time and agriculture. We reap what we sow, and January 12 may be a day when we realize our economic silos are nearly depleted while our collective debts, including corporate liabilities, demand a balloon payment in full, a nation's bill come due.

As Saturn gives shape to Pluto's totalizing demands, all the things we've been shoving down and burying will rise up like Godzilla and take tangible form. For best results, acknowledge the denial and look for the lesson. There's a reason 12 Step programs call for a "fearless and searching moral inventory" in the process of overcoming addiction. In order to break age-old patterns, Saturn forces us to look at our fears and problems squarely in the eye. It isn't easy, but it's the first step toward building structures that can liberate us from restrictive circumstances. "The truth will set you free."

Maybe it's a "breakthrough insight" (like Galileo's telescope that allowed the discovery of Saturn) or a clarion call for a new world order. Whatever the case, things are going to be different as this new decade dawns. The Saturn-Pluto duopoly will pervade all realms, causing everything from a massive mindset shift to a radical update to our operational systems and social structures.

The Rage of Reformation

The last time Saturn and Pluto's paths crossed in Capricorn was in January 1518. Just three months prior, in October 1517, German monk Martin Luther released his doctrine *95 Theses*, which exposed financial corruption that had been rampant in the Catholic Church. Subsequently, this sparked the massive Protestant Reformation of Christianity. This is an example of the kind of transformation that can emerge when Plutonian secrets are revealed and a new Saturnian system is presented.

1518 is also the year when a bizarre "Dancing Plague" broke out in Strasbourg, France. Perhaps the first recorded example of a mass psychogenic illness (MPI) in history. MPIs are characterized by individuals, typically young females, suddenly exhibiting identical strange behaviors, which can spread virally to include a thousand or more. The Strasbourg dancing epidemic began with a few people in the public square and swelled to a crowd of hundreds over the next few days. Despite the blazing summer heat, the victims kept dancing without breaking for food and water. City officials and local medics promoted more dancing, in hopes that the group would shake off their "sickness." This continued for nearly a month, with many either falling over unconscious or literally dying from exhaustion and "hot blood."

As unreal as this sounds, it's a well-documented event. Did karmic Saturn draw out this obsessive "possession" from Pluto's transgressive vault? Or were the overwhelming forces of 16th century social repression, disease and poverty served notice by the indomitable human spirit emerging as a sublimated "fight-or-flight" response—and danced into being by a long-suffering French community? When Saturn applies pressure to Pluto, unknown forces can erupt from the depths.

Where are you being a little too obsessive for your own good? If you've been swept into a vortex of single-minded action, you could finally hit a wall. Saturn sets limits that are best obeyed. With both planets in tenacious, career-driven Capricorn,

   The AstroTwins' 2020 Horoscope

workaholic culture has become the norm. But destroying your health is never worth the price, even if you profit less. January 12 delivers a wakeup call to prevent breakdown and "dis-ease." To find that work-life balance, you may have to stop in your tracks and see the impact on your mental, emotional and physical wellbeing. Less can be more.

The Rise of the Transatlantic Slave Trade

The transatlantic slave trade, which began in the 15th century, took a nefarious turn in 1518, as Saturn and Pluto conjoined in the sign of the Sea Goat. That year, King Charles I of Spain signed a pivotal charter with Portuguese traders authorizing Spain to send slave ships directly to the Americas from Africa.

The Spanish king's mandate set off a brutal new phase in African slavery, the machinations of which would eventually account for an estimated 2.5 million African slaves sent to the burgeoning New World between 1525 and 1866, creating conditions for systemic racial conflict in both South America and North America that endure to this day.

This period of our collective history shows in stark geographic contours where Capricorn profiteering sank to a depraved low while underscoring the most diabolical aspects of Pluto, the ruler of purgatory, and Saturn, the planet associated with leaders and restricted freedoms—if not outright iniquity.

Privatized Prisons Under Scrutiny?

Shortly after Saturn and Pluto last joined forces in 1982 (in Libra), CoreCivic was established, the first corporation to privately own a prison. In 2020, CoreCivic is a publicly traded company on the New York Stock Exchange, reporting annual revenues of $1.7 billion. As Saturn and Pluto converge in Capricorn this January 12, the company (now rebranded as Corrections Corporation of America) is back in the news, scooping up government contracts at controversial ICE detention centers that hold asylum seekers in custody. A class-action lawsuit is also pending, alleging that the company forced labor in their detention centers, using inmates as a workforce instead of hiring local employees. As Saturn and Pluto conjoin, the ceaseless pendulum swing between government control and privatization will face deeper scrutiny. A more fundamental reform could be in order.

Even for those of us who are living free, life could feel like a giant power struggle near January 12, as we grapple with feelings of domination and invisibility. In mythology, Pluto, king of the underworld, falls madly in love with Persephone, abducting her from her mother, Demeter, forcing the maiden to live in the underworld as his wife for half of each year. Embedded in this mythology is the great cycle of nature and a seasonal ordering of life, death and rebirth. Where do we require a period of dormancy so that we maybe reborn? A January "fallow" period in which to self-reflect may be in order. (Medical astrology tells us that Saturn rules modes of depression and medicine as a whole, including the ancient pharmacopeia of herbs and compounds used in healing.)

But when we feel wronged, dominated or trapped by our lot in life, people on all sides of the socio-political spectrum may justify extreme beliefs and behaviors that are, in their own way, no different than the actions of our "enemies." At the Saturn-Pluto conjunction, contrarian perspectives could merit deeper consideration, rather than a contemptuous dismissal. (And yes, we know finding the line between "tolerance" and "taking a stand" is easier said than done.) But as 2020 dawns, any true responsibility to self and community is best served without dishing vengeful retribution. Healthier offerings are recommended.

> "Even for those who are living free, life could feel like a giant power struggle near January 12 as we grapple with feelings of domination and invisibility."

Conservation and Renewable Energy

Capricorn is the eldest of the zodiac's three earth signs and is associated with conservation. Our natural resources fall under its care, like the slow-growing (Saturnian) forests, which decompose into the subterranean fuels of coal, oil and natural gas, eventually claimed, and made part of, the vast repositories of Pluto. Historians have framed our age of fossil fuel use as the Petroleum Age, owing to the ubiquity of petroleum-based fuel and technologies powering the second half of the 19th century and the entire 20th century. Controversial though it may be, many predict that petroleum use will at least partially continue for the next two centuries, even as alternative energies, such as solar and wind power, become more affordable.

As Saturn and Pluto merge, the firestorm over our energy sources will intensify—a huge topic of the 2020 U.S. presidential elections. From a historical perspective, the cumulative benefits of the Petroleum Age directly raised living standards for billions while increasing human lifespans and ushering countless new technologies and medicines over the period.

Meanwhile, climate scientists continue to issue warnings about the effect of unchecked global fossil fuel consumption at the pivotal geopolitical moment when the energy-challenged economies of China, India, and the rest of the developing world mature as industrial powerhouses, providing the majority of global manufacturing through their dependence upon the oil infrastructure.

To compete—and even survive—many industries (whether in the east or west), are forced to adopt costlier production practices in order to comply with "sustainable" regulations. Yet, rapid developments in technology and declining profit margins present myriad challenges. This will continue until the overall economic system or legislation changes, or these corporations are offered incentives attractive enough for them to adopt new practices.

And if that doesn't happen? The global economy may well be subject to the ever-present dangers of economic deterioration. This could set the stage for the ultimate Plutonian plot twist—a "black swan event" a term to denote a random event occurring outside all known statistical modeling and or status quo perspectives, an absolute surprise, coined by the bestselling author, Nassim Nicholas Taleb in his 2007 book, *The Black Swan*, which is now credited with presaging the financial environment that led to the 2008 subprime mortgage collapse. Widely seen as the contrarian oracle of the financial markets, Taleb was born in 1960, when Jupiter and Saturn were in Capricorn.

On the consumer side of this mind-bending fiscal calculus, we want our gourmet sushi and beautiful status symbols (also ruled by Capricorn) and we want 'em for a good price! We also want our jobs, which for many folks have become service-based and or financed-based as the U.S. and other Western nations manage their own indebted, post-industrial economies, requiring a dependency on the supply chain of low-priced, factory-produced goods and related services arriving from an equally indebted Asia and elsewhere. Debt as a financial instrument is fundamentally driven by Saturn and Pluto, whether applied to the bond market, commodity markets (including precious metals like gold or silver), equities and so on. As Saturn and Pluto press us to gain new levels of financial literacy, we might be wise to "follow the money" and learn how our financial system has developed into the labyrinth it is today. Only then can we plot a different course.

But what about the impact on our ancient blue planet? Last year, raging fires tore through swaths of the Amazon rainforest in Brazil, producing a smoke signal of epic and varied meaning, redirecting the focus of the recent G-7 Summit in France away from the histrionics of our leaders back to the original and primary ecosystem we all belong to. To wit, in September 2019, energy scientists at Rice University announced a breakthrough in the technology repurposing the greenhouse gas, carbon dioxide (CO_2), and converting it to pure liquid fuel using renewable electricity. While Saturn and Pluto are in Capricorn, necessity can be the mother *and* the father of invention.

> "As Saturn and Pluto press us to gain new levels of financial literacy, we can plot a different course."

Of course, our conservation efforts need to move beyond a land-based perspective, even as Saturn and Pluto touch down in terrestrial Capricorn. Currently, environmentalists are dragging plastic out of the vast and unexplored oceans (which constitute two-thirds of the planet), some from the packaging wrapped around overseas, overnight deliveries. Distressingly, microfibers from laundering our outdoor adventure clothing, like those found in eco-activist Patagonia sportswear, are proving to be the most vexing of the plastic flotsam. Groundbreaking studies from 2011 on show microfibers accounting for up to 85 percent of human-made debris on coastlines around the world.

Perhaps the quintessential expression of Saturn and Pluto in Capricorn is the humanitarian crisis in Venezuela, a nation that literally sits atop the world's largest oil reserve. Under the reign of dictator Nicolás Maduro, who has positioned himself between the interests of China, Russia and the United States, Venezuela, a leading economy in the 1990s, is now enduring food, medicine and energy shortages. As the global superpowers fight for Venezuela's oil, more than 4 million people have fled the country—a refugee crisis second only

to Syria's, one that's outpacing the availability of international aid.

There *are* a few ingenious ideas blowing in the wind. In 2014, Denmark produced over 40 percent of its electricity from wind power alone. The proactive nation has targeted 2020 as the year where 30 percent of all its energy will come from renewable sources. In September 2019, 16-year-old Swedish environmental activist Greta Thunberg—a Capricorn born January 3, 2003—spearheaded the Global Climate Strike, a day of worldwide marches that included 4 million people in 163 countries.

As the planet of science, Saturn will team up with Pluto, the planet of the unknown, intensifying the search for more pivotal discoveries, leaving us questioning whether global leadership will align with these and other seemingly "alchemical" discoveries in 2020 and beyond.

Recession Proofing

Power brokers Saturn and Pluto share a mutual obsession with generating wealth—and more than ever while in success-obsessed Capricorn. It's no surprise that their meetups have often marked a shift in the global economy, including looming threats of a recession. The Saturn-Pluto unions of 1914-15 dovetailed with the start of World War I and stretched until the next Saturn-Pluto conjunction (in Leo) in 1947, which aligned with the end of World War II. During that time span, global powers emerged, battled for supremacy and created industrial economies and trade agreements which have set up the modern-day economy. In 1947, the International Monetary Fund (IMF) was established to foster worldwide fiscal cooperation.

On November 16, 1914, the U.S. Federal Reserve began operations as Saturn and Pluto (both retrograde) united at 1° Cancer. Right before that, the world was rocked by the Financial Panic of 1914. With impending war threatening global markets, spooked investors pulled out of their securities in a scramble for cash and gold. This led to an unprecedented shutdown of the London Stock Exchange for five months, and the U.S. Stock Exchange for four months. For six weeks during August and early September 1914—as Saturn and Pluto made close contact—almost every stock exchange in the world was closed.

The last Pluto-Saturn conjunction on November 8, 1982, coincided with the end of a brief recession as the Information Age unveiled itself across the blazing screens of the new "personal computer." Less than two months later on January 1, 1983, under the sign of Capricorn, the modern Internet was officially born when an agreement was reached to make TCP/IP the global network protocol, and researchers began assembling what is now the World Wide Web.

While the preparatory mapping of the Internet took place throughout the preceding year, 1982, the bestselling personal computer ever, the Commodore 64, arrived in stores nationwide, debuting at the Las Vegas Consumer Electronics Show, during the Capricorn-ruled month of January. Pluto and Saturn approached conjunction within 5°03' of each other in Libra on the opening day of the show (January 7), eventually setting sales records that remain unchallenged to this day. At one time, the Commodore 64 was selling a robust two million units per year, outpacing IBM, Apple and Atari, and accounting for 35 percent of personal

 The AstroTwins' 2020 Horoscope

computer sales! That's just Capricorn business as usual for the computational GOAT, the "C64."

Since then, the Internet has made virtually everything accessible for purchase. The last three decades have spawned a new class of technology billionaires, like Amazon CEO (Capricorn) Jeff Bezos, who will celebrate his birthday on January 13, one day after the 2020 Pluto-Saturn conjunction.

New Forms of Money & Economic Models

Will 2020 mark the end of capitalism as we know it? Or will sustainable industries emerge to steward humanity into the 21st century? Hard to say—especially as Saturn and Pluto point out the mounting complexities. How can we get safe, affordable and convenient goods without damaging the planet? Under this conjunction, something may have to "die" for a new system to be invented.

Near January 12, Saturn may reveal more of the shaky balance between self-interest and public benefit, especially in Capricorn-ruled industries such as banks, government and corporations. Case in point: Pluto's entry into Capricorn in 2008 leveled the global economy, ushering the disastrous sub-prime mortgage collapse that required a $700 billion government bailout of Wall Street commercial banks and mortgage lenders, what has come to be known as the Great Recession.

One thing's for sure, the *Game of Thrones* mindset that has threaded through the last few Saturn-Pluto conjunctions has had a resounding impact. The threat to the food chain may break open opportunities for the emerging technology of "blockchain," forcing us to explore new economic

models and attendant payment platforms. Nonetheless, Bitcoin and cryptocurrency are still, well, cryptic, to many.

That trend may change with Facebook CEO Mark Zuckerberg on a mission to win regulation for his proposed digital currency—aptly named "Libra." On the surface, Zuckerberg's blockchain-based initiative appears to challenge the old guard. But with crusty Saturn involved, we'd be wise to keep a grizzled eyebrow raised, especially as the Libra Association is currently stocked with members of the "one percent." Will Saturn and Pluto share the bounty with the rest of us? If history is any indication, it's unlikely. As of this writing, every bank in the world is busy creating blockchain-based payment interfaces. The decentralized could become centralized at this Saturn-Pluto summit.

Pluto is forging through Capricorn until 2024, which will accelerate developments for new money models over the next four years. Can a cashless society prevail? New alternatives are clearly needed—and cryptocurrency, which is arguably more efficient than cash, could certainly provide new funding pathways. Pluto's entry into Capricorn has given rise to new models such as the "gig economy" and crowdfunding, as people are forced to consider all means of trade and earning a living. The other side of the (bit)coin might suggest weaving in aspects of the barter system—the world's oldest method of trade—or to explore the "gift economy," a concept advanced by Capricorn Larry Harvey, the late founder of Burning Man, an experimental city that rises in the Nevada desert for a week each summer.

A Challenge to Patriarchal Systems

The patriarchy, which is ruled by Capricorn, will not likely escape the crosshairs of the Saturn-Pluto conjunction. Its specter has loomed like a hungry ghost since Saturn joined Pluto in Capricorn on December 19, 2017. From the crimes exposed by the #MeToo and #TimesUp movements to attempts to pass state laws restricting women's reproductive rights, it's hard to tell whether the clock is turning back or moving forward.

At the same time, we have solutions and strides to celebrate. The U.S. is enjoying a rise of women in business and government (with six female candidates in the 2020 presidential race). The demand for gender parity and female leadership is rippling through every institution, boardroom and industry. Internationally, female leaders are making an impact. At this writing, Capricorn-born Christine Lagarde, is slated to be the first woman ever to run the European Central Bank. We may expect to see more shake-ups to the leadership bodies of our most important institutions in 2020.

With structural Saturn and transformational Pluto both in Capricorn, the sign of masculinity and all things "male-identified," it's no surprise that gender identity has become a huge topic of reform. In 2020, we may see new developments in the expansion of legislation that acknowledges the non-gender binary population.

Saturn, ruler of governments, is already involved. In the United States, a rising number of states and companies are allowing people to label their gender as "X" on driver's licenses and IDs. The stars suggest that gender non-conformity will continue to gain public acceptance, even if the wins are still small for now.

Lifting the Social Mask

What do you reveal and what do you hide? We all have a social "persona," but what is it covering up? On a deeply personal level, the Saturn-Pluto conjunction will force us to deal with the "shadow" aspects of our personalities. These are the parts of ourselves we may disown, feel ashamed of, or even project onto other people, accusing them of the very qualities that we are acting out (but simply cannot admit to having).

Since these planets are meeting in status-conscious Capricorn—a sign that likes to "keep up appearances"—it won't be easy to drop the mask. With composed Saturn getting body-checked by intense Pluto, circumstances may force us to get real. Look out! Like a volcano erupting, feelings you swore you'd never express could spew forth like hot lava. But here's the twist: The people who love you might actually feel closer to you once you ditch the control and show some raw humanity.

The Saturnian and Plutonic realms contain vast wealth, whether found in our external resources or collective archetypes deep in the human psyche. Are you tough enough to endure the challenge and not fall victim to "fake news" and groupthink? That will be one of the gauntlets 2020 throws down. As Capricorn journalist Maureen Dowd said, "The minute you settle for less than you deserve, you get even less than you settled for." ✹

The AstroTwins' 2020 Horoscope

SATURN IN AQUARIUS

Life turns communal as Saturn enters the sign of teamwork.
March 21 –July 1, 2020 and December 17, 2020 – March 7, 20203

Gather the thought leaders and call a global summit! From March 21 to July 1, Saturn lifts its nose from Capricorn's grindstone and takes a Hoverboard ride through Aquarius, the sign that rules progress, technology and collective action. The galactic guru hasn't stationed in the Water Bearer's realm for nearly three decades; in fact, its last visit was from February 6, 1991, to January 28, 1994. Humanitarian Aquarius rules the future while sensible Saturn is the master planner and guard. The world could use a large dose of the innovative strategizing this cosmic cycle brings. Can the citizens of Earth join together to architect a smarter future? Now is the time!

Saturn's tour through Aquarius from March 21 to July 1 is a preview of a longer cycle. On December 17, the structured planet settles back into Aquarius until March 7, 2023, opening up a two-year window for progress. Aquarius is the mad scientist of the zodiac, a sign that pulls off the paradoxical feat of being rational and idealistic at once. (Picture Aquarius Thomas Edison if you need a visual.) And while the process-driven planet's style may seem at odds with the laid-back Water Bearer, Saturn was actually Aquarius' ancient ruler, before Uranus was discovered by a handmade telescope in 1781. The ringed taskmaster feels quite at home in Aquarius, and that means nothing is impossible in 2020! After all, rainbows can be measured along the ROYGBIV spectrum and unicorns could reasonably exist using VR technology.

Can we all get along? Maybe, maybe not. But regardless of our differing views, we will have to write some new rules for how to share this planet. In 1991, during Saturn's last jaunt in Aquarius, the Madrid Conference was co-sponsored by the United States and the Soviet Union as an international attempt to negotiate an Israeli-Palestinian peace treaty. NAFTA, the North American Free Trade Agreement, was signed by Canada, the United States and Mexico weeks before Saturn left Aquarius in January 1994. Perhaps there's hope to resolve these border crises and international trade wars yet.

Saturn rules time and, in contemporary astrology, is known as the Lord of Karma. Wherever he lands, chickens come home to roost. While touring Capricorn since December 2017, Saturn has exposed the shadow side of nationalism, mass consumerism and authoritarian world leadership. Can Saturn in Aquarius serve up a solution from left field…or the quantum field? We're not ruling out space or interdimensional travel as options either. (One ticket to Pleiades, please. Do you take Bitcoin?)

From the Internet to the IoT (Internet of Things)

Artificial intelligence, augmented reality, virtual everything…while Saturn's in tech-savvy Aquarius, the geeks (not the meek) shall inherit the Earth. In fact, the World Wide Web came to life during the last Saturn in Aquarius cycle. On April 30, 1993, the "www" source code was released by CERN, making the software free and available to anyone. A year before that, in 1992, futurist (and Aquarius!) Ray Kurzweil's book about A.I., *The Age of Intelligent Machines,* essentially forecast the wild popularity of the 'net as we know it!

When Saturn orbited through Aquarius back in 1962, *The Jetsons* premiered, ABC's first animated, color TV series, about a family living in the Space Age. The Hanna-Barbera producers imagined an "impossible" world where people could talk to each other on video screens, food could be programmed to come from a machine and robots worked as household servants. In 2020, we're well-versed in video chats on Google Hangouts and FaceTime, and our Roombas are cleaning the floors like Rosie the Robot of *Jetsons'* fame. Currently, the Internet of Things (IoT) is revolutionizing the ways we use technology. As thumb-sized computers with tiny sensors are being programmed to make our devices "smart" and our homes totally automated, we may never have to push another on/off button again. (Alexa, find me my slippers!)

While many people worry that A.I. developments could make human labor obsolete, pragmatic Saturn cautions against spiraling into doomsday thinking. Nevertheless, the ringed planet wants us to hustle and bring our skills up to snuff. Get trained on the software, apps, social media and whatever technological advances are happening in your industry. In 2020, this won't be a luxury; it will be a necessary step in staying relevant.

Relationships Reconfigured

From pansexual to polyamory, monogamish to heteroflexible, a new crop of relationship labels is being added to the conventional coupling model that's been based on survival of the species for eons. Saturn in Aquarius can rewrite the "rules" for how to partner, and the sky might be the limit. Even one-on-one types are exploring options like the L.A.T. model—Living Apart Together—to accommodate geographical shifts in industries that may prevent them from working (and living) together full-time in the same city.

The Aquarian "one love" mantra puts the A in androgyny (and LGBTQIA). With Saturn here, we may add more gender checkboxes to the list—or do away with the category altogether on many forms. At time of this writing, 12 states in the U.S. allowed "X" to be checked as a third gender option on drivers' licenses. We expect this trend will expand after March 21, but with conservative Saturn involved, it may receive a fair amount of pushback.

Madonna's infamous photo book *Sex* went on sale when Saturn was in Aquarius in 1992. Controversial for its time (and still titillating to date), the black-and-white coffee table hardcover was shot by Steven Meisel and featured the singer in various erotic configurations. Within a few days of release, *Sex* sold out its limited 1.5 million print-run.

Communes and Co-Sharing Spaces

As the world adapts to climate change and shifting economies, we may need to pool more of our resources. But how to do so fairly without destroying the vibrancy of free will that is so essential to an Aquarian transit? Interesting fact: On November 6, 1991, nine months after Saturn entered Aquarius, the Communist Party of the Soviet Union and the Soviet KGB was dismantled. With repressive Saturn in Aquarius, we have to be mindful not to confuse "equal" with "identical."

The gig economy will continue to flourish with app-based services like Uber and TaskRabbit; however, Saturn in Aquarius is likely to demand greater regulation. Drivers may have to go through a certification program, especially in cities like New York and Paris where the taxi and livery companies are in fierce competition.

In modernized nations, the nuclear family is no longer considered the ideal option for many folks. Statistics are reporting significantly fewer babies being born in countries like the United States each year. With lower birthrates, the co-living model has grown in popularity. In cities like San Francisco, people are renting individual bedrooms in buildings with communal facilities like kitchens and lounges. According to Greek mythology, the Water Bearer (the symbol for Aquarius) was a young man named Ganymede who was the object of Zeus' affections. He served cups of H_2O to the gods in exchange for eternal youth. While "adulting" is mandatory under mature Saturn's reign, extending the dorm-style life into the 30s, 40s and beyond might become another "new normal" now.

On the corporate front, coworking spaces like WeWork and The Wing continue to open new locations, proving that this trend of collectivism shows no sign of slowing down. As "always be prepared" Saturn lends its organizing principles to the communal Aquarian equation, co-sharing facilities may begin offering more essential group services as part of their package. Think: affordable health insurance, all-access urgent care clinics and on-site childcare.

In 2020, as Saturn weaves in and out of Aquarius and Capricorn, three titans of industry—Amazon's Jeff Bezos, Berkshire Hathaway's Warren Buffet and JPMorgan Chase's Jamie Dimon—are developing Haven, a free-market effort to reform health care in the United States. Will these billionaires be able to hit the mark while Saturn is in "power to the people" Aquarius? Their idealistic plans could go through another round of R&D between March 21 and July 1.

Upzoning and Space Travel

When it comes to purchasing homes, stabilizing Saturn in Aquarius may shift the type of real estate we invest in. Rising sea levels, along with intense weather patterns like hurricanes and wildfires, could push populations into denser, inland urban areas that have access to fresh water and food supplies. As a result, land parcels may become less available, forcing cities to build upward and owners to invest in air space—which makes sense, considering that Aquarius is one of the zodiac's three air signs.

Buildings with renewable energy, like wind and solar, will also become more attractive with sustainable Saturn in Aquarius, the sign that rules electricity. Under the Water Bearer's influence, developments may occur around water desalinization—a potential key area of interest for impact investors.

Maybe it's time to join the 600 people (at time of this writing) who have reserved a seat on Sir Richard Branson's Virgin Galactic for a flight into outer space? In July 2019, Virgin Galactic announced a merger with Social Capital Hedosophia to create the first-ever publicly traded commercial human space flight company. Space travel as big business? When mogul-maker Saturn launches into Aquarius, this trend could really catch on.

Back when Saturn buzzed Aquarius in 1962, M.I.T. sent a TV signal by satellite for the first time to Astronaut John Glenn, who became the first American to orbit Earth. Project Apollo—NASA's lunar landing program—was being developed in earnest. In 1992, another Saturn in Aquarius cycle, Mae Jemison was the first African American woman to visit space aboard the Endeavor STS-47.

A New Wave of Social Justice

Humanitarian Aquarius is the zodiac's Utopian idealist, and Saturn helps bring those visions into form. Some of modern history's most influential developments in social justice happened under this transit. As we enter 2020, the left and right are more divided than ever. Will Saturn in Aquarius help us lay down our swords (and step away from our Twitter feeds) in order to give peace a chance?

The answer is yes, very possibly…if history repeats itself. But first, there may be further uprising as people push back against the systems that they feel are treading on their rights.

On March 6, 1991, one month after Saturn moved into Aquarius, four police officers were caught on video beating Rodney King, an African American resident of Los Angeles who was pulled over for speeding. Despite the visible evidence, a jury acquitted the officers, who were being tried for excessive use of force. Six days of uprising broke out in L.A. in April and May of 1992. In the melee, 63 people were killed, over 2,000 injured, and more than 12,000 arrests were made. A month later, Rodney King gave an impromptu media conference and coined the ubiquitous (and very Aquarian) phrase, "…can we all just get along?"

Between 1962-64, while Saturn was doing a similar dance and threading between Capricorn and Aquarius, another King was in the headlines. On August 28, 1963, Dr. Martin Luther King, Jr. delivered his "I Have A Dream" speech at a Civil Rights March to the Lincoln Memorial in Washington, D.C. Subsequently, the Civil Rights Act and Voting Rights Act were signed into law, passing after an 83-day filibuster in the U.S. Senate. When Saturn returned to Aquarius 29.5 years later, the Martin Luther King Jr. Day holiday was observed in all 50 of the United States for the first time, on January 18, 1993.

In South Africa, a similar social justice pattern is traceable through Saturn's cycles in Aquarius. In June 1963, anti-apartheid revolutionary Nelson Mandela was sentenced to life in prison. Thirty years later, during Saturn in Aquarius' 1993 tenure, Mandela was awarded the Nobel Peace Prize for laying the foundation which brought an end to apartheid and a new Democratic South Africa.

Saturn in Aquarius has historically brought developments for women's rights, too. On June 10,

1963, President John F. Kennedy signed the U.S. Equal Pay Act into law to "prohibit discrimination on account of sex in the payment of wages by employers." Later that year, Dorothy Hodgkin was the first British woman to be awarded the Nobel Prize in Chemistry for her work on penicillin and Vitamin B12. Carol Moseley Braun, the first African American woman to be elected to the U.S. Senate, claimed her seat in November of 1993 when Saturn cycled back to Aquarius. On June 14, 1993, Justice Ruth Bader Ginsburg was appointed to the United States Supreme Court and took her oath of office in August of that year.

> "The spirit of progress will be in the air for the final two weeks of 2020, as The Great Conjunction of Jupiter and Saturn arrives."

With the U.S. Democratic Party's presidential primary elections taking place from February through June of this year—a period partially covered by Saturn in Aquarius, from March 21 on—it's no surprise that issues of equity are on the table. Some candidates are campaigning for reparations, a restitution payment to the descendants of African slaves brought to the United States. Policies are being outlined to protect women's reproductive rights, and to ensure equal pay and paid family leave mandates. With a record number of female and POC candidates running for office, 2020 has the potential to be a tide-turning and historic year. Voting in the U.S. primaries will be a determining factor, as Saturn will be back in traditional Capricorn during the November presidential election.

The Great Conjunction of Jupiter & Saturn

Whatever the outcome, the spirit of progress will be in the air in the final two weeks of 2020. On December 17, Saturn heads back into Aquarius, followed by boundless Jupiter two days later, on the 19th. The two planets will co-pilot through the Water Bearer's zone on and off until December 29, 2021, combining their paradoxical powers.

Circle December 21, 2020—also the Solstice—as a major date on the calendar! For the first time since May 31, 2000, Jupiter and Saturn will meet up at an exact degree in the sky, at 0°29' Aquarius. Astrologers call this event The Great Conjunction, an alliance that only happens once every 20 years!

Although they're as different as night and day, Jupiter and Saturn make quite the dynamic duo. Jupiter is the abundant growth agent, blessing us with the Midas touch and a gambler's instinct. Saturn is the cautious auditor, calculating risk and making sure we invest wisely. Their meetup this December 21 will get us thinking: What should we hang onto and where can we let go, in order to catapult ourselves into a new league? Philosophical Jupiter opens our minds and Saturn creates a structure for our thoughts to become tangible actions. And carried on the wings of liberated Aquarius, the spirit of revolution will be in the air! ✳

the *12* SIGNS IN *2020*

ARIES
2020

Yearly Highlights

LOVE

As Jupiter, Saturn and Pluto activate your goal-oriented tenth house, you might feel as if you're married to the job. Penciling in blocks of quality time will be essential. Or, team up with your S.O. on a professional mission! Start a business together or join forces where your careers dovetail. With Venus in flirty Gemini from April 3 to August 7, a coworker crush could heat up; or Cupid could reveal a keeper in your friend zone. Lusty Mars, your red-blooded ruler, spends an extra-long time in Aries, from June 27, 2020, to January 6, 2021. During this time, your magnetism will be amplified. Be discerning about who you draw close while Mars is retrograde from September 9 to November 13.

MONEY

Express elevator to the top! A power-pack of Capricorn planets, plus a lunar eclipse, pours rocket fuel into your tenth house of career. Feeling lost? A purpose-driven path could emerge. If you've been developing a venture in earnest, financial backing can come from well-heeled funders, or through a brand partnership. Thanks to expansive Jupiter joining impresarios Saturn and Pluto in Capricorn, corporate Rams could rise through the ranks swiftly. Welcome to the executive wing!

WELLNESS

Solo marathon or team sports? Vitality-booster Jupiter will spend most of the year in Capricorn, firing up your #FitnessGoals. Plus, with your ruler, daredevil Mars, on an extended tour through Aries, from June 27 to January 6, 2021, you're pumped for a challenge. Your body is capable of far more than you give it credit for, Aries. (Just get some coaching so you don't get injured!) Driven Saturn swings into communal Aquarius from March 21 to July 1. Jump into a summer league, like softball or soccer, or join a 30-day challenge at your yoga studio. Being part of an online support group can help you break a bad habit or revamp a few eating habits.

LEISURE

Your social life is ablaze during the first part of 2020, as affable Venus hangs in Gemini and your zone of peers from April 3 to August 7. A "friend crush" could evolve into a real-deal romance, or you could partner up with a sibling on a project or business idea. When two Cancer eclipses charge your home and family zone in January and June, relatives could require extra attention. If it's time to move, renovate or relocate, these eclipses can speed up the process. When both Saturn and Jupiter enter Aquarius after December 19, form an inspiring friend circle comprised of the fierce individuals (and quirky characters) your sign adores. ✳

The AstroTwins' 2020 Horoscope

ARIES

2020 HOROSCOPE

2020 Power Dates

ARIES NEW MOON
March 24 (5:28am ET)

ARIES FULL MOON
October 1 (5:05pm ET)

SUN IN ARIES
March 19 – April 19

Whoever said Aries are better at starting projects than finishing them hasn't met the 2020 version of you! Can-do Jupiter has officially joined disciplined Saturn and transformational Pluto in Capricorn, and this persevering trio supplies the unwavering focus to take it all the way. This year, you'll have bottomless refills of stamina, provided you don't spread yourself too thin.

Your 2020 success blueprint revolves around setting one or two epic goals and giving that mission all of your blood, sweat and tears. Resist FOMO and narrow the field, Aries. That's how you'll finish out the year with a fedora full of feathers!

Since Capricorn rules your tenth house of career, you'll be obsessed with figuring out your soul purpose. If you're already marching along your path, scale up your mission or expand into new territories. Long hours at the office won't bother you at all; in fact, you might just set up a workspace at home this year so you don't have to sacrifice all your family time to achieve your goal.

That said, nailing the elusive work-life balance will be a worthy challenge in 2020. With three final

---

eclipses hitting the Cancer/Capricorn axis between January and July, you could get pushback from loved ones if you skip too many family gatherings—or bring your laptop to the kitchen table so you can work through dinner.

With all this high-profile energy afoot, renegade Rams will have to set aside punk-rock ways and learn to play by the corporate rules…at least some of the time. But from March 21 to July 1, sensei Saturn lunges into rebellious, team-spirited Aquarius, giving you a chance to bend (or rewrite) a few of those laws. Before you go there, push yourself to gain a fundamental understanding of these directives. They do have a purpose, even if you consider it archaic. Saturn will return to Aquarius again from December 17 until March 7, 2023, so don't get overly hung up on changing the game this year. It's more important that you learn how said game is played—and what makes the players tick!

On December 19, 2020, daredevil Jupiter will join Saturn in Aquarius until December 29, 2021. Just in time for the holidays, your popularity shoots through the roof. You'll find yourself at the center of a buzzing community of activists, thought leaders and disruptors. (Home sweet home!) Your charitable holiday donations may be heftier than usual, as this Aquarian energy stokes your idealistic nature.

Romance gets a revamp for everyone in 2020, too. Venus turns retrograde from May 13 to June 25, a cycle that happens every 18 months. This time, the love planet backs through Gemini and your friendly, flirty third house. Lines could blur in ways that are both beguiling and a tad troubling, so don't let your rash nature guide your moves. The third house is the realm of coworkers and neighbors, two groups of people you should think twice about fooling around with. What might feel like a convenient spring fling could leave you feeling beyond awkward around your office or apartment complex. On a positive note, Venus' backspin could give you the courage to admit that your feelings go beyond friendship for someone who makes you swoon. Coupled Aries can use Venus retrograde to strengthen communication. Are you insisting on autonomy at the expense of harmony? See where you can compromise and cooperate more.

If love feels like a low-priority (or sidelined) agenda item in the first half of 2020, no stress! On June 27, your ruler, lusty Mars, pops off an extended tour through Aries that lasts all the way until January 6, 2021! Your "sex magick" will be a strong brew, Aries, and without even trying, you'll have fans clamoring for your attention. Use this magnetism judiciously. The goal is to attract multi-dimensional people into your orbit—the types who won't bore you once the flattery wears off.

Besides, Chiron (the "wounded healer" comet) is spending its first full year in Aries, where it will hover until April 2027. Since April 2018, when Chiron briefly popped into your sign, you've been deepening your connection to your shadow nature, learning how to powerfully turn some of your so-called stumbling blocks into your own healing gifts. For this reason, it's even more important to surround yourself with people who won't let you get away with being anything less than your fullest, truest self!

Jupiter, Saturn & Pluto in Capricorn.

The Trio: December 2, 2019–March 21, 2020; July 1, 2020–December 17, 2020

Ambitions ahoy! The galaxy is the limit for Rams this year, as Jupiter, the planet of luck and adventure, joins masterful Saturn and strategic Pluto in Capricorn and your tenth house of success. The red-spotted planet only visits this zone once every 12.5 years, which could make 2020 among the most fortune-filled periods you've had in over a decade.

Workhorse Saturn's been hustling in Capricorn since December 19, 2017, and strategic Pluto's been whirring away in the Sea Goat's suite since November 27, 2008. You've no doubt had some big plans in the works over the past 12 years. But now, enterprising Jupiter will turn the key in the ignition, accelerating your elevator ride to the top. Tangible, visible progress will be a hallmark of 2020—along with some well-deserved accolades. Those steady "wins" will keep your instant-gratification-loving sign motivated.

For many Rams, the past two years have felt like professional boot camp, as staunch Saturn refused to let you take a single shortcut. Even if you were passionately hustling away at your dream job, you've probably put in your share of long hours. Good help has been hard to find since late 2017, forcing you to pick up the slack, and maybe work the job of two (or three) people.

One Aries we know owns a successful talent agency. In 2019, she temporarily downsized her staff, which forced her to act as both the CEO and the booking agent for a few months. She admits that it was inspiring to get back in the trenches; in fact, doing so was instrumental in shaping her hiring decisions for her current (and upgraded) staff. But she's also happy to be back on her throne in 2020, running the show and having time to breathe and enjoy traveling with her son.

> "For many Rams, the past two years have felt like professional boot camp."

Like our friend, the past two years have probably tested your professional will. How badly do you really want to get your mission in motion? If you're still in the game as this new decade dawns, you'll be in it for the long haul!

With Saturn traveling astride power-broker Pluto for the past two years, it's possible that you made a big investment in a business. Some Rams dove into learning about financial projections, revenue models, HR manuals and other such "corporate" things. Maybe you took out a loan or raised a round of capital to bring a vision to life. After being laid off from a tech company, one Aries we know used her severance package to buy her favorite local bar from its original owner, remodeling the place with Ram panache. Her collection of ironic velvet paintings canopies the pub's vintage wallpaper, while unique craft cocktails and trivia nights have turned the locals into regulars.

On the other end of the spectrum are Aries who forked off the independent contractor path to work for a company, in the name of stabilizing your finances. While the nine-to-five grind isn't your ideal setup, you do like having steady funds in the bank to cover your spontaneous lifestyle.

Wherever you are on the career continuum, since December 19, 2017, you've been forced to evaluate your efforts from a pragmatic perspective. For you, "living the dream" means doing something you're passionate about. But Saturn's presence may have put a damper on your capricious gambling style. If you rushed headlong into a project or business idea, it's possible that you hit a wall over the past couple years. Inconvenient realities, like working capital shortages or untrustworthy staff, could have put a damper on your enterprising spirit.

But now that #Blessed Jupiter is in the picture, your Midas touch returns. The bountiful planet tours Capricorn from December 2, 2019, until December 19, 2020, giving you an entire year to tap that rich vein of gold. Since the tenth house sits at the very top of the zodiac wheel, it's the most public and status-boosting part of your chart. With auspicious Jupiter pumping up your prominence, you could catapult to the peak of your game—or serendipitously walk right into the Next Big Thing for your life.

Your innate leadership skills will be in high demand this year. Recruiters may start calling, luring you into the executive chambers. Suit up and circulate among the cognoscenti. Even if you'd rather go straight home, hit the important events, spread positive energy and make good on your promises. Think: less Netflix, more networking. This is the year to establish yourself as the capable chief you were born to be.

Saturn-Pluto conjunction: Uphold Ideals.

December 2019–February 2020
(Exact on January 12)

Power struggle or power surge? On January 12, transformational Pluto and structured Saturn make direct contact, meeting up at the exact degree of Capricorn and combining forces in your tenth house of career, fathers, and men. These two planets only share the stage every 33 to 38 years, so yes, it's definitely a big deal. While Pluto governs what's hidden below the surface, Saturn is the architect who turns the abstract into the concrete. This dynamic duo could exhume one of your burning ambitions, helping you project-manage your purpose-driven path into something you can share with the world.

Powermonger Pluto is on a long roll through the Sea Goat's realm, from 2008 to 2024. For the past 12 years, the mythic god of the underworld has been working behind the scenes to help you discover your soul's purpose. Suffering through a clock-punching gig may have felt like a living hell on some days, especially if you had to answer to an authoritarian boss. Private Pluto isn't necessarily comfortable in the tenth house, which is the zone of status and public image. But executive Saturn is right at home here—and in Capricorn, which is the zodiac sign that it rules. Since the ringed planet landed in Capricorn on December 19, 2017, he's been slowly nudging Pluto out from the shadows, and, in turn, helping you to position yourself strategically as the masterful teacher, leader or expert.

So, Aries, are you ready to be the boss? The union of alchemical Pluto and karmic Saturn will hand you a gleaming sword. You can use this as a protective shield and uphold an honorable ideal, or as a weapon to dominate others and start a war. That's a lot of power and responsibility! Yes, you are the zodiac's warrior, but that doesn't mean you have to rush into battle like a bloodthirsty Viking on a cathedral raid. Instead, think of yourself as a divine protector. Great leaders prevent wars, they don't start them. The choices you make near January 12 could affect your public standing for the coming five, ten, even 20 years. The trick is to avoid getting threatened by the so-called competition, which can suck you into a morass of vengeance.

Although the Saturn-Pluto conjunction will push you to go public with your goals, be highly selective about what you share on January 12. It's not uncommon for your visionary sign to be ahead of the curve, by years, if not decades. An Aries family friend has extolled the virtues of yoga since the 1970s. She still goes barefoot on the mat (with purple-polished toes) and can't help but roll her eyes at people who "discover" this ancient practice 50 years later…some who pooh-poohed her decades ago. Another Aries we know married a Columbian shaman and co-hosts plant medicine ceremonies with him around the world. While you may know, down to your bones, that your obsession will evolve the human race, the more conservative factions of the population—governed by Saturn—could take exception to your cutting-edge techniques. With underground Pluto in the mix, some people may judge your well-intentioned pursuits as nefarious.

> **"This could be the year you get the huge promotion or step into a position of power."**

You'll have to be strategic, Aries, or your game-changing mission could draw scrutiny from less-enlightened souls. Hiring a publicist could be a savvy move, since putting the right spin on your story will be essential.

The tenth house rules men. With Saturn and Pluto merging forces, you might cement an undefined relationship, for business or pleasure, near January 12. Since Pluto governs your blind spots, however, you could find yourself unconsciously seeking approval from the archetypal daddy…or railing against him. Your actual father might not even be part of the drama. Pluto is the "projector" planet, and you may unconsciously be taking out those bottled up emotions on your boss, your boo, or someone else who seems to be dominating you.

If you've become overly dependent on a provider type, reclaim your independence (or interdependence) in January. So maybe your other half is earning a bigger paycheck, or you have to live with your folks while you repay a university loan. Contributing in-kind services or support, for example, can restore equilibrium to these lopsided connections. Conversely, are you feeling like the sugar momma or daddy, as people get high on your supply? This is your cue to send a cutoff notice to anyone who's been draining your hard-won resources without restocking the collective pond.

Jupiter-Pluto conjunction: Join forces.

April 4, June 30, November 12

If that's not enough to fire up your enterprising engines, don't fret. In 2020, "can't stop, won't stop" Jupiter makes three exact conjunctions (meetups) with transformational Pluto. The first, on April 4, will set off the trilogy, as Jupiter shines a massive spotlight into Pluto's hidden vault of treasures. They'll meet again on June 30, when both planets are retrograde, giving you a second look, albeit a head-scratching one. Then, on November 12, these heavy-hitters will connect again, with both in direct (forward) motion.

Live-out-loud Jupiter and private Pluto can make uncomfortable companions. Jupiter is wild, capricious and a massive gambler. Pluto is stealthy, competitive and insanely strategic. Their odd-couple mashups in Capricorn and your professional tenth house can churn some push-pull dynamics for your career. At the same time, both of these planets love power; they just tend to rule from different places. King Jupiter (AKA Zeus) puts your accomplishments on the mythological mainstage. Pluto, who rules the underworld, helps you quietly pull strings and creep up on the competition. Sneak attack for the win!

With both of these powerhouses in your most aspirational zone, get ready for massive professional growth and evolution. This could be the year you get the huge promotion, make a bold career change or step into a position of power. Even if you fancy yourself a renegade, your shoot-from-the-hip leadership style could land you at a large,

Fortune 500-style corporation or a promotion into a management-level or executive position. Your responsibilities might multiply along with your pay, which could cut into your cherished free time. But the benefits will make it worth the sacrifice—or at least, your full consideration of any offers.

Jupiter was last in Capricorn from December 18, 2007, to January 5, 2009. Reflect on that time for clues of what might come back around now. Did you launch a business or change your role at work? Maybe you assumed new responsibilities with your family. If you're just starting out on your path, connect with people who are established and willing to show you the way.

The tenth house rules mentors, and a seasoned pro in your industry may take you under their wing. Be the humble ingenue and do what it takes to prove your dedication. In turn, these influential people could recommend you for opportunities or make valuable introductions. Since Jupiter also rules higher education, you might return to school to earn an advanced degree or to gain important credentials that position you for better opportunities.

In late 2008, Pluto parked in Capricorn. What skills and expertise have you been developing since then? Jupiter's presence will provide the courage to share your gifts with the world. Most people would label you as confident, Aries, but what they don't know is this: You can be reticent about sharing your deep-down passions.

It's not that you're insecure! On the contrary, you know your value, and you can be highly protective of your intellectual property. But what good is guarding this treasure trove really doing? The clock is ticking, Ram, and 2020 is the year to bring those buried gems into the light of day. Lawyer up and get them copyrighted and trademarked. Just don't procrastinate, because April 4 and November 12 are two dates that could be timely for a release—and, of course, a release party!

If you have a business (or an inkling to start one), keep everything polished and pro-level. Make it easier for people to discover your talents and offerings—and spell out the value in black and white. This could be the year to launch an online store or invest in marketing materials and headshots. Carry yourself like the next opportunity is right around the corner, because this year, it actually could be.

> "Treat your contact list like a precious natural resource."

With your polished tenth house activated, image matters. We're not saying you have to walk around in Chanel suits 24/7; but hey, maybe it's time to replace a few of the thrift store finds with some upscale vintage? You never know who might be in the elevator or at that "random" party you attend.

If you've been working in your field for a long time, you could receive an award or be recognized as an expert. Leverage the attention as a building block for your next mission. You might even market yourself as a keynote speaker…and get paid the big bucks for those rousing TED-style talks you give at luncheons and conferences. Use this to your advantage, because after December 19, Jupiter won't return to Capricorn again until 2031.

The tenth house rules fathers and men, and your relationship with an important guy may undergo a big evolution. If there's a conflict to resolve,

the Jupiter-Pluto combo won't let you stuff it into the dark corners of your unconscious. Whether you're working it out with a therapist or having a confronting (yet ultimately healing) dialogue with your dad, this is the year to get it sorted out.

Since maturing Saturn will be accompanying Jupiter and Pluto during their April 4 and November 12 meetups, you may finally begin an adult-to-adult dynamic with your parents. If you've been playing the "dutiful son" or "doting daughter," those roles will feel stifling. Time to transform and rebuild! Even if you're super close to your family, your relationship could still be up for some important growth. A generous man could play an inspiring and supportive role in your life this year, especially with regard to your career.

Got #PatriarchyProblems? With alchemical Pluto and avant-garde Jupiter firing up your changemaking spirit, you could find yourself on the front lines of the battle for gender equality, like Aries Gloria Steinem. Instead of founding a magazine, you could enlighten people on how to shift away from the culture of toxic masculinity and bring forth the divine masculine—a responsible, balanced energy that is lovingly supportive instead of oppressively domineering.

To take this all beyond gender, the tenth house rules "yang" energy: action-oriented, results-driven and to the point. With Jupiter and Pluto mashed up in Capricorn, your spirited sign could be drawn to challenging activities like extreme sports, boot camp or a hobby that requires skill and concentration. If you didn't think you had the patience for a long, detailed undertaking, you might find out otherwise.

Your innovative mind is ultra-sharp in 2020, so use it to plot, plan and make some savvy power moves.

Saturn in Aquarius: Level up your social circle.
March 21–July 1, December 17, 2020–March 7, 2023

Who are the people you call "squad," Aries? The call to collaborate will lure you out of your hibernation cave starting March 21, as serious, status-driven Saturn darts into Aquarius and your eleventh house of groups and society until July 1. Then, on December 17, the ringed planet makes a more long-term shift into Aquarius, where it will hang tough until March 7, 2023.

From activism to after-hours extracurriculars, Saturn in Aquarius will give your social life a sleek, sophisticated upgrade. When any planet buzzes through your eleventh house (even slow-moving Saturn!) your circle of influence expands. Don't waste a second of time trying to win popularity contests or boost your Instagram likes. Under discerning Saturn's influence, quality reigns over quantity on Team Ram. You can team up with a cutting-edge crew that's all about social impact and change. Spending time in the company of other thought leaders can spark inspiring initiatives.

With status-driven Saturn here, you may be invited to join an elite organization. It's not that you can't (or won't) still be "down for the people," Aries. But surrounding yourself with heavy hitters, even some from the old guard, might advance your cause in

surprising ways. As the saying goes, your network determines your net worth. A progressive mentor with deep pockets might just want to fund your trailblazing launch or killer app idea.

During the March 21 to July 1 "preview phase" of Saturn in Aquarius, take stock of your inner circle. Are the people around you elevating your standards or keeping you stuck in a small-minded rut? There are folks who flatter you and pander to your ego… but do they actually have your best interests at heart? Tough-love Saturn doesn't want you hanging out with a pack of enablers who collude with self-destructive behaviors or encourage a victim mindset. Sure, it's important to have a support network that will be there for you when the chips are down. But extract yourself from those "misery loves company" entanglements. Saturn's directive: Take responsibility for shaping your future. No more excuses!

As you open the space, new people could appear in your life who are powerful messengers and mentors—even if you resist their tough love advice at first. No Aries wants to be finger-wagged and told what you can and can't do. But with Saturn in Aquarius, you may find that you're ready to be "coachable," and receive some hardcore advice. You've never been one to mince words, so why would you want anyone to sugarcoat their message to you? As our uncle once said, "Do you know the difference between a friendly person and a friend? A friendly person tells you what you want to hear; a friend tells you the truth."

While Saturn dips its toe in Aquarius' rational waters, you'll discover a new resiliency for letting people call you on your BS. As long as you know they have your best interests at heart, don't resist! You have everything to gain from these honest dialogues. And how much better will that be than having to treat each other with kid gloves, or worse, gossiping behind each other's back?

Between March 21 and July 1, the "real talk" types could become your favorite people. With accountable Saturn playing social director, you'll thrive by holding yourself and your crew to higher standards, whether that's with your longtime friends or your work teammates. You might need to have some straightforward conversations, like, "Hey, I know we've bonded over our nightmare dating experiences or snarked about our coworkers' annoying traits, but let's challenge ourselves to talk about more positive things."

Warning: Some friends could hear this as a criticism, so prepare for a little pushback. Plus, studies have shown that bonding over a common enemy can be one of the most powerful unifiers among people. But if you're going to get your knickers in a knot, let it be for a good cause. Saturn in Aquarius will rouse your activist spirit and support you in planning the revolution. Over the coming three years, your vision for a better world could easily evolve into a full-force movement.

The catch? Saturn is the planet of tangible action and has zero tolerance for armchair revolutionaries. You say you're fed up about an important issue? Well, Aries, what are you going to do about it? That question could weigh heavily on your mind. Don't get lost in rumination. Start somewhere, like door-to-door campaigning for a 2020 political candidate or volunteering at a neighborhood non-profit.

Before Saturn finishes up its tour of Aquarius on March 7, 2023, you might even jump into the race and run for office yourself! The eleventh house rules technology, so you could combine real-time efforts with social media and digital marketing strategies to raise awareness.

No matter where you channel your prodigious energy, collaborating with the right partners will be a crucial component of your success. Treat your contact database like a precious natural resource—which it is!—and you'll find everything you need right there within a degree of separation.

Take an unblinking look at the way you participate in communities, especially when you're not the reigning royal. Do you give the leaders a hard time, rebelling at every turn and ignoring ground rules? Sure, you believe you have a better solution, but Saturn serves an eye-opening realization about the impact of uncooperativeness. People love your spunky vibes, but if you're going to rock the boat in 2020, try not to capsize it in the process.

Footnote: The cosmic Lord of the Rings only visits this part of your chart every 30 years; it was last here from February 6, 1991, to January 28, 1994. Scan your archives (if you're old enough) for clues of similar patterns and lessons from that time. They could repeat this spring, or near the holidays.

Jupiter in Aquarius: Expand your social reach.
December 19, 2020– December 29, 2021

Although this year demands focus and hustle, it will end on a much lighter note. On December 19, free-spirited Jupiter liberates you from the grind when it joins Saturn in Aquarius and your eleventh house of friendships and collaborations, hanging out here until December 29, 2021. This jovial 12-month cycle proves that "all work, no play" could never really be the Aries M.O. But along with that comes a challenge: Give up your "my way or the highway" schtick and learn how to be a genuine team player—or get benched on the sidelines!

Even if you burn some midnight oil in your lamp this December, Jupiter in Aquarius reminds you that many hands make light work. If you're worried about crushing Q4 deadlines, call for backup! Even if you have to skim some cream from your profits—or barter services with the hired guns—at least you won't miss the Aquarian-fueled holiday celebrations. They will be weird, wonderful and packed with as many bizarrely entertaining characters as your favorite offbeat series!

With Jupiter in Aquarius, tap the hive mind for inspiration. Crowdsource and crowdfund your most innovative schemes. Surely, you've heard the expression, "it takes a village." Well, with Jupiter buzzing through Aquarius until December 29, 2021, you could go one step further. Reprise your own version of The Village People and team up with a wacky, mischief-making crew to unleash your creativity on the world. (Can we get a YMCA-men, Aries?)

Many Aries are media mavens, and with publisher Jupiter logging in to your eleventh house (AKA the tech sector of the zodiac wheel), you could make a huge name for yourself in the digital domain. Do friends consistently compliment your inventive fashion choices? Start that style blog or Etsy store and plant your flag as an Instagram influencer. Many Rams have a knack for public speaking. Spread your message far and wide with a YouTube channel or IGTV episodes. Are you a long-form writer? With all the self-publishing tools available, you don't have to wait for some old-school literary bastion to offer a book deal. Upload the manuscript, hire a graphic designer and cover illustrator, and get your words in print by yourself. You never know: A bigger publisher could pick it up for a second printing!

Romantically, Jupiter in your eleventh house can unleash your experimental nature. Suddenly, even the pickiest Aries could be puckering up to a totally unexpected prospect…or pondering unconventional options in your relationship. With expansive Jupiter in liberated Aquarius, monogamy could be challenging. If you don't want to stray from a "one and only," you may have to loosen up regulations in other ways, like, say, exploring more independent extracurriculars…and letting yourself flirt (within limits!) while you're out mingling. Single Rams will likely diversify your friendship and dating portfolio during this 12-month circuit. Even if you swore off Tinder earlier in the year, don't rule out Bumble, Hinge or another app. Digital dating could bring a lucky swipe, and Jupiter the gambler will reward you for taking a chance on romance.

The Great Conjunction: Jupiter & Saturn unite.
December 21

The winter solstice this December 21, 2020, comes with an added twist! As Jupiter and Saturn band together at 0°29' Aquarius, they herald a rare cosmic event known among astrologers as the Great Conjunction. These mashups only happen once every 20 years; the last was on May 28, 2000.

Say-anything Jupiter and buttoned-up Saturn

might just be the most awkward bedfellows of all the planets—polar opposites in agenda. But when fine-tuned, they are complementary forces, creating a solid structure that can turn your visions into reality. The question is, how can you expand and contract at the same time? Saturn curbs some of Jupiter's "act first, think later" impulses, sparing you public embarrassment, both online and IRL. In exchange, risk-taker Jupiter lends Saturn's low-key plans the hit of showbiz razzle-dazzle that makes the public take notice!

With the Great Conjunction converging in your community-spirited eleventh house, who you mingle and jingle with near the holidays could be a huge topic of discussion. While open-minded Jupiter in Aquarius wants you to throw your arms around the world, reserved Saturn will make you anything but a hugging saint. How can you satisfy your need for social experimentation while also protecting yourself from the users and losers? Saturn asks: Which side of the family do you actually want to spend time with over the holidays—if any? Jupiter counters: Could you just ditch the celebrations and travel to one of the Greek Isles?

Navigating social obligations when you thirst for personal liberation could create quite the conundrum near December 21. You don't have to memorize the map before you go meandering. Just be strategic about the direction you start off in. You could walk right into a group of incredible people or discover a town that's built on the kind of eleventh house utopian ideals you crave as 2020 winds down.

Have you already found your high vibe tribe? During the Great Conjunction, you could take on a more prominent role, but not necessarily as the leader. As the year's Capricorn influence fades

out, you may prefer to be an organizer instead of a mouthpiece. Think of yourself as "crew glue," the one that keeps the band together through thick and thin.

Venus & Mars Retrograde: Relationship review.

Venus Retrograde: May 14 – June 25

Mars Retrograde: September 10 – November 13

How effectively do you articulate your needs—and how well do you listen? Does sharing come easily to you or do you struggle to cede control? In 2020, Venus will hold up the mirror as she takes an extended voyage through Gemini and your third house of communication and cooperation. From April 3 to August 7, the celestial diplomat sashays through the sign of the Twins, bringing a simpatico vibe to your partnerships.

Then, trouble arrives in paradise. From May 13 to June 25, Venus slips back into her once-every-18-months retrograde, sending pleasantries out the window. Politeness has its place, but not at the expense of honesty—an Aries law of the land. Venus is the planet of harmony, and you're ruled by warrior Mars. Unlike most zodiac signs, you don't mind a little dissonance.

Should tension escalate, take the cue for more real talk with your people, especially the folks you deal with on the day-to-day: siblings, coworkers, neighbors. If you've slipped into a selfish behavior pattern, Venus retrograde will not let you get away unscathed. Return to mutuality, Aries!

The third house governs platonic love. If you're not feeling all hot-and-bothered for your S.O. while Venus vacates the building, don't panic. The rush of spring fever will return right after the Summer Solstice. While the heat is off, work to strengthen the friendship aspect of your bond. Open up a safe space to talk about topics that might feel scary to broach. That's what you'd do for one of your BFFs, right? Even if the "say anything" discussions reveal different points of view, you'll be glad to have the truth out on the table.

Looking for love? The friend zone may deliver between April 3 and August 7. But advance carefully while Venus is retrograde—and this could get much more complicated than you expect. Not sure anything will come of this? Keep your lusty feelings in the "secret crush" category and see if they're still burning after June 25. Single and searching? You could attract people who are charismatic but not exactly available—a mirror for your own indecision about being "tied down." Stay off that slippery slope. It's all fun and games until someone gets hurt.

In all types of relationships, Venus retrograde tasks you with improving your communication style. You're known for being direct to a fault. Soften the blow of your truth hammer and you'll get your point across more effectively. Practice buffering your critiques in a "praise sandwich," beginning and ending with a genuine compliment.

> "Not feeling all hot and bothered? The rush of spring fever will return right after the Summer Solstice."

Next: Strap on your jetpack and get ready for liftoff! On June 27, your ruler, make-it-happen Mars, launches an extended orbit through Aries, which lasts until January 6, 2021. If your 2020 mojo got off to a slower start, fear not. Stalled personal projects accelerate at lightning speed once Mars comes home to your sign.

Fortunately, you're the zodiac's speed demon and you'll relish the supersonic tempo that Mars supplies. As an Aries, you'd much rather be overwhelmed than bored. There will be lots of moving parts to coordinate and many cats to herd after June 27. The trick to winning this game? Use your innate leadership skills and delegate.

Normally, Mars visits each of the zodiac signs for about seven weeks. But due to a retrograde from September 9 to November 13, he'll stretch out his mission for six months. The last time the red planet entered your realm was hours before the New Year's ball dropped on 2019, where he hung around until Valentine's Day. Revel in the celebratory vibes that will invariably spark up when your planetary ruler swings by for a kiki. Bartender! A round of "momentum moonshine" shots for everyone!

If you've been dying to make an epic life change, courageous Mars pushes you off the ledge after June 27. The tough part? You might be leaving behind something (or someone) you love, at least temporarily. As the zodiac's most independent sign, you need to step out of life to get in tune with your thoughts, feelings and intuition. After that, you always know how to act.

Just don't cut off your nose to spite your face. Rash Mars might convince you that it would be easier to just burn it all down and start from nothing. But as history has shown (repeatedly), destructive moves have a way of catching up to you. Wherever you go, there you are…but maybe this time your allies and loved ones could be there too? Don't push people out of your life just because you need some space. Instead, how about engaging them as supporters for your semester-long vision quest? That balanced approach would be a win-win as 2020 winds down.

On September 9, Mars pulls the emergency brake on some of your fast-moving progress when he shifts into a low-power retrograde until November 13. Ground Control to Major Ram! You'll likely experience frustration during this cycle, especially if a pet project was just achieving liftoff and then—wham!—it comes to a seeming standstill. Try to see the silver lining: This is a rare chance to hit pause in the middle of the action and review your progress to date. How viable is this? Will it scale? What's left to do? Can you legit make a living doing this?

Few things are flawlessly executed right out of the gate. Find something you can improve, and get busy tweaking, revising and perfecting your formula! As Oscar Wilde quipped, "Experience is just the name we give our mistakes." Embrace the spirit of revision and reach out to people who have pulled off a similar feat. By the time Mars corrects course on November 13, you might actually hit on a faster, smarter or more economical way of accomplishing this vision.

Edgy Mars in your sign could spark a yearning for a radical personal makeover. But when the red planet is in reverse, you really don't want to do anything irrevocable. While the hair you chop off will grow back, tattoos are hard (and expensive) to modify. Get inspired by other people's style and see what small changes you can make that will add up to the feeling of a significant shift. (And put all the other ideas onto a Pinterest board to reconsider after November 13.)

If you rushed to embrace a new identity or path in 2020, Mars' backspin reminds you not to throw out the baby with the bathwater. There are aspects of your "former life" that are worth keeping around. Use the retrograde to rebalance.

Cancer/Capricorn Eclipses: Restore work-life balance.
January 10, June 21, July 5

How do you balance your personal life against the demands of your career? Since July 12, 2018, you've been seeking that very equilibrium, thanks to a series of eclipses on the Cancer/Capricorn axis. Capricorn rules your tenth house of men and fathers, while Cancer governs your fourth house of women and mothers. Over the past couple years, you may have dealt with changes regarding your parents, kids or family of origin. The people living under your roof may have behaved unpredictably, or maybe you dealt with shifting responsibilities at your job. It hasn't been easy to figure out the flow!

Because Cancer and Capricorn are the two signs that form a square (90-degree angle of tension) to your Sun sign, there have been some bigger adjustments to make, especially with regards to your public image and relationships. We know several Rams who spent 2019 in career limbo—

partly by choice, because they wanted to develop a path that truly felt like a calling.

In 2020, there will be three more Cancer/Capricorn eclipses, on January 10, June 21 and July 5. What's ahead, Aries? Maybe you'll become a parent, deal with empty-nest syndrome as a child moves into a different age bracket or travel to your ancestral homeland to explore your roots. The struggle for "work-life balance" may rattle you until July.

Fortunately, you're also starting to see tangible results for your efforts. After two years of surrendering control, releasing the past and obsessing over your life purpose, clarity is incoming! The first full moon of the year, on January 10, marks the lunar eclipse in Cancer. A lingering family issue could be resolved in a surprising way. Perhaps an estranged relative will offer an olive branch, or you finally let go of a long-standing grudge. Just like that, you're back in communication again. Sweet serenity!

With karmic Saturn and Pluto opposing this eclipse, there could be a "meant to be" pregnancy, or miraculous baby news from a loved one who has struggled with fertility. You might have a vivid dream that reveals a suppressed memory, paving the way for deep healing in 2020. Are you stuck in a pattern that seems to predate your childhood? You could try a past-life regression or hypnotherapy session near this eclipse.

Other Aries might delve deeper into discovering your roots, from a DNA testing kit to meeting cousins on another continent. With investments highlighted, you could receive a surprise inheritance, family support or just the emotional conviction to make a courageous move toward security. A home-based business might be part of that plan. Set up that kitchen-table side hustle, stat!

The final Cancer eclipse is a solar (new moon) eclipse on June 21. With your domestic fourth house ablaze, some Aries could move, renovate or buy property. Pregnancy, adoption or a change to your family structure might also be on the agenda, and you'll have the clarity to move forward.

Eclipses can reveal a shadow, so the choices you make near these dates may come with a hidden clause. During the July 12, 2018, solar eclipse in Cancer, an Aries friend sold her home and moved into a larger space with a voluminous garden. She's currently installing heated floors and a second bathroom, but since she's further out from city center, she's also adjusting to not having the amenities she loves within walking distance. That convenience, admittedly, worked well for her as a spontaneous Ram, and she hasn't quite gotten over having to drive to grab a dozen eggs and a six-pack of IPAs. But she's come to see that this transition was worth every penny, especially since she sold her house for almost double its listing price.

The July 5 lunar (full moon) eclipse is the only one this year in your ambitious tenth house. Changes to your professional path and goals that launched near January 5, July 16 or December 26 in 2019 (the dates of last year's Capricorn eclipses) could see another wave of action. You might make a radical change to your career, accepting an unanticipated job offer that also demands a lifestyle change or a literal move.

A leadership role, promotion or changing of the guard at your company could also be in order. If you've been searching for the most fulfilling way to earn a living, these illuminating beams could finally crystallize the solution. Get into action, even if that means starting from the bottom so you can learn the ropes of a new industry.

One Aries we know spent a good part of 2019 packing up his childhood home after his father (who passed away from Alzheimer's days before one of these eclipses) moved to a memory care center. Simultaneously, he was shuttering a ten-year business, which also involved a major cleanup mission. It was a lot to handle at once, but as the new decade dawns, he's writing a fresh chapter on a blank slate, and feeling a new sense of excitement about his life. He's also set up a home office, which keeps the overhead low as he develops his next big dream.

Gemini/Sagittarius Eclipses: Reveal your message.
June 5, November 30, December 14

Lift the gag order! When you "call it like you see it," Aries, there's no denying your ability to hit the nail on the head. But your unvarnished delivery can be a little, er, direct for some folks. After getting burned a few times, you may have become careful about what you express, or how readily you speak your mind in groups. But in 2020, a new eclipse series begins in loquacious Gemini and Sagittarius, waking up your communication axis until December 3, 2021. In 2020, three lunations—on June 5, November 30 and December 14—will unleash a flood of visionary ideas and sharpen your ability to articulate your plan with impact.

Eclipses pull you beyond the familiar, revealing new facets of yourself, even when you're not looking for them. If your lens on life has gotten a tad narrow, the June 5 lunar eclipse in worldly Sagittarius will switch you back to a wide-angle view. Since Sagittarius rules your philosophical and nomadic ninth house, this game-changing full moon could guide you to live or study abroad. Whether you're enrolling in a summer university program or an immersive surf camp is up to you, Ram. But if you're planning to travel in June, go beyond sipping umbrella drinks on the beach and find something that stimulates your intellect, athleticism or spirituality.

Are you feeling the pull to relocate? Under the shadowy beams of this eclipse, start testing the waters. Organize an apartment swap or do a short-term rental in your desired destination. Of course, the Cancer solar eclipse on June 21 might further spur you on to find a new home. But maybe this address works better for a vacation property, one you can rent out for income or even turn into a future retreat center (a dream for several of our visionary Aries friends).

The "think globally, act locally" maxim rings true with these eclipses, especially on November 30, when the Gemini lunar (full moon) eclipse activates your third house of community, socializing and self-expression. Are people misinterpreting your intentions, perhaps seeing you as intimidating or hard to read? The time has come to make a conscious change. Craft and deliver a powerful message, perhaps through channels like social media, a website or in-person events. A close friendship could turn into an exploratory business partnership. Take it slow and team up on a small project to test the waters.

The third house is also the zone of peers, coworkers and neighbors. Want to strengthen these bonds? Organize an icebreaker event, like a holiday party after work. Or, if you're already close, deepen your connections with a fundraising drive, or a powerful gathering, like a vision-boarding moon circle within a month of November 30. With this eclipse in expressive Gemini, you'll be sharing stories and even a few secrets. A casual friend could become a BFF-grade kindred spirit, or a project partner you work with in 2021. Your relationship with a sibling could grow beyond a rivalry or outdated childhood dynamic.

On December 14, a second Sagittarius eclipse arrives, this time as a solar (new moon) eclipse. Plans to be home for the holidays could suddenly shift into something a lot more adventurous, like visiting friends in a charming seaside village or ringing in 2021 in a jungle retreat center overseas. And how about a round of truth serum to chase down that cup of cheer? Powerful conversations can create new openings with the people you love, as you settle your differences or begin discussions about a co-branded venture that you can begin to develop next year. ✳

         The AstroTwins' 2020 Horoscope

January

January 3-February 16: Mars in Sagittarius

The sky's the limit during this bold transit as lusty Mars races through your worldly ninth house. Adventure awaits, and you could go somewhere totally new, solo or with an intriguing stranger who's different from your usual type. Couples could take a dream trip or first (or second!) honeymoon.

January 10: Cancer full moon (lunar eclipse)

The first eclipse of 2020, an emotional full moon that illuminates your domestic fourth house, makes it safe to show your sensitive, vulnerable self. Don't even *try* to keep your true self bottled up! Home and family come into the spotlight, and the next few weeks could bring exciting baby news for some Aries of the childbearing set.

January 13-February 7: Venus in Pisces

These three weeks are perfect for letting your guard down and allowing your imagination to get a bit carried away. With amorous Venus in your twelfth house of dreams and fantasy, it may be hard *not* to go there!

January 26: Venus-Mars square

During this one-day clash of the love planets, you might see a different side of a romantic interest—or just lose interest! But if you can resist overreacting, you might catch a glimpse of something important that you can work on—without having to call the whole thing off.

January 27: Venus-Neptune meetup

Let fantasy reign today! With the dreamiest planets in cahoots, your romantic imagination will be on fire. Don't hold back your feelings—you couldn't if you tried—but make sure anything you share is draped in kindness and compassion.

January 2: Mercury-Jupiter meetup

Don't like the terms of an agreement? Negotiate! Under this adaptable mashup, people will be eager to seal the deal, and if you're the squeaky wheel, you *will* get the grease! Be strategic and stick to your guns, and you should be able to walk away with a feather in your cap.

January 3-February 16: Mars in Sagittarius

With self-determining Mars marching through your visionary, indie-spirited sector, you won't be a big fan of the hivemind. This is your nudge to do

50

things your way, on your timeline. This realm also rules travel, education and entrepreneurship, any or all of which areas could become more important over the coming six weeks.

January 10: Uranus retrograde ends

If you've struggled to get your finances in order the past several months, you'll be relieved to learn that things could start to improve today, as disruptive Uranus ends a five-month retrograde that's been wreaking havoc in your money and security zone since August 11, 2019. Now that it's moving forward, you—and your plans—can, too!

January 12: Mercury-Saturn meetup

Mixing shoptalk with personal conversation could actually be kind of sexy today, Aries—and certainly good for business. Which is a great thing, because thanks to the mashup of the communication planet and career-focused Saturn, you might not be able to avoid it!

January 12: Mercury-Saturn-Pluto meetup

Big, sudden changes could be afoot at work today, and since you may not see them coming, the best thing you can do is stay flexible! A transformational team-up of radical Pluto and messenger Mercury in your professional zone could lob a curveball your way. Whatever comes out of this, don't walk away until you find the "lesson" or silver lining. Be honest: Were you secretly hoping for a way out? With today also bringing a rare (once every 35 years) meetup of Saturn and Pluto, examining your motives will be key, especially around authority figures and whatever may unconsciously drive your ambition.

January 13: Sun-Saturn-Pluto meetup

Buckle your seat belt! On top of the extremely rare

Saturn-Pluto alliance, a once-a-year Sun-Pluto merger electrifies your professional tenth house with so much wattage, you might not know where the chips are going to fall for at least another day (or longer). If you've felt underappreciated in any area of your job, take a firm step toward turning that around now. This transit supports a bold power move or aligning yourself with an influential VIP. You may need to strategically shift into a position of authority. Are you resisting leadership or responsibility in any area of your life? The Sun's mashup with daunting Saturn could rattle your confidence. Rather than spiral into self-doubt, take honest inventory of where you might need more training and credentials. But don't let it stop you in your tracks.

January 16-February 3: Mercury in Aquarius

Today, collaborative Mercury blasts into digitally savvy Aquarius and your eleventh house of teamwork and technology. Got a big project to tackle? Partner up with like-minded folks to save work, time and possibly even money!

January 18: Mercury-Uranus square

Where's the fire, Ram? Don't rush into anything before you've had a prior chance to evaluate the whole situation. Your mind might be way ahead of your physical abilities under this antsy square. And with Mercury in your collaborative zone, don't over-rely on a colleague who might not be up to the task—or might only be out for themselves.

January 23: Sun-Uranus square

Think big, but don't mistake "visionary" for "realistic." You might be stoked about a brilliant new brainstorm, but until it's ready to actually be worked on, you'll need to manage your expectations.

Pace yourself, Aries: That part of the project could take weeks or even months.

January 24: Aquarius new moon
Chinese Year of the Metal Rat

Do you have everything in place to launch a thrilling new initiative—except your dream team? Today's auspicious lunar lift in your eleventh house of collaborations and technology can lead you to a new crew *or* the perfect app to help you blast off. Make sure you plan your execution carefully. Today also kicks off the Chinese Year of the Metal Rat, and as the first animal of the Chinese 12-year cycle, the Rat is auspicious for well-crafted beginnings.

January 28: Mars-Neptune square

You're ready, willing and able to make things happen, but with hazy Neptune in the frame, it might prove difficult to take something that last step from "close" to "done." Don't sulk if you have to return back to the drawing board. One more pass could get this thing in shape for the big reveal.

February

FEBRUARY: LOVE HOTSPOTS

February 7-March 4: Venus in Aries

Whether you were looking for a romantic reboot or not, you're likely to enjoy the infusion of fresh energy that comes when the love planet returns to your sign after being AWOL for a year. Venus gifts you with the "It" factor, so enjoy flirting, turning heads and playing with a bold new look.

February 9: Leo full moon

This once-a-year full moon in your fifth house of passion, amour and creativity could spark chemistry that's palpable—and combustible! It could also unleash some pent-up emotions, so mind your temper as you sidestep heated conversations and people who push your buttons—to the degree possible.

February 16-March 30: Mars in Capricorn

Your ruler, hot-blooded Mars, marches into your tenth house of structure, future planning and reputation over the next six weeks. You could become fixated on where a relationship is heading—but resist the push to make things official. This time is better spent discovering whether your long-range goals align and hammering out compromises where they don't.

February 23: Venus-Jupiter square

Fantasy can wait. While you'd love to get lost in one, reality beckons. Expansive Jupiter may be egging dreamy Venus on, but from its perch in your career corner, it's reminding you of all your other responsibilities. After you take care of business, you're free to indulge in some spicy sexytime!

February 23: Pisces new moon

Even if you have to postpone a steamy dream, you can stay in touch with your emotions today. The year's only new moon in empathic Pisces is powering up your romantic twelfth house, giving you direct access to your softer, nostalgic side. Enjoy this sweet change of pace and lead with your more receptive feelings.

February 28: Venus-Pluto square

You'd love to be an open book about your feelings, but today's planetary face-off could make communication a struggle, as peacekeeper Venus battles manipulative Pluto. One of you might feel like the other is being controlling, making a levelheaded discussion all but impossible. Retreat to neutral corners and try again in another day or so.

FEBRUARY: CAREER HOTSPOTS

February 3-March 4: Mercury in Pisces

Today, mental Mercury begins its annual downshift through your restful, imaginative twelfth house. Crunching numbers and analyzing hard data may not be the best activity now as you're apt to confuse fact, opinion and fantasy. These next three weeks are far better for creation than implementation.

February 9: Leo full moon

Open your heart! The year's only full moon in your passionate, lusty fifth house could open the floodgates of desire. A budding attraction could consummate into a full-blown love affair and couples could feel their mojo rising fast. Careful, though: Tempers and knee-jerk reactions can also reach peak levels just as quickly.

February 16-March 9: Mercury retrograde

Despite Mercury being retrograde in dreamy Pisces and your twelfth house of hidden enemies, you can move forward with certain projects—but vet them twice as carefully! On March 4, when the messenger planet backflips into Aquarius and your collaboration zone, you may get a second chance on a group initiative. Use this introspective time to review all your work and double-check everything before you share it with the world.

February 16-March 30: Mars in Capricorn

Your professional star is rising as your galactic guardian, motivated Mars, blazes into your ambitious tenth house, dialing up the desire to succeed. Your secret for these next six weeks is being very clear about your goals and where (if anywhere) you're willing to compromise. But note: You won't be the only one on a mission, so be prepared for out-and-out stiff competition.

February 21: Mars-Uranus trine

Want it? Push harder for it! An empowering sync-up of your ruler and game-changing Uranus supports your taking a bold (yet calculated) risk. Have supporting evidence ready for the naysayers, and they'll see you as an innovator—rather than a loose cannon.

March

MARCH: LOVE HOTSPOTS

March 3: Venus-Saturn square

Traffic cop Saturn could check your speed on the romantic highway today as it forms a restrictive square with vixen Venus. But that's not necessarily a bad thing! If you've been speeding along without checking a roadmap, you might look up and not have a clue where you are. You *can* redirect a relationship, but use a gentle touch. Single? Loosen up your ideas of who your "perfect" partner should be and meet people where they're at.

March 4-April 3: Venus in Taurus

Pull out the stops when it comes to upscale dates and sensual details! Today, decadent Venus grooves into her ultimate comfort zone: your second house of practical luxury. "Too much of a good thing" sounds about right for the four weeks, so enjoy!

March 8: Venus-Uranus meetup

Your love life may take a sudden detour, or an unexpected expression of desire (on your part or someone else's) could take you by surprise when disruptor Uranus hooks up with amorous Venus. Unattached? This could feel heaven-sent. But if you're in a relationship that's been on shaky ground, these seismic shifts might topple it.

March 20: Mars-Jupiter meetup

In your mind, you may have your future all mapped out. But hello…there's another person's desires to take into consideration! Before you get carried away, have a discussion with your love interest to see how *they* feel about these big ideas!

March 27: Venus-Jupiter trine

Sometimes there's a fine line between a stable commitment and a stranglehold. Today, you can put your relationship to the test to see if your level of attachment makes you feel free yet grounded—or like you're gasping for air. A calm and loving discussion could help you restore the balance. Single? Set off traveling or enroll in a class. You don't need to start with a partner to end with one!

March 28: Venus-Pluto trine

Reality check: Just because your S.O. isn't pulling down a heavyweight income doesn't mean they're not right for you. Today, as the love planet falls into the clutches of status-hungry Pluto, you could start to "compare and despair." Stop and reassess, focusing on everything you adore about them, and don't go there!

March 30-May 13: Mars in Aquarius

The line between platonic and erotic could get blurry over the next six weeks as lusty Mars treks through your eleventh house of friendship and technology. It's your call whether to "dabble" or not, but since this is your digital domain, finding a love connection online might be a smarter approach, since you won't risk losing an important relationship.

March 31: Mars-Saturn meetup

How ready are you to introduce a new love interest to your inner circle? If you're hesitating because you fear someone won't like the other, get over it! You're a grownup, and the most important opinion here is *yours*. Under this social sync-up, couples will enjoy going out with mutual friends, but choose your company carefully because people may have very different ideas about how to spend an evening.

MARCH: CAREER HOTSPOTS

March 4-16: Mercury in Aquarius

Inquisitive Mercury kicks off a short but intense sprint through innovative Aquarius and your eleventh house of teamwork and technology. Buddy up with eclectic pioneers and you can accomplish tremendous things—in record time!

March 9: Virgo full moon

If you've rushed through an assignment recently, this Virgo full moon—the only one of the year—will power up your detail-minded sixth house and illuminate any important tidbit you may have glossed over. Going over things with a fine-toothed comb is not your favorite activity, but you will appreciate being super-organized when you finish your review!

March 16-April 10: Mercury in Pisces

Analytical Mercury returns to Pisces and your dreamy twelfth house after a confusing three-week retrograde. Now you can take some of those creative ideas and see which are doable. But you might have to bend the rules a little.

March 20: Mars-Jupiter meetup

You might want to don some protective gear as this transit can shatter the last remnants of a glass ceiling: Driven Mars (your ruler) only teams up with supersizer Jupiter once every other year, and it can take a decade—or two—for them to reconnect here, in your professional tenth house. If ever there was a day to take those blue-sky possibilities seriously, it's now. And don't be too quick to accept "no" for an answer. The only limits are the ones in your imagination.

March 21-July 1: Saturn in Aquarius

This is a big-deal planetary movement, since Saturn hasn't brought its inimitable brand of structure and planning to your eleventh house of teams and technology since 1991! This is "Phase One" of the operation since Saturn will be retrograde for almost five months this summer and fall. But then it'll be in full effect until March 7, 2023. This move can shift your focus from all-career-all-the-time and remind you that there is a life outside of work. Over the next three years, think about strategic networking and partnering up with people on your wavelength with whom, together, you'll be greater than the sum of your parts.

March 23: Mars-Pluto meetup

Your power and charisma are peaking, so make that big ask—or that audacious move. Once every other year, your ruler, assertive Mars, aligns with power player Pluto. For a span of approximately

16 years, this summit meeting takes place in your career corner. Don't sit around waiting for someone to reach out to you; make it happen!

March 24: Aries new moon

This cosmic birthday present hands you a golden opportunity for a fresh start in any area of life where you've felt stuck. Where do you want to initiate change? Set some bold intentions and map out a few concrete steps you can take over the next two weeks (peak manifesting time). Then set one of them as your destination point and don't stop till you get there!

March 30-May 13: Mars in Aquarius

With the energizing planet marching through your collaborative zone, you can be an agent for getting people back on the same page. But don't emphasize the differences of opinion. Help everyone focus on shared goals and what they stand to gain by working together. During this six-week cycle, you could get involved in some very exciting team projects.

March 31: Mars-Saturn meetup

Speed check! Motivated Mars makes you eager to kick off a new collaboration, but restrained Saturn insists you slow down enough to conduct due diligence. Someone might have a hidden agenda that won't mesh with others'. While there is indeed strength in numbers, that's only true when you've got the right people on your team.

April

APRIL: LOVE HOTSPOTS

April 3-August 7: Venus in Gemini

No one will need to tell you to "lighten up" during this extended cycle (thanks to a retrograde). With the love planet on a long, slow cruise through breezy Gemini and your house of communication, you'll find all kinds of ways to express yourself when it comes to amour. Single? You may be far more interested in "casual" than "committed," which is fine, provided you're upfront with people about how serious you're willing to get. Attached? This is a highly social period, so loosen up any bonds that hold you together a little too tightly.

April 4: Venus-Saturn trine

Boundaries! If you're struggling to communicate something a little heavy to a love interest, it can help to treat it like a professional relationship. Sometimes, when you're too close, it's easy to "dump" on them or speak disrespectfully. Imagine you don't know them that well, then have a fair-minded and caring dialogue. Single? A casual conversation could lead to something provocative and worthy of pursuit!

April 7: Libra full moon

The year's only full moon in Libra electrifies your partnership house and spotlights a key relationship. You could take a hoped-for next step or bring things to a head if you're not seeing eye-to-eye. Single? These next two weeks are rich for manifesting a person with real potential. But you have to put yourself out there—and be a little vulnerable.

APRIL: CAREER HOTSPOTS

April 3: Mercury-Neptune meetup

It's not your brainpower that will be your secret weapon today. It's your ability to read the tea leaves. With a mashup of analytical Mercury and psychic Neptune in your twelfth house of divine downloads, you'll notice things that aren't expressly on the page. Don't second-guess yourself; trust this!

April 4: Jupiter-Pluto meetup

What do you stand for on a fundamental level—and how can you express that in your career and worldly accomplishments? At this once-every-13-years alignment between visionary Jupiter and power-seeking Pluto, you'll be asked to deeply examine the motives behind your professional path. Is it time for a radical leap of faith? If you're not operating from a truly powerful and soul-centered place, work could feel unbearable. Consider it a demand from the universe to make the real transformation you've been circling and tiptoeing around. This is the first of three Jupiter-Pluto meetups this year; the next two will arrive on June 30 and November 12. By the end of the year, you could be operating from a completely new realm of status and leadership.

April 7: Libra full moon

If you've been thinking about partnering up with an individual or a company, this illuminating lunation will either give you two enthusiastic thumbs up—or it will shine a light on certain issues you hadn't been aware of. Rose-colored glasses off: It's time to go either all in or out!

April 7: Mars-Uranus square

It's unrealistic to think everyone will always get along. Even solid teams have differences of opinion. Today, even if unwieldy group dynamics threaten to undermine a project, stay with it. Your calm voice of reason might be the very thing that rights the ship.

April 10-27: Mercury in Aries
With brilliant and capable Mercury forging through your sign for the next two weeks, you don't need to dim your light for others to shine. Just turn up *your* wattage and let everyone else take responsibility for themselves! Got a message to deliver? Don't overthink it; just share it!

April 14: Sun-Pluto square
No matter how justifiably upset you are about something, keep it to yourself. Under this aggro mashup, you don't want to risk alienating an ally or authority figure. You don't need to be the one to bring them down a notch. Truth has a funny way of getting revealed.

April 15: Sun-Jupiter square
Try to balance your swagger with a dose of realism today, as the confident Sun in your sign squares off with fearless Jupiter. If you're feeling butterflies in your stomach, that's normal—and it could be protecting you from going too far. Tap your team for support and go forth. Just be careful not to bite off more than you can chew.

April 21: Sun-Saturn square
Your upbeat, confident energy could get thwarted by a colleague or client today, so have a backup plan for moving ahead. Under this tense square, there could be divergent opinions that make it impossible to come to a meeting of the minds. If you try and try but no one's budging, drop it and get back to work on something you *can* control.

April 22: Taurus new moon
This practical and grounded moon of fresh starts lands in your second house of money and security. Where are you hoping to turn over a new leaf? Opportunities will present themselves over the next two weeks, so meet the universe halfway by putting yourself—and your desires—out there so people can find you!

April 25: Mercury-Pluto square
Power struggles could arise at work under this willful clash. Don't fan the flames by projecting your resistance onto authority figures. If you've got personal issues to deal with, handle them on your own time. The one place they don't belong is on the job!

April 25: Mercury-Jupiter square
A new wave of excitement might have you raring to get started on something, but curb your enthusiasm! You're in it for the long haul, and you don't want to risk running out of steam before you even really get going. It's all too easy to get carried away under the influence of supersizer Jupiter, so let methodical Mercury run the show.

April 25-October 4: Pluto retrograde in Capricorn
Just when you were about to shift into high gear, control freak Pluto hits the manual override and slows your roll. Knowing this retrograde will last for five long months can help you create more realistic new deadlines and conserve your energy. The one thing to watch for during this cycle is hot-headed confrontations with an authority figure on a power trip. To keep the peace, you might have to let them (think they) win.

         The AstroTwins' 2020 Horoscope

April 26: Sun-Uranus meetup

Make it rain! A big dream can become a reality over the next six months thanks to today's electrifying sync-up in your second house of work and money. Uranus is the impatient disruptor of the zodiac, so don't wait for fame and fortune to come knocking. Seek them out with your signature audacity!

April 27-May 11: Mercury in Taurus

When mental Mercury forays into your financial zone, you won't be able to ignore the warning signs. Before you sink (further) into debt, make the necessary adjustments to your spending and saving habits. Step one: Figure out where you're "leaking" money and plug that hole!

April 28: Mercury-Saturn square

Unless you actually *enjoy* banging your head against the wall, this planetary face-off may finally convince you to walk away from a hopeless situation. Some people just like to be contrarian for the sake of exerting their own will. Today's clash between the communication planet and resistant Saturn will make that obvious. Focus instead on something you actually can make headway on.

April 30: Mercury-Uranus meetup

Today can be a turning point for you financially, as these two game-changing planets unite in your work and income sector. Think (and seek!) outside the box for new job or moneymaking opportunities.

May

MAY: LOVE HOTSPOTS

May 3: Venus-Neptune square

You may be tempted to talk about your feelings today, but you might find that words fail you, thanks to a tense angle between communication planet Mercury and emo Neptune. And that's perfectly fine! It's a good excuse to let yourself connect to how it feels without trying to articulate it, which could take you out of the pure state.

May 7: Scorpio full moon

This once-a-year event in your erotic eighth house turns up the heat on your love life as it increases passion *and* intimacy. But at the same time, it can dredge some deeply buried emotions, which may need to be processed over the next two weeks.

May 13-June 27: Mars in Pisces

As action planet Mars shifts into low-power mode in your twelfth house of rest, healing and fantasy, you could get swept away by a quixotic or even clandestine attraction. Part of you will relish getting caught up in these wild feelings, but deception (including self-deception) could be in play. Attached? This transit is ideal for a couple's spa retreat or long-overdue forgiveness work.

May 13-June 25: Venus retrograde in Gemini

The love planet makes an extended backspin through your communication center, disrupting the easy flow in relationships and triggering arguments. You may not be able to talk this out just yet. In the meantime, you can journal about your feelings and talk to a confidante or therapist.

May 22: Mercury-Venus meetup

This one-day sync-up of articulate Mercury and amorous Venus in your communication center sets the stage to diplomatically broach a touchy topic—or tell someone how much you care.

May 28-August 4: Mercury in Cancer

The messenger planet beams into your sentimental sector for an extra-long visit because it'll turn retrograde from June 18 to July 12. You might have a discussion before June 18 and *think* you cleared the air only to find that one of you interpreted things a little differently from the other. Pro tip: Wait till after July 12 to even try to untangle that!

MAY: CAREER HOTSPOTS

May 7: Scorpio full moon

Investments and joint ventures could be unexpectedly profitable over the coming several weeks, thanks to this lunar lift in your eighth house of shared resources and wealth. Need a jumpstart? Talk to an adviser and consider new ways to make your money work (even) harder for you, perhaps with some form of passive income.

May 9: Mercury-Pluto trine

Stepping into your power will be second nature under this charismatic sync-up. You'll know exactly what to say to convince people to join your team or fund your venture. Back it up with data and solid projections and people will find it impossible to say no to you.

May 10: Mercury-Jupiter trine

Under this supportive alignment, a person in a position of power gets your vision and is genuinely interested in your ideas. Down a cuppa courage and pitch away! With Jupiter in cahoots with the messenger planet, you'll know exactly how to communicate your big ideas and how much enthusiasm to unpack!

May 11-September 29: Saturn retrograde

Try as you might, you can't always be racing ahead in fifth gear. Today, the planet of structure and long-range planning kicks off its annual retrograde—this year in your eleventh house of teamwork and technology. There will be delays, and they will be frustrating, but there's also a silver lining. This is the chance you probably wouldn't otherwise avail yourself of to go back to the drawing board and give everything a thorough review.

May 11: Mercury-Mars square

With Mars dialing up competitive vibes at work, it's hard to feel much team spirit or camaraderie. But try! Under this communication-inspiring alignment, you're urged to open up a conversation with colleagues or clients about ways to reduce the pressure you're all feeling. Since everyone is in the same boat, people might actually be amenable to a discussion about splitting up responsibilities differently.

May 11-28: Mercury in Gemini

The mental planet makes its annual foray into your articulate third house, shifting your mind into high gear. Ideas will come a mile a minute over the next few weeks, so be ready to capture the best of 'em. No need to go this alone. You've got more support than you realize.

 The AstroTwins' 2020 Horoscope

May 12: Mercury-Saturn trine

Team up FTW! Your best resources are other people, and there are plenty of folks who'd love to join forces. But be selective about who you link up with. The right people will make your work easier and more brilliant; the wrong ones will only bring frustration.

May 13-June 27: Mars in Pisces

As your ruler, energizing Mars, slips into your restful twelfth house—where he hasn't been in two years—it's time to give your creative right brain a shift at the wheel. It may be hard to focus and do highly analytical work. But with your imagination dialed up, you could devise the most innovative ideas of your whole year!

May 14-September 12: Jupiter retrograde in Capricorn

Just as you're about to reach your cruising altitude, you may be forced to slow down or go back to the drawing board. Jupiter has been spurring you on professionally, but during this annual retrograde, you get your first chance to review your work to date. Rather than let this frustrate you, consider it an opportunity to make sure everything is as good as you want and need it to be.

May 15: Sun-Pluto trine

You can put your personal stamp on a big project and still get advice from a manager or consultant. In fact, bringing them in on a minor level could inspire them to promote you and champion some of your even bigger ideas.

May 20: Venus-Neptune square

Not sure how to "sell" something today? Being too literal in your descriptions might not be appropriate, and it could be better to play up the emotional aspects. Turn to the hivemind and see how they feel about this.

May 22: Gemini new moon

Under this once-a-year cosmic brainstorming session, your communication skills will be at peak levels. Use this cosmic catalyst to explore potential synergies by examining all the possibilities on the table. A conversation with like-minded folks could develop into a sweet synergy over the next six months.

May 22: Mercury-Neptune square

You don't have to express every thought that pops into your head today. In fact, it's best to keep any unclear notions on hold until this foggy square passes. You may think you're onto something brilliant only to realize you haven't a clue how to communicate it.

June

JUNE: LOVE HOTSPOTS

June 2: Venus-Mars square

Wires get crossed today and signals seriously scrambled as the cosmic lovebirds play tug o' war. You probably won't get an accurate read on people's motives, and since you might struggle to own your true feelings, it's probably better to resort to good old reliable body language.

June 13: Mars-Neptune meetup

Oh, sweet surrender! Your imagination is on fire as lusty Mars teams up with fantasy-fueler Neptune in your twelfth house of yearning. It'll be easy to get swept up in daydreams and maybe a clandestine encounter. All's fair in love, but be realistic about believing people's promises.

June 18-July 12: Mercury retrograde in Cancer

The messenger planet flips into retrograde motion in your domestic center, which, TBH, you might consider blessed relief after a few weeks of hosting hyperkinetic Mercury in your social sector. Just watch for a few moody moments, when you'll have a hard time separating feelings from facts.

June 21: Cancer new moon (annular solar eclipse)

This special lunation can help you start writing a whole new chapter when it comes to your romantic life and domestic dreams. Eclipses bring things out of the shadows, so someone might surprise you with a few unexpected announcements. One thing you can count on: Home base and a sense of emotional security will be top priorities over the next six months.

June 23-November 28: Neptune retrograde in Pisces

During nebulous Neptune's lengthy annual retrograde, things may not be as they seem at first. It'll be tempting to believe them and rush into something, but for the sake of your heart, be slow to get into new relationships or commitments. Got some unresolved emotional issues? This is a great time for processing them!

June 27, 2020-January 6, 2021: Mars in Aries

Talk about making up for lost time! Your passionate ruler hasn't visited your sign for two years, but when he comes marching in today, he'll stick around for an extra-long time because of a long, slow retrograde from September 9 to November 13. Not only will this ramp up your mojo and give you major head-turner status, but you'll speak with confidence and authority, building trust (and burning desire) in anyone you bring into your orbit.

JUNE: CAREER HOTSPOTS

June 5: Sagittarius full moon (lunar eclipse)

You can't dream too big under the glowing beams of 2020's only Sagittarius full moon in your visionary ninth house—which also happens to be a game-changing lunar eclipse. What are your most inspiring goals for the rest of the year? Of course, think professionally, but don't leave out travel and your lofty bucket-list wishes!

June 17-July 12: Mercury retrograde in Cancer

Mercury shifts into reverse in Cancer and your domestic zone. If you do any work from Chez Ram—or outside the office—make sure your passwords are strong and not used for multiple sites. This is a good time to back up all your important files—and if you're traveling, to triple-check reservations!

June 27, 2020-January 6, 2021: Mars in Aries

With motivator Mars paying an extra-long visit to your sign (because of a retrograde from September 9 to November 13), you'll have all the drive and energy you need to pursue a passion project or a solo endeavor with gusto!

 The AstroTwins' 2020 Horoscope

June 30: Jupiter-Pluto meetup

The second of this year's three rare conjunctions between expansive Jupiter and powerhouse Pluto lands in Capricorn and your ambitious tenth house. Look back to April 4 for clues of a major transformation to your career path and goals. Then start plotting your biggest move yet for the grand finale on November 12.

July

JULY: LOVE HOTSPOTS

July 8: Mercury-Mars square

You've been holding some important emotions inside and it's taking a toll to stay mum. Today, as retrograde Mercury butts heads with forthright Mars (in your sign), it will be nearly impossible to bottle those up any longer. Just beware that communications could come across as defensive or just plain combative under these stars. You're also extra thin-skinned today, prone to taking things personally. Maybe it would be better to write a draft of your thoughts before simply unloading. These two planets will meet again on July 27, when Mercury is longer retrograde. Perhaps you'll have more fully-formed thoughts to share then.

July 20: Cancer new moon

This rare second consecutive new moon in your domestic zone opens up a six-month opportunity to realize some exciting lifestyle dreams. If you didn't take action on them last month, you're prodded to do so now, whether you're pining for a house with a white picket fence, an urban pied-à-terre, or being sexy global citizens with a fellow nomad. After all, "home" is ultimately a state of mind.

July 27: Venus-Neptune square

Feel rather than think your way through a situation today. Since words may fail you, don't make matters worse by saying the wrong thing. It'll be better to show than tell under this foggy mashup anyway!

July 30: Mercury-Neptune trine

Ask and receive! Today, as thoughtful Mercury taps into Neptune's mystical frequency, your intuition may be borderline psychic. You'll know exactly how to act to get your needs met.

JULY: CAREER HOTSPOTS

July 1-December 17: Saturn retrograde enters Capricorn

Restrained Saturn pulls the emergency brake on the runaway train in your career house, but rather than seeing this as purely frustrating, look for the silver lining. It's possible that you were going a bit too fast for your own good—or headed down the wrong track. By slowing down and reviewing your work, you might find errors you would've overlooked. Or you might hit upon another approach that's even better or more cost-effective.

July 5: Capricorn full moon (lunar eclipse)

This once-a-year event could signal a peak moment in your professional year! Full moons indicate completions and turning points, and in your career corner, this might be cause for a major victory celebration. Take a moment to share the glory with your team, but keep the momentum going by coming up with your *next* big set of goals.

62

July 15: Sun-Pluto opposition

Try not to take things personally today. With power-tripping Pluto throwing shade at the ego-driven Sun, you may feel underappreciated. If possible, let the powers that be know what your contributions to a project were, but don't come off as desperate. Think about what you could do next time to affect a different outcome.

July 20: Sun-Saturn opposition

Reality check! There are only so many hours in the workweek, and this clear-eyed opposition urges you to be more pragmatic about what you pile onto your plate. Saturn rules time and structure, so if you want to turn in your best possible work, you have to settle for producing a little less.

July 30: Mercury-Jupiter opposition

You can't please all the people all the time, but hopefully you can make it up to them later! Under today's home-work juggling act, you may have to make some sacrifices with your inner circle for the sake of a major deadline. But after it's done, let your manager or client know where your limits are.

August

AUGUST: LOVE HOTSPOTS

August 4-19: Mercury in Leo

Don't hold back! As the messenger planet parades through your passionate, expressive fifth house, it's a perfect time to let someone know how you feel about them. If they're pretty clear about that, how about sharing some of your secret desires or fantasies?

August 7-September 6: Venus in Cancer

As affectionate Venus spins through your nurturing fourth house, it's a good time to assess where you are in a relationship. Is it finally time to meet each other's family—or exchange keys? Solid couples can deepen your connection with talk of next steps, whether that's a major home-reno project or starting or expanding a family.

August 17: Mercury-Mars trine

How will they know how you feel if you don't just say it already? With a new or budding relationship, confident Mars' nudge to Mercury in your self-expression house can give you the shot of courage you need to open your heart—and your mouth! Attached? What message have you been stuffing down? Out with it!

August 18: Leo new moon

The year's only new moon in your zone of romance and courtship can bring a wave of fresh energy to your amorous ties, regardless of your status. Single? Stay open to people who seem different from your usual type, especially if chasing that "type" hasn't produced any worthy candidates. This realm also rules fertility, so dive in, or double up on protection accordingly.

August 25: Venus-Jupiter opposition

While attraction and affection are important, to go the distance with someone, your long-term goals need to align. Today could bring an eye-opening epiphany. A partner's neediness or dependency may suddenly feel too heavy—or maybe you're the one having a clingy phase. Refocus on *your* ambitions, and talk through your shared ones. If either of you has been in workaholic mode, hit pause and emotionally reconnect.

August 27: Venus-Neptune trine

With love planet Venus sweetly synced up with fantasy-fueled Neptune, let yourself slip into a reverie about your S.O. or ideal mate. This is hardly a waste of time or energy: The stronger you can feel the emotion of your desires, the more likely you are to manifest exactly what your heart is dreaming of.

August 30: Venus-Pluto opposition

Buckle up for safety! Your emotions may take you on a roller-coaster ride as intensifier Pluto opposes gentle love goddess Venus. While there's a side of you that craves peace and harmony, part of you is addicted to the drama. Do your best not to fan the flames or project any baggage onto others.

AUGUST: CAREER HOTSPOTS

August 1: Mercury-Pluto opposition

Your best strategy at work: Keep a low profile and don't rock the boat. With manipulative Pluto yanking on the messenger planet's strings, you can expect power struggles and sketchy dealings, which are the *last things* you want to get entangled in! Resist the triggers.

August 2: Sun-Uranus square

You always take the high road, but there could be a wolf in sheep's clothing prowling the low road today. This silver-tongued devil might be saying all the right things—while trying to undermine you at every turn. Protect yourself as best you can, but do *not* stoop to their level.

August 3: Aquarius full moon

The year's only full moon in your eleventh house of teamwork and technology is a perfect opportunity to get involved with an elite group. But don't wait to be invited! Reach out to a crew you've had success with in the past or a new one that's working on something you can uniquely contribute to.

August 3: Mercury-Saturn opposition

You might struggle to stay on-task today as mental Mercury in emo Cancer opposes restrained Saturn in your work corner. If you need to have a conversation, have it, but then set a time limit for "obsessing" and get back to work!

August 4-19: Mercury in Leo

As nimble Mercury marches through Leo and your creativity zone, this is a good time to advance one of your passion projects. Obviously, you'd love to garner some social media attention, but getting too attached to the outcome can detract from the quality of the work.

August 4: Mars-Jupiter square

You may waver on how far to push a personal agenda item today, and there's no easy answer. If you find yourself at loggerheads with a client, boss or another authority figure, weigh the pros and cons. On the one hand, standing up for yourself will show them you have backbone—and maybe make them reconsider your point. On the other, they might see you as a loose cannon and decide they don't want the headache. What you *don't* want to do is lose your temper, which will cost you their respect.

August 10: Mercury-Uranus square

You might need to scale back on an ambitious goal today since certain key players may be impossible to rein in. To avoid ending the day feeling frustrated or held back, set one modest objective and be satisfied if you can pull that off.

August 13: Mars-Pluto square

Temper, temper! Fiery Mars forms an irreconcilable square with shadowy Pluto in your work sector, and trying to stand up to a power-tripping colleague will only backfire. Attempt to handle things diplomatically—and if you can't make any headway, talk to a supervisor or someone in HR.

August 15, 2020-January 14, 2021: Uranus retrograde in Taurus

When the unpredictable planet makes a five-month reversal through your second house of work and money, you might not have the tightest grip on your finances. Since the only thing you can reasonably expect is the unexpected, make a point of keeping extra cash on hand. See if you can earn a little extra income by taking on a freelance project or becoming an eBay or Etsy vendor.

August 19-September 5: Mercury in Virgo

Meticulous Mercury hunkers down in your efficient sixth house for the next few weeks, helping you bring order to the Aries court. As you streamline your systems and tidy up your whole life, take note of how much time—and energy—you're saving!

August 24: Mars-Saturn square

With your ruler, driven Mars, in your sign lighting a fire under you (and keeping it stoked until early January), you're motivated to accomplish *a lot*! But today's speed-checking clash with restrictive Saturn could slow your roll. Realize that you can't keep the accelerator floored the entire time, and when you do have to adjust your pace, welcome it as a chance to perfect your project.

August 25: Mercury-Uranus trine

Don't question solutions that come quickly. Under today's quicksilver alignment, your thoughts are sharp and organized. If you need to make a presentation or lead a meeting, you can do so with confidence. Just be sure you've crunched all the numbers and anticipated people's questions ahead of time.

August 29: Mercury-Jupiter trine

Your secret weapon today: the ability to combine big-picture thinking with a solid strategy. As the quick-thinking and expansive planets unite in your career zones, you could captivate a decision maker or map a simple plan to take an idea viral. Set yourself up for success by putting innovative concepts into a structure, complete with timeline, budget and action steps!

August 30: Mercury-Neptune opposition

It may be hard to keep all the details of a complex project in your head today—so don't! Use a spreadsheet, mind map or just good old-fashioned notebook. You need all your brainpower to stay alert and responsive in the moment.

September

SEPTEMBER: LOVE HOTSPOTS

September 2: Venus-Saturn opposition

You know the importance of firm boundaries, yet passion might get the best of you today. Need some emotional shoring up? Talk to a friend who can offer a more objective perspective—and don't do anything rash!

September 2: Pisces full moon

Surrender and release! The annual full moon in your fantasy-fueled twelfth house can bring untold pleasures. The trick? You'll have to let go and receive. If you've been unclear about someone's true motives, la luna could reveal crucial information. But don't leap to conclusions before you have all the facts. Playing amateur detective or psychoanalyst could come back to bite you.

September 4: Venus-Mars square

You might be at cross-purposes with a love interest today, but you don't need to be in lockstep 24/7. Enjoy a little time apart, letting your hearts grow fonder. Single? Show your interest, but don't come on too strong. Under this signal-jamming sync-up, people might misinterpret your intentions.

September 5-27: Mercury in Libra

Expressive Mercury wings into your partnership house, making it a little easier (and way sexier) to talk about your feelings and desires. This is a perfect opportunity to flex those flirting muscles!

September 6-October 2: Venus in Leo

Ready for a romantic reboot? Today, the love planet commences her annual catwalk through flamboyant Leo and your passionate fifth house. Not only are you encouraged to put yourself out there but also to make sure you always look the part. The number one thing that will attract the right people is your confidence. Couples should take this as a poke in the ribs to get into the habit of regular date nights—*à deux!*

September 9-November 13: Mars retrograde in Aries

Your ruler, impassioned Mars, makes a U-turn for the next two months as it reverses through your sign. See this as a chance to tone down any over-the-top or inappropriate behavior. With the red-blooded planet off-course, jealousy and anger can flare. Watch that you don't come on too strong or lapse into self-centered behavior. If you rushed into a romance that you're now unsure about, you'll have a chance to walk it back several steps!

September 15: Venus-Uranus square

Romance and relationships are usually high priorities for you, but under today's liberating alignment, they could feel a little claustrophobic. Note: There's a way to enjoy your freedom without straying outside agreed-upon borderlines. As long as you're acting with integrity you'll be fine.

September 24: Mercury-Mars opposition

"My way or the highway" won't get you far with a love interest today. Even if you don't see how you'll get on the same page, don't issue any ultimatums—unless you're truly prepared to walk. Negotiation and compromise are key to making a relationship work, but under this feisty opposition, neither of you will likely back down. Call a time out!

September 27-October 27: Mercury in Scorpio

Communicator Mercury pays its first of two visits to your erotic eighth house—and an extra-long one owing to the fact that the messenger planet will be retrograde from October 13 to November 3. During its trek through this private sector, you may be inspired to share some secrets and previously unexpressed desires in the name of ever-hotter sex!

September 28: Venus-Mars trine

With the love planets hooking up in sizzling fire signs—and the most sensual parts of your chart—it's safe to express your emotions without trying to protect your heart. Of course, you won't fully believe that until you let down your guard and try. The result could be a stunning outpouring of love and support.

SEPTEMBER: CAREER HOTSPOTS

September 1: Mercury-Pluto trine

Listen to your gut! Your intuition is razor-sharp today, and you'll be able to read people like a large-type book. But don't just listen to their words; the real clues will come from their tone of voice, facial expressions and body language.

September 3: Mercury-Saturn trine

You have the perfect blend of innovation and solid data to take your idea to the top! Memorize the important details so you can speak with passion—and be sure to look people in the eye when you talk to them. They need to feel the connection.

September 5-27: Mercury in Libra

You can get a flailing collaboration back on track by giving some premium grease to the "squeaky wheel" and suggesting some compromises. With communicator Mercury sailing through your partnership house, this is a perfect time to renegotiate a deal or team up.

September 9-November 13: Mars retrograde in Aries

Energizing Mars slams on the brakes for a two-month backspin in your sign. The "lesson"? Despite your strong desire to be in control of everything, you aren't. So kick back and let things unfold at a natural pace and don't try to force or rush anything.

September 12: Jupiter retrograde ends

And you're back! Good luck charm Jupiter resumes forward motion after a four-month retrograde in your career corner. Things should continue to accelerate until December 19, but you won't benefit from taking any shortcuts. It's your diligence and hard work that will pay off in quantum professional advancement.

September 14: Sun-Pluto trine

If that major breakthrough isn't getting any closer, hang in there. Under today's galvanizing mashup, you can make a giant stride forward. When all else fails, stay focused on your highest goal.

September 17: Virgo new moon

The year's only new moon in your sixth house of dedication and service may inspire you to look beyond your own needs and go the extra mile for someone. Carve out time today—and over the next two weeks—to set new career objectives and map out everything needed to get you there, from timelines to budgets to the division of labor.

September 17: Mercury-Jupiter square

Getting on the same page with a collaborator about your long-range goals could prove an exercise in futility today. But rather than try to persuade them to see things *your* way, make a point of actually

The AstroTwins' 2020 Horoscope

listening to their core concerns. If you can agree to compromise on a few key points, you both may feel more inclined to accede to the other.

September 21: Mercury-Pluto square

Silence is golden! Under this slippery square, someone might be misrepresenting their power. But don't fall for their ruse and inadvertently give away any state secrets. Better to listen and ask questions—and hold your cards close to your vest.

September 23: Mercury-Saturn square

Catch yourself acting overly stubborn or argumentative today. It's one thing to defend a position you're passionate about, but if you find yourself resisting something "on principle," take a look at what that might really be about—and hit "pause" for a few days.

September 24: Mercury-Mars opposition

You know what *you* want, but your ideas might be diametrically opposed to what other key players have in mind. There's no easy way around this. Trying to convince people to do it your way will make you look stubborn and rebellious, and giving in will make you feel weak. Accept that you're going to have to compromise somewhere, and hopefully you can choose your battles.

September 27-October 27: Mercury in Scorpio

People may be withholding information when the messenger planet journeys through your secretive zone. Stay calm even if things slow down or slip away while the deal-making planet is retrograde from October 13 to November 3. Use that time to double- and even triple-check your work before

you take it public. You'll get another shot at this when Mercury returns, in forward motion, from November 10 till December 1.

September 29: Mars-Saturn square

Make sure you've dotted all your "i"s and crossed all your "t"s before you challenge anyone in a position of authority. You could well be right—and your point of view might save the company money or embarrassment. But under this tense square, they may not exactly welcome your concerns with open arms.

September 29: Saturn retrograde ends

Ready, set, exhale! Taskmaster Saturn wraps up a frustrating five-month retrograde in your career house. You might not be able to count the times you've gone back to the drawing board around goals and plans, but now your course corrections should start to pay dividends. Looking for a new gig? Some exciting options could open up now.

October

OCTOBER: LOVE HOTSPOTS

October 2-27: Venus in Virgo

Amorous Venus commences her annual visit to your sixth house of self-care and wellness, which could make "healthy loving" your new priority. If you're in a relationship, team up on a commitment to improve your meal selections, exercise together and pamper yourselves during this inspired cycle. Single? Switch from vino to fresh juice for the next few weeks—and try to get an extra hour of sleep—then see how your body feels.

October 10: Venus-Uranus trine

Under this leash-loosening trine, you'll enjoy a little more freedom in your life, which doesn't mean inviting anyone else into it. Simply adding more spontaneity can do you a world of good. Single? Today is better for flirting and having fun than looking for someone who ticks all your boxes.

October 13-November 3: Mercury retrograde

Communication planet Mercury begins its backspin in your private eighth house, which could inspire you to share some secrets and previously unexpressed desires in the name of ever-hotter sex! From October 27 to November 10, it'll sojourn through Libra and your partnership corner, which might bring back someone from your past.

October 16: Libra new moon

The year's only new moon in your partnership zone offers an opportunity to hit refresh in your closest unions and really think about what you want and need in a relationship. Whether you're single or attached, you can gain valuable insight, work through a sticking point and move into a new phase of even deeper commitment.

October 18: Venus-Neptune opposition

Taking off the rosy-hued glasses may not give you the clear vision you're hoping for. But you're not doing anything wrong: The bewildering mashup of fantasy-fueled Neptune and romantic Venus could blur the picture for anyone. When in doubt over what someone is saying, take it with a grain of pink Himalayan sea salt. Big decision? Sleep on it.

October 19: Venus-Jupiter trine

You're feeling pragmatic and optimistic about romance or a certain relationship, and without the dreamy vibes that can cloud reality, you can bring about a desired shift in your dynamic. You could restore a healthy balance of give-and-take or meet someone who's all about fair play in a union.

October 21: Venus-Pluto trine

Under this rare, twice-a-year mashup, you can rekindle the flames with a longtime partner: Doing something a bit wild or out of your "norm" could be very exciting! You may have to take the lead, but you'll enjoy it! Single? If it's not blatantly breaking company policy, have another look around the office. That favorite colleague might suddenly feel like serious dating material.

October 24: Venus-Saturn trine

Don't overthink things today! This grounding alignment can help you get back on *terra firma* with a love interest or discern the keepers from the creepers if you're on multiple dating sites. If you start to feel overwhelmed, ask yourself what your most logical friend would do, then do exactly that.

October 27-November 21: Venus in Libra

Mighty Aphrodite kicks off her annual visit to your seventh house of committed relationships. Longtime couples can bring back the balance and reconnect to the love you felt when you first met. During this three-week cycle, a budding relationship could turn serious. Enjoy dreaming about a shared future with someone you adore. If you've been on the fence about someone, you'll soon figure out which side to jump onto.

OCTOBER: CAREER HOTSPOTS

October 1: Aries full moon

The only full moon in your sign for 2020 is like your own private New Year's party! This can signal the completion of a project or a phase you've been immersed in for the past six months. Even if there's still a little bit left to be done on it, you should make a point of basking in the spotlight—for a moment. But then go back and get 'er done so you can move onto your next big thing!

October 4: Pluto retrograde ends

Power up! After a five-month reversal through your career sector (since April 25), alchemist Pluto resumes forward motion. All that professional soul-searching is about to pay off. Now that you know what you want, your next step is figuring out how to manifest it.

October 7: Mercury-Uranus opposition

You don't have to go along with someone's ideas about spending or investing money today. In fact, trusting your own instincts may prove the smartest move of all. (Note: You also don't have to justify your decision.) This cosmic collision sends your mind into overdrive, but hold your tongue. In this case, the first thought probably isn't the best thought. Just quietly follow your gut. Mercury and Uranus will face off on October 19 and November 17, when you'll be tasked with navigating this erratic energy again.

October 9: Mars-Pluto square

Watch your temper today because it could flare up without much warning! Fiery Mars, your ruler, spins into a tense square with volcanic Pluto in your work sector, and your argumentative streak could alienate the wrong person. Try to handle things diplomatically, perhaps by speaking to a supervisor or someone in HR. If that's not an option, save any heated emails to your drafts folder.

October 13-November 3: Mercury retrograde

Intentionally or otherwise, people may be withholding information when the communication planet journeys through your secretive zone. Don't hit the panic button if things slow down or even backslide while the deal-making planet is retrograde. Use that time to double- and even triple-check your work before you take it public.

October 15: Sun-Pluto square

A delicate situation may cause you to doubt yourself. You know what's right, yet someone's control issues could make it impossible to move the needle. Rather than spin your wheels, make a few constructive suggestions that get you to "yes."

October 16: Libra new moon

An opportunity to team up for business or a creative venture bodes well under today's new moon in your partnership realm. Don't get carried away by exciting synergies, though. You want to make sure this has staying power.

October 18: Sun-Saturn square

Slow and steady may win the race, but the challenge is to keep moving forward when self-doubt threatens to sideline you—like under today's restrictive Sun-Saturn square. If you feel stuck, you might find it helpful to reconnect to the reason you're doing this in the first place.

October 19: Mars-Jupiter square

If you can't come to an agreement with a boss, client or authority figure, don't back down—or go all passive-aggressive on them. Dial up the courage to take a stand for yourself. But speak only in positive terms: what you believe in, the greater good, the higher mission. What you *don't* want to do is lose your temper, which could get you kicked off the island.

October 31: Taurus full moon

Trick or treat! This once-a-year lunation in your work and finances sector could bring a huge opportunity for advancement at your current job or shine a light on a more ideal position. If you don't have any leads at the moment, tap your social network (discreetly) and let people know you're in the market. You might benefit from a few sessions with a career coach.

November

November 3: Mercury retrograde ends

Smooth sailing once again! As communicator Mercury ends a dicey backspin that started October 13, you'll get back on the same page with your S.O. or relationship plans. If an ex resurfaced during this time, you'll soon have a clear read on whether to give this person another chance.

November 9: Venus-Mars opposition

A relationship (or dating effort) could hit a speed bump today as the love planets spin into a tense opposition. Control issues, finger-pointing and a "victim" mentality could be just some of the drama that erupts under this gloves-off sparring match. Part of you wants to pull the other person's strings; another side just wants to run away. Under these fraught skies, defer and delay action!

November 10-December 1: Mercury in Scorpio

Talk dirty to me! Loquacious Mercury makes its second trip through your sizzling and intimate eighth house. Thanks to its recent retrograde, mixed signals made it hard to trust. With Mercury in forward motion this go-round, you can bare your soul and start expressing those private desires without all the chaos.

November 13: Mars retrograde ends

You can breathe a sigh of relief as your ruler, intensifying Mars, resumes forward motion after a couple months of spinning backward in your sign. You might have felt like your personal projects were getting shot down one after another—for no discernible reason. See if you can find any "teachings" in the experience, but don't waste too much time on that. You've got two-plus months of lost time to make up for!

November 15: Scorpio new moon

Romance reboot! The year's only Scorpio new moon fires up your eighth house of intimacy and eroticism and could almost single-handedly bring sexy back. If it never went AWOL, you can use this extra blast of passion to take things to an even deeper level, perhaps aligning the physical and the emotional (and maybe the spiritual). Unattached? Let yourself get more vulnerable: Is it time to let someone play a bigger role in your life?

 The AstroTwins' 2020 Horoscope

November 15: Venus-Pluto square

It may be hard to tell if someone is trying to manipulate you, or if it's just your imagination? While you probably won't get to the bottom of this mystery today, simply by expressing your concerns, you'll let someone know where your boundaries are. But before you do anything rash, give them the benefit of the doubt.

November 16: Venus-Jupiter square

With Venus parked in your relationship sector, you may be craving more—or closer—companionship. But a tense angle to excessive Jupiter in your future-planning zone could make you too fixated on the long-term. Slow down and let this unfold naturally. Applying too much pressure could cause this to go sideways. Stay engaged and loving, but don't micromanage things.

November 19: Venus-Saturn square

If you've been racing full steam ahead in a new relationship, pump the brakes. As cautious Saturn speed-checks dreamy Venus, you might have some doubts or reservations. But this is a good thing. It's a chance to make sure you're on the same page and still share the same goals.

November 21-December 15: Venus in Scorpio

When Venus joins Mercury in your seductive eighth house today, there's no telling what might go down! Warn friends that you could be MIA for the next few weeks—and let roommates know to take that "Do Not Disturb" sign seriously.

November 23: Mercury-Neptune trine

So much for those boundaries you were going to put in place. Emotions—including lust—could get the better of you under this sexually charged alignment. While there's nothing wrong with pursuing an irresistible attraction (if you're both available), it's a different story if you've made a commitment to someone else. Couples should unplug and silence devices and tune in only to each other.

November 27: Venus-Uranus opposition

You might need some "space" in a suffocating relationship under this liberating alignment. Be honest about your feelings—and respectful of your love interest's. Strong emotions could threaten to disrupt your connection, but if you remember that this intensity will likely pass as quickly as it came on, you might be able to resist temptation.

November 28: Neptune retrograde ends

Communication will be easy once again as fog machine Neptune resumes forward motion in your hazy twelfth house. If you've felt like every time you tried to have a serious relationship conversation since mid-June, your messages came out scrambled, you'll have more success now.

NOVEMBER: CAREER HOTSPOTS

November 1: Mercury-Saturn square

This challenging square is the first of a one-two punch (the same formation will recur on November 6, when Mercury is direct) that can show you where you're being excessively rigid or stubborn. If you find yourself resisting something "on principle," take a look at what that might *really* be about. Are you afraid of losing control or being exposed as not having all the answers? Keep the "imposter syndrome" in check by doing all your homework.

November 3: Mercury direct in Libra

Are you in or out? With contractual Mercury retrograde since October 13, it's been hard to know who was on Team Aries. Now that the messenger planet resumes forward motion, you can evaluate contenders with a much clearer mind. Perhaps key information surfaced over the last couple weeks. Factor it in—this may be a blessing in disguise.

November 10-December 1: Mercury in Scorpio

Money talks! Mental Mercury makes its second trip through your eighth house of joint ventures, long-term finances and wealth. Could you merge your assets or talents for mutual gain? Book a strategic summit. A year-end review with a financial advisor could reveal an opportunity to shrewdly invest or save on taxes. Sit down with a pro and you could close out 2020 with a surprise bonus!

November 12: Jupiter-Pluto meetup

Career transformation or bust! Visionary Jupiter and power-player Pluto make their third and final conjunction in your career sector. Break down the barriers and push past your resistance, because a new level of success awaits. These two luminaries only connect every 13 years, so don't squander the chance to go after your dreams in a big way. For clues of what may reach its pinnacle today, look back to the two prior Jupiter-Pluto meetups on April 4 and June 30.

November 13: Mars retrograde ends

Welcome news comes on the professional front: Your ruler, energizing Mars, resumes forward motion after a two-plus-month retrograde. Now you can tie up all those loose ends as you prepare to blast into an exciting new chapter.

November 15: Scorpio new moon

This annual lunar lift widens your perspective on investments and moneymaking opportunities that involve other people. But the first step to financial reinvention (and independence) is paying off debt or diversifying your assets. Make that your priority for the coming six months, even as you create a game plan for earning and saving more.

November 30: Gemini full moon (lunar eclipse)

Check your voicemail and inbox regularly. A full moon—also a scene-stealing lunar eclipse—in your communication corner could bring the big news you've been waiting for. And if you do land that A-list client or score the big gig, don't be shy about broadcasting news of your coup. You've worked hard to pull this off, and your network will be eager to show their support. Any messages you want to put out there will be well received and acted on.

December

December 5: Venus trine Neptune

Sensual Venus and dreamy Neptune unite in two of the most fantasy-fueled zones of your chart, delivering high romance. You can resist everything except temptation under these stars. Either place yourself strategically close to the mistletoe…or stay far away if willpower is needed.

December 15, 2020-January 9, 2021: Venus in Sagittarius

Love planet Venus commences her annual horizon-widening sojourn through your expansive ninth house, and things could get very interesting over the next three weeks. Whether you're solo or attached, you'll be in "high adventure" mode. Single? An exotic trip could tick *multiple* things off your bucket list. Attached? A romantic getaway—or sexy staycation—will get your juices flowing.

December 29: Cancer full moon

Under this emotional lunation in your domestic fourth house, your best fashion statement will be wearing your heart on your sleeve. Go ahead and reveal your sensitive side, and good luck trying not to get all misty-eyed and mushy. Home and family are in the spotlight for the next few weeks. For some, this lunation could bring baby plans or a visit from the proverbial stork.

December 30: Venus-Neptune square

As thick-skinned as you might feel, under this tenderizing mashup, an old wound or heartache might slow your lusty roll. With hypersensitive Neptune in your unconscious zone squaring off with amorous Venus, anxiety or self-doubt could surface. But rather than brush it off, call a timeout and track the feeling down to the deepest level. You could finally clear this out for once and for all.

DECEMBER: CAREER HOTSPOTS

December 1-20: Mercury in Sagittarius

Dream it, do it! As the messenger planet jets through Sagittarius and your expansive ninth house for the next three weeks, you'll be able to articulate some of your grandest dreams. But don't waste your best material on people who don't get it. Wait until you find the perfect audience to share your genius.

December 13: Mercury-Neptune square

You may feel pulled in two very different directions under this left brain-right brain clash. Analytical Mercury is convinced that facts and figures tell the whole story, but intuitive Neptune knows there's more here than meets the eye. Try to hold off until you can get definitive answers.

December 14: Sagittarius new moon (total solar eclipse)

The new moon in your visionary ninth house—which is also a galvanizing solar eclipse—invites you to set "practicality" aside and indulge in some unfettered blue-sky dreaming. Don't get hung up on whether the details are doable. There'll be plenty of time to figure that out—after your genius is recognized and the project gets green-lighted!

December 17, 2020-March 7, 2023: Saturn in Aquarius

Who are the people you call friends? As structured Saturn makes its long-term entry into Aquarius and your eleventh house of groups, you'll spend the next couple years upleveling your squad goals—and your inner circle. Not only will you meet some inspiring "who's who" types, you'll also have a chance to meaningfully contribute to your community, even a social or political cause. The best news? Saturn is departing your career zone, meaning you get to graduate from "boot camp" and watch your professional efforts take flight. If you've paid your dues, prepare to be handsomely rewarded!

74

December 19, 2020-May 13, 2021: Jupiter in Aquarius

Hopefully you took full advantage of the opportunities and good fortune that supersizer Jupiter brought over the last year as it toured Capricorn and your tenth house of career and public image. Today, it kicks off a new yearlong chapter as it marches through Aquarius and your eleventh house of teamwork and technology. Are you looking to get more involved with professional groups or become more digitally savvy? Before you rush in willy-nilly, set some attainable goals. And get ready to become a networking force to be reckoned with!

December 20, 2020-January 9, 2021: Mercury in Capricorn

You'll have the upper hand at most negotiation tables as expressive Mercury lends its gift of gab to you in all professional matters. The best part? You won't have to write or memorize a script. Come in prepared, and you'll know exactly how much to share and what to hold back.

December 21: Jupiter-Saturn meetup (the Great Conjunction)

Expansive Jupiter and restrictive Saturn may be astrological opposites, but once every 19 years or so, they unite in the same sign. Today, this event—called The Great Conjunction—happens in your eleventh house of teamwork and technology. Your most visionary ideas could be catapulted skyward with the combination of Jupiter's enthusiasm and Saturn's hardscrabble integrity. Prepare for a wave of popularity and the opportunity to move the masses with your message and leadership.

December 23: Mars-Pluto square

Watch your temper—and a know-it-all tendency—today, because it could spark up without much warning. Your galactic guardian, impassioned Mars, locks into a tense square with inflammatory Pluto in your career corner, and your combativeness could alienate the wrong person. If diplomacy isn't an option, vent to a friend—or your journal!

December 25: Mercury-Uranus trine

Granted, not much work happens on Christmas Day, but this is a such a rare and brilliant alignment that you're certain to have some a-ha moments that you won't want to forget. If inspiration does hit, politely excuse yourself from the festivities to capture the main points on paper or in your Notes app. You don't have to act on the idea now. Just make sure you can remember enough to articulate it when you return from the holiday break. ✷

TAURUS
2020

Yearly Highlights

LOVE

Cupid takes you on an international tour in 2020, thanks to a posse of planets occupying your global ninth house. Single? Diversify your dating portfolio instead of sticking to the same old type. Coupled Bulls may explore unconventional arrangements, possibly living long-distance from each other for part of the year. Traveling and romance make happy bedfellows, so bring on the "baecations," and maybe a far-flung fling!

MONEY

Money may come to you in unexpected ways this year, thanks to a series of Gemini/Sagittarius eclipses waking up your financial axis. You could invest in real estate or pick a winning stock. With enterprising Jupiter's touring your startup sector, you may work remotely, score gigs as an independent contractor, or get your own indie biz off the ground. From March 21 to July 1, stable Saturn rises to Aquarius and your executive tenth house. Recruiters could call, or you may be tapped for a leadership role at your company. Balancing freedom and responsibility will be the challenge!

WELLNESS

Ah, do you feel that spring in your step? Robust Jupiter joins regenerative Pluto in Capricorn until December 19, boosting your vitality and powering up your athletic streak. Jump into a sports league or hiking club, especially if it means spending more time outdoors. Or turn yoga and meditation into a legit practice. With nervous Uranus spending its first full year in Taurus, moving around is essential to burning off stress. Detoxify your diet and consider a cleanse while Mars is retrograde in your twelfth house of healing from September 9 to November 13.

LEISURE

While you'll never stop supporting the ones you love, in 2020 someone else is going to have to be the rock. With your free-spirited ninth house lit by Jupiter, Saturn and Pluto throughout the year, you need room to roam and explore your solo interests—without playing caretaker or entertainment director. When Saturn darts into Aquarius from March 21 to July 1 (and again after December 17) you'll be more focused on your kin. Plan family vacations and visits back home during this spell. ✵

The AstroTwins' 2020 Horoscope

TAURUS

2020 HOROSCOPE

2020 Power Dates

✳

TAURUS NEW MOON
April 22 (10:25pm ET)

TAURUS FULL MOON
October 31 (10:49am ET)

SUN IN TAURUS
April 19–May 20

Check your rearview mirror, Taurus. Can you see your comfort zone fading to a distant blur? Ever since radical Uranus shifted into your sign on May 15, 2018, you've been propelled into uncharted terrain. On many days, the floor beneath your loafers feels more like quicksand than reclaimed wood. Even wilder? In order to ground yourself, you've had to stay in perpetual motion…at times, with no clear idea of your actual destination!

Keep a bag packed, Bull. With Uranus twerking through your sign until April 26, 2026, the reinvention tour wages on this year. And with a trio of planets—Jupiter, Saturn and Pluto—journeying through Capricorn and your nomadic ninth house in 2020, "citizen of the world" could become your new handle.

For a fixed earth sign, this irregular rhythm can feel mind-boggling, to say the least. You're the pillar amongst your peeps, the dependable rock. But try as you might to uphold traditions, your old way of life is steadily slipping away. The pressure to evolve may feel downright Darwinian at times—adapt or become a dinosaur. Fortunately, you are the tenacious *toro*, as capable of metamorphosing as the rest of us. But you'd better start adding spontaneity into your steadfast equation in 2020. Then, fasten your seatbelt and get ready for a wild and exhilarating ride!

With your enthusiastic and expansive ninth house lit, 2020's planets help you face your changing circumstances with a rare sense of enthusiasm… and, dare we say, *joie de vivre.* That might also mean scrapping your meticulous ten-year plan or cashing in on an investment before it's reached full maturity.

One Taurus we know is standing at this very crossroad. Twenty years ago, he rolled up the sleeves of his *guayabera* shirt and built an eco-chic hotel on an unpopulated strip of Mexican beach. Guided by his Venus-ruled aesthetics, an elegant ring of *cabañas* rose from the sand. With gleaming white stucco walls, thatched roofs, and ritual art gathered from Goa, India, his boutique BnB was a breathtaking vision against the backdrop of turquoise sea. When hurricanes struck each year, his Taurean persistence did not waver; he simply rebuilt. Loyal customers, warmed by his exceptional hospitality, returned each year for beachfront yoga and the artfully plated organic meals, often hand-served by our Taurus friend himself.

But in recent years, this best-kept secret of a beach town became Instagram famous. Noisy bars wedged in between serene healing centers, and $700 caftans crowded out the folksy embroidered textiles. Preserving the oasis-like sanctuary of his space has become our Taurus friend's newest challenge. He now finds himself questioning everything: Will the rustic charm of his *cabañas* be "enough" for the new waves of tourists—or must he cave and add luxury amenities that attract the celebutante sun worshippers? Is it time to cash out and start over on

a virgin coastline? He's clear that change is coming, but the details remain opaque.

Should you find yourself suspended between two worlds like our hotelier *amigo*, do not panic. With horizon-broadening Jupiter in Capricorn and your open-minded ninth house until December 19, you'll be shocked by your own versatility. This is the year to be a student of life, opening your mind to discoveries. Since Jupiter is the galactic gambler, your play-it-safe nature won't hold you back when it's time to leap. Risky moves you would never have considered in the past might seem sane and logical in 2020. Both Jupiter and Uranus have a teenage quality to them, and in 2020, you could feel as fearless (and frisky) as a 15-year-old!

Simultaneously, structure-obsessed Saturn and control-freak Pluto will travel alongside Jupiter in Capricorn, providing some semblance of a safety net. These powerhouse planets have been settled in Capricorn's realm for a while—Saturn since December 19, 2017, and Pluto since November 27, 2008. Fear not, Taurus, you haven't lost all touch with your common sense. Even if you do have moments where you just want to escape off the grid, status-conscious Saturn and Pluto won't let you give up all worldly possessions to follow a guru across the globe. (A three-month stint in an ashram, however, is not out of the question in 2020.)

It doesn't hurt that career-focused Saturn is heading to the top of your chart, activating your professional "true north." From March 21 to July 1, the ambitious planet darts into Aquarius and your tenth house for a quick warm-up before retreating into Capricorn and taking a final lap. This three-and-a-half month preview will get you thinking seriously about the direction of your future. And (huzzah!), since Saturn is naturally at home in the tenth house, this short spell will re-energize your planning powers, giving you one of the best windows of 2020 for getting a profitable mission off the ground.

When Saturn finally drops anchor in Aquarius from December 17, 2020, until March 7, 2023, you'll be ready to embrace the mantle of leadership once again. But will you play the role of the executive superstar, Taurus, or would signing your own paychecks be your cup of oolong? (Or maybe a mix of both?) As entrepreneurial Jupiter rises to Aquarius and joins Saturn in your tenth house this December 19, you may feel pulled in both directions.

Two days later, on the winter solstice, there will be an ultra-rare and exact alignment of Jupiter and Saturn at 0° Aquarius. This meetup, which only happens every 20 years, is called The Great Conjunction. Given that it's taking place in the most ambitious zone of your solar chart, you could make yet another "shocking" move near December 21, kicking off your Havaianas and stepping into a pair of power pumps. If you felt adrift with your career earlier in 2020, don't freak out. The Great Conjunction will help you harmonize the polarities of Jupiter's free-spiritedness and Saturn's demands for structure. In the meantime, your exploratory missions are the best possible form of research you can do this year. It's not often that your routine-driven sign is this liberated from the proverbial box. In 2020, trust that all your meandering has the potential to guide you into a fulfilling future. The more "purposefully uncomfortable" you can make yourself, the stronger and wiser you'll feel when the ball drops on 2021.

Your ruler, value-driven Venus, will also keep the coffers full in 2020, along with a new series of eclipses which falls on your financial axis. From April 3 to August 7, Venus shakes her moneymaker in Gemini and your second house of daily bread. Due to a retrograde from May 13 to June 25, Venus spends four times longer than average in this zone of your chart. The boost probably won't be enough to afford you a private island, but it will keep steady cash flowing in, which is music to your security-loving ears. (Especially while Jupiter and Uranus make you feel like a space cadet and interdimensional traveler for most of 2020.) Think outside the nine-to-five box, Bull. Two eclipses will jangle your eighth house of big money on June 5 and December 14, which could bring a fruitful sale of property, a deal that pays you in royalties, or a chance to be a ground floor investor in a savvy startup.

Since Venus is the ruler of love, she'll institute a firm "no romance without finance" policy this year. Single Bulls will have little tolerance for a Tinder date who doesn't reach for their wallet when the check comes (as an act of generosity as opposed to archaic gender roles). And if they have no plans for building a stable future, it's an instant "bye!" Between April and August, coupled Taureans could come into cash as a result of your S.O.'s good fortune, through their income, an inheritance or a mix of both. Serious talks about spending, saving and investing must be had in 2020. Fortunately, Venus is the cosmic diplomat, which makes it easier to discuss the "taboo" topic of money.

And should all the fast-moving energy of 2020 necessitate a major life change, courageous Mars has your back. The warrior planet will hold an extended pose in Aries and your twelfth house of healing, transitions and endings from June 27, 2020, to January 6, 2021. During the retrograde phase, which lasts from September 9 to November 13, you may need a time-out to grieve a transition. What's a fantasy and what's an illusion? You could spend time grappling with this question in the fall. Want to pen a poetic farewell? You'll be a regular Rumi in the second half of 2020. Just be careful not to let guilt overtake you! Mars in Aries hastens your departure. When it's time to move on, you simply must, Bull, or else you'll stagnate. Instead of thinking of this as the end, how about, "until we meet again?"

Uranus in Taurus: Transformation Station.
May 15, 2018 – April 26, 2026

Ever since radical disruptor Uranus started buzzing through your sign on May 15, 2018, the Chaos Theory has become an operating principle for your life. Gone is your desire for perfect order. You've accepted that "disturbances in the field" are essential to evolution and control is a myth.

Do you even recognize yourself? Probably not. This transformational spell comes once in a lifetime (or every 84 years), when Uranus pops into your sign for a portion of the decade. Try your best to enjoy the planet's seven-year sabbatical in Wonderland. When Uranus moves on to Gemini on April 26, 2026, you'll truly miss the unbound sense of liberation this rare transit brings.

In 2018 and 2019, Uranus bobbed back and forth between Aries and Taurus, a tumultuous tango that

made it harder to fully incorporate its innovative, enlivening rush. In 2020, the side-spinning planet is officially plugged into the Taurus grid, where it will generate a fast-moving current of power. Bulls born between April 22 to 30 will feel the strongest charge from Uranus' electrifying charge this year, as the planet travels between 2° and 10° of your sign, making contact with your natal Sun.

Exhilarating? Absolutely. But if you're still freaking out about it all, we're not surprised. Uranus is in "fall" in Taurus, which is its least comfortable position. No wonder you've earned a reputation for stubbornly resisting change! Taurus Sigmund Freud had his own theory on this paradox: "Freedom involves responsibility and most people are frightened of responsibility."

Maybe that's true, but as one of the zodiac's most industrious signs, you happen to love anything that involves responsibility. So why not embrace this liberation front as if it were your duty? An epic lifestyle shift could pluck you out of your comfortable existence in 2020. With innovative Uranus spinning through your first house of identity, you could radically change your appearance, shocking everyone with a purple pixie, a sleeve tattoo or a totally new partner on your arm!

Disruptor alert: Suddenly, you're no longer the traditionalist, but rather, the game-changing badass who shakes up the system. With activist Uranus firing up your idealism, you could become the face of a movement, like 15-year-old Taurus Alexandria Villaseñor. Every Friday in 2019, the determined teen would "strike" from school, sitting on a bench outside the U.N. to demand that world leaders address the climate crisis. At this time of writing, her organization Earth Uprising has helped fuel a

The AstroTwins' 2020 Horoscope

movement in over 47 countries, drawing attention from Barack Obama and other global luminaries.

As a tenacious Taurus, embracing radical change isn't necessarily part of your basic nature. But in 2020, the call for transformation will be too loud to ignore. Kicking back and taking the easy route? No thanks. Kabbalists refer to those unearned victories as "bread of shame." You'll struggle to accept or enjoy those kinds of wins because you didn't gain them on merit. Keep your silk sleeves rolled up, Bull, and hustle away on more complex missions. The struggle is real—and oh-so rewarding—in 2020!

Jupiter in Capricorn: Call of the wild.

December 2, 2019–December 19, 2020

Rise from repose, Taurus, and fix your gaze on greener pastures. In 2020, Jupiter, the planet of risk-taking, expansion and new horizons, treks into Capricorn and your worldly ninth house. Until December 19, no fence or ceiling can hold you—not when you're ready to charge off on a thrill-seeking mission! Growth will be your operative word as you embrace one of the most horizon-broadening years you've had in over a decade.

With your can-do ninth house activated by joyful Jupiter in Capricorn, happiness is more than an elusive goal—it's an essence you'll weave into your daily rituals and routines. In astrological lore, Capricorn is represented by the mythical Sea Goat, with the head of a satyr and the tail of a mermaid.

With daring Jupiter in this sign, you're sure to set some depth *and* height records for yourself.

In 2019, you were willing to make sacrifices if it meant supporting family or building a nest egg. In 2020, you'll have zero tolerance for stultifying circumstances. Determined to live your truth, there will be days when you'd sooner bail on everything you've built than limit your potential. But this is where you'll need to check your gut and the facts, so you don't become the proverbial destructive bull in the China shop.

Jupiter is in "fall" in Capricorn, which can be a tricky position to navigate. When you plunge into mystical pursuits, be sure to swim up to the surface for periodic reality checks. And when you ascend new mountain peaks, tie some trail markers as you go, so you can find your way back down to base camp. If you keep at least one hoof planted on terra firma, you won't go wrong. And even if you stumble here and there, this optimistic energy will help you quickly turn any "mistake" into a powerful lesson.

Jupiter is the global ambassador of the skies, and under 2020's nomadic influence, you could reside in more than just one zip code…or country code! Like the wise, ancient tortoise who carries her home on her back, embrace the concept of "Wherever I go, there I am." And if this quest happens to rack up frequent flier miles and passport stamps, all the better.

No matter your GPS coordinates, this is the year to bond intersectionally and diversify your social portfolio. Like a cultural ambassador, take it upon yourself to unite friends from all walks of life. Thanks to "one love" Uranus' tour through Taurus since May 2018, we're betting you've become BFFs with everyone from the hostess at your favorite wood-fired pizza joint to the investment banker you chatted up at the gym. They might never meet one another without your guiding hand—and impossible-to-resist dinner party invitations. Carpe diem! Rather than cleaving to societal conventions, in 2020, you'll thrill at the opportunity to witness your "Odd Squad" click.

When it comes to love, Jupiter in the ninth house opens your mind and heart. Fire up the Duolingo app and ditch those stubborn notions about who your "type" actually is. Cross-cultural dating, long-distance relationships and other unconventional arrangements are all on the table. You could enjoy some legendary "bae-cations" in 2020, so include your plus-one on journeys whenever possible.

Long-term relationships might take an unscripted turn for coupled Taureans, especially if independent pursuits lead you and your S.O. in dueling directions. One Bull babe we know is in the midst of this very scenario. Shortly after Uranus entered Taurus in 2018, she organized a three-month sabbatical with her husband and two grade-school-aged kids. In record time, she bonded with a group of incredible women, and was tan and radiant from spending 80 percent of her time in the fresh air. She even joined a musical circle that allowed expats to play alongside the indigenous locals.

Upon returning Stateside, she shocked her entire friend group by putting her manicured Craftsman on sale and announcing the build of a dream home in this enchanting, overseas town. This year, she'll enroll her kids in the area's school and give international living a whirl. Her husband, who works in tech, finagled a part-time remote office arrangement. He will travel back and forth as they explore this totally unprecedented family arrangement. For a play-by-the-rules Taurus, this is a huge deal. But for a change, she is following her heart instead of asking for other people's blessings. (Thanks, Jupiter and Uranus!)

> "This could be the year to apply for grad school, take up yoga teacher training or delve into personal growth."

Love where you live? That doesn't mean you'll be forced to stay put. Raise your hand when your boss asks for a representative to work a Vegas convention or oversee the opening of the London office for a month. You may also travel in the figurative sense in 2020, as the red-spotted planet revs up your thirst for knowledge. Both Jupiter and the ninth house are associated with higher education. This could be the year to apply for grad school, take up yoga teacher training, or delve into a personal growth curriculum.

With Jupiter the traveler in the mix, your studies could be incorporated into a retreat. A university that offers both live and online sessions will make it easier to cover tuition, since you won't be forced to quit your day job. Are you the student who has become the master? In 2020, you may develop your own unique curriculum to share your skills and put money in the bank.

Speaking of which, your entrepreneurial spirit will be stoked by Jupiter in Capricorn, an energy that isn't always so readily available to the steadfast, security-loving Bull. You prefer the consistency of a paycheck, but in 2020, you may realize that you're limiting your earning potential by playing it so safe. No need to quit your day job before you have another gig lined up, of course. (As if!) But do start developing that side hustle you keep buzzing about, be it a food truck or a 3D printing empire. Bonus: Under Jupiter's golden guidance, profits could roll in quickly. Hoping for more flexibility without sacrificing stability? Switching from employee to independent contractor might be your best bet. Sure, you'll spring for your own health insurance, but reclaiming your time could make the trade-off well worth it.

Got a podcast or a novel brewing in your brain? Both Jupiter and the ninth house rule publishing and broadcasting. 2020 is an amazing year to build a platform. With all the incredible tools available, from IGTV to print-on-demand books, getting your work into the world is easier than ever. Invest in a high-quality webcam and Bluetooth mic—and maybe a talented graphic designer or audio engineer to help with the final mix—and boom, you're in business! Don't feel pressured to monetize this, of course. What matters is that you're getting your message out to the world. When you speak your truth, you naturally attract fans and followers, especially with authentic and inspiring Jupiter spurring you on.

Jupiter's last sail through Capricorn was from December 18, 2007, to January 5, 2009. Flip back in your mental memoirs: The scene that plays out in 2020 may encapsulate similar storylines. Did you move to a new zip code, get a startup business going, publish your own blog?

With Jupiter fanning the flames of your indie spirit until December 19, you'll be feeling equally unbound. This surge of starry-eyed optimism might irk a few skeptics and haters, especially if they've always relied on you to be their rock. Trust that your enthusiasm will be contagious. Liberate yourself from obligation and live your best life!

Saturn-Pluto conjunction: No shortcuts to the top.
December 2019–February 2020 (exact on January 12)

While no one's clipping your wings in 2020, at times you'll fly with heavy cargo strapped to your back. You can thank sober Saturn and shadow-dancer Pluto for that. Throughout 2020, the two karma cops will accompany Jupiter on its tour through your philosophical ninth house.

You'll feel their weighty influence on January 12, when the two heavy-hitters unite at 22° Capricorn, a conjunction that only happens once every (approximately) 35 years. You may have to face some harsh truths in early 2020 or pay off debts you accrued due to hasty actions in 2018 and 2019. Don't dodge the responsibility! The sooner you deal—or hash out a settlement—the sooner you'll be free for good! Can you start your New Year off meditating on a mountaintop or gathered in circle with a Peruvian shaman? That would be pretty ideal, given all the hidden truths that could surface when Saturn meets Pluto on January 12.

84

Furtive Pluto, the planet that rules the unseen, has been shacked up in Capricorn since November 27, 2008. Over the past decade-plus, you've traded your hardcore realism for a more metaphysical perspective—perhaps even with a surprising side of woo! Your formerly 3D world has a few more dimensions to it since the mystical planet began its 16-year trek through your ninth house. Self-development studies may have transformed your outlook on life since 2008, raising your emotional intelligence to a higher "EQ."

Saturn first moved into Capricorn, its home sign, on December 19, 2017. Since then, your daring schemes have been checked by the ringed taskmaster's stern policies. While Uranus in Taurus started revving up your gambling instincts in May 2018, Saturn's been running interference all the while, insisting that you pay your dues. That's not to say you haven't had any victories. Take Taurus rapper Travis Scott, who has collaborated with everyone from Drake to Stevie Wonder, all while keeping billionaire makeup mogul and baby-mama Kylie Jenner at his side. Or your signmate Jojo Siwa, whose platinum blonde side-pony and unflappable cheer catapulted her from Dance Moms reality star to YouTube luminary. Like these hardworking Bulls, you've undoubtedly burned your share of midnight oil to achieve every win.

Did you take shortcuts or get pulled into a "get rich quick" scheme along the way? We hope not! With Sgt. Saturn overseeing affairs, rash actions hit you hard in the cryptocurrency account…not to mention your pride. (Case in point, former U.S. E.P.A. Chief, Taurus Scott Pruitt, whose private plane rides and $43K soundproof office got him booted unceremoniously from the cabinet.) Or maybe you simply got swept up in a guru's sales pitch, handing over your power and some hard-earned "tuition" to a compelling Svengali who led you down the garden path. Whatever the case, Bull, the tide is turning in 2020. These teachable moments are part of the journey to mastery. Humble yourself and integrate what you learned from your mistakes. If you do, you'll turn any setbacks into a springboard for success.

As a down-to-earth Taurus, you have a mechanical mind. You like to understand how things operate, why they exist, and what functionality they serve. That linear thinking will come in handy near January 12, thanks to Saturn's pragmatic influence. But merged with shadowy, esoteric Pluto, don't expect to find any easy answers. The rare Saturn-Pluto conjunction brings eye-opening insights about the challenges you're facing in life. These won't be easy to digest! Keep supportive sounding boards close on January 12! With outspoken Jupiter hovering nearby, you will need to talk it all out—extensively! You might even enlist a coach or therapist to help you make sense of the jumbled thoughts that come pouring out.

While you're at it, open up a voice memo and hit record. Your "processing" will contain some serious wisdom, Taurus, even if it feels nonsensical in the first quarter of 2020. Listen back to that footage a little later in the year, especially when Saturn takes a hiatus from Capricorn from March 21 to July 1. You could write about your discoveries, or use them as the underpinnings of a curriculum, documentary or some other serious work!

     The AstroTwins' 2020 Horoscope

Jupiter-Pluto conjunction: Seeking wisdom.
April 4, June 30, November 12

Once Pluto passes through the eye of Saturn's needle this January 12, the lessons get a lot easier—and dare we say it, downright enjoyable! On April 4, June 30 and November 12, bright spirit Jupiter will make three exact connections to the shadowy dwarf planet. Like a klieg light shining into a dark cave, you'll have some major epiphanies as you ponder life's bigger questions.

With both planets parked in earthy Capricorn, your mind may ruminate on larger issues, like, *Why have we designed a world economy that's so harmful to Earth's natural resources? What can we do to stop the abuses of power?* Or, on a more personal level, *Why is this all happening to me?* But what's most important to ask yourself is, *What am I meant to learn from this?* Shift from complaining to curiosity and the breakthrough insights will roll in.

A master teacher could appear to Sherpa you along this introspective journey. You might seek out a spiritual community or philosophical school that offers a mind-expanding curriculum, the kind that probably isn't taught in universities. The ninth house favors experiential learning: This is the year to travel (alone, even!) to an energetic vortex like Sedona or Maui. You might sign up for an intensive teacher training at a metaphysical retreat center, or volunteer at a utopian festival like Burning Man. The Jupiter-Pluto conjunctions are a lot like vision quests, especially on April 4 and November 12, while both planets are in direct (forward) motion.

During the second conjunction on June 30, Jupiter and Pluto will both be retrograde. For your summer vacation, how about revisiting a place that has served as a powerful portal for your development in the past? You could discover new meaning on this follow-up visit, especially if you combine the journey with some sort of self-development work.

Pluto is associated with sexuality, particularly the parts of your erotic nature that you may hide… or only reveal behind closed doors. Jupiter's truth-telling presence could expose your buried desires and help you get real about what turns you on. You may feel bolder and more experimental than ever near these three dates. Will your lusty moves leave jaws on the ground? Possibly so! But if your libido's been slower than a lazy river, you'll be determined to bring a fresh current into the mix, even if that causes temporary turmoil with your partner. Keep a respectable privacy policy in place, however, since reporting your escapades to your friends could violate trust with your lover.

Venus & Mars Retrograde: Relationship review.
Venus Retrograde: May 14 – June 25

Mars Retrograde: September 10 – November 13

Venus and Mars, the legendary love planets, both undergo a retrograde cycle in 2020. These reverse commutes can be as nostalgic as they are nerve-wracking, as old chapters reopen and paramours from your past reappear. Reuniting with a childhood sweetheart can be a touching affair, especially if wonky timing was the only thing keeping you apart. Running into your ex and their new partner at a music festival? You could do without that. Since Venus is your ruling planet, her backspins tend to affect you more than the other zodiac signs. Highlight May 13 to June 25 on the calendar. While your galactic guardian retreats through Gemini, you'll need to chill and be still instead of reacting to every disruption in the field.

Venus first cruises into Gemini on April 3, extending a "buffer zone" prior to the May 13 retrograde. When the backspin ends on June 25, the love planet will hang out in the sign of the Twins until August 7, giving you an integration period to make sense of any changes that arise. That means Venus will hover in Gemini for one-third of 2020, which is also four times longer than its usual lap through a single sign.

What's a Taurus to do? For starters, light the tea candles and set your Spotify to the John Legend station. Gemini rules your sensual (but sensible) second house, which is the part of the zodiac wheel that's naturally associated with your sign. Under this slow-jamming spell, you'll catch an early case of spring fever. Revel in it! And not just because you love all night sex-a-thons and gourmet breakfast in bed. Before Venus pivots on May 13, you want to flood your "emotional bank account" with as much feel-good energy as possible. Get all those "Where is this relationship going?" conversations hashed out prior to that date, while you're in a more

> **"You'll catch an early case of spring fever. Revel in it!"**

levelheaded space. Insecurities could snowball quickly after that, which is not a good look.

When Venus shifts in reverse, abandonment issues may flare. Instinctually, you'll feel like clutching on to your amour. But don't! Being smothering and needy will only push bae away. Should the "You're going to leave me!" fears strike, enlist levelheaded counsel to talk you down from the tree. This will be a whole lot more effective than making teary demands for reassurance. Stubbornness and righteousness could also interrupt your peaceful coexistence between May 13 and June 25. You'll have to try harder than usual to be a better listener, even if you have smoke pouring out of your ears during the talk.

If you're the rare Taurus who backs down too quickly from a fight, this retrograde might just fortify your backbone. While Venus is in verbose Gemini, you'll have the debating skills of a corporate defense attorney and the diplomacy of a U.N. ambassador. But all politeness goes out the window during the retrograde, and you'll need to temper your aggression. The goal is to assert yourself, not to rage on people you love.

This is also a crucial moment to review your finances. Have you been so swept away in a fairy tale that you've forgotten to keep your glass slippers on solid ground? (And, uh, how much did you spend on those clear heels anyway?) While Venus backs up through Gemini and your sensible second house, dial down the splurges, and devise tricks to get the books back to black. It's fine to be fanciful, sensual and decadent, but in 2020, you might have to "summer" on a budget.

Above all, remember this: While you can't control what other people say and do, you can take command of your own life. Step away from the complainers and tea spillers and surround yourself with uplifting friends. Eat clean, get eight hours of beauty (and sanity) sleep nightly, drink two glasses of water for every mug of coffee you down. Move your body daily and make sure you break a serious sweat at least three times a week. If others want to act the fool, well, that's their business. Buffer yourself against their shenanigans by taking excellent care of yourself.

A month after Venus corrects course, Mars starts perfecting his backstroke through Aries and your twelfth house of transitions. From September 9 to November 13, the red planet's retrograde churns up buried anger and resentment. Did you rush to make peace with someone who did you wrong? Fail to put up solid boundaries with an energy vampire? The retrograde will force you to rectify that. Don't stuff down your anger, but do find a healthy outlet for release, like the boxing gym, yoga shala or even a private karaoke room where you can belt out fierce ballads without having to share the mic.

Like Venus, Mars will also spend an extended time in one sign, holding its warrior pose in Aries from June 27, 2020, to January 6, 2021. During this entire cycle, you may find yourself sorting through the past, figuring out what should stay and what should go. With Mars in fearless Aries and your twelfth house of transitions, you could finally muster the courage to close an expired chapter of your life. Keep the tissues handy and allow yourself to grieve. Sob, scream, punch a pillow, whatever it takes to process those feelings.

During the intensified Mars retrograde, you can achieve some deep regeneration. Any kind of therapeutic treatment will be favored, so if you've been waiting for a "sign" to work with a holistic practitioner or counselor, this is it. In this highly receptive state, you might have stunning results with hypnotherapy, shamanic journeying or energy work. Conversely, if you've been doing all that and more and have hit a plateau, take a time out. Immerse yourself in nature and art instead, and let time do its bit with this healing.

Saturn in Aquarius: Rise through the ranks.
March 21–July 1, December 17, 2020–March 7, 2023

Ambition ablaze! From March 21 to July 1, success-obsessed Saturn shifts into Aquarius, leading a homecoming parade through your aspirational tenth house, its natural domain. Then, on December 17, the ringed mogul makes Aquarius its long-term residence until March 7, 2023. This should be music to your security-loving ears, and yes, your bank account. As much as you'll enjoy the free-flowing ninth house transits of 2020, you could be feeling a little twitchy about the lack of a solid plan. When Saturn rises to the top of your chart (the tenth house), as it does every 29.5 years, you won't merely discover your true north. You'll also be fixated on turning it into a profitable mission.

With slow-and-steady Saturn in your tenth house, you don't have to sprint to the executive suite. Instead, ascend toward your throne in a regimented way. Aquarius is the sign of innovation, community and large organizations. With Saturn dropping anchor here, you may spend 2020 researching developments in technology. What are the industry standards in your field, and what do trend forecasters predict for the future? Knowledge is power, Taurus.

When Saturn parks in Aquarius, rolling up your sleeves and hustling won't be enough to raise the bar. Aquarius is the sign of community, underscoring the old chestnut that it's all about who you know. Call in the pros! Align yourself with experts who have legit credentials under their belts. Entrepreneurial Bulls should take the emotion out of your hiring (and firing) practices—yes, even if you work at a family-owned firm. Your cousin Sheila was a fine bookkeeper in 2019. In 2020, aim higher. Either send her to accounting school, or upgrade to a legit CTA who understands tax laws and can advise on high-level financial decisions.

Ready to soar through the ranks at your day job? Even if you're the obvious next-in-line for a promotion, Saturn in Aquarius will still put you through paces. The interviewing and HR process could be aggravatingly slow. Don't lose your determination! Greet every challenge with humility and confidence. Sure, your work speaks for itself, but you will still have to speak up for yourself and be proactive. Organize and polish your professional materials. At a moment's notice, be ready to prove that you're the perfect candidate for the gig—even if that means stepping away from a party to help your boss out of a jam.

The Great Conjunction: Jupiter & Saturn unite.
December 21

Even if #MogulMode escapes you while Saturn makes its first lap through Aquarius from March 21 to July 1, by the time December 17 rolls around you'll be a full-on contender in the game of thrones. But wait, there's more! On December 19, enterprising Jupiter joins Saturn in Aquarius, blessing you with the Midas touch for a full year—until December 29, 2021, to be exact.

On December 21, 2020—the Winter Solstice—Jupiter and Saturn will make an exact connection in the skies, a union that only happens once every 20 years. Astrologers refer to the power-pairing of expansive Jupiter and restrictive Saturn as The Great Conjunction. Although these planets are basically polar opposites, their combined energies bring the loftiest visions into tangible form. And since they are conjoining in your career-driven tenth house (at 0° Aquarius), you could wrap 2020 with a fedora full of feathers!

Do your gift shopping early this year, Taurus. With the Great Conjunction arriving just before Christmas, professional progress could interrupt plans for a chill holiday celebration. You'll be too busy burning the midnight oil to toss the yule logs on the fire. Or strike a compromise and work remotely under the twinkling   lights.

With worldly Jupiter accompanying Saturn through your ambitious tenth house for a year, you could rack up frequent flier miles as a business traveler. Or, you may find gainful employment at an international firm, interfacing via webcam with colleagues in different time zones. Since Jupiter rules higher education, you might spend the holiday break filling out college applications or applying to a specialized training that will bring your skills up to snuff for this new decade.

The tenth house rules men and fathers. With Jupiter refreshing your perspective and Saturn bringing the wisdom of maturity, you could heal some old pain around your dad—or the cultural impact of "toxic masculinity." This is also a call to celebrate the "divine masculine," which is the healthy expression of male energy that doesn't include domination, ego or force. As the year winds down, surround yourself with men you admire and respect. They'll be among your greatest allies in 2021!

When it comes to love, experimental Jupiter and serious Saturn are quite the odd couple. Single? Fire up the dating apps, as Aquarius is the sign associated with technology. Be patient with the process. You might have to weather a few agonizing coffee dates before you hit the *right* right swipe. Attached? As you snuggle under the mistletoe, begin discussions about the future. Are your goals aligned? Is there an adventure on your shared bucket list that you've always wanted to pursue? It might involve traveling, taking a sensuality workshop or even starting a business together. Explore!

Cancer/Capricorn Eclipses: Find your kindred spirits.
January 10, June 21, July 5

Your social life continues to expand in intriguing ways, as scene-shifting eclipses make landfall on the Cancer/Capricorn axis for the third year in a row. Since July 2018, these lunar lifts have made you a lot more vocal and fearless in your self-expression. But you've also learned important lessons about not tweeting every unpolished thought or 'gramming all your #iwokeuplikethis selfies.

A final trio of Cancer/Capricorn eclipses continues to crystallize those lessons in 2020. On January 10, the lunar (full moon) eclipse in Cancer and your cooperative, communicative third house confirms who your kindred spirits really are. If you've tested the waters successfully on several projects, your dynamic duo could morph into an official alliance. Since the third house rules neighborhood activity, you may adopt a new role in your zip code, maybe as the chair of a community board or as a local politician. A writing or broadcasting project could become more than just a hobby. Stay busy in early 2020 by enrolling in workshops—or even teaching a class!

On June 21, the final Cancer eclipse in the series—a new moon solar eclipse—could make you a solid fixture on the community scene. Although you probably didn't expect to step into such a prominent role, your planning powers make you a natural choice as an organizer. You might also realize that you've outgrown some of your hanging buddies. If so, branch out! This eclipse will reward your exploration, bringing a fresh crop of BFF-grade homies into your world.

Finally, a full moon (lunar) eclipse in Capricorn and your ninth house of travel and expansion will wrap up this series of lunations on July 5. Maybe it's time to embrace the concept of multi-city living, Bull. A "home away from home" could be more than just a favorite place to visit. Perhaps it's time to invest in a pied-a-terre or to rent an Airbnb for few months to test the relocation potential of a second city. If you're stuck in a groove, this eclipse will spur you to make a change, and in a big, bold way, like applying to grad school or taking a job on the opposite coast. Progress unleashes at a galloping pace, and once you've set your mind to it, there will be no turning back!

Since the ninth house is nakedly honest, the July 5 lunar eclipse could bring a powerful moment of truth. While it won't be easy to bare your soul, you need to know where people stand. Keep it real, even if others insist on putting on airs. Take a stand for diversity. You know that "people are people," but the fearful minds in your midst might still be clinging to ridiculous stereotypes. Show them that we can all get along. You could become a powerful agent of change in the process, healing age-old divides and building bridges.

Gemini/Sagittarius Eclipses: Money, sex, power.
June 5, November 30, December 14

On June 5, a new group of security-focused eclipses starts up on the Gemini/Sagittarius axis, igniting your second and eighth houses of security and sensuality until December 4, 2021. During this 18-month cycle, you'll reform your approach to money management—and you'll bring sexy back in surprising ways.

In 2020, three eclipses will land here, beginning with the June 5 lunar eclipse in Sagittarius and your eighth house of merging, sex and shared resources. Nothing light and fluffy here, Taurus! If you've invested (or co-invested) wisely, this supercharged full moon could bring a windfall, like the sale of property or a large royalty check. Since eclipses always yield a modicum of surprise—and an accelerated timeline—negotiations could be fraught with "extra-ness," like bureaucratic riders and clauses.

Intimate relationships will be thrown in the spotlight near June 5, and surprises could emerge. Maybe an antique diamond engagement ring will be delivered in your tiramisu. But your partner may drop a jarring revelation on you, leaving you shook. As the 12-Steppers say, "You're only as sick as your secrets." If the June 5 eclipse throws your steady relationship a curveball, it will be a blessing in disguise. Maybe you've slipped into old-marrieds mode, forgetting to stoke the erotic fire of your bond.

Esther Perel's *Mating in Captivity* could be essential reading for you in 2020. As the Belgian modern relationships expert advises, "Love rests on two pillars: surrender and autonomy. Our need for togetherness exists alongside our need for separateness." Breathing room is a good thing, Bull! If you've been trying fruitlessly to turn a bad romance into a happily-ever-after (or a frenemy into a BFF), the June 5 eclipse sweeps in like an

The AstroTwins' 2020 Horoscope

intervention coach to break it off for good. Sob into that pint of Ben and Jerry's if you must, but block their number before you lose your resolve!

On December 14, the solar (new moon) eclipse in Sagittarius reveals new ways to thrive cooperatively. Pool funds for a shared investment, like a two-bedroom rental property or an original work from an up-and-coming artist. When it comes to love, you can make all the lists and "relationship requirements documents" in the world. But you might just rip them to shreds mid-December when the eclipse reveals a superior plan to the one you concocted. And, ooh la la, Taurus! A mistletoe moment could rock your world, illuminating a hidden crush—or a surprise to celebrate with your S.O. like a pregnancy or two tickets to spend NYE in Fiji.

Only one of these eclipses, a lunar (full moon) event on November 30, falls in Gemini. This one activates your second house of income and daily routines. Out of the blue, a recruiter could message you with a job offer, or you might turn your passion for knotting macramé wall pieces into a holiday gifting side hustle. The second house rules self-worth and value, and events can transpire that force you to advocate for yourself. Your sign rules the throat, so use your powerful voice, Taurus. If you don't speak up for what you deserve, who will? ✳

January

JANUARY: LOVE HOTSPOTS

January 3-February 16: Mars in Sagittarius

Call in those intimate and erotic vibes! Lusty Mars blasts into your eighth house of sex and permabonding for the first time in two years. If things have been a little cool around the Bullpen, this could be exactly the temperature reset you've been hoping for. Enjoy the sizzle but note that the red planet can also heat up jealousy and possessiveness.

January 13-February 7: Venus in Pisces

As upbeat Venus makes her annual romp through your free-spirited eleventh house, you're encouraged to take things at a casual pace (if you're unattached) and enjoy checking out your options. Under these social vibes, couples will enjoy hanging with your separate crews, or in a mixed group setting, instead of forcing any intentionally romantic encounters.

January 26: Venus-Mars square

You might feel at cross-purposes under this confusing face-off of the love planets. Venus is trying to keep things light and breezy, but Mars is playing for keeps. If you really can't call it, ease off the throttle and let things unfold naturally. Pro tip: Don't push it, and definitely don't try to control it!

January 27: Venus-Neptune meetup

Keeping a certain relationship platonic may be a tough line to toe as amorous Venus hooks up with quixotic Neptune in your friendship corner. Fantasy wins out over realism, and you could surprise *both* of you with the feelings that well up today. Pisces and your eleventh house also rule the digital universe, meaning a new dating app could be the pathway to true romance!

JANUARY: CAREER HOTSPOTS

January 2: Mercury-Jupiter meetup

When communicator Mercury aligns with outspoken Jupiter in your truth-telling ninth house, you can't help but be direct and honest. And why not be? Sharing from heart is the best way to make an exciting idea go viral.

January 3-February 16: Mars in Sagittarius

As the action planet fires up your eighth house of wealth, investments and joint ventures, you may be ready to make a big financial or business move. While things could happen at light-speed, they might also come with a side of competitiveness or resentment. Talk things out and be extra transparent with partners. You don't want to watch

The AstroTwins' 2020 Horoscope

a potentially good thing tank because you can't agree about control or money.

January 10: Cancer full moon (lunar eclipse)

If you need to clear the air or have been waiting for the right moment to share an exciting idea with a potential collaborator, this full moon/lunar eclipse could be your moment. Full moons bring things to completion and signal turning points, so you might get the answer you've been waiting for in the next two weeks—prime "manifesting" time for this lunation.

January 10: Uranus retrograde ends

Forward! Unstable Uranus ends a five-month backspin through Taurus that's been disrupting your personal projects and initiatives since August 11, 2019. Dust off a trailblazing idea that got relegated to the back burner. Then, assume your role as the captain of this thrilling voyage!

January 12: Mercury-Saturn meetup

This planetary pairing urges you to think before you speak today. With restrained Saturn in cahoots with the communication planet, your verbal skills will not fail you. Don't let the details trip you up. Just explain the big picture and what you're proposing—playing up what others stand to gain—and they'll be queuing up to sign on!

January 12: Mercury-Pluto meetup

Your mind is racing about 100 miles ahead of everyone else's, but patience, Bull. Let people catch up to you and be ready to hit 'em with your sharpest elevator pitch the minute they do. Score!

January 13: Saturn-Pluto-Sun meetup

What a huge moment! Structured Saturn and transformational Pluto make their once-every-35-years conjunction, and the bold Sun will ping both planets today, too. Talk about a power surge, Taurus. With all three luminaries in Capricorn and your visionary ninth house, you could break through to a new level of power and status. Stay humble, and you might receive priceless advice from an industry insider or entrepreneurial pioneer. Under this once-a-year merger of the radiant Sun and disciplined Saturn in your visionary zone, you can test the practicality of a business idea. If it looks solid, you could earn a rep as a trailblazer in your field. Meanwhile, the annual mashup of the creative Sun and game-changing Pluto helps you peer beyond the obvious to catch a long-sighted glimpse of what's possible. A powerful person may be intrigued by your ideas, but get them to sign a nondisclosure agreement first. (It's your intellectual property. If they're professional, they'll understand.) Play your cards right, and this could open doors to a prestigious opportunity.

January 16-February 3: Mercury in Aquarius

Speak up, Taurus! Over the next three weeks, mental Mercury will soar through your tenth house of career ambition, helping you analyze a big move you want to make or propose. During this high-profile transit, don't keep your innovative ideas to yourself. But take the necessary time to research and polish your plan before delivering it to the decision makers.

January 18: Mercury-Uranus square

You're not generally a rule-breaker, Bull, but as the saying goes, they were made to be broken! And today, when messenger Mercury faces off with disruptor Uranus, you won't have the patience to wait for permission to test-drive some of your big ideas. You can always explain yourself later when (and if) they catch up.

January 23: Sun-Uranus square

You're raring to get going on an initiative, but check the pulse of the room first. Under this erratic starmap, you might butt up against someone's outsized ego today. Don't take the bait. Focus on what you can do, and then let them crash and burn without you on board.

January 24: Aquarius new moon
Chinese Year of the Metal Rat

Career goals: check! This annual new moon powers up your professional zone and helps you map out a grand plan for your brilliant future! Work backward: Where do you want to be by the corresponding full moon on August 3? Change starts with your vision, and the clearer you get about that now, the richer opportunities you'll set yourself up for. This is an auspicious day to send out resumes or follow up with promising leads. Today also kicks off the Chinese Year of the Metal Rat, and as the first animal of this modality's 12-year cycle, the Rat bodes well for all well-thought-out new beginnings.

January 28: Mars-Neptune square

Keep a few cards close to your vest today, especially if you sense that someone might be looking to take advantage of *your* hard work. How well do you know that colleague who's always buzzing around your desk? Before you sign on any dotted lines, thoroughly research the situation.

February

FEBRUARY: LOVE HOTSPOTS

February 7-March 4: Venus in Aries

As love planet Venus plunges into your twelfth house of fantasy, you could easily be swept off your feet. While you adore getting lost in enchanting daydreams, at least *try* to be realistic about this person's prospect. In an LTR? Be more vulnerable, receptive and supportive during this sensitive annual transit.

February 9: Leo full moon

You won't be able to keep a lid on powerful emotions that gush up under today's full moon in your sensitive and domestic fourth house. Just try not to overwhelm anyone with your enthusiastic "sharing." An important female could figure prominently in the day's events. For some Bulls, news of a pregnancy, change of residence or another major personal life transition might be in the cards.

February 16-March 30: Mars in Capricorn

Lusty Mars returns to your adventurous ninth house after a two-year hiatus, putting the "lust" in "wanderlust." If you're single, these next six weeks should dangle some exciting prospects, both at home and away. Cross-cultural attractions or long-distance chemistry might heat up. Couples can "feel the burn" of that amplified passion by traveling or exploring new interests together.

February 23: Venus-Jupiter square

With Jupiter in your truth-telling sector, you're eager to set the record straight. But thanks to its tense square with love planet Venus in your hazy twelfth house today, things might not come out the way you intend. You may not realize that your emotional investment is causing you to overstate your feelings—or someone else's role in the situation. Best idea? Think on this a little longer and wait another day or two to have *that* conversation.

February 28: Venus-Pluto square

Under this eye-opening clash, you may be forced to see someone for who they truly are, not who you want them to be. If you've put them up on a pedestal, cut through the illusions. When it comes to dating, keep your skepticism intact and make people earn your respect!

FEBRUARY: CAREER HOTSPOTS

February 3-March 4: Mercury in Pisces

Mercury will activate group ventures as it cruises through your eleventh house of teamwork and technology for an extra-long stay, as it will be retrograde from February 16 to March 9. Don't get too frustrated if initiatives you begin this month stall or even seem to vaporize. The solid ones *will* resurface or pick up speed at the end of March.

February 16-March 9: Mercury retrograde

Just when you thought you were getting an exciting project off the ground, the messenger planet goes and turns retrograde. You know the drill: Hurry up and wait! From now until March 4, when it's back-spinning through Pisces and your collaborative zone, you'll likely experience a raft of delays, miscommunications and technological glitches.

(From March 4 until March 16, it'll disrupt things in your career corner.) Since you can't micromanage things outside your control, use this time to review your work, research more deeply and reconnect to people you've lost touch with.

February 16-March 30: Mars in Capricorn

You're eager to expand over the coming six weeks, and lucky for you, the universe (or at least the red planet) has your back! Go ahead and take a leap of faith. As ambitious Mars sails through your ninth house of growth, your priorities may involve travel, study or being part of a stimulating startup. Push yourself to work outside your comfort zone. Should a long-distance opportunity in another time zone fall into your lap, get an inflatable pillow and stock up on melatonin.

February 21: Mars-Uranus trine

Fortune favors the bold, and with this planetary pairing of red-hot Mars and anything-goes Uranus in your sign, you'll be a force to be reckoned with.

February 23: Pisces new moon

This once-a-year reboot in your eleventh house of teamwork and technology gets the creative juices flowing! If you know you want to do something but you're not sure exactly what it looks like, take it to the hivemind. Talking it through with someone who's done something similar—or with a business coach—can help you get the ball rolling.

March

MARCH: LOVE HOTSPOTS

March 3: Venus-Saturn square

A little fantasy goes a long way, so set some limits with your daydreaming! Your ruling planet, amorous Venus, is sailing through your misty-eyed twelfth house, which can send you off to Cloud Nine. But today's reality-checking square from restrained Saturn may pull you right back down to *terra firma*. Keep those rose-colored glasses off your face and deal with the actual person who's right in front of you.

March 4-April 3: Venus in Taurus

You can look forward to a magical, magnetic four weeks as your planetary protector, charming Venus, shimmies through your sensual sign. You'll feel beautiful and flirty again, and as a result, you'll effortlessly earn official head-turner status. Whether you're single or attached, if you want your desires to be met, let them be known!

March 8: Venus-Uranus meetup

If you've been hoping for a change in your romantic status, your prayers could be answered under today's curveball-throwing mashup. Singles can meet someone with potential; and a wobbly union could resolve itself one way or another. If you're actually happy with the status quo, you might want to go to great lengths to keep the peace since there's no telling what disruptor Uranus might do when it makes its annual collision with the love planet.

March 9: Virgo full moon

Love wins! This annual lusty lunation in your fifth house of glamour and *amour* can do wonders for your romantic life, regardless of your current relationship situation. Take the lead and let someone know exactly how you feel. If there's no one to share that news with, get out and flex your flirting muscles. These next two weeks are prime time for erotic manifesting!

March 24: Aries new moon

The only Aries new moon of 2020 may stir things up in your twelfth house of healing, release and transitions over the next two weeks. It's not easy for your resolute sign to let go of things (and especially people), but this once-a-year new moon of fresh starts is the perfect opportunity to move on from something that's been holding you back. Release with love and compassion, then get ready to blast into your exciting new chapter!

March 27: Venus-Jupiter trine

Under this grounded, earthy alignment of romantic Venus in your sign and lucky Jupiter, take a chance on love! Things could definitely go your way. This sweet sync-up is also a perfect time to compliment or thank someone you care about—no strings attached.

March 28: Venus-Pluto trine

Be bold! Even if part of you is holding back a little, this empowering planetary pairing supports you in expressing your true feelings. And if you'd like to push things a little further, faster—lean in to the powers of transformational Pluto. Single? See what happens if you put your desires out there. You could have an appealing taker!

The AstroTwins' 2020 Horoscope

MARCH: CAREER HOTSPOTS

March 4-16: Mercury in Aquarius

Today, as clever Mercury blasts into innovative Aquarius and your career-oriented tenth house, you'll be a Bull on a mission! For the next two weeks, you'll accomplish more by focusing on your goals and embarking on a concrete plan of action. Recruit the right colleagues and there's no telling what you might produce!

March 16-April 10: Mercury in Pisces

Mercury begins its second visit to your eleventh house of teamwork and technology after briefly retrograding out of it earlier in the month. Now that it's back, you can pick up where you left off. Finish an exciting future-forward project and send it out into the wider world.

March 20: Mars-Jupiter meetup

This mashup is perfect for taking a bold risk on an entrepreneurial venture or getting some advanced training in your field. With confident Mars and optimistic Jupiter pooling their resources in this expansive and candid zone, you could pull off a major coup simply by sharing your unabashed opinions with a decisionmaker.

March 21-July 1: Saturn in Aquarius

For the first time since 1991, the planet of solid foundations, Saturn, returns to Aquarius and your professional tenth house, kicking off a new three-year cycle. This is the first phase of the transit—Saturn will retrograde back into Capricorn and your ninth house for a few months—but plans you start working on this spring will bear fruit between now and March 7, 2023. This is the chance you've been waiting for to restructure and revamp your career trajectory and prepare yourself for the really

big leagues. Don't wilt at the inevitable tests and challenges that will crop up; they're designed to make you stronger and more resilient!

March 23: Mars-Pluto meetup

Under this intensifying one-day transit, things could spiral out of control at work, so do your best to slow things down to a more manageable pace. Because intense emotions might arise among your teammates, be prepared to handle irrationally jealous or competitive people. Have a plan to redirect the crew if you can't get them back to a shared vision.

March 30-May 13: Mars in Aquarius

Today kicks off a new chapter in your professional life, one in which you have the energy and motivation to initiate something really big over the coming months. And the universe will meet you halfway by dangling some juicy opportunities! This is not the time to slow down or pull a disappearing act. People will be taking notice of you, and you want to give 'em something to talk about!

March 31: Mars-Saturn meetup

Your feet may not know whether to hit the gas or pump the brakes under this bewildering mashup of energizing Mars and cautious Saturn in your professional corner. Since you won't be able to predict what'll come at you, try to pace yourself to conserve your energy. Frustrating as it may feel at times, if you can find the perfect combination of this stop-start energy, you could hit a new milestone!

April

April 3-August 7: Venus in Gemini

Upgrade? Yes, please! As amorous Venus commences her annual visit to your luxurious second house, enhance any aspects of your lifestyle where you've been cutting corners, especially on dates and in your boudoir. But no need to do anything rash. The love planet will be retrograde from May 13 to June 25, and as a result, will enjoy an extra-long time in this realm. Slowly but surely add some luxe touches that will make you feel (even) more beautiful, sophisticated and pampered. Single? Boost your game by frequenting more "upscale" social spots.

April 4: Venus-Saturn trine

Stability can be sexy! Don't believe it? Just wait for this future-focused alignment of the love planet and "playing-for-keeps" Saturn in two of your most grounded houses. It's a good day to talk about where things are going, but…*tranquilo*! If this is meant to last, you don't need to push it along. Single? Don't rule out a slightly older prospect or a responsible person you might have (prematurely) written off as boring.

April 10-27: Mercury in Aries

Go on and utter those sweet nothings! With talkative Mercury in your surrendered twelfth house, sharing a fantasy and speaking with compassion are the order of the day. Let yourself be vulnerable and tell them how you really feel.

April 3: Mercury-Neptune meetup

Teamwork *can* make the dream work! Several brilliant ideas will come out of collaborative brainstorming sessions today, but don't get so carried away by the exuberant energy that you overlook obvious problems. Stay present in the moment, taking good notes; you can run them through the reality filter later.

April 4: Jupiter-Pluto meetup

At this once-every-13-years alignment between visionary Jupiter and power-seeking Pluto, you can suddenly imagine limitless possibilities becoming yours. Break out of any confines and blast past barriers. This rare duo in your ninth house of travel, entrepreneurship and study could find you doing business long-distance, launching a startup or even returning to school. What will bring the biggest transformation, Taurus? Explore there. This is the first of three Jupiter-Pluto conjunctions in 2020; the next ones will be on June 30 and November 12.

April 7: Libra full moon

This once-a-year lunation in your house of hard work and organization gives you the focus and the drive to tackle a major project that will ultimately make your work life more efficient. But in the meantime, you've got to get through a ton of small stuff before you can tackle the bigger aspect. Today, come up with a master plan, and slowly but surely plow through it over the coming few weeks.

April 7: Mars-Uranus square

This rare clash between two of the most stress-inducing planets can bring a work situation to a head. While you'll be grateful for *some* kind of resolution, if you aren't 100 percent pleased with the outcome and you can't change it, make your focus finding a way to live with it. And then go meditate or take a hike in nature!

April 10-27: Mercury in Aries

These next few weeks will present repeated opportunities to practice leaning in to your intuitive and creative right brain hemisphere (rather than over-relying on your analytical left). With the mental planet out of its element in your introspective twelfth house, you'll benefit more from paying attention to your dreams, journaling, meditating and vision-boarding than letting yourself get caught up in "analysis paralysis."

April 14: Sun-Pluto square

Someone may be playing fast and loose with the truth under today's shadowy clash between the forthright Sun and master manipulator Pluto in your honesty sector. Since you probably won't be able to separate fact from big claims, just listen politely and hold off making any binding decisions.

April 15: Sun-Jupiter square

No, Taurus, you're not being a naysayer if you follow the old "if it sounds too good to be true, it probably is" rule today. With these overconfident planets at odds, someone who's talking a good game may ultimately be full of hot air. Save yourself some stress and take it with a grain of Himalayan pink salt!

April 21: Sun-Saturn square

Don't go into a tailspin if a pet project bangs into some obstacles or your support squad is nowhere to be found. With taskmaster Saturn squaring the optimistic Sun in your sign today, you might feel like you're working on your own. The truth is, you're not. But you might have to come out and ask for help.

April 22: Taurus new moon

The year's only new moon in your sign brings the chance to start writing an exciting new chapter in your life. But before you put pen to paper (or pedal to metal), stop and reflect on what you need to release in order to make a new beginning. Set some intentions for the rest of the year, then lower those horns and charge ahead!

April 25: Mercury-Pluto square

Don't take things at face value today. Someone may not be the supportive ally they claim to be, but even if you come up with hard evidence, don't call them on it just yet. Under this dodgy square, they could find a way to skirt accountability or even start a vendetta against you. Keep your distance and your dignity—*and* a paper trail for possible future reference.

April 25: Mercury-Jupiter square

Sure, you're feeling optimistic, but be careful what you sign on for or promise today. Under a wildly optimistic mashup, it'll be easy to overestimate your abilities. This tense squareup also prompts you to double-check all facts, figures and deadlines.

April 25-October 4: Pluto retrograde in Capricorn

When alchemical Pluto swings into reverse direction in your visionary zone, you might start to doubt yourself. Rather than go into panic mode, see this as your cue to go back and make sure things are truly what you want—and 100 percent doable.

April 26: Sun-Uranus meetup

Expect the unexpected today, as this once-a-year cosmic curveball lands in your sign and shakes things from the foundation up. The change you've been praying for could finally come—or someone might pull the rug out from under you. Either way, trust that whatever comes next is for your own highest good.

April 27-May 11: Mercury in Taurus

The communication planet commences its annual jog through your sign, pulling you up on the stage and handing you the mic: What message do you want to put out to the masses? Or what big ask do you need to make? Over the next two weeks, get ready to make some bold and assertive moves.

April 28: Mercury-Saturn square

Speaking your truth is a good thing, but there's also the little matter of who you are addressing. Today, as the messenger planet squares off with restrictive Saturn in your career corner, it might not be politically wise to unload to a superior who holds a different perspective. For now, keep your wild ideas and opinions to yourself until you know it's safe to share them.

April 30: Mercury-Uranus meetup

This is the first of a series of such alignments over the coming seven years, when your mind will be racing with innovative ideas and clever ways to express or execute them. And with Mercury and Uranus both in your grounded sign, you'll have the patience and foresight to plan well and see the right ventures through to completion. This is how you turn a dream into a reality.

May

MAY: LOVE HOTSPOTS

May 3: Venus-Neptune square

If you find yourself confused about a love issue today, one thing you do *not* want to do is go running to your inner circle for answers. Ask three people, and you'll get six opinions! Under this emotional and perplexing mashup, it's better to tap your own higher wisdom. The more you do this, the stronger the guidance will become. You'll get another chance to check in when Venus squares Neptune again (this time while retrograde) on May 20.

May 7: Scorpio full moon

The year's only full moon in your partnership zone could be a "make it or break it" day when you (or they) finally decide whether to go all in or cut bait. Scorpio plays for keeps and needs the "whole enchilada," and this lunar lift will strengthen you in your resolution. Single? These moonbeams could light a path to a prospect with soulmate potential.

May 13-June 25: Venus retrograde in Gemini

You'll get to host the love planet (and your galactic guardian) in your second house of sensible sensuality and upscale pleasures for an extra-long cycle thanks to a six-week retrograde that begins *today*. Security with all the frills, yes please! Single? Search harder—or consider a prospect you passed over before, maybe even an ex. Attached? Work together to get your budget on track—but be sure to add a line item for "date nights and romantic excursions."

May 22: Mercury-Venus meetup

As the planets of *amour* and communication align, you'll have the confidence to express your feelings clearly without getting overly emo or demanding. In fact, speaking up for your needs and values could attract someone who shares them. For couples, it could bring you closer.

MAY: CAREER HOTSPOTS

May 7: Scorpio full moon

No need to toil away on your own when this annual lunation shines a light on a like-minded collaborator! There are probably *many* options out there—provided you're willing to compromise, which is not exactly your strong suit.

May 9: Mercury-Pluto trine

Your big-picture thinking will come in handy today, especially if there's a juicy deal you're eager to close on. Bring the parties together around the conference room table and let the negotiations begin!

May 10: Mercury-Jupiter trine

Watch those truth hammers today, Bull! Of course you want to speak with candor, but "pre-edit" so you don't inadvertently hurt or offend anyone. When faced with a choice, always take the high road and talk in a positive way rather than tearing anything (or anyone) down!

May 11-September 29: Saturn retrograde

Today, as the planet of time and structure makes his annual course reversal—this year starting in your career zone then backing into your visionary ninth house on July 1—you may realize that you need to scale back or roll something out in phases. Luckily, "slow and steady" is a Taurean specialty!

May 11: Mercury-Mars square

A little competition is healthy, but dial down the killer instincts. This may not even be coming from you but from someone on your team. Be careful about getting pulled into rivalries, and seriously limit your exposure to people who are all about bickering.

May 11-28: Mercury in Gemini

This annual transit of the mental planet through your money zone puts financial matters front and center. Don't just "wing it" or let your funds languish in a no-interest account. Do some research, talk to an adviser, and make your money work as hard for you as you do for it.

May 12: Mercury-Saturn trine

Solidifying Saturn grounds quicksilver Mercury, helping you to see things clearly and get a firm grasp of the big picture. This is a perfect moment to share your visionary ideas for expanding a team project. Don't hesitate to step into the role of ad hoc leader if things start going off the rails.

May 12-June 27: Mars in Pisces

When driven Mars blasts into your eleventh house of teamwork and technology, you may be working more closely with some of your colleagues. While this probably signals "compromise ahead," it also means that you don't have to burn the midnight oil!

May 14-September 12: Jupiter retrograde in Capricorn

You've been making quantum leaps all year, but once the expansive planet commences its annual retrograde in your growth sector, it's time to slow down and integrate some of those developments.

Use this time to review what you've been doing and tweak your next wave of big plans so you can hit the ground running when Jupiter straightens out at the end of summer.

May 15: Sun-Pluto trine

When the Sun in your sign makes its annual merger with game-changing Pluto, one of your ideas could take off if it's developed properly. How much are you willing to risk on this, Bull? Take one telling step today to see how viable it is. This could be the moment people realize what a creative visionary you truly are!

May 22: Gemini new moon

Woot! The year's only Gemini new moon powers up your second house of security and finances, inspiring you to turn over a new leaf (if necessary) and start writing an exciting chapter in your fiscal life. In social Gemini, la luna prompts you to reach out to people who can help you get a toe in the right door, and once that door opens, be prepared to lunge through it!

May 22: Mercury-Neptune square

Want to get a better handle on your finances? Stop hanging out with your "high-roller" friends! Maybe they can afford top-shelf everything (and maybe they can't). But if you're trying to grow your nest egg, you need to apply self-discipline. This hazy square could dangle temptation, but stay focused on your goals—and stay strong!

May 28-August 4: Mercury in Cancer

As inquisitive and creative Mercury sails through your communication corner, brainstorms should come fast and furious. Get some power lunches on the books and schedule a few idea-generating meetings. Carve out time to advance a personal writing, media or video project.

June

JUNE: LOVE HOTSPOTS

June 2: Venus-Mars square

Venus in your security sector intensifies your desire for stability in a relationship, but today's tense square with Mars (and his legendary lusty appetite) could lead you into temptation. Stay mindful, and don't do anything you can't walk back.

June 5: Sagittarius full moon (lunar eclipse)

The year's only Sagittarius full moon not only powers up your erotic, seductive eighth house—it's a transformational lunar eclipse! If you're ready to take your next step toward commitment, this lunar light can light a path for getting there. The next two weeks are ideal for deep emotional bonding, even if that means becoming a little vulnerable. On the flip side, if a relationship isn't going anywhere, you have an opportunity to call it quits with minimum collateral damage.

June 27, 2020-January 6, 2021: Mars in Aries

Surrender and release! Energizer Mars will spend the rest of the year in Aries and your spiritual, closure-focused twelfth house, thanks to a retrograde backspin from September 9 to November 13.

If you have unsettled issues from the past, Mars will embolden you to do the necessary work to heal and deal. With the lusty red rover in your secretive twelfth house, a past love connection could resurface or you might be drawn to a clandestine affair.

The AstroTwins' 2020 Horoscope

Careful, Taurus: Things may not be as they seem and that includes people's motives. For longtime couples, adding a touch of fantasy will spice things up in the boudoir.

JUNE: CAREER HOTSPOTS

June 5: Sagittarius full moon (lunar eclipse)

This once-a-year lunation in your eighth house of wealth, investments and shared resources could bring your efforts of the past six months to an exciting tipping point. And because it's also a transformational lunar eclipse, it might illuminate certain aspects that have been lurking in the shadows. Sagittarius is the sign of openness and transparency. If you've got any questions, come right out and ask!

June 13: Mars-Neptune meetup

Networking is the key to advancement, and motivated Mars in your collaborative zone is eager to get out there and meet new people. But the red planet is aligned with hazy Neptune, so you might not be able to get an accurate read on anyone. Do the chitchat and elbow-rubbing, but spend more time with (and Google) anyone you're considering teaming up with professionally.

June 18-July 12: Mercury retrograde in Cancer

Watch your words! Communication planet Mercury makes a tricky about-face in your third house of information and interactivity. For the next three weeks, be careful what you say—and to whom. Back up your data and protect your intellectual property. Avoid people who try to bait you into spreading rumors or sharing anything you're not ready to spill. If you're in the market for a new computer, phone or car, hold off until after this cycle if possible, as it can challenge technology and transportation in particular.

June 21: Cancer new moon (annular solar eclipse)

This eclipse in your expressive third house helps you fuse head and heart in your professional communications. Tap the compassionate Cancer energy and really listen in conversations. Catch yourself starting to interrupt or formulating your response before the other person even finishes. Let coworkers share their ideas without feeling the need to edit or judge. Once innovative ideas are on the table, you can always fine-tune them in the coming months.

June 22-November 28: Neptune retrograde in Pisces

As "emotional sponge" Neptune turns retrograde in your collaborative eleventh house, limit your exposure to "difficult" people. This might be easier said than done, since plenty of folks present themselves as fair and reasonable, but give 'em an inch, and suddenly you're sucked into their dramas or being recruited to save them. If you're having second thoughts about working with someone, put the project on hold until December.

June 27, 2020-January 6, 2021: Mars enters Aries

Easy does it, Taurus. You may be fighting fatigue for the rest of the year, as energizer Mars plunges into your restful twelfth house. Instead of pushing yourself past the point of burnout, try to go with the flow. Tend to your health with plenty of self-care and consider taking a short sabbatical if time and budget allow. With Mars in this imaginative zone, this could be a richly creative time that opens up your artistic side. Healers will also get a special boost from motivator Mars, so if you're in the spiritual services business or any kind of "maker," get ready for a renaissance! Mars normally spends about six weeks in each sign, but a retrograde from September 9 to November 13 will extend its stay. Book those two months to do a lot of cleanup work or to finish a lingering project for once and for all. On January 6, 2021, the red planet will blaze into *your* sign. Clear the decks so you're prepared for liftoff!

June 30: Jupiter-Pluto meetup
The second of three rare (once every 13 years) mashups of expansive Jupiter and transformational Pluto arrives, stoking your desire to go big! As these two powerhouses unite in your ninth house of travel, learning and entrepreneurship, you're ready to launch a purpose-driven idea into the world. But wait—both planets are retrograde at this point, so you're better off tweaking, testing and refining your ideas. Look back to the first conjunction on April 4 for clues—and plot your big reveal for the third alignment on November 12, when both planets are direct (forward).

July

JULY: LOVE HOTSPOTS

July 8: Mercury-Mars square
If something's bothering you, find a way to discuss it diplomatically. Just watch that "raging Bull" temper of yours, which could be easily triggered today—and again on July 27, when this challenging alignment repeats. With Mercury retrograde in your communication house, it may be impossible to sweep strong feelings under the rug. But a clash with hotheaded Mars (also retrograde) in your twelfth house of unfinished business makes this even trickier. You could be tempted to bring up every past resentment instead of sticking to the issue at hand. Shocking information may surface that also throws you off your level-headed game.

July 27: Venus-Neptune square
This is the third and final square of this series, the first two of which occurred on May 3 and 20. Hopefully by now, you've gotten some clarity around a certain union—or how you "do" relationships in a general way. But under this final hazy hookup, you're better off not taking any decisive action. Better to observe from the sidelines and make your final call later in the week.

JULY: CAREER HOTSPOTS

July 1-December 17: Saturn retrograde enters Capricorn
Structured Saturn backs into Capricorn and your entrepreneurial ninth house for a limited-run final hurrah. If you feel like you missed the boat in launching a business, returning to school or traveling for work, you'll get a second chance now. But this time, don't hesitate! Saturn will be retrograde until September 29, a good time to revisit what worked (and didn't) the last time, and to carefully consider what's needed to make this a success.

July 5: Capricorn full moon (lunar eclipse)
This once-a-year event powers up your expansive ninth house, which would be exciting on its own. But because it lands alongside a trio of heavyweight

105 The AstroTwins' 2020 Horoscope

planets—supersizer Jupiter, alchemical Pluto and disciplined Saturn—you might finally achieve liftoff with a visionary or entrepreneurial project you've been trying to get off the ground. And since this is also a potent lunar eclipse, certain previously hidden bits of intel might finally come to light to aid in your decision-making process.

July 12: Sun-Neptune trine

You've got some big ideas that you're eager to share, but under this empathic pairing, you're very tuned in to what others are thinking (and feeling!). To win the respect—and trust—of potential collaborators, make a point of letting them speak first and showing them what a team player you truly are.

July 15: Sun-Pluto opposition

Watch where you aim those truth hammers! Words can be crushing today, as Pluto faces off with the ego-driven Sun across your communication axis. With the "master manipulator" in the picture, it won't take much for power struggles to erupt or a shady character to try to advance their own self-interested agenda. But regardless, *you* want to take the high road!

July 20: Cancer new moon

The new moon in your house of communication and the intellect—the second of the year—makes this a perfect day to brainstorm, discuss synergies and pitch ideas that could unfold over the next six months. Focus on fresh branding, social media, marketing and writing projects.

July 20: Sun-Saturn opposition

Once a year, boundary-hound guard Saturn issues a warning, insisting you protect your personal limits. This goes for people who might try to cross a line with you *and* for you! Make sure you're not

promising more than you can deliver, and if you did (whoops!), be direct and see if you can get a little more time or assistance.

July 30: Mercury-Jupiter opposition

Does the "Tower of Babel" ring a bell? Under this noisy face-off, it may seem like everyone is carrying on their own conversations—yet nobody's hearing anyone else. Let other people talk over one another, but if you want to accomplish anything, step away from the fracas, slip on your headphones and focus on your own affairs.

July 30: Mercury-Neptune trine

This intuitive mashup bestows a special superpower: You'll be able to read people like a large-print book today! With Mercury and Neptune pinging each other from your interpersonal houses, it's a perfect day for meetings, pitches, interviews and shoring up your most important professional relationships. Networking events can turn up surprising serendipities.

August

AUGUST: LOVE HOTSPOTS

August 4-19: Mercury in Leo

Busy much? Finally, after a few hectic weeks of being out and about, you'll have a chance to slow down, get quiet and process any heavy emotions that came up in July. With the communication planet gliding through your private fourth house, you can dive into sensitive topics and even get a little teary-eyed or nostalgic. Drop your practical, logic guard and let your sentimental side out.

August 7-September 6: Venus in Cancer

This monthlong transit of amorous Venus through your third house of socializing and local happenings can bring fun and lightness to your romantic life. Singles might see a platonic pal in a new light or have a titillating chat with someone you meet hanging in your 'hood. Attached? Bring more levity to your shared world by going to more live performances: music, theater or comedy.

August 17: Mercury-Mars trine

Motivated Mars lends his passionate touch to Mercury's message, so if you want to share something with an intimate connection, speak from your heart, not your head. Even if you're feeling some anger or resentment, focus on what you love about them before you talk. That'll have the effect of greasing the emotional wheels.

August 18: Leo new moon

This once-a-year lunar lift in your fourth house of emotional foundations can clarify your desires around home, family or your domestic lifestyle. You may decide you're ready to buy (or sell) real estate or to start (or expand) your family. Check in with yourself to ensure you're acting out of your own authentic desire, not any external pressure.

August 19-September 5: Mercury in Virgo

When chatty Mercury makes its annual sweep through your passionate and fun-loving fifth house, you may feel like an uncaged songbird, so let the witty and flirty banter begin! Don't worry where something is "going," but how it feels in the moment!

August 25: Venus-Jupiter opposition

Speak your truth or protect your heart? You may be confused about how to act under this signal-scrambling mashup. If you're single, you could contract a wicked case of "grass is greener" syndrome: The person you *didn't* say "yes" to suddenly seems better than the one you did. Just stay in the flow and don't try to nail down your entire future! For couples, a conversation could go sideways, leaving you both frustrated. Stick a bookmark in it and deal with it another day.

August 27: Venus-Neptune trine

"Platonic" could lose its meaning as Venus aligns with dreamy Neptune in your friendship houses. You won't need much to get you charged up—provided there's plenty of deep and provocative conversation!

August 30: Venus-Pluto opposition

This could be a highly emotional day as the love planet faces off with intensifier Pluto. While part of you is eager to connect on a deeper level, another part might be resisting out of fear or old patterns rearing their heads. If this is a fairly solid relationship, open up to your partner and let them know what you're feeling so they don't misinterpret your behavior.

AUGUST: CAREER HOTSPOTS

August 1: Mercury-Pluto opposition

It's what people *aren't* saying that has you on tenterhooks today. What seemed crystal-clear yesterday may feel riddled with hidden agendas and mixed messages today. Do your best to read between the lines, but ultimately don't come to any final conclusions. Things could be totally different again tomorrow!

August 2: Sun-Uranus square

Someone may be trying to push your buttons or test your limits under this ego-clashing square. It may be hard not to react, but that's exactly what you should do to elude their clutches. Step back and see if this person mirrors any old family dynamics for you. If you can "name" it, you can claim it—and transcend it!

August 3: Aquarius full moon

This might be one of the most exciting days of your professional year! The year's only Aquarius full moon powers up your house of career success and could signal a culmination of your past six months of hard work—or a turning point. You may finally receive the recognition you deserve for your talents and accomplishments. Accept it graciously, but don't stop now! This lunar lift can help you write your next round of intentions.

August 3: Mercury-Saturn opposition

Ease off the gas, Taurus! Eager as you may be to launch a big project, this opposition to Mercury from restrained Saturn reminds you that you don't want to risk doing so prematurely. Better to take a little more time to get it "picture-perfect" than have to go back to the drawing board.

August 4: Mars-Jupiter square

When one door closes, another *will* open—and hopefully drop you off in an even better place! This square may force your hand in letting something go. Sure, it can be painful, but honest Jupiter will help you see the inevitability of closure. If you have any forgiving to do, this is a good time, provided you can do it sincerely. (If not, wait.)

August 10: Mercury-Uranus square

Curb your enthusiasm! You're psyched about an issue today, but make sure you're not getting carried away. Be passionate and truthful, but you don't want to risk losing your audience because you got a little *too* dramatic.

August 13: Mars-Pluto square

You'd love to hang out in the shadows and do your work behind the scenes, but this titanic clash may require you to stand up to a manipulative or harshly authoritative person. Be strong and insistent without stooping to their level—even if they try to push your buttons.

August 15, 2020-January 14, 2021: Uranus retrograde in Taurus

As the cosmic disruptor kicks off its annual five-month backspin—this year in your sign—you have an extended opportunity to review a potentially game-changing project. Even if you're dying to launch this into the world, you know a little tweaking can only make it stronger.

August 24: Mars-Saturn square

Don't force it! As impatient Mars and cautious Saturn butt heads, the next few days could feel like you have one foot on the gas, the other on the brake. People may not be ready to discuss your ideas or commit to any grand visions. Give them the information they need and time to digest what you're offering. Proceed with caution before sharing any big ideas or plans. Not everyone can be trusted to keep your information private.

August 25: Mercury-Uranus trine

Big ideas are flowing like champagne at a wedding today, but your job is to sift through them to

108

find the most doable—and original! Thanks to a harmonious hookup of transformative Uranus and communicator Mercury, you'll be operating at your sharpest. You don't have to put anything into production now; just pick a few winners to work on for the rest of the year.

August 29: Mercury-Jupiter trine

The key to success today is thinking *way* outside the box. Even if the powers that be are hung up on following protocol, if you can find a way to present your brilliant ideas as beneficial to them, you could have a rapt audience!

August 30: Mercury-Neptune opposition

You want to be fair, but it's not always appropriate to let everyone have a vote. Well, not if you want to actually get anything done. Today, close the opinion polls, make a firm decision and let the team know how to proceed. If you're working solo, screen out distractions and get busy. You could get a lot accomplished—if you stay focused.

September

SEPTEMBER: LOVE HOTSPOTS

September 2: Venus-Saturn opposition

Don't let your temper get the better of you under this provocative face-off. While you should express your true feelings, you don't want to let things devolve into name-calling or taking cheap shots. If you don't think you can keep your emotions under control, table this for another day.

September 4: Venus-Mars square

Unconscious feelings or old programming could scramble communication as the love planets lock into an uneasy square. You can't trust that you're accurately tracking someone's motives—because they may be deliberately trying to conceal their intentions. Truth be told, *you* may be equivocating a bit yourself! The best thing to do might be to retreat to neutral corners and ride this out.

September 6-October 2: Venus in Leo

Today, when the cosmic coquette shimmies into passionate Leo and your domestic quarters, you may not have to leave the house to do your romancing. If you're attached, this is a great cycle for in-home entertaining—with friends and especially *à deux*! Talk could turn to meeting each other's relatives, exchanging keys or moving in together. Singles should take your dating apps a bit more seriously and line up a few "low-stakes" meetings.

September 9-November 13: Mars retrograde in Aries

As lusty Mars spins into reverse in your foggy twelfth house for the next two months, some of your jokes and flirting efforts may miss their mark. In relationships, jealousy and resentment can flare. Stay mindful that you don't come on too strong or lapse into self-centered behavior. If you rushed into a romance that you're having second thoughts about now, tap the brakes!

September 15: Venus-Uranus square

Feelings may run hot and cold under this disruptive face-off, so do your best to not react to them. Unpredictable Uranus squaring sensitive Venus could leave you prone to emotional outbursts. Since you might not be able to keep a lid on them, steer clear of people you know have a way of pushing your buttons.

September 17: Virgo new moon

This annual lunar lift in your passionate fifth house could usher in a promising love connection, but only time will tell if it's a keeper or not. Couples should clear the decks for a night of fun, just the two of you. If you've been thinking of starting (or expanding) a family, this fertile lunation of new beginnings could be your lucky star!

September 27-October 27: Mercury in Scorpio

Messenger Mercury will enjoy an extended tour of your partnership house, thanks to a retrograde that begins October 13. Before and after those three weeks is an ideal time to talk about the balance of your union and whether you're both getting your needs met. Single? Meet and greet! But don't be disappointed if a promising person ghosts you when the communication planet goes retrograde.

September 28: Venus-Mars trine

A beautiful day to open your heart arrives as loving Venus and passionate Mars join hands in the most sentimental zones of your chart. Couples can bond with a nostalgic date somewhere the two of you always loved to go. If you're thinking of meeting each other's families, starting one of your own or spending quality time with the clan you've created, there's hardly a better day.

SEPTEMBER: CAREER HOTSPOTS

September 1: Mercury-Pluto trine

You'll know better than to take things at face value since this rare alignment dials up your intuition to laser levels. You're able to read people like a book—but not from listening to their words. Your insight will come from watching their body language and picking up on other subtle cues.

September 2: Pisces full moon

The year's only full moon in your house of technology and teamwork could bring a long-running group project to a celebratory conclusion. Enjoy a moment (or a whole day) of glory with your cohorts, and don't be shy about alerting the media and other influencers, or posting "viral content."

September 3: Mercury-Saturn trine

Your mind is racing with innovative ideas, but what will seal the deal today is being able to back things up with solid facts and figures. If you've got the ear of a decision maker, have a clear explanation prepared for how this can advance *their* interests.

September 5-27: Mercury in Libra

When mindful Mercury swings into beautifying Libra and your house of health and self-care, the message is clear: Take care of Numero Uno before you tend to others! Stop putting off those medical appointments. Get a massage on the books—better yet, buy a package. During this short but significant cycle, start paying more attention to what goes into your mouth, how much exercise you're getting—and getting proper sleep!

September 9-November 13: Mars retrograde in Aries

You can't control everything, Bull. And today, when go-getter Mars hits the brakes for a two-month backspin, you will learn firsthand that it's actually better to let things unfold at an organic pace and not try to force or rush anything.

September 12: Jupiter retrograde ends

As expansive Jupiter resumes forward motion after a four-month backspin in your visionary ninth house, it's safe to hit the gas on an entrepreneurial venture that stalled, or to book that epic vacation you've been waiting all year to take!

September 14: Sun-Pluto trine

Turn up your light and let it shine! With the creative Sun and transformative Pluto in sync, your innovative ideas could have a positive and far-reaching impact. Don't be afraid to color outside the lines, even if no one else is. Here's a five-star opportunity to lead by example.

September 17: Mercury-Jupiter square

With chatty Mercury in your judgmental sixth house—squaring loose-lipped Jupiter in your candid ninth house—your critical side could make an unscheduled appearance. Unless you can take what you dish out, don't open a can of worms. In fact, keep all your opinions to yourself, unless someone asks for them. And even then, tread lightly.

September 21: Mercury-Pluto square

You might be tempted to give someone an unfiltered piece of your mind, but if you're not prepared to deal with the consequences, restrain yourself! While it might feel good in the moment, "mouthing off" is liable to only churn up bad blood.

September 23: Mercury-Saturn square

Rein it in or let it rip? You're pulled in dueling directions under this vexing square. And naysayer Saturn may win out over clever Mercury. But no need to scrap all those visionary plans! Just lean in to Saturn's mature, restrained energy to find any weak spots or anticipate objections to your proposal, then zip back to the drawing board.

September 24: Mercury-Mars opposition

Loose lips could sink more than ships today, so be extra mindful of what you share in public. Your thinking may be a bit emotional, and you could make a knee-jerk reaction when a calculated judgment is called for. Hold off on big decisions: You're likely to regret them.

September 27-October 27: Mercury in Scorpio

Thanks to a retrograde mid-October, eloquent Mercury will spend an extended period in your partnership house. Got a big deal to hash out or negotiate the terms of? Do so before and after those three retrograde weeks and you should be pleased with the outcome. Been on the outs with a colleague? Get back on the same page.

September 29: Mars-Saturn square

It's a "hurry up and wait" kind of day as speed demon Mars clashes with cautious Saturn. Someone could be trying to micromanage you, or they might be pulling a power play by being overly concerned with protocol and procedure. Tap your trademark patience, and if you reach the end of your rope, focus on something you do have control over.

September 29: Saturn retrograde ends

Back in action! After a frustrating reversal in your

visionary, entrepreneurial ninth house, Saturn resumes forward motion. Hopefully you've used these past few months to put together a game plan and are ready to set it into motion. Calculated risks could pay off handsomely now!

October

OCTOBER: LOVE HOTSPOTS

October 1: Aries full moon

The year's only full moon in your twelfth house of closure and healing—in the sign of bold Aries—can help you walk away from a painful or untenable situation. Call in support and cut the cord. With la luna also igniting your fantasy fires, you might consummate a connection with a soulmate or let down those ironclad walls. Whatever happens, you're more than ready for it!

October 2-27: Venus in Virgo

Vixen Venus (your ruler) makes her annual visit to your fifth house of *amour* and glamour. You won't be a modest mouse during this seductive cycle! Whatever your relationship status, get ready for some autumnal canoodling!

October 7: Mercury-Uranus opposition

It's great that you want to speak your piece, but there's a time and a place—and a way—to say it. Blurting without thinking can create unnecessary chaos. If you "need" some changes to occur for you to continue a relationship, get yourself calm and centered, then ask the other person when a good time would be for them to have a dialogue. Remember to hand *them* the talking stick, too.

October 10: Venus-Uranus trine

Anything goes under this electrifying alignment of your ruler, amorous Venus, and unpredictable Uranus in your sign. Single? A casual convo could quickly spark into seductively flirty banter, which could lead to…who knows? Attached? Cue up a sexy surprise for tonight!

October 13-November 3: Mercury retrograde

With the mindful planet sailing through your relationship realm, it's only natural that you're wondering where things are going. With Mercury retrograde, this rumination could turn into a mini-obsession. Before *that* happens, try to get a clear understanding around your commitment or have an honest talk about the futures you each envision.

October 18: Venus-Neptune opposition

Emotions may be stronger than usual, but under today's hazy face-off between your ruler, amorous Venus, and fantasy camper Neptune, the object of your affections may be impossible to get a read on. Avoid doing anything extreme or irrevocable. If necessary, throw yourself into a personal project or deep-cleaning mission.

October 19: Venus-Jupiter trine

Today's rare connection can blow your heart wide open and make you feel extra generous toward your partner or love interest—or perhaps toward everyone! If you've been hanging out on the sidelines, get back in the game. Couples might plan to make it official or renew their vows—destination ceremony, anyone?

October 21: Venus-Pluto trine

Sensual *and* stable: Is there anything sexier than that? Under today's alchemical connection, you could find (or realize you already have found) intense passion with a grounded, reliable partner. Single? Hold out for that mind-body-soul connection because you just might feel it with someone today.

October 24: Venus-Saturn trine

Fantasy interrupted? It's okay, Taurus. You can get back to them later in the week. Today, solidifying Saturn brings its unblinking clarity to a romantic situation, and if you can let go of ungrounded hopes, you'll actually be grateful for the reality check. If you are about to move forward, you want to be sure you're not imagining anything.

October 27-November 21: Venus in Libra

When your celestial ruler, beautifying Venus, returns to your sixth house of wellness and self-care for an "encore" performance (as it backflips into the sign of the Scales), you may find yourself at the crossroads of fitness and romance. Attached? Inspire your partner to do more active things together, like a fall hike or long bike ride. Single? Lose the earbuds. You could strike up a conversation with an intriguing—and available—person at the gym or while out running errands.

OCTOBER: CAREER HOTSPOTS

October 4: Pluto retrograde ends

Transformational Pluto wraps up a five-month retrograde in Capricorn and your risk-taking ninth house. If your enthusiasm and optimism took a hit, they'll come flooding back now that Pluto is moving forward. Anything that stalled during that time can pick up speed—in fact, this is a great day to really hit the gas!

October 9: Mars-Pluto square

If you have to stand up to a controlling authority figure today, make sure you don't stoop to their level. Think before you speak—or put it in writing—and try to find a "high-vibe" way to approach them.

October 13-November 3: Mercury retrograde

As savvy Mercury zips through your partnership house—in reverse—you'll have a chance to renegotiate a deal or hash out even better terms. But get it in writing! Retrogrades have a funny way of giving people amnesia.

October 15: Sun-Pluto square

Just because you see something doesn't mean you're required to say something! In fact, under today's slippery clash, it's better to keep your observations to yourself. With manipulative Pluto pulling the strings, it could turn out that the person you go running to is the mastermind of the whole scenario. Take notes for (possible) future reference, but for now, keep them private.

October 16: Libra new moon

This once-a-year lunar lift powers up your sixth house of organization, helping you get a sprawling project back on track. During the next six months, you could reach a major goal—if you can find a way to banish the distractions and stay focused. You might need to invest in a specialized service provider, but the time (and mistakes) you save will be worth it!

October 18: Sun-Saturn square

Some days are full of sexy, visionary projects, but under today's grounded mashup, it's more about hunkering down and doing the grunt work. But this is what dreams are built on!

October 19: Mars-Jupiter square

Are you tenaciously clinging to something that you know in your heart is done and over with? Maybe it was a pet project of yours that wasn't viable or an employee who never quite got up to speed. Letting go can be painful, but it's in your best interests to cut bait and move on—and trust that something better is just around the corner.

October 19: Mercury-Uranus opposition

Blurt alert! It might feel impossible to hold something in, yet speaking or writing without proper vetting could lead to unforeseen (and undesired) consequences. Even constructive criticism will go over like a lead balloon. Jot down your thoughts so you don't lose them, but wait until later in the week to share them—if you still feel the need.

October 31: Taurus full moon

Happy cosmic birthday! The year's only full moon in your sign can bring much-deserved kudos for your efforts of the past six months, but don't make them come and find you. Step out from the shadows and assume your rightful place at center stage. Take however many curtain calls you need, but then get busy formulating your next big set of goals!

November

NOVEMBER: LOVE HOTSPOTS

November 9: Venus-Mars opposition

Love may get confusing as the cosmic lovebirds stare each other down from introspective chart sectors. Part of you feels like you've got one foot on the gas, craving more of your beloved, while the other is on the brake, as you secretly hope for things to simmer down. Take a day to yourself to think this through.

November 10-December 1: Mercury in Scorpio

When the thoughtful planet returns to your relationship realm, you may come to some important decisions about what you want, need and are *not* willing to put up with in a relationship. With the cosmic communicator in intense, passionate Scorpio, you'll find a way to express your feelings in a strong way—just be sure not to lay blame or dump your stuff on your love interest.

November 13: Mars retrograde ends

As fierce Mars wraps up a two-month retrograde, the heavy vibes will lift—and not a moment too soon! You might have reached the point of erupting over something, but now you could feel clearheaded enough to forgive someone's immature behavior. Of course, if you're concerned that it wasn't a onetime flare-up, it may be time to move on.

November 15: Scorpio new moon

The year's only new moon in your committed partnership house can give you the courage and inspiration to make a big leap of faith. In this heart-centric zone, la luna will help you write a new chapter in your personal book of love! Set some intentions for a happy, healthy bond and read it daily until you manifest it. For couples who have gotten out of sync, you can get back into a balanced groove in the two weeks following this lunation.

November 15: Venus-Pluto square

Avoid the trap of being overly focused on a love interest's flaws and foibles and how you can "fix" them. That's a recipe for frustration and disappointment. Instead, shift your thinking and retrain your vision on their positive qualities. Do they have enough of those to keep you satisfied? If the scales keep tipping the wrong way, you've got some serious rethinking to do.

November 16: Venus-Jupiter square

You love 'em, you're not *sure* if you love 'em… Don't let yourself get into a futile "chasing your tail" quandary about the ultimate future of a certain relationship. With supersizer Jupiter poking the love planet in the ribs, you may unconsciously be playing out scenarios far into the future when it's extremely premature. Stay in the here-and-now and do your best to focus on this person's most endearing characteristics.

November 19: Venus-Saturn square

Under this speed-checking transit, you may realize a budding relationship is accelerating too quickly or that you're unsure of someone's intentions for the future. Saturn can help you downshift or, if you've been going *under* the speed limit, look at your blocks to reaching the next level of closeness.

November 21-December 15: Venus in Scorpio

When your ruler, charming Venus, makes her annual move into your partnership house, you might start giving serious thought to how you want your current union to evolve or what you're hoping to draw into your life. Putting more conscious effort into your dating strategies or communication style will pay off big-time.

November 27: Venus-Uranus opposition

Things could turn on a dime under this capricious clash. But you haven't lost *all* sense of control. Step back and examine *your* role in a key relationship:

Are you being overly accommodating to someone to avoid confrontation? Compromise is essential in all successful relationships, but if you're living with resentment on a daily basis, it's time to get things out in the open.

NOVEMBER: CAREER HOTSPOTS

November 1: Mercury-Saturn square

This is the second of three Mercury-Saturn squares this season (the first was September 23, and the final one occurs on November 6, when Mercury resumes forward motion). The theme for you is reconciling your "sensible" side (Saturn) with the part of you that "dares to dream" (inquisitive Mercury). It doesn't *have* to be a tug of war. There are times and situations where one approach is preferable to the other. This thrice-occurring transit can help you find that balance.

November 3: Mercury retrograde ends

Back to work! Communicator Mercury resumes forward motion in your systematic sixth house. Time to get healthy, organized and on track with your priorities.

November 10-December 1: Mercury in Scorpio

Expressive Mercury returns to your partnership house, clearing a path for an exciting collaboration to move forward. Check in with your Spidey senses: If they're tingling in a *good* way, you should feel confident about proceeding!

November 12: Jupiter-Pluto meetup

Ignite your visionary ideas! The third and final conjunction of wide-angle Jupiter and potent Pluto sweeps through Capricorn and your expansive

The AstroTwins' 2020 Horoscope

ninth house. This only happens every 13 years, so it's not to be squandered. Look back to April 4 and June 30, the first two meetups, for ideas of what could surface now. If you've been working on a groundbreaking idea for a business, dreaming of long-distance travel or considering an education-based project, this starmap lends special support.

November 13: Mars retrograde ends

The stress and so-called "healthy" competition of the past two month evaporate as aggro Mars completes a retrograde in your introspective twelfth house. If there's someone to forgive (or forget), take the first step and get it over with already. When the red planet fires up your sign at the beginning of 2021, you don't want any loose ends holding you back!

November 15: Scorpio new moon

Partner up for the win! The year's only Scorpio new moon beams into your house of committed relationships and contracts. Got a deal to ink before the year wraps? Do it now!

November 17: Mercury-Uranus opposition

Resist the temptation to blurt out something that may make you feel good in the moment but then terrible in the aftermath. If this can affect the outcome of a team project, talk to a supervisor and let them handle it. If it's of a more personal nature, vent to an insightful colleague and take the most diplomatic approach.

November 23: Mercury-Neptune trine

You've got the gift of gab *and* the ability to tap into your intuition and come up with the perfect language for your message. One thing to be aware of, though: When you're this receptive, you need to shield your field. Your empathy can weaken your personal boundaries, so be careful not to absorb other people's energy and drain yourself.

November 28: Neptune retrograde ends

When shady Neptune ends a five-month retrograde in your eleventh house of teamwork and technology, the fog lifts and you'll be able to clearly see who's been pulling their weight and who hasn't. No more putting up with slackers!

November 30: Gemini full moon (lunar eclipse)

This once-a-year lunar lift in your second house of work, security and money can bring the successful completion of a long-running project—or a big payday! You could see an immediate bump in your income, or it might take up to six months to materialize. In any event, you're moving into a new level of prosperity. If you're a newbie at investing, talk to a few different pros to learn the basics and understand your own risk tolerance.

December

December 1-20: Mercury in Sagittarius

With thoughtful Mercury cruising through your eighth house of intimacy and eroticism, you may not be happy with just a casual fling, or an on-off relationship. Since Mercury gets conversation flowing, you'll be able to express a few of these thoughts, as well as some secret desires and fantasies. The holidays just got hotter!

December 5: Venus trine Neptune

Enchantment awaits! Romantic Venus and dreamy Neptune converge in your interpersonal houses, lending friendships and relationships a touch of magic. Someone you never thought of "that way" could suddenly appear oh-so alluring. For couples, it's a perfect night to make holiday party rounds or to plan something special with your mutual friends.

December 14: Sagittarius new moon (total solar eclipse)

The year's only new moon (symbolizing fresh starts) in your seduction sector can deepen your current bond or attract a different kind of person into your orbit. And because this is a solar eclipse, things could happen fast! In the sign of truth-telling Sagittarius, you may have to lay your cards on the table and get vulnerable. It's a time to be completely honest—with other people, but especially with yourself.

December 15, 2020-January 9, 2021: Venus in Sagittarius

As vixen Venus shimmies into your seductive eighth house, things are sure to heat up in your romantic life. A budding relationship could advance to the next stage of commitment, solid ones could deepen emotionally, and single Bulls may find themselves in a dating frenzy!

December 30: Venus-Neptune square

Even as your head is being pulled into the clouds, it's important to keep at least one boot on terra firma. This fantasy-inducing face-off heightens sensitivity and intuition, but it can also distort facts and leave you confused, jealous and even paranoid. Take a timeout from the dating game and meet friends for some lighthearted IRL fun instead.

DECEMBER: CAREER HOTSPOTS

December 1-20: Mercury in Sagittarius

There's no such thing as too much research under this hyper-focused transit. With mental Mercury in your investigative eighth house for the next few weeks, a captivating idea could take you to near-obsessive levels. Make the most of your enhanced powers of concentration, but watch out for tunnel vision. You can accomplish a lot before everyone clocks out for the holidays, so screen out those distractions!

December 13: Mercury-Neptune square

You're eager to launch a new initiative, but Neptune is making it hard to get the info you need to move forward—and today's bewildering square could really throw you into a tailspin. Keep doing your part, but table "liftoff" until everything is nailed down.

December 14: Sagittarius new moon (total solar eclipse)

The year's only new moon in your house of shared resources and joint ventures is also a potent solar eclipse, planting seeds for mutually beneficial long-term investments. But remember: This is a marathon, not a sprint. You may not see immediate results, but that's okay because you're in this for the long haul.

December 17, 2020-March 7, 2023: Saturn in Aquarius

Roll up your sleeves, Taurus. Structured Saturn begins its longer journey through your ambitious tenth house, bringing slow but steady growth to your career sector. It's time to get your hustle on—in the name of your biggest goals. This visit only happens every 29 years, so major shifts could come to your career and professional path. Don't let any challenges or roadblocks deter you. You're being prepared for the big leagues now!

December 19, 2020-May 13, 2021: Jupiter in Aquarius

Finally: The career news you've been waiting 12 years for! Auspicious, expansive and optimistic Jupiter blasts into your tenth house of professional success. All things are achievable now as the planet of possibilities helps you shatter the glass ceiling— *and* your own limiting beliefs. Set some lofty goals and make sure you're willing to put in the effort. Start by envisioning what you'd like your career to look like a year from now. Then map out the steps you can take to get there by the fastest and most scenic route!

December 20, 2020-January 9, 2021: Mercury in Capricorn

When the winged messenger sails into your expansive ninth house, you'll find inspiration outside your comfort zone, which will be helpful if you hit a creative plateau. A good place to start? By approaching your most challenging problem from a wildly different angle! This is also a good time to research and register for a workshop to get 2021 off to a stimulating start.

December 21: Jupiter-Saturn meetup

A rare and powerful moment for career growth arrives as expansive Jupiter and structured Saturn unite in your professional tenth house. Normally these two are strange bedfellows: Jupiter wants growth and risk while cautious Saturn flees from it. At this Great Conjunction, which only occurs every 20 years, you can strike the sweet spot, taking a

calculated risk that sends you soaring to new levels of leadership and success.

December 23: Mars-Pluto square

This is the final face-off of these feisty, fiery planets, and today could bring a "test" of what you learned during the previous two earlier this year. Will your temper get the better of you, or have you found a way to take things in stride and not give people the reaction they want? Lean in to your Taurean cool, and steer your ship in the direction *you* want!

December 25: Mercury-Uranus trine

This rare mashup gives you a flash of insight but also the practical thinking to actually make the dream happen. Don't worry what others will think. If you know in your heart that this is the way to do things, hit the gas and *go*. Just don't get so excited that you forget it's also Christmas!

December 29: Cancer full moon

Not everyone has gone AWOL for the holidays. And if you've got an exciting idea you want to share with a potential collaborator, reach out. This full moon—the second one in Cancer this year—brings your efforts to completion, and you could get the answer you've been waiting for before the calendar turns. ✳

Tools from The AstroTwins
for your 2020 PLANNING

Visit all year long for
new updates & additions!

www.astrostyle.com/2020tools

Yearly Highlights

LOVE

A scintillating year is in store as wild-child Jupiter joins seductive Pluto in your erotic eighth house until December 19. Since this is the zone of perma-bonding, you could truly live the dream of having a passionate partner who also wants a committed relationship. With your libido fired up to max settings, you'll be a freak in the sheets and maybe also on the streets! There's no shame in your sensual game in 2020, especially while ardent Venus takes an extended tour through Gemini from April 3 through August 7. But that doesn't mean you should barrel ahead on every impulsive whim. Venus will be retrograde from May 13 to June 25, which could bring back an ex or lead you on a regrettable detour down temptation's trail.

MONEY

No piddling pocket change will do for you in 2020. This year, enterprising Jupiter joins power brokers Pluto and Saturn in your eighth house of big money. Funds could flow in from an investment, or you could earn other passive income through royalties or a rental property. If you're in debt or need to settle up with the tax man, this cosmic trio helps you clear your credit record and get back in the black. Two eclipses in Cancer, on January 10 and June 21, land in your second house of fiscal foundations which can lend support with steadier income streams—or vault you into a gainful job that helps you cover baseline bills.

WELLNESS

Fold in those social butterfly wings. For the first half of 2020, buzzy Geminis will prefer quality over quantity in your interactions. As you draw a tighter radius around your inner circle, some BFF-grade superstars will emerge. Your popularity gets an epic boost come June 27, when accelerator Mars shifts into Aries for six months and sends your clout soaring. With the red planet retrograde from September 9 to November 13, you could sync up with squads from your past, and even get the band back together.

LEISURE

Healing is an inside job in 2020, as planets plunge you into a deep exploration of the connection between mind, body and spirit. You may be "guided" to work with a holistic healer, shaman or metaphysical practitioner. Therapy, meditation, and even hypnosis, can help you drill down to the root of an issue that's affecting your physical body. Reproductive health may require your attention, or you might need to balance blood levels with specific vitamins and supplements. Disciplined Saturn darts into your vital ninth house from March 21 to July 1, which can help you get back on the wellness wagon and engage in a fitness modality that is both effective and fun. ✷

GEMINI 2020 HOROSCOPE

2020 Power Dates

✴

GEMINI NEW MOON
May 22 (1:38 PM ET)

GEMINI FULL MOON
November 30 (4:29 AM ET) Lunar Eclipse

SUN IN GEMINI
May 20 – June 20

How close is too close, Gemini? As the zodiac's Twin, sharing is a basic instinct. But in 2020, you could bounce between poles. At moments, your urge to merge will be insatiable. Other times, you'll want oceans between you and anyone demanding a commitment.

As you plunge into deep waters, then swim to the surface for huge gulps of air, you'll volley between two extreme realities. Thankfully, your dualistic sign enjoys variety, though you probably haven't experienced it quite so palpably.

Superficial relationships are a no-go in 2020, and it will be impossible to hold loved ones at arm's length this year. On December 2, 2019, expansive Jupiter embarked on an extended night swim through Capricorn and the mysterious, alluring waters of your eighth house of joint ventures, perma-bonding and sexuality. With intrepid Jupiter exploring this esoteric reef until December 19, 2020, you'll discover hidden dimensions of your own psyche.

And what's the good of unearthing a buried treasure if you can't share your findings with everyone in your life? You're ruled by messenger Mercury, Gemini, and you're wired to spread information like a viral campaign. Deep discoveries lead to even deeper conversations in 2020. Alchemical Pluto accompanies Jupiter in Capricorn all year, along with authoritative Saturn for most of 2020. With all that mastery and magnetism at your behest, you could move the masses as an influencer. Just be careful not to turn your cult of personality into a literal cult, Gemini!

Although your popularity will soar, hosting this cosmic trio in Capricorn and your intimate eighth house can bring out your rare introverted streak. Set up a sacred oasis at home—your own Virginia Woolf-style "room of one's own." You'll need to have your own little retreat center where you can journal, meditate and create when you need a cathartic outlet from the intense feelings that planets in the eighth house can churn up this year.

Intimate, one-on-one relationships are also the eighth house's domain. And we're not talking "one and done" hangouts either, Gemini—even though you've broken speed records for creating "I feel like I've known you for my entire life" connections. (What's the difference between 15 minutes or 15 years when you click, right?) This year, partnerships could become permanent—and hella sexy, too! But nothing less than a mind-body-soul connection will do. You'd rather have no one than the wrong one in 2020, especially since you'll find so much richness in your own company.

Financially, sharing assets and joining resources can help you stabilize…and flourish! With three eclipses in Cancer and Capricorn activating your money axis in the first half of 2020, you could drum up capital from surprising sources. An investor might offer to put dollars behind your dreams. Maybe you'll explore a business loan or crowdfund a

campaign. If you need to repair your credit or get a handle on debt, these eclipses speed up progress.

Fueling your charm offensive in 2020 will be vivacious Venus. From April 3 to August 7, the celestial seductress takes an extended tour through Gemini, ratcheting up your sensuality and sex appeal. Creative downloads will be epic, so if you're working on a novel, a painting series, or an EP, don't overbook yourself during this four-month window. You never know when the muse might strike!

Normally, Venus hovers in a single sign for four weeks, but she's posted up in Gemini for so long because from May 13 to June 25, the love planet will take her biennial retrograde. With the cosmic coquette reverse-commuting through your sign for nearly six weeks, there could be crossed signals in the game of love. During the backspin, be careful not to rush into a commitment, make assumptions about your S.O. or invite a toxic ex back into your life. If you play your cards right, Venus retrograde can be a bountiful time, helping you find diplomatic ways to work through conflicts with the ones you adore. Ultimately, Venus wants peace, love and harmony—but that doesn't mean making an emotional bypass over tough issues.

On May 5, the lunar North Node will shift into Gemini, its first visit to your sign since April 2003! This special point in the sky directs our collective destiny. The world will hum at a Gemini frequency until January 2022—a huge advantage for Twins! Your stellar intellect and communication skills will give you the leading edge. And with your first house of identity lit, you could "rebrand" yourself with a fresh career path or a totally unprecedented style (or both). This is a time to develop your gifts and invest in personal growth.

Another nudge towards independence comes from March 21 to July 1, as Saturn darts into Aquarius and activates your ninth house of travel, expansion and higher learning. You'll begin breaking free from suffocating entanglements during this three-and-a-half-month window, but it might take until the end of 2020 before you truly liberate yourself. On December 17, 2020, the ringed planet shifts into Aquarius until March 7, 2023. Two days later, on December 19, jovial Jupiter will join Saturn in the Water Bearer's realm—and on the Winter Solstice, December 21, they'll make an ultra-rare connection at 0°29' Aquarius.

This tete-a-tete, which astrologers have dubbed The Great Conjunction, only happens every 20 years. Power up for a major mission, Gemini! With Jupiter activating your enterprising spirit and Saturn providing the structure to bring big ideas to life, this day is like a launchpad for your dreams. With your global ninth house in the Great Conjunction's crosshairs, you might need a plane ticket or an international visa to get this one into orbit. Have vision, will travel!

Jupiter, Saturn & Pluto in Capricorn.

The Trio: December 2, 2019–March 21, 2020; July 1, 2020–December 17, 2020

Power suit or wetsuit? In 2020, a dive boat of planets—which includes Saturn, Pluto and Jupiter—drifts through Capricorn and the mysterious waters of your solar eighth house. This is the zone of wealth, sexuality, death and rebirth.

You'll be rolling in the deep this year, Gemini, from the boardroom to the bedroom (and back again!).

To maximize the gifts of the eighth house, think joint ventures. In 2020, you'll plunge below the surface in relationships, exploring the art of "interdependency." Keep your Brené Brown audiobooks queued up: You're going to need regular pep talks on the power of vulnerability, especially since Jupiter accelerates your urge to merge. To give and receive freely, without keeping score, can leave you feeling wide open and raw. But the payoff is so worth it, as you expand your capacity to care for another soul.

As the zodiac's Twin, you're no stranger to pairing up; in fact, you can lock down a BFF or bae in record time. But how real are these connections? Are they built to last? The eighth house doesn't do "microwaved" bonds, Instagram besties or anything superficial. This is all-or-nothing terrain, where trust must be earned through a complex series of loyalty tests. For a sign that loves variety as much as yours, the prospect of giving one person your all can be daunting. It's not that you're incapable, Gemini; in fact, when you choose to devote yourself to someone—for business or pleasure—you're all the way involved. But you can also suffer from bouts of extreme buyer's remorse. As soon as the ink is dried on the deal you worked so hard to seal, that little voice of doubt can start whirring away. *Did I make the right decision? What if I'm stuck here? Will it still be this good in five years?*

But we're also happy to report that your knee-jerk, runaway bride reflex has been tempered over the past two years. You can thank wise Saturn for this evolution. The seven-ringed general has been marching through Capricorn and your solar eighth house since December 19, 2017. This has definitely changed the pace for your quicksilver sign. For the past two years, you've been earning a Master's degree in patience and persistence, developing sterling integrity as you go. Every time you stayed put when you wanted to bail, apologized for starting drama when you wanted to defend yourself, and finished a project even when it seemed "too hard," Saturn decorated you with another star. You'll have more opportunities to strengthen your staying power, as Saturn weaves in and out of Capricorn throughout 2020.

Alchemist Pluto has been stoking through your eighth house from 2008 to 2024, a 16-year journey that lured you away from the logical, left side of your brain. The icy dwarf planet feels right at home in the eighth house, a blessing for Geminis with an interest in esoterica. Over the past 12 years, life may have taken a turn towards the mystical. Perhaps you're working in an eighth house field, which spans the range from witchy pursuits to investment banking! (Sounds paradoxical, sure, but both require powers of intuition and an ability to predict what's coming next.)

One Gemini friend has found a new way to play "double agent." After a decade of working as a hairstylist, she returned to school to be certified in a healing bodywork technique and is now offering sessions. Simultaneously, she opened the doors of her own metaphysical boutique, selling a gorgeous array of wares from crystals to rare divination decks. Another Gemini we adore launched a career as an herbalist and released a successful series of books with a major publishing house.

> "Your knee-jerk runaway bride reflex has been tempered over the past two years."

With entrepreneurial Jupiter entering the fray, your mystical—or musical—talents could bring even more lucky strikes! The eighth house is a deeply creative zone. Divinely inspired visions could rouse you from your bed to produce your magnum opus while the rest of the world sleeps. (The art of the power nap will be your saving grace in 2020!) But don't let a little sleep deprivation deter you from sharpening your goddess-given arsenal of skills. Jupiter only visits this zone of your chart once every 12.5 years. The last run was from December 18, 2007, to January 5, 2009. Flip back to that time period to see what themes may repeat for you in 2020.

While you'll enjoy the passionate provocations of 2020, the frenetic emotional activity thrusts you outside of your cool, intellectual comfort zone. It's not that you don't love a probing conversation. You just prefer to keep the focus upbeat and positive (with an occasional side of tea-spilling snark). You are visual and tactile; the eighth house rules things you can't see or touch. You prefer instant downloads, snap decisions and shoot-from-the-hip (and lip) spontaneity. The eighth house is suspicious, strategic and slow to reveal. At times, you may feel like an astrological expat, fumbling around on foreign soil, relying on translation tools for the simplest of conversations… which will not be easy for you, the zodiac's super-communicator.

With the eighth house, it's helpful to picture the number "8": Leaning on its side, it forms the infinity symbol, representing the continuous flow of energy that we put in and receive back. This trio of planets will deliver a-ha moments around everything from shared money to sex to power to deeply-buried emotions. You may abruptly join forces or part ways as a result of these pot-stirring transits. Strong feelings can erupt like a dormant volcano becoming active.

But the payoffs of an eighth house transit can be mighty! You can reinvent your life from the ground up, should you choose. Money flows to you in large lump sums and you can have the best sex of your life! You just have to accept that you'll be living 2020 according to the Law of Polarity. In order to reach a new high, you have to be willing to carve out space for some deeper lows. Without darkness, there can be no light. *C'est la vie.* No one emerges from an eighth house transit as a one-note singer…or even a two-note chord striker. With your expanding emotional range, you'll compose a symphony of sensitivity—and sensuality—before the year is through.

Saturn-Pluto conjunction: Grow your money.
December 2019–February 2020 (exact on January 12)

Hello, money magnet! On January 12, karmic Saturn and power-broker Pluto host a rare, exact meetup at 22° Capricorn. These two heavy-hitters only conjunct each other once every 33 to 38 years, and when they do, you can't help but evolve. Saturn rules time and all things that stand the test of it. Over the past two years, the ringed planet's tour through Capricorn has been an eye-opener for your restless sign. Instead of reaching for the low-hanging fruit, you're embracing the ripening process. There's a reason that savvy financial advisors refer to the growth of assets as a "maturing." They know that remaining patient and non-reactive is the way to ride out market fluctuations and reap the true wealth. This is true for finance and romance, and by now, you've likely learned that lesson a few times over. On January 12, you'll have an opportunity to put those skills to the test.

Power broker Pluto's been on a long roll through elite Capricorn, since November 2009. With Saturn ringing his bell this January 12, it's "blue chip or bust." (Sorry, Gemini: Day-trading penny stocks ain't gonna cut it in Q1.) Under this planetary pairing, you could rethink your entire budget. In order to create legitimate wealth, you may have to sacrifice a few non-essentials or raise your rates! Then, put the extra cash into a high-interest-yielding investment, like a mutual fund, perhaps one that includes a few socially responsible stocks.

If you've never done more than drop money into a basic savings/checking account, January 12 is a call to raise your fiscal IQ. With this cosmic duo activating your eighth house of big money, think outside the nine-to-five box. You don't have to quit your day job, but how about collecting royalties (or dividend) checks along with your standard paycheck? Instead of hustling harder, add a passive income generator to your portfolio. This could span the range from a rental property to a downloadable product to a well-managed 401k.

If you've been living beyond your means, this is your wake-up call to pivot. You could downsize or embrace the sharing economy, and say, bring in a roommate for a few months while you get back on your feet. Maybe you've attached your identity to an image, like "bohemian artist" or "front-lines activist," which is fine—except when you cut off your supply to the wealth that wants to flow in your direction. Who says artists have to be "starving" to produce great works? Or that denying yourself pleasure and abundance will bring about social justice? Take care of yourself in a responsible way, and you'll have far more energy to pour into your passions.

Here's some good news: For your mentally alert sign, transformation can be as simple as changing your mind. Once you retrain your brain to focus on the positive, you become a highly attractive force. Work with mantras, vision boards and all the "woo" tools at your disposal. But pragmatic Saturn insists that you also learn some budgeting skills. Enlisting a financial coach or planner might seem like yet another expense, but if it means getting off the "feast or famine" hamster wheel, the ROI could be worth it.

For Geminis in solid relationships, January 12 is an epic day for co-creation! You could combine resources for a powerful purpose, one that benefits both of your lives—and perhaps a community in need. Maybe you'll pool your savings to buy (or rent) a starter apartment in an emerging neighborhood or scout beachfront property for a spiritual retreat center. If it's not money that you merge, it might be your creative talents. Could you and your S.O. record an album or co-write a manifesto this winter? It's possible!

Jupiter-Pluto conjunction: Join forces.

April 4, June 30, November 12

What happens when guarded Pluto bumps into high-exposure Jupiter…and in your sexy, secretive eighth house? We can feel the frissons of intrigue and tension already, Gemini. Three times in 2020, these fractious entities will hook up at the exact degree of Capricorn on April 5, June 30 and November 12. Jupiter and Pluto's high-strung mashups can reveal a treasure trove of buried, and burning, desires.

Can we get a "meow," please? You'll feel sultrier than you have in ages, that's for certain. And when you launch your charm offensive, the response will be instantaneous. To call you magnetic would be an understatement. But as quickly as you attract people, you may soon feel repelled by them—and the "come here, now go away" dance could wage on throughout the year. It's not that you don't want people to be close to you. In fact, you'd like some skin-on-skin contact, please and thank you. But what happens when they start forming (cough) expectations? This is where commitment always gets tricky for you. It's one thing for people to swoon over your charming ways, but quite another for them to start making demands. You like to have an "out" clause, a rear window, an escape hatch. Even more confusing? You've been known to get obsessed with the very same person who annoyed you, the minute they finally get fed up with the games and pull away. Argh!

Indie-spirited Jupiter understands this. Security-obsessed Pluto does not. You'll need to negotiate the dueling desires for free love and unwavering commitment in 2020. Thank goodness your sign is so comfortable with paradoxes, Gemini, because this planetary activity will pull you between extremes.

It's a lot like taking an adventure dive into an underwater cave. In astrology, Pluto rules the underworld, and is associated with the shadow side of our personalities; often the traits we reject within ourselves. The icy dwarf planet is perfectly comfortable paddling around the murky waters of the eighth house. But high and mighty Jupiter? Not so much. He sits on an elevated perch, beaming a stadium-sized spotlight down to expose the truth. But have you ever tried shining a light into water? That's a good metaphor for what happens when Jupiter attempts to illuminate the watery depths of the eighth house. The beam refracts, the view is distorted. Colors fade to a blue-grey and distances are hard to determine. In some instances, you simply see a reflection.

> "You could travel, return to school or launch an indie business venture. "

In other words, Gemini, what you see is not what you get in 2020—especially when it comes to binding relationships. You may think you're reading people like a library book only to discover that you've misinterpreted the manuscript. In fact (glug), you might be projecting some of your own hidden fears onto others, which is one of manipulative Pluto's favorite defense mechanisms. Are you seeing them, the reflection of your own shadow…or both? It really is that complex in 2020. Before the year is through, you could be versed in all of Carl Jung's archetypes. But hey, it was Jung who said, "Even a happy life cannot be without a measure of darkness, and the word 'happy' would lose its meaning if it were not balanced by sadness. It is far better to take things as they come along with patience and equanimity."

Despite the push-pull dynamics, this activity in your eighth house of perma-bonding can help you cement meaningful partnerships…and keep them hot! This year, you'll learn that commitment can be an adventure—and an erotically (or financially)

charged one at that! Regulating the balance between autonomy and connection will be a key component in this dance. That might mean letting go of your #twinning fantasies and giving your beloved some space! Or, you'll have to engage in independent activities that fortify a strong sense of self. As *Mating in Captivity* author Esther Perel advises, "Allow yourself to feel more deeply the otherness of your partner. You never really possess each other. You just think you do."

Has a relationship run its course? If you're still holding on, praying they'll have a change of heart, Jupiter could pry your Plutonian grip loose, possibly by putting a sizzling new person in your path. You'll have to let go of the old fantasy, Gemini, especially if you've been living in a lonely promise of what might materialize…someday. Longtime couples could explore spirituality or attend therapy to dismantle any deeper blocks you've been avoiding. Bonds will be reinvented, and you can gain a renewed connection to your own sexuality.

If you struggle to integrate this part of yourself, you might even create an alter ego for your sensual self. This is one of the core concepts of Sheila Kelly's S-Factor, an empowering movement practice that incorporates pole dancing. Students are guided to discover their "erotic creature," the persona that emerges when we allow raw, sexual desire to take hold. As a Gemini, getting in touch with your multiple selves can help you embrace the multi-dimensional wholeness of your being.

And oh, the places that "creature" could go! Pluto will guide you into some seamy depths while Jupiter is always up for experimentation. The (not-so) secret freak in you could be unleashed by the Jupiter-Pluto conjunctions. Private Pluto prefers that you keep things behind closed doors…or maybe away from home base. That's fine by globe-trotting Jupiter, who can help you master the art of the vacation fling or a passionate "baecation" with your long-term love. Have protection, will travel.

With lucky Jupiter joining investment banker Pluto in your eighth house of wealth, assets and passive income, you'll continue to magnetize money this year. Financial windfalls may arrive in large chunks, perhaps through a bonus, a real estate sale or an inheritance. You might take a gamble on an investment, as your risk tolerance increases tenfold. Some Geminis may part ways from a longtime business or romantic partner, and this year could be about dividing up shared assets.

The eighth house rules power and the way we share our resources. Are you hoarding all your "toys" or are you putting a portion back in the communal pot? Are you playing the sole provider or are you allowing others to contribute their fair share? Wield any newfound influence with care. Under the year's eighth house influence, let the continuous loop of giving and receiving be your guiding energy.

Taxes, dividends and other lump sum payments also fall under eighth house rule. If you've been dodging the IRS or delaying your filings, it's time to play catch-up. Geminis who are behind on credit card bills, student loans or other principal payments might work out a settlement. Most lenders (and even the IRS) just want to get some of their money back and are often willing to negotiate a lower payoff amount. You'll be in a good position to advocate for this near the April 4 Jupiter-Pluto conjunction. We recommend that you deal with debt before the second Jupiter-Pluto confab on June 30, when both

planets will be retrograde and could leave you at risk of penalties. If you need to clean up your credit—or simply want to raise your credit score—this is the year to restore your good standing. By lowering your monthly bills and beginning to consistently pay them on time, you can already start to rebuild.

Pluto and the eighth house are associated with loss and the afterlife. And with curious Jupiter joining in, you may find yourself fixated on the spiritual nature of death. Where do we really go when we leave this mortal coil? This doesn't have to be a morbid exploration, Gemini. Delving into past-life regression books like Michael Newton's *Journey of Souls,* Dolores Cannon's *Between Death and Life,* and Brian Weiss' *Many Lives, Many Masters,* can bring you an amazing sense of peace. Or, perhaps you'll resonate with a spiritual tome, like *The Tibetan Book of Living and Dying.* If you're grieving a loss, you will find reads like these comforting during this karmic year.

The green-eyed monster will be sitting on your shoulder often, so don't let envy become the deadly sin that delivers the *coup de gras* to your friendships and relationships. If anything, learn to use envy as a map, as suggested by Julia Cameron, author of *The Artist's Way.* Rather than coveting thy neighbor, remix your own version and do it up Gemini-style.

Since you'll be pinging between the poles often during 2020, it's probably best to embrace the Kabbalistic concept of "restricting your reactions." Instead of going off the rails at a moment's notice, the goal is to become proactive, taking steps that will resolve a conflict, rather than conflating it by heaping more fuel onto the fire. That won't be easy for your impulsive sign, but every time you pause for a beat, you'll gain more power…and save yourself from the guilt and shame that comes each

 The AstroTwins' 2020 Horoscope

time you spontaneously combust before you have all the facts. Practice makes perfect, Gemini.

Venus & Mars Retrograde: Relationship review.

Venus Retrograde: May 14 – June 25

Mars Retrograde: September 10 – November 13

Mirror, mirror on the wall. Who's the hottest zodiac sign of them all? You don't need to peer into the looking glass to figure that out, Gem. In 2020, radiant Venus beams into Gemini and your first house of identity from April 3 to August 7. This extended cycle blesses you with added magnetism and allure. Everyone you meet will be charmed and captivated by you, and your popularity will soar.

But ahh, there is a catch: From May 13 to June 25, Venus pivots retrograde in your sign. This six-week intermission flips the lens inward. Have you been people-pleasing, telling lovers (and friends) what they want to hear instead of what you truly believe? Or maybe you've overdosed on togetherness and feel like an involuntary inmate in the couple bubble. (Help…air!) While you don't want to punish your boo for behaviors that you instituted, draw back for some self-reflection during this cycle. Conversely, the temporary uncertainty that arises during the retrograde can turn you from confident to clingy. Check yourself before firing off 30 consecutive "Where RU?" texts to bae! (Who is probably in a meeting.)

Oscar Wilde summed it up best, "To love oneself is the beginning of a lifelong romance." This extended Venus in Gemini cycle is all about cherishing yourself, with or without a partner or any sort of outside validation. But that's not the easiest thing for you. As the sign of the Twins, you may struggle to find your identity when it's not being reflected back to you by another person. Trouble is, that leaves you "relationship dependent," rather than in control of your own happiness.

A little alone time can go a long way this spring! Single Geminis might take a Tinder timeout between May 13 and June 25, an opportunity to reconnect to your own needs and desires. Since Venus is the cosmic creatrix, use this slower window to develop an artistic or musical project that keeps getting shuffled back on your priority list. Just don't make yourself so busy that you fail to notice the needs of your partner or the fine specimen who's checking you out from across the room.

Want to go deeper? If you've kept things superficial, Venus retrograde helps you plunge into more intimate terrain. But if you see red flags, don't ignore them. This backspin can draw you toward dangerous liaisons and people with pasts so shadowy, you couldn't find their souls with a stadium light! If you're already committed elsewhere, beware the lure of an emotional affair between May 13 and June 25, which, for you, can feel as erotically charged as the act itself. You'll know you're blurring lines if you can't stop thinking of excuses to send helpful tips to a "friend," or if you're counting down the minutes until you are together in the office/class/band practice, etc. Boundaries, Gemini: They are a must!

Hold off on any cosmetic updates like chopping your hair or getting inked between May 13 and

June 25. Radical changes could lead to regrets with beauty queen Venus in reverse. Put your plans on a Pinterest board and review after six weeks. Same goes for any major purchases: With values-driven Venus in reverse, your fiscal decisions may be muddled, especially if you let your fluctuating emotions dictate spending. (Retail therapy is all too real during this cycle.) Since retrogrades rev up the past, you might tap into a fresh income stream by reviving an old passion!

Here's a fascinating tidbit about Venus: Every eight years, she returns to one of the same five zodiac signs for a retrograde, until she cycles through all 30 degrees of that sign and moves on to the next one. You, Gemini, are among the "lucky" ones who gets to host backspinning Venus in this lifetime. She's been pinging back through your sign since 1932—and will do so until 2088! So you might as well learn to appreciate these once-per-decade relationship review periods.

On that note, flip back to 2012 when Venus last moonwalked through your sign from May 15 to June 27. Recurring themes may arise in 2020. Maybe you'll get a second chance to make things right with someone who was in your life eight years ago. If that old flame isn't rekindled, you could meet someone who stokes the same embers. Coupled Geminis may have to rehash an issue that you thought was buried. But don't exhume those skeletons just to keep things interesting. If you're feeling restless, stop obsessing over your partner and go develop one of your gifts instead.

At the same time, teamwork does make the Gemini dream work in the second half of 2020, as momentum-builder Mars glides into Aries and your collaborative eleventh house for a prolonged visit, until January 6, 2021. Normally, the red planet hangs in a sign for seven weeks, but every other year, a retrograde cycle stretches out its stay. In 2020, Mars will make its reverse commute from September 9 to November 13.

Before the Mars backspin, assemble your ideal cast! You have between June 27 and September 9 to make these superstars official members with some sort of contract. Commitment isn't your favorite word, Gemini, but the last thing you need is anyone jumping ship midway through a project because you kept everything too loosey-goosey.

Since the eleventh house also governs science and tech, adventurous Mars in Aries could turn you on to the latest gadgets and software. Could your work be more productive—and moreover, profitable—if you upgrade? Does your website need professional dev support? If so, the investment could be worth it. Mars may turn you into a bona fide YouTuber, Instagram influencer or legit online celebrity.

Your activist streak will also be aroused in the second half of 2020, just in time for the U.S. Presidential elections. Have bullhorn, will protest! (Or work the phone bank, ring doorbells, whatever.) Your silver tongue could be the secret weapon a political candidate or important cause has been waiting for.

The only bummer of this cycle? Progress could grind to a halt—or even backslide—starting September 9. Until November 13, you might experience slowdowns or even work stoppages on a joint project. While pushing, arguing and cajoling might feel good in the moment, none of that is likely to have a positive effect. Yet assuming a passive (or passive-aggressive) attitude is probably worse. Pick your battles carefully: If someone isn't carrying their fair share of the load, take them aside and firmly but kindly let them know exactly what needs to change. Spell out the consequences of not doing so. This may be a little challenging with forthright Mars in reverse. If you can't find the words, prepare a short "script" that you can memorize and recite rather than trying to think on your feet, when you might get a case of the jitters.

Since retrogrades rule the past—and the eleventh house is also the domain of groups, social activism and innovation—you may reconnect with old friends or colleagues who are involved with world-bettering programs. In your personal life, with Mars retrograde, you might prefer to stay more insulated with your innermost circle between September 9 and November 13. Huddle up and enjoy the cozy "hygge" season vibes!

Saturn in Aquarius: Calculated risks.

March 21–July 1
December 17, 2020–March 7, 2023

Now for a relief from all that intensity! On March 21, taskmaster Saturn shifts out of Capricorn and your hyper-focused eighth house, springing into compatible air sign Aquarius for a brief window. With your freedom-loving, world-traveling ninth house getting some action until July 1, you could plot your next epic adventure. Maybe that looks like applying for an artist's residency in Florence… or going on a guided shamanic journey through Peru. Whatever fantastic voyage calls your name, Gemini, Saturn's planning powers can lend an assist with manifestation.

No matter your GPS coordinates, Saturn's tour of Aquarius will activate your quest for knowledge, truth and your highest purpose. Since the ninth house rules higher education, consider a return to school or seeking formal training in your field. Credentials count under Saturn's rule, and hey, it never hurts to strive toward professional advancement. Strengthen any weak areas with a mentor or through formal training. Have you already developed mastery in a topic of interest? During Saturn's tour of the ninth house, you could create your own curriculum or author a book. Travel for business or steady work with a long-distance client are both possible. Some Geminis will take concrete steps to launch an indie venture.

It's enough to take preliminary steps this spring and summer, since Saturn slips back into Capricorn on July 1 before resuming a longer trek through Aquarius in December.

There's also a paradox to navigate, because Saturn restricts and the ninth house expands. How can they settle this difference? Think of the ways that structure can set you free. Visualize yourself building a solid container, one that's designed to hold your dreams. After all, a vision that has no plan or direction won't manifest into tangible form. The trick is not to suppress your ideas or stifle your creative process. Respect it and give it room to breathe. Allow space for blue-sky dreaming before you start asking things like, "Will my partner support me with this endeavor?" or "When can I quit my day job and do this full time?" By the same token, don't run willy-nilly like a three-year-old on a sugar high. Otherwise, you'll just end up scattering your energy and burning out fast.

It may be enough for you to merely know that freedom and expansion are right around the corner for you, and by the end of 2020, they'll feel like your birthright again!

One of the best things about a planetary transit in the ninth house is that it can inspire some long-overdue physical activity. If you've been in a sedentary slump, having the personal trainer planet (Saturn) move into your ninth house on March 21 is a timely boost for your spring training goals. Saturn loves a program and a plan—and you, Gemini, thrive when you work with a supportive community. Consider joining a 60- or 90-day challenge at the gym or yoga studio; or jump into a wellness coach's online boot camp. By the time Gemini season rolls around on May 20, you'll be feeling like your best self again. Photo shoot!

Jupiter in Aquarius: Freedom & adventure.
December 19, 2020– December 29, 2021

Sweet freedom! On December 19, Jupiter will jailbreak from Capricorn's restrictive cage to join Saturn in Aquarius and your liberated ninth house. As the year wraps, you'll feel like a free-spirited Gemini again. It's as if someone handed you a limitless airline voucher and said, "Go forth and explore!"

After groping around in the eighth house's hall of mirrors for most of 2020, it might take you a minute to get your bearings again. But not too long! Worldly Jupiter is right at home in the international ninth house, which is its favorite cabaña in the horoscope wheel. This transit, which lasts until December 29, 2021, will bless you with abundant good fortune, radiant vitality and an intrepid spirit. If you've been thinking of going back to school, starting your own business or moving to another part of the world, Jupiter will pour rocket fuel into your tanks.

Jupiter was last in Aquarius from January 5, 2009, to January 18, 2010. Look back to those times: Did you take any major risks or widen your perspective? With this growth-driven sector activated once again, you could travel, return to school, launch an indie business venture or swing far outside your comfort zone. As you make your 2021 resolutions, think big. Jupiter in this no-limits zone will stretch your perceptions of what's possible!

With Jupiter buzzing into your ninth house, you'll feel a burst of vitality, as if you downed a celestial smoothie—powered up with raw cacao, maca and live greens. Just in time for the holidays, this jovial year-long cycle will turn you from brooding "elf on a shelf" to volunteer Santa Claus in 0.2 seconds. Thankfully, people are used to seeing you pull these whiplash-inducing switcheroos. It might be you who has some eleventh-hour adjustments to make. Did you plan on a low-key celebration to ring in 2021 at home, by the fire? *Boooooooring!* Snag those last-minute tickets to visit far-flung family (and see your favorite DJ on tour while there). Or nab the spot that just opened up in a friend's beach town Airbnb rental…or ski-lodge suite. Your active, adventurous side is back with a vengeance as 2020 wraps, such sweet relief after this introspective year.

The Great Conjunction: Jupiter & Saturn unite.
December 21

On December 21, 2020, a rare (as in once every 20 years) cosmic event called The Great Conjunction arrives with the Winter Solstice. For the first time since May 28, 2000, Jupiter and Saturn will make an exact connection in the skies. This time they'll meet at 0°29' Aquarius, hitting your ninth house of worldwide expansion, the higher mind and adventure. With Saturn's potent planning powers, and Jupiter's can-do zeal, you could see a clear way to make even the most daunting dreams come true.

In many ways, Jupiter and Saturn are opposites, but they can be perfectly complementary forces. Jupiter is the gas and Saturn is the brakes, and every vehicle needs both. Saturn can curb some of Jupiter's high-rolling instincts, helping you determine which risks are savvy and which ones could send you to the poorhouse. Simultaneously, jovial Jupiter lifts melancholy Saturn out of the doldrums and inspires the planetary engineer to be more innovative. As this cosmic coupling can teach us, mindful gambles are necessary for growth. Learn the art of calculated and well-timed moves and your dreams will gain staying power. As Nelson Mandela said, "It is only impossible until it's done."

With Jupiter and Saturn both in Aquarius, a compatible fellow air sign, you'll feel like your old self again. Better still? In this position, they form a flowing trine (120-degree angle of harmony) to your Gemini Sun. Late December 2020—and all of 2021—can be a powerful time for taking decisive action around your dreams. Being daring and discerning all at once is the way to win with Jupiter and Saturn here.

If you don't have your bags packed for a New Year's Eve vacation—or plans to host an otherworldly feast to fete in 2021—get busy. Decadent Jupiter rules the ninth house, so you'll get a double dose of hedonism and spontaneity as 2020 wraps. While Saturn can restrain your appetite, it also adds clout and stamina. One of your wilder ideas may actually gain traction, even if it seems like "too much." If you're dreaming of going big, you'll have the follow-through to turn your visions into reality. Strike the word "impossible" from your vocabulary—it has no place there now.

North Node in Gemini: Solo spotlight.
May 5, 2020– January 18, 2022

Now for some truly exciting news! In 2020, destiny is calling—and it has your name stamped all over it. On May 5, the lunar North Node returns to Gemini for the first time since April 14, 2003. This special point in the sky is associated with the higher calling, transformation and dharma. It's the stretch we must make to evolve as spiritual beings. During this fateful and fortunate cycle, which lasts until January 18, 2022, the world will be tuned to the Gemini frequency. You'll have a clear advantage over the other 11 signs in most competitions—provided you stay true to your values. If you bend to another person's whims or compromise your ideals, you could find yourself adrift.

Navigating this solo energy will create some dissonance, since there's such a planetary pull to join forces in 2020. Make sure you've carved out space for "me, myself and I," along with all those shared ventures. Call it your path, your purpose, destiny…whatever the case, the North Node in Gemini is here to help you make your unique mark on the world.

One caveat: The North Node, which we like to refer to as "the zone of miracles," is not a familiar place. Even when this point in the sky corresponds with your sign, you may still feel like you're trekking on foreign soil with only a temporary visa. Having a solid support network is essential to keep you from scurrying back into your comfort zone.

Start making a budget, Gemini, because after May 5, you may want to invest in coaches, mastermind groups, specialized trainings and degree programs. Or hey, apply for a scholarship: With so much luck on your side, you'll easily snag those funds. Do whatever it takes to get your meant-to-be mission in motion—and keep you on that road for eighteen months! The North Node only visits your sign every 18.5 to 20 years, so you don't want to miss this crucial window for self-development.

The last time the North Node visited Gemini was between October 14, 2001 and April 14, 2003. If you're old enough to remember what was going on then, you might see some recurring themes crop up.

> **"Your laborious 2019 efforts could finally pay off with legitimate earnings. "**

Cancer/Capricorn Eclipses: Money makeover
January 10, June 21, July 5

Pennies from heaven? If they don't start raining down, you could discover new ways to "make it rain" as three of 2020's six eclipses strike gold across your financial axis. These are the last three eclipses in a series that began with the Cancer new moon on July 12, 2018, and waged on with four more on the Cancer/Capricorn axis in 2019. Ever since then, you've been transforming your approach to earning (and burning) money. Although these lunar lifts can bring hidden opportunity, they also open your eyes to habits you need to change.

On January 10, the first full moon of 2020 arrives as a shadowy lunar eclipse in Cancer and your second house of financial foundations. Your laborious efforts of 2019 could finally pay off with some legitimate earnings. Out of the blue, a job offer could land in your inbox that's too good to pass up. Or you could make a sudden (and only halfway expected) exit from a gig that was sucking your soul. In the sign of the emotional crab, this lunation might bring in a bounty or a shake-up, or a mix of both. Either way, on January 10, a new way of dealing with your finances will come to light.

On June 21, the solar eclipse arrives with the new moon in Cancer. You could have an epiphany about your career path or discover a money-making opportunity that was hidden in plain sight. Is it time for a raise? The second house rules self-worth, and this eclipse will give you a strong nudge to advocate for yourself. If you don't speak up for what you deserve, who will?

The final burst in this two-year series comes on July 5, when a lunar (full moon) eclipse lands in Capricorn and your eighth house of merging, intimacy and shared resources. This throws the spotlight on your closest ties and reveals how you can meld your superpowers for gain. From crowdfunding to bartering, these eclipses uncover new ways you can thrive cooperatively. If it's time to break free of a draining partnership, this eclipse lights the exit ramp. You're either in or you're out—no half-stepping!

Gemini/Sagittarius Eclipses: Me or we?

June 5, November 30, December 14

How much self-care do you need, and how do you fill your love tanks? Beginning June 5, a new series of eclipses will galvanize the Gemini/Sagittarius continuum. Until December 3, 2021, these lunations will be shaking up the balance between your personal first house (Gemini) and your seventh house of partnership (Sagittarius).

It begins with an eye-opening lunar eclipse that arrives with the full moon in Sagittarius this June 5. With these moonbeams activating your interpersonal seventh house, don't be surprised if dashing and dynamic people appear like forces of nature. This could "eclipse" an important person

into—or out of—your life. If you've been hovering on the fence about whether to stay or go, your deliberating days are over. Vital information could be revealed, helping you make the right choice. Some Twins could feel impulsive and compelled to take action, rushing off to City Hall to say "I do"—or making a swift and sudden exit from a union. An exciting business deal may come together or completely fall apart.

Lunar eclipses can be especially disorienting, since they deal with transitions and turning points, so give yourself a few days to adapt before doing anything hasty and irreversible. Whatever's (truly) meant to be around this day, shall be.

Only one eclipse, the November 30 lunar (full moon) eclipse, will fall in Gemini in 2020. As you go through seismic changes, questioning everything from your beliefs to your lifestyle to your past choices, it's only natural that your relationships will undergo big transformations, too. It's an adjustment process: As you evolve, some people will adapt to that, while others just might not groove with Gemini 2.0. You may change your terms of engagement (for example, shifting from romance to friendship—or vice versa!) or separate if you're not on the same wavelength. But rest assured, some compatible new cronies and collaborators will fill that blank space pretty quickly!

On December 14, the solar (new moon) eclipse in this cluster could bring an important decision about the future of a relationship or a business deal straight out of the gate. Lawyer up and draft those contracts. Things could get official fast! ✹

January

JANUARY: LOVE HOTSPOTS

January 3-February 16: Mars in Sagittarius

The lusty planet returns to your partnership house for the first time in two years, kicking off an electrifying two-month adventure. Couples can bring sexy back, but to keep it there, make a promise to not fight or even bicker all week. Single? Things could get hot fast—and, if you both wanted it, semi-official!

January 10: Uranus retrograde ends

Disrupter Uranus resumes forward motion after five unstable months of reversing through your twelfth house of healing and transitions. You've probably shed a lot of emotional baggage, but what's left to forgive or transmute into gold? If you're ready to release resentment or cut the cord on a toxic behavior, radical Uranus will help you break that addictive pattern.

January 12: Mercury-Saturn-Pluto meetup

In a rare and groundbreaking three-way mashup, the messenger planet merges with future-oriented Saturn and alchemical Pluto in your eighth house of intense feelings. While you might be tempted to blurt out a confession or reveal a secret fantasy, remember that a little intrigue keeps things spicy and unpredictable. Speak from your heart when you do share, but don't feel compelled to tell everything.

January 13: Sun-Saturn-Pluto meetup

Feelings you've been burying could break the surface as this exceptional cosmic alignment forms in Capricorn and your eighth house of intimacy. If you've hid your feelings or held in a secret desire, you could find the confidence to boldly let it out. A relationship that's riddled with ego and power struggles could reach a breaking point.

January 13-February 7: Venus in Pisces

Amorous Venus begins the year in your house of long-term goals, meaning the next three weeks are ideal for setting some new resolutions about what you want for the future—either with a potential new partner or the one you're with! Who knew that making a five-year plan could be so sexy?

January 26: Venus-Mars square

With the cosmic lovebirds out of sync, your romantic plans could get derailed. While Venus is having rosy dreams of the future, pushy and rebellious Mars could be applying too much pressure to commit or throwing up obstacles where there's actually no conflict. Tread lightly today!

January 27: Venus-Neptune meetup

Daydreams dominate as the love planet merges with fantasy agent Neptune in wistful Pisces and your future-oriented sector. While there's nothing wrong with dreaming up romantic plans, it's important to make sure that you and the other person are actually on the same page. Otherwise, you could be in for a bit of a letdown.

JANUARY: CAREER HOTSPOTS

January 2: Mercury-Jupiter meetup

Nothing wrong with a little blue-sky dreaming, but make sure the logistics work on paper. And before you do anything on your own, sit down with all partners and collaborators. Initiate honest conversations about your mission statement, strategy and how to make big bucks.

January 3-February 16: Mars in Sagittarius

Partnerships can heat up and move quickly into official status over the next few weeks, so make sure you know what your bottom line is. With the passionate planet heating up your dynamic-duos realm, you could feel energized by a creative cohort but also a little stressed out by their "demands." If it's really bugging you, tell them you do better with suggestions.

January 10: Cancer full moon (lunar eclipse)

The first full moon of 2020 is also a lunar eclipse, which could bring all your efforts of the past six months to a culmination. You might get the answer you've been waiting for or, if you're lucky, be cashing a nice bonus since it lands in your money zone. This lunar lift can herald a surprise job offer or moneymaking opportunity. Since eclipses can throw wild curveballs, you may suddenly leave a job or experience an unplanned change at your workplace. Expect the unexpected!

January 10: Uranus retrograde ends

Changemaker Uranus corrects course after five unsteady months in your introspective zone. You've had plenty of time to think through a job offer or new business plan, and now it's time to put your money where your mouth is. A creative venture could rocket forward.

January 12: Mercury-Saturn-Pluto meetup

This super-rare merger helps you think strategically and plot your next moves. With mental Mercury and serious Saturn conjunct Pluto in your calculating eighth house, it's a great day for mapping out intricate plans or negotiating like a master chess player. And power broker Pluto gives you the confidence to move forward without looking behind you—or even around you.

January 13: Sun-Saturn-Pluto meetup

The bold Sun and plumb-the-depths Pluto align but one day a year, and Saturn and Pluto only connect once every 35 years, so this mega-merger could be major! For three consecutive years, this summit takes place in your eighth house of joint ventures (and strong emotions), so set aside the latter to successfully navigate the former. Block out the distractions and feel your own power surge. You're a master strategist, Gemini, and if you plot your moves carefully, you could lead the troops to a rousing victory.

January 16-February 3: Mercury in Aquarius

When your galactic guardian beams into fellow air sign Aquarius for the next three weeks, you won't need any prodding to think outside the box or go all in on a calculated risk with a potentially massive payoff. As the quicksilver planet blazes through your visionary ninth house, you'll be a step ahead of the pack and there won't be any catching you.

January 18: Mercury-Uranus square

While you're racing ahead, others might be resentful or even jealous to the point of trying to block you. Ignore the naysayers and just do you. And maybe make an impossible-to-copy move to leave 'em all in the dust!

January 23: Sun-Uranus square

It'll be hard to keep your opinions to yourself under this tongue-loosening clash, so if you must express them, make sure you have an appropriate audience. People who aren't familiar with your eclectic thinking and iconoclastic wit could take your words out of context and use them against you.

January 24: Aquarius new moon

This galvanizing new moon lands in your ninth house of education and entrepreneurial ventures. What ideas have you been kicking around that are finally ready to put into action? Today also launches the Chinese Year of the Metal Rat, which bodes well for all strategic new beginnings. Take your first bold move on the path to success!

January 28: Mars-Neptune square

Mars is all about taking decisive action, but with nebulous Neptune throwing major shade, the plan might not be as viable as it seems. Someone could be talking a big game but doesn't have the substance to follow through. Under this illuminating square, make sure that "someone" isn't you, Gemini!

February

FEBRUARY: LOVE HOTSPOTS

February 7-March 4: Venus in Aries

During romantic Venus' monthlong romp through your platonic eleventh house, the flames of passion could cool, and you might find yourself craving more breathing room. If you're not involved, keep dating efforts light and casual. Since this realm rules technology, a new app could be your best matchmaker. Or you could fall head over what-just-happened heels for a friend. Couples should go out and socialize together.

February 16-March 30: Mars in Capricorn

So much for cool and casual! Once lusty Mars blasts into your erotic eighth house for two months, an attraction blazes up. You could lunge into a steamy sitch or be tempted by a clandestine affair. Most important now is being honest with yourself about what you're getting into. For unhappy partners, things could get contentious, especially if you're splitting up. Even happy couples could fight about money or control, but there's a two-word silver lining: makeup sex!

February 21: Mars-Uranus trine

Under this rare connection of passionate Mars and unpredictable Uranus, sparks will fly, and if you're up for a boudoir bonfire, seize this anything-goes energy!

February 23: Venus-Jupiter square

When insatiable Jupiter dukes it out with amorous Venus, you might actually be craving freedom or a new conquest more than commitment. Since this is a fast-moving transit, avoid doing anything drastic.

February 28: Venus-Pluto square

You could get sucked into something more overwhelming than you expected under this mashup of the love planet and manipulative Pluto in your intense eighth house. No, Gemini, you're probably not overreacting, although good luck trying to keep a level head. Stay connected to your heart (and your gut) today. If you're feeling under attack or pressured, try to extract yourself or at least pull back a little.

FEBRUARY: CAREER HOTSPOTS

February 3-March 4: Mercury in Pisces

Mental Mercury kicks off its annual tour of your professional tenth house today, dialing up your ambitions. Have conversations about your goals with mentors and decisionmakers. Take the time to plot a master plan—and for best results, put it in writing!

February 9: Leo full moon

An illuminating full moon in your communication house inspires you to speak your truth and express yourself fully. If you find the words to post this on social media, your ideas could go viral. Over the next two weeks, you might receive long-awaited news or make a collaboration official.

February 16-March 9: Mercury retrograde in Pisces

When the messenger planet shifts into reverse in your professional tenth house, you could have second thoughts about your career path. Things that were starting to take off last month may suddenly wither on the vine. Use this time to reflect, review and reconsider. On March 4, Mercury will back into Aquarius and your truth-telling ninth house, a time to get honest with yourself and others about what you really want.

February 16-March 30: Mars in Capricorn

Stealth equals wealth as motivator Mars enters your shrewd eighth house, ramping up your negotiating powers. Turn yourself into a money magnet by aligning yourself with power players and keeping distractions to a minimum. A hit of healthy competition can move you to the head of the pack. But beware getting so obsessed with what your rival is doing that you take your eye off your own big goal.

February 21: Mars-Uranus trine

Today's supportive starmap reminds you that you don't have to do it all by yourself. If someone offers help, accept it and thank them graciously! Sometimes assistance comes in more subtle form, so pay attention to synchronicities and "coincidences" that give you assurance that you're on the right path.

February 23: Pisces new moon

This initiating new moon plants some quick-sprouting seeds in your career house. If you've been hoping for a change, this lunar lift can send you down a whole new path. But you'll need to keep an open mind and be willing to consider slightly more unusual offers that may come your way. Happy where you are? This lunation sparks a stimulating six-month cycle of professional growth and inspires you set some lofty new goals for the rest of the year.

March

MARCH: LOVE HOTSPOTS

March 3: Venus-Saturn square

Get hot and heavy—or play it cool? Your emotional temperature may be all over the thermostat as the love planet in your open-minded eleventh house catches shade from restrained Saturn in your perma-bonding zone. It's hard to talk about commitment and the future when all you want to do is have fun! Finding that delicate balance will take extra effort today.

March 4-April 3: Venus in Taurus

When amorous Venus dips into your twelfth house of introspection and release, you'll be ready to bring on the feels and surrender to sweet fantasies. Open your heart and let yourself be a little vulnerable. You'll be amazed at what happens when you don't try to control the situation.

March 8: Venus-Uranus meetup

This lightning-bolt jolt could bring a sudden soulmate or some other unexpected shift in your relationship status. If you've been the one holding back, you may finally decide to let a special someone get closer.

March 9: Virgo full moon

The year's only Virgo full moon illuminates your sentimental fourth house, bringing emotions to a full boil. But if you don't discuss your feelings with your partner or love interest, you'll never move the needle. Single? Over the next two weeks, you can get clarity around your deepest desires and what "security" means to you. Attached? Talk could turn to family planning, moving in together or making changes to your living situation.

March 20: Mars-Jupiter meetup

Intimacy and intense emotions could heat up quickly as inflammatory Mars and supersizer Jupiter unite in your sector of merging. If you've been holding back strong feelings, they could come surging up now.

March 23: Mars-Pluto meetup

This could be one of the steamiest or most emotionally intense days of your entire year! When these two lusty planets align in your erotic eighth house, serious chemistry is sure to get fired up. No sense holding back now!

March 27: Venus-Jupiter trine

This rare heart-opening alignment encourages you to take a risk in the name of amour and share from the deepest level of your being, even (and especially) if it makes you feel vulnerable.

March 28: Venus-Pluto trine

There's nothing casual about today's emo vibes. When the love planet in your introspective zone hooks up with smoldering Pluto in your eighth house of intimacy, you may not be able to hold in your deepest desires. Ready to take a bold next step? Go ahead and initiate a conversation about making things more official. Single? Stay open to different types. An appealing suitor might blip onto your radar screen without warning. Pursue!

MARCH: CAREER HOTSPOTS

March 4-16: Mercury in Aquarius

You won't need a poke in the ribs to think outside

the box or take a calculated risk on a project with a potentially big reward. With your quicksilver ruler jetting through your bottomless ninth house, you'll be miles ahead of the pack.

March 16-April 10: Mercury in Pisces

When the messenger planet blasts into your professional tenth house today, your career ambitions get kicked up a level. Use the next few weeks to firm up your plans, map out some even bigger goals and start talking to people who can help you turn them into reality!

March 20: Mars-Jupiter meetup

Under this rare (once every other year) merger of action planet Mars and Jupiter the gambler, you're stoked to take a risk and the leap of faith it requires. But no need to broadcast this news to less intrepid folks, who might be unsupportive (which could just indicate envy).

March 21-July 1: Saturn in Aquarius

The planet of structure and discipline returns to your visionary zone for the first time since 1991. These next three-and-a-half months are just "phase one" of the full transit, which is in effect until March 7, 2023. But now you can start pursuing your dreams one calculated step at a time. During this three-year journey, you'll have a higher tolerance for risk, and could travel for work, return to school or launch your own business.

March 23: Mars-Pluto meetup

Step into your power today! Call a spontaneous strategy session and map out some tactical moves. Listen to what others have to say: You could discover a potentially powerful ally or team up with a well-connected person who can usher you into an elite and influential circle.

March 24: Aries new moon

The year's only Aries new moon electrifies your eleventh house of networking and technology, connecting you with a group of eclectic thinkers or a cutting-edge "geek squad." Got a big idea you've been holding to your chest? Share selectively over the coming two weeks. You may discover that you don't have to reinvent the wheel to pull it off.

March 30-May 12: Mars in Aquarius

Passionate Mars returns to your adventurous ninth house for the first time in two years. If you've been waiting for the right moment to launch a project or expand in a more global way, this could be it!

March 31: Mars-Saturn meetup

Hit the gas—or the brake? You may experience bursts of energy only to feel totally exhausted a bit later under this uneasy alignment of driven Mars and cautious Saturn. Pace yourself so you don't burn out.

April

APRIL: LOVE HOTSPOTS

April 3-August 7: Venus in Gemini

This year, when the love planet blazes into your sign for her annual visit, it won't be the usual quickie stopover. Thanks to a retrograde from May 13 to June 25, you can look forward to an extended romantic power surge! Your magnetic sex appeal will be off the charts. Single? Enjoy the attention but try not to let it go to your head. Couples can do a few intentional things to strengthen the ties that bind. What might your next step look like?

April 4: Venus-Saturn trine

A couple times a year, the love planet gets into harmonious formation with future-focused Saturn, and when she does, you may instantly tire of mind games and commitment-phobes. If you're ready (or close to ready) to take the plunge, stop talking and do something about it! Already attached? It's a great moment to discuss shared future plans.

April 4: Jupiter-Pluto meetup

Deep-seated emotions you weren't even aware of could suddenly come into the open as revelatory Jupiter and penetrating Pluto make a rare (once every 13 years) union in Capricorn and your intimate eighth house. A simmering attraction could hit a boiling point. Are you imagining that it's mutual...or not? You could certainly find out now, or at the two other conjunctions on June 30 and November 12.

April 7: Libra full moon

The year's only full moon in your fifth house of glamour, amour and creativity is a great reason to celebrate! Since full moons bring things to culmination, this one could point to a major tipping point in a certain relationship. In articulate Libra, this lunar lift can help you communicate some of your deepest feelings and desires.

April 22: Taurus new moon

Are you about to shut the door on a certain chapter and move on? Before you do, is there something you need to release or someone you need to forgive (or make amends with)? The annual new moon in your house of transitions and healing can help you balance that accounting and get on with your life, whether solo, with your current partner or a new, improved candidate!

April 25-October 4: Pluto retrograde in Capricorn

Just when things reached cruising altitude, the alchemical planet kicks off its annual backspin in your intimacy zone. This could force you to downshift—or pull the brake if things are too speedy. Either way, you're being given a beautiful opportunity to explore trust issues or devote quality time to processing some old wounds. This will ensure that you don't project your past onto a new union. A tempting but potentially toxic ex could resurface. Proceed with caution.

APRIL: CAREER HOTSPOTS

April 3: Mercury-Neptune meetup

Talk about a winning combo! Today, analytical Mercury teams up with the planet of intuition and imagination, amping up your communication skills. Add little creative flourishes to your presentations and speak to everyone with genuine compassion.

April 4: Jupiter-Pluto meetup

At this once-every-13-years alignment between visionary Jupiter and transformational Pluto, a calculated risk could deliver a financial windfall or catapult you into new levels of mastery and power. These two luminaries will unite in Capricorn and your eighth house of merging three times this year. Today's strategic moves could pay off at the other two Jupiter-Pluto conjunctions on June 30 and November 12.

April 7: Mars-Uranus square

The answers you seek may not come from traditional sources today, so let "serendipity" guide you. Meet the universe halfway by watching for unexpected connections to develop out of the blue. But resist your analytical sign's tendency to try to interpret them. Observe and be prepared to act, but don't do anything rash under this unpredictable aspect.

April 10-27: Mercury in Aries

When your ruler, articulate Mercury, buzzes into your networking sector for its annual three-week pollination session, you can build or strengthen new professional alliances, possibly with folks from different departments or with fresh perspectives. Trailblazing Aries could inspire something totally progressive—and impressive!

April 14: Sun-Pluto square

Strength is found in numbers, but so is disagreement and discord as this twice-annual clash can remind you. Sniff out potential manipulators and power-trippers and cut them a wide berth. If you do discover that someone is pushing a selfish agenda, diplomatically let them know you're onto them.

April 15: Sun-Jupiter square

There are confident and helpful people in your world, and then there are cocky and self-interested folks. Under this aggrandizing clash, it may be hard to tell them apart. Watch for outsized egos and unbridled jealousy to flare up today, and do your best to stay out of the fray.

April 21: Sun-Saturn square

Ignore that little voice that's doing its best to undermine your confidence. That's an old program that's running, Gemini, and it's no longer relevant in your life. Stay on guard for people who press your buttons. They don't deserve your high-vibe energy!

April 22: Taurus new moon

Stuck on a seemingly unsolvable problem? Stop thinking about it and use your imagination! The year's only new moon to power up your subconscious zone can spark genius. Try looking at this from different perspectives. During the next weeks, ask your mind to manifest answers as you're falling asleep. A surprisingly brilliant idea could strike—in dreamtime!

April 25: Mercury square Jupiter and Pluto

Oversharing alert! Watch out for TMI today as verbally nimble Mercury locks horns with larger-than-life Jupiter and manipulative Pluto in your "chamber of secrets." You might be feeling bold and confident, but until you're 100 percent sure of the people you're about to reveal sensitive information to, it's probably better to keep it locked in the vault.

April 25-October 4: Pluto retrograde in Capricorn

A joint venture could hit a speed bump in the coming few months, but as they say, forewarned is forearmed! How can you guard your intellectual property and assets? It's never a bad idea to run things past an attorney with experience in this area. Be transparent, but also self-protective.

April 26: Sun-Uranus meetup

When the creative Sun forms its annual merger with inspired Uranus in your dreamy twelfth house, your ideas will be nothing short of genius. Don't worry if people don't get it. You might be too far ahead of the curve to explain this. Dive into your process and let the results speak for themselves.

April 27-May 11: Mercury in Taurus

When your ruler, mental Mercury, dips into your introspective twelfth house for the next few weeks, take a step back from a team project and

turn inward. This is a good time to give your imagination free reign. Don't worry about what's "doable." Just capture your best ideas and plan to refine them when Mercury buzzes into your sign later next month.

April 28: Mercury-Saturn square

Feeling overwhelmed by a project that's ballooned out of control? That's a sign that you need to set some limits and enforce your boundaries! The best way to manage expectations is to break things down into smaller chunks, and then take one methodical step at a time.

April 30: Mercury-Uranus meetup

The annual summit of these inventive planets in your dreamy twelfth house cranks your creative machinery up to peak operating capacity. After a long gestation period, you're in the home stretch of a huge ideation phase. Get ready to start making these dreams a reality.

May

MAY: LOVE HOTSPOTS

May 3: Venus-Neptune square

This is the first of a series of clashes between amorous Venus in your sign and dreamy Neptune in idealistic Pisces. While it can dial up the fantasy and loving vibes, it will also make it hard to see a situation clearly. You may be processing things one way while the object of your affection could be on a totally different page. Unfortunately, trying to talk about it can only worsen. Sleep on it.

May 9: Mercury-Pluto trine

Under this sweet sync-up of the messenger planet and alchemical Pluto, things could get deep and intense without a lot of warning. Open up and be more vulnerable. And don't be caught by surprise if your mate or a new love interest also decides to bare their soul.

May 12-June 27: Mars in Pisces

And you're off! When the action planet zooms into your future-oriented tenth house, you'll be on the fast track to making a commitment official. Exciting, sure, but you could also feel pressured to agree to something before you're ready. Examine your resistance as well as their pushiness. This is a good time to talk it about and find a comfortable balance.

May 14-September 12: Jupiter retrograde in Capricorn

If a relationship has been speeding ahead at vertigo-inducing rates, this annual reversal of expansive Jupiter—this year in your eighth house of intense emotions and sexuality—gives you a moment to tap the brakes, catch your breath and reflect. Take the necessary time to consider a specific connection but also how you "do" intimate relations.

May 14-June 25: Venus retrograde in Gemini

The love planet begins her once-every-18-months backspin today—and this time, it's happening in your sign. This could cause you to feel misunderstood, underappreciated and self-critical. Venus retrograde can disrupt the easy flow of all relationships. With the planet of beauty reverse-commuting in your first house of image, put off any radical changes to your appearance or style.

The AstroTwins' 2020 Horoscope

May 22: Mercury-Venus meetup

How deep is your love? Tell them in no uncertain terms! Under this harmonious hookup of verbal Mercury and seductive Venus in your sign, you'll find the perfect words to express how you feel. And, if you'd like to see some changes in your relationship, this cosmic combo helps you articulate that diplomatically.

MAY: CAREER HOTSPOTS

May 7: Scorpio full moon

Order in the Gemini court! The full moon in your administrative sixth house helps you tie up those lingering loose ends and tune up your systems. Pinpoint any inefficient processes and update them with better technology or communication flow. Are there weak links in the chain? Make sure everyone is trained properly. Maybe it's time for a team check-in?

May 10-September 29: Saturn retrograde in Aquarius

When the cosmic ruler of time and structure makes his annual pivot—this year in your visionary ninth house—you may realize that you need to scale back or roll something out in phases. Saturn trains you to think "slow and steady" rather than trying to rush your ideas into production. It'll be worth it in the long run.

May 10: Mercury-Jupiter trine

Facts and data are important, but much has been written about "how to lie with statistics." Under today's alignment, what you're really waiting for is a thumbs-up from your gut. Your intuition will be sharp, so rally some creative minds and have an impromptu brainstorming session.

May 11: Mercury-Mars square

You didn't want it to come to this, but if the backbiting and bickering hasn't stopped on its own, you may need to step into the role of referee (or tough-love parent). It's time to put an end to any unprofessional behavior on your team. Aggression and bullying are a no-go.

May 11-28: Mercury in Gemini

Speak up! With your ruling planet, expressive Mercury, now in your sign, holding back your ideas would be a waste of everyone's time. Start spreading the news, gauging interest and finding people who want to get on board with your clever concepts.

May 12: Mercury-Saturn trine

Ideas are a dime a dozen, but if you want them to succeed, they need a timeline and structure. Under this solidifying alignment, get your thoughts on paper and share them with a well-connected person who might be interested in funding it or perhaps even partnering up.

May 12-June 27: Mars in Pisces

As the cosmic master of motivation blasts into your successful tenth house for the next six months, your ambitions will be on fire. You've got the drive, inspiration and energy to reach some of your biggest professional goals. Hit the gas and don't slow down till you get there!

May 14-September 12: Jupiter retrograde in Capricorn

Retrogrades always sound like bad news, but when lucky Jupiter shifts into reverse (something it does annually for four months), it's an invitation to review your long-range financial goals and shared resources, at least this year when it's touring your house of investments and joint ventures. If you're carrying debt, make an effort to whittle it down this summer!

May 15: Sun-Pluto trine
Trust your gut today as the bold Sun and insightful Pluto sharpen your instincts. Tune in to people's body language and pay attention to what they're *not* saying. Those subtle cues could say more than the words that come out of their mouths.

May 22: Gemini new moon
The year's only new moon in your sign is one of the best days of 2020 to rethink and regroup on any projects that aren't turning out like you'd hoped. The world's your oyster for the next few weeks… so set a lofty goal and really stretch to reach it!

May 22: Mercury-Neptune square
Truth is stranger than fiction today as communicator Mercury (in your sign) forms a slippery square with hazy Neptune in your tenth house of career and long-term goals. Before you share your big ideas with anyone, protect your intellectual property. If you have any hesitation about whether someone can be trusted, either keep your concepts under wraps or have them sign a non-disclosure agreement. Think twice before being overly frank with clients or higher-ups today. Better to respect the pecking order than to come across as rude or entitled.

May 28-August 4: Mercury in Cancer
As analytical Mercury zooms into your second house of work and money, you'll be in the driver's seat when it comes to pitching new prospects or leading a negotiation. This pivot is extra-long because the winged messenger will be retrograde from June 18 to July 12. Meaning: no need to rush anything!

June

JUNE: LOVE HOTSPOTS

June 2: Venus-Mars square
Don't cave to external pressure under today's clash between the cosmic lovebirds. Mars always wants more—and sooner—but Venus is retrograding through your sign and enjoying the scenery (and the prerogative of changing her mind) The only thing "required" is honesty. Beyond that, you get to decide at what pace you want to roll.

June 5: Sagittarius full moon (lunar eclipse)
Ooh, baby! The year's only full moon in Sagittarius lands in your seventh house of partnership, which could bring a simmering attraction to a rolling boil during the next two weeks. That said, if it's a lukewarm connection, the flame might die out on its own. But before you do anything permanent, check in with your heart and make sure your expectations are realistic.

June 13: Mars-Neptune meetup
When motivational Mars merges with murky Neptune in your future-oriented tenth house, be careful not to get carried away with your dreams. Single? This is a good time to get clear about what you're seeking in a partner. Couples, on the other hand, have *carte blanche* to live out their fantasies or try something decidedly not vanilla.

June 27, 2020-January 6, 2021: Mars in Aries
Ambitious Mars blasts into your eleventh house of teamwork and technology. Because of a retrograde from September 10 to November 13, you've

The AstroTwins' 2020 Horoscope

got a lovely, extra-long stretch to embark on a collaboration or launch a digital venture. Just don't let Mars push you into doing anything prematurely!

June 30: Jupiter-Pluto meetup

Your quest for emotional transparency gets another lift today as the second of 2020's three rare Jupiter-Pluto conjunctions lands in your intimate eighth house. With truth-seeker Jupiter illuminating Pluto's shadowy depths, someone's unconscious motives could become clear—or clearer, anyway. Since both Jupiter and Pluto are in pensive retrograde, probing your own psyche could lead to powerful insights. Examine your motives and make sure they're above-board. If you're caught in an addictive or obsessive pattern, Jupiter's wisdom can help set you free.

JUNE: CAREER HOTSPOTS

June 5: Sagittarius full moon (lunar eclipse)

The full moon in your dynamic-duos zone can advance a partnership or convince you to finally ink a deal. And since it's a game-changing lunar eclipse, offers could come out of the blue—with little time to think them over before an answer is needed. As the original "twinning" sign, you're keenly aware of how the right alliances can take your efforts to a level you could never reach on your own. Don't deliberate too long—a golden opportunity may not remain on the table forever.

June 13: Mars-Neptune meetup

As assertive Mars and enchanting Neptune unite in your career and leadership zone, today calls for being an "iron fist in a velvet glove." Deliver any commands with compassion and sensitivity, while still being firm about your boundaries. If you give clear instructions and set people up to win, they'll do your bidding…with pleasure!

June 17-July 12: Mercury retrograde in Cancer

With the mental planet reversing through your financial sector, keep a close eye on your money and an extra-strong grip on your plastic! During this signal-scrambling period, it'll be easy to overlook an expense or lose hours of valuable work to a computer crash. While you may not be able to avoid that, you can hit "save" often and load important files to the cloud for insurance!

June 21: Cancer new moon (annular solar eclipse)

This first of two rare back-to-back new moons in your financial sector could bring some exciting news on the job or money front (or both!). And because it's a solar eclipse, you might get some insider info that helps you make a major professional leap forward. On a personal level, this lunation and its follow-up on July 20 can herald the beginning of a new approach to handling your finances and establishing greater fiscal security!

June 22-November 28: Neptune retrograde in Pisces

When mystical and profound Neptune kicks off its annual five-month slowdown in your career sector, you might find yourself asking questions like "Am I serving my life's purpose?" and "What is this all for?" But you won't get any solid answers if you don't step back from the rat race at least a little to reflect. While you're pondering your next phase, look for ways to infuse your goals with some soul.

June 27, 2020-January 6, 2021: Mars in Aries

Settle in for the long haul! With motivated Mars slow-jamming through your collaborative, tech-savvy zone for an extended run (thanks to a lengthy retrograde from September 10 to November 13), you can take your sweet time getting a passion project just right. If you need some professional input, hiring a top pro could be a smart investment.

June 30: Jupiter-Pluto meetup

Where do purpose and power align? Today brings the second of this year's three Jupiter-Pluto connections in Capricorn and your strategic, wealth-minded eighth house. Since both planets are retrograde, it's a powerful time to review your financial goals and to take stock of your assets. By the time the third meetup arrives on November 12, you could make a savvy investment or ink a major joint venture.

July

JULY: LOVE HOTSPOTS

July 1-December 17: Saturn retrograde enters Capricorn

Cold feet and second thoughts? Today, as structured Saturn returns to future-oriented Capricorn, you can start to work through your issues around trust and vulnerability. Over the coming months, you could get serious about cohabitation, long-term merging and even marriage. But note, relationships on shaky foundations will be put to the test. Single Geminis may decide to resist casual sex or online dating in search of the real thing.

July 5: Capricorn full moon (lunar eclipse)

This intense full moon, which is also a game-changing eclipse, powers up your erotic zone and sets the stage for one of the sexiest days—and nights—of the year. In your "chamber of secrets" zone, it might even inspire you to confess one of your deepest desires.

July 27: Venus-Neptune square

Don't push for a "final answer" under this hazy hookup. With amorous Venus in your sign out of sorts with bewildering Neptune in your future-oriented tenth house, your idea of where things are heading could be 180 degrees away from how your love interest is seeing things. Manage your anxiety, and definitely ride this one out!

JULY: CAREER HOTSPOTS

July 1-December 17: Saturn retrograde enters Capricorn

When slow-and-steady Saturn backs up into your eighth house of joint ventures and long-term wealth for almost the rest of the year, you could reach a new level of power and financial security—but it won't happen overnight. Plan to put in the hard work and stay alert to important lessons about making people earn your trust and not handing it out like business cards at a networking event!

July 5: Capricorn full moon (lunar eclipse)

If you've been building up trust in a new deal or partnership, things could finally come to fruition under this grounded lunar eclipse. Give it six months to fully reveal its potential. With the potency of these moonbeans cranked up, this could be a game-changer!

July 8: Mercury-Mars square

Tension could flare today over shared finances or work duties as communicator Mercury, which is retrograde in your finance house, butts heads with incendiary Mars. If you stay open instead of getting defensive, perhaps you'll broker a more equitable arrangement. Everyone deserves to feel appreciated and compensated fairly for their work. Heads-up: This transit will repeat again on July 27 when Mercury is no longer retrograde. Hash things out now and you'll be in a better place to compromise then.

July 12: Sun-Neptune trine

Conduct all the due diligence you need, but under this intuitive alignment, your secret weapon is your ability to visualize what you want and then manifest it! With the self-assured Sun supported by mystical Neptune, you'll be on fire. It's a great moment to do something that can actually make a difference in other people's lives.

July 15: Sun-Pluto opposition

This once-a-year alignment may reveal the dark underbelly of a deal or person you're thinking of partnering up with. While the potential to make big money is there, so is very real risk. If you're still tempted, research this one thoroughly—and have an out!

July 20: Cancer new moon

This rare second consecutive new moon in your financial sector comes on the heels of a powerful June eclipse. It could bring a job offer or an unexpected opportunity for a major money move. Maybe it will just prompt you to create a brand-new budget that sets you up for success over the coming six months.

July 20: Sun-Saturn opposition

During this annual face-off between the Sun and long-term-planner Saturn on your money axis, you'd do well to call a timeout and take a financial reality check. While el Sol may be eager to advance a project, this warning signal from Saturn urges you not to rush into anything. Take the time to double- and even triple-check your numbers.

July 30: Mercury-Jupiter opposition

Expansive Jupiter is putting the spurs to your sides to sign a contract or launch a partnership with someone who seems promising. But mental Mercury is prompting you to hit pause and play out a few different scenarios, including "worst-case." Before you invest any time or money, get the assurance you need that this person can deliver the goods.

July 30: Mercury-Neptune trine

The devil is in the details, but sometimes your greatest guidance comes from your gut. If you have to make a financial decision today, follow your intuition. As cerebral Mercury harmonizes with perceptive Neptune in your work and money zones, you'll be tuned in to nuances that others might miss.

August

AUGUST: LOVE HOTSPOTS

August 4: Mars-Jupiter square

Under this conflicting starmap, it might be better to sit out a dance or two until you get clarity around what you truly desire. It won't be fair to you or an admirer to give false hope. Attached? Don't

The AstroTwins' 2020 Horoscope   150

feel guilty if you're not in the mood for romance. Everyone's entitled to their off days!

August 7-September 6: Venus in Cancer

As amorous Venus settles down in your grounded second house for the next four weeks, you'll be craving stability, which can lead to more certainty about what your heart desires. Singles should be clear and direct with the object of your affection: Better to know for sure than keep barking up the wrong tree. Solidly together? Upgrade your dating style to include a little more luxury—and definitely more sensuality!

August 15, 2020-January 14, 2021: Uranus retrograde in Taurus

Just when you thought you had a solid grip on a certain person or an aspect of your relationship, disruptor Uranus shifts into its annual five-month reversal—through your surreal twelfth house of transitions, release and healing. But no finger-pointing. During this backspin, you may need to acknowledge a codependent relationship or an addictive behavior of your own.

August 19-September 5: Mercury in Virgo

For the next three weeks, your ruling planet will moonwalk through your sensitive fourth house, prompting you to trust your heart more than your head. But be subtle and sensitive to the emotional climate. If you show that you care about someone else's feelings, you'll build trust, which will make it easier to ask for their support in the future.

August 25: Venus-Jupiter opposition

Under this once-a-year smackdown, you could experience a surge of jealousy or possessiveness that threatens to destabilize a relationship. If you've

lapsed into a boring rut, there are better ways to spice up the union than by doing things that could break your bond of trust. How about planning a sexy vacation or test-driving some new moves in the boudoir?

August 25: Mercury-Uranus trine

Under this lip-loosening alignment of spontaneous Uranus and the messenger planet, you can broach a subject you've been keeping under wraps. Step out of your rigid roles and have a heart-to-heart. You can wind up stronger and more connected as a result of it!

August 27: Venus-Neptune trine

Twice a year, the love planet connects with enchantress Neptune, dialing up your compassion and capacity for empathy. You don't need to set any "relationship goals" or create an agenda. Just be there to listen without trying to solve or fix anything.

August 29: Mercury-Jupiter trine

A budding relationship quickly turns deep under this supersizing alignment. Make sure you know what you want because you won't have time to think once things get going. Couples can talk through what their next big steps might look like—anything that enhances merging is supported!

August 30: Venus-Pluto opposition

This once-a-year manipulative mashup could reveal someone's ulterior motives—possibly yours. Pay attention to what you're saying. You might not realize you're being passive-aggressive until someone points it out. Then, instead of getting defensive, catch yourself and nip it in the bud before you do regrettable damage.

 The AstroTwins' 2020 Horoscope

AUGUST: CAREER HOTSPOTS

August 1: Mercury-Pluto opposition

Be slow to jump onto any deals that involve money—especially when it's yours. With manipulative Pluto throwing shade at cerebral Mercury across your financial axis, be extra-cautious about joint ventures and shared investments. And definitely think twice before lending or borrowing, especially if it comes with high interest or other strings attached.

August 2: Sun-Uranus square

Blurt alert! Under an edgy face-off of rash Uranus and the ego-boosting Sun in your communication corner, you could be tempted to utter some angry, uncensored things. But bite thy tongue, Gemini! And if you feel yourself slipping, a walk or a workout could do wonders to calm you down.

August 3: Aquarius full moon

Whatever you've been working on for the past six months could finally reach a culmination point under this visionary full moon. You've paid your dues; now you're ready to launch yourself into the stratosphere! The next six weeks are especially auspicious for travel, furthering your education or debuting an entrepreneurial idea.

August 3: Mercury-Saturn opposition

If you've been burning your income as fast as you're earning it—or can't get a handle on mounting debt—today's stern starmap inspires you to investigate some different approaches. Tightening your belt is an obvious place to start, but you may need to find a side gig or work with a financial coach to help you identify and eradicate any deep inner blocks.

August 4: Mars-Jupiter square

You might not see eye-to-eye with a key associate or collaborator today, which may or may not spell trouble. Every team has its ups and downs; your job is to figure out whether they're just having "one of those days" or they're not a good match. If it's the latter, don't be afraid to cut ties and move on.

August 4-19: Mercury in Leo

Break out the voice recorder apps and multimedia equipment: You'll be hosting your celestial ruler in your innovative third house for the next two weeks, and brainstorms could come a mile a minute. Get the best of the bunch out of your head and recorded somewhere so you can begin to turn them into a reality.

August 10: Mercury-Uranus square

Your words could push someone's buttons unwittingly today, leading to an argument. Or maybe they'll trigger a sore spot for you. With volatile Uranus involved, it's likely that everyone will be caught off guard here. Catch yourself if you start reacting—and don't be afraid to swallow your pride and apologize. Sometimes, the best words you can are utter are, "You know what? You're right."

August 13: Mars-Pluto square

Steer clear of an authority figure who's mounting their high horse or playing power games today. Not only are they annoying and distracting, but if their dictates go against your principles or challenge the integrity of a project, you owe it to the team to shut them down—or at least walk away.

August 17: Mercury-Mars trine

You've got the mic: Do you know what message you want to deliver? If you do, stand proudly and speak loudly! People will gather to support you. Not clear on your talking points? Sit down and map 'em out now while you've got this cosmic tailwind!

August 18: Leo new moon
The year's only new moon in your communication center fills your head with so many ideas for fresh initiatives that your only challenge will be figuring out which to tackle first! During the next two weeks, prioritize projects that benefit a worthwhile cause or help you get more immersed in the culture.

August 24: Mars-Saturn square
Trying to get people on the same page may be an exercise in futility today, so quit while you're ahead (or at least not at wit's end!). But here's a worthwhile question to ask yourself: Have you assumed more responsibility than necessary? Do your part—and do it impeccably—but then hold others accountable for their contributions.

August 30: Mercury-Neptune opposition
Your head and your heart may pull you in dueling directions today, so try to avoid making any irreversible decisions. If you find yourself overthinking this, stop and sleep on it.

September

SEPTEMBER: LOVE HOTSPOTS

September 2: Venus-Saturn opposition
If your heart is saying yes but your head isn't sure, check in with a deeper, wiser part of your psyche. You might not realize that a love interest or partner is triggering an old wound that has nothing to do with them. If it feels right after you've processed that, pursue—slowly and cautiously.

September 4: Venus-Mars square
Your desire for stability in a relationship could be undermined by Mars' lusty appetites. Part of you is content with the status quo, yet another side is craving excitement. Enjoy the passionate wave but find an outlet for it that doesn't mess up an important bond.

September 5-27: Mercury in Libra
When the cosmic communicator flits into your romantic fifth house, you won't be able to hide or deny your desires. Use this expressive transit to speak from the heart. Playful banter could turn into something more.

September 6-October 2: Venus in Leo
When vixen Venus commences her annual peacock strut through regal Leo and your third house of communication, your ultimate aphrodisiacs will be (sincere) flattery and conversation that's stimulating—on all levels!

September 9-November 13: Mars retrograde in Aries
As lusty Mars shifts into reverse for two months, a relationship could get wobbly or an ex could resurface and attempt to sweep you off your feet. Try to see past the moment. Whatever happens now is temporary, and come mid-November, the winds of change will shift direction yet again. Make sure whatever you choose is setting you up for long-term happiness, not "live for the moment" thrills.

September 12: Jupiter retrograde ends
Back in action! After four months of slowdowns,

missed connections and crossed wires, auspicious Jupiter resumes forward motion in your eighth house of sex and intimacy. Singles might meet someone with keeper potential, couples can deepen their bonds, or, if you've been wavering about a certain relationship, you'll have more clarity about how to proceed.

September 14: Sun-Pluto trine
The rare and intensifying merger of the confident Sun and transformative Pluto in your most private chart sectors could send you spiraling inward—or you might find the courage to reveal a secret. Don't worry that it will make you seem "flawed"; it's your vulnerable and messy humanity that people are attracted to!

September 15: Venus-Uranus square
You might feel on edge under this uncomfortable mashup, but don't push yourself too hard. You could develop a case of grass-is-greener syndrome today or wonder what (and who) else is out there. Don't beat yourself up for those thoughts—it's not like you have to act on them. Chances are, they could help clarify your deepest desires.

September 17: Virgo new moon
This once-a-year lunar lift lands in your fourth house of home and family, putting those issues front and center for the next six months. What changes are you hoping to achieve by next March? Whether you're looking to move, meet each other's families or make babies—start taking steps in that direction during the next two weeks.

September 21: Mercury-Pluto square
You may be itching to blast forward with a relationship (whether brand-new or longstanding),

but this edgy square urges caution. You may think you know this person—and you might—but they could be going through something that has nothing to do with you. Trust can be challenged, so soft-pedal your approach. And try not to take things personally today.

September 23: Mercury-Saturn square
You're not out of the "trust-challenging" woods yet as chatty Mercury in your effusive fifth house catches major shade from tight-lipped Saturn in your chamber of secrets. Better to keep a few details under wraps than risk making yourself too vulnerable.

September 28: Venus-Mars trine
Share the love! As the amorous planets form a flowing trine in the friendliest and most communicative zones of your chart, you could have a heart-opening conversation with someone you adore. Friends can introduce you to their friends and you could meet someone special online. Who knows where chatting could lead? Just make sure they're fully available before you get carried away.

September 29: Saturn retrograde ends
Not a moment too soon, stoic Saturn concludes its annual retrograde—this time, through your eighth house of intimacy. For the past five months, this may have tested you on a deep level but also, ironically, opened you up emotionally, spiritually and sexually. If you've been on the fence, could it finally be time to make things official?

SEPTEMBER: CAREER HOTSPOTS

September 1: Mercury-Pluto trine
The ability to read people like a book is your

superpower today as observant Mercury and penetrating Pluto form an investigative tag team. Pay attention to subtle cues like body language, and if you get a hunch that something's off, ask incisive questions—or quietly take note.

September 2: Pisces full moon

This once-a-year galvanizing event in your professional zone can set you up for a major success in the coming two weeks. You've done a good job of setting the bar high: Now that you're reaching this milestone, it's time to reset it for another lofty goal. Don't compromise on your ambitions for the next half-year. You can earn the recognition you want—and deserve—but it will require you to put yourself out there more and ramp up the self-promotion.

September 3: Mercury-Saturn trine

Game on! Under this sober yet inquisitive merger, you can balance your analytic and creative sides and find a perfect way to pull off a special project. With sharp-witted Mercury in cahoots with structured Saturn in emotionally astute chart sectors, just follow your instincts. But make sure you've got the "evidence" to make it up in case you're challenged.

September 9-November 13: Mars retrograde in Aries

When the action planet goes off-course in your house of teamwork and technology, things could get wonky. Back up all your data to the cloud and an external hard drive. Change your passwords, too. Watch for normally mild-mannered people to reveal their unabashedly competitive sides. Be slow to confide in anyone till the red planet corrects course mid-November. And then, use the intel you collected during this pivot to be more selective about who you collaborate with.

September 12: Jupiter retrograde ends

After four frustrating months of backtracking through your shared-resources realm, auspicious Jupiter resumes forward motion, and all sorts of joint ventures get back on track. It's finally safe to pick up where you left off last spring with a budding deal or partnership. Things might go more in your favor after this forced "review" period!

September 17: Mercury-Jupiter square

Save your big reveal for another day. Under this sketchy clash, you might not be on the same page as the other party. Too much isn't being said, so wait until you get a clear green light.

September 24: Mercury-Mars opposition

It won't take much to spark tempers under this combustible sky map. You or someone on your team might be in particularly argumentative spirits, which isn't setting up the "all for one" vibe you'd prefer. Think twice before teaming up, and if you do join forces, take your time to carefully choose the right players.

September 27-October 27: Mercury in Scorpio

Your ruler, cerebral Mercury, zips into your hardworking, service-oriented sixth house for an extended stay (thanks to another retrograde from October 13 to November 3). Though retrogrades can be frustrating at times, there is an upside: You can use this slowdown to get any unorganized areas of your life back in order. Tackle your digital life and your personal space, and you'll be ahead of the game when it straightens out!

September 29: Mars-Saturn square

Today's stars pose a tough question: Are you

taking on more responsibility than necessary? With enthusiastic Mars at odds with the planet of firm boundaries, you could learn a valuable lesson about not enabling people. Even if their work affects yours, let them sink or swim on their own accord.

September 29: Saturn retrograde ends

You can exhale now! After a tough four-month retrograde in your eighth house of shared wealth and long-term investments, cautious Saturn swings back into forward motion and lifts some financial restraints. An outstanding bill or business obligation may have consumed a lot of your resources, but starting today, you can get back on track and start refilling those coffers!

October

OCTOBER: LOVE HOTSPOTS

October 2-27: Venus in Virgo

When tender Venus lands in your domestic fourth house for the next several weeks, your sentimental side will lead the way. Singles may have to push themselves to go out more, but if you can leave your inner critic at home, you could meet a worthy suitor. Ready to take a next step with your partner? This thoughtful period may prompt you to share your thoughts about moving in together or starting or expanding a family.

October 4: Pluto retrograde ends

Heaviness: lifting! You can breathe more easily now that intensifier Pluto is concluding its annual five-month retrograde cycle in your sex and intimacy

house. If any dark or not-pleasant emotions surfaced during this time (like anger, jealousy or trust issues), things should finally start to settle down.

October 10: Venus-Uranus trine

When curveball-throwing Uranus fist-bumps the love planet in your most internally focused sectors, take a risk by dropping your emotional guard and sharing a secret or confessing strong feelings. Single? Being this open and vulnerable could attract a soulmate type from out of the blue.

October 16: Libra new moon

This once-a-year lunar lift in your passion corner hits the refresh button on all relationships! New moons bring opportunities for fresh starts, and this one, in partnership-oriented Libra and your amorous fifth house, can help you find love or take your union a new level during the next two weeks.

October 18: Venus-Neptune opposition

You might be extra emotional under this hazy hookup of the love planet and nebulous Neptune, so avoid making any irrevocable decisions. What you're feeling and what's really going on could be miles apart. Let things simmer but ride this one out.

October 18: Sun-Saturn square

This speed-correcting square can slow things down if someone is getting too close too fast—or help you see things in a clearer light if you're the one trying to rush ahead. There's an appropriate way to move forward, and this alignment can be useful for finding that balance.

October 19: Venus-Jupiter trine

This auspicious alignment gives your relationship a mojo booster shot. If you're ready to go deeper,

take a next step toward long-term commitment or renew your vows, there's no better tag team than amorous Venus and expansive Jupiter!

October 19: Mars-Jupiter square

If you're feeling a little claustrophobic in a certain relationship, open a window and let in some air! Under this freedom-craving clash, you may suddenly need breathing room. Nothing wrong with that, but don't say or do anything that could give your love interest the false impression that you're trying to bolt. Single? Don't be so hasty to write someone off just because they get on your nerves—which are pricklier than usual today.

October 21: Venus-Pluto trine

You could feel a potent connection with someone who seems to "get" you without your even uttering a word. It won't matter whether this person shares your background or is from a totally different culture. When you feel each other on a soul level, there's nothing like it. For couples: Wade out of the shallow end and dive into deeper waters by sharing something you've never revealed.

October 24: Venus-Saturn trine

Let bygones be bygones! This solidifying alignment can pull your relationship over any rough patches and get you back on terra firma. Talk through any unsettled issues but focus on the love and your shared future hopes.

October 27-November 21: Venus in Libra

You'll be in your element when vixen Venus grooves into fellow air sign Libra and heats up your flirtatious fifth house. During this sizzling and seductive cycle, you could meet a soulmate type or take an important next step. One caveat: Mercury retrograde backs into Libra today as well, which

could scramble signals and cause messages to be misinterpreted.

October 31: Taurus full moon

The year's only Taurus full moon illuminates your twelfth house of fantasy, which can be wonderful for a new or rock-solid relationship. But if things have been on shaky ground, this full moon can lend the willpower to pull the plug.

OCTOBER: CAREER HOTSPOTS

October 1: Aries full moon

This annual lunar lift in your sector of teamwork and technology powers up all group efforts and could herald a shared victory. Not on the same page as your squad? This full moon might plant the idea that it's time to move onto a whole new project or crew. But take the next two weeks to think through that decision before you entirely cut the cord.

October 4: Pluto retrograde ends

A partnership deal or joint venture might have gotten sidelined over the past five months while game-changing Pluto was reversing through your eighth house of shared finances. But now that it's moving forward again, relevant discussions can resume. Don't be afraid to be the one to bring it up!

October 7: Mercury-Uranus opposition

Since this impulsive meetup could loosen your lips, don't be too quick to trust unfamiliar faces around the conference table. They could be perfectly fine, but unless you've worked with them in the past, they (and their motives) are still wild cards. Today might be better for listening and gathering information— as well as on October 19, when these planets clash again while Mercury is retrograde.

       The AstroTwins' 2020 Horoscope

October 9: Mars-Pluto square

Keep your eyes peeled for someone who may be on their high horse today, thinking it's acceptable to bark out orders and let everyone else do the heavy lifting. Staunch Mars in your teamwork zone won't take kindly to that, and thanks to a push from controlling Pluto, you might just let this person have a piece of your mind. But be careful not to cross a line yourself!

October 9: Mars-Jupiter square

If you see something, say something! Even if you only sense that a situation is about to go off the rails, speak up. While it may seem totally obvious to you, it's entirely possible that no one else notices and that they'll be more than grateful you spoke up. Heads up: This transit will occur again on October 19 and November 17.

October 13-November 3: Mercury retrograde

Cerebral Mercury reverses course in your organized, detail-oriented sixth house until October 27, when it backflips into Libra and your creativity sector. Use this three-week slowdown to get any out-of-control areas of your life back on track. Mercury retrogrades can make a mess of communication, but they're a perfect time for planning big initiatives—like your next career coup!

October 15: Sun-Pluto square

You might not be able to keep a low profile today, thanks to the rib-poking antics of an office provocateur. But no one says you have to take their bait! Screen them out or excuse yourself from any interactions before you get hooked.

November

NOVEMBER: LOVE HOTSPOTS

November 1: Mercury-Saturn square

Here you go again? This is the second of three squares between chatty Mercury and cautious Saturn in 2020—and this time Mercury is retrograde. An important message may finally get clear. Hold off on any big debuts until things are 100 percent ready. While Mercury in your effusive fifth house wants you to be an open book, timekeeper Saturn knows the value of waiting for the perfect moment. A little restraint goes far!

November 3: Mercury retrograde ends

Messenger Mercury ends a challenging retrograde that may have brought back an ex or caused old issues to flare. Been toying with the idea of a reunion? Now you can decide whether to give that person another chance. For couples, drama should die down. Hopefully, any heated emotions helped you forge a compromise.

November 9: Venus-Mars opposition

Once every other year, the love planets face off in opposite houses, inviting—or maybe forcing—you to stop and reevaluate things. Are you accepting less than you deserve or making excuses for someone who can't get their act together? Try to focus on the big picture. Just because you have feelings for each other doesn't mean you want the same things for the long haul. Find out!

November 12: Jupiter-Pluto meetup

Will the truth set you free…or seal your bond? Probing Pluto and adventurous Jupiter make their third and final alignment (the other two were on April 4 and June 30) in your intimate eighth house. All year, you've been exploring themes of lust and trust, taboos and temptations. Today, you could have a moment of deep insight about an important relationship. Should you make this a permanent arrangement? Do you want to get emotionally involved, or is it better not to go there? Jupiter and Pluto only conjoin every 13 years, so this burst of clarity should not be squandered.

November 13: Mars retrograde ends

When passionate Mars resumes forward motion in your house of friendship and technology, you might start to see a platonic pal in a whole new (and lusty) light. Online dating, once a dreaded activity, suddenly feels like a newly-stocked fish pond. Bait your rod and cast away!

November 15: Venus-Pluto square

Under this intense alignment of the love planet in your romance sector and shadowy Pluto in your eighth house of heavy emotions, your only fantasies might be of the "revenge" variety. Don't keep this bottled up. Talk to a friend, a therapist or your journal. Just steer clear of the object of your acrimony until this emo wave passes.

November 16: Venus-Jupiter square

Don't get carried away by your (overactive) imagination. Jupiter is like a funhouse mirror, and what it's reflecting back to the love planet is probably highly distorted. At the end of the day, the person you're putting on a pedestal is still human, and like you, has their strengths and weaknesses. So just deal with them like a regular mortal.

November 19: Venus-Saturn square

This edgy clash could leave you feeling conflicted about your love life or a budding interest. Venus in your flirty fifth house wants to get everything out in the open—or least get things going!—but guarded Saturn is riding the brakes. Ask yourself: What would be the most honest and direct way to get your romantic needs met?

November 21-December 15: Venus in Scorpio

When the planet *d'amour* invades intensifier Scorpio and your organized sixth house for a three-week journey, she may decide it's time to bring some sweeping changes. Whether you initially approve or not, trust that they're for your own good! This is an excellent period for getting your house in order—literally and figuratively—as well as addressing any health or energy issues that might be hounding you.

November 27: Venus-Uranus opposition

Expect the unexpected today as compassionate Venus opposes unpredictable Uranus. You might receive surprising information that initially throws you for a loop. While you're tempted to react impulsively (or stew in silence), stay neutral and try to get more insight into what's really going on.

NOVEMBER: CAREER HOTSPOTS

November 10-December 1: Mercury in Scorpio

Your ruler, analytical Mercury, returns to Scorpio and your detail-minded sixth house after a two-week retreat into Libra and your creativity zone. Now that it's back in forward motion, you can move ahead on some of those inspired downloads you might have gotten during the retrograde. All systems go!

 The AstroTwins' 2020 Horoscope

November 12: Jupiter-Pluto meetup

Keep your freedom or make it official? Restless Jupiter and entangling Pluto make their third and final union of 2020—in your eighth house of merging, shared property and joint ventures. Since as far back as two other meetups, on April 4 and June 30, you may have been considering an investment. But will this offer bring more breathing room or leave you feeling suffocated? Today's insightful alignment can deliver the info you need to make that judgment call.

November 13: Mars retrograde ends

Action planet Mars wraps up a frustrating retrograde that began on September 9 and powers forward in your eleventh house of technology and teamwork. Update your software, buddy up with a complementary force and get ready to take your next mission to a mind-blowing new level!

November 14: Scorpio new moon

This annual event in your sixth house of work, service and organization brings opportunities to make some fresh starts in any (or all!) of those areas of your life. This is also your zone of helpful people, and over the next two weeks, you might get clarity around the fact that you don't actually have to do it all by yourself. It might finally be time to call that highly recommended service provider.

November 17: Mercury-Uranus opposition

This is the third and final face-off between these two mentally agile planets, and this time, communicator Mercury is in forward motion. If you've been biting your tongue or sitting on your hands, this might finally be your moment to make that proposal or reach out to a power player. Nothing ventured, nothing gained!

November 23: Mercury-Neptune trine

Work doesn't have to be completely removed from your personal values, so take advantage of this heart-opening alignment to add some soul to your goals. Jot down any creative brainstorms that come today—they could be the makings of a lot more.

November 28: Neptune retrograde ends

Clarity returns as the nebulous planet concludes its annual reversal through your career corner. You may have been entertaining some larger-than-life notions over the past five months, but starting today, you can figure which if any of those dreams and schemes are doable.

November 30: Gemini full moon (lunar eclipse)

The year's only full moon in your sign is a cosmic half-birthday present. Because this potent lunar eclipse lights up your first house of self, you'll have the pluck to pursue a solo venture or work on your magnum opus. For the next few weeks, all eyes will be on you, so put extra effort into pitches or presentations you have to make. You could win some influential new supporters!

December

DECEMBER: LOVE HOTSPOTS

December 1-20: Mercury in Sagittarius

Mindful Mercury kicks off its annual tour of your seventh house of relationships, turning your thoughts to the qualities that make for a good partner—and a solid partnership. What do you need to be happy? And, on the other side of the coin, how can you be an even more supportive and adoring mate? An open dialogue about this could reveal insights.

December 5: Venus trine Neptune

Lean into the love language "acts of service" today, as Venus in your helpful sixth house sends a kindhearted beam to compassionate Neptune in your leadership zone. Ramp up the romance and the do-gooding with tickets to a holiday benefit party. Or keep the glamorous goodwill flowing by shopping for gifts that donate a portion of their proceeds to organizations you admire.

December 14: Sagittarius new moon (total solar eclipse)

This annual lunation in your relationship house signals new beginnings, and because it's also a total solar eclipse, you have a double dose of galactic gusto to manifest your dreams. What will you write in this fresh chapter of your personal book of love? Let your desires guide you!

December 15, 2020-January 9, 2021: Venus in Sagittarius

It just keeps getting hotter and hotter in your relationship realm! Today, when vixen Venus makes her annual arrival, you'll be ready for a romantic reboot or to take a major next step. Single? Be sure you actually want a full-time commitment before you go looking for one. In the sign of the autonomous Archer, Venus might prefer to play the field.

December 25: Mercury-Uranus trine

What better day than Christmas to speak openly about your feelings or forgive someone and move on? This mashup helps you find the perfect way to articulate something that's been kicking around in your noggin for a while. As long as you keep compassion in the mix, it'll all come out right.

December 30: Venus-Neptune square

With Venus in your relationship house locking horns with dreamy Neptune in your future-oriented tenth house, you might struggle to discern fantasy from reality—and keepers from players. Protect your heart by staying in observer role as you get a handle on what your heart really desires.

DECEMBER: CAREER HOTSPOTS

December 1-20: Mercury in Sagittarius

As your ruler, articulate Mercury, roars through your seventh house of contracts and partnerships, you could seal a deal or iron out any lingering points of dissent. Got a proposal to put forward? Don't wait, negotiate!

December 13: Mercury-Neptune square

Uncross your fingers and take an unblinking look at the current situation. Are you trying to bring someone to the bargaining table who isn't willing to compromise? Let it go—for now. Focus on work you can personally control and save the negotiations for the new year, when people will hopefully feel refreshed and ready to make a deal!

December 14: Sagittarius new moon (total solar eclipse)

This annual lunar lift—also a powerful total solar eclipse—electrifies your partnership sector and bodes well for any mergers over the coming six months, especially those inked over the next two weeks. Focus on mutual benefit, and if you sense

 The AstroTwins' 2020 Horoscope

there might be an imbalance of power, negotiate now to ensure that doesn't happen.

December 17, 2020-March 7, 2023: Saturn in Aquarius

If you can dream it (and plan it), you can do it! Cautious and calculating Saturn spends the next couple years in Aquarius and your visionary ninth house. After a short visit from March to July, the ringed taskmaster settles in here for a long run that only happens every 29 years. Between now and early 2023, you might go back to school, start an independent business or travel for work.

December 19, 2020-May 13, 2021: Jupiter in Aquarius

Auspicious Jupiter returns to your expansive ninth house for the first time in more than 12 years, supercharging your imaginative goals for much of next year. Where others see only obstacles, you see limitless possibilities! Aim high and keep reaching, and you might just touch the stars. In between all that jetting-ahead, be sure to build in plenty of time for blue-sky dreaming.

December 20, 2020-January 9, 2021: Mercury in Capricorn

When your ruler, messenger Mercury, blasts into your eighth house of wealth and financial planning, you may need to make some weighty decisions about your own investment strategy and any joint ventures you're involved in. Don't be short-sighted. Capricorn's gift is the ability to sacrifice now for long-term payoffs.

December 21: Jupiter-Saturn meetup

Your recipe for unstoppable success? Dream big and back it up with a plan. Today's mashup of abundant Jupiter and structured Saturn—known as The Great Conjunction—happens roughly every 19 years. This go-round they'll meet in Aquarius and your ninth house of limitless possibilities. Is it time to give your big ideas the investment of time and energy they deserve?

December 23: Mars-Pluto square

In this third and final Mars-Pluto scuffle, you can finally get the "warring tribes" to come to the table and help people see eye-to-eye. You may not have total success today, but if you emphasize the mutual benefit of working together, you might at least get everyone to agree to continue discussing this.

December 29: Cancer full moon

The year wraps on a big-money note as 2020's second Cancer full moon lands in your financial sector and brings your labors of the past six months to a culmination point. You could finally get the green light on your big initiative—and possibly a hefty bonus check for your efforts—before you've even made your New Year's resolutions. ✳

Tools from The AstroTwins
for your 2020 PLANNING

Visit all year long for
new updates & additions!

www.astrostyle.com/2020tools

The AstroTwins' 2020 Horoscope

CANCER
2020

Yearly Highlights

LOVE

Your most important duos get more dynamic in 2020 as jovial Jupiter sails alongside committed Saturn and Pluto, both in Capricorn and your seventh house of partnerships. Serious relationships don't have to feel like a giant weight on your shoulders. Enough of that, please! Free-spirited Jupiter, along with three final eclipses on the Cancer/Capricorn axis, will help you strike the right balance between "me" and "we." When Saturn and Jupiter shift into your seductive, stick-it-out eighth house in late December, important bonds will be cemented, both for business and pleasure.

MONEY

Pair up for the win! As fiscally savvy Saturn and Pluto team up, you'll be a magnet for magnates. People with complementary skillsets can launch your moneymaking missions into a new league. During Saturn's brief visit to Aquarius from March 21 to July 1, you could make a savvy investment in real estate, fund a start-up or begin regular contributions to your retirement fund. Your career kicks into high gear after June 27 when motivator Mars lumbers into Aries and lights up your ambitious tenth house for the rest of the year!

WELLNESS

You're the nucleus of your friend group and the nurturer of your family, Cancer, but it's time to pass the baton. In 2020, the emphasis is on building stronger one-to-one connections instead of always bringing the crew together. Take a fun-loving, responsible trainee under your wing, like a BFF or beloved relative. Share your secret recipe for event planning, group hangs and festive holiday gatherings. Sure, Cancer, you can still get involved, but this year, it will be a relief to let someone else be in charge.

LEISURE

Ready, set, de-stress! Beginning June 5, an 18-month series of eclipses in Gemini and Sagittarius galvanizes your health and healing axis. Build self-care into your weekly rituals and dial down any workaholic ways. Wellness is an inside job this year, so work on releasing old patterns that keep you stuck and anxious.

CANCER
2020 HOROSCOPE

2020 Power Dates

✳

CANCER NEW MOON
June 21 (2:41am ET) Solar Eclipse
July 20 (1:32pm ET)

CANCER FULL MOON
January 10 (2:21pm ET) Lunar Eclipse
December 29 (10:28pm ET)

SUN IN CANCER
June 20–July 22

No Crab is an island—a fact that will be proven true in 2020, as planets sail through the most relationship-focused houses of your solar chart. As a highly sensitive water sign, you're not just susceptible to picking up vibes from other people, you absorb them like a (sea) sponge! Pulling back into your shell can be a matter of self-preservation. But as the new decade launches, it's time to learn some non-isolating techniques for navigating the world. Can you retain safe borders while enjoying soul-centered partnerships? The planets in 2020 give that a resounding "Yes!"

As the year begins, growth agent Jupiter is co-piloting through Capricorn alongside stable Saturn and transformational Pluto. With this cosmic consortium in your seventh house of committed relationships, you'll shift into pairing mode. From project partners to long-term love matches, you're a highly attractive force! And with worldly Jupiter logged in to this zone, your signals will travel, drawing intriguing prospects from a wide radius. While logical Saturn ensures that you won't stray too far from what's sensible, seductive Pluto and daring Jupiter save you from falling into ennui. It was Cancerian Selena Gomez who crooned,

"The heart wants what it wants." In 2020, you're more risk-tolerant when it comes to relationships, willing to take chances on partnerships that come with complex circumstances, like living in different cities, states…or countries!

Another reason to peek out of your shell? Throughout the year, Saturn, Jupiter and Pluto will mix and mingle, meeting up at exact degrees of Capricorn and Aquarius, where they'll combine their formidable strengths in your intimate relationship zones (the seventh and eighth houses). These cosmic combos are extremely rare: The Saturn-Pluto meetup, which occurs on January 12, 2020, only happens every 33 to 38 years. This year's three Jupiter-Pluto connections (on April 4, June 30 and November 12) occur every 12 years, and the "Great Conjunction" of Jupiter and Saturn this December 21 takes 20 years to repeat! Just one of these planetary power-couplings in a single year would be jaw-dropping. Having all three marks a unique moment in astrological history—even if some uncomfortable stretching is required to maximize the benefits.

Need to set better boundaries, Cancer? Or, for the more tenderhearted among you, learn what a boundary actually is? Loving Venus will spend an extended cycle in Gemini and your sacrificial twelfth house from April 3 to August 7. Because of a retrograde from May 13 to June 25, the congenial planet will linger here four times longer than usual. Melodie Beattie's *Codependent No More* could become a dog-eared, yellow-highlighted bible on your nightstand as you learn how to rein in some of your enabling ways. Do you struggle to stay centered when others are close? Learn about the four main attachment styles (Amir Levine and Rachel S.F. Heller's *Attached* is a must-read) and find out if

you've been an "anxious" attracting "avoidants," or vice versa.

Relax, Cancer, you'll still enjoy some sacrosanct solo moments in 2020. Two of the year's six eclipses land in your sign, activating your first house of autonomy and individual expression. The inaugural full moon of the year, on January 10, is a Cancer lunar eclipse—an auspicious way to launch the new decade! You'll enjoy rapid manifestation as this lunar lift corresponds to the galvanizing solar (new moon) eclipse of July 2, 2019. On June 21, the final Cancer eclipse in this two-year series pairs with a new moon. This solar eclipse is like a ribbon-cutting ceremony for your important dreams; maybe one that you've been developing since as far back as July 2018. But wait, there's more! In 2020, you get a "bonus" new moon in your sign. On July 20, a second new moon in Cancer will echo the themes of the June 21 eclipse, giving you another launchpad for your one-Crab missions.

The power of partnership extends to your career, especially between March 21 and July 1, when Saturn darts forward into Aquarius, lending gravitas to your eighth house of investments and joint ventures. The ringed taskmaster hasn't visited this part of your chart since January 1994, but his arrival will get you serious about creating long-term wealth. The eighth house is the sexiest sector of the zodiac wheel (sharing similar qualities to Scorpio, the eighth sign). Gaining command over your finances will make you feel like one powerful vixen! But Saturn is slow-moving and deliberate so forget about turning into the Wolf of Wall Street. This spring and summer may find you focused on paying off old debts and balancing your books. When Saturn springs back into Aquarius for a longer tour, from December 17, 2020, until March

   The AstroTwins' 2020 Horoscope

7, 2023, you'll be ready to start playing the market and building your portfolio. And you'll get a helping hand from fortuitous Jupiter, who joins Saturn in Aquarius from December 19, 2020, to December 29, 2021.

Another boon for your career comes on June 27, when maximizer Mars lumbers into Aries and your tenth house of success. Normally, the red planet visits here for seven weeks every other year. But due to a biennial retrograde from September 9 to November 13, Mars lends a potent charge to your ambitions that lingers through January 6, 2021! Build as much momentum as you can between June 27 and September 9, then handle backstage developments during the reversal. You could have something awe-inspiring to launch after November 13. Is leadership calling? Mars in aggrandizing Aries calls for boldness. If you've earned your stripes, step forward as an expert or authority in your field before the year is through.

Jupiter in Capricorn: Adventures in partnership.

December 2, 2019 –
December 19, 2020

Two is Cancer's magic number in 2020, as free-spirited Jupiter joins stalwarts Saturn and power-player Pluto in Capricorn and your seventh house of partnerships. This trio of heavenly heavyweights hasn't assembled in the sign of the Sea Goat since 1285 C.E.! (So yeah, this is kind of a huge deal.) Cancel any plans to retreat into a monk-like existence. As the new decade dawns, relationships will be your raison d'etre. But who says you have

to follow a traditional template when it comes to dating and mating? As progressive Jupiter elbows conservative Saturn and Pluto, you don't have to give up your independence and precious solo time for the sake of companionship.

With the celestial supersizer here from December 2, 2019 to December 19, 2020, relationships will be fertile ground for expansion, allowing you to grow and blossom like a wisteria vine. During this 13-month spell, you'll meet friends, business associates and romantic prospects who complement you beautifully—and open your mind to fresh perspectives.

But get ready, Cancer: With this planetary trio opposing your Sun sign, your mates will be your mirrors, reflecting back both your best qualities and the aspects of yourself that could use some fine-tuning. Projection, projection? The traits that annoy you most about others may echo the ones you've rebuffed within yourself. Don't be too quick to cut people off because they get under your skin. You might be banishing your best teachers in the process.

Relationships haven't exactly been a lighthearted affair since serious Saturn rooted in this realm on December 19, 2017. And it hasn't helped that intense, possessive Pluto has occupied your partnership zone since November 27, 2008. Over the past decade, the people you've attracted have been anything but casual encounters. It's as if you had predestined soul contracts to fulfill, whether for a reason, a season or a lifetime.

One Cancer we know made a life-changing connection when she "randomly" decided to take herself out to a nice dinner and sit at the bar. Days earlier, she'd finally screwed up the courage to leave a secure but claustrophobic relationship with a man who was also her business partner—and she was hardly looking for a replacement! But when an intriguing man on the adjacent bar stool struck up a conversation, the chemistry clicked on too many levels for our friend to ignore. He lives overseas, but they've managed to see each other regularly, despite his visa issues. In many ways, she explains, this is an ideal arrangement. She gets to enjoy her sacred alone time in her new apartment, nesting and decorating to her own tastes, while filling her calendar with adventurous travel. She already has plans to meet her new beau in two countries she's never visited, a perfect way to scratch the itch of nomadic Jupiter in her seventh house.

Other Crabs have not only solidified deep and abiding connections, but you've also formalized them since traditional Saturn moved into its home sign of Capricorn December 19, 2017. Maybe you got engaged, bought a shared home or blended your families. Or perhaps you have plans to do so in 2020. As the new decade dawns, you could be busy handling all the preparations, from securing a wedding venue to changing your official address.

If you've been in self-imposed romantic isolation, this is the year to gently wade back into the dating pool. Since late 2017, Saturn and Pluto have supported you with grieving a loss or breaking a toxic pattern that drew you to unfulfilling mates. While there's truth to the assertion that "it's better to have no one than the wrong one," be honest, Crab. Have you erected a fortress around your heart? Whimsical Jupiter can help deconstruct that wall, giving you the galactic green light to take a few more chances in romance.

> "Open-minded Jupiter invites you to sample the range of options instead of one specific type."

Whether you're scouting a spouse or a song-writing partner, infuse some fun into the "casting call." Open-minded Jupiter invites you to sample the range of options instead of going after one specific type. Solo Cancers might be drawn to someone wildly different than your usual jam—perhaps from another cultural background or religious upbringing than yours. Since Jupiter can expand your heart chakra across the miles, a long-distance relationship might give your privacy-loving sign the right amount of "me" and "we" time as you grow closer, step by step. This could be the year for proposals and engagements, even for Crabs who swore they'd never walk the aisle (again)!

But above all, Jupiter wants you to stretch beyond the familiar. Novelty is an aphrodisiac—it activates the brain's reward centers and triggers a rush of dopamine, which makes you feel excited and alive. If you've been with the same person for years, break out of any stultifying routines and choose a new adventure. Experiencing things together for the first time can be a sexy bonding agent!

Existing relationships will enjoy a growth spurt, along with a few growing pains. Live-out-loud Jupiter lobbies for transparency and vulnerability, which can be a mixed bag for your private sign. It's not that you won't share your feelings, Cancer. But you reserve the right to sequester yourself when you're working through raw emotions. Trouble is, when you draw back (and even disappear temporarily) your loved ones feel abandoned. Let your people in on the process—at least some of it—even if it makes you squirm. You aren't burdening anyone and you're not being needy! After all, aren't you the "first responder" when they need someone to dry their tears? What goes around should come around.

If you've hit a plateau with your partner, shake things up. As the galactic global ambassador ignites your long-term relationship zone, you can put the "lust" in "wanderlust." Set fare alerts and start researching "baecation" rentals in your bucket-list destinations. Maybe you'll renew your vows in a charming stone house in the English countryside. Some couples will take a class, learn a foreign language or start an indie business together. When you combine your superpowers, who knows what could happen?

With the seventh house's emphasis on balance and equality, strive to make your relationship feel more mutual. You may switch roles in the relationship this year. For example, the higher earner takes a sabbatical from their cushy job to write a novel and the other person goes back to the corporate grind to support the household. Or, just give it some breathing room—enjoy more independent pursuits, then come together for shared moments. You don't have to be together 24/7 to prove that you love each other!

Jupiter's visit to Capricorn will also transform your platonic relationships. From your closest friendships to your "work spouse" to promising business allies,

you'll attract people who help you grow. At the office, pair up with people who challenge you to think outside your shell. Summon intelligent, experienced types who aren't afraid to push back on your knee-jerk emotional responses. This will help you break past your limits. (Which, if you're being honest, are probably just your fears having a field day.)

But as you enjoy this uncharacteristically #YOLO year, don't just race ahead on feel-good vibes...or start doing business with handshakes. The seventh house rules contracts, and Jupiter happens to be in "fall" in Capricorn, meaning it's one of the planet's weaker positions. Stick to calculated risks, especially since cautious Saturn is still weaving in and out of Capricorn all year. Lawyer up and put it all in writing. Who's responsible for what, how are you dividing up money, and how much risk are you each willing to take? Both parties should have skin in the game and be fairly compensated for your efforts.

Jupiter rules higher education and entrepreneurship. Ready to uplevel your skill set? You'll flourish in an interactive class that allows you to engage with other eager pupils. And, not for nothin', you could fall head over high-tops for your study buddy. If you have a business venture in progress, you can attract an avalanche of interest. Or you might sign with a representative, such as an agent, headhunter or publicist, who helps further your goals. A complementary partner could help you take an idea from your kitchen table to the marketplace.

Most people find it hard to peddle their own creative works, so having a fearless rep do the hustling for you might be the key to finally gaining visibility (and profitability!). Don't get hung up about "losing" money by investing in business support. If you find someone who increases your revenues, you'll have a bigger pie to slice from.

Jupiter was last in Capricorn from December 18, 2007, to January 5, 2009, so look back to that time: Did you make a career or romantic partnership official? Did you exit one relationship or begin a new one? Themes from that last Jupiter circuit could repeat themselves, and bonds that you forged during that window may now be up for review.

Jupiter-Pluto conjunction: Join forces.
April 4, June 30, November 12

As lovely as it sounds, Jupiter in Capricorn and your partnership sector won't be all rainbows and unicorns. Three times this year, shadow-dancer Pluto lures the red-spotted planet into his dark cave. On April 4, June 30 and November 12, Jupiter and Pluto meet at the same degree of Capricorn, combining their palpably paradoxical strengths. Jupiter is an unflappable optimist, always ready to view the world through a rose-colored filter. Suspicious Pluto, on the other hand, puts everyone through a mobster-level loyalty test.

Near these three dates, certain relationships could hit a snag. With Jupiter shining its high beams into Pluto's chamber of secrets, you might discover something difficult (or downright troubling) about a person you adore…information which was possibly hidden from you. While this could jolt you out of a romantic reverie, it doesn't necessarily portend doom. Jarring events have been known to bring couples closer, if you're both equally committed to working through the impact. If you're doing all the heavy lifting while your lover or business partner slacks off, the Jupiter-Pluto conjunctions can help you turn the tide.

As you set boundaries and stand up for your self-worth, you may realize the person who needs the most training is *you*, Cancer. Learn to reel in the compulsive caretaking, which has enabled this bad behavior. Unless people explicitly ask for your support (and even then), let them work through their struggles first. That's how they'll earn—and strengthen—their wings.

Have you felt stuck in a dead-end relationship? Sometimes, even longtime lovers can outgrow each other. Liberated Jupiter in Capricorn can offer a jailbreak from confining alliances. But with possessive Pluto hovering in the frame, you may get pushback. To slip away smoothly, you'll need a strategic exit plan. April 4 or November 12 might be ideal days to stage your farewell. Avoid June 30, however, while Jupiter and Pluto are both retrograde. If you do end a relationship, you can attract an even better match pretty quickly, so don't plan on holding onto your single card for long!

Saturn-Pluto conjunction: Relationship restructuring.
December 2019–February 2020 (exact on January 12)

Ready to do some relationship repair work? Haul in the cranes on January 12, when alchemical Pluto meets architectural Saturn at the same degree of

Capricorn. These two load-bearing planets only conjoin once every 33 to 38 years, and when they do, old habits die hard. Even the most stable partnerships could get a foundational shakeup while this transit lingers through February.

If you've been auto-piloting through a commitment, some jarring alerts could snap you to attention near January 12. Change-averse Saturn rules tradition, but transformational Pluto has a visceral edge. As this duo merges in the skies, you'll find that your reflexive way of functioning and reacting won't achieve the same reliable results. You don't have to reinvent your entire operating system, Cancer, but you may need to install some upgrades. For example, you might discover that the "gut feelings" you get about people aren't as reliable a barometer as they have been in the past. There's a chance you've been cutting others off a little too quickly in the name of "self-preservation." Or maybe you've unconsciously kept loved ones at arm's length, even if you're physically present in the room.

It makes sense, symbolically: The side-stepping Crab is a vulnerable creature that's wired for self-protection. Proximity to people might even feel like a threat to your survival! That raw instinct might just be your best *and* worst trait. When the alarm bells start chiming in your head, listen up but question them as well. While Pluto may traffic in secrecy and suspicion, inspector Saturn conducts a thorough audit before drawing conclusions. So put on your headlamp, Cancer, and find the cracks in the foundation. Buried pain could be the culprit behind your defense structure, and this cosmic duo will push it to the surface. Like hot lava bubbling up from a volcano, the realizations might sting at first. Get it all out into the light where you can properly examine it. The sooner you deal, the faster you'll heal—and ready yourself to *truly* let people into your heart.

> **"Your must-have spring accessory: a levelheaded person who can snap you back to reality."**

If power dynamics have been lopsided, this is your cue to adjust. Perhaps you signed a deal that just wasn't in your best interest over the last two years. As Saturn and Pluto have inched closer and closer together in the sky since December 19, 2017, you've discovered how resilient you really are. (Impressive!) But starting January 12, you can protect your own best interests while also forging win-wins. Be willing to walk away from a situation that requires you to bend like a Cirque du Soleil acrobat. Flexibility is one thing, but contortionism is quite another!

Although this transformational energy may cause temporary turbulence, there's a silver lining to putting your shearling bootie down. On the other side of this struggle, you'll find a more fulfilling way to engage with your fellow humans, one that's based in respect and reciprocity. As it turns out, Cancer, you don't have to handle so much on your own. Sweet relief! And speaking of engaging, the Saturn-Pluto merger could light the pathway to a long-term commitment. You might put a ring on it...or ink a contract that makes a business arrangement exclusive.

Venus & Mars Retrograde: Relationship review.

Venus Retrograde:
May 14 – June 25

Mars Retrograde:
September 10 – November 13

Another opportunity for heart healing comes from May 13 to June 25, 2020, when affectionate Venus slips into a six-week retrograde. As the planet of love and beauty retreats through Gemini and your twelfth house of boundaries, healing and forgiveness, you'll drill down to the root of an ongoing block.

Have you never *really* dealt with a particular breakup, loss or disappointing experience from your history? Swaddle yourself in support for this process—but get ready for a deluge of feelings. Your heart may take a little longer than your head to resolve this, so don't push yourself to "get over it" faster than is humanly possible.

Here's an unconventional idea: Instead of trying to push away all thoughts of the situation, create an integration ritual to move through the pain. What parts of this person or experience will you always yearn for and really miss? While Venus is in reverse, set up a temporary altar with photos or objects, allowing yourself to feel the pain of the loss fully as you sit before it. You could visualize a chamber in your heart where you put these happy memories, then imagine them dissolving and becoming part of your being forever. Feel free to mourn as needed—

but remember, you can keep the happy memories without being tortured by them.

By June 25, when Venus goes direct (forward), you might even be ready to build a fire and do a ceremonial burning of a few of those mementos—or to pack them away in storage. If visual evidence of the past is too triggering, set aside a block of time each day to read healing books, write in your journal, and give your emotions space to unleash. The fastest way to get over this kind of pain is to go through it fully.

Coupled Crabs won't be able to sweep issues under the rug. And why should you? This deep-diving Venus retrograde can bring some incredible insights for you both. Book a therapy appointment or find another outlet where you can work together to heal issues and support one another through your self-discovery.

For single Cancers, Venus' backspin can skew your judgment and even lure you towards the troubled types, such as old hookups who seized your heart then ghosted because they weren't "ready" (or some other manufactured excuse). Has someone been a consistent force of chaos in your life? Whether you want to rip their head—or their clothes—off (or both), you may realize that it's time to say a final farewell or put up an uncrossable boundary.

Keep the rose-colored glasses off your shopping list between May 13 and June 25. If there's any must-have accessory for the spring, it's a levelheaded wingperson who can snap you back to reality before you race off to rescue a wounded bird. Retrogrades can act as do-overs, too. If you ended a connection prematurely, you may get a second chance between May 13 and June 25. Venus lingers in Gemini and your twelfth house from April 3 to August 7, and it might take this entire period before you can figure out if the sequel is a great idea or a terrible one. Check in with yourself, always: Is this "let's make it work" urge coming from a true desire or does it stem from a fear that you may never find a soulmate? If the latter is the case, consider a time-out from dating while Venus is retrograde.

Got goals? Um, do you ever! Starting June 27, you'll be en fuego around the office, when go-getter Mars zooms into Aries and your tenth house of ambition and success. Normally, the red planet pings a sign for seven weeks, but due to its biennial retrograde—from September 9 to November 13—you'll get a six-month supply of rocket fuel for your career!

Aiming high is only half the equation while Mars hovers here until January 6, 2021. You also need to focus like a laser, sharp and direct. There's no time for playing small when Mars visits Aries every other year. Whether your idea of the big leagues involves an office in the executive wing or the freedom to run your business while on a surf vacation in Costa Rica, you'll take huge strides towards your dream scenario in 2020.

But your big leap may also be proceeded by a modest step backwards on September 9. That day, Mars slams on the brakes and shifts into reverse until November 13. It's not like you to sleep on the job, but with the motivational planet spinning retrograde for over two months, a work project may slow down, or you might endure a protracted period while you wait for signoffs, permits and paperwork.

The silver lining? During this forced Q3 and Q4 slowdown, you might finally get a chance to review what you've accomplished YTD. If it makes

sense, enlist a business coach who can help you streamline your goals and polish your presentation. Or apprentice alongside an industry pro. What you'll learn from the hands-on experience will be priceless! Though you won't be operating at the manic pace you ended the summer with, you'll have a chance to dot every "i" and cross all those "t's" instead of rushing to the finish line.

Use the retrograde to nurture all your professional relationships. Strong bonds with colleagues and decisionmakers can make all the difference—and it's your sensitive sign's superpower! Also, this respite falls smack in the middle of cuffing season. The slower pace allows you to focus on other important missions: your personal life, a romantic attraction and time spent with family. Ready, set, exhale...

Saturn in Aquarius: Power moves.
March 21–July 1
December 17, 2020–March 7, 2023

Your money moves can do more than just pay the bills this year, Cancer. They can set you up for long-term security, and *that* should be music to your stability-loving ears. From March 21 to July 1, ambitious Saturn darts forward into Aquarius, heating up your eighth house of intimate bonds and long-term finances. Then, on December 17, the ringed guru will head back into this same zone for a longer tenure, until March 7, 2023.

The eighth house rules quite a complex gamut: sex, emotional bonding, spirituality, mysticism and joint finances. It governs the life cycle from birth to death to reincarnation, and the "unseen" realm of spiritual mysteries. With karmic Saturn here, the mood could feel heavier between March 21 and July 1, but that's not necessarily a bad thing! As one of the zodiac's three water signs (along with Scorpio and Pisces) you like to punctuate the cheer with a perfectly moody grey day. It's what gives life dimension—something the depth-plumbing eighth house is all about. Saturn visits this part of your chart every 28 to 29 years, and it was last in Aquarius from February 6, 1991, to January 28, 1994.

Financially, the eighth house covers the way we share money, time and resources with others—everything from debt to passive income to property and assets. Money matters could fluctuate this spring and summer, but don't panic! Wise Saturn wants you to start "adulting" around your finances, and that might involve creative (but sound) co-financing. How can you join forces for mutual gain? Merging assets and sharing resources could increase your influence and build your empire during this Saturn cycle. Get serious and strategic about the company you keep. Surround yourself with people who are savvy with their coin. They'll rub off on you quickly, Cancer, and before you know it, "playing" the market might become your favorite online game.

Regardless of who's around you, sober Saturn demands greater rigor around your discretionary income. Over the next few years, you could see a serious uptick in your nest egg by flowing finances into a diverse portfolio of investments, like buying real estate in a developing neighborhood and funds that yield compounding interest. While you'll always need *some* sort of a cultural activities budget, you may start spending less on food and beverages and more on the market!

Between March 21 and July 1 (and again at after December 17), you may feel the burden of a large expense or debt, or you may have to financially support a partner. If you're divorcing or in the midst of a business breakup, dividing assets could be a laborious process that may require legal expertise. Saturn in Aquarius could bring a few lean times and hard lessons as you learn to make better financial choices—and shake off any scarcity beliefs.

Need to pad your earnings to pay some bills? Look for (legitimate) ways you can make passive income, such as through affiliate or direct sales. Is there a network marketing business that could enhance the services you already offer? From essential oils to plant-based beauty products, this might be a natural upsell that your customers want. Or perhaps you'll create a downloadable product that generates royalties. Start out slowly as a side hustle, but don't ride the brake. If you're passionate about what you're creating, the sales will be dinging on the virtual cash register while you sleep!

During this Saturn cycle, the Law of Attraction is fully the rule of the land. In other words: You'll get back what you put in. Everything you do must be conscious and soul-centered for it to work. Whether that's financial, sexual, emotional or spiritual, Saturn in the eighth house teaches you lessons in discernment. Remember, however, that with Saturn it's a marathon, not a sprint—and the March 21 to July 1 circuit is just a warm-up lap for the real race, which begins December 17, 2020.

 The AstroTwins' 2020 Horoscope

Since the eighth house is the realm of permanent bonding, one or two key relationships could really be locked and loaded before 2020 is through. This is the zone where "two become one," and as we've mentioned, that's not exactly comfortable for you. While you're easily swept up in the idea of romance, your vulnerability alarm bells start chiming when people "invade" your personal space. It's never a bad idea to know where your escape routes are, but don't let your inner runaway bride steal your good sense. Sitting through the discomfort of intimacy is better than burning bridges with someone you love, then living in endless regret.

The eighth house is all about trust, and if there's even a whiff of a betrayal or breach (past, present or future), you won't be able to brush that aside. With Saturn in this intuitive house, your inner guidance system is dialed up. You can be the most forgiving person on the planet when you love someone, but if you've been lying to yourself about their character, Saturn will shut down that narrative. While it can be painful to face facts, your relationships must be built on honesty, even if the truth is hard to swallow.

And hey, it's up to you to decide what constitutes "the end." Many couples go through scandals such as cheating or lies and come out stronger once they both do the emotional heavy lifting. We're fans of modern-love expert Esther Perel's book *The State of Affairs,* in which she takes an unflinching look at why people cheat. Her theory is that we're trying to reconnect with a lost part of ourselves through an infatuation. And it makes sense! If you've drifted from your sensuality, stopped experiencing uncensored joy or sidelined your creative hobbies, use this time to reclaim them!

Jupiter in Aquarius: Dive into the depths.
December 19, 2020– December 29, 2021

Mistletoe magic gains some seriously sexy momentum on December 19, when lusty Jupiter shifts gears, slinking into Aquarius and your erotic eighth house, for over a year. Be careful where you plant yourself, Cancer, because sparks will fly under those sprigs! In fact, your kundalini may rise to "dangerously" elevated levels while the red-spotted planet simmers here until December 29, 2021. Ooh la la! With daring Jupiter in this zone of perma-bonding, it's essential to be selective. People won't be keen to leave once you magnetize them into your orbit. You, on the other hand, might feel attraction and repulsion in equal measure. This extreme energy will definitely have Cancers running hot and cold.

If you're not feeling the power of your purr, start moving your body. Athletic Jupiter leads you to all kinds of energizing fitness modalities, from Peloton clubs to pole-dancing workouts like S-Factor which help you tune in to your "erotic creature," the sexual persona that is stowed in your psyche. Because this Jupiter cycle can turn you into a night owl, you might switch from being a sunrise yogi to a moonlight devotee. And you're never too old to dance on the bar, Cancer…at least as far as Jupiter is concerned!

Fortunately (or not), discerning Saturn will ride shotgun with rowdy Jupiter for its entire tour through Aquarius. This will help you keep at least one clear-heeled pump on terra firma. And on December 21, Jupiter and Saturn will meet at the exact degree of Aquarius (0°29'). This rare event, which astrologers call The Great Conjunction, only happens every 20 years! (The last one happened in May 2000.) This pairing of planetary opposites can fine-tune your "picker," guiding you to relationships that deliver security and excitement in equal measure. From the boardroom to the bedroom, The Great Conjunction will remind you that yes, you can have it all. And you might just find that "total package" near this date.

The question is, Cancer, do you actually want to be linked for life to that certain someone? Jupiter and Saturn in Aquarius bring gravitas to the commitment conversation. If you're feeling the love, you could take things to a more permanent level. Whimsical Jupiter will want to book a chapel and elope before the New Year, but traditional Saturn insists on at least a few formalities, like say, inviting your BFF and mom to attend your City Hall nuptials. Already "all in" with your plus-one? If Jupiter in Capricorn was the proposal or the ceremony, then Jupiter in Aquarius is the post-honeymoon period, when lives merge and you realize that there's no turning back! But if your heart is still sending out lukewarm signals, this watershed day may herald a breakup or at least, more time to evaluate how long this should last. Be as gentle as possible without falling into a guilt trip.

If you've been playing Al Green's "Let's Stay Together" on auto-repeat, your holiday season could be cozy, sexy and ideal. Nestling into the couple bubble will feel like an aphrodisiac after December 19, and with experimental Aquarius governing this part of your solar chart, you may stray from the conventional. Tuck a new toy in the nightstand drawer, sign up for a couple's "playshop" or drop into a tantric workshop. What's your pleasure, Cancer? That's an open-ended question as 2020 winds down, and one that could guide some titillating discoveries.

Got some end-of-year business to plow through? With energizer Jupiter in this laser-focused zone, you could get wrapped up in an all-consuming project, one that requires rapt attention to detail. You may crave extra privacy while you focus on building your empire or bringing a creative vision to life. If your friends start sending out smoke signals, don't be surprised! Speaking of your squad, under this discerning Jupiter-Saturn cycle, you'll go back to your "quality over quantity" social M.O. As the year winds down, pick one or two relationships that you really want to develop. Adjust your schedule so you can give these special people focused one-on-one time. (How about slipping off for a special NYE together?) Everyone else will have to see you at a group hang!

Cancer/Capricorn Eclipses: Solo dreams ignite.
January 10, June 21, July 5

By now, it's crystal-clear that 2020 is a year made for tag team efforts, but that doesn't mean your personal goals have to languish. Two of the year's six eclipses will touch down in Cancer and your first house of self and identity, igniting into your solo missions. You've been experiencing eclipses in your sign since they began striking the Cancer/Capricorn axis on July 12, 2018. Although this lunar series ends on July 5, 2020, you're still in the throes of this "reinvention tour" for the first half of the year.

On January 10, the first full moon of the decade announces itself as a Cancer lunar eclipse—an epic cosmic coming-out party for you! Forget about making halfhearted or superficial New Year's resolutions. Radar in on what you want and take concrete action to manifest it. The eclipse will give you a nice, galvanizing boost. An opportunity that involves leadership, status and responsibility could arrive out of the blue as 2020 begins. This may be the culmination of events sparked by the July 2, 2019, solar eclipse, making the impact even more powerful. Your own needs, desires and dreams get top billing (ready or not). There will be no more holding back or hoping someone else will do it for you. The spotlight's on you, so claim your status as trailblazer, influencer and alpha.

Have you put your own plans on the back burner to support other people? That's not unusual for your nurturing sign. But January 10 is no day to be a martyr! With heavy Saturn and controlling Pluto opposing this full moon, you'll need to pull away from all the people who depend on you (and there are many) so that you can tune in to your inner guidance. Since this eclipse falls on a Friday, start the weekend early, treating the 10th like a daylong one-Crab retreat. Spend the afternoon at a spa, soaking in pools and napping in a jade-tiled sauna. Or book a night (or three) at a holistic retreat center where you can do yoga, meditate at a sound bath, and fill up the first pages of your 2020 journal.

The summer begins with a moment of bold self-discovery, as the June 21 solar eclipse lands in Cancer, prompting you to get deeply in touch with your desires again. This superpowered new moon will jump-start any big solo ventures or goals. Opportunity could present itself and you'll have to act fast, perhaps putting your needs (gasp) above everyone else's. Eclipses push us off the indecisive fence and force us to take concrete action. If you've been waffling about pursuing your dreams, you may be forced to make some accelerated decisions.

While we're not suggesting you damage an important relationship or resort to selfishness, this final Cancer eclipse in the two-year series could deliver rewarding fruits for all your labors. Along with that may come an offer that's too good to refuse…but also has some challenging circumstances attached. For example, you could land a dream job that requires you to travel for a week of each month just as you're settling into a joyful routine at home. Or maybe you score a book deal, but the publisher wants the manuscript in a nail-biting three months instead of six. How badly do you want this to happen, Cancer? Eclipses only come to your sign every eight years, so don't sleep on a rare opportunity simply because it requires some stretching and temporary discomfort.

On July 5, the series finale—a Capricorn lunar eclipse—arrives with the full moon, activating your seventh house of partnerships. This lunar lift could formally secure an exciting romantic or business alliance—or launch you into new levels of intimacy and collaboration. You might make a relationship official or perhaps decide to call things off. Either way, you'll want to turn to a clean page and get all your bonds aligned. Look back to January 5, 2019, when the first Capricorn eclipse in this series touched down here. The next round of big developments could take flight now.

Gemini/Sagittarius Eclipses: Lean in or let go?

June 5, November 30, December 14

Seize control or surrender? The line between leaning in and letting go is one you'll be navigating for the next two years, as a new eclipse series activates your health and healing axis. Between June 5, 2020, and December 3, 2021, these electrifying lunar liaisons are touching down in Gemini (custodian of your twelfth house of closure and release) and Sagittarius (sentry of your sixth house of health, fitness and organization). Some parts of your life could use more focused attention and crispness, while others will reveal themselves as soul-sucking struggles that you need to leave behind.

Two of 2020's eclipses will land in Sagittarius and your systematic, salubrious sixth house. Taking care of business—and your body—is a non-negotiable now. The first, a lunar (full moon) eclipse on June 5, will motivate you to incorporate regular exercise and healthy eating into your daily routines. Working with a trainer or a certified nutritional advisor can yield big results this year. Book those checkups now, too, and don't leave any nagging pains undiagnosed. Since eclipses reveal what's hidden, you might have to quickly handle a health issue in order to nip it in the bud. If that's the case, don't stall, Cancer. Book any procedures for right after July 12, when Mercury is done with its retrograde; or, if there is a cosmetic procedure involved, once Venus ends its retrograde after June 25.

Since the sixth house rules helpful people, you might delegate some duties to capable assistants and service providers. Upgrade Team Cancer a notch or ten! You may hire or fire, change jobs or make a huge lifestyle shift in the name of wellbeing. This eclipse ratchets up stress levels, revealing the need for more support or a better system for managing and tracking. This could be your prompt to start talking to recruiters or circulating on Monster.com and LinkedIn.

On November 30, a lunar eclipse lands with the Gemini full moon, and activates your transitional twelfth house. A situation you hoped would work out may not be in your best interests. If you're tangled up in codependent dynamics, get ready to cut the cord—abruptly. Sometimes, the universe actually has a better plan, one that won't be revealed until you stop trying to force it.

If you're dealing with any health issues—emotional, physical or psychological—consider this your cue to seek help, from getting tests to dealing with recovery around an addiction or vice. As the saying goes, "If you can feel it, you can heal it." If you've encountered a loss that you haven't grieved or processed, strong feelings might come up near this day, ready to be washed away in a healing stream of tears.

The final solar eclipse of 2020 arrives with the December 14 new moon in Sagittarius. This galvanizing lunar lift will help you finish the year strong! Like the legendary Hanukkah menorah, you could be burning every last drop of oil in your own reserves—for eight days or the two last weeks of the year. But you'll have plenty of incentive since there may be a lucrative carrot dangling for your career. Your savvy sign isn't one to leave money on the table, so give it one more push and set yourself up for even greater success in 2021! ✳

January

JANUARY: LOVE HOTSPOTS

January 2: Mercury-Jupiter meetup

Open up dialogue with your S.O.—or someone who could be a candidate for that role. With garrulous Mercury and outspoken Jupiter united in your relationship zone, no topic should be off-limits. Creating some shared goals for 2020 with your sweetheart can leave you both inspired!

January 12: Mercury-Saturn-Pluto meetup

In a highly unusual—and potentially game-changing—three-way collision, Mercury aligns with goal-oriented Saturn and transformational Pluto in your seventh house of committed relationships. It's hard to say exactly what will transpire on this intense day, but it's safe to assume something will shift in a major way. Under the influence of those heavy hitters, the messenger planet is pushing you to speak up and share your feelings and needs. It may not be the breeziest conversation you'll have this month, but once you get it off your chest, you're going to feel a whole lot lighter!

January 13-February 7: Venus in Pisces

When the planet *d'amour* enters dreamy Pisces and your adventurous ninth house, she extends her invitation to open your mind—and your heart! Singles could meet a prospect quite "off-type" as sparks fly with someone from a different background or culture. A long-distance romance may heat up. Couples can break out of a rut by doing anything new and different. And if you can travel over these next three weeks, do it *a deux!*

January 16-February 3: Mercury in Aquarius

Sharing secrets? Chatty Mercury enters your erotic and confidential eighth house, a time to reveal a fantasy or open up about your deeper emotions. It's a good time to do some soul-searching. Process those bottled-up feelings and look beyond the surface. Working with a therapist or healer could lead to a-ha moments.

January 26: Venus-Mars square

Are you having that same fight again? Today, as the love planets lock into their annual square, you and a close connection might struggle to get on the same page—or even in the same book! But before you go pointing any fingers, stop and reflect on what's really bugging you. Might you be projecting your frustration with yourself onto someone who doesn't deserve it? If you catch yourself being overly critical, nip it in the bud!

January 27: Venus-Neptune meetup

When it comes to amour, the "tried and true" won't float your Love Boat today, thanks to the annual alignment of romantic Venus and Captain Fantasy (AKA Neptune) in your expansive ninth house. If you can't fly to Paris for a weekend, find something close to home that's exotic—and erotic—enough to get your pulse racing.

JANUARY: CAREER HOTSPOTS

January 2: Mercury-Jupiter meetup

Don't step away from that negotiating table until you've secured the terms you want! Under today's merger-minded skies, you can wheel and deal with the best of 'em. But make sure you actually care about what you're discussing and not just playing for a win. This magnanimous mashup can lead to some visionary thinking and high-minded action.

January 3-February 16: Mars in Sagittarius

Don't let the details overwhelm you! Step back, take a deep breath and find a way to break a major project down into smaller, more manageable chunks. And then lean into the wave of organizational motivation you're getting thanks to the return of driven Mars to your systematic sixth house for the first time in two years!

January 10: Cancer full moon (lunar eclipse)

It's not going to be business as usual under the first of 2020's two full moons in Cancer—especially since this one is also a potent lunar eclipse! This is the best possible way to welcome in a new year. Consider today your private astrological coming-out party, and get crystal-clear on your intentions before you blow out any candles. A project you've been working on since your birthday might come

together with a flourish over the next two weeks, or a client or partner you've been wooing will finally seal the deal.

January 10: Uranus retrograde ends

The cosmic disruptor has been retrograde in your house of group endeavors and technology since August 11, 2019, and it would be an understatement to say it's made a royal mess of things. But starting today, you can get projects and collaborations back on track, even if there's a lot to mop up and apologies to extend. The second they're done, you're back to work!

January 12: Mercury-Saturn-Pluto meetup

You're on the verge of nailing a huge deal, but under this intensifying three-way mashup, you need to be extra cool and dispassionate—not the easiest thing for your sensitive sign. But they say whoever loses their temper first loses, and you don't want it to be you! Give yourself a pep talk in the mirror, listen to an empowering meditation, talk to a friend who always knows the perfect thing to say. Bottom line: You've got this, so just act like it's already happened.

January 13: Sun-Saturn-Pluto meetup

Strength in numbers! Under this rare and empowering merger, it's more important than ever to team up with the right person or group. If you've got that locked down, this is the day to make a decisive move together. Still searching for that missing puzzle piece? Put out word for exactly what you're seeking, envision it, and keep doing your own impeccable work till they appear.

The AstroTwins' 2020 Horoscope

January 16-February 3: Mercury in Aquarius

As the cosmic communicator dances through your chambers of secrets, hold your cards tightly to your chest. Not all friendly faces should be trusted. If you're not sure of someone's motives, make them prove their integrity—and loyalty—before giving away any state secrets!

January 18: Mercury-Uranus square

Watch for a frenemy bearing gifts who's really just trying to wrest important intel out of you. Ask yourself what you have to gain by going along with their ruse—and what you stand to lose! Your intellectual property is a treasure, and you need to protect it like a hawk!

January 23: Sun-Uranus square

With the self-directed Sun forming one of its twice-annual clashes with disruptive Uranus in your collaboration zone, someone could pull a fast one and undermine your best efforts without any warning. You don't have to be paranoid, but there's no harm in keeping a tighter grip on your own proprietary ideas.

January 24: Aquarius new moon

A joint venture with the right partner could take your brilliant ideas to new heights over the next six months thanks to a new moon in your eighth house of mergers and acquisitions. Today also kicks off the Chinese Year of the Metal Rat, a time of great productivity. So, what are you waiting for?

January 28: Mars-Neptune square

Under this dualistic face-off, part of you will be thinking big-picture—which is great for planning—but to pull it off, you'll need a well-honed plan. The challenge today is finding the right balance between keeping things under control while allowing room for spontaneity.

February

February 16-March 30: Mars in Capricorn

Galvanizing Mars returns to your partnership realm for the first time in two years, lighting a fire around committed relationships. A new connection could blaze up out of the blue, couples could deepen (or reheat) their bond. Or, if the union was built on shaky ground, you might finally be ready to pull the plug. Just watch for strong emotions, like jealousy, resentment or anger, which the red planet has a way of churning up.

February 23: Venus-Jupiter square

Don't fall into the "too much, too fast" trap! A certain relationship has been accelerating, but you need to learn what this person is about. Besides, the "getting to know you" part is the most romantic of all! Couples will benefit from a candid conversation about unmet needs and hopes for the future.

February 28: Venus-Pluto square

Even happy couples have "off" days, and you could hit a speed bump under this flashing yellow light. Step back and make sure you're happy with where you're at, and if there's something major to discuss, find a gentle way to broach the subject. Big changes could come from this if handled diplomatically! No partner? No problem. Think about how you can switch up your dating style, whether with a new app or getting very clear on what you want to call in.

182

FEBRUARY: CAREER HOTSPOTS

February 3-March 4: Mercury in Pisces

Unleash your big ideas on the world! With mindful Mercury spending the next month in your philosophical and growth-oriented ninth house, you're thinking in supersized terms. Explore all the blue-sky possibilities and don't limit yourself. Next month, you can map the keepers to a strategic plan.

February 9: Leo full moon

The year's only full moon in your second house of work and finances could bring a big payday for your efforts of the past six months. If you've been looking for a new gig, give it one huge push over the next two weeks—peak manifesting time. Let people know you're in the market. This is also a good time to review your 2020 budget and make any needed tweaks.

February 16-March 9: Mercury retrograde

Don't be discouraged if you need to tap the brakes on a larger-than-life initiative. The planet of communication and connection shifts into reverse in your expansive ninth house, which can help you "right-size" something that may have ballooned out of proportion. Use this backspin to ensure you've crossed all your "t's" and dotted every "i"!

February 16-March 30: Mars in Capricorn

The action planet brings its legendary motivational energy to your partnership corner for the first time in two years. If you've been hoping to connect with a like-minded collaborator, put the word out—and keep the bar high! You might reel in the perfect wing person.

February 21: Mars-Uranus trine

Team up FTW! This "strength-in-numbers" mashup could make you twice as effective—and with way less effort! Kick around some big ideas with a colleague to inspire each other to think outside of the box, which will be easier thanks to the blend of confident Mars and quirky Uranus.

February 23: Pisces new moon

If you land on a brilliant new idea today (or over the next two weeks), run with it! The year's only new moon of fresh starts lands in your visionary ninth house. It's worth following up on anything that seems like it might succeed, especially if it's so original there's nothing out there to compare it to.

March

MARCH: LOVE HOTSPOTS

March 3: Venus-Saturn square

Don't feel pressured to accelerate a budding relationship or make a deeper commitment than you feel comfortable with. Saturn's speed-checking square to the love planet reminds you that you really have all the time in the world to get to know this person and make your decisions one day at a time.

March 4-April 3: Venus in Taurus

When the amorous planet grooves through your eleventh house of friendship and technology, your dating apps may start blowing up, or you could see a whole new (and appealing!) side to a platonic pal.

March 4-16: Mercury in Aquarius

Retrograde Mercury backs into your intense eighth house for a short second trip. Jealousy alert! Your mind could drift into paranoid terrain, so be careful not to fling accusations. With Mercury heating up your erotic eighth house again, add more intrigue and mystery to your love life, especially if you've been an open book.

March 8: Venus-Uranus meetup

Things could change on a dime when the radical disruptor merges with the love planet. Stay open to new possibilities because they arrive unexpectedly! If you're attached and suddenly feeling the need for some breathing room, be honest with yourself—and your partner. But bear in mind this is a very fast-moving one-day transit!

March 20: Mars-Jupiter meetup

This rare (every-other-year) mashup of forward Mars and expectant Jupiter in your relationship zone may inspire a bold, confident move toward the next level of commitment. You may not have time to deliberate since Mars is the planet of swift and decisive action. Just make sure you've at least considered possible outcomes.

March 21-July 1: Saturn in Aquarius

In this first phase of a lengthy transit (which lasts until March 7, 2023), serious Saturn will lumber through your intimate eighth house, something that hasn't happened since 1991. It's not always going to be easy or fun, and if you have issues around trust and vulnerability, Saturn can help you work through them. During this cycle, you could get serious about cohabitation, merging assets or marriage. Conversely, relationships on shaky ground may not survive three years of tremors and shock waves.

March 23: Mars-Pluto meetup

Once every other year, these two powerhouses align, and since 2008, the summit meeting has been occurring in your house of committed relationships. Things could get super-intense fast with a new love interest, or you might achieve power-couple status. But these inflammatory planets can churn up competition and possessiveness, so work on strengthening your trust above all else.

March 27: Venus-Jupiter trine

If you can lower your unrealistic standards and be more accepting, you might experience blistering chemistry with someone from a different background or with decidedly different interests from yours. Just accept—and embrace—your unique personalities and how much you enrich each other's worlds.

March 28: Venus-Pluto trine

Under this electrifying alignment, love could heat up quite unexpectedly, or you could suddenly realize how strongly you feel for someone. Single? That can change on a dime, so get out and hobnob with the most elite group you can find.

March 30-May 13: Mars in Aquarius

When lusty Mars returns to your intimate, erotic eighth house for the first time in two years, the sexual chemistry will be palpable! But the red planet also cranks up not-so-wonderful emotions, like jealousy, paranoia and competitiveness. Catch yourself if you start to slide down that slope and channel thaeenergy into a sweet and sultry seduction.

184

March 31: Mars-Saturn meetup

If it feels like you're simultaneously hitting the gas and the brakes, it's because of this rare (once every other year) mashup of driven Mars and restraining Saturn in your intimacy corner. Part of you is ready to go all-in and do something a little impulsive, yet another side is holding back. Rather than swing between extremes, can you find a happy medium?

MARCH: CAREER HOTSPOTS

March 4-16: Mercury in Aquarius

With the messenger planet cruising through your privacy sector for the next three weeks, it's not a bad idea to hold your cards close to your vest. You'll get the most done by working behind the scenes, researching like a fiend—and keeping your intel under lock and key.

March 9: Virgo full moon

All hands on deck! The year's only full moon of completions lands in your communal zone, giving you a chance to review and streamline your systems and make sure everyone is working to max capacity. Take the next two weeks to make necessary adjustments, then go!

March 16-April 10: Mercury in Pisces

Messenger Mercury pops back into your expansive ninth house today after a brief retrograde through Aquarius. Now you can get back into visionary mode and start to develop some of those lofty ideas you may have set aside in February.

March 20: Mars-Jupiter meetup

Keep your eyes and ears peeled for an inspiring partnership opportunity, but don't sign on the dotted line till you've done adequate due diligence.

Combined, these impulsive planets could spur you to jump into a commitment prematurely.

March 21-July 1: Saturn in Aquarius

For the first time since 1991, the planet of long-range planning and structure returns to your eighth house of joint ventures and wealth. The name of the game from now until March 7, 2023, is slowly but steadily growing your nest egg and positioning yourself for a new level of power and financial security. It's a realistic goal, but it's going to take effort and stick-with-it-ness.

March 23: Mars-Pluto meetup

Thanks to the game-changing mashup of these two powerful and charismatic planets in your partnership house—something that only happens every other year—you could team up with an impressive partner. Don't exclude someone you once considered a rival. This may be the key to your success!

March 24: Aries new moon

The year's only new moon in your career corner could guide you to an exciting opportunity that you hadn't considered even last month. But don't sit around waiting for it to fall from the sky. Doors can indeed open, but you need to step boldly through them—and bring your A-game to every meeting.

March 30-May 13: Mars in Aquarius

As activating Mars marches through your eighth house of investments and shared ventures, you could team up with someone who has your missing puzzle piece. Not sure what your next move is? Schedule a consultation with a financial pro to offer some appropriate suggestions.

March 31: Mars-Saturn meetup

You're eager to realize some ROI on a big project, but good things come to those who wait. And this rare (every other year) mashup of proactive Mars and guarded Saturn could act like a speed check, helping you slow down or lower unrealistic expectations.

April

APRIL: LOVE HOTSPOTS

April 3-August 7: Venus in Gemini

Thanks to a retrograde from May 13 to June 25, the planet *d'amour* will spend an extra-long time cruising through your fantasy zone. While it's fine to get a little lost in your daydreams, if you want to manifest something concrete, you'll need to come down from Cloud Nine and make some real-life efforts on planet Earth!

April 4: Venus-Saturn trine

Your most romantic wishes could be granted under this rare and solidifying sync-up of the love planet and reality-focused Saturn in your house of permabonding. Coupled? Let your partner support you emotionally. If they're not sure what you need, don't beat around the bush—tell them in plain English!

April 4: Jupiter-Pluto meetup

Curveball? The first of 2020's three rare (every 13 years) alignments between illuminating Jupiter and secretive Pluto lands in Capricorn and your seventh house of relationships. Information could come to light about a partner or you may suddenly realize that your feelings for someone are anything but casual. This conjunction will occur again on June 30 and November 12. Don't rush to conclusions—things may take a few months to fully unfold.

April 7: Libra full moon

The year's only full moon in your sentimental fourth house can tug on your heartstrings, but don't settle for a good cry. Over the coming two weeks, use this lunar energy to get closer to someone or share what you're feeling. Attached? You might move in together, take a major step on a joint long-range goal or even buy real estate together.

April 25-October 4: Pluto retrograde in Capricorn

Intensifying Pluto kicks off its annual reversal in your partnership quarters, which could stir up strong emotions, resentments and insecurities. But widen your perspective and take the high road. These next five-plus months can help you take an unflinching look at some key relationships and, most interestingly, give you an objective glimpse into how you "do" relationships. Hint: They're the ultimate mirrors of your own issues.

APRIL: CAREER HOTSPOTS

April 3: Mercury-Neptune meetup

Under this empowering mashup of thoughtful Mercury and inventive Neptune, you can blend analysis with creativity and outshoot the competition. No need to explain your thought process. For one thing, you probably can't; for another, no one would be able to copy it!

April 4: Jupiter-Pluto meetup

Strategic alliances spark today as effusive Jupiter and power-player Pluto make their first of 2020's three conjunctions in your partnership house. You could feel an instant connection with someone—a meeting of the minds that's also got a kindred spirit click. Could this chemistry create the perfect formula…or just combust? Two more conjunctions—on June 30 and November 12—will reveal that. In the meantime, explore freely, but keep some intel under wraps. You can have an open heart without being an open book.

April 7: Mars-Uranus square

With competitive Mars in your intense eighth house clashing with disruptive Uranus in your teamwork zone, anger and jealousy could rise up out of nowhere and spark dissent on a group project. Assuming you're not the one causing it, be prepared to take a lead role in calming people down. You might need to confront a bully. If you do, have an outcome in mind so you don't wind up stooping to their level and fighting fire with fire.

April 10-27: Mercury in Aries

While strategic Mercury lopes through your tenth house of career ambition, you've got nearly three weeks to set some new goals and map out a game plan to get you there. No need to rush, though: Slow and steady will win this leg of the race.

April 14: Sun-Pluto square

Your star is rising at work, but that might not be received as good news by everyone. While plenty of people are rooting for you, there are a few dissatisfied souls who aren't happy unless they can gain the upper hand. Under this manipulative mashup between the proud Sun and shady Pluto, watch for a frenemy in team colors.

April 15: Sun-Jupiter square

This is one productive starmap, but to make the most of it—and not stress yourself out—don't bite off more than you can realistically chew. Jupiter thinks on a grandiose scale, but trying to accomplish the impossible will only leave you frustrated.

April 21: Sun-Saturn square

You might be a touch sensitive today as taskmaster Saturn crosses swords with the ego-driven Sun. An innocent comment from a coworker could activate your emotional defense system. Before you go into meltdown mode, ask the person point-blank what they meant, being careful not to go on the attack yourself.

April 22: Taurus new moon

Don't wait to be personally invited to drop in on meetings where you actually have more than two cents to add. The year's only new moon in your group-activity zone inspires you to become a joiner, both at work and in your personal life. There's strength in numbers, even if you occasionally have to yield a point or two.

April 25: Mercury square Jupiter & Pluto

It's great that you're willing to stand your ground on a matter close to your heart, but don't set yourself up for inevitable defeat if there's a way around it. Today, as thoughtful Mercury squares off with controlling Pluto and supersizer Jupiter, your best ideas may be challenged by someone who doesn't fully understand them or see the big picture. But rather than waste your breath (and precious time), put it all in an email—and cc your boss and/or HR!

 The AstroTwins' 2020 Horoscope

April 25-October 4: Pluto retrograde in Capricorn

Don't just assume (or hope) that a problematic situation with a colleague will work itself out. Shady Pluto is turning retrograde for nearly half a year, a time to work out any off-balance dynamics with colleagues and collaborators. Another idea? You can screw up your courage and handle the matter like the true professional you are.

April 26: Sun-Uranus meetup

Good managers know when to take the credit for group projects and when to pass the kudos on to the team. Today, regardless of whether you're a savvy supervisor or "just" a team player, you'll instinctively know when to showcase others' contributions and when to take a one-Crab curtain call!

April 27-May 11: Mercury in Taurus

Stuck on a vexing issue? Follow collaborative Mercury's lead and turn to your team for inspiration. A colleague might have faced the same problem in the past, or the synergistic buzzing of the hivemind could come up with a creative solution!

April 28: Mercury-Saturn square

You're just one person, and there are only so many hours in the day! Don't be daunted by an unrealistic deadline or attempt to pull off a miracle without adequate resources. It's entirely possible that the powers that be don't realize you're underfunded or understaffed. Type up a memo explaining the situation and spelling out exactly what's needed to bring this to a successful conclusion.

April 30: Mercury-Uranus meetup

Brainstorms come fast and furious under this once-a-year mashup in your house of teamwork and technology. But the real strength is found in collaborative efforts. Call together a few colleagues and strategize about ways you can take those groundbreaking ideas out of your head and into production!

May

May 3: Venus-Neptune square

Under this confusing clash of the most romantic planets, you could confuse intuition with wishful thinking. Stay mindful so you don't misinterpret someone's signals and jump to erroneous conclusions.

May 7: Scorpio full moon

Siz-zle! The only full moon of 2020 to activate your fifth house of passion and romance sends your libido into overdrive. In sexy Scorpio, it's spurring you to act on a smoldering attraction or share a secret fantasy. Why keep things to yourself when, by expressing them, you could get your deepest desires met!

May 11-September 29: Saturn retrograde

Starting today, relationships—and how you think about and act in them—come up for review as Saturn, lord of structure and future planning, kicks off its annual backspin, this year through your partnership sectors. Not to worry, Cancer: You won't spend the next four and a half months on the sidelines (unless you want to). This is an excellent opportunity to observe and reflect on your behavior, including how you go about getting your needs met. If there's "relationship repair" work to do or you fancy a romantic reboot, get busy!

May 13-June 25: Venus retrograde in Gemini

When the planet *d'amour* shifts into reverse for a six-week backspin in your unconscious zone, you may have moments of feeling lost at sea on the emotion ocean. You could be unsure of the future of a union or be forced to deal with old hurts or trust issues that come out of nowhere. Beware the return of an ex bearing gifts, especially if things didn't end well.

May 14-September 12: Jupiter retrograde in Capricorn

A speedy relationship could slow down when supersizer Jupiter kicks off its annual backspin—this year through your relationship house—but ride it out. Even in reverse, the auspicious planet is still your friend. During this "correction" cycle, you'll have a chance to reevaluate and make sure you weren't rushing in prematurely...or perhaps not taking action when you should be!

May 22: Gemini new moon

The year's only new moon in your twelfth house of reflection, release and reinvention is a time to surrender to your own higher wisdom. The next two weeks are perfect for letting go of any old wounds you're still nursing or to forgive someone and move on. This can also crank up the romantic vibes and plunk you down in fantasyland. Enjoy the view, but make sure you come back to reality.

May 22: Mercury-Venus meetup

When the love planet meets articulate Mercury in your twelfth house of secrets, you'll be eager to share your feelings—and fantasies—with a special someone. But be careful not to be swept off your feet by a seductive sweet talker.

MAY: CAREER HOTSPOTS

May 9: Mercury-Pluto trine

With collaborative Mercury buzzing through your teamwork zone and aligned with alchemical Pluto, your secret weapon is the hivemind. You don't have to do it all by yourself; in fact, when you check in with colleagues, you may find some are ready and willing to pitch in.

May 10: Mercury-Jupiter trine

Team up FTW! Communication is the key to your success under today's collaborative confab of the messenger planet and candid Jupiter in your people houses. Call an impromptu brainstorming session; take the crew out for lunch and an ideation meeting. The point isn't to nail down details, just to get some creativity flowing.

May 11-September 29: Saturn retrograde

As the future-oriented planet spins into its annual reversal and illuminates the seriousness of a potential partnership, slowing down is best. This is a great period for researching, asking questions, doing due diligence. Take your time committing.

May 11: Mercury-Mars square

Just when you thought everyone was on the same page, competitive Mars throws a curveball, and you're back to square one. Stay alert for petty bickering and mean-spirited backstabbing, and when you catch a whiff, do what you can to nip it in the bud.

May 11-28: Mercury in Gemini

Today marks the messenger planet's annual arrival to your internal, imaginative twelfth house. Leave the detail-driven aspects of an assignment for later and turn your attention to more creative or people-oriented parts. Got a critical decision to make? Stall!

May 12: Mercury-Saturn trine

Here's a good day to tackle the more left-brain aspects of a project! When cerebral Mercury syncs up with systematic Saturn in your emotional centers, you need only tune in to your heart to find the right approach. Trust your instincts—but have the data to back up your proposal.

May 13-June 27: Mars in Pisces

You could be packing your bags for a business trip or cashing in some of that accrued vacation time while the adventurous planet jets through your travel sector. Some enterprising Crabs may finally be ready to launch your own start-up!

May 14-September 12: Jupiter retrograde in Capricorn

A prospective deal may vaporize before your eyes as accelerator Jupiter shifts into reverse in your partnership arena for the next four months. But you don't have to stagnate. Get your own ideas up and running, and if you need to go back to the drawing board, this is the perfect time.

May 15: Sun-Pluto trine

This potent pairing can lead you to a kindred spirit who has equally grand ideas and the same work ethic as you, plus complementary skills. Team up and crush the competition—in a friendly way, of course!

May 22: Mercury-Neptune square

You won't be thinking at your rational best today, so avoid making any decisions you can't easily undo. With cerebral Mercury in your hazy twelfth house squaring befuddling Neptune, the natural ruler of that zone, you'll be happier clocking out early for the weekend or gazing at the stars than analyzing spreadsheets.

May 28-August 4: Mercury in Cancer

When the winged messenger planet alights in your sign, it'll put down deeper than normal roots because of a retrograde from June 18 to July 12. If you're honing a message, don't rush to share it with the world, especially when Mercury is in reverse. You may think it's ready to broadcast, but you could be overlooking some detail—or a key piece of info may change dramatically in the coming weeks. Timing is everything, so trust that waiting can only help you. In fact, if you've flirted with doing a "digital detox," this is a perfect opportunity!

June

JUNE: LOVE HOTSPOTS

June 2: Venus-Mars square

They say forewarned is forearmed, so consider this your official heads-up. A few times a year, the love planets lock horns, as they'll do today. You might be overly emotional, prone to taking things personally or to overreacting. The best tack? Take it on the chin and redirect your attention. This will pass by tomorrow.

June 30: Jupiter-Pluto meetup

Romantic renovations? Insightful Pluto and illuminating Jupiter, both retrograde, make their second of 2020's three rare unions in your committed partnership zone. The truth could set you free today—either into honest new terrain with a partner or completely out of a toxic relationship. But don't be too quick to pin blame on the other party. The person who pushes your buttons the most might be the most important teacher you've ever had. Look back to the first meetup on April 4—and ahead to November 12—when a third conjunction will help it all make sense.

JUNE: CAREER HOTSPOTS

June 5: Sagittarius full moon (lunar eclipse)

This annual "manifesting" full moon in your sixth house of work, service and helpful people supports you in getting your systems shipshape. Over the next two weeks, step back and evaluate where you can make changes, what you can let go of altogether and how you can streamline the whole operation.

June 13: Mars-Neptune meetup

If an exciting idea hits you from out of the blue today, run with it! This rare (once every other year) merger of creative Neptune and activator Mars in your visionary zone can spark original thinking. Don't get hung up on the details. Just get everything down on paper or in an app and trust you'll work it all out later.

June 18-July 12: Mercury retrograde in Cancer

When the messenger planet shifts into reverse in your sign for the next few weeks, you may feel like no one understands you or is willing to take the time to try. Before you slip down a paranoid rabbit hole, remind yourself that you've survived these periods before and you'll do it again. Then pick a few high-priority items that you can work on by yourself, and lower your nose to the grindstone and get busy. Your focused productivity will be the perfect consolation prize.

June 21: Cancer new moon (annular solar eclipse)

Talk about auspicious! Not only is this the first of a rare, back-to-back pair of new moons in your sign, but it's also a potentially game-changing solar eclipse! And, because la luna is your celestial caretaker, for the rest of the year you'll draw from a deep well of support for all your new ventures.

June 23-November 28: Neptune retrograde in Pisces

When the quixotic planet shifts into reverse in your visionary zone, your head will be full of big ideas. Inspiring? Of course. But if you're serious about trying to implement any of them, run 'em through a reality filter first. Or, start small!

June 27, 2020-January 6, 2021: Mars in Aries

Motivated Mars returns to your tenth house of power, status and career for the first time in two years, so get ready for a turbo-charged ride to the top! This will be an extra-long visit thanks to a retrograde from September 9 to November 13. But don't sit around waiting for the influencers to notice you. Put yourself out there, shell out the bucks for the right VIP events, and wherever you go, dress to impress. When you smell opportunity, pounce!

The AstroTwins' 2020 Horoscope

June 30: Jupiter-Pluto meetup

Even dynamic duos need repair work from time to time. As truth-teller Jupiter and insightful Pluto unite in your partnership house, pause to deeply assess your "interpersonal affairs" department. This is the second of three rare meetups in 2020 (the first was April 4; the next is November 12), and this go-round, both planets are in reflective retrograde. Examine which relationships are a balanced give-and-take and which could use more compromise. Not sure whether to ink your name to a contract? Wait it out. Between now and the next conjunction in November, a lot more information could become clear.

July

JULY: LOVE HOTSPOTS

July 1-December 17: Saturn retrograde enters Capricorn

Future-oriented Saturn, which turned retrograde in Aquarius on May 11, backflips into Capricorn and your partnership house today, giving you a chance to review what you've learned. Consider this extended visit a "stress test" of sorts, showing any cracks in a new union's foundation or in longtime bonds. If things don't "pass," it may be time for a trial separation or to do some repair work with a coach or counselor.

July 5: Capricorn full moon (lunar eclipse)

The year's only full moon to light up your partnership zone is also a potent lunar eclipse! This cosmic event is transformational, it can spark some life-altering moments and, for some Crabs,

bring a relationship turning point. No one on your romantic radar screen? Get out there more and stay positive. In grounded Capricorn, these lunar high beams can illuminate worthy prospects who can go the distance.

July 15: Sun-Pluto opposition

Warning: This won't be a light and breezy day. The annual opposition of the ego-driven Sun in your sign and alchemical Pluto in your dynamic-duos zone will serve up a strong brew of mixed emotions. If you've been keeping things to yourself because you're afraid of rocking the boat, ask yourself which is better: Suffering in silence or taking action that could potentially improve the situation?

July 27: Venus-Neptune square

This is the year's third clash between these two idealistic planets while they are in Gemini and Pisces, respectively—and this one may be hardest of 'em all. By now you probably think you're seeing a situation clearly, but chances are you're still projecting your hopes (or fears) onto it. Don't do anything rash with a love interest—just try your best to keep things calm, cool and casual!

July 30: Mercury-Jupiter opposition

You and your partner (or a new "person of interest") might be on the same page, but don't rush to the conclusions. Part of the fun is getting to know them and exploring all those fascinating differences. A good way to find them is to listen more than you talk.

JULY: CAREER HOTSPOTS

July 1-December 17: Saturn retrograde enters Capricorn

When solidifying (and skeptical) Saturn pivots back into Capricorn and your seventh house of partnerships and contracts, the message is clear: Don't rush into anything! While its return could attract some heavy hitters into your orbit, that doesn't necessarily mean they're appropriate teammates for you. Take your time getting to know them, their values, work ethic and culture. If this is meant to go the distance, you need to do the research and background checks now. A solid offer won't evaporate overnight. And if it does? Question just how real it was in the first place.

July 5: Capricorn full moon (lunar eclipse)

As today's Capricorn full moon/lunar eclipse brings a metamorphosis to your partnership sector, a deal that had been in the works could come together with a drum roll today or over the next two weeks. You might receive info or insight into an alliance you've been iffy about—which will send you running either toward them—or to the nearest exit!

July 8: Mercury-Mars square

Keep that contrarian streak in check, Crab. Talkative Mercury, which is retrograde in your sign, clashes with hotheaded Mars in your tenth house of career and authority. Mind the pecking order, even if you think it's unfair. Or, should you choose to fight that battle, be prepared for any outcome, including an irreparably burnt bridge. Got a hot idea to share? Know that you might not have the most receptive audience today. This transit will repeat on July 27,

but then, Mercury's retrograde will have ended. You'll be able to express your dissenting opinions and pioneering ideas to decision-makers without as much pushback. Be prepared to answer their tough questions anyway!

July 12: Sun-Neptune trine

Under this twice-yearly sync-up of the creative Sun and free-styling Neptune in your expansive ninth house, you won't see the obstacles or limitations—only limitless opportunities! Start capturing some of these downloads before you lose 'em, and gather fellow visionaries to help you really think outside the box. Don't worry how far or how fast you're going; just enjoy the sensation of leaving the naysayers in your wake.

July 15: Sun-Pluto opposition

Teamwork makes the dream work, but too many chefs in a tiny kitchen also spoil the broth. Sometimes you just have to uplevel and be the boss. Today, as these powerhouses oppose each other, you might meet with some resistance, but if you've got the pool cue, you get to call the shots.

July 20: Cancer new moon

This "repeat" new moon in your sign reaffirms some of those grand intentions you set last month and brings even more opportunities to get them off the ground. By all means, get going, but no need to skip any steps. You've got six months to realize these golden dreams!

July 20: Sun-Saturn opposition

You're pretty clear on your game plan, but if you need others' support or backing, make sure you have a convincing (and palatable) way to present it. Under this stubborn face-off, someone may resist you just to exercise a little power. What you need to do is to show them the undeniable win-win benefits of your vision.

July 30: Mercury-Jupiter opposition

Think, dream, plan, bounce ideas off teammates… just don't put anything into motion today. Cerebral Mercury is stationed in your unrealistic twelfth house and at odds with hyperbolic Jupiter. What feels doable in the moment may prove to be a giant disaster when you actually try to enact it.

July 30: Mercury-Neptune trine

Your Spidey senses are working overtime thanks to this tuned-in alignment of analytical Mercury and perceptive Neptune. If you get a "funny feeling" that something is about to go off the rails, by all means, speak up before a problem occurs. This will save everyone time, frustration and possibly money—and make you the hero of the day!

August

AUGUST: LOVE HOTSPOTS

August 1: Mercury-Pluto opposition

Romantic tension can ratchet up excitement—which might eventually lead to epic makeup sex—but all that is so draining. Surely there are healthier and less extreme ways to rekindle sparks in a sleepy union (or get the party started)? Think: boudoir toys, cosplay and maybe a little Kama Sutra. If that's not your thing, a change of location could add some sexy novelty.

August 3: Aquarius full moon

The year's only full moon in your intimacy zone may inspire you to take a bold step toward deeper commitment, or get you carried away with erotic vibes. If you're not ready to move in together or talk long-term, enjoy where you're at now. Note that full moons can bring turning points, like parting ways or changing your "rules of engagement."

August 7-September 6: Venus in Cancer

Today, as the planet *d'amour* blasts into your sign, it's time to stop dimming your love light and let it shine brightly. If you're in a union, be more playful while also being supportive. Single? Maybe a subtle style or hair makeover will make you feel like the flirtatious minx you were born to be.

August 25: Venus-Jupiter opposition

Don't let your attraction get the better of you. Under this larger-than-life amorous alignment, you may entertain some wild fantasies. While there's nothing wrong with pursuing them, make sure you're not trying to wrangle a unicorn. Couples should talk through conflicts with love and compassion. Set an intent to get through it and you'll become stronger as a result.

August 27: Venus-Neptune trine

Go ahead and leave those rosy-hued aviators in place all day! Under this glowing trine, you'll be feeling generous and loving, and will see the good in people before any flaws poke through. Share this dreamy idealism with your beloved or let it show with a brand-new person of interest.

August 30: Venus-Pluto opposition

You're either all in or ready to bounce under today's obsessive mashup of the love planet and

inexorable Pluto. A new relationship might feel like The Real Thing—but give it time to fully reveal itself. Everyone has a shadow side, and nothing will pry it from the shadows like a Pluto transit. Couples might want to consider a night apart to restore a little of that lost perspective.

AUGUST: CAREER HOTSPOTS

August 2: Sun-Uranus square

Someone is hellbent on disrupting your peaceful bubble today, so keep your antennae up and don't take anyone's bait, no matter how irresistible. While you might need to have a private word, if you can keep your wits, there's no reason for this molehill to blow up.

August 3: Aquarius full moon

The year's only Aquarius full moon illuminates your region of joint ventures and shared resources. Since this can indicate an upcoming windfall, you need to position yourself properly now. If you're close to teaming up with an inspiring new partner or investing in an impressive startup, don't trust your gut alone. Do the research to make sure it—and they—will be a safe bet.

August 3: Mercury-Saturn opposition

Make your pitch but don't oversell yourself or your ideas. People will either get it or they won't, and all the fancy dancing in the world won't change their minds. In fact, under this "less-is-more" mashup, they'll see through any false fronts, and you could lose their respect. By the same token, if someone's giving you the hard sell, cut 'em off quick before they suck all the air out of the room.

August 4: Mars-Jupiter square

Not everyone will be on the same page today, so don't waste any time trying to herd feral cats. With Mars blazing through your success zone, you don't have time to stop and try to explain things to people—possibly for the third time. Thanks to a boosting angle from passionate Jupiter, you'll find the right support from the ideal person—exactly when you need it most!

August 4-19: Mercury in Leo

The cerebral planet makes its annual trek through your financial sector—and because it's a quick trip this time around, you'll need to get the story fast and be prepared to make a snap decision. But no worries: Mercury in confident Leo is more than ready to step up to the plate!

August 10: Mercury-Uranus square

If you sense that someone hasn't been carrying their weight—or is undermining a team effort—don't wait for a "smoking gun" to appear. In this case, strong circumstantial evidence could be enough to draw them out of their shady cave and into the light. Give them one chance to come clean and make amends. If they can't or won't, have no qualms about showing them the door.

August 13: Mars-Pluto square

Sometimes butting heads feels inevitable—as it might under this power-tripping meetup. But given the intense and shifty nature of these planets' subterranean energies, you're better off sidestepping the actual issue and letting someone higher up handle it directly.

The AstroTwins' 2020 Horoscope

August 15, 2020-January 14, 2021: Uranus retrograde in Taurus

Don't lock yourself into a rigid timeline for the rest of the year. Erratic Uranus, which is in your house of teamwork and technology for the next six years, kicks off its annual course reversal. With the cosmic disruptor gone rogue, there's no telling how long a group project might take. You can try to break it down into phases (many small ones) but even then, let the people you're accountable to know there are too many variations to guarantee the deliverables.

August 17: Mercury-Mars trine

Money can be an awkward subject, but sometimes there's no getting around talking about it. Try to make it impersonal—perhaps using euphemisms or colorful examples—and don't worry if you're making others slightly uncomfortable. If this is part of getting a job done, then out with it!

August 18: Leo new moon

The news you've been waiting for could come within two weeks of this annual new moon in your second house of finances and security. But don't kick back and wait for the phone to ring. What can you do to speed the manifesting process, from cold-calling executives to planting media stories to just rubbing shoulders with the VIPs at important industry functions?

August 19-September 5: Mercury in Virgo

When articulate Mercury treks through your expressive third house, give your communication style a quick review. How eloquently—and passionately—do you present your best ideas? This isn't about peppering your speech with superlatives, but rather, leaning in to your authentic love of what you do or are promoting. This is also an enhanced social period, so put yourself out there and explore synergies with a whole range of creative types!

August 24: Mars-Saturn square

With motivational Mars revving through your career zone, you're amped up and ready to hit the gas. But thanks to a brake-tapping square from taskmaster Saturn, you may feel like you're being held back. First: Don't take it personally! Second, take action on what you can, but trust that this brief holding pattern won't put you behind the 8-ball.

August 25: Mercury-Uranus trine

Combine your superpowers and let synergy flow! Under this harmonizing meetup, the smartest thing you can do is pool your resources. And with that kind of talent surrounding you, you won't have to look far to find your dream team.

August 29: Mercury-Jupiter trine

No sweating the petty stuff today. With mental Mercury mashed up with expansive Jupiter in your communal houses, take the high road and let minor grievances roll off your back. When your eye is on such a lofty goal, you don't want to slow yourself down by stooping too low.

August 30: Mercury-Neptune opposition

There's no shortage of big ideas today under this visionary alignment. Write them down, flesh them out, but bear in mind that you're in more of an ideation than a "get 'er done" mindset. There's a time and a place for everything.

September

SEPTEMBER: LOVE HOTSPOTS

September 2: Venus-Saturn opposition

Before you can get too carried away with a romantic fantasy, clear-eyed Saturn in your partnership zone steps in and snaps you back to reality. With Venus in your sensitive sign, you're prone to a little imagination overload, so don't take this as "raining on your parade" but maybe an invitation to get to know someone better before you start ordering monogrammed towels.

September 4: Venus-Mars square

When the cosmic lovebirds sing out of harmony a few times a year, you might be tempted to act rashly or with vengeance. But this is a fast-moving transit, and by this time tomorrow, you may be back in the throes of passionate love—or least lust, so pick your battles (or just skip 'em).

September 6-October 2: Venus in Leo

Every year, the cosmic stylista settles into your sensual second house for a few weeks, elbowing you to up your game. You're no slouch in this department, but beautifying Venus wants to add more luxury and self-care into your life. When you look good and feel good, you're simply irresistible!

September 9-November 13: Mars retrograde in Aries

When the forward-moving planet flips into reverse in your future-minded zone, you could get stuck in a rut, unsure which direction to move in. It could be a lack of "action" in your romantic life—or it may be too many good options, including a simmering attraction to a colleague. Read the company policy manual before you go there!

September 12: Jupiter retrograde ends

Romantic reboot! After a seemingly endless retrograde through your relationship house, optimistic Jupiter corrects course and hits the reset button on your love life. It's safe to pick up where you left off four months ago, whether you were making holiday plans with your honey or free-diving into the dating pool.

September 15: Venus-Uranus square

Close that polling station! Your friends' opinions don't matter nearly as much as how you feel about someone, so stop soliciting their input. Today's clash between the planet *d'amour* (or at least de flirting) and independent Uranus prompts you to think for yourself—and trust your own gut.

September 17: Mercury-Jupiter square

With the cosmic communicator in your sentimental fourth house aligned with courageous Jupiter in your partnership sector, take a risk and let someone know how you really feel. Already solidly attached? What one sweet or even over-the-top gesture can you make that will show much you care?

September 23: Mercury-Saturn square

A close friend, relative or love interest's needs might impose on your time today, but before you act, weigh the pros and cons. Giving up too much of your precious time won't help anyone, yet doing nothing could cause resentment. Set some boundaries around what you're willing to do and for how long. Later, when you've got more wiggle room, check back in and see how they're doing.

 The AstroTwins' 2020 Horoscope

September 27-October 27: Mercury in Scorpio

The winged messenger planet alights in your romance sector for its first of two trips in 2020 (owing to a retrograde from October 13 to November 3). This pours rocket fuel in your confidence tanks and may inspire you to share some strong (and sexy) feelings and desires. Single? Don't wait to be talked to. If you catch the eye of a friendly-looking person, strike up a convo. What have you got to lose?

September 28: Venus-Mars trine

Lean in to love! This harmonious hookup of the romance planets in your most stable chart sectors bodes extremely well for relationships. A romantic risk could pay off abundantly!

September 29: Saturn retrograde ends

This cosmic newsflash is auspicious indeed! Cautious, restraining Saturn has been retrograde in your dynamic-duos zone for the past five months, slowing your progress or, in some cases, throwing curveballs at every turn. But now that it's back in forward motion, you can move ahead, too. Plot a course, pick your co-pilot and soar!

SEPTEMBER: CAREER HOTSPOTS

September 1: Mercury-Pluto trine

You can outwit—and outrun—the competition under today's brain-boosting cosmic mashup. Mercury in your mental third house dials your strategic powers way up, and a twice-a-year supportive beam from transformative Pluto can launch you into the professional stratosphere!

September 2: Pisces full moon

The year's only full moon to land in your visionary and global ninth house pushes you to think bigger! The sky may literally be the limit if you've got business travel plans on the books. During the next six months, you can expand your personal, brand's or company's reach beyond your wildest dreams. Just don't get hung up on details.

September 3: Mercury-Saturn trine

Less is more today as circumspect Saturn keeps chatty Mercury in check. Listen to what others are saying and don't be too quick to give up valuable intel. Your ability to think like a boss is your superpower. Show your strength by being discernng about how much you share.

September 5-27: Mercury in Libra

Pause for the cause! Over the next few weeks, don't jump right into work talk or barking instructions. A personal touch will go further in keeping the wheels greased than all the elbow grease in the world! This is one of the most soulful transits of the year, so tap into the harmonious vibes and enjoy the deeper sense of connection.

September 9-November 13: Mars retrograde in Aries

You've been on fire at work, but when the action planet shifts into reverse in your professional sector, you'll have a chance to slow down, catch your breath and review what you've accomplished in a few short months. Before you blast into the next phase, make sure you're on pace with projections and still passionate about the mission.

September 12: Jupiter retrograde ends

With the planet of abundance back to full strength, you can blaze ahead on a deal or partnership that was just gaining momentum when Jupiter backflipped in your dynamic-duos zone on May 14. Get ready to hit the gas because there are people who've been patiently awaiting your return.

September 14: Sun-Pluto trine

You've got the seed of a potentially brilliant idea, but you'll go farther faster if you team up with someone (or a group) that has the know-how and the resources to get this off the ground. Why bother reinventing the wheel if someone's already got a warehouse full of 'em?

September 17: Virgo new moon

For the two weeks following 2020's only new moon in your communication zone, your mind will be racing with original ideas and ways to package your message. This is a great time to experiment and see what works best. You want to get this right because if you unexpectedly get the ear of a key decisionmaker, you need to be able to wow them on the spot!

September 21: Mercury-Pluto square

Limits are called for under this line-in-the-sand-drawing clash between social Mercury and restrictive Saturn. You could fall for someone's hard-luck story—but don't! Your time is important, and you don't have enough to waste on someone who probably isn't going to change. Give them your vote of confidence then move on!

September 24: Mercury-Mars opposition

Even as the pressure mounts at work, don't let it get to you. When your stress levels climb, you don't think as clearly. Under today's adrenaline rush of an opposition, you might think you need to work harder or faster than is actually required. Get the info from the horse's mouth so you can work at your optimal pace.

September 29: Mars-Saturn square

If you're having doubts about an aspect of a complex project or someone working on it, don't ignore it. Under today's cautionary angle between speedy Mars in your professional zone and restrained Saturn, it's worth following up on any of those suspicions so they don't undermine your efforts.

September 29: Saturn retrograde ends

And you're back! After five months of back-pedaling through your partnership realm, structured Saturn corrects course. You may need to go back to the drawing board, but it is safe to resume talks about an exciting deal or joint venture.

October

October 2-27: Venus in Virgo

With harmonious Venus in your communication sector for most of the month, you can get a wobbly relationship back on track. In Virgo, she'll bring an objectively analytic approach and help you develop a thicker skin, which might make all the difference in the world.

October 4: Pluto retrograde ends

You've endured five months of mixed signals and dodgy dealings; now, with shadowy Pluto back in forward motion, you can integrate some of the lessons you've learned and work on getting a relationship into the shape you want. And if your love interest can't—or won't? You should have the fortitude to move on with confidence.

October 10: Venus-Uranus trine

What are you waiting for? Whatever you've been waffling over, today's action-spurring alignment of amorous Venus and spontaneous Uranus can push you off the fence. Be the one to break the ice or say yes to someone's offer! With your social sectors lit up, couples can enjoy an upbeat, drama-free night out on the town—or stay home and light some indoor fireworks!

October 13-November 3: Mercury retrograde

Love on the run? Communication planet Mercury makes a three-week backspin through the emotional parts of your chart. Until October 27, the cosmic messenger will reverse through Scorpio and your passionate fifth house, which could stir up drama or draw an ex back into the picture. Tread carefully before going there. After that, Mercury backs into Libra and your emo fourth house, which could send your moods all over the map. Honor your feelings, but don't let them hijack every situation.

October 16: Libra new moon

Though a dark sky, the year's only new moon to land in your sentimental fourth house can shine a light on emotional needs you might be ignoring—or are afraid to pursue. If you're in a relationship, these next two weeks are ideal for sharing your deepest desires with your mate—and listening to theirs. Single? Getting a handle on your emotional triggers is a prerequisite to creating the kind of mature partnership you crave. This lunar lift can help you begin writing a new whole new chapter.

October 18: Venus-Neptune opposition

Quixotic and romantic vibes? Check! A good day to make a potentially course-altering decision? Not so much. With the most romantic planets activated in your idea centers, you should assume there's some wishful thinking going on. Ride out the fantasy and then, later in the week, revisit that plan.

October 19: Venus-Jupiter trine

Today's biggest challenge? Choosing from among your bounty of awesome options! Thanks to the expansive alignment of abundant Jupiter and Venus, you are squarely in the amorous driver's seat. Before hitting the gas, offer up a little prayer of gratitude.

October 21: Venus-Pluto trine

Under this profound pairing, you won't be happy with small talk and casual connections. Couples could talk about next steps—or emotional stumbling blocks—and if you're unattached, take a moment to really visualize the kind of partner you're hoping to attract. And then, don't settle for less!

October 24: Venus-Saturn trine

Just like that, a simmering attraction could flare up and catch you both by surprise—in the sweetest way. Keep your eyes wide open, but if you're feeling it, don't hold your breath. Fire needs oxygen to burn brightly!

October 27-November 21: Venus in Libra

Home base can become a sacred (and sensual) sanctuary for the next three-plus weeks as Venus sets up shop in your domestic fourth house. Make your place a private retreat for you and your beloved. If you live together, talk about things you can do together to make it even cozier. Singles should make sure there's physical and energetic space for someone else to occupy. You could be blocking love inadvertently.

OCTOBER: CAREER HOTSPOTS

October 1: Aries full moon

All those months of hard work and logging long hours were not in vain! Today, the year's only Aries full moon electrifies your tenth house of professional success. Your star is solidly on the rise, and even if your phone isn't blowing up yet, trust that the right people are taking notice. Help your cause with some strategic self-promotion and developing the knack of being in the right place at the right time.

October 4: Pluto retrograde ends

Backbiting and stealthy competition begone! Today, as shadowy Pluto wraps up a five-month retrograde in your partnership sector, it's safe to proceed with a collaboration that may have stalled since April. You might even have developed the courage to confront someone who was blatantly challenging or manipulative. No matter how frustrating their behavior was, don't stoop to their level!

October 7: Mercury-Uranus opposition

This is the first of three of these impulsive angles, so if you don't handle this one the way you'd like to, don't worry: You'll get two more chances to get it right! The quickest-thinking planets align, spurring you to rush into action or say something regrettable. And it'll happen so fast, you might not be able to stop yourself. But pay attention to what happens as a result, and if you need to make amends in any way, you should get a chance during Mercury's return trips on October 19 and November 17.

October 9: Mars-Pluto square

Even if you are in a position of power, that doesn't mean you should wield it over others. People will actually respect you more if you take a gentler, more diplomatic approach to dealing with personnel issues. Of course, with reckless Mars clashing with strongman Pluto, that may be easier said than executed.

October 15: Sun-Pluto square

It's a nice idea, in theory, to extend the benefit of the doubt. But today, there's a chance someone might actually be trying to pull a fast one. Don't feel compelled to "play nice." This isn't your first rodeo, and if you catch even a whiff of shadiness, call them on it before they take it too far.

October 18: Sun-Saturn square

Keep a low profile under this cautious mashup. You might be in an emotionally volatile or agitated state, and you don't want to risk damaging your sterling reputation by being an oversharer or by remotely acting unprofessional. If you've got a door, close it and get to work!

October 19: Mars-Jupiter square

You're on a professional tear, but a colleague may require a little hand-holding today. While it's frustrating to have to slow your pace to give them a jumpstart, think of this as "paying it forward." Eventually, we all wind up lagging behind in the

The AstroTwins' 2020 Horoscope

slow lane, and it's nice to think someone will stop for us when we need a little roadside assistance.

October 31: Taurus full moon

Today's Taurus full moon (the only one of 2020) activates your eleventh house of teamwork and technology—and the lunar lift it brings indicates that a major group victory is at hand. Celebrate, promote your success and bask in the sense of accomplishment that comes from a job well done (especially a drawn-out one!), but then prepare to get right back to work. This is the time to ride the momentum—not rest on your laurels!

November

NOVEMBER: LOVE HOTSPOTS

November 3: Mercury retrograde ends

After a choppy backspin that began on October 13, the cosmic communicator corrects course. If you've been confused about how you feel or your emotions have obscured your better judgment, those clouds will soon be parting.

November 9: Venus-Mars opposition

The different "personalities" of the love planets are highlighted under their rare face-off today. Every other year they meet like this, and it can be confusing, to say the least. You may not be sure if what you're feeling is love or lust (and frankly, you may not care). Mars wants instant gratification, but Venus is all about a long, sexy buildup. Make a game of trying to walk a middle line today.

November 10-December 1: Mercury in Scorpio

Eloquent Mercury returns to your seduction center for its second visit this year (because of a retrograde from October 13 to November 3). On this follow-up transit, you may have a renewed interest in sharing some secret fantasies, and zero shyness about sexy pillow talk—which will actually be a potent aphrodisiac.

November 12: Jupiter-Pluto meetup

All the way in…or out? Honest Jupiter and deep-diving Pluto make their third and final connection of 2020 in your relationship house, and you could reach a crucial epiphany around a commitment. These two luminaries only unite every 13 years. Leave no stone unturned if you're considering a partnership decision. Coupled Crabs may have been working through some intense emotions since the first Jupiter-Pluto alignment on April 4. Your diligence and devotion could pay off now.

November 13: Mars retrograde ends

Forward! Passionate Mars has been retrograde in Aries and your goal-focused tenth house for the past two months, making it hard to see a clear path ahead. Work stress may have impacted your relationships or cut into quality time. You could have reached an impasse around next steps or discovered you didn't want the same thing for the long haul. As the red planet corrects course, fighting ends and tension clears up. If you've been the one feeling pressured to commit, you may abandon your resistance and warm up to the idea.

November 15: Scorpio new moon

Hoping for a reboot in your love life? Then today's annual new moon (foreshadowing fresh starts) in your zone of courtship and creativity will bring a welcome energy. But it's not magic, Cancer. You need to do your bit to help things along, whether that means sitting down and hashing things out with your mate or getting back in the dating game for real. Sincere efforts will be rewarded!

November 15: Venus-Pluto square

No matter what someone close to you says or does today, resolve to keep your cool. It sounds easy now—but wait. Under this provocative pairing, a power struggle might ensue, and it could catch you totally off-guard. Don't react immediately. If a few moments of reflection don't help you ground yourself, let them know they caught you at a really bad time and you'll respond as soon as you can.

November 16: Venus-Jupiter square

Tap the brakes! If you realize you're getting ahead of yourself in a certain relationship, slow down to assess. This aggrandizing alignment isn't good for reality-checking, though it has been known to dial up the fantasy factor to unprecedented levels. Step back and at least try to get an accurate read. And if you can't? Delay taking any major steps.

November 19: Venus-Saturn square

Another speed-checking transit occurs today as cautious Saturn throws major shade at loving Venus. Suddenly you're not sure whether you should go all in—or even go any further at all. Doubts and suspicions haunt your every step. This is precisely why you should slow down and take emotional inventory of your own feelings.

November 21-December 15: Venus in Scorpio

The love planet kicks off her annual sultry sweep through intensifying Scorpio and your seduction center. Strong feelings and desires may overtake you, barely giving you a chance to catch your breath. Since there will be mistletoe moments at every turn during the next three weeks, you might as well relax and enjoy the ride!

November 27: Venus-Uranus opposition

Under this disruptive transit, you could learn something that's a potential game-changer for a certain union. Venus wants to keep the peace, but she's in passionate Scorpio—and getting jolted by Uranus—so you might struggle to keep your composure. Deep breath!

November 30: Gemini full moon (lunar eclipse)

Just in time for the holidays, an empowering full moon—also a galvanizing lunar eclipse—lights up your twelfth house of release, endings and healing. What better way to enter this season of love and forgiveness than by letting something go that's been an emotional albatross? If that "something" is a toxic relationship or an ex you're still carrying a torch for, comfort yourself knowing that this is a necessary step to clear your field and call in a more appropriate partner.

NOVEMBER: CAREER HOTSPOTS

November 1: Mercury-Saturn square

This is the second of three squares between these thought-provoking planets, and it can challenge some basic values. While you want to be there for a person in need, you also know you only have so much time (and, frankly, patience) for the same old story. Tough-love Saturn reminds you that sometimes the best way to help people is not enabling them and instead, giving them the confidence to handle their own issues. This could come to head on November

The AstroTwins' 2020 Horoscope

6, at the next and final square, when Mercury, which is retrograde now, will be once again be moving forward.

November 12: Jupiter-Pluto meetup

Let's make a (strategic) deal! Powerful alliances that have been simmering since the spring could become official as expansive Jupiter and penetrating Pluto unite in your partnership zone. This is 2020's third and final alliance (the other two were on April 4 and June 30), so give any promising offers your full consideration, even if they involve a measure of risk. Jupiter and Pluto only meet like this every 13 years or so. Strike while the iron is white-hot!

November 13: Mars retrograde ends

Back to the fast track! After a stressful couple of months in your professional sector, action planet Mars zips forward in his home sign of Aries, bringing your career ambitions along with him.

November 17: Mercury-Uranus opposition

Rather than get involved in some unsavory group dynamics today, mind your own business and flit above the fray. Not only will you get more accomplished, others will respect your self-restraint.

November 23: Mercury-Neptune trine

Let the bean counters worry about the pragmatic details of a project. Under this visionary alignment, you're already thinking of ways to take some aspect of it to another level. If you get a chance for business travel, seize it. There might be even more opportunities there than meets the eye.

November 28: Neptune retrograde ends

Neptune can be disorienting enough in forward motion, and in reverse, it's a total wild card. And over the past five months, as the foggy planet retrograded through your expansive and boundless ninth house, you might have felt like you were spinning your wheels more than gaining traction. But now that it's back on course, you can hit the gas on some of your lofty plans, whether to travel or launch your own start-up!

December

DECEMBER: LOVE HOTSPOTS

December 5: Venus-Neptune trine

Under the spell of these two hyper-romantic planets, you could get swept up in a serious fantasy. And we're not saying that's a bad thing! Bask in this rarefied emotional high, and see where going with the flow takes you.

December 15, 2020-January 9, 2021: Venus in Sagittarius

Healthy is sexy! For the next few weeks, as beautifying Venus makes her annual visit to your wellness zone, you and your partner could deepen your bond by cooking nutritious meals or working out together. Single? Maybe don't wear earbuds every time you exercise or go hiking. You never know who you might meet and strike up a conversation with!

December 17, 2020-March 7, 2023: Saturn in Aquarius

How deep is your love? As serious Saturn begins the longer leg of its three-year journey through your intimate eighth house, some of your ties could be tested. Cautious Saturn can slow the pace. If you've rushed to commit or handed your trust to someone who hasn't fully earned it, Saturn may send you back a few steps to do the crucial foundation work. And if you've been the one reluctant to commit, prepare for a new odyssey into the realms of true soulmate-level merging.

December 19, 2020-May 13, 2021: Jupiter in Aquarius

Hang that Do Not Disturb sign! Today kicks off a heart-and-soul-deepening phase as auspicious Jupiter begins a yearlong trek through your eighth house of intimacy, eroticism and shared resources. The expansive planet hasn't touched down here in 12 years, and during this leisurely tour, you'll have plenty of chances to put all those hard-earned love lessons to good use and manifest the personal life you've always dreamed of.

December 20, 2020-January 9, 2021: Mercury in Capricorn

Here's the chance you've been waiting for! Articulate Mercury wings through your dynamic-duos zone, helping you put some strong (if hazy) feelings into words. Broaching a sensitive topic is never easy, but if you need an answer—or some key changes—this is the most direct path.

December 21: Jupiter-Saturn meetup

Hearts and souls unite as idealistic Jupiter and realistic Saturn make their rare union—known as the Great Conjunction—in your eighth house of sex, intimacy and merging. Taking a calculated risk could seal your bond for the long haul. A "twin flame" connection may be revealed.

December 30: Venus-Neptune square

If you're unhappy in a relationship—or unhappy not being in a relationship—look at your role in this. With dreamy Neptune mashed up with Venus in your critical and micromanaging zone, you'll get a clear view of where your standards might be a tad unrealistic. People are only human, meaning there's going to be something less than ideal with everyone. Prioritize your highest values and resolve to let the other stuff slide.

DECEMBER: CAREER HOTSPOTS

December 1-20: Mercury in Sagittarius

You'll be in an industrious mindset for the next few weeks as organized Mercury sweeps through your hard-working, detail-oriented sixth house. With the holiday deadline in sight, you'll sail through assignments and maybe even get a head start on 2021 goals. Stay focused, and you can break for the festivities with a clear conscience.

December 13: Mercury-Neptune square

Other people's lack of planning is not your emergency! Today, as hazy Neptune casts shade on productive Mercury, don't allow someone else to dump their problem on you. If they persist, let them know you wish you could help out, but you've got your own tight deadlines to manage!

December 14: Sagittarius new moon (total solar eclipse)

The year's only new moon to activate your organized and service-oriented sixth house is also an empowering solar eclipse, which motivates you to get serious about wrapping up 2020 business so

The AstroTwins' 2020 Horoscope

you can "holiday" with a clear conscience. And when you are in vacay mode, spend a little time envisioning your next big career coup!

December 17, 2020-March 7, 2023: Saturn in Aquarius

Time to get serious about your financial future. Ambitious Saturn starts its longer trek through your eighth house of assets, mergers and investments. In the next couple years, you could buy or sell property, earn revenue through passive income or start making your money work harder for you. But cautious Saturn warns against cutting corners or rushing into anything. Avoid harsh lessons or losses by slowing down. When in doubt, get advice from a professional.

December 19, 2020-May 13, 2021: Jupiter in Aquarius

Risk-taking Jupiter returns to your eighth house of joint ventures and shared resources for the first time in 12 years. The hardest part of this yearlong transit will be pacing yourself and trying to not make it all happen at once. Just keep putting one foot in front of the other, and watch the magic unfold!

December 20, 2020-January 9, 2021: Mercury in Capricorn

You'll be in rare negotiating form as the cosmic communicator lights up your partnership zone. But before you approach the bargaining table, make sure you know what you need to walk away with—which will leave you plenty of wiggle room.

December 21: Jupiter-Saturn meetup

Calculated moves could pay off as risk-taker Jupiter and cautious Saturn unite in your eighth house of wealth and investments. This rare event, known as the Great Conjunction, encourages you to take a savvy step out of your comfort zone. Someone could float an offer to merge your assets or launch a joint venture, with the possibilities of mutual gain. Make sure your dream team has the right blend of experienced wisdom and visionary pioneer.

December 23: Mars-Pluto square

These two heavenly hotheads form their final square of the year, which may test your patience. You've been watching a certain situation and holding off taking action, but someone might finally push you too far. If you must assert your authority, bear in mind that the effects might be irrevocable. Think before you do anything rash.

December 25: Mercury-Uranus trine

The year ends on a professional high note as the zodiac's most original thinkers hold their final summit meeting. True, it's Christmas, but if you finally hit on the perfect solution to a nagging project or download a brilliant project to kick off 2021, get it on paper so you don't totally forget it during all the holiday revelry.

December 29: Cancer full moon

The second Cancer full moon of 2020 (the first was on January 10) could stick one final feather in your cap as you put finishing touches on something you've been toiling on for a while. If this is "it," celebrate your coup and share the news with people who'll appreciate it—and are eager to share in your success! ✷

Tools from The AstroTwins
for your 2020 PLANNING

Visit all year long for new updates & additions!

www.astrostyle.com/2020tools

The AstroTwins' 2020 Horoscope

LEO
2020

Yearly Highlights

LOVE

With love planet Venus logged into your tech sector from April 3 to August 7, you'll be the belle of Bumble and the headmaster of Hinge. But, like the Supremes crooned, you can't hurry love. From March 21 to July 1, enduring Saturn hunkers down in Aquarius and your seventh house of relationships, its first visit there since January 1994! Coupled Leos could make serious future plans, or you may decide to restructure your entire approach to relationships. Saturn returns to Aquarius for two-plus years on December 17, joined by lucky Jupiter from December 19, 2020, to December 29, 2021. As the year ends, you'll be in your amorous element!

MONEY

Do the hustle! With a trio of planets powering up your industrious sixth house, your 2020 professional goals demand some serious elbow grease. To avoid feeling more like a drone than hive royalty, put savvy systems in place. Efficiency is the name of the game in 2020. Having the right support staff backing you is a must. Only work with qualified people who have the skills to take things off your overflowing plate and execute them with competence. You may travel for work or return for schooling when action planet Mars zooms into your worldly ninth house from June 27, 2020, to January 6, 2021.

WELLNESS

Bring it on! With vitality boosting Jupiter joining personal-trainer Saturn and transformational Pluto in your wellness zone all year, you're ready to get into fighting shape. Mix up your workouts so that they're fun, not punishing. You could revamp your eating plan, go vegan or heal a nagging condition through a dietary change. From MDs to massage therapists, self-care isn't a luxury in 2020—it's a necessity!

LEISURE

A lion is nothing without its pride, but in 2020, you may have to opt for quality over quantity when it comes to time with your loved ones. (Unless, of course, they work with you!) We know you're busy, Leo, but make sure you aren't treating family like boxes to tick off your to-do list. You could meet friends through a service group or "voluntourism" trip. Since fitness will be a big focus this year, how about turning your inner circle into workout buddies? Catch up over energizing hikes instead of energy-zapping brunches. ✴

LEO 2020 HOROSCOPE

2020 Power Dates

LEO NEW MOON
August 18 (10:41pm ET)

LEO FULL MOON
February 9 (2:33am ET)

SUN IN LEO
July 22–August 22

A green juice toast to your health, Leo! (And a round of blue spirulina tonics for all your friends.) The new decade is off to a salubrious start as vital Jupiter cannonballs into Capricorn and joins powerhouses Saturn and Pluto in your sixth house of wellness and work. These three planets haven't synced up like this since 1285 C.E. so this is major news! Some long-overdue restructuring is order, as you hack away habits that drain your life force and replace them with processes that support your radiance.

Whether you're in decent shape or dealing with some health challenges, this cosmic trio raises the bar. Are you tending to mind, body and spirit? In 2020, you could become a meditation maven, a plant-based practitioner or a guru of all things green, clean and serene.

Efficiency is the name of the game if you want to reach your lofty 2020 goals. This is the year to organize everything from your closets to your calendar, scaling back on your caretaking ways and reserving ample time for creativity. Get honest: Where are you "leaking" energy, Leo? With two final eclipses hitting Cancer and your boundary-challenged twelfth house on January 10 and June 21, and one more in Capricorn and your systematic sixth on July 5, you'll need to draw sharper lines with people in your world. If you don't, your magnanimous nature could infect you with resentment—never a good look for a sunny Leo!

Thankfully, a socially supportive starmap is also ahead in 2020. From April 3 to August 7, convivial Venus embarks on an extended tour through Gemini and your eleventh house of community, technology and activism. Get out and circulate, even if your Instagram and Facebook friend lists runneth over. The zodiac's jungle ruler can never have too many acquaintances…as long as they can match your generosity! While Venus is retrograde from May 13 to June 25 (an every-other-year event), you may have to banish a few energy vampires from your realm.

With love goddess Venus logged into your tech-savvy eleventh house, April through August could bring some lucky swipes on the dating apps. (And maybe the Return of the Disappearing Tinder Date during the May 13 to June 25 retrograde. Proceed with cautious optimism!) Coupled Lions should circulate more as a power couple, knitting together your friend groups and organizing dinner parties, weekend trips and other fun for the people you both adore.

But you may feel like getting, ahem, un-Hinged, starting June 27, when lusty Mars moves into Aries for an extended tour through your worldly, independent ninth house that lasts until January 6,

2021! The red planet will also pivot retrograde in 2020, from September 9 to November 13. During that time, even happily partnered Leos will have to navigate some fiery emotions. Pro tip: Absence makes the heart grow fonder! Waiting for your partner to join you on an adventure could mean missing out on a life-changing opportunity. Don't limit your own expansion, Leo. Do your thing, and you can share all the magic with your mate when you return to the lair.

Relationships will take a turn for the serious from March 21 to July 1 when enduring Saturn settles into Aquarius and your seventh house of committed coupling. Lighthearted love affairs could hit a "will we or won't we" turning point, and you won't be content to play the field. On December 17, the ringed planet will park in Aquarius for a longer spell (until March 7, 2023), putting partnerships through some endurance tests. Thankfully, jovial Jupiter will keep the spirit of romance alive, joining Saturn in Aquarius from December 19, 2020, until December 29, 2021.

A new series of eclipses begins this year on the Gemini/Sagittarius axis, which will illuminate the balance between being a team player and stepping forward as the star. You're an ace at both when you want to be, but no need to pull the modesty card. The two Sagittarius eclipses, on June 5 and December 14, stir things up in your fifth house of fame, passion and romance. You're quite the head-turner on the average day, Leo, but your star qualities will be in rare form under these two lunar lifts. You could end the year with a powerful mistletoe moment, or with something fabulous to debut to your ever-growing fanbase!

Jupiter, Saturn & Pluto in Capricorn: A return to vitality.

The Trio: December 2, 2019–March 21, 2020; July 1, 2020–December 17, 2020

Ready to restore yourself to roaring good health? Self-care isn't a #treatyoself indulgence in 2020; it's a habit-forming lifestyle shift. Since December 2, 2019, vital Jupiter has been power-spinning alongside disciplined Saturn and transformational Pluto in Capricorn and your salubrious sixth house. Ditch the deprivation mindset, Leo! This Jupiter cycle, which lasts until December 19, will turn you into a healthy hedonist.

For the past two years, karmic Saturn and Pluto have been co-piloting through Capricorn. These planets inspect the unseen, revealing shoddy structures that need to be replaced in order to support your best life. Their presence in your wellness zone may have put the kibosh on a Dionysian habit…one that has been hard as hell to break! (You may still be struggling.)

Maybe a gluten sensitivity forced you to part ways with the patisserie that served the best Petite Madeleines this side of the Seine. Or perhaps those champagne nights and black coffee mornings stopped delivering the same one-two punch…and, you're so over the hangovers. While you might not feel like the life of the party, the Saturn-Pluto buzzkill has also been a blessing, since it pushed you to take better care of your body. If a routine exam revealed less-than-optimal numbers, get proactive! Vitality-boosting Jupiter is on your side.

Even healthy Leos will hear the call to level up. And with fun-loving Jupiter in the mix all year, turn your workouts into "playouts." (You can leave the boot camp routines for the other no-limit soldiers.) This is the year to reconnect with the childlike joy you felt when you were running around at recess. Join an indoor league or hit the trampoline park once a week. You might even take your fitness to a literal playground, using the monkey bars for pull-ups and doing triceps dips on a bench. If you're up for the athletic challenge, try Parkour, a training discipline that turns an outdoor urban environment into an obstacle course.

Worldly Jupiter could lead you to African dance, Five Rhythms or the theatrical (and oh-so Leo) Japanese Butoh. Or, since Jupiter loves variety, get a Class Pass and sample studios on every side of town. Just don't overdo it! Jupiter in the sixth house can make you overly optimistic, and that might lead to injuries. Stretch, warm up and humbly start with the beginner's class, even if your competitive streak wants to earn an Olympic gold medal on day one.

Since Saturn rules time (and aging), you may be a little obsessed with maintaining a youthful glow. And Jupiter, the planetary Peter Pan, is so on board with your "forever young" mission. But before you spend thousands at the medical esthetician's office, work on igniting your inner pilot light. There's an art to aging gracefully, Leo, which means looking your best for the stage of life you're in—and embracing it!

The sixth house shares qualities with Virgo, the sixth sign of the zodiac, so anything natural and holistic will serve you well in 2020. In fact, this posse of planets encompasses mind (Jupiter), body (Saturn) and spirit (Pluto). This year, make sure your wellness plan hits all three realms. We're not telling you to ignore your Western MD. There's a place for modern medical wonders along with ancient remedies and the "woo." Functional medicine might be your jam in 2020: This approach to care involves treating the root cause of disease instead of just the symptoms. But do consult a qualified doctor before weaning yourself from any prescriptions.

Since the sixth house governs the digestive system, tending to gut health could power up your immune system. From colon cleanses to microbiome tests to popping a daily probiotic, it's all about your intestines in 2020. Whenever possible, eat clean and plant-based, making sure you're getting as much of the protein, vitamins and other building blocks as possible in your diet. We're not saying you have to become a raw vegan, Leo, but follow the 80/20 rule of healthy consumption. In the words of Greek physician Hippocrates, "Let food be thy medicine and medicine be thy food."

The sixth house is the "administrative affairs" department of the zodiac wheel, and with Jupiter joining Saturn and Pluto here until December 19, this is a year for sorting, downsizing and revamping your routines. Are you feeling like a prisoner of your possessions? Leos can be power-shoppers who always want the best of the best. You'll sample fifteen mascaras before choosing your wand, or get really into sneakers and suddenly stack your closet to the ceiling with vintage Jordans and high-tops. And let's not even talk about all the products you purchased to support your friends' retail start-ups. But if your storage spaces runneth over, this is the year to clean the castle from bottom to top.

Has an area of your life grown messier than you'd like? Instead of just straightening, set up an actual system. Create a neatly categorized folder system for data and a storage system for physical objects. One friend of ours borrowed from the corporate world and made an "operations manual" for her life: She organized all her most important phone numbers, passwords, appliance instructions and go-to recipes into a Google Doc and also an easy-access three-ring binder. Knowing that she could find what she needed on a moment's notice gave her a sense of inner peace.

Pick a goal for each quarter and add some entertainment value by giving it a name, like Destination: Inbox Zero or The Closet Makeover Challenge. Nothing motivates a Leo more than the reward system. How about booking a spa treatment for every milestone achieved? You'll have your storage unit cleared out in no time. Feeling overwhelmed? Try setting "microresolutions," a technique from the book *Small Move, Big Change* by Caroline Arnold. (Why not listen to the audiobook while you organize the bathroom vanity and paint a coral accent wall?) For example, rather than attempt to clean your entire basement, you tackle one small area per week. As you grow comfortable with a new habit, it creates a snowball effect.

Career-wise, Saturn and Pluto continue to push for stability, while Jupiter seeks greener (and more profitable) pastures. When the red-spotted planet visits the sixth house every 12.5 years, people yearn for the kind of work that makes a difference. You could find luck in the service sector, or within a "green" or wellness industry. Need to boost your skill set? Since Jupiter rules higher education, you may enroll in short certification courses that position you for a salary increase. Consider taking a low-pressure "bridge job" that pays the bills while you devote your best brain cells to learning. One friend worked the desk at a yoga studio and did light admin work while she earned a computer coding certification.

If you're happy in the field that you're in, you may update to greener, leaner methodologies. Many companies are adopting an "agile" approach to staffing, allowing employees to work remotely from any city. The virtual conference room is replacing the board room, as presentations are made by screen-sharing instead of projector. This might be the ideal scenario for you, Leo, at least part-time.

Conscious Leo business owners can earn carbon credits by cutting back on flights, transportation and the emissions produced by heating and cooling an office. That said, your social sign should not go too long without human contact. Join an office co-share or appoint yourself Sustainability Lead, putting compostables in the coffee room and encouraging the company to go paperless…or solar!

Three days this year will be particularly fruitful for Leos on the professional prowl. On April 4, June 30 and November 12, power broker Pluto and lucky Jupiter unite at the same degree of Capricorn, combining their strengths. Since Pluto rules the unseen and Jupiter is like a giant cosmic spotlight, hidden opportunities could be illuminated. Random acts of kindness may be bestowed upon you, as a near-stranger takes interest in your offerings. Or, someone who you've hooked up in the past could scratch your back in return.

> **"Someone you've hooked up in the past could scratch your back in return."**

While Pluto and Jupiter are both retrograde on June 30, a deal that was off the table may show new signs of life. Get negotiations underway and see what gives the second time around. While it might take until the final Jupiter-Pluto conjunction on November 30 to hammer out all the details, trust that this offer returned for good reason.

During this bustling year, dialing down stress may be the most crucial component to wellness. That nightly puff or sip might help you power down, sure, but escapism ultimately catches up to you, Leo. Instead of slipping into denial, gain command of your "spinning thoughts" by tuning in. If you don't have a meditation practice (or a meditation app), 2020 is the year to get the ball rolling. Neuroscientific findings are proving that meditation literally transforms your brain, decreasing anxious "fight or flight" responses that cause you to sweat the small stuff. Set up your cushion and close your eyes; record your insights in your journal. When you can't sit still, try moving meditations, like yin yoga and analog nature walks.

Pets fall under the sixth house domain—and hey, cuddling a cute creature has been shown to reduce blood pressure and have all kinds of psychological benefits. Adopting a canine or kitty companion can be a lot of responsibility at first, but the unconditional love will make it worthwhile. If you're already a pet owner, like many Leos, you and your furry friend could become Instagram-famous in 2020!

Saturn-Pluto conjunction: Restructure your support system.
December 2019–February 2020 (exact on January 12)

On January 12, give the world service with a smile… or a furrowed brow if you prefer! This game-changing day is one that astrologers have been counting down to for months, as astro-architect Saturn syncs up with alchemical Pluto at 22°46' Capricorn. These two heavenly heavyweights only connect once every 33-38 years, and when they do, entire systems are transformed.

This is a day where one simple act could alchemize your entire universe. Don't judge a book by its cover, Leo, and treat every stranger with dignity. That "rando" in the fleece and Tevas could be a Silicon Valley tech entrepreneur who wants to fund your genius app idea. Free advice you share on LinkedIn could shape a younger person's career path, and this anonymous "mentee" could one day return the favor with a game-changing connection. Or, you may simply pay it forward with a charitable deed and get yourself on the right side of the karmic food chain.

Where could you use some support, Leo? Sure, you're capable of being a one-lion show, but imagine the difference you could make if you were reigning over a dream team? Since the sixth house rules service providers, give up the notion that good help is hard to find. Perhaps you need to put a better process in place for choosing qualified associates…

or clients! As a heart-centered sign, following your feelings is essential. But it's equally important to measure those intuitive hits against your intellect. Outlining what you want and need will help you make smarter decisions about the mission-oriented aspects of your life. Perhaps it's just one "project manager" type who can sit by your side and bring all your dreams to fruition through an organized game plan.

Warning: This depth-plumbing alignment could shine a light on unhealthy relationship dynamics. Have you been laying your pearls before swine, as the saying goes? Generous Leos love to shower your people with (thoughtfully chosen) gifts. But if you don't pay attention to the flow of give and take, relationships can become seriously lopsided. Rein in your magnanimous spirit this January, even if it hurts a little to hold back. It's not about keeping score, Leo, it's about giving people an opportunity to return your many favors…before resentment creeps in.

Venus & Mars Retrograde: Commit with caution.
Venus Retrograde: May 14 – June 25

Mars Retrograde: September 10 – November 13

Toast of Tinder? Headmistress of Hinge? You'll proudly claim such titles between April 3 and August 7, when alluring Venus spins through Gemini and your tech-savvy eleventh house. If you've been complaining about your single status, tap that app, Leo. If you're in a relationship, this four-month circuit may reinvigorate your social life as a couple. Your sex life, too! It's anyone's guess what kind of toys or trysts will enter your bedroom while Venus buzzes through this experimental zone.

There is, however, a blackout period: From May 13 to June 25, Venus will be retrograde, a six-week signal-jammer which could short-circuit your better judgment. Have you been exchanging messages with a catch…or a catfisher? Eek! You know the drill. You have to message a lot of frogs before Prince(ss) Charming shows up. Between May 13 and June 25, run a thorough Google search on anyone who makes it to IRL date status, and check their social media feeds. (Those memes can be telling…) Better to be safe than sorry when la love planet turns into Sleeping Beauty, a tricky transit that happens every 18 months. You'll have to follow due process—which ain't easy for a passionate Leo! Slow down and think about dating multiple people instead of rushing into monogamy.

The eleventh house rules the future, so careful not to put the cart before the horse this spring. If you've only gone on a handful of dates, for example, stop tormenting yourself with questions like, "Could this be The One?" If you're gonna get freaky, choose a "safe word" and talk through boundaries and comfort zones thoroughly before you pull anything battery-operated from your nightstand drawer.

If you've had an unrequited crush on someone who keeps popping in and out of your life, this would be the time to be more hardcore—with yourself. Limit the time you spend with the stringer-alongers. That way, you can open up space for someone who is actually ready to commit. Plus, you know what they say: Absence makes the heart grow fonder.

Coupled Leos may have some real negotiating to do about your shared future, which could be a lively exploration. But get ready, because if you really probe, your partner might reveal some independent desires that don't easily dovetail with your own. You might even have some strong emotions about it, feeling caught off guard, angry or upset. Try to remember that everything is a negotiation. Maybe your partner wants to move to Berlin and you just accepted a job in San Francisco, or suddenly one of you wants a baby, when last year, you were both sure that adopting a French bulldog was the next big move. Life paths don't always line up perfectly even when you love someone, and this Venus retrograde may reveal a fork in the road. But that's what "playing the long game" looks like, right? Things like this don't have to be the end of the road, but perhaps the beginning of an adventurous new chapter. Get it all out into the open!

On a lighter note, Venus' extended tour through Gemini from April 3 to August 7 opens up an ideal window to reconnect to a beloved friend group… or get the band back together for a reunion tour. Venus is the pleasure planet, so why not upgrade? Think about doing something decadent, like meeting up in Miami for a weekend of margaritas and massages—or renting an Airbnb in the heart of the forest with a giant room that you can use as a rehearsal space.

There's no such thing as "too much" in the world of a Leo, but your over-the-top ways could go from three- to six-ring circus starting June 27! That day, thrill-seeking Mars blasts into its home sign of Aries, cannonballing through your "no limits" ninth house for an extended tour, until January 6, 2021. Normally, Mars holds court in a sign for seven weeks. But this year, a two-month retrograde (from September 9 to November 13) will keep Mars swinging on Aries' trapeze for six months!

Ready to play Where's Waldo? If so, you'll be rocking the red Breton stripes, Leo, as friends follow your global wanderings via social media. (Unless you choose to disappear off the grid for a portion of time after June 27, that is…) This motivating Mars cycle could send you back to school to finish your degree, or into a specialized training that allows you to teach something that you love. Enterprising Leos will enjoy the wind this Mars cycle puts in your sails. Your startup could become a reality before 2020 is through!

Just know this: After September 9. you may need to downsize or temporarily hold off on a few of grandiose plans as Mars turns retrograde until November 13. It's not like nothing will happen for this two-month window—you'll just have to be thorough with your timeline and diligent in your pursuits. (And be ready with contingency plans!)

If you're looking to launch a freelance business or an entrepreneurial project, this retrograde cautions against taking unnecessary risks. Don't oversell yourself: If anything, lowball your projections and what you can deliver. It's better to pull off 50 percent of a project and have it shine brilliantly than turn in something complete but shoddy.

As the expression goes, "When you fail to plan, you plan to fail." Heed that, because if you want to pull off any outsized missions, you're going to have to run a tight ship. And if you're developing that aforementioned entrepreneurial project, Mars' backspin cautions against shooting from the hip or taking too many gambles. You may need to do some additional research, training or schooling before you can confidently step out with it. Better you should delay your launch until Mars shoots forward again on November 13 than to put an untested product on the market just to meet a deadline.

Temper your words with tact. Brash Mars in the ninth house can make you honest…to a fault! You could detonate bridges with your truth bombs, and those will be hard to rebuild. Rule of thumb between September 9 and November 13? If you don't have something nice to say, don't say/text/tweet anything at all.

If you're thinking of a fall getaway, you might prefer to revisit a favorite destination rather than check out someplace unfamiliar. One tiny caveat: With adventurous Mars in reverse, you'll want to exercise total caution and pay attention to your surroundings. Daredevil Mars in snooze mode could skew your judgment. Wandering into dangerous neighborhoods or arriving at an international port without any hotel reservations is unadvisable during this window, even if you think you can handle it. But with proper planning—plus your fire sign charisma—you may quickly be adopted as a beloved ersatz citizen of buzzing metropolises and charming hamlets around the world!

Saturn in Aquarius: Royal courtship turns serious.
March 21–July 1
December 17, 2020–March 7, 2023

Time for a couple's coronation ceremony? Your regal sign was born to reign, but you prefer a multiplayer game of thrones. If it's been lonely at the top (or in your bed), that could change in a big way on March 21, when structured Saturn breaks free from the Capricorn cluster and sprints forward into Aquarius and your seventh house of relationships until July 1. During this three-month window, business and romantic alliances take a turn for the serious. And this is merely a prelude of what's to come, Leo! On December 17, 2020, Saturn parks in Aquarius for a longer tenure. You'll have until March 7, 2023, to "lock and load" a royal boo or take that next major step with your long-term love.

The last time Saturn waded through the Water Bearer's rivers was from February 6, 1991, to January 28, 1994. If you're old enough to remember that period of time, take a look back. Recurring themes and lessons may arise that shape the next few years of your life, especially with regards to partnerships.

This serious Saturn cycle could help you make a relationship official. Are you blocked by an old fear that you'll be hurt, rejected or abandoned? While Saturn visits Aquarius, you could do the deep inner work to heal that. An engagement, wedding or vow renewal is possible, but it's just as likely that you could call nuptials off if you've rushed in. Single Leos may be drawn to people significantly older or younger, as Saturn rules age and generational differences. You could meet someone through work—but check company policy on intra-office dating before you invite the VP of Marketing out for cocktails.

Loving the single life? Although you may enjoy stalking the Serengeti for no-strings jungle loving, while in Aquarius, serious Saturn strengthens the allure of your purr. The person you pigeonholed

as a random right swipe while you were "playing Tinder" (as our Leo friend Shaun calls it) could end up sticking around for the long haul. Given the karmic nature of Saturn's lessons, this might happen due to a lack of planning. For example, a one-night hookup could produce a love child (oops!)—but you might also decide to go forward with the pregnancy. Or a newish partner you're fairly certain could be your missing puzzle piece may be dealing with a challenging set of circumstances, like a kid from a former marriage and a contentious ex.

Existing relationships may feel heavy with Saturn here, and some weighty decisions lie ahead for Leos. Maybe you'll consider marrying your expat partner so they can stay in the country. Your spouse could be offered a plum job on the opposite coast, right after you renovated your dream home. Coupled Leos may go through a rough patch, where you feel out of sync with a partner or you can no longer sweep problems under the Persian rug. Take a deep breath, square your shoulders and call the relationship therapist if you can't seem to sort this out yourselves. If nothing else, you'll emerge so much stronger as a duo, knowing you can make it to the other side of tough times and prevail.

Mature Saturn rules tradition, and its job is to enforce rules and regulations. There will be tests with the most important people in your life, ones that can strengthen resilient relationships and topple those built on a flimsy foundation. Dynamic duos that are constructed on terra firma could end this Saturn phase perma-bonded for the long haul. But first, you may need to call in the pros to help you hash out your differences.

With Saturn here, some Leos might take a short trial separation. Or, you could literally be kept apart due to a heavy work and travel schedule, family demands or other "adulting" responsibilities. Saturn sets hard boundaries, and it can create actual physical distance. Long-distance love isn't your affectionate sign's ideal arrangement, but don't rule it out. Even if you share a home address, maybe you need a little more space for yourself on certain days? Don't forget, Leo, you are a fire sign, which makes you fundamentally creative. But in your desire to please people, you can tamp down your own blazes in the presence of others (or get hooked on their applause and approval ratings.) Having a pied-à-terre may be a hidden blessing, offering you a private little studio where you can develop your dreams without giving a damn what anyone else thinks.

Aquarius is your opposite sign, and we'll be honest: It can be bracingly eye-opening when tough taskmaster Saturn makes this harsh 180-degree angle to your Sun. (It only happens every 28 to 30 years, thankfully!) Leos born from July 23 to 26 will feel Saturn's stress the most in 2020. You may be forced to renegotiate the terms of a partnership, or you could deal with challenging people who throw roadblocks and resistance in your path. But Saturn rules restraint, and herein lies the key to your breakthrough. Learning to be proactive (rather than reactive) in the face of adversity will mark you as the leader you were born to be.

All kinds of experts fall under Saturn's domain. If you're a performer, maybe you'll retain an agent to represent you and shop your work around. Or if you're a behind-the-scenes Leo, you could help a talented ingénue live out their "A Star Is Born" dream. Team up with the right people for win-win scenarios like these. Check references before you sign on with anyone though—with cautious Saturn here, you can't be too careful!

Professionally, your playful sign craves variety within your routines. But this can leave you in a perpetual cycle of "one and done" clients or task-based work that never really leads anywhere. With Saturn parked in Aquarius, it's time to start investing in relationships that will go the distance. Move on from contracts and collaborators who string you along but sporadically come through. The chasing games will just exhaust you. With Saturn in this balancing part of your chart, surround yourself with colleagues whose skills and strengths complement yours.

A powerful partnership could emerge, but with cautious Saturn here, screen potential collaborators thoroughly. You might even do a personality assessment test, like the Myers-Briggs or Gallup StrengthsFinder, to see how your skills will dovetail. No need to rush this process. Trial runs between March 21 and July 1 can be eye-opening.

If you decide to keep the magic going in 2021, don't just seal it with a handshake or a verbal agreement. Saturn insists on formalities. Lawyer up and draft an actual contract. Sure, this might feel awkward, especially if your project partner is an old friend or even a relative. Reframe those worries, Leo. Spelling out the terms is the best insurance policy you can buy the relationship, increasing the likelihood that you'll be sharing a champagne toast a year (or five) from now, instead of sitting in arbitration over who owns the intellectual property rights to your co-created invention.

The Great Conjunction: Jupiter & Saturn unite.
December 21

Lighten up, Leo! All the process-driven drudgery will lift as 2020 draws to a close. On December 17, Saturn settles into Aquarius until March 7, 2023. Two days later, on December 19, Jupiter follows suit, joining the ringed taskmaster there until December 29, 2021. With these two "attractive opposites" co-piloting through your seventh house of partnerships for over a year, you'll attract the sorts of people who are both exciting and stable. Talk about an ideal energetic blend! And that, Leo, is because you'll be feeling that way yourself.

With optimistic Jupiter and realistic Saturn in cahoots, you'll have a clear-eyed view about who to pair up with. And if that means backing out of certain engagements, you won't spend too much time ruminating. Abundant Jupiter reveals a bounty of options. The grass might literally be greener on the other side of the state, country or world!

Global Jupiter spurs you to journey, which could lead you to a long-distance relationship or a cross-cultural connection in your own neck of the woods. When the chemistry is this potent, what are a few miles or time zones between you? Your WhatsApp and FaceTime could be on heavy rotation, perhaps also due to a business opportunity that arrives from afar. Cast a wide net with all your relationships as 2020 ends, and (if you read this in time) book a New Year's getaway at a bucket-list destination, preferably with your favorite plus-one!

Meanwhile, pragmatic Saturn keeps you from going off the romantic rails. No one holds the torch for fairy-tale love more than you, Leo. But let's be honest: You've probably deluded yourself about someone's "potential" more than once. We've dabbed the tears for many a Leo friend, knowing that all we could say was "there, there," while they unspooled, realizing that the boundless energy they poured into their good-for-nothing exes was not enough to create a miraculous transformation. And what fools those players were to turn down the adoration of such a loyal mate as you! But alas, it's time to give up the rescue missions, Leo, and find a partner who's ready to be a royal now.

Take heart, Lion Kings and Queens: Saturn and Jupiter in Aquarius will recalibrate your "picker," helping you make smarter selections. The Winter Solstice (December 21) will be a particularly tide-turning day for relationships, when Jupiter and Saturn make an exact connection at 0°29' Aquarius. This mashup, which only happens every 20 years, is known among astrologers as The Great Conjunction. Consider this your leap into a new league! As legendary Leo Mae West quipped, "I like restraint, as long as it doesn't go too far." That basically sums up the push-pull dynamic of Jupiter and Saturn. Position yourself strategically under those mistletoe sprigs!

Even if you're single with no option in sight during the December 21 Great Conjunction, make a symbolic gesture. One idea: Marry yourself! Buy flowers, dress up and treat yourself to an important piece of jewelry. Commit to a practice of doing at least one adoring thing for yourself every day. (Saturn will love that!) Heck, even if you are in a relationship, this would be an amazing habit to implement, since self-love is the crucial building block for a healthy partnership. Once again, Mae West said it best, "I never loved another person the way I loved myself." Amen to that!

Cancer/Capricorn Eclipses: Health and healing.
January 10, June 21, July 5

Motivate or meditate? In 2020, three game-changing eclipses touch down in Cancer and Capricorn, activating your health and healing axis. There's a time to lean in and a time to let go, Leo. You've been navigating those extremes since this lunar series began in July 2018. Some parts of your life could use more focus and integrity, while others have felt like soul-sucking struggles. In the first half of the year, you'll decide which are worth the elbow grease, and which to leave behind. On January 10, June 21, and July 5, you'll get three more opportunities to nail the "work-life balance" equation.

Instead of crashing after you soar, what if you could make a softer landing? Well, Leo, you absolutely can. "Flight school" begins on January 10, when the first full moon of the decade—a lunar eclipse—beams into Cancer and your twelfth house of soulful surrender. After a bustling holiday season, you may feel too exhausted to pivot into super-achiever mode. And that's fine! Give yourself a longer runway for ramping your resolutions.

Despite having a pack of planets in your pragmatic sixth house, January 10 is one day where you won't find answers by trying to control the material plane. Step away from the spreadsheets and head to the spa…or a vibrational sound healing. Or maybe book a shamanic soul retrieval with an energy worker who can help you reclaim an abandoned part of yourself. Anything that touches on the woo and helps you to relax will fill this eclipse's prescription. Once you've connected with the relaxed side of yourself, you'll know how best to act.

The twelfth house rules endings, and January 10 may herald an important transition. If a situation from 2019 just isn't working out as you hoped, stop pushing and forcing, Leo. That's wasted energy that could be channeled elsewhere, like into a cathartic creative project. The struggle is real, but it could also be the inspiration for a future EP, a collection of poems or a series of paintings.

Remember this: Releasing your worries to the universe isn't the same as giving up! Eclipses reveal shadows, and there may be a hidden solution waiting in the wings. But you won't see it until you close your eyes, let go and stop fixing your gaze in the same direction.

January's deeply healing eclipse can help you process stuck emotions. Have you fully grieved a loss? You might think you're past the pain, but a wellspring of feelings could surface. While you hate to lose your composure, don't sob alone in your lair. Compassionate people—like "earth angel" friends, therapists and holistic healers—could appear to Sherpa you along your journey. Miraculous messengers may also arrive in unexpected forms. Be open to the wisdom of strangers, or perhaps the kindness of an "overbearing" person who you pushed away in the past. Have you been considering a support group? This eclipse could lead you to a healing circle, 12-step program, or transformational retreat where you can dive in, deal and heal.

If you're tangled up in codependent dynamics, this eclipse will cut that cord. Or, you could part ways with 90 percent of the stuff in your storage unit that's made you feel like a prisoner of your possessions. Downsize, declutter and free yourself from the past! After January 10, you'll feel like traveling with a lighter pack.

Another chorus of "let it go, let it go" resounds on June 21, with the new moon in Cancer. This one is a galvanizing solar eclipse, which accelerates progress. Are you ready to remap your creative and spiritual landscape? Spend the Summer Solstice at a retreat writing a memoir, dip-dying fabrics or learning how to play quartz singing bowls. With your dynamic range, the hardest part will be picking which of your passions to focus on first.

On July 5, this two-year eclipse series ends with a lunar (full moon) eclipse in Capricorn. The spotlight is on your health, so book any checkups and deal with nagging aches and pains before they snowball into something bigger. Capricorn is the sign of experts. Working with a nutritionist, personal trainer or holistic healer can get your body back to fighting shape.

If you've been implementing self-care strategies all year, you may be proudly showing off your "dangerous curves" this summer, in the spirit of Leo Jennifer Lopez. But no matter what you look like, this is a cue to love yourself unconditionally, inside and out. Your worth cannot be measured by a number on a scale. As if!

Work chaos that's dogged you since July 2018 (or early 2019) could resolve near July 5. You may have struggled to find good help or a job that could hold your interest. Clarity arrives now to help you map what your ideal customer, client or workflow looks like. Write it down, Leo! Gut feelings aren't to be dismissed, but this eclipse calls for logic. If you're responsible for hiring, for example, write up a job description and circulate it among your networks. Don't just employ the first person you like. Give yourself the gift of options. You might discover someone whose traits outshine your expectations!

You're a tenacious fixed sign, but this can leave you stuck in an old way of doing things. If you've been resisting a new process or ignoring protocol, you've probably made your work ten times harder than it needs to be. Wave the white flag on July 5, Leo. Using a financial tracking app, for example, can actually be liberating once you orient yourself to its functionality. The brain space you free up by not having to store everything in your head can be used for better things…like making art or love!

Gemini/Sagittarius Eclipses: Step into a starring role.
June 5, November 30, December 14

Curtains up! This year brings a new series of eclipses that will fall on the Gemini/Sagittarius axis from June 5, 2020, to December 3, 2021. Their mission? To help you learn when to step forward as the star and when to collaborate with an ensemble cast. This year, two eclipses in Sagittarius will activate your fifth house of passion, creativity and fame; one will arrive in Gemini and your collaborative, innovative eleventh house.

The first one, a Sagittarius solar (new moon) eclipse on June 5, fires the starting gun, making it impossible to not pursue your passions. With your slumbering creativity springing to life, you could uncover a new obsession or be recognized for a talent that you've been quietly developing behind the scenes for years. The fifth house rules love, glamour and self-expression. This eclipse can attract a fervent fanbase while also giving you the courage to boldly "do you."

Summer love could come with a few surprise twists and turns near June 5. You may discover a burning attraction for someone who is supposed to be off-limits—perhaps because one (or both) of you is otherwise engaged. While you don't want to just act on those feelings, especially under the charged influence of an eclipse, they are worth examining since they may portend a passion that's missing from your life. Of course, you could find ways to scratch that itch that don't jeopardize existing relationships. But you may feel torn and a bit out of sorts near June 5.

Ready to make a big leap with your partner? You might solidify a romantic relationship, making things official near June 5. A casual connection could get suddenly serious, perhaps with baby news or a deep conversation about carving out quality time. If you're a performer, this eclipse pushes you onto center stage. We don't have to tell a Leo to give 'em the show of a lifetime. Wherever you find yourself on this day, there's only one rule: Hold absolutely nothing back!

On November 30, the year's lone Gemini lunar eclipse may bring exciting friendships and affiliations, or an opportunity to team up around a cutting-edge cause. Adopt a collaborative approach; the combined superpowers of your squad could bring a Level: Dom Perignon victory. This eclipse could rouse your inner activist. You could become the surprising "voice of the people," championing a cause or getting more politically active than you've been in years.

If you've been resisting Cupid's calling for a while, you may finally surrender to some right swipes in time for Cuffing Season. While the dating apps will deliver near November 30, hover near the mistletoe on December 14, when the solar eclipse in Sagittarius stitches your heart onto your sleeve. Strong feelings surge up, and there will be no stemming the tide once the floodgates open. A romantic relationship could rocket to the next level or fizzle out completely. This eclipse once again might bring baby news or a special piece of jewelry to show off with your NYE formalwear.

Ready to make a name for yourself? The December 14 eclipse (or within a month of it) is an ideal window for dropping an album, debuting a new look or sending your audition video to a casting director. It's time to hear your zodiac sign's three favorite words again: lights, camera, action! ✳

monthly hotspots

January

JANUARY: LOVE HOTSPOTS

January 3-February 16: Mars in Sagittarius

Fiery Mars returns to unbridled Sagittarius, heating up your lusty (and fertile!) fifth house for the first time in two long years. Over these next eight weeks, you can make up for "lost time." Question: What does your heart truly desire? Set that as your bullseye, and keep your aim true.

January 10: Cancer full moon (lunar eclipse)

This intensifying lunation is the first of two Cancer full moons that will land in your twelfth house of introspection, release and healing (the next is on December 29). Because it's also a potent lunar eclipse, you may be pushed to let go of a relationship, behavior or limiting belief that's blocking your forward progress. Surrender doesn't come easily to your take-charge sign, but sometimes it's the only way to bring about the shifts you crave.

January 13-February 7: Venus in Pisces

When vixen Venus swan-dives into your eighth house of intense emotions, sexuality and intimacy, there will be no such thing as casual. You'll prefer to go all the way in—or get out while you can. There's no part-way under this transit.

January 16-February 3: Mercury in Aquarius

When the cosmic communicator wings into chatty air sign Aquarius and your relationship house, the best possible aphrodisiac for you will be spicy, intelligent pillow talk. But don't rush to the sheets. Enjoy the slow, passionate build-up of flirting, teasing and anticipating. This works just as well for solid couples!

January 24: Aquarius new moon

This once-a-year Aquarius new moon can cause budding relationships to heat up, solid partners to take a next step toward commitment and for singles to meet people with keeper potential. But trust that if something is meant to be, it'll unfold organically—during the next few weeks or even six months. Today also kicks off the Chinese Year of the Metal Rat, a strategic cycle that could have "power couple" written all over it.

January 26: Venus-Mars square

Once a year, the cosmic lovebirds fall out of harmony, which can spark anxiety, anger or confusion about how to react. The trick is to not overreact. Step back far enough to see things in a wider perspective, and you'll realize that this is just part of the natural ebb and flow of relationships. It could actually be a good thing if it nudges you to talk about a subject you've been keeping to yourself.

January 27: Venus-Neptune meetup

This annual mashup invites you to unhinge from buttoned-up reality and let yourself get a little lost in a fantasy—alone or *à deux*! Sometimes it's valuable to blur the edges and think (or do) things outside your normal comfort zone. Just don't buy anyone's snake-oil miracle cure!

January 28: Mars-Neptune square

Warning: Love does not conquer all, and under today's fog machine of a square between passionate Mars in your zone *d'amour* and befuddling Neptune in your erotica sector, you might be sending and receiving very mixed messages. Watch out for strong reactions to flare up as a result. Your best policy? Make no assumptions and think twice before you blurt!

JANUARY: CAREER HOTSPOTS

January 2: Mercury-Jupiter meetup

This once-a-year mashup gives you the rare ability to both drill down to the tiniest detail—and widen your lens so you can focus on the big picture, like visioning, branding and global outreach. Pro tip: Don't try to do them at the same time!

January 3-February 16: Mars in Sagittarius

When the planet of motivation blazes into your creativity corner, you'll tap a rich vein of innovative energy. The red planet only touches down here every other year, and in candid and confident Sagittarius; it may force you out of hiding.

January 10: Uranus retrograde ends

Curveball-throwing Uranus ends a five-month retrograde (since August 11, 2019) in your professional corner that may have interrupted your forward progress. Hopefully you took advantage of the opportunity to review, rethink and reinvent—because now that it's marching ahead in this ambitious chart sector, distractions should lessen, and you'll be confident enough to take a gamble on one of your more outré ideas. Hey, you can't win if you don't play!

January 12: Mercury-Saturn-Pluto meetup

This super-rare "triple play" can get you motivated to put some smart new protocols into place, take a few hours out to do all needed software updates and then, when all systems are go, take a deep dive into a complex project. The combo platter of cautious Saturn, analytic Mercury and intensifying Pluto will make you a serious force to be reckoned with!

January 13: Sun-Saturn-Pluto meetup

On the heels of yesterday's empowering mashup, today's galvanizing "triple header" of a pile-up, in your efficient sixth house reveals opportunities to bring some fresh blood onto a team project. Age and experience are valuable, but sometimes a younger person can bring a whole new perspective that you never thought of.

January 16-February 3: Mercury in Aquarius

Two heads are so much better than one, a truism you'll call upon time and again over the next three weeks as the cosmic messenger powers up your seventh house of dynamic duets. Focus on playing to each other's strengths and win-wins and you'll save a ton of work—and have way more fun!

January 18: Mercury-Uranus square

Don't waste precious time or energy trying to get colleagues on the same page today. People will be too opinionated and unable to see the value of compromise. Just let the chips fall where they will and focus on your own piece of the puzzle.

January 23: Sun-Uranus square

With your ruler, the self-possessed Sun, in your partnership house at loggerheads with unpredictable Uranus in your career corner, don't worry about what anyone else is up to. They might be keeping their cards too close to their vest for you to get an accurate read.

January 24: Aquarius new moon

Two is your magic number for the next two weeks thanks to the fresh-start energy of the year's only Aquarius new moon in your partnership house. Simply shifting your mindset from "me" to "we" could spark an exciting new connection. Today also marks the Chinese New Year in the sign of the shrewd Metal Rat, which bodes well for strategic alliances.

February

FEBRUARY: LOVE HOTSPOTS

February 3-March 4: Mercury in Pisces

The cosmic messenger spends an extra-long time in Pisces and your erotic, intimate eighth house this year because it will go retrograde from February 16 to March 9 and flip back into Aquarius for a few days. If relationships start to stall (or even disappear) during this time, take time to review what you really want. Things should get back on track once Mercury resumes forward motion.

February 7-March 4: Venus in Aries

When the love planet swings into your candid and cosmopolitan ninth house, you'll naturally become (even) more honest in matters of the heart. Single? You could meet someone while traveling, or perhaps an intriguing visitor to your town will catch your eye! Couples can rekindle their connection with a romantic getaway or taking a workshop together.

February 16-March 30: Mars in Capricorn

The energizing red planet returns to your sixth house of health, self-care and organization for the first time in two years. You'll get motivated to tackle a life-improvement project, alone or with your partner. While it's great that you're taking your wellbeing seriously, don't slip into obsessiveness or perfectionism. This is a journey to enjoy!

February 16-March 9: Mercury retrograde

The celestial communicator kicks off a three-week reversal through your eighth house of intimacy and merging, which could disrupt the harmony of a certain bond. Trust might be tested, and you may be forced to address issues you've been ignoring. Since retrogrades rule the past, watch for the tempting return of an ex. But even if you think you see all green lights, proceed with utmost caution.

February 21: Mars-Uranus trine

This is a great confluence to get a stalled relationship back in gear. But don't resort to the same old tactics. Disruptor Uranus has some new tricks up its sleeve, and lusty Mars is pretty good about picking up on hints. Don't worry about being subtle.

February 23: Pisces new moon

This once-a-year "fresh starts" new moon in your eighth house of sexuality and intimacy could throw you overboard from the Love Boat, and plunge you smack into the sea of love. Whether you're hoping for a reset on your current relationship or to meet someone with keeper potential, own your part in this, and take any and all necessary action!

February 23: Venus-Jupiter square

Are your amorous "eyes" bigger than your "stomach"? You might not be seeing things in the most realistic light under this supersizer transit. Are you conveniently overlooking someone's unsavory behavior? Or might you be confusing love and lust? Tap the brakes and wait for clarity to return.

February 28: Venus-Pluto square

This one-day, intense clash could reveal a structural flaw in the foundation of a certain relationship, and once that genie is out of the bottle, there will be no stuffing it back in. Pluto's hits are never fun, but if you're playing for keeps, you *are* going to want to know about this. Of course, even solid couples hit speed bumps. As long as you're not in denial, you'll know how to proceed.

FEBRUARY: CAREER HOTSPOTS

February 3-March 4: Mercury in Pisces

The cerebral planet will hang out in Pisces and your eighth house of joint ventures for an extended visit thanks to a retrograde from February 16 to March 9. Use this time to research and get clear on long-term financial plans. During the backspin, things that started to build momentum may unexpectedly stall, or someone might bail on a commitment. Stick it out: The right thing will come along to replace it.

February 9: Leo full moon

This once-a-year powerful lunation shines its high beams on you, setting the stage for a powerful "coming-out" moment over the next two weeks. Get ready for your big reveal—perhaps involving a creative sideline gig you're launching.

February 16-March 9: Mercury retrograde

As the messenger planet turns heel in your eighth house of shared resources and long-term investments, a deal or sale could be put on hold. Hold off signing contracts or financial agreements until Mercury resumes forward motion—and if possible, give it another three weeks for safe measure.

February 16-March 30: Mars in Capricorn

As the action planet marches through your sixth house of streamlining and organizing, you'll be motivated to throw yourself into a project that previously felt too messy and overwhelming to take on. But now that you're fired up, you'll be eager to jump into it. Tip: Break it down into smaller chunks so you don't get frustrated and quit halfway through!

February 21: Mars-Uranus trine

You're in the zone today, under this auspicious trine that gives you a leg up on the competition. But really, when you're this hot, the concept of "competition" is just theoretical. Don't think about it: Just hit the gas and go!

February 23: Pisces new moon

This annual new moon in your house of shared resources could shine a light on a solid investment partner, but you need to be very thorough in your background checks and due diligence. Pisces energy dials up the idealism, which is great for creative ventures. But if money is involved, you can't be too careful!

March

March 3: Venus-Saturn square

You might be excited by the "big picture" of a certain person or relationship, but when you narrow your focus and consider the little day-to-day things, you may realize you're not as content as you'd like to be. Today, get as much clarity as possible on what you need, but wait for Venus to swing out of Saturn's force field to discuss it.

March 4-April 3: Venus in Taurus

Vixen Venus commences her annual tour of sensual Taurus and your future-oriented, status-conscious tenth house, upgrading your desires. Dates in dive bars and the nosebleed seats won't cut it for the next month. Singles will be in the mood for sophisticated romancing, and if you're attached, you're ready to step out as the power couple you are!

March 4-16: Mercury in Aquarius

When the cosmic communicator makes its annual visit to articulate air sign Aquarius and your relationship house, your greatest turn-on will be intelligent, seductive repartee. You'll feel comfortable enough to share your feelings, secret fantasy or even broach a sensitive subject.

March 8: Venus-Uranus meetup

Mix it up! When unpredictable, excitable Uranus hooks up with voluptuous Venus in sensual Taurus, a little spontaneity will get the blood racing! Single? Check out some new venues or change your "swiping" strategies. And because this is your future-minded house that's being activated, couples can have fruitful talks about upcoming plans.

March 16-April 10: Mercury in Pisces

The messenger planet returns to Pisces after dipping back into Aquarius for almost two weeks. You've had a chance to talk through nagging issues—or decide whether you want to pursue something. Now with the messenger planet in your permabonding zone, it's time to seal the deal with some soulful nonverbal communication.

March 21-July 1: Saturn in Aquarius

For the first time since 1991, solidifying Saturn lends its gravitas to your partnership house, which could act like a stress test for longtime bonds. This is the first phase of a three-year transit (until March 7, 2023). Separation is a possibility, but so is true commitment! Single? Set the bar high and you could attract someone who shares your most cherished values.

March 27: Venus-Jupiter trine

This auspicious and empowering mashup can give you the optimism to pursue something your heart is pounding over. If you're feeling hopeful about a new or solid union, be bold and propose what you truly desire. Single? You may not be for long!

March 28: Venus-Pluto trine

Under this rare (twice-a-year) intensifying alignment, you can plumb the depths with a lover or get to know someone much better! While electric chemistry is irresistible, what will act like Gorilla

Glue over the long haul is shared values and goals. Make sure that's there before you go all in.

March 30-May 13: Mars in Aquarius

The lusty planet is setting up shop in your partnership zone, which can add a supercharge to all relationships (hot!), but it can just as quickly trigger jealousy or competitiveness (not!).

March 31: Mars-Saturn meetup

When the cosmic accelerator (Mars) bangs into its counterpart, the celestial brakes (Saturn), you might feel like someone killed your engine just as you were reaching cruising speed. Don't panic! This is a one-day "correction," so take advantage of this opportunity to check in and see if you like the direction you're headed.

MARCH: CAREER HOTSPOTS

March 4-16: Mercury in Aquarius

When the winged messenger flits into your partnership realm, you might have a white-light realization about a mutually beneficial alliance. Choose someone whose skills and talents dovetail with yours, rather than overlap. When interviewing, don't shy away from asking the tough questions.

March 9: Virgo full moon

The year's only Virgo full moon illuminates your financial sector, shining a light on the way forward. This could bring a long-running project to completion, but don't cling longer than is necessary. If you can stay open to what comes, the next two weeks (even six months) could bring you to a possible career turning point. Ask for the money you deserve!

March 16-April 10: Mercury in Pisces

When analytical Mercury returns to your eighth house of long-term wealth after a retrograde and brief return to Aquarius, you may watch some of your investments get resuscitated, or an iffy partner could finally be ready to ink the deal. Things that were building momentum then stalled should get back on track. Number one requirement? Patience!

March 20: Mars-Jupiter meetup

Even if you try to work on the nitty-gritty details today, you may find it impossible to focus. That's because big-picture Jupiter is getting frothed up by energizing Mars in your organized sixth house. Widen your angle and think about the super-structure of a project and how all the moving parts come together—not who's working on which tiny component. Leave that to the bean counters.

March 21-July 1: Saturn in Aquarius

Serious Saturn kicks off phase one of its new incarnation in Aquarius and your partnership and contracts house, priming you for the big leagues between now and March 7, 2023. The planet of time and structure can help you weed out any draining people or counterproductive habits and help you attract heavy hitters into your orbit. Anything built on a shaky foundation will fall apart in the months and years to come, but solid collaborators will more than pull their weight.

March 23: Mars-Pluto meetup

This is a powerful day for you professionally, with these two heavy hitters forming a rare (once-every-other-year) merger, this time in your realm of problem-solving, organizing and parsing complex issues. If you've been sitting on a volcano about someone's less than impeccable behavior, either have a word stat, or be prepared to erupt.

March 24: Aries new moon

Do it! If you've been mulling a gamble involving a business venture, this annual new moon of fresh starts in your expansive ninth house prods you to take action. And because the ninth house rules travel, education and startups, if any (or all) of these things are involved, don't even hesitate!

March 30-May 13: Mars in Aquarius

Team up for the win! Go-getter Mars zooms into your seventh house of contracts and collaborations, heating up your partnership sector. Dynamic duos could move quickly. With combative Mars here, negotiations could get tense, especially if you feel rushed into signing on the dotted line. You may need to iron out a few sticking points with an existing collaborator or client, too.

March 31: Mars-Saturn meetup

When high-octane Mars merges with cautious-to-a-fault Saturn in your dynamic-duos department, part of you will be ready to link up with a creative bigwig—but another part knows it's vital to protect your intellectual property and all your interests. This is not the time to rush! If anything, hire an attorney to review all the fine print.

April

APRIL: LOVE HOTSPOTS

April 3-August 7: Venus in Gemini

Levity returns during this extra-long, three-month transit—and just in time if you've been unable to find a happy middle ground with a love interest. You won't have the bandwidth to engage in protracted finger-pointing and are much more in the mood to have fun for fun's sake! And with Venus touring your eleventh house of platonic pals, you could reconnect to the BFF side of your partner or, if you're single, catch a glimpse of a friend in a whole new light.

April 4: Venus-Saturn trine

This solidifying sync-up of the love planet in your social sector and commitment-minded Saturn in your dynamic-duos zone underscores the friendship part of your bond. After all, shouldn't you be able to tell your S.O. everything? For single Leos, this could illuminate a certain platonic pal who might actually have partner potential!

April 7: Mars-Uranus square

Things took off at breakneck speed, and now you're getting flashed a cautionary yellow light. Under this one-day clash, a fast-moving relationship could make a sudden U-turn, or you might be forced to admit your future plans aren't in sync. Couples may diverge on summer-vacation ideas. Don't poke at it now. Set it aside and revisit it another day.

APRIL: CAREER HOTSPOTS

April 3: Mercury-Neptune meetup

Look beyond the spreadsheets and what people are telling you. Your intuition is way more accurate than data reports. Under this insightful merger of analytical Mercury and perceptive Neptune, you'll know exactly what your best next move is, even if it feels counterintuitive to others.

April 4: Jupiter-Pluto meetup

Systematizing is powerful! Expansive Jupiter and transformational Pluto make their first of three rare hookups. As they unite in Capricorn and your sixth house of efficiency and service, you're called to do work that makes a difference. Streamline your processes and trim the excess. A junior employee you take under your wing could become your "secret business weapon." Stay tuned for two more Jupiter-Pluto conjunctions on June 30 and November 12.

April 7: Libra full moon

The annual Libra full moon lights up your communication corner, encouraging you to boldly share your ideas to a group and maybe take a gamble with a new client. The next two weeks are perfect for launching a social media campaign or making that big-deal pitch. You've got this!

April 7: Mars-Uranus square

Just because a person is on your team doesn't automatically make them a team player. Today, someone may show their true colors by blatantly trying to advance a selfish agenda. But don't waste precious time or energy waiting for the perfect public moment to cut them down to size. Have a private word, and let them know that one more step in the wrong direction is all you need to report them to your mutual boss or HR.

April 10-27: Mercury in Aries

Leave the details to the others. During the next two and a half weeks, your talents will be best used by engaging in blue-sky thinking (ideally way outside the box) and concentrating on your highest personal goals. A business travel opportunity may come up in this time frame. Be ready to pack a bag on a moment's notice!

April 14: Sun-Pluto square

You don't need everyone's support, Leo—just get a few key collaborators on board. Under this fast-moving but disruptive clash, you may need to sidestep someone who isn't carrying their weight or, worse, is secretly undermining your best efforts. Ignore them as long as you can, but if their meddling starts to take a toll, speak up.

April 15: Sun-Jupiter square

Know-it-all alert! Make sure you back up your lofty claims with facts and figures—and demand the same in return. Opinions are valid to a point, but swagger won't sway the true decision-makers.

April 21: Sun-Saturn square

As you're shattering glass ceilings and catching the eye of some important influencers, you're feeling good about your accomplishments. But not everyone is quite so pleased on your behalf. Today's harsh square could reveal someone in your inner circle who'd happily see you stumble or fail. Don't stoop to their level. Just be your best self and don't let their negativity enter your field.

April 22: Taurus new moon

You've been waiting a year for this moment: the beginning of the next exciting phase of your career—and it promises to be incredible! The only Taurus new moon of 2020 powers up your house of professional ambitions, opening doors that had previously been closed off to you. Note that to open a new door you probably have to close another, so don't shed too many tears on your meteoric ascent up the company ladder. Setting goals for the coming six months is a perfect activity for the next two "manifesting" weeks.

April 25: Mercury square Jupiter and Pluto

You may feel like David fighting a pack of Goliaths today, but don't throw down your slingshot and head for the hills. Those behemoths might be putting up a tough front because they know you've got the goods and they don't want to give up an iota of their power. Pay attention and wait for your moment to either team up with like-minded "little people" or for the big guys to come clean. You've got integrity on your side, and that counts for a lot.

April 25-October 4: Pluto retrograde in Capricorn

It's a mark of a good manager and clever creator to periodically hit pause, call a team meeting and review...everything. On small projects, you could bang this out in a day or two. But to really air out a large, complex system that many people operate from, it might take some time, and you can't afford to rush. Today, as astute and transformative Pluto flips into reverse in your sixth house of organization and helpful people, it's the perfect time to find any bugs in the master plan, weak links in the personnel chain and where you yourself might be "leaking" energy. Take a few months to put the necessary fixes in place.

April 26: Sun-Uranus meetup

This once-a-year meetup of your ruler, the creative Sun, and inventive Uranus can spark downloads that will make you look like a genius! Dangle teasers to get their interest, then propose the terms you want so you get full credit for your brilliant ideas!

April 27-May 11: Mercury in Taurus

No more idling in neutral. Quicksilver Mercury flits into your tenth house of career ambition and advancement today. This two-week professional power surge can illuminate the perfect strategy for getting your name out there. Speak up in meetings, offer your unsolicited two cents whenever you can—while being aware to not sound like a pushy opportunist!

April 28: Mercury-Saturn square

You can't hit it out of the park every time, so don't take it personally if a decisionmaker doesn't green-light your first draft of a proposal. Assume they know what they're doing—or at least what the client or boss wants—and listen attentively to their constructive criticism. Reframe it as free, high-level mentoring!

April 30: Mercury-Uranus meetup

Your patience may be tested as others around the table struggle to keep up with your presentation. Just because your mind is racing like an Olympic sprinter doesn't mean the uninitiated can follow along. Learning how to get your point across to people who aren't on your level is a valuable lesson, so you might as well perfect it now!

May

MAY: LOVE HOTSPOTS

May 3: Venus-Neptune square

Don't jump to amorous conclusions under this foggy face-off, during which it will be easy to confuse someone's being nice with their being interested. (Awkward!) Worse: You might think your intuition is right on, but in reality, you could be a victim of the fantasy vibes that a Neptune square is famous for! (Note: You'll get two more "doses" of this medicine when Venus goes retrograde in Gemini, then corrects course, on May 20 and July 27, respectively.)

May 7: Scorpio full moon

Keep the tissues handy! The year's only full moon in your sensitive fourth house could trigger a passionate confession or leave you feeling emotionally raw. Couples who've been thinking of exchanging keys or moving in together could take a decisive step during the next two weeks.

May 11-September 29: Saturn retrograde

Relationship repair time? Structured Saturn backs through Aquarius and your relationship zone until July 1, then makes one last dip into Capricorn, where it will perform a rigorous audit of your health habits and wellbeing. Make sure stress levels aren't spiking—and that the people who are there to support you are performing up to par! Some Leos may decide to take a break from a partnership to do some important soul searching. If your bond can endure the separation, it might just last for the long haul. Other couples could spend time apart due to heavy responsibilities from work or family duty. Choose quality over quantity if you're faced with such circumstances.

May 13-June 27: Mars in Pisces

Lusty Mars returns to your eighth house of seduction, intimacy and emotional bonding for the first time in two years. Things could heat up quickly. But don't lose your rationality in the face of sexual chemistry, even when it borders on Tantric. For as much as Mars cranks up the libido, he also dials up jealousy and obsession.

May 13-June 25: Venus retrograde in Gemini

When the love planet commences a six-week backspin, a relationship that was heating up nicely might cool off. Couples can argue more, and singles may feel like the dating pool has been stocked with mediocre fish (especially online). Hang in there, Leo. This is just a natural "correction"—a chance to catch your breath and ensure you like the path you're on. If you're looking for a total reset, use these six weeks to change your own vibration so you can attract someone more suitable.

May 22: Mercury-Venus meetup

Friend, lover: Why not toggle between those distinctions if you're both single and feeling a strong mutual attraction? Today's hookup of amiable Mercury and amorous Venus in your social eleventh house refills your drinks and pushes your bar stools a little closer together. (Or serendipitously puts you in very close quarters with a kindred spirit.) Either way, if there's truly nothing to lose by testing the waters—then there's no reason not to go for it. Coupled? This is a great day for you and your partner to communicate with loving intentions.

May 28-August 4: Mercury in Cancer

You'll be hosting cerebral Mercury in your introspective, restful twelfth house for an extra-long period because it will turn retrograde from June 18 to July 12. During this long, creative stretch, you're encouraged to plumb the depths of your imagination and do as little "heavy mental lifting" as you can get away with. Some old issues can resurface and you'll have to talk them through yet again, thanks to the communication planet doing the backstroke through that dreamy twelfth house. Hopefully it isn't you who's gone into denial or refusing to deal with a pressing matter!

The AstroTwins' 2020 Horoscope

MAY: CAREER HOTSPOTS

May 9: Mercury-Pluto trine

Under this electrifying trine, you'll be firing on all cylinders, so screen out the distractions and throw yourself into today's assignment. The work you do behind the scenes will have a powerful effect on the larger mission, so don't think you're toiling in vain!

May 10: Mercury-Jupiter trine

If you know you're onto something huge, go ahead and take an inspired risk today. Not totally sure? Test the waters with a trial balloon and gauge the reaction. Pay attention to what people say to you as well as what they're privately discussing. They might be so blown away they want to find a way to co-opt your idea without you knowing it!

May 11-September 29: Saturn retrograde

If you've been picking up the slack for a so-called partner, drop that like it's hot! There's a reason you signed on to work together—and it wasn't for you to do all the heavy lifting and for them to sit back and cash their checks. As stern Saturn spins into reverse in your dynamic-duos zone, you can correct imbalances, have tough talks and get things back on a fair and even keel. It might take a few weeks (or months), but after this, you won't be taken advantage of again.

May 11: Mercury-Mars square

Don't expect everyone to be on the same page today—and don't waste one minute trying to herd those cats! Competitive Mars is clashing with inventive Mercury in your career house, and anything you say or do will only pour gasoline on this dumpster fire. Mind your own business, and give the provocateurs an extra-wide berth.

May 11-28: Mercury in Gemini

As cerebral Mercury cruises through its home sign of Gemini and your collaborative zone, your thoughts will be laser-sharp and you'll be focused on working synergistically with fellow creatives. Anyone whose ego is larger than life won't fit in with your dream team.

May 12: Mercury-Saturn trine

Sit out the big meetings and deal with people on a one-to-one basis today. You'll have a special ability to connect on a personal level, which will be lost in a crowded room. You know what you're trying to accomplish, so make a point of drawing out others' opinions. There could be gold in those nuggets!

May 13-June 27: Mars in Pisces

Whether you're handling only your own long-term finances or a company's, it behooves you to check in with a professional adviser over the next six weeks to make sure your money is working as hard for you as you are for it. You also need to know you've got enough liquidity to cover an unexpectedly large expense or a downturn in your cash flow.

May 14-September 12: Jupiter retrograde in Capricorn

Even if all your incredible forward progress of the past few months comes to a grinding halt, look for a silver lining. You can't go gangbusters 24/7/365 without eventually hitting pause and coming up for air. This annual reversal, while annoying, is a valuable opportunity to review anything you might have slapped together in haste. Now you can take the time to do it properly.

May 15: Sun-Pluto trine

You've got more support than you may realize, so don't worry that you're doing this entirely on your own. Penetrating Pluto is propping you up from behind the scenes even if you feel like you're a one-Leo act. Turn to a trusted mentor or coach and get a pep talk. That's all you need, because you've got the goods!

May 22: Gemini new moon

If you've been harboring resentment toward a certain colleague, today's new moon of fresh starts can wipe the slate clean. Without going back over the past, you can move forward with genuine optimism and confidence. All kinds of group activities will crop up over the next few weeks, so come out your hole and partner up strategically!

May 22: Mercury-Neptune square

You may be prone to paranoia or unfounded fear under this hazy mashup. Analytical (sometimes to a fault) Mercury is at odds with dreamy Neptune in your house of intense emotions. It's entirely possible that you're blowing up a molehill into an Everest. Talk to a rational friend and ask for her most clear-eyed reality check.

May 28-August 4: Mercury in Cancer

Try as you might, you won't be at your sharpest over the next couple months, especially from June 18 to July 12, when the cerebral planet is spinning backward—in your hazy twelfth house, no less! While this isn't a great time for crunching numbers and advancing career objectives, it's an incredible time for healing and forgiveness work and tending to old wounds. If you've wanted to start or get back into therapy, this would be an ideal time.

June

JUNE: LOVE HOTSPOTS

June 2: Venus-Mars square

You might be caught up in a budding fantasy, but today's brake-slamming square may splash some cold water in your face. Take a moment to reconnect to what you really want and not just go along for the ride (however pleasant it may be). If something has gotten hot and heavy a little too fast, use today to adjust your speed to a less vertigo-inducing pace.

June 5: Sagittarius full moon (lunar eclipse)

The year's only Sagittarius full moon lands in your fifth house of passion and romance, turning up the heat on a developing relationship or sending couples into serious talks of what's next. Under Sagittarius' truthful beams, you may be inspired to share your feelings and desires without worrying what "they" think about them. But of course you'll want to take your love interest's needs into account and give them equal consideration.

June 13: Mars-Neptune meetup

Who wants facts when you're caught up in the sweetest fantasy? Passionate Mars reconnects with dreamweaver Neptune in idealistic Pisces and your eighth house of intimacy and eroticism for the first time in two long years. You might be ready to go all in at the drop of a hat, but hold back a little until you're sure who you're getting into bed with. Couples, on the other hand, could experience a powerful sexual or emotional healing if they can loosen up the need for control.

     The AstroTwins' 2020 Horoscope

June 18-July 12: Mercury retrograde in Cancer

As the cosmic messenger shifts into reverse in your murky twelfth house, you won't be thinking clearly, and even your emotions could be a bit exaggerated or distorted. Retrogrades rule the past, so a tired old problem may resurface. Challenging as it may be, stay conscious and don't slip into denial or ignore an important issue. Now is the time to deal and heal.

June 21: Cancer new moon (annular solar eclipse)

The first of the year's two back-to-back Cancer new moons supercharges your sensitive twelfth house, giving you the rare ability to see and feel things from others' perspectives. Since this one is a solar eclipse, it can spark sudden and intense changes that you didn't see coming. What do you want to release, and what are you hoping to call in? Make these things your primary focus for the next few weeks and watch them manifest!

June 23-November 28: Neptune retrograde in Pisces

Are you enjoying a well-deserved, toe-curling romantic rendezvous—or wandering around lost in a confusing fantasy that may not amount to anything you can take to the emotional bank? "Hard to tell" is actually a correct answer, if not a terribly confidence-boosting one. That's the thing with nebulous Neptune—especially when it's retrograde in your house of permabonding and sexuality. Your ability to think things through in an objective manner dialed down for five months so research, observe and take it slow.

June 27, 2020-January 6, 2021: Mars in Aries

You'll be in adventurous spirits for an extra-long period as the passionate planet makes an extended trip through your worldly ninth house. You might take a bucket-list trip, complete with many romantic interludes, or connect on a deep level with someone who's a wildly different "type" or hails from a different cultural background. Couples will enjoy traveling together and exploring in both literal and figurative ways. Anything you've never tried is sure to get the blood pumping!

JUNE: CAREER HOTSPOTS

June 13: Mars-Neptune meetup

This rare combo (which only occurs once every other year) is so unique and packed with practical magic that if some golden opportunity doesn't present itself, you should seek one out! And go big, Leo. You've got the vision, drive and manifesting mojo to make this happen. Pick a top goal and home in on it!

June 18-July 12: Mercury retrograde in Cancer

You might want to leave a breadcrumb trail to find your way back to "what was I just doing?" For the next several weeks, Mercury is retrograde in your daydream sector, which can muddle your thoughts and send you off on long tangents. While you won't be at your sharpest, you can do some inspired visioning work around a big upcoming project.

June 21: Cancer new moon (annular solar eclipse)

This first of a rare pair of Cancer new moons powers up your internally-focused twelfth house. You might need a little time on your own to work through problems or come up with the next killer campaign—so don't feel guilty taking it. And since this is a solar eclipse, initiatives started now and over the next two weeks could have "mega success" written all over them.

June 23-November 28: Neptune retrograde in Pisces

Confusion may set in regarding shared resources, joint ventures or investments as hazy Neptune embarks on its annual reverse-commute through your eighth house. The upside? This is a perfect opportunity to take a step back and assess your finances. See if any adjustments are necessary.

June 27, 2020-January 6, 2021: Mars in Aries

Action planet Mars returns to your empire-building ninth house for the first time in two years. Get ready to go big! Have you been talking about a startup venture—perhaps with an overseas presence? That would be ideal when your ninth house of entrepreneurship, travel and growth is being stoked by the red-blooded planet! Just watch for jealousy or competitiveness in people you thought were friends. Mars normally visits a sign for six to eight weeks, but due to a two-month retrograde starting mid-September, you'll have his galvanizing presence here for the rest of the year.

June 30: Jupiter-Pluto meetup

When outspoken Jupiter and furtive Pluto merge their superpowers, it's anyone's guess what will be revealed. Today marks their second of three rare hookups in 2020 (the first was April 4 and the last will arrive November 12). This time, both planets are retrograde in Capricorn and your analytical sixth house, prompting a deep-diving audit of your systems, processes and workflow. Who are the rock stars on Team Leo and who's been slacking? A frank performance review may be in order. Does your career feel meaningful on a soul level? If not, this could be an undeniable wakeup call.

July

JULY: LOVE HOTSPOTS

July 20: Cancer new moon

The second in a pair of new moons in your twelfth house of compassion and healing helps you see things from a "higher" perspective and makes forgiving (a little) easier. And that's a wonderful thing. Just don't let a "user-friendly" type take advantage of your generous nature.

July 27: Venus-Neptune square

In a relationship, one of you may be trying to hit the gas while the other is pumping the brakes. Talk about emotional whiplash! Take this as a sign to slow down and reassess. This is not the best day for couples to attempt to have any serious talks that have long-range consequences. Keep it light, and if things get tense, do something fun!

JULY: CAREER HOTSPOTS

July 1-December 17: Saturn retrograde enters Capricorn

After a few months of testing the Aquarius waters, the planet of structure backflips into Capricorn and your wellness sector. If you've been working 'round the clock and not taking care of yourself, this long retreat may insist you start. There's no shame in admitting you need a break, so find ways to reduce stress, get more rest, eat nutritious meals—and just be kind to yourself!

July 5: Capricorn full moon (lunar eclipse)

The year's only full moon to land in your sixth house of work, organization and service could be a game-changer for you! In the sign of the hard-working Goat, this lunar lift can bring major kudos for a project you've been toiling away on for months. And, because it's also a lunar eclipse, it could serve up fame, fortune—and perhaps a high-profile new position. Focus on what you want because you can now manifest it.

July 8: Mercury-Mars square

Don't overpromise or talk up a big idea if you don't have the facts straight. You could come across as wildly overconfident—and amateur—if you try to speak on a topic without expertise. Devote the day to creative visualizing and brainstorming, not pitching. These planets will align like this again on July 27, after Mercury retrograde ends. You may have a clearer idea of how to share your vision by then, but if you don't, wait until next month.

July 12: Sun-Neptune trine

Stuck on a knotty problem? Shift from left-brain to right-brain function and tap into your own higher wisdom. Under this potent alchemical alignment, your secret weapon is your ability to creatively visualize and work the Law of Attraction to manifest clarity and abundance.

July 15: Sun-Pluto opposition

Trust and giving people the benefit of the doubt is a wonderful way to be in the world, but under today's shadowy clash, you actually want to stay on guard for double talkers, slackers and traitors. Your ruling star, the resplendent Sun, is a force to be reckoned with, but the dwarf planet packs a mighty punch. Pay attention, and don't apologize if you lead with your skepticism.

July 20: Cancer new moon

You don't need a mentor; you need to shut off all that buzzy stimulation from the outside world and tune inward! Today's rare second new moon in your intuitive twelfth house can put you in direct touch with your own higher wisdom. But if your mind is racing with ideas and plans and projects, you won't be in the proper state to receive it. Whether you're looking for guidance on dealing with a difficult coworker or hoping for a creative brainstorm, you'll find it within yourself.

July 20: Sun-Saturn opposition

Looking to scale up? Make sure your core brand is rock-solid. Today's opposition of structure fiend Saturn and your ruler, the ambitious Sun, can reveal where you may be trying to go too big, too fast. Being a visionary is important, but what's needed now is realism—not idealism.

July 30: Mercury-Jupiter opposition

Yet again, bigger isn't better, and faster isn't necessarily more efficient. Today, as detail-minded Mercury clashes with supersizer Jupiter, your vision may not be sustainable. Dream, brainstorm and research, but hold off on taking any concrete steps until you've got a clearer sense of the big picture.

July 30: Mercury-Neptune trine

If you can call in sick (or "well"), this is a perfect day for a creativity refresh! With cerebral Mercury in a flowing formation with intuitive Neptune in your most intimate and imaginative chart sectors, you can tap into the depths and manifest like a pro! The important first step is having a vision of what your heart desires most.

August

AUGUST: LOVE HOTSPOTS

August 3: Aquarius full moon

This is an exciting day for your romantic life: The year's only Aquarius full moon illuminates your seventh house of committed partnerships, which can signal a turning point in solid unions or burgeoning romances. Some Leos may be ready to officialize a bond while others will recognize it's either time to address those recurring conflicts at the root or amicably part ways.

August 7-September 6: Venus in Cancer

When the love planet cozies up in your dreamy twelfth house, your preferred fashion accessory will be rosy-hued aviator sunglasses! Affection could quickly turn to love—or at least potent lust—and possibly veer into obsession. Enjoy your quick visit to Cloud Nine, but remember, you will be needed back on *terra firma* in a month.

August 25: Venus-Jupiter opposition

Don't get carried away with a fantasy or hand your power over to someone whose offer to "help" could be an unsubtle ploy to gain control over you. Since this opposition flows in both directions, make sure you're not the one pulling this emotionally-manipulative string.

August 27: Venus-Neptune trine

This otherworldly mashup was made for getting lost in a sweet fantasy! If you're in a fairly solid twosome, this is a great day (or, even better, night!) to talk about your hopes and dreams—and maybe share some steamy desires. Single? You can't help but lead with your heart…just be careful not to leave it totally defenseless.

August 30: Venus-Pluto opposition

Under this earth-shaking throwdown between the love planet and alchemical Pluto, the only thing not to expect is a calm, peaceful, business-as-usual kind of day in your romantic life. You could fall head over heels for someone new, but you might also discover something shady about a love interest or do your own personal amorous about-face. Trust could be challenged, and "hard evidence" might be in even shorter supply. Ride this out without doing anything too radical and irrevocable.

AUGUST: CAREER HOTSPOTS

August 1: Mercury-Pluto opposition

Since people aren't likely to be saying what they mean—intentionally or otherwise—if you need to get clarity on a situation, you're going to have to read between the lines. But with communicator Mercury at loggerheads with shifty Pluto, even body language and subtle cues may only lead you down the primrose lane.

August 2: Sun-Uranus square

You won't be in the mood to "go along to get along" at work today, especially if someone is trying to advance an agenda that doesn't make sense to you—or to anyone else! With your ruler, the virtuous Sun, at odds with wild child Uranus

The AstroTwins' 2020 Horoscope

in your career corner, you may have to stand up to someone whose behavior is so shocking or offensive that you're not even sure how to talk to them. If this is, in fact, "above your pay grade," let the proper person in management handle it.

August 3: Aquarius full moon

If you've been trying to come to terms on a big deal or ink a partnership agreement, today's annual Aquarius full moon in your seventh house of dynamic duos could bring things to a mutually beneficial conclusion. If you haven't actually been looking, someone may reach out to you in the next two weeks with an offer you can't refuse.

August 3: Mercury-Saturn opposition

Be as transparent as possible today in all your business dealings. Under this BS-calling opposition, anything you say or even imply that isn't 100 percent accurate will be found out—and brought to light. It's not like you're trying to pull the wool over anyone's eyes, but sometimes if you don't do your full due diligence, you wind up passing along false or incomplete information.

August 4: Mars-Jupiter square

If a little is a good thing, that doesn't necessarily mean that more is better! Today's over-the-top clash between supersizer Jupiter and go-getter Mars could tempt you to overreach a goal or take on a little more work than you can realistically handle. While your intentions are good, you need to make sure you don't say "yes" one too many times and then have a project suffer as a result.

August 4-19: Mercury in Leo

When the cosmic communicator makes its annual visit to your sign, your tongue will be gilded and you'll know exactly how to pitch an idea or wow your audience. Take a risk and put your creative talents on display during the next three weeks. Feeling a little inhibited? Don't think of it as ego but as sharing your gifts with people who could actually benefit from them.

August 10: Mercury-Uranus square

There's a time and a place to fall in line, and then there are moments when disrupting the status quo is actually the better course of action. But it might be hard to know which approach to take today since no one is clearly right or wrong. Under an action-provoking mashup of verbal Mercury in your sign, and rebellious Uranus, you won't be happy not taking action. But you don't want to risk making a public scene or getting upset over something that's not even...a thing.

August 13: Mars-Pluto square

You may clearly see where someone is barking up the wrong tree or taking the perfectly wrong tack, but under this temper-triggering tiff between aggro Mars and manipulative Pluto, your "help" may backfire. People will be on edge and not amenable to well-intended advice. Unless they're about to do something really stupid (or with expensive consequences), zip your lip.

August 15, 2020-January 14, 2021: Uranus retrograde in Taurus

You can't keep charging forward forever without a break, and ready or not, you're about to be given one. Every year around this time, curveball-throwing Uranus shifts into reverse for a five-month backspin, and for the second of seven years, this will happen in your career corner. This doesn't mean you'll lose your momentum, but this is a time to stop and reevaluate your progress to date and make sure you're still heading in the purposeful direction you want.

August 17: Mercury-Mars trine

If someone asks for your opinion today—and really wants it—don't demur. Your mind and the hivemind are very much in sync, and your creativity could do wonders for a team project. Share freely, but don't hand over your most treasured intellectual property and ideas.

August 18: Leo new moon

Happy cosmic New Year! The only Leo new moon of 2020 plugs you into an infinite power source and hands you the mic. If you've been keeping a low profile, it's time to answer this question for yourself: What's the primary message you want to put out into the world? You could get your name on the map for your own talents or hop up on a soapbox and let people know about a special cause that's close to your heart.

August 19-September 5: Mercury in Virgo

Money talks, and when the cosmic communicator enters your financial sector, it's time for you to talk about money. Your discretion is admirable, but unless you have all the answers (which no one does), you can only benefit from a sit-down with a professional adviser. Think about your goals and risk comfort level before you meet, since those subjects will pave the way for your investing strategy.

August 24: Mars-Saturn square

Excited about a new assignment? Force yourself, if necessary, to do some big-picture analysis before you dive headfirst into it. Enthusiasm is great, but it will only get you so far. With Saturn speed-checking excitable Mars from your detail-minded sixth house, easing into it slowly with all the background info digested can only help.

August 25: Mercury-Uranus trine

Speak up in meetings and share your experience freely. Someone more junior than you could really benefit from your wisdom and innovative thinking. Your generous sign is happy to give without a quid pro quo, but the sweet thing about today's trine is that, directly or indirectly, you may be richly rewarded for your selflessness.

August 29: Mercury-Jupiter trine

Could the only thing holding you back be limiting beliefs or negative self-talk? Wipe the mental slate clean and tell yourself that you can solve any problem that comes up today. The best part? It's true! This rare and empowering alignment is like Miracle-Gro for your brain.

August 30: Mercury-Neptune opposition

Money could get a little funny under this blurring opposition, so avoid making any major financial decisions today. Cerebral Mercury is in your income and security zone, but a confusing signal from hazy Neptune could make it hard to get a firm grasp of the specifics. It's not necessarily that you're missing anything; it's possible that the other party is deliberately obfuscating.

September

SEPTEMBER: LOVE HOTSPOTS

September 2: Venus-Saturn opposition

Consciously, you may feel ready to get involved with someone or go deeper in an existing relationship. But if you keep doing odd little things that seem to sabotage your best efforts, it's likely that some unresolved (and maybe unacknowledged) childhood issues are still tripping you up. This once-a-year clarifying opposition might be what it finally takes to get you to take a deep dive into your subterranean inner world—ideally with a professional guide.

September 2: Pisces full moon

The year's only Pisces full moon shines its intoxicating high beams in your eighth house of intimacy, eroticism and permabonding. If you're ready to go all in with someone, you could officialize things within the next two weeks. Single or not ready? It's safe to say that things could get really intense for the rest of the month!

September 4: Venus-Mars square

This disruptive transit only lasts one day, but you might be tempted to hit the panic button, fearing that a relationship is about to go off the rails. That's just Mars doing his intensifying job, whereas your job is to ride this out. The silver lining is that it may force you to acknowledge some issues that you've been sweeping under the hooked rug. They probably need to come out—just not today!

September 6-October 2: Venus in Leo

Hello, head-turner! This is your annual "high season," and with the love goddess herself shimmering through your sign, you'll be at the center of buzzing hives. Single? Treat prospects with as much respect as you like to be treated with. Attached? Direct all this juicy mojo to each other.

September 9-November 13: Mars retrograde in Aries

Passion isn't a steady, linear feeling: It ebbs and flows like everything else in life. Starting today, for the next seven weeks, your energy and mojo might not always be at your usual high levels. But it's nothing to worry about! If your sweetie starts questioning your loyalty, let them know what you're feeling. Really frustrated? Try more intense workouts and maybe taking sensual dance classes.

September 15: Venus-Uranus square

You might have a wandering eye under today's provocative clash between amorous Venus and indie-spirited Uranus. Look all you like, but before you cross any lines, do some soul-searching and imagine all possible consequences. Is this worth the risk.

September 28: Venus-Mars trine

Everything feels possible as the love planets embrace in a golden trine. Even better? Romantic Venus is in your sign, beaming at passionate Mars in your ninth house of risks and growth. Take a chance on someone who might be different than your usual type. For couples, stretch out of your comfort zones through travel or explore new interests together to feel like you're meeting each other over again. Swoon!

242

SEPTEMBER: CAREER HOTSPOTS

September 1: Mercury-Pluto trine

You may not realize it, but your superpower at work today is your intuition (not your left brain)! Trust your instincts and do something that feels very right to you—even if it doesn't follow the normal protocol. Taking a low-risk gamble could put your name on the company map.

September 2: Pisces full moon

Long-term wealth is your focus over the next two weeks—"manifesting time" for today's annual Pisces full moon in your eighth house of investments and shared resources. If you've been thinking about buddying up with a major person in your industry, that alliance could prove to be a mutual win-win.

September 3: Mercury-Saturn trine

You've had some exciting creative downloads lately, and today's solidifying trine between mental Mercury and structured Saturn can help you get a few of those ideas into concrete form. Not all of them are going to fly; that's the whole point of sketching them out and crunching the numbers.

September 5-27: Mercury in Libra

Networking opportunities abound for the next three weeks as a "perfect storm" of the messenger planet in eloquent Libra gathers in your communication corner! You won't have to sugarcoat your message or play up the positive qualities. Your sincerity, clarity and charisma will have people eating out of your hand. Make sure you know exactly what you're selling because folks will want to buy!

September 9-November 13: Mars retrograde in Aries

When motivated Mars snaps into reverse for the next seven weeks and loses power, you might feel more stressed than usual because you won't have adrenaline as a buffer. With the red planet off-course, people could have shorter fuses and get all snippy. Try to be an observer rather than a participant and do your best to not engage—even when provocateurs press your buttons.

September 12: Jupiter retrograde ends

Back to work! After an annoying four months of backpedaling, expansive Jupiter resumes forward motion and is eager to make up for lost time. You can extract yourself from a quagmire of details and petty arguments and resume that favorite activity, big-picture scheming!

September 14: Sun-Pluto trine

If you've been looking for ways to raise your bottom line, this game-changing, twice-a-year mashup could shine a light on an exciting one! The Sun is your ruler, and because it's in your financial zone this month, it suggests that money will come from something close to your heart—and probably a creative venture. This rare alignment with transformational Pluto can bring opportunities out of thin air. Imagine how it will feel when you're doing this, and then magnetize it to you!

September 17: Virgo new moon

What timing! Just days after the Sun aligned with alchemical Pluto, the year's only Virgo new moon fires up your financial sector, helping you turn a page and start writing a whole new chapter in your book of personal wealth. But it's not magic, Leo. Do your bit by letting people know what you're looking for and make a list of all the aspects of the new gig you desire, from location and work scope to salary and flex time.

September 17: Mercury-Jupiter square

Guard your ideas like a mama bear! You might be lured into spilling some beans that are better left sealed up in an airtight canister. With boundary-challenged Jupiter poking at chatty Mercury, you could veer into TMI territory, without even realizing what you're saying!

September 21: Mercury-Pluto square

The concept of "the whole truth" can be a moving target when revealing too much could give a competitor an unfair advantage. You've worked hard to accomplish what you have, and it's perfectly natural—and fair—to protect it. Today, don't feel compelled to say more than you care to. And by the same token, don't assume other folks are telling you everything!

September 23: Mercury-Saturn square

Your words pack a punch today, so wield them carefully. With solemn Saturn running interference with verbal Mercury, people will be parsing every word, looking for hidden meanings. Be clear and reveal as much as you want, and when you've said it all, let the other party know in no uncertain terms that the most important thing is to support your mutually agreed-upon goals.

September 24: Mercury-Mars opposition

You may think you've got all the answers, but this challenging clash sends you racing back to Google. Stay humble, and if you're not 100 percent sure of something, admit it. People will respect you more for your honesty than if you BS them.

September 27-October 27: Mercury in Scorpio

When the communication planet treks through intense Scorpio and your foundational fourth house, you need to speak your highest truths and not waver to appease people. This is an extra-long visit because Mercury will be retrograde from October 13 to November 3 (and dip back into articulate Libra for two weeks). You may not win everyone's favor, but people who do support you could become friends or associates for life.

September 29: Mars-Saturn square

Where's the fire? If you're about to embark on a new mission, it's worth taking the time to get a rock-solid structure in place and ensure that you've got the human and financial resources lined up to pull this off. Cautious Saturn inspects to protect. Do the work!

September 29: Saturn retrograde ends

You can start to mop up the messes that may have ensued when serious Saturn went on a walkabout in your sixth house of work and service for these past five months. Hopefully you did any and all necessary restructuring and are now ready to hit the gas and blast ahead!

October

OCTOBER: LOVE HOTSPOTS

October 2-27: Venus in Virgo

It's an upscale, lavish month as dazzling Venus shimmies through your luxe second house, upgrading your wining, dining and sartorial choices. Couples should make the most of these ritzy vibes by splurging on a few high-end dates, like dinner in a chic hotel restaurant then spending the night upstairs. Single? You'll be attracted to well-mannered folks who appreciate how you roll. Choose selectively!

October 10: Venus-Uranus trine

There's no predicting your amorous moods today as the love planet catches spontaneous vibes from capricious Uranus. You could fall in love (or lust) with someone as suddenly as you lose interest. Or you might see your longtime love in a whole light—for better or worse! Avoid doing anything you can't easily undo because this is a one-day transit, and things could be back to status quo tomorrow.

October 13-November 3: Mercury retrograde

When the messenger planet pivots into reverse in your moody fourth house, you might be surprisingly sensitive, taking things personally that have nothing to do with you. Don't make any major changes to your living situation now—no gut renos, no big moves, no moving in (or kicking them out)! You'll be feeling very differently next month.

October 18: Venus-Neptune opposition

If something seems too good to be true…you know how that ditty ends. And today, it goes double as idealistic Venus clashes with fantasy-fueled Neptune, making it near impossible to tell a sweet daydream from reality. Play it safe by playing it cool.

October 19: Venus-Jupiter trine

Do something nice "just 'cause" for your love interest or crush (or would-be date). As the most buoyant planets align in a harmonious angle, you'll feel good knowing your simple act makes someone else so happy.

October 21: Venus-Pluto trine

You could get surprisingly close to someone today simply by sharing authentically from your heart. With transformational Pluto in a rare (twice-a-year) harmonious angle with affectionate Venus, you'll feel safe enough to be a little vulnerable and reveal some deep feelings. Even if this is brand-spanking-new, you can get tighter faster.

October 24: Venus-Saturn trine

So much for those hot bad boys and girls! Thanks to today's twice-annual sync-up of amorous Venus in your security zone and solidifying Saturn in your grounded sixth house, what's more likely to float your boat is someone with a good job and minimal drama in their life.

October 27-November 21: Venus in Libra

The love planet makes her annual visit to your communication corner, a perfect time for single Leos to practice the fine art of flirting. Even if you're only window-shopping, plan to get out more and chat up strangers who you catch a vibe from. Attached? You can look forward to three weeks of lighthearted fun together as Venus brightens this social sector.

OCTOBER: CAREER HOTSPOTS

October 1: Aries full moon

Whether you're actually planning your world domination tour or just joking dreaming it, the only Aries full moon of the year will power up your worldly ninth house, getting you excited about broadening your horizons. The next couple weeks are perfect for a last-minute work-related trip, picking up a freelance gig or taking a high-end webinar. Wherever you feel down a quart, that's the place to "fill 'er up"!

October 4: Pluto retrograde ends

After five months of watching—and possibly being dragged into—power struggles and navigating people's control issues, life and all its drama will settle back into an easier groove. With transformational Pluto moving forward again, you can focus on getting all your systems and paperwork in order and ending the year on a high note!

October 7: Mercury-Uranus opposition

Today marks the first of three anxiety-producing clashes between these two quicksilver planets. (The next are October 19 and November 17.) Big ideas might be bandied about, and before you know it, some of them will be put into immediate effect without anyone doing any real-time assessing. Remain flexible and be ready to adapt to change.

October 9: Mars-Pluto square

Resist the urge to micromanage today, even if you "know" the best way to approach things. Tempers will be short and easily triggered. Someone might not be showing their true colors. There's too much guesswork to make a momentous decision, so lower your expectations and have your own personal Plan B handy to save face.

October 15: Sun-Pluto square

Choose your battles carefully today! When your ruling star, the confident Sun, lock horns with shady Pluto, someone might try to goad you into a time-suck of a debate over something ridiculously trivial. Neither of you has time for this, so see it for what it is (a power play) and don't take the bait!

October 16: Libra new moon

Strategic alliances are highlighted under this collaborative, fair-minded Libra new moon. The trick is finding someone whose talents dovetail with yours and whose values and work ethic align, as well. You've got six months to make this happen, so don't rush, and cast a very wide search net.

October 18: Sun-Saturn square

Don't let your disappointment show if you don't get what you want today. Reality-checking Saturn squaring your ruler, the enthusiastic Sun, can certainly be a buzzkill, but look for the silver lining. Is it possible that your proposal wasn't up to snuff? Or that you yourself were only lukewarm about it? Leave your ego at the door, take any constructive criticism to heart, then go back to the drawing board with renewed passion.

October 19: Mars-Jupiter square

Your desire to do it all is admirable, but unrealistic. Boundary-challenged Jupiter is out of sorts with driven Mars, which has you believing you can handle (way) more than you can. There's no shame in letting people know you overestimated things.

And the sooner you admit it, the sooner everyone can move on.

October 31: Taurus full moon

This is a professional red-letter day, with the year's only Taurus full moon powering up your tenth house of career ambition and success. This can signal a turning point in a long-running project—or bring it to completion. Keep the manifesting spirit alive, because what's coming next is sure to be really exciting!

November

NOVEMBER: LOVE HOTSPOTS

November 9: Venus-Mars opposition

Under this disquieting clash, it will be hard to know whether to follow your desires or do your best to maintain the status quo. Singles might be irresistibly attracted to someone you know isn't good for you (and yet…). Couples could fight over silly things, like a clearly innocent comment or, more seriously, the balance of power in the relationship.

November 13: Mars retrograde ends

Finally! After two irritating months of hosting a backward-spinning (and very frustrated) Mars in your expansive ninth house, the red planet corrects course and with it comes your motivation, optimism—and libido! Singles will be open to romantic adventures, and couples can restoke the embers with a sexy getaway.

November 15: Venus-Pluto square

You may feel like you're riding an untamed stallion today as manipulative and shadowy Pluto ruffles amicable Venus' feathers. You love the excitement of these passion surges, but you don't like the feeling of being so out of control. You might need to put yourself in the "timeout corner" to make sure you don't get into any actual trouble.

November 16: Venus-Jupiter square

If no one wants to hear about all your amorous options, Leo, keep the juicy recaps under wraps. A rare conflict between the "benefic" planets could open up the romantic floodwalls. If you're single, enjoy being the center of attention—for as long as it lasts. Attached? Focus your affection on your sweetie, no matter how irritated you might be. These loving vibes can help you forgive and maybe even forget.

November 19: Venus-Saturn square

Chemistry is a good start, but to keep the home fires burning for the duration, you need to know you're in sync with someone on the (even) more important issues. If you're newly dating, surf Saturn's serious wave to ask some tough questions, like whether they ever want to settle down, have a family, etc. Couples can also raise some matters they've somehow never discussed, like where and when they might buy a home or even eventually retire.

November 21-December 15: Venus in Scorpio

When sensual Venus touches down in sizzling Scorpio and your domestic fourth house for her annual home stay, things could get hot at Chez Leo without you ever touching the thermostat. You may grow closer to your love interest, move in together or, if you're single, speed up the getting to know you process.

November 27: Venus-Uranus opposition

With curveball specialist Uranus at odds with romantic Venus in your home camp, work demands could eat into personal time or affect your romantic life. You may need to do some hardball negotiating to not get sucked into a crisis that shouldn't have anything to do with you. Another possibility? An office attraction could teeter on "culmination." Tread cautiously!

November 28: Neptune retrograde ends

You can get emotions back under control—for the most part anyway—as hazy Neptune ends a befuddling five-month retrograde through your eighth house of seduction and bonding. Strong feelings might have welled up out of nowhere, tossing you between ecstasy, jealousy and rage. Trust issues may have flared, and it might take a little while—and a lot of honest dialogue—to get back on steady footing.

NOVEMBER: CAREER HOTSPOTS

November 1: Mercury-Saturn square

Under this obstinate face-off—the second of three this season—willfulness will be the theme of the day—in you and your colleagues. No one seems open to giving an inch, so forget about meeting in the middle. You might simply have to table this for another day—but wait until after November 6, when these expressive planets square each other one last time (and this time, messenger Mercury will be direct).

November 3: Mercury retrograde ends

Back to business! As expressive Mercury straightens out in your third house of communication, stalled negotiations and troubled talks could get back on track. Shopping for new office equipment? With the planet of technology acting right again, it's safe to upgrade your gadgets and devices.

November 10-December 1: Mercury in Scorpio

As the cosmic communicator makes a quick run through emotional and intense Scorpio, don't waste your time on small talk. If you've got something important to discuss, just jump in feet-first. People will appreciate your candor—and your acknowledgement of their intelligence.

November 12: Jupiter-Pluto meetup

Master plan: unveiled! As visionary Jupiter and calculating Pluto make their third and final union in your systematic sixth house, the dots finally connect. You can map out a master agenda to turn a dream into reality. Choosing the right people for Team Leo is critical. Look past flattery and personal preferences, and start with a good old-fashioned job description. You need sharp and dedicated players who are perfectly suited to the job. Look back to the other two Jupiter-Pluto alignments on April 4 and June 30 for clues of what could surface now.

November 13: Mars retrograde ends

A grand vision may have had to be scaled back when go-getter Mars flipped into reverse. But now that the red planet is back to full strength, you can pick up the ball where you left it and run it all the way in for a score. With your passion so palpable, people will be eager to volunteer for your team!

November 15: Scorpio new moon

With the year's only new moon of fresh starts powering up your foundational fourth house, you may want to negotiate a little more work-from-home or general flex time. You're starting to see the real cost of being away from your loved ones so many hours a day. If you can't get that, see if you can shift your hours or score a little more vacation time. It never hurts to ask!

November 23: Mercury-Neptune trine

Statistics aren't "facts"; they can be manipulated to prove almost any claim anyone wants them to. If you're in the middle of important negotiations today, ignore the bean counters. Listen to the real decision-makers, and let your heart be your guide. If you can rearrange your to-do list, devote time to the more creative or social aspects of your work.

November 28: Neptune retrograde ends

If your investments have been on autopilot for more time than you care to admit, you can—and should—do something about that, stat. Now that hazy Neptune is back on course, you can stop the flow of red ink and get a handle on your finances again. Not sure of the best strategy for you? Don't try to guess; hire a professional to guide you through the process.

November 30: Gemini full moon (lunar eclipse)

The year's only Gemini full moon lights up your eleventh house of teamwork and technology, helping you work smarter, not harder. Because it's also a lunar eclipse, the momentum now will be even more potent! Gemini energy is all about strategic social networking. And as the original multitasker, "the Twins" know better than anyone how to mix business with pleasure.

December

DECEMBER: LOVE HOTSPOTS

December 1-20: Mercury in Sagittarius

You can have a flirtatious holiday, thanks to the frisky messenger planet racing through your passionate and playful fifth house. Singles won't need to park under the mistletoe. Just aim your 100-watt smile at a person of interest, and you'll be taking sexy-elf selfies together in no time flat! Couples will enjoy dressing up in party costumes almost as much as undressing.

December 5: Venus trine Neptune

Hearts and souls unite as these two enchanting planets align in deeply emotional zones. Drop your guard and be vulnerable. Couples might talk about starting a family, moving in together or making a shared investment (perhaps in something shiny…). Meeting each other's families over the holidays? Today's softhearted sync-up is perfect for winning over those tough-customer relatives.

December 13: Mercury-Neptune square

Don't fall for someone's well-rehearsed pickup lines! With foggy Neptune throwing shade at the cosmic communicator, it'll be hard to know who means what. Therefore, your safest course of action is to believe no one! The good news: This is a one-day transit, and after spending a full day rolling your eyes, you'll have extra appreciation for a person of quality when you do meet one!

The AstroTwins' 2020 Horoscope

December 14: Sagittarius new moon (total solar eclipse)

The year's only Sagittarius new moon—also a potent total solar eclipse—electrifies your zone d'amour and revs your romantic engines. Seek and you will find! Attached? If you're hoping for a relationship reset, don't bother with those cliché little boudoir "tricks." Change your mindset to one of gratitude for all the wonderful things about your partner. This would be an excellent list to make and check twice.

December 15, 2020-January 9, 2021: Venus in Sagittarius

The year ends on a high note, with the smoldering love planet hunkered down in your passionate fifth house. Single Leos should dress to the nines and venture out to all the mistletoe-bedecked venues. By the time the calendar turns, you should have a few attractive options. Couples will enjoy glamming up and hitting the holiday-party circuit!

December 17, 2020-March 7, 2023: Saturn in Aquarius

Time to get serious about a commitment? Saturn, the planet of endurance and maturity, returns to your seventh house of partnerships. For the next couple years, your most important ties could be tested. Does your relationship have the resilience to go the distance—or is there repair work in order? Inspector Saturn will assess the state of your union and reveal the weak spots. Single? Don't waste time settling. Better to hold out for the real thing than to accept less than you deserve!

December 19, 2020-May 13, 2021: Jupiter in Aquarius

Some Leos have been waiting 12 long years for the return of auspicious Jupiter to their relationship realm, and you'll have a full year (with a two-month retrograde break in the middle) to bask in the warm glow. When Jupiter alights in your dynamic-duos zone, you'll have renewed hope about meeting a life partner—as well as plentiful opportunities to reel in that person. If you've already found each other, this expansive energy will inspire you to take some major next steps—perhaps living together, putting a ring on it or hatching a brood. In other words, everyone's a winner!

December 30: Venus-Neptune square

As you're bouncing on the edge of the high dive, preparing to plunge into the emotion ocean, the last thing you're thinking of is that you might get hurt. While that's a wonderful, proactive attitude to take, that fear serves a purpose: It keeps you from being too impulsive. Today, the choice is yours—but maybe don't totally ignore that little voice?

DECEMBER: CAREER HOTSPOTS

December 14: Sagittarius new moon (total solar eclipse)

With the annual Sagittarius new moon turbocharging your creative juices as it lands in your playful fifth house, you'll be back in your element. And because this one is also a total solar eclipse, you're encouraged to throw out the old playbook and go from your gut. Your spontaneity and willingness to take a (calculated) risk are among your greatest assets now.

December 17, 2020-March 7, 2023: Saturn in Aquarius

Long-term partnerships could become your new thing as structured Saturn settles into your committed seventh house for the next couple years. The ringed taskmaster won't accept any half-steppers, though. Make sure anyone you consider getting financially involved with can carry their weight equally. If you team up with anyone who's less than an equal, you'll be the one to pay a hefty price. Screen thoroughly!

December 19, 2020-May 13, 2021: Jupiter in Aquarius

Team up FTW! With confidence-boosting Jupiter marching through your dynamic-duos realm for a year (with a two-month retrograde break in the middle), you will be led to an ideal partner who can either take some of the work off your plate or expand your sphere of influence. Be discerning about who you align with, though. This person will reflect on you, and you can't risk damaging your hard-won, sterling reputation.

December 20, 2020-January 9, 2021: Mercury in Capricorn

No task will be too trivial, no detail too drab for you to drill down! As the eagle-eyed messenger planet soars through your minutiae-minded sixth house, you'll be laser-sharp. Take your time and don't attempt to multitask, and you'll score a major coup by early next year.

December 21: Jupiter-Saturn meetup (The Great Conjunction)

Powerful partnerships could ignite as expansive Jupiter and restrictive Saturn—the ultimate odd couple—merge their superpowers in your companionship zone. You could take one small but definite step toward making things official today. Or, test the waters of a promising connection to see if there's real-deal potential. This alignment only happens every 19 years, so all offers that arrive around this date should at least be considered.

December 23: Mars-Pluto square

Pushing or rushing will only backfire under this exacting square. While Mars wants to hurry up and get 'er done, Pluto's legendary powers of concentration require you to scrutinize this until the bitter end! This transit only lasts one day, and when you wrap this up and put a bow on it, you can duck out for your holiday break with a clear conscience—and a giant smile on your face.

December 25: Mercury-Uranus trine

Even if there's no one to call or share your brilliant brainstorm with, you'll know you just hit the creative jackpot. But don't assume you'll remember every detail in another week or so. Excuse yourself from any holiday celebrating, jot this down, sketch it out, research and email yourself relevant links. Once it's all captured in black and white, you can return to your regularly scheduled programming.

December 29: Cancer full moon

The year's second Cancer full moon in your house of hidden agendas and unconscious thoughts may not bring fun times, but it can shine a light on a mutineer or BS artist. You want to give everyone the benefit of the doubt, but when you see incontrovertible evidence with your own eyes, you will be forced to take tough action. Ease any guilt by reminding yourself that it's for everyone's greater good. ✴

VIRGO
2020

Yearly Highlights

LOVE

Passion isn't just percolating in 2020, it's spilling into every corner of your life. With effusive Jupiter sailing alongside serious Saturn and seductive Pluto until December 19, this year brings epic romantic highs. Whether you're proclaiming undying love, getting engaged or pregnant—or enjoying the sweet, experimental freedom of single life—you'll be (uncharacteristically) ready to throw that Virgo caution to the wind. Sexy vibes go from warm to exothermic on June 27, when Mars conducts a chemistry experiment in your erotic eighth house that burns until January 6, 2021. We can already feel the power of your purr!

MONEY

Passion projects take precedence over "plug and chug" duties for much of this year, thanks to a planetary posse—plus a July 5 lunar eclipse—touching down in your fifth house of creative expression and fame. As you attract a wider following, you'll be well-positioned to be an influencer, performer or emergent thought leader. Be as wildly experimental as you can, because after December 19, both Jupiter and Saturn will move on to your systematic sixth house, putting your focus back on the more mundane aspects of producing your dream.

WELLNESS

Early this year, some hedonistic habits creep in, but drill sergeant Saturn won't abide by that for long. When the ringed taskmaster darts into Aquarius and your salubrious sixth house from March 21 to July 1, you'll have bountiful discipline for your spring training goals. Give group fitness classes a go! Two eclipses, on June 5 and December 14, could inspire a nutritional overhaul. Bring on the fermented microbiomes and non-GMO goodies!

LEISURE

Family martyr no more! Generous, caring Virgos are always rushing in to "stage mother" your peeps, but the tables are turned in 2020. Be receptive, not resentful. Your community has your back, but it's your responsibility to ask for what you need—and also to set limits with the demanding folks in your crew. Ambitious Mars could inspire a real estate purchase after June 27, but no matter where you're living, you could end the year with an adorable new pet curled up by your side. *

VIRGO

2020 HOROSCOPE

2020 Power Dates

VIRGO NEW MOON
September 17 (7:00am ET)

VIRGO FULL MOON
March 9 (1:47pm ET)

SUN IN VIRGO
August 22–September 22

The Pleasure Principle is alive and fully operational for Virgos in 2020 as a planetary posse sashays down the step-and-repeat of your fifth house of fame, decadence and heart-thumping romance. Anyone who is still laboring under the delusion that your sign is quiet or boring (or…cough…virginal) is about to get schooled! Your flamboyant side will not be repressed; in fact, this year, it will spill out like a glorious and colorful cascade. Embrace your role as a showstopper! As the new decade dawns, you'll burst onto the scene in a shower of glitter, sequins and confetti to claim your crown.

For the first time since the year 1285 C.E., lucky Jupiter, stabilizing Saturn and transformational Pluto are traveling in close alignment through Capricorn and your theatrical fifth house. Throughout the year, they'll mix and mingle, meeting up for rare conjunctions in the sky. On January 12, Saturn and Pluto sync up for the first time in 35 years. This could bring a game-changing moment that shifts the course of your romantic future or positions you as a spotlight-stealing luminary. Because these serious stars don't mess around, you could make your first momentous (decision right after the New Year.

Your romantic palette expands in colorful ways, as dazzling Jupiter and seductive Pluto dance cheek-to-cheek three times this year, on April 4, June 30 and November 12. Presently unattached? Since Jupiter is the galactic globetrotter, it's anyone's guess on which coast or continent true love awaits you. No matter your GPS coordinates, the landscape of your love life will be punctuated by romantic highs. Attached? This is the year to tick that epic "baecation" off your shared bucket list.

The only catch? Heavenly heartthrobs Venus and Mars both turn retrograde in 2020. These are less-than-optimal periods for planning anything romantic, from that trip to Fiji to your destination wedding. Black out May 13 to June 25 while Venus is in reverse, and September 9 to November 13 while Mars is off course. Already booked the chapel or the romantic getaway? Forewarned is forearmed, so be prepared to navigate a few curveballs if you do anything ceremonial during those dates. If marriage is on the docket during Venus retrograde, plan on renewing your vows in 2021 at your one-year anniversary. Since the cosmic lovebirds only go retrograde every other year, rest assured that the renewal ceremony will not suffer a fault in the stars.

Saturn leaves the Capricorn party for a short window, lunging forward into Aquarius and your sixth house of work and wellness from March 21 to July 1. You'll have your nose to the grindstone—and your feet in statement sneakers—as you pound the pavement, hustling to achieve your grander ambitions. A fitness practice could get you in fighting shape, whether you do sun salutations or spin. Saturn is the taskmaster of the skies, and while he tours this industrious zone, you run the risk of burning the candle at both ends. Thankfully, a two-year Gemini/Sagittarius eclipse series begins on June 5, helping you create better work-life balance.

Professionally, 2020 serves up both passion and productivity. While celestial charmer Venus takes an extended tour through Gemini and your career zone from April 3 to August 7, you'll be living proof that it's all about who you know. Strategic socializing helps you dart ahead of the competition and you'll be keen to collaborate with other creatives. This is a power-couple cycle, so pairing up with another luminary (perhaps even the one who shares your bed) could bring a huge win! Just make sure you don't step on their toes when Venus backs into a challenging retrograde from May 13 to June 25.

With driven Mars also on extended tour through your eighth house of investments from June 27, 2020, to January 6, 2021, you could leap on a fortuitous opportunity, like buying real estate in an emerging neighborhood or funding a startup in exchange for stock that quickly rises in value. Be mindful during the red planet's retrograde from September 9 to November 13, however, because this shadowy nine-week period could bring sketchy deals and fast-talking hucksters.

The year wraps with a major astrological event called The Great Conjunctions, which falls on December 21 alongside the Winter Solstice. As Saturn and Jupiter station themselves in your sixth house of healthy routines (on December 17 and 19 respectively), they'll meet up at 0°29' Aquarius, combining their paradoxical powers. Jupiter expands and Saturn contracts. Together they create the perfect system of checks and balances for one another. Just in time for the holidays, your legendary planning powers resume! As Saturn hands you the project manager's baton and exuberant Jupiter fuels your ideals, we can bet you'll be dreaming of a Christmas (or Hanukkah or Kwanza) in your sign's favorite hue: lush and leafy green!

Jupiter in Capricorn: Step into the spotlight.

December 2, 2019 – December 19, 2020

Lights, camera, Virgo! We don't have to tell the Zodiac's Most Responsible that life is not a dress rehearsal. The question is, are you ready for prime time? As an unapologetic perfectionist, you never really feel 100 percent prepared to perform. But sorry, Virgo: Dodging the spotlight is not an option in 2020. As lucky Jupiter blazes through Capricorn and your fifth house of fame and self-expression until December 19, your lesser-known flair for the dramatic will be on display. And since the celestial supersizer blows everything up to epic and entertaining proportions, expect to draw a larger crowd of adoring fans and followers.

Whether you've dreamed of seeing your name on a theater marquee or rolling in the credits of a film, this is the year to raise your profile. We live in an era when "influencer" is a respected job title, and you, Virgo, are perfectly positioned to capitalize on this trend. Not only do you look and sound fabulous on camera but, like Virgos Bernie Sanders and Jada Pinkett Smith, you provoke a fascinating cultural dialogue. Despite the baffling (and utterly false!) legend that Virgos are boring, you are a striking character to behold. Cue Pose star Billy Porter's Oscars tuxedo dress or Beyoncé's thigh-baring leather onesies.

The challenge? Go beyond the requisite bio and headshots and cultivate a brand. Have a videographer follow you around for a "day in the life" shoot. Set up your own IGTV or YouTube channel to share your findings and techniques.

Who knows? Like stylist Rachel Zoe or sassy child star Honey Boo Boo, both Virgos, you could be an emerging reality star. Even if you prefer to make your mark behind the scenes, this is the year to stop playing Best Supporting Castmate and become the Executive Producer or Director.

Fashion-wise, you may be ready for a complete overhaul. Maybe you'll snip your locks into an edgy bob or shimmy into body-con pieces that turn heads. If you're already a maximalist, try a striking makeunder. Because restrained Saturn has been steering your style choices since December 19, 2017, it's possible that you "leaned in" to a more professional look. And thanks to metamorphic Pluto in your fifth house since November 2008, radical makeovers—even surgical alterations and body-modifications—may have been a thing for some Virgos. But now that bawdy Jupiter's joining the chorus, you'll feel like adding some playful elements back into your "lewk," even if you're simply layering statement accessories over a monochrome jumpsuit or blazer.

Romance burns with promise and pleasure under hot-blooded Jupiter's tour through your true love zone. The galactic gambler can nudge even the most reticent Virgo to take a chance on romance. But in early 2020, you'll have some baggage to unload. Since late 2017, Saturn and Pluto have added gravitas to your love life, weighing down even the lightest connections. Your love life may have plodded along with a series of stops and starts. Perhaps you fell for someone who seemed great on paper, but wound up feeling like their parent/secretary/handmaid. Maybe you've been holding a torch for a potential soulmate who still hasn't come around. Even Virgos who met The One might still have to navigate "circumstances," like a jealous ex or planning a wedding with someone from a wildly different cultural background. Exasperating!

Coupled Virgos may have taken on a big commitment together, like buying a house or opening a joint venture. One of Tali's favorite Seattle hangouts is co-owned by a Virgo and her Gemini partner. Shortly after getting married, this duo rented a space and divided it into a coffeeshop and a hair salon. While the Gemini styles tresses, the Virgo curates beans and makes killer oat milk lattes (one of which is being sipped at the time of this writing).

In 2020, relationships can be built on pleasure and reciprocity—not desperation or obligation. If you're hustling overtime to make a relationship work, you're doing something wrong, Virgo. And while we hate to spew clichés, the old, "If you love someone, set them free…" rule applies. No begging, cajoling or convincing people to be with you, got it?

The Saturn-Pluto merger set some Virgos up for a real deal relationship, however. Case in point, one of our dear Virgo friends manifested her mindful mate in the middle of 2019 under this karmic duo's watch. After filling at least three journals with angst-filled revelations and performing an intricate full moon ritual in early 2019, she was ready to open her heart again. In early summer, she activated her dormant dating app profile and met her guy a week later. But still…Saturn's mantra of "anything worth having is worth working hard for" hung in the air. Dueling travel schedules kept the lovebirds long-distance for the first two months, relegating communication to daily WhatsApp calls. Their connection withstood the miles, and she passed Saturn's test. She has now relocated to explore their bond and help him launch a retreat center on his wooded land…a dream of her own for years!

Love stories like these can really heat up in 2020, thanks to jovial Jupiter's participation. It may simply be a matter of making different choices. This year, your patience for a partner who can't commit will be so thin it's transparent. And if they're not bringing their best to the table, deliver one final warning and be prepared to walk. But here's the rub: Gallivanting Jupiter can be a fickle figure. This year, you could be the one with feet so cold that you need three pairs of wool socks every time the word "commitment" comes up.

If you're on the fence, three pivotal 2020 dates could expedite the decision-making process. On April 4, June 30 and November 12, liberated Jupiter syncs up with Pluto at the exact same degree of Capricorn. As Jupiter's highbeams shine into Pluto's shadowy underworld, hidden truths emerge.

Jupiter is shameless; Pluto is mysterious. When these polarizing planets team up every 12 years, it's a lot like watching two awkward junior high kids at a school dance—with all the stammering, blushing and "adorkable" confessions. Pining for a secret love interest? Show your hand on April 4 or November 12. Coupled Virgos could make a bold investment together as high-rolling Jupiter merges with investor Pluto. Maybe it's time to open a shared bank account or buy that fixer-upper Victorian?

On June 30, both Jupiter and Pluto will be retrograde, which could exhume the ghosts of your romantic past. If an old flame comes back 'round for review, they might be worth considering. Sometimes people really do change, Virgo. If you still have love for each other—and you've both done the (deep) inner work, be cautiously optimistic and see how the sequel plays out. By the final Jupiter-Pluto conjunction on November 12, you'll have clarity.

Time to cut your losses? The trio of Jupiter-Pluto conjunctions supports a speedy (and stealth, if necessary) departure. Don't drag out a long goodbye if things have gotten truly toxic. Life is too short to mix up a bad batch of lemonade from sour lemons! Of course, sometimes couples just grow apart as a matter of course. With laid-back Jupiter cooling down Pluto's vengeful streak, you might pull off the miraculous by ending a relationship amicably… and even becoming the best of friends.

If you're single as 2020 dawns, don't complain! In fact, you might want to hang on to that status for a while, and taste Cupid's sampler platter. Jupiter widens the berth of everything it touches, and that includes your romantic palate. You're notoriously picky, but this year, you might find yourself drawn to a whole new range of bedfellows. Jupiter pushes you to open up to someone who's not your usual "type." You may find yourself in a long-distance love affair or having a vacation fling for the books (cross that off your 2020 bucket list, Virgo!).

While the fifth house is the love zone, it's also the part of the chart that governs that first blush of romance. (The seventh house rules commitment—and Jupiter won't arrive until December 29, 2021.)

You may indeed get to the happily-ever-after part this year, but first, you're looking for excitement and fun—and a few rom-com inspired highs. Just roll with it! A palpable attraction that makes your pulse quicken is not a bad thing. Allow yourself to be treated and adored…by more than one hopeful admirer, if the fates allow. Keep your mind open and your morals, er, flexible.

Couples can bring back the honeymoon vibes in a relationship that's fallen into a mundane groove. First step? Spoil each other! Instead of making everything about the kids, work or bills, get proactive about enjoying your "just the two of us" time. Dress up like a glamorous duo and hit the town for live music and art openings. Since Jupiter rules travel, pack your bags and take that dream trip to Tokyo, Tulum or Tahiti. Invite more novelty into your lives—it will activate the release of dopamine, the brain chemical that stimulates excitement. It's never too late to stoke those lusty flames again.

You might duck out of the spotlight for a bit while Jupiter is retrograde from May 14 to September 12. During this slowed-down time, you may have second thoughts about a budding romance or you could be busy with other obligations. Retrogrades can bring back the past, and this one might involve the return of an ex or an unresolved drama.

Note to Virgo: Even if your partner is your favorite sounding board, don't take advantage of their generous listening by complaining about work over candlelight dinners. Playing life coach can be a romance killer, too, so back off if you've fallen into "fixer" mode. Challenge yourself to talk about new things. If you need fresh subject matter, find it by going on cultural activity dates. Awkward silence could turn into buzzy dialogue about the pop-up art show or independent film you just saw. This is when the Virgo "critic" is at its best, and hopefully, you chose a partner who appreciates your witty and nuanced analyses.

The fifth house is associated with the childlike energy of creativity and play. Throw on some old clothes and get messy painting a mural in your bedroom or dipping clothes into plant-based dyes. Take dance breaks or pick up a paintbrush instead of scrolling through social media feeds during your free time. Or use the medium proactively and sharpen your photography skills by setting up shots for Instagram. With knowledge-seeking Jupiter in this expressive zone, you might enroll in a digital photography class or hire a speaking coach to help you develop a TED-style talk. And no, you don't need to have any aspirations for fame—though it may come anyway with Jupiter in this attention-grabbing zone.

If you're looking to grow your followers and fans, Jupiter brings a global draw. A creative project could attract attention from a wider audience or a new demographic. Yes, this could be the year that you become a smashing success in Asia or attract a cult following in South America. Jupiter rules media, education and publishing. If you've mastered your craft, you could land a book deal, develop a workshop or pilot a show for a TV network or an online channel like Facebook Watch.

Fertility also falls under the fifth house domain, and abundant Jupiter here can also mean procreating. Virgos of the childbearing set may find themselves sourcing organic cotton baby blankets and pondering home births. (And with abundant Jupiter acting as your metaphorical stork, there could be multiples…) Virgo parents will enjoy spending more quality time with the kids you already have. Take them on an unforgettable family vacation; it will be epic in 2020! You'll enjoy field trips to puppet shows, petting zoos and science museums as much as your little ones do—if not more.

Jupiter only visits each sign every 12.5 years; it was last in Capricorn from December 18, 2007, until January 5, 2009. Look back to that time: Did you have a legendary love affair or a prominent moment in the public eye? Maybe you were famous around town for your purple hair and vintage leopard coat, or you performed your one-Virgo show; or you just vocalized your beliefs more often. Themes

from back then are repeating, so reprise the vibrant and self-expressed parts of yourself that may have slipped by the wayside.

Saturn-Pluto conjunction: Love and creativity get serious.

December 2019–February 2020 (exact on January 12)

Have you been following your true north star, Virgo? Or was that actually a slow-moving satellite drifting through the ether? Doubts will be removed (or revealed) on January 12, when karmic contractors Saturn and Pluto make an ultra-rare connection in your fifth house of fame, creative expression and romance. The two planets have been communicating on a back channel since Saturn crept into Capricorn in December 2017. (Pluto's been there since November 2008.) What you thought you desired may shift—especially while this duo travels in ultra-close contact from December 2019 through February 2020.

January 12 is the day of their clearest connection, when they conjunct at 22°46' Capricorn. This interstellar exchange can shake the ground beneath your shearling-lined booties. Pluto is the transformer, tearing down what no longer serves us. Strict Saturn is the astrological architect, rebuilding everything back up to code. If you've drifted from your core values, this planetary pairing could come in like a wrecking ball, destroying something that was erected on false or unhealthy premises. Chalk it up as one of life's necessary losses and don't cling. A new range of possibility will emerge…but it won't show up on your radar if you're fixating on the past.

If you've been building your dreams on a solid foundation, you'll get clear confirmation, because your vision will be unshakeable. Talk about passing a serious test! Creative ideas that have been bubbling below the surface for over a decade may start to take concrete form. A true love connection might become "officially official." And after January 12, developments could accelerate. But Saturn demands a plan, so don't hit the gas until you've worked out the budgets, timelines, venue and other crucial details.

If you've been finessing your already-perfected plan forever, stop polishing and start promoting! Progress requires actionable steps. Take the first one near January 12 and you'll be amazed how quickly things develop. The media could come knocking or you might be tapped for a front-facing leadership role. It's time to make your first mark of the new decade.

Venus & Mars Retrograde: Relationship review.

Venus Retrograde:
May 14 – June 25

Mars Retrograde:
September 10 – November 13

When it comes to love, the Future (with a capital F) will be at the top of your mind between April 3 and August 7, when romantic Venus embarks on an extended voyage through Gemini and the seas of your goal-driven tenth house. Some of your long-held romantic dreams could come to life, Virgo! With Venus in communicative Gemini, speak up about what you want. For example, there's no sense in playing along with a Peter Pan type if you know you want to start making babies within a year. Articulate your vision and you'll soon find out if you have a willing co-pilot or someone who's just gonna waste your time.

Alas, it won't be all smooth sailing during this four-month window. From May 13 to June 25, Venus dips into retrograde, a backward journey she takes every 18 months. During this time, discuss your dream scenario in broad strokes instead of trying to map out "happily ever after" on an Excel spreadsheet or pressuring your partner to pick a wedding date. Getting too detailed while Venus is in reverse is just a buzzkill and can lead to frustrating loggerheads. If you simply can't hold back, have these talks in smaller bites.

Pro tip: Set up systems that keep you on the same page as your sweetie, like a shared calendar that syncs with your cell phones. Pick one or two nights a week that are sacred "just the two of us" time. In 2020, your career objectives might not mesh perfectly with your mate's. Before you bail, try to work out compromises—and if need be, book a few couple's therapy sessions to help you hash out a better plan.

For single Virgos, Venus retrograde could leave you ruminating over the one that got away. It's easy to glorify the past, but there was a reason you broke things off. However, if it was merely bad timing that messed things up, Venus' backspin might provide a do-over. Just take things slowly because you won't get a clear read until after June 25 (more like mid-July). If an ex keeps interfering with your dating goals, you may need to put the "let's be friends" thing on hold for a while so you can actually move on with your life!

Venus in Gemini can be a golden time for your career, especially when it comes to nurturing business relationships. During the May 13 to June 25 retrograde, reconnect with colleagues from your past. Your current paths may dovetail beautifully—and profitably—in 2020! Be sure to navigate professional relationships with greater care while Venus is in reverse. Make a point of building stronger bonds with your boss or key clients—and using cautious diplomacy in your interactions. You don't have to treat them with kid gloves but check those eye rolls when you disagree with their policies. (Oh, you thought they didn't notice?)

Virgo business owners might have to dig deeper—both for client leads and creative inspiration—in May and June. Take on the challenge! Head to the networking events or just go out to places where you can mingle with people who you'd consider your ideal customers or collaborators. One fateful connection could change everything!

Your mojo and magnetism skyrocket beginning June 27, when white-hot Mars starts a searing voyage through Aries and your erotic eighth house. Your seductive charms will be in rare form in the second half of 2020 and randy Mars will provide plenty of opportunities to wield them.

Normally, Mars spends seven weeks in a single sign, but every other year, a retrograde will extend his passage. Lucky you, Virgo! The lusty star will be parked in Aries from June 27, 2020, until January 6, 2021. This is certain to be sexy, but also intense.

Monitor your neurotic tendencies, especially if you start to freak out about the future. Be careful not to heap pressure onto a relationship, like trying to force someone to commit before they're ready. And don't let anyone rush you to move before you've made up your mind.

This is especially crucial while Mars pivots into retrograde from September 9 to November 13. During this two-month flip, a developing relationship could sputter, or you might lock horns over trifles. Toss in eighth house emotions, like anger, jealousy or resentment and things could get ugly. Yikes! Having a great support network (one that may include a skilled therapist) will keep obsessing at bay during the red planet's retreat.

Since retrogrades rule the past, an ex could reappear from out of the blue this fall. Tempting as it might be, give yourself a refresher course on why this didn't work out in the first place. (Yes, even if it was the best sex of your life.) And don't fool yourself into believing you can "just be friends" if there's still chemistry. You may feel like you're in control—but Mars retrograde in your relationship zone is famously deceptive.

You could find out a secret about someone you adore during this period. Get all of the facts before you react, Virgo. It's easy to make mountains out of molehills between September 9 and November 13. While Mars' reversal can slow down a relationship that's been speeding along too quickly, this measured pace is an opportunity to create more meaningful intimacy with the object of your affections. You might just pop open the Kama Sutra, take a tantric workshop, even explore a little role playing as a sexy, er, bonding experience. Meow!

Saturn in Aquarius: Order in the Virgo court.

March 21–July 1
December 17, 2020–March 7, 2023

Structured Saturn is on the move in 2020, shifting into Aquarius and your sixth house of health, organization and daily work. Although Saturn's lessons can be harsh, the sixth house shares similar qualities to Virgo (you're the zodiac's sixth sign), making this cycle smoother sailing than usual. In 2020, the ringed taskmaster will weave in and out of the Water Bearer's realm, visiting first from March 21 to July 1, then taking up a longer residence from December 17, 2020, until March 7, 2023.

Virgos can be leisurely, but at the end of the day, you relish a little discipline. Taskmaster Saturn is the "what doesn't kill you makes you stronger" planet. Like a tough personal trainer, he pushes you past so-called limits—an uncomfortable process, but one that produces long-term results. The body is a messenger, and with Saturn in this health-conscious zone, yours may issue strict orders to get serious about exercise, proper nutrition and stress reduction. Old habits are hard to break, and new ones can be even tougher to adopt. But your efforts will pay off over time and lead to lasting vitality.

So, Virgo, what will your next practice be: hot Pilates, holotropic breathwork (with crystal bowl meditations), aerial silks? When you commit to a program, you not only give it your all, you become

its loudest evangelist. If you feel overwhelmed at the thought of picking just one thing, spring for a Class Pass and sample different studios between March and July. By Saturn's second pass on December 17 you'll know just the modality (or two) that suits your style. And don't miss the point, which is to get moving. Since Aquarius is the community sign, Saturn's tenure here can make you a devotee of group classes, from Peloton to Pure Barre. Turn your friend group into an army of wellness warriors!

Saturn rules mastery and expertise: From trainers to specialists, get your advice from the pros this year. While you've been known to self-diagnose holistic remedies, don't rely on Dr. Google to be your naturopath. Consult a board-certified doctor (M.D. or N.D.) for check-ups and procedures. As an earth sign, your body often responds best to natural treatments and anything plant-based. Look for someone who integrates traditional medicine with acupuncture, Chinese herbs or CBD remedies.

The sixth house rules digestion, and Saturn's extended visit may reveal gut health as a possible culprit of any wellness issues. You might try a daily probiotic, a cleanse or intermittent fasting. (Do the words "intestinal flora" mean anything to you, Virgo? Discuss with your doc.) If you're of the age for a routine colonoscopy, make an appointment. Greek physician Hippocrates advised, "Let thy food be thy medicine and thy medicine be thy food." A dietary overhaul could restore your glow. Bring on the microbiome-rich fermented foods, like tempeh, kimchi and kombucha!

With Saturn in this systematic zone, this is a year to get organized and efficient. Another myth about Virgo is that you're a neat freak. While you can be a tad obsessive about your décor, you're also a notorious collector, which can invariably clutter your space. Saturn in Aquarius helps you tidy up without killing off your curatorial flair. Spend time between March and July sifting through the crates. Could you sell a few of those rare titles at the used book store, or the wrong-sized couture on eBay? Whittle down and lighten your load.

Don't sleep on the little ways you can make your environment clean, green and serene. Bless your house with exotic plants and switch to eco-friendly cleaning products. Get an air filter, essential oil diffuser and energy-efficient appliances. Assemble satin meditation cushions in a circle on the floor and pipe mood-lifting music through a Bluetooth speaker system. Maturing Saturn here can help you feel grounded and responsible enough to adopt a pet, which could lower your blood pressure and give you a source of unconditional love.

The sixth house rules day-to-day work: Not so much your grandiose career goals, but more the administrative, back-office type of duties that keep life humming along. Bring on the life hacks! Orderly Saturn helps you upgrade your systems and learn to delegate. Weed out any draining projects that make you feel more like a martyr than a maven. Streamline your schedule and leave some white space on the calendar.

The sixth house rules your support staff and service providers. With masterful Saturn here, you'll require some pros on the team. Have you been relying on interns or a college kid who will do the grunt work for peanuts? Throw yourself a lifeline and upgrade your shoestring budget! Time is money, Virgo, and you may be ready to outsource to a capable and experienced freelancer. With the cosmic inspector in charge, there's no cutting corners or making excuses for shoddy work.

Job hunting or pondering a big career change? While Saturn tours this service-oriented sector, you'll be more "Virgo" than ever, looking for ways to give back or do work that has real social impact. Some Virgos can benefit from taking classes to build your skillset. Even if you already "know everything," you still might need to go back and earn an official certification. Start with a spring semester class, and if you're into it, consider enrolling in a longer training in 2021, when Saturn will be solidly in Aquarius for two years.

Jupiter in Aquarius: Adventures in wellness.

December 19, 2020 –
December 29, 2021

Chestnuts roasting on an open fire? Well, if they're sustainably farmed, organic and non-GMO—sure! On December 19, vitality-boosting Jupiter zooms into Aquarius, embarking on a yearlong visit to your sixth house of natural health, organization and daily work. Just as everyone else starts mainlining brandied eggnog and rum cake, you're ready to eliminate refined sugar and go keto. But easy on the proselytizing, at least until after the New Year. If you're going to use the holidays as a teachable moment, show, don't tell. Use your kitchen wizardry to demonstrate the plant-based power of vegan side dishes and the salubrious sweetness of raw desserts.

Of course, you might be too busy frolicking in the snow to bother playing food police. (Here's hoping…) As athletic Jupiter rappels through your sixth house, sluggishness melts away. Anything that slows you down or zaps your energy has got to go! You want to feel alive and in tune with your physicality. Get your heartbeat up in the winter wonderland: Learn how to snowboard, barter ski instructor services for time on the slopes, become the ice queen of the local outdoor rink.

At work, this Jupiter cycle could bring a surge of forward moving momentum—and it might propel you overseas. Pick your favorite airline and set up a frequent flyer account, if you haven't already. As the galactic globetrotter sails through this realm until December 29, 2021, you could rack up miles on your corporate card. Entrepreneurial Virgos might work with contractors and consultants all over the world this year, from Melbourne to Mumbai. Or maybe you'll live the digital nomad dream. There could be worse things than producing online content from a remote workstation overlooking the Caribbean, right?

Exuberant Jupiter will be in interesting company in Aquarius, lumbering alongside stoic Saturn for the entire yearlong journey. And these two planets are off to quite a monumental meet-and-greet! On December 21, they sync up in the skies at 0°29' Aquarius—an event so important that astrologers have dubbed it The Great Conjunction. This only occurs once every 20 years, so mark your calendar.

Saturn and Jupiter are essentially opposites: Saturn contracts while Jupiter expands. Saturn is cautious and conservative; Jupiter is a capricious risk taker. At optimal equilibrium, The Great Conjunction can bring an eye-opening audit that reveals the weak spots and your strengths.

With the Great Conjunction landing in your solar sixth house, you could get a wakeup call to take better care of yourself and to find a healthier work-life balance. Ignoring or neglecting your wellbeing is no longer an option. Cut out stress, ask for help (and allow yourself to receive it!) and treat your body like the temple it is. While Saturn lends discipline, Jupiter pours jet fuel in your tanks. If you've fallen off the wellness wagon, this driven duo will hoist you back on. At work, Saturn helps you put savvy systems in place so you can enjoy the blossoming that Jupiter brings without burning out!

Cancer/Capricorn Eclipses: Step into a starring role.
January 10, June 21, July 5

Play it cool or fire up the fierce? Regulating your emotional temperature is a challenge you've been mastering ever since an eclipse series began rippling across the Cancer/Capricorn axis in July 2018. In 2020, three final lunations will round out this two-year cycle. Capricorn rules your fifth house of passion, self-expression and fame, while Cancer (its opposite sign) governs your cool-headed eleventh house of teamwork and technology. Eclipses can push us to extremes or bring unexpected events and sudden changes. If we've been wishy-washy or procrastinating, an eclipse may force your hand.

On January 10, the first full moon of the decade—a lunar eclipse in Cancer—could reorder the rank and file of your squad. You could formalize a collaboration group that's been assembling since the July 2, 2019, solar (new moon) eclipse. Write the charter and create your mission statement! Or

264

if you know in your heart that you've outgrown a crew, you may descend from the metaphoric Mardi Gras float and stop raining on your own parade.

Since this lunar lift occurs in near-exact opposition to Saturn and Pluto, you may need to confront some simmering group dynamics or distance yourself from a toxic clique. Just remember that Saturn and Pluto are karmic messengers, and they hold up a two-way mirror. Before you write off one group as "negative" or "judgmental" look for the deeper lesson. That said, you never have to stick around to soak up draining vibes. Banish the energy vampires from your force field before they drive a stake through your heart.

On June 21, the first in a back-to-back pair of Cancer new moons will unveil the year's first solar eclipse. Your role in a group could transform from passive bystander to powerful voice of change. Even though you may hover in the background at times, your luminous light will be impossible to hide. No more dimming your radiance, Virgo. It's time to share it with the world! That said, boundaries may need to be established in a friendship or working relationship, or you'll want to make sure everyone's expectations are crystal clear to avoid a major misunderstanding. As politics dominate the headlines, this eclipse may activate your activism. You could devote a chunk of your summer to ringing bells and dropping off flyers to promote a presidential candidate.

The last eclipse in this two-year series rolls in on July 5, with the Capricorn full moon. This lunar eclipse casts its shadowy glow into your fifth house of self-expression and romance. Harness your inner fame monster! Ready or not, you could find yourself standing in front of a crowd, with mic or musical instrument in hand. During this peak creative day, you may be struck with a brilliant download that breaks a longstanding block. Rush to your "studio" to capture the visions that are rolling in! They've been swirling in your mind's eye for two years and they're finally ready to evolve into something concrete!

For lovestruck Virgos, July 5 could be a day for the history books. But if not, see what develops in the month that follows. You and your love interest could be making your relationship "Instagram official" or announcing another milestone, like an engagement or pregnancy. Someone could step forward from the friend zone, professing true love. It's anyone's guess what can emerge under the mysterious light of a lunar eclipse. Embrace the element of surprise.

Gemini/Sagittarius Eclipses: Reinvent work-life balance.
June 5, November 30, December 14

Get ready, Virgo: Big changes are coming to both your personal and your professional sectors. This year brings the activation of a two-year eclipse series on the Gemini/Sagittarius axis that's running from June 2020 to December 2021. These game-changing lunations will revolutionize your home, family, career and goals, as they touch down in your (Gemini-ruled) tenth house of success and your (Sagittarius-governed) domestic fourth house. Because Gemini and Sagittarius are the two signs that form a square (90-degree angle of tension) to your Sun sign, there will be some adjustments, both to your own identity and your most important relationships.

Gemini rules your tenth house of men and fathers, while Sagittarius governs your fourth house of women and mothers. Not to genderize astrology, but it's quite likely you'll deal with changes around your mom, dad or family of origin. Maybe you'll become a parent, deal with empty-nest syndrome as a child moves into a different age bracket or explore your roots. The struggle for work-life balance is realer than ever these days, and these eclipses will help you navigate your attempts to pursue your goals while also nurturing your closest bonds.

On June 5, the lunar (full moon) eclipse in Sagittarius touches down in your domestic fourth house. This could bring a sweeping change to your home life, like a move or a renovation. Your landlord may announce that she's selling your rental—and you could boldly put an offer on the table to buy the place! Maybe you'll purchase land or a fixer-upper. Since eclipses have a shadow, be sure to have any real estate thoroughly inspected to avoid unpleasant "surprises." The last thing you need is to discover that your lakeside cabin is built on a water table and floods every winter (and is showing signs of black mold). Near this eclipse, there could be a new cast of roommates and relatives under your roof. Pregnancy, adoption or a change to your family structure could also be on the astro-agenda.

This is also a time when old family dynamics and demons could crop up. The eclipse's revelatory influence may uncover a secret or bring up some triggering parts of the past, nudging you to work through that old pain in individual or family therapy. You may have a vivid dream about a departed relative that feels like a visitation (who's to say it isn't?) or you'll get serendipitous "signs" and guidance. Stuck in a pattern that seems like it predates your childhood? You could try a past-life

regression near this eclipse. Other Virgos might delve deep into discovering your roots, from trying an Ancestry.com-style DNA kit to visiting your family's country of origin.

The November 30 Gemini lunar (full moon) eclipse is the only one this year in your ambitious tenth house. You might make a radical change to your work, receiving a surprise job offer that also demands a lifestyle change. A leadership role, promotion or changing of the guard at your company could also be in order. If you're in that weird, in-between career phase of hating your current job but having no clue what you want to do, get serious about your soul-searching (and goal-searching) as the year winds down.

Finally, on December 14, the year's final solar eclipse touches down in Sagittarius. With your domestic fourth house electrified by these moonbeams, the holiday season could come with a few plot twists. A family feud might escalate, potentially rerouting your plans—or you may reconnect with an estranged relative after years of not talking. This could finally be the year that you host the celebrations, Virgo, your long-awaited chance to deck the halls to Pinterest perfection. A real estate deal may close just in time for the New Year, or maybe you'll hand your love interest a spare key. The cozy company of a pet could be something you just can't live without, and a fluffy companion may be your 2020 Christmas miracle! ✷

January

JANUARY: LOVE HOTSPOTS

January 2: Mercury-Jupiter meetup

Start the year off with grand gestures of affection! Expressive Mercury and larger-than-life Jupiter rendezvous in your romantic and dramatic fifth house, helping you put your passions into words. Make it a dialogue and not a monologue, leaving space in the conversation for your beloved to respond.

January 3-February 16: Mars in Sagittarius

Mars fires up your domestic and emotional zone, amping up the passion and driving you to take action on home-related issues. The red planet can be a bit impulsive, so be sure to think through any major decisions, whether it's a move or plans to expand your family. Watch your temper for the next few weeks as you can be a bit thin-skinned and reactive.

January 12: Mercury-Saturn-Pluto meetup

If you don't let people know you're attracted to them, you can't expect them to read your mind. Today's extremely rare mashup of structured Saturn and powerhouse Pluto helps you put your desires into words. It doesn't hurt that articulate Mercury is also in the mix, giving you persuasive powers—especially in the game of love. Does that person like you or is it your imagination? You could find out today, perhaps because they confess…or you work up the courage to finally ask.

January 13: Sun-Saturn-Pluto meetup

The bold Sun makes its once-a-year lineup with both pessimistic Saturn and power-player Pluto. As they all converge in Capricorn and your expressive fifth house, you'll command attention from a few admirers by unapologetically being yourself. But every fan doesn't have to get a backstage pass. This cosmic combo is all about being discerning and holding out for a compatible co-star. No groupies allowed, Virgo!

January 13-February 7: Venus in Pisces

The love planet lands in your seventh house of relationships, turning your focus toward commitment. Existing couples can get back in harmony with each other. Dating? Focus on prospects who have long-term potential. Whether you're coupled or single, pamper yourself during this transit and dress up more. Your grace and elegance won't go unnoticed.

January 26: Venus-Mars square

Tension with a loved one could arise when Venus

The AstroTwins' 2020 Horoscope

feuds with hotheaded Mars. Even your best intention to keep the peace could get derailed by someone's passive-aggressive reactions. Feeling needy or jealous? Head to neutral terrain until your roiling emotions taper off. While it's not a bad idea to address the problem directly, you may find it hard to stay calm and collected today.

January 27: Venus-Neptune meetup

There's magic in the air as idealistic Neptune and amorous Venus connect in your relationship house. Express your appreciation and be receptive to your S.O.'s sentimental gestures. Single? You can get swept up in a modern-day fairytale without pausing to question if it's real. On this fantasy fueled day, you don't even care!

January 28: Mars-Neptune square

Assertive Mars is raring to go, but a harsh angle from dreamy Neptune could make it hard to discern reality from fantasy. Are you being naive or too idealistic? Run it by a friend who can give you a neutral perspective.

JANUARY: CAREER HOTSPOTS

January 3-February 16: Mars in Sagittarius

Emotions are amplified in the coming weeks as ramped-up Mars moves through your fourth house of feelings and inner foundations. Monitor your mood swings and be careful not to dump any stress on your nearest and dearest. That said, watch for overgiving and trying to take care of others at your own expense.

January 10: Cancer full moon (lunar eclipse)

The first full moon of the year is also a potent lunar eclipse, illuminating your teamwork and technology sector. A stunning collaboration could suddenly coalesce, or the eclipse could bring about an unexpected career development. Just getting started on a big idea? Form a mastermind group to meet regularly, supporting one another's projects. A mentor or well-connected person could open doors—be prepared to walk right through!

January 10: Uranus retrograde ends

Innovative Uranus ends its extended backspin through your expansive ninth house today, helping you get big ideas back on track. Uranus is in this part of your chart until April 2026, so visualize how you'd like your life to look by then. Start immediately by taking a bold action. This house rules travel, publishing, entrepreneurship and education. Keep your eyes open for opportunities in these realms.

January 16-February 3: Mercury in Aquarius

Your organized sixth house gets a visit from methodical Mercury, aiding your efforts to streamline and systematize. Revamp your workflow for greater efficiency and you'll make more time for fun and fulfillment. Since this sector rules service, you may be inspired to volunteer or lend a hand in your community.

January 18: Mercury-Uranus square

Know your audience, Virgo. Your colorful comments might not be appreciated by the more conservative crowd in the room today. But an encounter between quick-witted Mercury and radical Uranus could make it hard to hold your tongue. Express your authentic views without alienating others.

The AstroTwins' 2020 Horoscope   268

January 23: Sun-Uranus square

The most well-intentioned feedback could be misconstrued under today's tense alignment of the ego-driven Sun and volatile Uranus. Only offer constructive criticism to those who ask for it, and don't waste your time doling out unsolicited advice. If you're pitching an idea, back it up with facts and figures. Uranus brings surprises, so come prepared!

January 24: Aquarius new moon

The year's first new moon pings your service-oriented sixth house. This launches the Chinese Lunar Year of the Metal Rat and helps you streamline and strategize for the coming months. Declutter and organize your physical space before tackling your inbox or digital files. Research apps for greater efficiency or try tracking your time. Most importantly, take breaks! You'll be at your most productive when you're well-rested and have time to play or socialize.

February

FEBRUARY: LOVE HOTSPOTS

February 3-March 4: Mercury in Pisces

The cosmic messenger makes the first of two trips into your partnership zone, thanks to an upcoming retrograde from February 16 to March 9. Prior to this, communication flows easily between you and your S.O. Single? Take your time talking with prospective partners to root out any red flags and see if they have long-term potential.

February 7-March 4: Venus in Aries

February turns fiery as amorous Venus shimmies into your erotic eighth house, right in time for Valentine's Day. Chemistry could be off the charts, but watch the burn rate of jealousy, possessiveness or illicit temptations. Don't settle for anything less than what you want.

February 9: Leo full moon

The year's only Leo full moon sheds light on your twelfth house of endings, closure and healing. What do you need to release in order to move forward? You might need to forgive and forget or discard limiting beliefs that are holding you back.

February 16-March 9: Mercury retrograde

Mercury makes its first retrograde of the year, a time notorious for foiling communication, technology and travel. The cosmic messenger will back through Pisces and your relationship sector until March 4. An ex could resurface unexpectedly, or you might take stock of your love life and how you can make better choices. From March 4 to 9, Mercury will reverse into Aquarius, disrupting your health and organization zone. Keep stress in check and watch for a critical streak with your partner.

February 16-March 30: Mars in Capricorn

Ardent Mars leaps into your passionate fifth house, upping your magnetism and boosting your confidence. The red planet is "exalted" in Capricorn, so its lusty energy will be extra strong and resonant. Your charisma and confidence can be off the charts now. Don't be surprised if you attract a few lusty admirers who aren't afraid to make their attraction known. Mars only visits this playful and pleasure-driven zone every two years, so get busy living each moment to the fullest!

February 21: Mars-Uranus trine

When's the last time you were truly spontaneous? Swerve out of your comfort zone today as an adventurous Mars-Uranus alliance activates your impulses. Channel this high-octane energy into something physical, whether that's an experimental boudoir romp or something extreme and outdoorsy. A last-minute getaway could add a frisson of excitement. Invite your favorite plus-one along—or, if you fly solo, be open to meeting a sexy co-pilot.

February 23: Pisces new moon

The annual Pisces new moon in your relationship realm supercharges all duos. Open a fresh page in your partnership playbook. Single and looking? Make a list of qualities you want in a mate and get clear on why each one is important to you. Then, let friends know what kind of person they should match you up with. Coupled Virgos can add adventure with a shared hobby or goal. Stuck squabbling over the same intractable issue? Give up trying to win and be "right"—and listen instead.

February 23: Venus-Jupiter square

Your powers of discernment might be temporarily offline, as two of the zodiac's most idealistic planets clash. Venus in your house of merging and bonding is ready for a commitment, while expansive Jupiter in your romance sector wants to roam free. Acknowledge both urges and be honest about where you're at.

February 28: Venus-Pluto square

Harmonizer Venus quarrels with controlling Pluto, causing power trips and unnecessarily strong reactions. You could unintentionally act out an old narrative or wound with a partner. Already healed that issue? See if there's another layer of the onion that needs to be peeled off. If you need time alone to process, ask your beloved for a little space.

FEBRUARY: CAREER HOTSPOTS

February 3-March 4: Mercury in Pisces

Mercury makes the first of two trips through your partnership house, due to an upcoming retrograde from February 16 to March 9. Need a hand (or four) on an upcoming endeavor? Scroll through your contacts to see who would be a great fit. If you're working with friends or new partners, thoroughly vet them to make sure everyone's work styles and expectations align.

February 16-March 9: Mercury retrograde

Collaborative endeavors could come to a halt when the messenger planet backs into your partnership house for three weeks. Mercury will spend the last few days of its retrograde in your organized sixth house, helping you fine-tune any little details you may have missed before moving forward. Be patient and communicate clearly.

February 16-March 30: Mars in Capricorn

All eyes are on you when self-assured Mars lands in your expressive and dramatic fifth house. You can make strides toward significant change when you speak up. Connect to the larger vision or mission so you avoid coming across as arrogant. While the red planet lights up this creative sector, an artistic medium could become your favorite new outlet.

February 21: Mars-Uranus trine

Start before you're ready! Courageous Mars in your passionate and expressive fifth house links up with innovative Uranus in your growth sector. Take a creative risk. Infuse more imagination into your work. Since the ninth house rules higher learning, sign up for a course or workshop to expand your horizons. Or launch one of your own!

February 23: Pisces new moon
The only Pisces new moon of 2020 highlights your partnerships, lending a fresh start. You could meet a co-conspirator and seal a promising deal within the next two weeks. What happens at new moons can take six months to unfold, so map out a plan for where you want to be by the end of summer.

March

MARCH: LOVE HOTSPOTS

March 3: Venus-Saturn square
Are you and your partner heading in the same direction? Cautious Saturn in your romance house confronts amorous Venus in your intimacy corner, your cue to check in. Hold a "state of the union" to get on the same page and set the right pace to move forward. Quit wasting your time guessing and get crystal clear.

March 4-April 3: Venus in Taurus
Sensual escapades await as Venus moves into earth-goddess Taurus and activates your jet-setting ninth house. Traveling together can catapult you out of the winter blahs and straight to spring fever. Under this independent transit, you'll be attracted to people with big ideas and adventurous spirits. If you're solo, set off into the wild unknown. You could get swept into a vacation romance or embark on a long-distance love affair.

March 8: Venus-Uranus meetup
There's no holding back your truth today. Authentic Uranus pings amorous Venus in your outspoken ninth house and helps you voice what's on your mind. A heartfelt conversation could revitalize a tepid connection or launch a budding relationship into a whole new stratosphere. Take spontaneous jaunts outside your comfort zone as these planets unite in your travel and growth sector. Book a weekend getaway, sign up for a workshop or snag tickets somewhere neither of you has been before.

March 16-April 10: Mercury in Pisces
Ready to make things official? Communicator Mercury makes its second trip of 2020 through your seventh house of committed partnerships. If relationships got rocky while Mercury was retrograde from February 16 to March 9, correct course and move forward with any pending decisions. Whether you decide to stay, leave or change the terms of engagement, you'll be better able to articulate your needs.

March 20: Mars-Jupiter meetup
When confident Mars and ebullient Jupiter rendezvous in your romance sector, it will be hard to contain those passionate desires! Nobody will have to guess how you really feel today. In fact, this larger-than-life combo can make you come on stronger than you think. No need for skywriting, though you may be inspired to make a grand declaration of love or present your *amour* with a lavish gift.

March 23: Mars-Pluto meetup
Intrigue, passion and power plays! Scintillating Pluto hooks up with passionate Mars in your smoldering fifth house, calling forth a sexy surge.

The AstroTwins' 2020 Horoscope

An infatuation could verge into obsession, so watch out for unrealistic expectations.

March 24: Aries new moon

Plunge into the deep end! The new moon in your eighth house of merging and intimacy boosts your bonds and births a new level of emotional closeness. This moon phase signifies beginnings; an attraction gets off to a steamy start, or an existing relationship reaches red-hot levels.

March 27: Venus-Jupiter trine

Freedom is an aphrodisiac! The zodiac's most loving, idealistic planets (known as the "benefics") align today, helping you connect over shared passions and adventurous plans. Communicate openly with your partner or love interest. Challenge yourself to be as honest as you would be with a close friend. This is no time for evasiveness or mind games. Your generosity of spirit will set the tone.

March 28: Venus-Pluto trine

An adventurous Venus pings Pluto in your passion corner, notching up the intensity. Explore a fantasy that pushes you past your usual bedroom routine, and perhaps even edges into the taboo. You could be attracted to someone who exudes a certain air of power and mystery.

March 30-May 13: Mars in Aquarius

A critical streak could flare as the red planet swoops into your perfectionistic sixth house. Watch out for codependent dynamics where you end up playing amateur therapist to your partner or beating yourself up. Picking at every little issue will only make it worse. The true culprit could be your own exacerbated stress levels. Ramp up self-care and get the support you need to stay balanced.

MARCH: CAREER HOTSPOTS

March 4-16: Mercury in Aquarius

Bye, bye, baggage! Minimalist Mercury re-enters your systematic sixth house, where it visited in January. Revisit any decluttering missions you didn't finish and review what still needs organizing. Make a plan while Mercury is retrograde through March 9, but hold off execution until it corrects course. Since this area of your chart also rules service, see where you can give back to your community.

March 9: Virgo full moon

The year's only full moon in Virgo shines its stadium lights on you! A solo project could take flight and you might get a burst of can-do energy that helps you promote yourself. A wish you've been trying to manifest could come to fruition within the next two weeks. You may finally be recognized for your hard work of the past six months. Bask in the appreciation instead of being overly modest. You've earned it!

March 16-April 10: Mercury in Pisces

Mercury starts its second visit to your partnership house this year—the perfect time to break bread after a choppy retrograde from February 16 to March 9. If a group project lost steam, progress will resume or new collaborators could emerge from the woodwork. Keep your options open and thoroughly vet any possible teammates.

March 21-July 1: Saturn in Aquarius

Structured Saturn kicks off the first installment of its two-and-a-half year transit through your sixth house of health, organization and systems. Start streamlining your workflow and delegating unnecessary tasks. You might also find a community organization to support, one that could potentially become a base to offer your services. Saturn only comes to each sign every 30 years or so; it was last in Aquarius in 1991. If you work in wellness, media or information, Saturn can help you rise to slow and steady prominence. No cutting corners, though! Self-care and stress management are an essential part of this plan.

March 24: Aries new moon

The year's only new moon in trailblazing Aries fires up your eighth house of joint ventures and investments. Do you have a solid support system to reach your goals? Find a financial advisor or reconnect with yours to make sure you're on track. Get clear on how you want to grow your wealth within the next six months and the steps it will take to get you there.

March 30-May 13: Mars in Aquarius

All systems go! Put solid strategies in place as energizer Mars bursts into your methodical sixth house. Review your schedule: Do you have enough time for rest and self-care? Efficiency shouldn't come at the cost of your wellbeing. Resist the urge to take on too many projects as Mars here can cause stress levels to skyrocket.

March 31: Mars-Saturn meetup

Today's biannual merger of go-getter Mars and serious Saturn hits your service-oriented and organized sixth house. A situation could come to a head and demand to be addressed with a solid strategy. If you've been working yourself to the bone on a big project, you might have no choice but to take a much-needed break. Are members of Team Virgo pulling their weight? A stern chat could be in order if someone's performance has

suffered. But first, make sure that your people are clear on expectations and instructions. Maybe you just need to spell it out for them.

April

April 3-August 7: Venus in Gemini

The love planet steps into your tenth house of long-term planning, turning your attention toward the future. You and your S.O. could decide to make things official, or revisit talks of your shared goals. Single Virgos who've been enjoying an early bout of spring fever might crave a more stable arrangement. This area also rules work and career, so you might meet someone at a professional gathering. RSVP "yes" to that industry event—you never know who you may meet over passed hors d'oeuvres or between conference sessions.

April 3: Mercury-Neptune meetup

Signals could get scrambled when dreamy Neptune encounters communicative Mercury in your partnership sector. Be patient if you don't understand your love interest and pause to organize your own thoughts before expressing them. The good news? This combination of Neptune's compassion and Mercury's objectivity can help you handle sensitive topics gracefully.

April 4: Jupiter-Pluto meetup

Staying mum about an attraction will be hard to pull off! Outspoken Jupiter and smoldering Pluto make their first of 2020's three rare conjunctions in Capricorn, setting your passionate fifth house ablaze. A simmering connection could reach a boil. This cosmic combo can magnify any intensity or drama. Keep that in mind if emotions get heated today, and at the two other Jupiter-Pluto meetups on June 30 and November 12.

April 4: Venus-Saturn trine

Put an action plan behind all of your big hopes and dreams. With romantic Venus and structured Saturn aligned in practical zones, shared goals are sexy! Completing a project as a couple could help strengthen your bond. You might meet someone through work or a charitable effort. A helpful person who truly has your back will be especially attractive under these stars.

April 10-27: Mercury in Aries

Bring on the seduction! Chatty Mercury glides into your erotic eighth house, spicing up your pillow talk. The next couple weeks could produce a flurry of suggestive texts and DMs (just make sure your privacy settings are strong!). With the cosmic communicator in this probing zone, you'll unearth any psychological blocks to intimacy or untangle complicated feelings you've been trying to process for a while. Vulnerability can open the door to deeper bonding.

April 25: Mercury square Jupiter & Pluto

Talking about your feelings could open up a can of worms today, as Mercury in your intense eighth house battles outspoken Jupiter and calculating Pluto in your romance sector. You could be privy to a secret or information that makes you question someone's trustworthiness.

April 25-October 4: Pluto retrograde in Capricorn

Shadowy Pluto makes a reverse commute through your romance zone for the next five months. Bravely sort through buried emotions that emerge and confront limiting beliefs that keep you playing small in love. A tantalizing ex could resurface, someone whose charms (and hooks) may be hard to resist. Careful: This could also invite drama into your life. Craving attention? You may have some epiphanies about what you really need to feel satisfied. Tune in to your desires instead of sweeping them under the rug.

APRIL: CAREER HOTSPOTS

April 3: Mercury-Neptune meetup

Do their actions match their words? Reasonable Mercury teams up with intuitive Neptune in your interpersonal sector, heightening your powers of perception. Pay attention to subtle cues like tone of voice or body language. Someone might not even be aware of what they're doing, so be compassionate without coddling them.

April 7: Libra full moon

Your industrious sign reaps the benefits of your efforts when the full moon lights up your second house of work and money. Take credit for what you've accomplished! The reward you've been expecting may come with an unexpected windfall. If extra cash is burning a hole in your pockets, find ways to invest or save it.

April 7: Mars-Uranus square

Even though every step is laid in stone, someone might suddenly rearrange or add to the plan. Unrealistic or impractical asks could push you over the edge. Take a minute to cool down before addressing all the reasons this won't work.

April 10-27: Mercury in Aries

Zoom in on the details for the next couple weeks, as clever Mercury burrows into your research-oriented eighth house. Focusing on one subject at a time will help you concentrate and master the material. If you're in negotiations, Mercury in this zone of shared interests encourages you to not give it all away. A little mystery can fuel people's interest. Make sure to craft a solid win-win where everyone will be rewarded commensurate with their contributions.

April 14: Sun-Pluto square

Are you resistant to pursuing a partnership? Even if this seems like a home run on paper, something is nagging at you to investigate further. Today's tense Sun-Pluto square makes it difficult to discern if your hesitation is valid. Are you just reluctant to renounce control? If you're feeling "off" about any relationship, journaling or meditation could help you get to the core. But think twice about sharing these concerns with anyone who's not a truly trustworthy sounding board. You don't want to start drama—especially if there may not be anything to worry about!

April 15: Sun-Jupiter square

Careful how much you share today. The Sun in your private eighth house is at odds with outspoken Jupiter in your attention-seeking fifth house. You could spill confidential intel (yours or someone else's). Even if you package it as a joke, that doesn't mean it should get out into the public sphere.

April 21: Sun-Saturn square

Cautious optimism is the name of the game today as the hopeful Sun and risk-averse Saturn clash. Even if people are rushing you to sign on the dotted line, press pause so you can ensure every little detail is in place to make this successful. The right support systems and a solid start can make a world of a difference.

April 22: Taurus new moon

The year's only new moon in your expansive and visionary ninth house invites you to take a leap of faith. Far-fetched dreams could seem within reach now—or they will soon enough. Plant the seeds for what you want to manifest within the next six months. You may have to take a risk, but who knows what you'll find when you cross the border of your comfort zone?

April 25: Mercury square Jupiter and Pluto

Power struggles might erupt today, especially if you pry into someone's business. Mercury in your insightful eighth house is on a fact-finding mission, but as it butts heads with both blustery Jupiter and secretive Pluto, you could run into supersized egos. Think twice before getting overly personal. If someone gets a little too familiar with you, resist the temptation to air all your dirty laundry. Be careful how much you promise or reveal today.

April 26: Sun-Uranus meetup

Innovators aren't always appreciated, but today's visionary starmap could bring an a-ha moment. Acting on your inspiration may lead you to a major breakthrough today. Embrace the most improbable ideas and ignore the skeptics. Your contagious enthusiasm could attract a few pioneering supporters who are also ahead of the curve.

     The AstroTwins' 2020 Horoscope

April 27-May 11: Mercury in Taurus

Bring on the brainstorms! You're everyone's go-to for great ideas as mental Mercury camps out in your inspired and inventive ninth house for the next couple weeks. Keep a notebook handy to capture any divine downloads. When Mercury moves into your career zone May 11, you can concentrate on which ones to pursue.

April 28: Mercury-Saturn square

Don't be discouraged if your brilliance goes unappreciated today. People might be so fixated on the practical details that they can't see the big-picture vision. It's okay to slow down to get them on board, but some folks might never be open-minded enough to understand. If complaints or criticisms arise, acknowledge them. But don't pull the plug on your big idea. Soon enough, those naysayers may get on board!

April 30: Mercury-Uranus meetup

Eureka! Cerebral Mercury meets up with disruptor Uranus, supercharging your ideas and bringing your grand scheme to a whole new level. Your mind is moving quickly today, so pause between thoughts. You could accidentally blurt out something tactless—or let proprietary intel slip—if you rush ahead. An opportunity to travel or make progress on a visionary idea could spark up out of the blue. Be ready!

May

MAY: LOVE HOTSPOTS

May 3: Venus-Neptune square

Values-driven Venus has you ready to start planning your romantic future, but a sucker punch from nebulous Neptune could throw indecision into the mix. Let yourself dream without needing to figure out all the details. This transit will repeat again on May 20 when Venus is retrograde. Details you sweep under the rug today might seem suddenly pressing when that happens. Take your time instead of rushing in!

May 13-June 27: Mars in Pisces

Summer gets off to a sizzling start when red-hot Mars heats up your partnership house. Single and attached Virgos alike will feel fierce and magnetic—and you'll attract sexy prospects who also have long-term relationship potential. Warning: Couples can argue more with combative Mars here, though you can also settle your differences in the bedroom. Learn how to handle stress and manage conflict, two issues tempestuous Mars can provoke.

May 13-June 25: Venus retrograde in Gemini

The love planet backspins every 18 months, and this year she retrogrades through your tenth house of long-term plans. If your relationship has hit a plateau, use this time to review and renegotiate the terms of your union. Instead of planning every miniscule detail, hold a series of exploratory talks with your S.O. about your desires and fears. Single? A workplace spark could become a tantalizing distraction.

May 14-September 12: Jupiter retrograde in Capricorn

Growth-oriented Jupiter makes its annual retrograde and reverses through your romantic and creative fifth house. A feverish but distracting flirtation could cool down enough to allow you to focus on other matters. Use this time and energy to concentrate on personal growth projects. An adventurous ex, perhaps one who moved far away, might resurface. Could a reunion trip be in order to explore if the chemistry's still there? Proceed with caution, rather than excessive optimism. With Jupiter's penchant for learning, this is a great time for a workshop on dating, seduction or relationships.

May 22: Mercury-Venus meetup

When the zodiac's communicator pairs up with amorous Venus in your tenth house of goals, schedule a "state of the union" to talk about expectations, boundaries and the future. Not sure if you're on the same page for the long haul? Ask clarifying questions instead of assuming you have all of the answers. Take turns listening so each party feels heard.

MAY: CAREER HOTSPOTS

May 7: Scorpio full moon

Clarify your message and deliver it to the world! As the annual Scorpio full moon turns up the volume in your communication corner, the floor is yours. Share your novel ideas or make an important pitch. Who in your immediate network might be a valuable ally? Brief them on your vision and welcome them aboard. By merging your superpowers you'll create a win-win! A savvy collaboration could gain traction within the next few weeks.

May 9: Mercury-Pluto trine

Planetary PSA: Not every thought should be expressed out loud. Practice discernment and only share what's absolutely necessary. When you stop voicing every little opinion or critique, people give your carefully-delivered viewpoints the weight and attention they deserve. Try it!

May 10: Mercury-Jupiter trine

You could try to tackle a problem alone, but why do things the hard way? Today's cerebral starmap brings brilliant ideas from unexpected sources. Gather a group and mine the collective brain power for gold. Putting a call out to your social networks could also spark novel solutions and approaches.

May 11-September 29: Saturn retrograde

Staying organized will take extra effort over the next couple months (yes, even for you, Virgo), as regimented Saturn turns retrograde. Until July 1, the cosmic curmudgeon will backspin through Aquarius and your systematic, health-conscious sixth house. Your discipline might slip or you could find yourself struggling to stay on top of stressful projects. Reach out for proper (and skilled) support, and get the slackers on Team Virgo in line. Your own skillset might be due for an upgrade. From July 1 to September 29, Saturn will rear into Capricorn and your creative, expressive fifth house. You may revisit an artistic project or get serious about cutting those distracting drama queens off—at least, during peak productive hours!

May 11: Mercury-Mars square

It's tempting to put someone in their place, but a tense transit between articulate Mercury and aggressive Mars could come back to bite you. Is it really your job to respond? If not, bite your tongue.

 The AstroTwins' 2020 Horoscope

May 11-28: Mercury in Gemini

Your cosmic ruler, sharp-witted Mercury, soars into your professional tenth house for the next couple weeks. You're brimming with bright ideas and eager to get them green-lighted! No need to hard-sell; just keep your message simple and elegant. Pitch with an air of authority—and the substance to back up your claims. Who could refuse you?

May 12: Mercury-Saturn trine

Do your dreams have a solid structure for success? Create a game plan when the zodiac's professor, Saturn, sits down with its best student, Mercury. With both planets in systematic sectors of your chart, you've got the formula for mapping both the big-picture vision and the day-to-day execution.

May 13-June 27: Mars in Pisces

Launch a new collaboration or revive an existing one as confident Mars visits your partnership zone for the next few weeks. Use this self-assured energy to reach out to an influential person whose work you admire. The two of you could be teammates in no time! If you're not seeing eye-to-eye with a partner or close colleague, use this assertive transit to hash out differences and create a smarter way to work together.

May 14-September 12: Jupiter retrograde in Capricorn

Has the muse gone MIA? When expansive Jupiter reverses through your artistic fifth house, your creative passions could be pushed onto the backburner. Progress might slow significantly, or you may be tempted to throw the whole endeavor out. Don't let your inner critic sabotage this, Virgo. Putting forth the effort when you're not feeling inspired is what separates the amateur from the professional. Chip away a little at a time. If you need a break from your magnum opus for a couple weeks (or even months), that's okay. Just put it in a safe place so you can come back with fresh perspective…and still find it there!

May 15: Sun-Pluto trine

Inspiration unleashed! Your charm and persuasion are turned up under today's magnetic mashup. Work that to your advantage. Fine-tune your talking points but don't overthink this. The magic will happen when you connect with people energetically. Practice your pitch so you don't need to read from a script. Focusing on your audience will get them emotionally engaged—and invested—in your vision.

May 22: Gemini new moon

Your career gets a reboot when the new moon activates your ambitious tenth house. Revisit your 2020 professional goals to see if you're on track—or even still inspired by those. Feel free to recalibrate or start fresh today. Already crossed the big ones off your list? Visualize what you want to accomplish by the end of the year. Write that down and get into action!

May 22: Mercury-Neptune square

Are they on Team Virgo…or aren't they? People are talking in circles under today's confounding clash between logical Mercury and obfuscating Neptune. Your accomplices could run hot and cold, and your attempts to make sense of the situation will only further your confusion. Hold off on binding decisions today. Outline the pros and cons and sleep on it! With dreamweaver Neptune in the mix, your subconscious might just hash out an answer while you rest.

May 28-August 4: Mercury in Cancer

Gather your brain trust! Expressive Mercury sails into your eleventh house of teamwork and technology for an extended stay. The quicksilver planet helps you gather the people and the resources you need for greater efficiency. From networking to masterminds to cutting-edge collaborations, there's power and possibility in numbers. But forge your alliances fast! When the cosmic messenger turns retrograde from June 18 to July 12, a team could temporarily lose steam.

June

JUNE: LOVE HOTSPOTS

June 2: Venus-Mars square

The love planets are at odds today, with fervent Mars in your relationship corner sparring with amorous Venus in your sector of long-term plans. What you want could be in conflict with what you need. Take a deep breath before you start a fight that's not worth having.

June 5: Sagittarius full moon (lunar eclipse)

Brace yourself for a wave of powerful feelings as the annual Sagittarius full moon—also a groundbreaking lunar eclipse—lights up your sentimental fourth house. This heart-opening lunation could take you by surprise. If you've lost touch with a loved one, reach out and reconnect. Open up to your current S.O. and infuse an extra dose of tenderness in your interactions. Single? Be vulnerable with prospective partners and surround yourself with supportive friends.

June 13: Mars-Neptune meetup

Fiery Mars meets up with idealistic Neptune in your relationship house, fueling your fantasies. Your magnetism is off the charts, so reconnect with your beloved and see what you two can manifest together. Single? These fortune-filled skies are perfect for homing in on what kind of relationship you're seeking.

June 23-November 28: Neptune retrograde in Pisces

When hazy Neptune makes its annual five-month retrograde, it'll backspin through your partnership house. This could actually give you more clarity, so look past illusions. As the fog lifts, so could your denial or uncertainty surrounding a certain someone. Step back from the situation to see it more clearly. If a former lover pops up with a bouquet of empty promises, be on guard. Do their words align with their actions? Or are they still crooning the same old song?

June 27, 2020-January 6, 2021: Mars in Aries

Hang the "do not disturb" sign! Passion is dialed up until the end of the year, as sizzling Mars heats up your intimate and erotic eighth house. It's an extra-long transit thanks to an upcoming retrograde in September. Until then, enjoy the ardor without slipping into jealousy, possessiveness or obsession.

June 30: Jupiter-Pluto meetup

The second of this year's three rare alignments (the others are April 4 and November 12) once again lands in your fifth house of passion and attraction. This time, however, both planets are retrograde. An old flame or an unresolved romantic drama could resurface. A buried secret could come into the open. What have you been suppressing? Anything from an aching sexual desire to legitimate anger might bubble up like a dormant volcano. With emotions this potent, you're not exactly using a filter. Go easy on 'em, even as you express your deep-seated truth.

JUNE: CAREER HOTSPOTS

June 13: Mars-Neptune meetup

Power up your partnerships! Go-getter Mars joins forces with the zodiac's master manifestor, Neptune, in the area of your chart that rules dynamic duos. Evaluate all future (or current) collaborators to ensure your work styles and visions match up. Those "gut feelings" are extra strong today. What does your intuition tell you? Consider that in your vetting process.

June 18-July 12: Mercury retrograde in Cancer

Back up your devices and practice careful communication. The cosmic messenger turns retrograde in your eleventh house of teamwork and technology for a couple weeks, bringing chaos and confusion to all interpersonal affairs. Contracts can be impacted, so wait to ink any new deals until Mercury resumes its forward motion in July.

June 21: Cancer new moon (annular solar eclipse)

The first of 2020's rare double-header of Cancer new moons is also a potent solar eclipse. Today, it sweeps through your collaborative eleventh house, kickstarting group projects or bringing big news by email or text. An exciting opportunity to join forces could arise within the next two weeks. Tread carefully since Mercury's retrograde here—but explore every possibility!

June 23-November 28: Neptune retrograde in Pisces

Are you too quick to trust, Virgo? When nebulous Neptune turns backward in your partnership house, a sketchy situation may come to light. A contract could have complications, or the resources allocated to your project might be less than expected. Stand your ground. This passive planet makes avoidance sound enticing, but you'll want to clear up any misunderstandings or setbacks quickly.

June 27, 2020-January 6, 2021: Mars in Aries

Motivated Mars bursts into your wealth sector for the rest of the year. Chart your financial ambitions and hit the gas! Pair up on a joint venture and tap into other people's assets through investments, loans and pooling your resources. Speedy Mars can add tension or pressure. You may need to deal with a large expense, especially when the red planet turns retrograde in September. Address any stressful money matters head-on to avoid blowing them out of proportion. Get proactive by making a debt payment plan sooner rather than later—and curb any excessive credit card usage or borrowing.

July

JULY: LOVE HOTSPOTS

July 1-December 17: Saturn retrograde enters Capricorn

Doubts could arise when serious Saturn begins

its backtrack through your romantic fifth house. This plodding planet has a tendency to focus on the potential downside of everything. Are you being too hard on your love interest or partner—or romanticizing an ex who doesn't deserve that pedestal? Hang on tight to your optimism but keep your feet on solid ground. Since this zone rules fertility, Virgos who are trying to get pregnant might encounter a few slowdowns. Patience and regular practice are the key—but also consult an expert and make sure you're really ready for the major lifestyle change of a child.

July 5: Capricorn full moon (lunar eclipse)

Bring on the romantic renaissance! Today's once-a-year lunation in your amorous fifth house is also a dynamic lunar eclipse. These moonbeams supercharge your love life and spark sudden developments over the next two weeks. Prospects who aren't a good fit may be "eclipsed" away. True love might strike out of the blue (and you weren't even looking!). For couples, this eclipse could bring a declaration of devotion or a heartfelt conversation. While it may be uncomfortable, the truth will set you both free.

July 27: Venus-Neptune square

Where is this thing going? Love planet Venus in your accountable tenth house is playing the long game, but murky Neptune is making it hard to see how to move forward. Can't stop racking your brain? Let yourself get swept up in daydreams today and save the planning for tomorrow.

JULY: CAREER HOTSPOTS

July 8: Mercury-Mars square

Power struggles could break out in a group today, as attempts to reach consensus get thwarted by people's passionate stances. There are certain values people won't bend on today. Perhaps it feels too threatening to their ego or turf. Rather than "poke the bear," respect everyone's need to feel secure. Perhaps there's more research to be done before pitching a risky idea, especially since Mercury is retrograde for a few more days. Mercury and Mars will meet like this again on July 27, when the communication planet is direct (forward). If necessary, revisit these ideas again then.

July 12: Sun-Neptune trine

There's power in numbers! Take the initiative to connect with like-minded people and see what you can accomplish together. If you're tired of tapping into the same pool, reach out to creative folks in other departments, industries and zip codes for fresh perspectives. Out-of-the-box thinking like that can breathe new life into a project.

July 15: Sun-Pluto opposition

Can you be the bigger person today, Virgo? Instead of getting pulled into hostile power dynamics, revisit the topic when people are ready to cooperate. Trying to drag someone along while they dig in their heels won't get either of you very far.

July 20: Cancer new moon

The (rare) second full moon in Cancer this year galvanizes your group endeavors. Look back to what started at the Cancer solar eclipse on June 21. Talks that started then could crystallize within the next two weeks. Map the six-month vision and get everyone working on their part!

July 20: Sun-Saturn opposition

Even your idols deal with rejection, Virgo. The

mark of a truly successful person is how quickly and gracefully they can bounce back from a disappointment. An opposition between the optimistic Sun and severe Saturn may bring some tough lessons. Remember, any setback isn't a reflection of your worth. Glean what you need to learn and turn your attention toward the next opportunity.

July 30: Mercury-Jupiter opposition

A lively conversation might suddenly spiral into an argument, threatening to cause a rift. Hold your tongue in team meetings and refrain from sending your best ideas through any messaging apps. A self-serving associate could steal your plans and pass them off as their own.

July 30: Mercury-Neptune trine

Strengthen your professional ties, as talkative Mercury hooks up with idealistic Neptune in your interpersonal houses. Sign up for a networking event or host a mastermind group. Flex your facilitator talents and earn karma points by connecting two like-minded souls with complementary skillsets. Negotiations will go smoothly today, and you both can walk away with exactly what you want. If you've been admiring an influential figure from afar, reach out with a sincere note and an invitation to connect.

August

AUGUST: LOVE HOTSPOTS

August 4: Mars-Jupiter square

Issues could get blown out of proportion with today's tense mashup of aggro Mars and supersizer Jupiter. Avoid expressing contempt, even a seemingly innocuous eye roll, and steer clear of criticizing. It'll be easier to clean up the aftermath of a storm—or to avoid it altogether—if you're kind and compassionate.

August 7-September 6: Venus in Cancer

When Venus moves into your social eleventh house for a month, you're the belle of every ball! With the love planet shooting friendly fire, a platonic pal could suddenly spark your interest. If it won't ruin the relationship, you might consider adding a "benefits package" to the friendship. Attached? Throw a soiree so your social groups have a chance to overlap. Or check out a community event on a topic you both find intriguing.

August 13: Mars-Pluto square

Shady Pluto in your romance corner is conflicting with aggressive Mars in your mysterious eighth house. Don't get carried away with self-defeating thoughts rooted in jealousy, comparison or possessiveness. Check in with a friend to voice your concerns instead of giving in to unhealthy patterns with your partner.

August 18: Leo new moon

The Leo new moon in your restful and receptive twelfth house helps you let go of a grudge or resentment. If a limiting belief is holding you back, bring it out into the light so you can release it. What are you ready to create space for? If you're seeking a soulmate, write down the details of the relationship you want to call in under this lunation.

August 24: Mars-Saturn square

Whoa! If your relationship went from zero to 60

overnight, you can catch your breath when go-getter Mars gets the brake pulled by slow-and-steady Saturn. The chemistry may be undeniable, but is this really what you're looking for? The rush of moving too quickly could have caused you to overlook some red flags. Now that your romantic high has subsided, step back and review. At the very least, you'll create a more sustainable arrangement, a blessing in disguise!

August 25: Venus-Jupiter opposition

One moment you're gushing about how great they are and the next you're feeling claustrophobic. Maybe your S.O. is the one sending out hot-and-cold vibes. New prospects might write you epic poems one day and ghost you the next. What gives? Free-spirited Jupiter is at odds with romantic Venus, giving you a bout of whiplash. Don't try to figure out your feelings today. Take your time and view the fleeting emotions like you might watch a passing cloud.

August 27: Venus-Neptune trine

Just friends? Someone in your inner circle might want to take things beyond platonic territory. Boundaries could blur as nebulous Neptune in your relationship corner winks at Venus in your friendship zone. An online match could look extra promising, but don't get carried away before you actually meet. Make sure all parties are fully available before diving in.

August 30: Venus-Pluto opposition

Dial down the theatrics in your love life and watch a scripted series instead. As controlling Pluto in your dramatic fifth house opposes affectionate Venus, resist the urge to pick a fight or self-sabotage. Channel that passionate energy into pleasurable pursuits instead of courting conflict.

AUGUST: CAREER HOTSPOTS

August 1: Mercury-Pluto opposition

Good luck holding your tongue today, as hotheaded Mars comes up against power-tripping Pluto. Before you fire off that angry email, take a walk around the block to clear your head. Could this conversation be held in person or over the phone? Connect to your mutual purpose so the two of you can find common ground. Resist getting sucked into dicey group dynamics or taking sides.

August 2: Sun-Uranus square

That pile of paperwork didn't get there on its own, Virgo. Ask for help and outsource any assignments that don't need your personal attention. If you're the only steward on the ship, rearrange deadlines. Remember that "no" is a complete sentence.

August 3: Aquarius full moon

Shelve your excuses! The motivating full moon energizes your sixth house of work, service and health. If you've been putting off a new fitness regimen or a shift in your daily habits, now's the time to pick a goal and commit to it. Identify an inspiring core intention so you can come back to it when your enthusiasm wanes. Looking for a new job? Start circulating that resume!

August 3: Mercury-Saturn opposition

Other people might pressure you to make a decision without giving you all the facts. Not gonna happen! As cautious Saturn challenges analytical Mercury, press pause and do your research. Now's not the time to just "go with your gut." Double-check references and triple-confirm the numbers. You'll feel better knowing you left no stone unturned.

August 4: Mars-Jupiter square

Is everyone pulling their weight? A collaboration could come up for review when ambitious Mars scuffles with risk-taking Jupiter. One party may ask for more than their fair share without contributing what they'd initially agreed upon. Your industrious sign is quick to pick up the slack. Drop what isn't yours or else you'll continue to enable their laziness.

August 10: Mercury-Uranus square

A farfetched idea may arise when intellectual Mercury in your hazy twelfth house clashes with unpredictable Uranus in your big-picture ninth. Hold off on making any major decisions, as Mercury's normally sharp wit is inhibited by its foggy placement. Beware of shady figures, whether it's the obvious snake-oil salesperson or more subtle emotional manipulation.

August 15, 2020-January 14, 2021: Uranus retrograde in Taurus

Innovative Uranus starts a five-month reversal through your visionary and expansive ninth house. Delay major risks and focus on the long game. Now is a great time for learning, so sign up for a continuing education course or take a workshop that shifts your mindset. Instead of doing a full-scale launch, schedule a beta test or pilot program to gather feedback. Then, get ready to roll out something really big early next year!

August 17: Mercury-Mars trine

Mental Mercury in your intuitive corner heightens your powers of perception. If you get a great feeling about someone or have an instant click, follow that hunch! And on the flipside, heed your sneaking suspicions when someone gives you a weird vibe. If something doesn't add up, investigate it instead of trusting their word. While you're at it, button your lips and don't divulge any of your own intel.

August 19-September 5: Mercury in Virgo

Your intellect is razor-sharp as Mercury jets into your sign for two weeks. Use this time to capture your ideas and draft a plan of action. Be discerning about how many projects you juggle now. It will be tempting to split your attention on multitasking, but you'll be more productive if you tackle one item at a time. Other people might flock to you for insights to improve their ideas. Consider charging money for your savvy opinions!

August 25: Mercury-Uranus trine

Mind-blowing breakthroughs abound under today's "eureka!" transit. Through this combo of clever Mercury and ingenious Uranus, a cutting-edge message could go viral, inciting a dramatic change. Tap into every imaginable outlet to get the word out, from blog and social media posts to writing a "white paper" that might position you as a thought leader.

August 29: Mercury-Jupiter trine

Go for the gold! Quick-witted Mercury and fortuitous Jupiter are in cahoots today, so aim high. Practice your pitch and put yourself in the right places to meet power players. Your enthusiasm will be contagious. Present your message in a colorful way through storytelling or eye-catching visuals. If you can make people laugh or get misty-eyed, you'll have them eating out of your hand.

August 30: Mercury-Neptune opposition

Say what? Expressive Mercury is at odds with murky Neptune, obscuring your message or its meaning. Ask clarifying questions to make sure everyone's on the same page. If you're making a decision, know that you probably don't have all the answers yet. Hold off because getting a straight one could be a wild goose chase today.

September

SEPTEMBER: LOVE HOTSPOTS

September 2: Venus-Saturn opposition

Careful where you aim those amorous arrows! Vixen Venus in your friendly eleventh house is batting her lashes at steady Saturn in your love zone. Your flirtatious moves could lead someone on, but one of you might be feeling the attraction more than the other. Even if it's mutual, the circumstances of your lives might not smoothly align. Make sure you both want the same things before leaping in.

September 2: Pisces full moon

The year's only full moon in your relationship house ushers in welcome changes. If your current sitch feels a little stale or you're tired of the same-old dating drama, implement shifts over the next couple weeks. Single? The glow of today's moonbeams could reveal a radiant new partner! Coupled Virgos can deepen their bonds or take your commitment to an even more official level.

September 4: Venus-Mars square

A sultry stranger could cross your path, tempting you to swan-dive into a steamy liaison. Is this really what you're looking for? Or is this fast and furious fling a stand-in for a deeper longing? Pause and reflect before hurtling into potential heartache.

September 6-October 2: Venus in Leo

Fantasy takes the front seat when Venus slips into your twelfth house of illusions and escape. You could reveal a secret or perhaps discover hidden information. This zone also rules release and endings, so you may outgrow a connection that's run its course. Have things gotten so close they're codependent? It might be time to put a little healthy distance into a relationship.

September 9-November 13: Mars retrograde in Aries

Mars makes its biennial backspin through your intimate and intense eighth house. A rapidly-moving relationship or sexual attraction could slow down now, giving you a chance to catch your breath. Recalibrate any dynamics that are off-kilter and don't rush into (or out of) anything without careful consideration. Watch for old jealousy, resentment and trust issues that could flare. Your knee-jerk reactions may do more damage than you expect.

September 12: Jupiter retrograde ends

Just as Mars turns backward, romantic hope resumes as adventurous Jupiter ends its four-month backspin through your fifth house of flirtation and love. In three months, Jupiter will leave this part of your chart and won't return for another 12 years. Use the optimistic cosmic energy to define romantic goals and take action. Lead with your heart and open yourself up to new prospects, especially those who aren't your usual type. But heed the warning of Mars retrograde and don't rush into anything binding too quickly.

 The AstroTwins' 2020 Horoscope

September 15: Venus-Uranus square

Your rose-colored glasses could slip off today, revealing a sharp view of reality. Amorous Venus in your foggy twelfth house sows confusion, while disruptive Uranus might interrupt your reveries with a jarring bit of news. Instead of making a hasty decision, gather the facts! Misinformation could run rampant today.

September 28: Venus-Mars trine

Now that's more like it! The love planets entwine in the most erotic and dreamy sectors of your chart, setting the stage for fantasy. Carve out some intimate space to connect and just be present with your S.O. Single Virgos could meet a soulmate type today. Yearning to be understood and supported? Drop that armor and allow yourself to be vulnerable. Allowing people see you as less than "perfect" and composed will strengthen your bonds.

September 29: Mars-Saturn square

Too much too soon? If an attraction took off at breakneck speed, pump the brakes and let your mind catch up to your heart. Jealousy or possessiveness could rear its head under this tense transit. Hold off on addressing it until the coals have cooled. People may be stubborn and unwilling to listen today. When everyone wants to be "right," nobody wins.

September 29: Saturn retrograde ends

Relief! Restrictive Saturn ends its lengthy retrograde, which included a reversal through your romantic fifth house since July 1. A "sure thing" might have dropped off the map, or you could've been the one with second thoughts. For some Virgos, an ex resurfaced, throwing a wrench in the works. Saturn is the cosmic professor, teaching us what we need to learn. Say goodbye to ghosters—

and ghosts of love lives past. Apply the wisdom to a new chapter instead of repeating painful patterns.

SEPTEMBER: CAREER HOTSPOTS

September 1: Mercury-Pluto trine

Your powers of persuasion are on point! Get your ideas in front of the decision-makers and make a compelling case. If you're the one reviewing pitches and proposals, conduct due diligence before inking any deals. Trust your instincts and don't be afraid to make them earn your business! Asking the tough questions is the only way you'll feel truly confident moving forward.

September 2: Pisces full moon

Dynamic duos are in the spotlight as the year's only Pisces full moon ignites your partnership zone. There's strength in numbers, so ask for help if you have a lot on your plate. See someone else struggling with their workload? Lend a hand!

September 3: Mercury-Saturn trine

Being liked *and* respected is a rare combo, but you've got that cosmic mojo today! As whip-smart Mercury (in your sign) teams up with heavy-hitter Saturn in your charming fifth house, few can resist your powers. Pro tip: Back your clever ideas with meticulous research. Put that into a polished proposal then work your magic!

September 5-27: Mercury in Libra

Review your financial forecast over the next couple weeks as logical Mercury, your ruler, races into your money and work zone. Are you on track for your goals? If you recently slipped into an overspending spree, make a few small shifts to your budget. Looking for a new gig? Talk to as many people as you can who could have leads. Cast a wide net and spread the word about your skills. With social Mercury here, attending industry events could pay off with a few great leads.

September 9-November 13: Mars retrograde in Aries

Biting off more than you can chew—and afford? Slow your spendthrift roll for a couple months as manic Mars backspins through your eighth house of investments, property, and joint ventures. Step back from a big endeavor to reassess: Will your efforts pay off or did this project suffer from a case of "scope creep"? See if you can trim unnecessary aspects of the plan and reallocate resources. A real estate or legal matter may have a few loopholes that you didn't anticipate. Breathe through the frustration—and decide if the extra effort is worth it before you spend time or money.

September 14: Sun-Pluto trine

Voice your opinion without apology! As the confident Sun sends positive rays to powerful Pluto, you'll command the spotlight. Others will connect with your bright perspective, especially if you articulate it with your signature storytelling flair. Enjoy the attention when it comes your way. You've earned it!

September 17: Virgo new moon

Dust off that passion project and prepare to self-promote! The year's only new moon in your sign helps you go public with your big ideas. Or, you could take the first bold step toward actualizing your dream. Write out your vision under this lunation, including a clear outline of what you want to achieve in the next six months. But don't get too caught in the details—the important thing is to identify what your heart truly wants.

September 17: Mercury-Jupiter square

Leave your sentimental side out of negotiations today. A spat between cerebral Mercury and impatient Jupiter could exaggerate emotions and fuel an argument. If a project has stalled or your job search turns up meager prospects, don't take it personally. Look at where you might not be representing yourself powerfully, or where your skills need some polish. Being honest with yourself and soliciting advice may lead to a breakthrough. A colleague might try to push your buttons. Take the high road and walk away to recuperate in private.

September 21: Mercury-Pluto square

Someone could try to highjack your hard-earned accolades today and claim the trophies as their own. Stand up for yourself! Be graceful but firm. Loop in management or an ally to protect your proprietary ideas. If you have a budding concept, think twice before sharing it with anyone today.

September 23: Mercury-Saturn square

Tighten your purse strings, Virgo. Mindful Mercury in your money corner is throwing jabs at restrictive Saturn. Take a hard look at your finances and map out a simple plan for debt repayment, savings and wealth building. Working with an advisor or coach can help. If you slip into an old scarcity mindset, address your fears so they don't hold you back. Breaking goals into manageable pieces will make your workload more enjoyable.

September 24: Mercury-Mars opposition

Don't let petty squabbles and distractions derail your focus today. Someone could argue over insignificant costs or waste your time on trifling tangents. What do they really need? You can't make everyone happy but you can attempt to quickly determine what they're trying to accomplish. If you can't reach a conclusion fast, table it. You simply don't have time to get pulled off course.

September 27-October 27: Mercury in Scorpio

The cosmic messenger begins its first of two transits through Scorpio and your cerebral third house, sharpening your mental capacities. Blast through "boring" tasks and go headlong into creative problem-solving, an area where you naturally shine. If nothing sparks your interest at work, start a side gig or passion project. Mercury will turn retrograde October 13 to November 3, giving you a chance to review and reassess your progress before its next dip into this area of your chart.

September 29: Saturn retrograde ends

Solid Saturn resumes forward motion in your creative fifth house, supercharging your artistic and expressive impulses. Add more of your signature style to your work projects. Establish yourself as an authority or influencer with a unique perspective in your field. Welcome the spotlight and promote your proudest accomplishments!

October

OCTOBER: LOVE HOTSPOTS

October 2-27: Venus in Virgo

The love planet spends the next few weeks in your sign, amping up your sex appeal and charm.

Single? Dress to feel like your most radiant and captivating self and watch as heads turn. During this indie-spirited transit, single Virgos can keep your options open and be honest about what you're looking for. Your sign is naturally prone to giving, so practice receiving compliments, support and gifts. (You might just get used to it!) Coupled Virgos can confidently express their desires and acknowledge their needs—then find a few sensual ways to bring those visions to life!

October 4: Pluto retrograde ends

Drama dwindles as power-hungry Pluto wraps up its annual retrograde. As the dwarf planet resumes forward motion in your passionate fifth house, you can say goodbye to guilt-trips, emotional manipulation or chaotic exes popping out of the woodwork. If you were the one churning the conflict, pinpoint how you might sabotage healthy relationships—and make a dedicated effort to break that pattern.

October 9: Mars-Pluto square

Watch that flaring temper! Emotions run high as aggressive Mars butts heads with potent Pluto. Impetuous decisions made in a moment of passion aren't always the soundest choices. Vent to a friend if you're feeling obsessive or jealous. They can talk you down from any potentially regrettable actions.

October 10: Venus-Uranus trine

If you need space, just ask! Your love interest is not a mind reader, so practice expressing your needs respectfully and clearly. It's perfectly acceptable to need some solo time—even in a larger dose than your partner does. Unattached? Speak in a straightforward manner. People will appreciate your authentic communication, and you won't leave anyone wondering where they stand.

October 18: Venus-Neptune opposition

Your usually grounded sign could get swept into a fantasy as amorous Venus opposes romantic Neptune in your relationship house. Just come back down to earth long enough to suss out whether this person has long-term potential. If they're unavailable, ask yourself what you were projecting onto them that represents an unmet need. This person could simply be a mirror, reflecting what you're seeking in a partner.

October 19: Venus-Jupiter trine

The zodiac's "benefic" (positive and helpful) planets sprinkle magic into your romance house today. When lucky Jupiter and loving Venus align, it could spark one of the most romantic days of the year. If you're currently coupled you can enjoy ease and passion with your partner. Single Virgos could manifest someone who takes your breath away. Whether it's a flirtation, a fling, or the real thing doesn't matter just yet. Enjoy the chemistry this transit ignites!

October 19: Mars-Jupiter square

Diva alert! This hotheaded mashup could provoke Oscar-worthy theatrics, but the award could come at the cost of your relationship. Try not to engage when someone pushes your buttons. Be careful not to poke any "triggers" yourself. Going there today won't be pretty.

October 21: Venus-Pluto trine

The chemistry is undeniable, but do you share the same long-term goals? If you're fine with something surface or short-term, go for it! But if you want this to last, spend some time identifying whether you two have enough in common to go the distance.

October 24: Venus-Saturn trine

Vivacious Venus in your first house of appearances links up with Saturn in your passionate fifth house, making you feel secure and radiant. Finally tell your longtime love interest how you feel, or flirt with an intriguing new person. Coupled? Pick a special spot for dinner and co-create your future together.

October 27-November 21: Venus in Libra

Make your move! Affectionate Venus floats into your sensual second house for nearly a month, bringing sophisticated sensuality to your world. Add more affection to your love life. Tap into your seductive side and infuse your escapades with slow and sultry pleasure. If you're seeking someone new, you'll have no qualms asking for what you want.

OCTOBER: CAREER HOTSPOTS

October 1: Aries full moon

The annual full moon in your eighth house of joint ventures and shared assets can attract prominent players into the fold. If you're prepared to relinquish a little control and credit, the accomplishment could be well worth it. Carefully vet any and all collaborators (especially the impressive-looking ones) to make sure they're really able to meet your high standards.

October 7: Mercury-Uranus opposition

Keep those comments to yourself when expressive Mercury locks horns with disruptive Uranus. It happens again October 19 and November 17, when rash remarks could put you in hot water at work. Even a seemingly clever response might come across the wrong way. Keep any trace of snark out of your communication!

The AstroTwins' 2020 Horoscope

October 9: Mars-Pluto square

It's great to love what you do, but when your "passion" pushes you toward a meltdown, you could alienate your clients or coworkers. How much work have you taken on, Virgo, and where could you get some help? Emotions run high under today's tense transit. Call a trusted sounding board before you make any impulsive decisions. This issue will blow over soon if you ride it out.

October 13-November 3: Mercury retrograde

Mercury backspins through your communicative third house, causing disruptions around travel and technology. Back up your data and schedule extra time for your commute. Missing a key meeting because of traffic or tech-related snafus would be a major bummer. On October 27, Mercury will lapse into Libra and your money zone, a good time to review your budget and keep a firm grip on funds.

October 15: Sun-Pluto square

An issue you thought you'd addressed or healed could come up for review when furtive Pluto throws shade at the candid Sun. If someone's passing comment cut you to the core, don't lash out or clap back with a caustic retort. Besides, you'll only be shooting the messenger. You're better off asking yourself: Why did this trigger me? Find the root issue instead of getting caught in verbal warfare.

October 16: Libra new moon

Ready, set, rock! The year's only new moon in your work and money house signals a fresh start for funding and could bring in new sources of revenue. Write down your fiscal target for the next six months and brainstorm innovative ways to reach it. If you're applying for a job or a raise, there's no better day to get that ball rolling.

October 18: Sun-Saturn square

Confidence and clarity will go far in your career today. If you're negotiating a new role or job, take the big picture into account. The salary is one aspect, but can they offer creative freedom, flexible hours or perks like working from home? How about a comprehensive benefits package? Identify your non-negotiables and stick to your list.

October 19: Mars-Jupiter square

Cracks could appear in the foundation of a collaboration under this power-tripping transit. An overbearing personality might be taking more credit while under-delivering, or stalling progress as a way to get what they want. Don't play into their attempts to gain attention or the upper hand.

October 31: Taurus full moon

Halloween is full of treats, not tricks! An opportunity to travel or publish your work could emerge within the next two weeks, as the full moon in Taurus illuminates your visionary ninth house. Entrepreneurial ventures and education get a boost from la luna, so take measurable strides toward your goal. Then get ready to reap the rewards!

November

NOVEMBER: LOVE HOTSPOTS

November 9: Venus-Mars opposition

A conflict between the love planets could throw your relationships off balance—or reveal where things went awry. You may feel like you're jumping from one extreme to the next, volleying between commitment and avoidance. Find a healthy way to

express your conflicting feelings or doubts. Think (or talk) things through before making any decisions.

November 12: Jupiter-Pluto meetup

In or out? Your love life could finally reach a decisive moment as expansive Jupiter and transformational Pluto make their last of three rare unions in Capricorn and your fifth house of passion. Look back to April 4 and June 30, the last two conjunctions, for clues of what might come full-circle today. If you've been on the fence about a pregnancy or working through an obsessive but hard-to-quit attraction to a toxic ex, you may get in touch with your deepest truth—at last!

November 13: Mars retrograde ends

Passionate Mars has been retrograde in your eighth house of intimacy and merging since September 9, sparking jealousy, obsession or a possibly painful reckoning with your deepest emotions. A strong sexual attraction you thought you'd overcome could have surged up, or complicated feelings may have surfaced. Passions may have cooled with a person you thought of as a soulmate, leaving you feeling confused or hurt. When the red planet resumes course, a combustible coupling might fire back up again. It will be easier to work through trust issues and even overcome a betrayal if you're both committed to this union. Stalled plans for pregnancy, engagement or moving in together could move ahead at warp speed, too!

November 15: Venus-Pluto square

Your insecurities could show up uninvited as shadowy Pluto stirs drama with a stability-seeking Venus. Suddenly, you feel unsure of where you stand, which may bring out a controlling impulse. But are you overthinking this? An innocuous comment might unintentionally trigger your fears and trust issues. Acknowledge your reaction without giving it power or the platform to make a scene.

November 16: Venus-Jupiter square

Today's overblown transit can provoke jealousy or neediness, and this upset can spiral into unnecessary theatrics. You or someone else could create a false narrative and use that as a reason to sabotage a good thing. Discipline yourself and don't go there, as tempting as it feels. Single Virgos should keep the bar high—but remember that nobody is perfect. You could develop a wicked case of "grass is greener" syndrome, setting standards that no mere mortal can possibly meet!

November 19: Venus-Saturn square

Amorous Venus in your security-minded second house goes to the mat with cautious Saturn in your romance corner. Are you playing catch-and-release, or for keeps? Figure out exactly what you're looking for before you reel anyone in. If you're on the receiving end of someone's affections, be sure you want what they're offering. A romance that keeps stopping and starting could threaten to fizzle out for good. If you're not feeling it, let it go!

November 21-December 15: Venus in Scorpio

Unleash your inner flirt! The love planet skips into your bubbly and communicative third house, turning every social occasion into a frisky meet-cute. Engage in witty banter with the latte line hottie or strike up a conversation with someone new. Attached? Fill your holiday season calendar with outings that include mutual friends, do some DIY decorating as a duo (followed by casual cocktail parties at your place) or explore a new shared hobby.

         The AstroTwins' 2020 Horoscope

November 27: Venus-Uranus opposition

Honesty is usually the best policy, but not if it's being used to emotionally manipulate or coerce someone. An offhand comment could have unintended consequences, leading to a fight or pushing one of you past the breaking point. Tread softly with the truth today.

November 28: Neptune retrograde ends

Finally! Foggy Neptune winds down its five-month retrograde through your relationship house, where it left its smudged fingerprints on even the tightest of bonds. Issues of guilt, secrecy and confusion may have left you unsure about a commitment. And if an ex drifted into the picture, that certainly didn't help! From today onward, you'll be able to get a clearer read on a commitment or would-be companion. The forward motion of this fantasy-fueled planet will help you separate fact from fiction.

NOVEMBER: CAREER HOTSPOTS

November 1: Mercury-Saturn square

Thoughtful Mercury, which is retrograde in your work and money sector, crashes into stern Saturn in your creative corner, delivering a reality check. It's the second of three transits this year, with the final one coming November 6. Use the last two months of 2020 to examine your year-end goals and create a realistic holiday budget. Pick up a side gig for some extra cash, or if you're drowning in work, offload assignments to colleagues.

November 3: Mercury direct in Libra

At last! Mercury's final retrograde of 2020 ends, and the clever planet charges forward in your work and money house. Make up for lost time (and revenue) with a novel idea that will boost your Q4 profits. From a freelance hustle to a flash sale to a viral email marketing campaign, your ideas could be worth their weight in PayPal profits!

November 10-December 1: Mercury in Scorpio

The cosmic messenger returns to Scorpio and your cerebral third house for its second visit, thanks to a retrograde from October 13 to November 3. Resume tasks you set aside during the slowdown, as your concentration emerges in full force. If you started a personal project that got sidelined for other priorities, pick it back up and add the finishing touches.

November 13: Mars retrograde ends

Reckless Mars ends its retrograde through your joint ventures and shared finances house, where it's been doing backflips since September 9. A tenuous dynamic could right itself and stressful negotiations may finally end. Get ready: Once they do, everyone will be eager to sign on the dotted line before the holidays! If you've been at odds with a close colleague or business partner, clear the air and restore any broken trust. Have you been questioning whether someone is trustworthy? You'll get a handle on their true motives soon enough.

November 15: Scorpio new moon

The annual Scorpio new moon lights up in your curious, communicative third house, raising lots of questions and sparking novel ideas. Talk it through! You could meet a kindred spirit who seems like a great potential collaborator. Test your chemistry on a trial project before making anything official. If your work ethics are as compatible as you hope, this synergy might evolve into a prosperous partnership.

November 23: Mercury-Neptune trine

Take advantage of your heightened intuition. Analytical Mercury clarifies and focuses as it speeds through your intelligent third house, while instinctive Neptune fine-tunes your ability to read nonverbal cues. As they meld their superpowers, you've practically got X-ray vision! The only downside is that you may absorb others' emotions that aren't yours to own. Imagine a golden bubble around you to keep your boundaries in place.

November 28: Neptune retrograde ends

When foggy Neptune finishes its five-month reversal through your partnership house, you can revisit discussions for collaboration. Now that you've had time to think it over, it'll be easier to decide whether or not it's beneficial to sign on long-term.

November 30: Gemini full moon (lunar eclipse)

The only full moon in your professional tenth house also happens to be a lunar eclipse, supercharging your career. Accolades and praise may come your way. Don't be so modest, Virgo! Own your accomplishments. By claiming credit for your hard work, you could open doors to new opportunities. A client, boss or key figure might be "eclipsed out" of your professional sphere, making room for a better fit.

December

DECEMBER: LOVE HOTSPOTS

December 1-20: Mercury in Sagittarius

Your mind is on domestic matters this holiday season when Mercury moves into your homey and family-oriented fourth house. Does your living space have room for two? Regardless of your status, set it up to invite companionship. Your sentimental side emerges now, so use articulate Mercury's powers to put those tender feelings into words. This social transit is perfect for entertaining. Tell your friends to bring their friends—you never know who might show up!

December 5: Venus trine Neptune

Words of love! This sweet embrace between the two most enchanting and romantic planets inspires you to gush about your feelings. You could make an unofficial declaration of devotion—or just tell your partner how deeply you adore and appreciate them. If there's a holiday engagement on the horizon, this is one of the best days for an over-the-top and amorous proposal.

December 14: Sagittarius new moon (total solar eclipse)

Ready to forge a fresh foundation? Today's new moon in your tender and domestic fourth house is also a potent solar eclipse. Create a nest that truly feels like home—or firmly commit to finding a new address in the next six months (if not sooner!). Figure out what you want to manifest, whether it's greater emotional security, a new place, or even a new addition to your family.

December 15, 2020-January 9, 2021: Venus in Sagittarius

Break out the tissues—and the tinsel—as tender Venus makes her annual visit into your sentimental sector. The holidays will be full of affection and nostalgia with Venus here. Add another round of decorations to your home, making it feel cozy and inviting. If you or your S.O. have a hard time with this season, surround yourself with your "chosen family." Single Virgos could meet someone through mutual friends or a relative. Make the rounds of those house parties this season—and keep an eye on the mistletoe.

December 20, 2020-January 9, 2021: Mercury in Capricorn

Provocateur much? The messenger planet streaks through your flirty and festive fifth house for the rest of the holiday season, making you quite the naughty elf. If you're feeling the love, let 'em know! You could be, er, rocking around the Christmas tree or ringing in the New Year together. If you're attached, dial up the pillow talk and tempt your mate with some coquettish conversation. Ramp up the romance with an "experience" gift, like tickets to a live show or a bucket-list destination.

December 23: Mars-Pluto square

"Green with envy" isn't your best look, but today's mashup of contentious Mars and Pluto, combined with holiday stress, could find you dressed in that unflattering verdant hue. And with combative Mars all worked up, you'll be primed for a fight. Vent about your anger to a levelheaded friend instead of making a rash move. This will pass in no time

and seem like a blip on the horizon. You'll be oh-so relieved you didn't lose your cool!

December 30: Venus-Neptune square

'Tis the season for giving, but you need to know when you've reached your limit. Today's stars set the stage for easy emotional blackmail if you're not careful. If you're feeling pulled in too many directions or sucked into the middle of a dispute, remove yourself—no guilt necessary.

DECEMBER: CAREER HOTSPOTS

December 13: Mercury-Neptune square

Are you bringing your best to the table? We all experience self-doubt or insecurity, but don't let it derail your work—or your confidence. Project poise when you walk into that meeting. By the end of it, you might even buy your own act! If you need a pep talk, call a friend instead of relying on coworkers. Keep business and personal matters separate!

December 17, 2020-March 7, 2023: Saturn in Aquarius

Time to put plans into place! Structured Saturn returns to Aquarius (it was here from March to July) for a long visit, its first since the 1990s. As the taskmaster marches through your organized and tactical sixth house, there will be no cutting corners. Luckily, Virgo's the natural ruler of this zodiac zone, so you'll be in your order-loving element. Managerial Saturn can make you a better leader, and since the sixth house rules employees, you'll learn a lot about delegating and running a team. Be vigilant with stress management, as it could take a toll on your health if you're not. Got a sedentary job? Book sessions with a trainer and set your alarm to get up and move every hour.

December 19, 2020-May 13, 2021: Jupiter in Aquarius

Expansive Jupiter joins Saturn in Aquarius, inspiring you to take more chances. Branch out and try a bridge job if you're not sure what your passions are. The next few months (or longer) encourage learning and personal development. Sign up to become a certified computer coder or commit to that 200-hour yoga teacher training. Get all your credentials up to date. This health-conscious transit also puts the spotlight on your wellbeing. If you're negotiating your salary, great medical insurance is a plus, especially if holistic or naturopathic providers are in the network.

December 21: Jupiter-Saturn meetup

If luck is where preparation meets opportunity, then today is like winning the lottery. As auspicious Jupiter and master-planner Saturn unite in your analytical sixth house, you'll see exactly how to turn one of your genius visions into a tangible plan. Map out a step-by-step agenda for an initial test version and see where it can go!

December 25: Mercury-Uranus trine

Forget about gift wrapping; Santa's bringing you brilliant ideas for Christmas instead! Even though the office is closed, your mind is running a thousand miles a minute. Hash out the genius concept in your notebook or a document draft (and maybe tease it to collaborators with a holiday message). Then kick up your heels, since you've already determined at least one of your New Year's resolutions!

December 29: Cancer full moon

All together now! The second Cancer full moon of the year glimmers in your teamwork house. Reflect on how far you've come since the first lunation on January 10. You now have another chance to strengthen a group connection or launch a promising collaboration. Full moons can bring endings and transitions. There may be a friendship or association that's no longer a great fit. Evaluate whether you want to put energy into this tie in the coming year. Ready to add a few fresh faces to your squad? Hit the holiday party circuit and you might meet some like-minded recruits!

Yearly Highlights

LOVE

The year starts off on a soft-filtered and sentimental note then gets a blazing hot by springtime! From March 21 to July 1, slow-burning Saturn heads into Aquarius, stoking a bonfire in your fifth house of amour. A relationship that's both stable and passionate could be in the stars, or you could take a serious step with your partner. This cycle strikes up again on December 19, when brazen Jupiter and Saturn team up in Aquarius for over a year. Fiery Mars blazes through your partnership zone from July until January, giving you the courage to commit! One catch: Couple's counseling might be needed during an emotionally-charged retrograde that lasts from September 9 to November 13.

MONEY

Stability is the key word for your 2020 finances, but that doesn't mean you need to suffer through a boring day job. Enterprising Jupiter joins power brokers Saturn and Pluto in Capricorn until December 19. A home-based business could take flight. You may travel for work or take on an "intrapreneurial" role at your day job which allows you more creative freedom. There couldn't be a better year for buying and selling real estate or making money through an investment or rental property.

WELLNESS

"You are what you eat" could be the guiding principle for Libras in 2020, as Jupiter, Saturn and Pluto pool in your fourth house of nourishment. A balanced diet can keep your mood and energy stabilized. During this gentler year, self-care should be a ritual, not a luxury. See what your health insurance might cover, from massage to acupuncture. A meditative practice that you can do at home will also keep you balanced. Give gentle movement like yin yoga a try.

LEISURE

Bless your nest! With your domestic zone warmed by a trio of planets, then activated by a galvanizing eclipse on July 5, home is where your heart will beat the strongest. Make sure your space feels like a sacred oasis and entertainment zone. Along with enjoying serene "me time," you're bound to welcome a nonstop parade of close friends and family. Keep a journal on your nightstand and snacks in the fridge! And if it gets too hectic under your roof, a short list of the best nearby hotels and Airbnbs could be handy, too. ✳

LIBRA
2020 HOROSCOPE

2020 Power Dates

LIBRA NEW MOON
October 16 (3:31pm ET)

LIBRA FULL MOON
April 7 (10:35pm ET)

SUN IN LIBRA
September 22 – October 22

Matters of home and the heart will be your priority in 2020, as planets weave in and out of your low-key fourth house and your luxurious fifth! Start collecting silk pajama sets, marabou slippers and cooling eye masks. The Libra lair will be the place to kick up your feet—and maybe even swing from the chandeliers with a titillating guest of honor!

For the past two years (since December 19, 2017, to be exact), rational Saturn and mystical Pluto have been co-piloting through Capricorn and your fourth house, lending their intense, karmic energy to home and family affairs. On January 12, 2020, they'll make an ultra-rare exact meetup (which happens every 33 to 38 years), which could start the year off on a powerful, emotional note! A matter involving real estate or a relative could come to resolution, as stabilizing Saturn helps to ground Pluto's transformational beams. Exhale, Libra, because you're bound to gain some major clarity about how to best support the people you adore.

Chateau Libra will be a buzzing hive of activity this year, too, since vibrant, venturesome Jupiter will also be in Capricorn until December 19. How can you set up your home so that it supports all your visionary dreams? Your kitchen table could become the birthplace of a thriving home-based business. Some Libras will start a family-owned company, and since Jupiter rules travel, you could work with people (even relatives) overseas. Three eclipses on the Cancer/Capricorn axis will accelerate any such events in January, June and July.

Your career will be #blessed by this eclipse series, so get ready for some well-deserved rewards for the past two years of hard work, especially near the January 10 lunar (full moon) eclipse in Cancer. On June 5, a new 18-month series of eclipses in Gemini and Sagittarius begins to rock your communication axis. You'll feel moved to get your message out to the masses—or at least to your corner of the world. Is there a book, workshop or documentary series bubbling around in your head? Maybe you've thought about becoming a coach or a teacher. Start exploring ways to share your vast knowledge with the world.

A new wave of energy comes in on March 21, when serious Saturn ambles into Aquarius and your fifth house of fame, fertility and true love until July 1. Some Libras could meet a long-term partner—for song-writing or baby-making—or finally commit to next steps. But don't stress if you get more mojo from the muse than you do from Cupid. This is an "advanced preview" of a longer circuit that begins on December 17, 2020, when Saturn flows into Aquarius until March 7, 2023. Even better? On December 19, no-limits Jupiter will also enter

Aquarius, pushing you into the limelight or a lover's arms…or both! If you're already living the dream, professionally and romantically, you'll be ready to manifest a bold and exciting new phase.

Mark your calendar for the Winter Solstice: December 21 is a power day. For the first time since the year 2000, Jupiter and Saturn will meet at the same degree (in Aquarius), sparking an event called The Great Conjunction. As these two heavy hitters exchange love notes, you could figure out how to map the elusive mix of excitement (Jupiter) and stability (Saturn). Yes, Libra, the two can coexist in a healthy, empowering way.

> "Between heavy work obligations, take time out for Numero Uno."

Your ruling planet, coquettish Venus, puts you in fine flirting form—and just in time for the spring. From April 3 to August 7, the galactic goddess of love and beauty zips through Gemini and your adventurous ninth house. Amore may arrive with a seductive accent, or you could finally book that "baecation" with your one-and-only. The catch? Venus will be retrograde from May 13 to June 25, which could bring mixed messages and blasts from the past. You won't want to leap capriciously during this challenging six weeks, but you might sign up for a few couples' therapy sessions or block your distracting ex's number.

Red-hot Mars will also be in your relationship corner this year, spurring you to get closer to a handful of key people, both in business and personal realms. From June 27 until January 6, 2020, the planet of lust, drive and motivation takes an extended tour through Aries and your seventh house of partnerships. Yes (sigh) this also includes a tempestuous retrograde phase from September 9 to November 13. You could lock horns with the people closest to you, but also unearth some of the long-standing issues that have been blocking you from true intimacy. Simultaneously, you may strike a dynamic duet with someone and shoot up the charts as a pair.

Bottom line? This year will bring tons of exciting developments, especially with the people in your life. But with so much planetary action in Capricorn galvanizing the foundation of your chart, you need deep enough roots to keep yourself grounded. From a peaceful home base to a supportive family (whether chosen or blood-related), remember, Libra: You don't have to do this alone!

Jupiter in Capricorn: Put down roots, expand your base.

December 2, 2019– December 19, 2020

Sprawling Victorian, tiny house or Airstream trailer? No matter what shape your four walls take, home is where your heart will blossom in 2020. Well, the right home, that is. Since December 2, 2019, adventurous, nomadic Jupiter has joined stable Saturn and metamorphic Pluto in Capricorn and your domestic fourth house, expanding your whole concept of nesting. As the red-spotted planet trots through the Sea Goat's realm until December 19, 2020, you'll discover limitless possibilities for living arrangements, from shared housing to solo dwelling. Jupiter only visits each sign every 12 years

and was last in Capricorn from December 18, 2007, to January 5, 2009. Look back to that time: Were there changes in your family structure or living situation?

The fourth house sits at the bottom of the zodiac wheel and represents your roots and foundations— from your nest to your nest egg. As galactic gambler Jupiter paces through this part of your chart, it can churn up quite the paradox. Hosting the planet of travel and risk in your fourth house of security doesn't exactly make settling down an easy feat! Yet, this transit could spur you to take a bold step like buying or selling property or investing in a vacation home. Some Libras will take a job that requires regular business trips or even relocation. If you're a student, you might take a semester abroad in 2020. In the market for a move? Cast a wide net. Your dream listing may be miles away from your current zip code! Already love where you live? In 2020, invest in making your space more functional for your lifestyle. Perhaps it's time to take out a home equity line of credit to finally put in that upstairs bathroom or replace a couple thrift store pieces with a plush sectional sofa or a rustic farmhouse table.

Don't be surprised if visitors drop in more frequently, now that jovial Jupiter (the legendary god of the feast) is lounging in your parlor. When your fancy-pants sign entertains, you spare no expense. But don't worry that you'll lose a fortune buying food and wine for a bloated guest list. With your sensitive fourth house lit by this trio of planets, you'll prefer more intimate huddles, from girls' nights in to home-cooked Sunday dinners. All the same, you might want to make a supermarket run and stock up on your favorite wine, artisanal cheese and crackers. Pro tip: Under this sleepy cycle, don't be afraid to gently escort your guests out the door when you're winding down, or need some time for yourself.

If you've become a homebody over the past few years, we wouldn't be surprised. Since December 19, 2017, restrictive Saturn has been parked in Capricorn and your fourth house of home, family and security, a three-year visit that winds down on December 17, 2020. Since then, you may have folded up your social butterfly wings to enjoy domestic bliss and quality time with your clan. Some Libras felt an added burden with Saturn here, perhaps playing caretaker to an aging relative, dealing with the demands of parenting or being pushed into a provider role.

Private, procreating Pluto has been cooling out in Capricorn since November 2008 and it will be stationed here until 2024. This has also kept many Libras tucked away behind closed doors, only popping out for cameos. But that doesn't mean your life has been a snore. (As if!) You've been plenty busy with nest-feathering and family responsibilities. During this Pluto span, Libra Kim Kardashian mothered three children and meticulously decorated her $60 million-dollar home, chronicling the journey to E! cameras in mesh-paneled leggings and Met Gala Givenchy.

Whether or not you have children of your own, your nurturing nature will take the wheel this year. As a partnership-oriented Libra, this can be a double-edged sword, especially if you fail to put up boundaries with the ones you adore. Martyrs are rarely given awards (or rewards). But with bottomless Jupiter in the mix, you could easily drain yourself trying to "be there" for others in 2020. To avoid burnout, extend generosity to yourself, too!

As cliché as it sounds, self-care needs to be part of your daily and weekly ritual.

With illuminating Jupiter exposing Saturn and Pluto's karmic lessons, buried family issues could come up for review before December 19. Your relationship with a female relative, possibly your mom or a mother figure, could go through a few (gentle) growing pains this year. A childish and age-old dynamic needs to evolve into a respectful adult-to-adult relationship. As hard as it is to break those deeply engrained patterns, you're ready to play a new role besides "bratty little sister" or "scapegoat son." Saturn's presence will also insist on healthy separation in relationships that are too (codependently) close for comfort. Absence can make hearts grow fonder—and also offer the necessary distance and breathing room to let those old patterns fall away.

Feeling disconnected from your heritage? Guided by Jupiter's love of learning and travel, you might take a voyage to your ancestral homeland, connect to long-lost relatives or trace your ancestry with a DNA kit. If you have elder kinfolk still around, turn on the video camera and document some of their stories for historical preservation. And don't forget the impact that your "chosen family" can have. A powerful and inspiring woman who's not a blood relation could open doors this year. At work, align yourself with heart-centered colleagues, the people who know how to lead with love—and do so effectively.

If you aren't feeling at home in your zip code, stop settling for less with your nest! If you could wave a magic wand, where would you wake up each morning, Libra? Start exploring and visualizing in early 2020. While skyrocketing rents and rising

       The AstroTwins' 2020 Horoscope

costs of living may be an issue, don't be seduced into joining this chorus of complaints. Where there's a will, there's a way! With Jupiter, the planet of good fortune, in your corner, your lucky listing could be as close as your next Zillow alert. We already know of one Libra who scored rent-stabilized housing in a thriving neighborhood while under the influence of recent Capricorn transits. How? By simply driving around her childhood bailiwick and striking up a conversation with her now-next-door-neighbor. Although the area had been gentrified since her youth, she held fast to the belief that she belonged back in the 'hood—even if the convenience stores had all turned into coffee shops selling lavender-infused lattes and artisanal donuts. (Which, she admits, is not really a bad thing, given her Libran propensity for all things gourmet.)

If investing in real estate is on the agenda for you, you're in luck. Three times this year, Jupiter and Pluto meet up at the exact same degree of Capricorn—on April 4, June 30 and November 12—spurring you to make a bold move. While Jupiter can attract the funds you need to, say, purchase a starter apartment, shrewd Pluto helps you suss out a home in an area where property values will rise exponentially. There could be epic developments near these three dates, but note that both Jupiter and Pluto are retrograde on June 30—a time better spent getting credit and paperwork handled so you can dash ahead with your initiative near November 12.

> "There's an undeniable link between food and mood, which may flare up this year."

Jupiter is the planet of entrepreneurship. Coupled with security-minded Saturn and investor Pluto, your home could be tied to your income stream in 2020. A kitchen-table side hustle may grow at an accelerated clip, incentivizing you to turn a spare room into an office—or to upgrade from a studio to a two-bedroom apartment so you can work or host clients from home. Got more space than you know what to do with? Keep the coffers full by renting out your basement to a tenant, or even building an A.D.U. on your property and turning it into an Airbnb.

How well do you nourish yourself? There's an undeniable link between food and mood, which may flare up this year. As the reigning beauty queens of the zodiac, many Libras are the earliest adopters of vitality-boosting trends, from adaptogenic mushrooms to CBD-infused balms. Gentle Libra souls may go vegetarian (or vegan) at a young age, as many of our friends born under this sign did while still in high school. (You'll take your pan-seared cauliflower steak paired with an earthy Syrah, thank you.)

Although you might be eating clean, are you getting the right nutrients for your age and stage of life? A plant-based diet is noble, especially when you consider the environmental impacts of over-fishing or too many cattle farms. But it might also mean supplementing your diet with vegan protein, for example. This is the year to set up a blood panel to test for food allergies and make sure you're not low on things like Vitamin D, which affects your energy level and thyroid function. If you get sleepy after meals, a Chinese medicine practitioner might blend you up some bitters, enzymes or other herbs to help with digestion.

As Libra John Mayer crooned, "Your body is a wonderland." Although he may not have been referring to the awe-inspiring functionality of your digestive system, a healthy gut is associated with everything from your immune system to your intuition. Salud, Libra!

Saturn-Pluto conjunction: Secure your foundation.
December 2019–February 2020 (exact on January 12)

It's inspection time, Libra! On January 12, time lord Saturn and transformational Pluto team up at 22°46' Capricorn, giving your foundational fourth house a shake. All realms of security—emotional, financial and domestic—will be put through an appraisal. Although this may feel as disruptive as an earthquake, don't bolt when the going gets tough! These cosmic karma cops truly have your best interests at heart. Think of them like strict parents preparing you for the "real world" by setting hardcore standards and challenging you to live up to them. You might hate when they enforce a curfew on school nights, but you'll thank them later when you're accepted to a prestigious university.

Pluto rules the unseen and mystical realms, while Saturn is the material manifester. If you've been working hard and saving responsibly, January 12 could serve up tangible gifts. For example, your beloved rental home might be offered to you for purchase, and at a price you can afford. HR could ping you about an exciting and well-deserved promotion.

On the other hand, if you don't feel prepared for the pressures of adulthood, this probably won't be your favorite date of 2020. But that's no excuse to sneak out and light up a spliff with the neighborhood derelicts. Saturn and Pluto only make an exact conjunction once every 33 to 38 years. In fact, the last one was in Libra in 1982! Don't miss out on the gift of this transit by rebelling against its stern demands.

We understand that it's no fun to go through an inspection (Pluto) and an audit (Saturn) at the same time. But if you're honest with yourself, wouldn't it be useful to know that you have leaky pipes in the basement? And moreover, don't you want to discover this before they burst and flood your home, bringing costly repairs, black mold and other nightmarish conditions that could have been avoided…if only you'd looked? We're speaking metaphorically here—although these planets are literally in your home sector, so a literal household inspection wouldn't be out of the question.

Near January 12, it would be wise to pop open the hood and take a fearless inventory of any area of life that could use a clean-up. So, Libra, here goes: Are you saving enough money for the future? Have you paid your taxes for the past few years? How's your credit score; does anyone owe you money? Are you living in a safe neighborhood with a great school district? Eating healthy meals at regular intervals? Building a strong base in your career and relationships?

We're not saying these are the boxes you necessarily want to tick—to each their own. However, it would be wise to create a crystal-clear definition of "security" for yourself, and then begin working toward that in earnest. While you'd rather spend on a sunny day than save for a rainy one, you may realize how much less retail therapy you'll need once you create a nest egg for yourself.

This won't always be the easiest process, but don't gloss it over. Shadowy Pluto rules all the buried secrets that are stuffed down in the underworld of your consciousness. Saturn is the engineer who helps you come up with sustainable solutions that resolve long-standing issues and actually work! But you can't make the necessary repairs if you keep covering up the problems. Examining these "weak spots" could actually be the most rewarding thing you've ever done for yourself. Since Saturn rules authorities, work with experts, like financial planners, debt specialists, family therapists, even lawyers, if you need help settling a case.

The fourth house is also the family zone. Pluto could churn up some karmic baggage near January 12, calling for levelheaded solutions from Saturn's vault. If a troubled relative has turned into an energy vampire (or even a "using" addict), the problem could compound near this date. Enforcing hardcore boundaries may be necessary. This is not just for self-preservation, but also for the serenity of everyone living under your roof. Draw the line: Destructive types are not welcome at Chateau Libra in 2020!

Older, wiser women could become pillars of strength for you near January 12. If you're working through some mother issues, or caring for an aging parent, it would be helpful to have a support network to lean on. If you don't have people like this around you, start scouting them out, perhaps by joining a community organization, a spiritual group or self-development circle.

It's actually a blessing that the Saturn-Pluto conjunction takes place just 12 days into the new year. This is a time when, universally, everyone is hyped on self-improvement fumes and ready to dig in and do the work. As you roll into this new decade, you'll feel inspired to set supercharged resolutions. Heed the call of "adulting" and get to work.

Venus & Mars Retrograde: Relationship review.

Venus Retrograde:
May 14 – June 25

Mars Retrograde:
September 10 – November 13

Cupid's casting a wide net for Libras in 2020, which could expand your vision of love from close-up to fisheye lens! From April 3 to August 7, your ruler Venus floats on an extended voyage through Gemini and your ninth house of travel, study and cross-cultural connections. With the planet of radiance and romance in this experimental position, your spring awakening might be a true eye-opener! Single Libras could tap into a totally new type when amour arrives in a very different packaging than your own. Keep your ears perked for intriguing accents. Don't rush to tie yourself down, either. During this independent four-month cycle, you'd be happy to entertain a few hopeful prospects, and maybe a casual lover or two.

Coupled Libras may put the old, "Absence makes the heart grow fonder" chestnut to the test. Be open to uncommon arrangements this spring and summer, like living in different cities part-time or kissing each other goodnight on Skype due to an accelerated work travel schedule. Although you're a relationship-oriented sign, you cherish your alone time, too. You love the dynamic tension of "the honeymoon phase," when everything feels charged with mystery and excitement. In that regard, time away from your partner can actually be a turn-on.

Too much distance, however, is not your cup of Earl Grey. Brace yourself, Libra, because from May 13 to June 25, Venus will be retrograde, which could keep you away from your beloved more often than you'd prefer. You're going to have to get creative about your "us time," perhaps commuting to each other's locations on alternate weekends or making certain compromises, like tagging along on your honey's work trip so you can get some legit facetime.

But don't pretend everything is "fine!" while Venus is reversing through your ninth house of truth this May and June. As much as you like to put on a happy face, you can't pep-talk yourself out of your honest feelings or put off speaking up because you don't want to rock the boat! Venus retrograde's gift is that it brings a golden opportunity to revisit the past and see where you can make things better. While broaching certain topics will be uncomfortable, once you open the floodgates, you'll feel so relieved!

In all your closest connections, it's time to put long-range goals on the table and see how they align. Though discussions may reveal that you want different things, this isn't the end of the line. Use Venus' four-month tour through Gemini (both while retrograde and direct) to cleverly brainstorm ways you can support each other's dreams. That might mean reconfiguring finances temporarily so one of you can afford to go back to school or finally get a start-up in motion. Put it all on the table and discuss!

Need help falling under Cupid's spell? Before June 25, revisit a location that makes you feel like your most beautiful and magical self. You can journey solo or with a plus-one, but the point of the exercise is to connect to your own power, and the sensual parts of yourself that you've neglected.

Relationships ramp up bigtime after June 27, when red-hot Mars barrels into Aries and your seventh house of partnerships until January 6, 2021. This should be music to your ears, Libra! There are few things your zodiac sign enjoys more than pairing and sharing.

This will be an extended journey for Mars, who usually only swings through your sign for seven weeks. But due to a retrograde from September 9 to November 13, the Sea of Love could get a little choppy midway through the voyage. During this two-month backspin, some of your closest ties might hit a rough patch. Don't pretend it isn't happening. Your sign is famously conflict-averse, but alas, burying your head in the sand will only inflate the issue. Fortunately, warrior Mars in Aries blesses you with bonus courage, making it easier to confront problems head-on. Pro tip: Address the simmering tension before September 9, while it's easier to tap into your gracious nature.

 The AstroTwins' 2020 Horoscope

On a cosmic level, this is essential for clearing out stagnant energy and rebuilding things on rock-solid ground. If rage or resentment arises, face it squarely and explore its roots (with the help of a therapist perhaps). The point is to recognize what's going on and nip that Mars-tinged anger in the bud before it has a chance to erupt into a full-on bonfire.

An old flame might rekindle while Mars is in reverse. Rather than waste energy obsessing over an ex, either resolve to walk away or give it a proper go. It's worth your while to figure out what it is about this person that has you in its thrall. Helpful hint: Mars can be lusty, so maybe it's not the who in the situation but the what. If it's just the way they make you feel (e.g., sexy and desired) but you know they're trouble, enjoy the innocent exchanges and use them for fantasy fodder instead of pursuing a serious relationship. Independent Mars reminds you that you don't have to get that kind of validation from anyone else. Try lighting your own fire with a burlesque workshop or a boudoir shoot.

Business partnerships are susceptible to the same tension while Mars is in reverse, so make sure wherever they're heading, you're taking the high road. You can use your Libran diplomacy to sidestep mixed messages and passive-aggressive behavior that could creep in before November 13. The sooner you amend lopsided agreements, the better! It may be necessary to lawyer up and get an actual contract on the table. This doesn't have to feel awkward or rude. Clarity breeds longevity!

Saturn in Aquarius: Emerge from the cocoon.

March 21–July 1
December 17, 2020–March 7, 2023

Even while you're planting deep roots in 2020, there will be days when "the ceiling can't hold you," to paraphrase rapper Macklemore. As a luxuriating Libra, you'd happily lounge in repose, summoning people with a "babe" or "darling" to fetch you a glass of Cabernet and some avocado toast. But you're also an outgoing air sign! Without ample time to flutter about socially, your temperament can go from "gentle breeze" to "multi-vortex tornado." It's never a pretty sight when the zodiac's peacekeeper loses that well-honed sense of balance. If you want to keep a healthy current flowing in 2020, you either need to get out more often or entertain regularly at Maison du Libra.

Fortunately, there will be a couple of prime windows to do just that. From March 21 to July 1, status-conscious Saturn lunges out of Capricorn and into Aquarius, activating your fifth house of glamour, romance and fame. This is a preview tour of what's to come on December 17, when the ringed taskmaster will strut into Aquarius for an extended red-carpet stroll that lasts until March 7, 2023.

All things considered, this should be a lively and flowing cycle. Like Libra, Aquarius is an air sign, and Saturn here will travel in a harmonious trine (120-degree angle) to your Sun, supporting your visionary ideas and your romantic goals. Libras born between September 23 to 28 will feel Saturn's influence the most this year.

If you're an artist or performer, Saturn in Aquarius wants you to get serious about your work. Enlist a private teacher, sign up for a masterclass—or lead one, if you're at that level. This Saturn cycle can help you polish your branding. Put the essentials in place—a demo reel, a website, headshots—whatever the industry standard is. After that, you might find an agent to represent your work or a publicist who can help you attract followers and mainstream press.

Patience, please: This is not the time to go "workshopping" your ideas to the public without practicing and perfecting them. Keep the raw material under wraps, even if it takes a few more drafts or additional time to get ready. When you make your grand debut, you want to have the basic kinks worked out. A mentor who's a veteran in your field could be invaluable now. Saturn here will also deliver a stern ego check. If you're only in it for the attention, money or instant gratification, you might receive humbling feedback.

Mindfulness in matters of the heart will be a must while Saturn weaves through Aquarius for three months. You'll feel the butterflies, but is it the real deal? Slow and steady Saturn is not a hit-it-and-quit-it kind of lover; but honestly, Libra, neither are you. Unlike many of the zodiac signs, you actually enjoy the whole dating scene: dressing up, trying new restaurants and cafes, chatting with new people… sending sexy photos? Yes, please! But when it comes to settling down, there's no rushing you. One Libra we know was nearly 50 before moving in with a girlfriend, despite being a serial monogamist since his 20s. Our own Libra grandfather, a handsome and worldly chap, didn't marry until he was 42—an age deemed "perma-bachelor" back in the 1940s.

It's not that you "vant to be alone," Libra. It's that your tastes—in everything from your wardrobe to your wine to your one-and-only—are utterly uncompromising. With Saturn in your fifth house of romance, passion and self-expression, you'll be even more inclined to conserve your creative and emotional energy, holding out for the best. Just make sure you don't become so picky that no mere mortal can lure you away from your open-plan loft and into a cohabitation station. And just because you're a hopeless romantic doesn't mean you play by a conventional, white-picket-fence playbook. But with traditional Saturn in your fifth house, you might be willing to bend on some of your "standards" in the name of enjoying a shared life.

> "Mindfulness in matters of the heart will be a must."

Already coupled? You won't be able to coast by on honeymoon fumes while restrained Saturn lumbers through Aquarius from March 21 and July 1. It will take a little something extra to feel frisky and turned on. (A good excuse to get those relaxing, weekly spa treatments!) Saturn loves to plan, so put non-negotiable date (and sex) nights on the shared calendar. While that might sound unromantic, relying on spontaneity could shortchange you of the quality time you crave with your partner. Plus, think of all the fun you can have surprising each other with tickets and researching the best places in town to hear live jazz, get hand-dipped ice cream or watch foreign films!

Trying for a baby? The fifth house rules fertility, and Saturn's maturing influence could help ready you for parenthood, or the addition of another child to your brood. Since Saturn is the planet that rules aging, this could involve freezing your eggs, IVF treatments or possibly a surrogate. Maybe you have to part with your beloved walk-up apartment, where you spent your formative halcyon days channeling Carrie Bradshaw, but get tired at the mere thought of lugging a travel stroller up four flights of stairs…even if you once dashed down them in Manolos!

But because nothing comes easily while Saturn's in the house, this transit could temporarily deter your efforts to conceive or adopt. If obstacles arise, take stock of your situation: Are there a few more pieces to put into place before you welcome in a new life? While nobody is ever 100 percent ready, make sure there aren't a few last oats you need to sow. Coupled Libras would benefit from prenatal counseling—and if you're already parents, perhaps a few family coaching or therapy sessions to learn healthy ways of navigating conflict.

Or perhaps you make peace with the decision not to have kids (or have more kids), and instead, redirect your energy towards a creative "child" instead. Let yourself go through this process, Libra—and don't rush. It might take you until Saturn is fully done marching through Aquarius on March 7, 2023, to arrive at a decision that feels right for you. As your deliberate sign knows, good things come to those who wait.

The Great Conjunction: Jupiter & Saturn unite.
December 21

Don ye now the sequined apparel! And let someone else throw a yule log on the fire. On December 19, you will reclaim your crown as the monarch social butterfly, when vibrant, adventurous Jupiter leaps into Aquarius and showers your festive fifth house with its jovial beams until December 29, 2021. After a year of domestic bliss, you'll emerge from the cozy confines of your casa—and spend a lot more time out and about!

With worldly Jupiter in this ardent zone, it's anyone's guess who you'll be snogging under the mistletoe. Single Libras could ring in 2021 with a sultry vacation romance, or a cross-cultural click that's too potent to ignore. Even if you've made (and refined) your "My Soulmate" manifestation list 100 times, Jupiter could expand your palette even further. Who knew you'd be into that person? Surprise!

Of course, the party season won't be a full-on rager as 2020 winds down. Measured Saturn pulls into the Aquarius lot on December 17, two days before Jupiter's arrival. The seven-ringed general will likely temper some of the red-spotted planet's joie de vivre. On the 21st, the two planets meet at the exact same point on the zodiac wheel—an event so rare that it only happens every 20 years.

Although stoic Saturn and live-out-loud Jupiter make an awkward pairing, their combined energy can be incredible. Saturn brings the sensible solutions; Jupiter delivers the visionary ideas. The Great Conjunction could herald all kinds of incredible developments, from a meant-to-be meeting of lovers to a massive creative breakthrough. Whatever the case, after December 19, dress as if your "major moment" could happen at any time (because it could). With outré Jupiter and classic Saturn teamed up in this stylish realm of your solar chart, you could also resume your mantle as the zodiac's sartorial royal. If style bloggers stop you on the street before the New Year, we wouldn't be surprised!

Cancer/Capricorn Eclipses: Restore work-life balance.
January 10, June 21, July 5

Since July 12, 2018, you've been busily rewriting your prescription for a happy and productive life. The reason? A series of changemaking eclipses has been sweeping across the Cancer/Capricorn axis, reshuffling affairs in your career sector (governed by Cancer) and your domestic fourth house (ruled by Capricorn). In 2019, there were four eclipses in these signs, which kept shaking up events both at work and home. In 2020, three final Cancer and Capricorn eclipses will wrap up this momentum on January 10, June 21 and July 5.

Eclipses can sweep away the expired and outmoded, creating space to usher in the new. Ready or not, the first full moon of 2020—a Cancer lunar eclipse—may bring a major transition or turning point professionally. Since this eclipse will oppose super-achiever Saturn and competitive Pluto, it could announce itself with intense power dynamics or even a Game of Thrones-style showdown. You may cut ties with a colleague who is undermining your efforts or trying to forward a hidden agenda. But watch your own cutthroat or controlling side, Libra! (Yes, even you, the zodiac's peacekeeper, have one.) It may come out in the heat of pressure. Are you hanging on to a toxic situation or allowing someone to derail you from your path? This lunar landing might "eclipse" away a client or responsibility that's been draining your vital energy. While that might cause temporary upheaval, have faith: Something much more suitable will show up soon, likely within a month of this eclipse.

No matter what plays out on January 10, a wave of exciting energy will sweep through your career zone this year. On June 21, the solar (new moon) eclipse in Cancer could bring an exciting opportunity or a major epiphany about your vocation. You might feel your own passion emerging from the shadows. While others are kicking back for the summer, you're just warming up. Bring on the poolside power lunches!

The final eclipse in this two-year series pops up on July 5, with a lunar (full moon) eclipse in Capricorn. This one activates your domestic fourth house, which could bring all kinds of new energy to your home life. There could be a move, a real estate purchase or a new family member to welcome. A job offer may have circumstances that affect your residential plans. If you're not required to relocate, you might have to set up a home office so you can work remotely. Alternatively, Libras who are toiling away at home-sweet-home may feel the desire for more work-life separation. Consider coworking spaces and office shares, which can bring the bonus of networking opportunities.

The AstroTwins' 2020 Horoscope

Gemini/Sagittarius Eclipses: Find your message.

June 5, November 30, December 14

Bring on the brainstorms! A downpour of brilliant ideas could flood your reward centers starting June 5, 2020. That's because a game-changing series of eclipses in Gemini and Sagittarius will fire up your axis of communication until December 3, 2021. Not only will you be swimming in brilliant thoughts, but you'll be far less inhibited about communicating these cutting-edge visions to the world.

Eclipses lure you far beyond the familiar and help you discover new facets of yourself—even when you didn't realize there was anything else to unearth! In June, November and December, you could have some major a-ha moments that arrive unexpectedly. This new 18-month eclipse series will help you clarify your message and evolve your mindset. Once you do, you might just go public with your novel concepts! By the time December 3, 2021, rolls around you could stake your claim as a media maven or thought leader in your niche.

Of course, harmonious Libras aren't strangers to the mindfulness movement. The more balanced among you were basically born with the ability to "Zen out," like Tali's high school boyfriend, who presented her with a copy of the *Tao Te Ching* at age 14 and regularly dropped existential George Carlin quotes into their teenage conversation. Libras who are fueled by adrenaline or anxiety (or both) learn quickly to develop a centering practice to maintain equilibrium. One of Astrostyle's Libra editors is also

a yoga teacher; another is our go-to for everything from veganism to shamanism.

Now for the 2020 challenge: How can you put your massive knowledge base into words? You could write a seminal book—or film the must-watch YouTube series—on the subject this year! What's most important is that you do something with all that wisdom stored in your head. Turn the internal monologue into a cultural dialogue! These eclipses—plus the lunar North Node's move into Gemini from May 5, 2020, to January 19, 2022, will push your ideas into the zeitgeist, and help you put a unique stamp on them.

The first of these eclipses, on June 5, will be a lunar (full moon) eclipse in Sagittarius and your third house of communication and media. Keep a capture tool handy because you might have to excuse yourself to go record song lyrics, write a stanza or film a deeply touching Facebook Live. Have you mastered your craft? Sagittarius rules higher education and this eclipse could inspire you to develop a workshop or share your knowledge through a podcast. If your path is still evolving, check the neighborhood continuing education outposts, which may be anywhere from an independent bookstore to the community college. Sign up for a short workshop or a summer semester mini-course. It might turn into a passion worth pursuing.

The third house also rules peers, like siblings, neighbors and coworkers. The June 5 eclipse could inspire you to strengthen relationships like these. As the zodiac's social butterfly, you're often fluttering in a thousand directions, which can leave people grasping to get more than a minute of your time. To build true connection, you need quality and quantity. Show up for office happy hours, and more than just once. Make a weekly or monthly standing brunch date with your sister. If you're super-inspired, you might even organize a summer block party, or become a regular at open-mic or pub trivia night.

But don't get too comfortable in your neighborhood's haute Pilates studio or craft cocktail bar, Libra. The November 30 lunar (full moon) eclipse falls in Gemini and your globetrotting ninth house, which will pull you out into the wider world. Exciting travel opportunities may crop up out of the blue, and you might just ring in 2021 on a Miami roof deck or meditating in a tiny Peruvian village. Open your mind to new perspectives. This year could anoint you a powerful "voice of the people" and an ambassador who bridges and heals divides. Commit to educating yourself first, then sharing that knowledge and insight with others.

A long-distance or cross-cultural connection may ignite near the November 30 Gemini lunar eclipse. Libras who cling to old-fashioned ideals may have a huge perspective change, as this eclipse widens your lens on the world. Your contact with people from vastly different backgrounds or upbringings might be downright transformational. An opportunity to travel, teach or launch a visionary project could also arise near November 30.

This eclipse can bring a powerful moment of truth, since the ninth house is the zone of candor. Being authentic can feel scary for conflict-averse Libras but consider the cost of keeping the peace "at any price." Any friendships built on falsehoods will be put to the test, forcing you to be honest about frustrations and resentments. Someone else might serve up the #RealTalk, causing you to confront where you've buried your head in the sand. Breathe through the temporary turmoil and stay committed to creating a harmonious solution. If you walk a mile in someone else's shoes, make sure you aren't giving yourself blisters in the process!

On December 14, the solar (new moon) eclipse slingshots you out onto the local scene again. Don't just mingle at the usual holly-jolly watering holes this holiday season. The exploratory energy of the Sagittarius new moon helps you diversify your friendship (and dating, if you're unattached) portfolio. Who are the thought leaders in your neighborhood? You could tap into a vibrant social community within a Lyft ride of your own front door. As the year winds down, you may adopt a new role in your 'hood: taking a city council seat or opening a pop-up shop. You've gotta admit, Mayor Libra has a ring to it! ✳

January

JANUARY: LOVE HOTSPOTS

January 3-February 16: Mars in Sagittarius

With impassioned Mars blazing a trail through your communication house for the next six weeks, you're supported in being more direct about your emotional desires and needs. (And fearless in sharing some steamy fantasies.) Mars also stokes competition and anger, so couples may argue more, but see it as an opportunity to get things out in the open. Single? You might crave variety under this liberated transit. And why race to commit when you're having so much fun out there playing the field?

January 10: Uranus retrograde ends

While volatile Uranus was reverse-commuting through your eighth house of seduction and intimacy (since August 11, 2019), your emotions might have been all over the map. Stability has been hard to come by, and you may also have had to contend with runaway jealousy, trust issues and possibly a surreptitious attraction—and not necessarily successfully! You'll be quite happy when the side-spinning planet resumes forward motion today and starts throwing curveballs you can actually catch!

January 12: Mercury-Saturn-Pluto meetup

Speak from the heart! It's a momentous day as serious Saturn and deep-diving Pluto unite in Capricorn and your fourth house of home, family and emotional foundations. These two luminaries only connect every 35 years, so it's kind of a big deal! With communication planet Mercury joining the party, you have feelings to express and they could run pretty deep. Talk may turn to expanding your family, buying property or making changes to your lifestyle. Or, you might make a dedicated effort to be a bit more transparent (and vulnerable) with the people closest to you.

January 13-February 7: Venus in Pisces

When beautifying Venus makes her annual tour of Pisces and your sixth house, the priority becomes healthy living—and loving! Couples can make getting in shape together one of their New Year's resolutions, which means working out and improving your eating habits. This realm also rules self-care, so get some (side-by-side) massages on the books. No partner? You could meet someone through fitness or volunteer pursuits.

January 16-February 3: Mercury in Aquarius

You'll have no problem breaking the ice with strangers during this chatty, flirty cycle. Single? Just being friendly could be the perfect "tactic." If you and your love interest haven't been on the same page, this lighthearted maneuver of Mercury's can dissipate the tension and bring back the fun!

January 18: Mercury-Uranus square

Stay on your toes today. Someone may be baiting you to overreact with outrageous accusations—or inappropriate advances. This is one unnerving clash, but if you know it's coming and stay in your power, you'll be able to transcend the troublemakers.

January 23: Sun-Uranus square

This difficult angle, which happens two days a year, can challenge you to the core—and push your buttons faster than you can formulate a higher-vibe reply. But even if you do take the bait, this could wind up being a good thing if it forces you to deal with a problematic situation you've been avoiding. Just beware that your emotions will be a bit raw, so do your best to not say things out of spite.

January 24: Aquarius new moon

Ooh baby! This is the year's only "fresh-starts" new moon to land in your lusty fifth house, so regardless of your relationship status, you can look forward to a scintillating six-month cycle for your love life. If you're harboring a grudge, set an intention to let it go and turn a fresh page. Couples might open up babymaking talks under this fertile lunation. Today also kicks off the Chinese Year of the Metal Rat, a time to be discerning with your choices. Power couple status: anyone?

January 26: Venus-Mars square

It's hard to know how you're really feeling about someone you thought was special under this soul-shaking clash of the cosmic lovebirds. Don't do anything irreversible today. You need to get more information and let the intensity die down. For the next couple days, retreat to neutral corners.

January 27: Venus-Neptune meetup

This once-a-year, fantasy-inducing merger of loving Venus and compassionate Neptune in your work and service sector could inspire some larger-than-life acts of kindness to your S.O. or someone else you care about. Enjoy how it feels without expecting anything in return.

JANUARY: CAREER HOTSPOTS

January 2: Mercury-Jupiter meetup

Want to get people excited about your big idea or pitch? Don't worry about impressing them with data. Rev up your own enthusiasm. When you're sincerely excited about something, your passion is contagious.

January 3-February 16: Mars in Sagittarius

Fiery Mars is racing through your expressive third house, helping you add more gusto to your communication. It can also fuel the urge to blurt out whatever's on your mind, which can be a good thing as long as your tactful. Try to self-edit those fast-moving thoughts before you say something regrettable.

January 10: Cancer full moon (lunar eclipse)

The first of a rare pair of full moons in Cancer is also a lunar eclipse, which can bring a major, long-running project to a turning point, possibly with quite a fanfare! Because it lands in your career zone, you could get your name on the map and be writing your own ticket within the next six months.

January 10: Uranus retrograde ends

Finally, you can begin to get ahead and gain a sense of stability about your long-term investments and retirement portfolio. For the past five months, volatile Uranus has been back-spinning through that zone but corrects course today. Give things a couple weeks to get back on track—but then, hit the gas!

January 13: Sun-Saturn-Pluto meetup

Even in tense business negotiations, it can be a wise tactic to drop your guard and share a little about your personal life today—but only enough to forge a warm human connection. This way, the other party may decide to not let it be all about the bottom line. In fact, if you can find the shared goals and values in this deal, you might reach a sweet win-win.

January 28: Mars-Neptune square

You may feel like you're being crystal-clear, yet when you ask others to repeat back what you just said, you realize that none of your message got through. When hazy Neptune throws shade at a decisive planet like Mars, trying to play by normal rules will only leave you frustrated. Instead, just stay present in the moment and say and do whatever seems most expedient.

February

FEBRUARY: LOVE HOTSPOTS

February 7-March 4: Venus in Aries

Vixen Venus, your heavenly helper, parades into your seventh house of committed relationships for the next three weeks. What does your heart desire?

That's your starting point. From there, you can work on manifesting it!

February 16-March 30: Mars in Capricorn

When forthright Mars returns to your domestic zone after a two-year hiatus, you could get a wild hare to make some big changes on the home front or, if you're in a serious relationship, talk about moving in together. Make an effort to stay calm and speak without rancor. You may not be aware that your tone is getting a little snarky.

February 21: Mars-Uranus trine

You don't always like to show your emotional hand, but under this provocative and intensifying trine, you might not be able to suppress some strong feelings you've been keeping under wraps. While this might come as a bit of shock (to both of you), it should also be a tremendous relief. Note: This activating angle can also rev up your libido, so consider yourself "on notice."

February 23: Venus-Jupiter square

Why do you care what other people think of your partner or your love life, Libra? Catch yourself slipping back into old patterns of looking for parental approval. Whether from family members or someone you admire.

February 28: Venus-Pluto square

You might be doing everything in your power to keep the peace at home or in a key relationship, but if the other party isn't willing to compromise, stop banging your head against the wall. This is a one-day transit, and while painful and frustrating, it will pass. Throw yourself into a project you have some control over and revisit this situation next week.

FEBRUARY: CAREER HOTSPOTS

February 3-March 4: Mercury in Pisces

When analytical Mercury swings into your streamlined sixth house for its first of two trips this year, you can begin to get a handle on all those admin tasks that always fall to the bottom of the heap because they don't have actual deadlines attached to them. But if you assign some, you're more likely to tackle things with speed and efficiency.

February 9: Leo full moon

The year's only Leo full moon powers up your eleventh house of teamwork and technology, helping you make easy work of a project that's been lumbering along in a low gear. Review who's pulling their weight, who's underperforming and where your software systems could use a serious upgrade. Over the next two weeks, take action based on these observations.

February 16-March 9: Mercury retrograde

The messenger planet kicks off the first of 2020's retrogrades, shifting from Pisces and your efficient sixth house back into Aquarius and your creativity zone on March 4. If you've got looming deadlines during this period, set some interim milestones so you don't get sucked into Mercury's morass and fall woefully behind.

February 23: Pisces new moon

Even if you don't think of Pisces as the most organized and efficient sign, a new moon of fresh starts in your sixth house can inspire you to declutter, get your systems in order and make sure you're using the most appropriate software for each project. You may need to invest a little money in updates, but the time you save in the long run will more than make up for it.

March

MARCH: LOVE HOTSPOTS

March 3: Venus-Saturn square

Watch for ancient fears or unhealthy family dynamics to rear their heads during this one-day romantic rift. Venus in your partnership zone is eager to hit the gas, but Saturn is up to his old tricks, a wise time to slow down and proceed with caution.

March 4-April 3: Venus in Taurus

Don't check your vents if the doors and windows in your bedroom suddenly steam up. There's nothing wrong with your HVAC system; it's your ruling planet, Venus, beaming into sensual Taurus and your erotic and seductive eighth house. No matter what the temps outside are saying, indoors, wherever you go, it's going to be hot!

March 4-16: Mercury in Aquarius

The mood in your love life should get lighter, breezier and friskier as the messenger planet wings through your fun-loving fifth house. Couples should add the concept of "play" to your "dates," and singles are urged to flirt with abandon. This is a great (short) cycle to really express yourself!

March 8: Venus-Uranus meetup

It's a day for surprises and sudden turn-arounds where your intimate life is concerned. Amorous Venus only meets up with unpredictable Uranus once a year—and in your seductive eighth house, whatever happens could be game-changing!

The AstroTwins' 2020 Horoscope

March 9: Virgo full moon

The only Virgo full moon of 2020 powers up your twelfth house of release, healing and transitions. If you've got some forgiving to do or if there's a situation to release to the universe, the next two weeks will be a supportive time. Turn to a wise friend if you need a little handholding. For couples, this is an opportunity to get vulnerable and share some deep feelings.

March 20: Mars-Jupiter meetup

You're feeling bold and ready to take an emotional risk, which might be the best thing to do under current circumstances. Honesty is key, but so is courge. Don't let fear hold you back.

March 21-July 1: Saturn in Aquarius

Your romantic life is about to take a turn for the serious as Saturn commences a long trek through your seventh house of committed partnerships. The structured and future-oriented planet hasn't been here since 1991, and you're a totally different person now than you were then. Note: This is the first phase of the full transit, which lasts until March 7, 2023. Over the next three years, you can weed out players and commitment-phobes and bring your own seriousness and maturity to bear on your union. Some Libras might decide to take a little break from casual dating, preferring to set the bar high and hold out for someone truly worthy.

March 23: Mars-Pluto meetup

When the two intensifying planets converge in your foundational fourth house, you might embark on an emotional excavation project: your own private big dig! Don't be afraid to dive into those old childhood wounds—everyone has them. But if things get rough, hire a therapist or energy healer to be your psychological sherpa.

March 24: Aries new moon

When the year's only Aries new moon electrifies your partnership realm, you can turn a page and start a whole new chapter in your personal book of love. Single? You might meet someone with keeper potential by hanging out in different venues or swiping in dating apps. Happy in your current coupling? Talk about the big, exciting next step you've been dreaming of.

March 27: Venus-Jupiter trine

Let your true feelings out under this confidence-boosting confab. You'll feel happy and generous, and it would be unfair to your partner or interested suitors to "hoard" this energy for yourself.

March 28: Venus-Pluto trine

You won't be able to hide your emotions or "walk it back" once you let the genie out of the bottle during this intensifying trine. With vixen Venus in your house of sensuality and intimacy fist-bumping alchemical Pluto, sex will be anything but casual (so choose selectively!). For couples, this could spark an all-night encounter.

March 30-May 13: Mars in Aquarius

You won't be hiding in the shadows once lusty Mars blasts into your passionate fifth house! You know you're hot stuff, and when you feel in your power, you're irresistible! A casual connection could heat up fast; couples can peel back another layer of intimacy. And because the fifth house rules fertility, babymaking may be on the docket over the next six weeks.

March 31: Mars-Saturn meetup

Talk about emotional whiplash! Your love life may feel like a stop-and-go affair as energizing Mars mashes up with stalling Saturn in your seductive fifth house. Feeling confused? Try shifting into neutral for a short spell.

MARCH: CAREER HOTSPOTS

March 16-April 10: Mercury in Pisces

After a three-week retrograde (February 16 to March 9) and brief pivot back into Aquarius and your zone of *amour* and creativity, efficiency expert Mercury revisits your sixth house of service and organization to wrap up 2020's visit. Here's your chance to tick off all those tedious yet essential admin tasks with ease and a sense of style.

March 20: Mars-Jupiter meetup

A work-from-home (or a café) day would be ideal if you've got that kind of flexibility. But if not, bring something that will make you feel a tiny bit more comfortable—like a favorite playlist or your house slippers, perhaps?

March 24: Aries new moon

Two's your magic number as the year's only new moon in your partnership house sets the stage for dynamic duets. Teaming up with someone whose skills dovetail with yours can help you both get farther faster. Before you ink any deals, do all the background and reference checks. This could be a brilliant—and profitable—new relationship!

April

APRIL: LOVE HOTSPOTS

April 3-August 7: Venus in Gemini

Romance is in the air—perhaps literally for Libras who have a jet-setting vacation planned for this spring or summer! While the love planet is cruising through your ninth house of travel and multicultural affairs, singles might develop an insta-attraction with someone from another culture or who just "breaks type" for you. Couples should either get away during this extra-long transit (thanks to Venus being retrograde May 13 to June 25) or have fun planning their next trip!

April 4: Venus-Saturn trine

Speaking your truth can do wonders for a dubious or wobbly relationship, and for solid couples, it might just be a foolproof aphrodisiac. Take it beyond "airing dirty laundry" and venture into "Here's a fantasy I've never shared with anyone before" then watch the windows steam up!

April 4: Jupiter-Pluto meetup

What do you think of as "home"? As global Jupiter and transformational Pluto make a rare union in your domestic fourth house—the first of three this year—you could shift into a whole new living or family situation. Perhaps you'll pull up the stakes and go explore the world. You might become deeply interested in your family's roots. This soul-supporting transit puts you in touch with your deepest emotional truths. Some might surprise even you!

The AstroTwins' 2020 Horoscope

April 7: Mars-Uranus square

Stubborn much? You might paint yourself into a corner today with your unwillingness to budge on a certain position. Worse, the other person seems to be just as intractable. Since nothing is going to shift today, table it and try to distract yourself.

April 10-27: Mercury in Aries

For the next few weeks, the cosmic communicator will be flitting through your relationship sector, making it a bit easier to initiate a discussion about "where's this going" or other personal sticking points. Unattached? Put some renewed energy into updating your dating profile(s) and photos and thinking about different places to hang out.

April 27-May 11: Mercury in Taurus

When eloquent Mercury deep-dives into Taurus, it stirs up some intense emotional waters in your eighth house of intimacy and eroticism. You may not be able to repress certain feelings or desires—and why would you want to? No plus-one at the moment? Let yourself be more vulnerable with new people, and when things start to get serious, be clear and direct about your non-negotiables.

April 30: Mercury-Uranus meetup

Ooh, baby! This once-a-year merger of the messenger planet and game-changing Uranus in your alchemical zone of soul-merging could bring a surprising opportunity to play out a wild fantasy or act on an attraction. You might suddenly want to do something very out of the ordinary. If everyone is open to that, why not give it a go?

APRIL: CAREER HOTSPOTS

April 3: Mercury-Neptune meetup

Ironically, the less you think about something, the more likely you are to hit on a brilliant solution! This rare (once-a-year) mashup of the zodiac's most analytical planet with the most intuitive planet can tap your unconscious to come up with an idea your thinking mind never would have landed on. Try this approach on some low-stakes problems first and, if it's working, then tackle some truly vexing issues!

April 7: Libra full moon

The year's only full moon in your sign lifts you up like a fairy godmothers, plunks you in the driver's seat and hands you the keys—destination to be determined by you! The sky's the limit for the next two weeks, full of opportunities to fine-tune your higher purpose and find ways to keep steering yourself close to your passions.

April 10-27: Mercury in Aries

You won't take "no" for an answer for the next few weeks as verbal master Mercury flexes its negotiating muscles in your seventh house of alliances and contracts. If someone is being stubbornly resistant, lean in to your world-class diplomatic skills and find the one thing that will bring them around. Take until April 27 if necessary.

April 14: Sun-Pluto square

Accept the fact that someone's bizarre behavior has nothing to do with you—but also that you don't have to have anything to do with them! Today's squirrely face-off between the high-integrity Sun and shadowy Pluto could keep the truth hidden. Cut them an extra-wide berth and disengage to the best of your abilities.

April 15: Sun-Jupiter square

Some days there actually is such a thing as being too optimistic. And today, as the creative Sun squares off with supersizer Jupiter, it's likely that your desire for a certain outcome is blinding you to the unpleasant reality of a situation. Best rule of thumb? Assume nothing (and go easy on the risks).

April 21: Sun-Saturn square

You may be eager to sign on the dotted line, but guarded Saturn is urging caution. When you merge resources, especially financial ones, you need to know you can trust someone 100 percent. If you're not there yet with a certain party, do more background sleuthing.

April 22: Taurus new moon

New beginnings await under the glowing spell of the year's only Taurus new moon in your eighth house of long-term finances. But in this slow-moving sign, you're advised to take your time and consider things from every possible angle. And really, there's no rush because this lunar lift will be influencing you for the next six months.

April 25: Mercury square Jupiter and Pluto

Loose lips can sink ships, and since it's your boat we're talking about, err on the side of withholding today. Even if you really believe you can and should trust this person, hold off at least one day. You might be glad you kept it to yourself.

April 26: Sun-Uranus meetup

Stuck on the fine point of a negotiation? Try another tack. With innovative Uranus teamed up with the Sun in your twosome zone, you should be able to find the perfect stratagy—if you keep at it!

April 27-May 11: Mercury in Taurus

You almost can't do enough research over the next few weeks as analytical Mercury saunters through your probing eighth house. Even if others try to pressure you to make a decision, resist! You'll get this done in your own sweet time.

April 28: Mercury-Saturn square

Trust issues could flare with someone you think you can rely on under this speed-checking face-off that urges caution. If anything, your resistance could be like a poke in their ribs, causing them to reveal something they'd been keeping hidden.

April 30: Mercury-Uranus meetup

Watch your own anxiety today, as this energizing encounter could cause you to act a bit rashly. Pull yourself out of the action and talk to a friend or mentor about how you're feeling. There are always other options, and if you step back far enough, you should see a few.

May

MAY: LOVE HOTSPOTS

May 3: Venus-Neptune square

This first of three face-offs while Venus is in Gemini may start to reveal where you're going to unrealistic extremes with a love interest. Either you're putting them on a pedestal or finding fault with everything they do. Hit pause and open an inquiry into whether this might, in fact, be a projection of something inside your mind and has nothing to do with them. Note, this will occur again on May 20 and July 27,

The AstroTwins' 2020 Horoscope

and hopefully by then, you'll have gained some valuable wisdom!

May 11-September 29: Saturn retrograde

Solemn Saturn kicks off its annual reverse-commute today, beginning in Aquarius and your romantic fifth house and then, on July 1, back-flipping into Capricorn and your domestic quarters. This is a time to slow down, take stock of what's working and not working in your personal life, and map out strategies for shifting course. You could experience delays with a budding romance or fertility. Even if you're in a solid union, you may have moments of doubt. Scratch beneath the surface to see what lessons are waiting there for you.

May 11: Mercury-Mars square

Your passions may be running so high that loving emotions could twist sideways and come out as jealousy or distrust. Some of this could be triggered by actual recent events, but if it feels like your feelings are an overreaction, chances are something else—older and deeper—is at the root of this. Call a timeout and work this through, on your own or with a therapist.

May 13-June 25: Venus retrograde in Gemini

As part of a much longer journey through your ninth house of travel, adventure and expansion, the amorous planet reverses direction today, which could feel like a slowdown—or even like you've come to a grinding halt! Take this as a cosmic cue to reduce your speed and rethink some of your fast-paced initiatives. During these six weeks, you can rebalance the power dynamics in a key relationship, and that alone will be worth the frustration!

May 14-September 12: Jupiter retrograde in Capricorn

When larger-than-life Jupiter commences its annual backspin—this year through your fourth house of family and foundations—you'll have one opportunity after another to step back and hit the emotional reset button. This is a time to nurture yourself and really reflect on unresolved issues in close relationships. By mid-September, you could be in a whole new, way happier place.

May 15: Sun-Pluto trine

If you're been parked on the fence over a budding (or stalling) relationship, this galvanizing merger should push you to one side or the other. Suddenly you'll know the contents of your heart, and you'll either be all in or all out. Penetrating Pluto helps you dive way beneath the surface, so whatever your status, you'll be willing to take a risk and see where it leads.

May 22: Mercury-Venus meetup

Keep it real with the ones you love! As chatty Mercury and harmonizer Venus unite in your truth-saying ninth house, you could take a risk and let someone know how you truly feel. A lovingly honest conversation may bring you closer today.

MAY: CAREER HOTSPOTS

May 7: Scorpio full moon

Your wealth isn't a product of luck, and today, the year's only full moon to light up your second house of money and security can provide insight into where you're either on the right path or undermining your own best efforts. Pay close attention to small things you do when presented with opportunities over the coming weeks. If you're ready to make a career move, get clear about it and don't let anything—or anyone—stop you!

May 9: Mercury-Pluto trine

Your brain will be in overdrive today as intensifying Pluto lends its alchemical superpowers to analytical Mercury. Take time out from your tasks to widen your focus and do some strategic long-range planning. Make sure to give yourself plenty of short mental and physical breaks throughout the day to stay fresh.

May 10: Mercury-Jupiter trine

If you can resist jumping into the fray and impulsively reacting, you'll be able to stay focused on your primary talking points and win over some fence-straddlers. Got an important email to send or pitch to make? Go forth post-haste because these stars have got your back!

May 11-28: Mercury in Gemini

Where others see roadblocks, you'll see unlimited possibilities for the next few weeks as quicksilver Mercury blazes through your ninth house of global expansion. This is a great time to take a workshop or class, or to start watching edifying videos. When presented with the opportunity for uncharted adventure, just say yes.

May 12: Mercury-Saturn trine

You're not just an idea machine today, but under this solidifying sync-up, you'll have the rare ability to give them structure and a realistic implementation plan. And your timing will be impeccable, because speed-checking Saturn will keep Mercury operating at just the right pace.

May 13-June 27: Mars in Pisces

As motivating Mars marches through your organized, service-oriented sixth house for the next six weeks, you may be fixated on getting your life (and health) in order. You've got some big ideas for friends and colleagues, too, but bear in mind, they might see your helpfulness as implying they need fixing and put up strong resistance. Here's a thought: Focus on you!

May 22: Gemini new moon

This once-a-year lunar lift can plant visionary notions in your mind, and it'll be hard to not try to act on them all at once. But that would be scattering your energy, and to pull off the loftiest of these plans, you need to conserve your energy and implement one at a time. Prioritize, consolidate your support and see which ones simply need to get done first.

May 22: Mercury-Neptune square

Did you accidentally sign on for something that sounded good in the moment and then in the clear light of "later" is looking like a Mission: Impossible? It may be important to get the info you need to proceed, so if you can't bail altogether…stall.

May 28-August 4: Mercury in Cancer

This is an extra-long trip for the messenger planet because it'll swing into retrograde from June 18 to July 12. During this phase, you'll have countless chances to rethink things you've started and walk them back if they're not feeling right. (In Cancer, Mercury works more from the heart—and gut—not the left brain.) The lesson here is to be patient and gentle with yourself and others. Give yourself until the next phase of this transit (from July 12 to August 4) to bring things to a culmination point.

Note that communication, technology and travel plans could be rife with glitches. Be extra-diligent about double- and triple-checking everything and always having a viable Plan B up your sleeve.

June

JUNE: LOVE HOTSPOTS

June 2: Venus-Mars square

Things could get intense today, with the cosmic lovers at loggerheads. Mars can make you both particularly intractable, so rather than dig yourselves in deeper, call a timeout. The silver lining? When you do (inevitably) reconcile, you'll have some toe-curling makeup sex to look forward to!

June 27, 2020-January 6, 2021: Mars in Aries

Lusty Mars returns to your relationship house for the first time in two years—this time, for an extended tour thanks to a retrograde from September 9 to November 13. Know what you want more than anything, because motivated Mars won't stop till it's successful. He's especially talented at reigniting sparks for couples who've been running hot and cold, and bringing exciting long-term prospects for single Libras.

June 30: Jupiter-Pluto meetup

Plant deeper roots or pull up the stakes? Adventurous Jupiter and possessive Pluto form their second of 2020's three rare unions. This astrological odd couple only pairs up every 13 years, and today, both happen to be in slowed-down retrograde. Turn your lens to the past. You could do some intense evaluating of childhood patterns and rethink your sense of home (in the world and within yourself). Couples might have an important—and brutally honest—conversation about your views on children, where you want to live and other deeply personal topics.

JUNE: CAREER HOTSPOTS

June 5: Sagittarius full moon (lunar eclipse)

The year's only Sagittarius full moon, which also happens to be a tipping-point lunar eclipse, powers up your house of communication and your gift of gab—which, let's face it, isn't so shabby to begin with. What big project or cause have you been waiting to promote more fully and actively? Take the next two weeks to apply finishing touches, then stop obsessing and get it out in the world, where it belongs!

June 13: Mars-Neptune meetup

Read the tea leaves today rather than mindlessly pushing your own agenda. This mashup of the most analytical and the most intuitive planet can help you tune in to the moment-by-moment shifts in people's energy. You know you've got a great product or service, but the way to sell it is to find that sweet spot when people are maximally receptive.

June 18-July 12: Mercury retrograde in Cancer

When the messenger planet shifts into reverse in your professional zone, it's sure to lead to some frustrating glitches in communication, technology and all kinds of future planning. Go to extra lengths to clarify, double-check—and have backup plans firmly in place for the duration.

June 21: Cancer new moon (annular solar eclipse)

This first of two Cancer new moons is also a powerful solar eclipse, and in your tenth house of professional ambition, it's grooming you for a higher level of success. But before you hit the gas, pull over and check your GPS coordinates. To accomplish everything you want, you need to know what your goals are. These next two weeks are perfect for formulating, clarifying and then acting on them, down to the smallest detail.

June 23-November 28: Neptune retrograde in Pisces

Details may be your nemesis during the next few months as nebulous Neptune backflips through your sixth house of organization and systems management. Since you may not be able to do much about that, head it off at the pass by delegating the smaller stuff to people who thrive on that and pour your energy into big-picture visioning and communications.

June 27, 2020-January 6, 2021: Mars in Aries

A onetime competitor could become your new BFF or a profitable partner if you can both take the high road and set aside past rivalries. And really, Libra, isn't that your guiding principle in life? As play-to-win Mars marches through your partnership zone for a very long time (thanks to a retrograde from September 9 to November 13), you'll be all about strategic alliances. Join forces with a synergistic partner FTW!

July

JULY: LOVE HOTSPOTS

July 1-December 17: Saturn retrograde enters Capricorn

Midway through its annual retrograde, structured Saturn backflips into Capricorn for one last hurrah through your fourth house of home and family. If you're still processing some old "mom" or motherhood issues of your own, these next several months can bring the clarity or closure you seek. Important now is setting healthy boundaries and getting certainty around your next step involving all-important foundational goals. You could get serious about buying or selling a home. And with restrictive Saturn here, downsizing might be on your mind, too.

July 5: Capricorn full moon (lunar eclipse)

The only Capricorn full moon of 2020 is also a partial lunar eclipse, and because it lands in close proximity to transformative Pluto in your domestic quarters, you may feel ready to make a major life change. Meeting your sweetie's family, moving in together—or perhaps one of you moving out—could be on the docket in the coming few weeks. This is also a great time for healing any wounds or rifts with close friends or relatives.

July 8: Mercury-Mars square

Sometimes, you just need to fight a little to clear the air. But as retrograde Mercury butts heads with combative Mars in your partnership zone, you're tempted to drag up past offenses. This could detonate a major fight, so be careful. If someone's apologized, keep it in the "bygones" category. And if you feel they've wronged you, make sure you don't come across as blaming or resentful. This aspect will repeat again on July 27 after Mercury corrects course. Things may not fully resolve until then.

July 27: Venus-Neptune square

This second clash of these hyper-sensitive planets might leave you feeling emotionally raw and confused about where a certain relationship is heading. At times you seem totally in sync, but when you get out of step, it feels like you're light-years apart. Continue being the observer, but don't take action yet.

JULY: CAREER HOTSPOTS

July 1-December 17: Saturn retrograde enters Capricorn

The return of Saturn (in reverse) to your domestic fourth house—a final hurrah of a three-year transit—is a perfect opportunity to consider going freelance, negotiating for more telecommuting flexibility or starting a home-based business. Feeling a bit fried? Make self-care a priority for the next several months.

July 12: Sun-Neptune trine

You may start thinking about your work as more than merely a paycheck-provider under this heart-opening angle. You'd love to use your gifts and talents to help others, so begin a search for ways you can build more service and giving into your daily routines.

July 15: Sun-Pluto opposition

Under this once-a-year provocative face-off, someone could push one of your buttons—and it might get stuck! But don't go pointing any fingers. Pluto can shine a light on things you've been ignoring, and if you're willing to be a little vulnerable, you may discover that the surface things that are bugging you to no end actually have way deeper roots in your own unconscious. Explore!

July 20: Cancer new moon

This rare second new moon in your professional sector (the first, an eclipse, was on June 21) can help you start to write a whole new and very exciting chapter in your career. Don't push yourself to accomplish everything this month. The influential period of this lunar lift is six months, so position yourself now for a raise or promotion (or job change) by the end of the year.

July 20: Sun-Saturn opposition

Not everyone can get along beautifully 24/7/365! If you and a colleague or work ally butt heads today, chalk it up to "the cost of doing business." Find a way to reach resolution—or agree to disagree for now—but whatever you do, don't take it personally.

July 30: Mercury-Jupiter opposition

Keep it professional! Today, as straightforward Jupiter in your home zone shoots a challenging beam to verbose Mercury in your career corner, make it your business to steer conversations away from personal subjects. This isn't to say don't share anything; just stay aware of what's appropriate in a work environment.

324

July 30: Mercury-Neptune trine

Sometimes rules really are made to be broken. Today, as tuned-in Neptune lends support to rational Mercury, trusting your intuition may be more useful than strictly following protocol. Even if you're guided to do something you can't immediately explain or justify, don't worry. The proof will be in the pudding!

August

August 3: Aquarius full moon

Confusion begone! Today's once-a-year full moon in your fifth house of love, creativity and joy may illuminate an area where you've been unsure what your next step is. New couples might decide to officialize things with a next step over the coming two weeks; solid unions could deepen in heart-opening ways. Single? Take the effort out of your dating initiatives and focus on having fun with interesting people. And in between outings, pour your energy into a passion project.

August 7-September 6: Venus in Cancer

Today, your galactic guardian, affectionate Venus, commences her annual visit to your future-oriented tenth house, which could intensify your musings over a certain relationship. But there's only so much you can accomplish thinking about things! If you're with someone, make time in the next four weeks to dispassionately discuss your hopes for a (shared) future. Single Libras should pay more attention to folks you meet at work-related events—and keep a very open mind!

August 13: Mars-Pluto square

Watch out for a random appearance of the green-eyed monster or the resurfacing of old family dynamics. You might really have to rein yourself in to not project childhood issues onto someone who wasn't party to the action. Silver lining? That "triggering" person may be holding up a mirror to facilitate your own inner work.

August 15, 2020-January 14, 2021: Uranus retrograde in Taurus

When unpredictable Uranus kicks off its annual retrograde—this year through your eighth house of soul-merging and eroticism—you'll get one opportunity after another to reflect on and process some heavy emotions—and their root causes—that still flare up in intimate relationships. Don't reflexively take the bait of a tempting-yet-disruptive ex. You may benefit from working with a therapist or energy healer during this intense transit.

August 25: Venus-Jupiter opposition

Even if you're involved with a caring, kind soul, today's starmap could trigger a wave of insecurity or old abandonment fears that send you reeling. Singles might experience a fleeting sense of loneliness. Find some time for your thoughts and feelings, allowing them to flow. Journaling or talking to a supportive friend could help.

August 27: Venus-Neptune trine

Stable and sexy? Why not? Under today's supportive alignment of two idealistic planets in the most grounded houses, discussing and planning your future will be a turn-on! Smoldering chemistry eventually fades, and what remains is your lifelong commitment and shared goals and values. Single Libras could meet a person of substance at work or through mutual friends. Look past appearances and really get to know them.

August 30: Venus-Pluto opposition

You may go deeper than you intended to with a close connection under this intensifying face-off. Venus prefers to focus on the affection and connection, but Pluto needs to keep peeling back those layers. Honesty and compassion can help you ward some of the inevitable tears—but they can be of joy as well as sadness!

AUGUST: CAREER HOTSPOTS

August 1: Mercury-Pluto opposition

Your goal today is establishing—and enforcing—better boundaries. People can be cagey with their hidden agendas, so rather than stay on high alert to weed out the self-aggrandizers, just let everyone know what you're willing and unwilling to put up with. That way you can go about your own business and get even more accomplished!

August 2: Sun-Uranus square

Not everyone will be true to their word today, a fact that never fails to disappoint you. Sadly, that's a reality and rather than get down about it, just be on-guard for someone whose enthusiasm is a little too zealous. Strengthen your true-blue alliances and have a plan ready to throw any mutineers off the island!

August 3: Mercury-Saturn opposition

Challenging as it may be today, try to keep your professional and personal lives separate. This annual face-off can bring domestic issues to the forefront during business hours—and it may not be so easy to leave work at the office. But don't berate yourself for being human! If that bothers a partner, roommate or colleague, just frame it as the price of being true to your head and heart.

August 4: Mars-Jupiter square

Someone you've been in negotiations with might suddenly get a little aggressive or unwilling to compromise. It doesn't necessarily mean the deal is off, just that one (or both) of you are feeling the effects of today's cosmic clash. Stand your ground, and if you have to save this for another day, so be it.

August 4-19: Mercury in Leo

If you've been working long hours by yourself to finish up an important deadline, tap into the strength that's found in numbers over the coming few weeks. As the chatty and agreeable messenger planet invades your collaborative eleventh house, people may appear out of nowhere to team up with and support you. Since this is also your "technology zone," it's a perfect time to launch a digital venture or just update your whole online presence.

August 10: Mercury-Uranus square

Diplomacy and tact may fly out the window under today's destabilizing square between the quicksilver communication planet and disruptive Uranus. Someone might think they're being helpful by unleashing an unedited torrent of complaints or criticisms. Take them aside and, as calmly as possible, point out the flaw in their logic.

August 15, 2020-January 14, 2021: Uranus retrograde in Taurus

When unpredictable Uranus begins its annual reverse-commute through your house of joint ventures and shared resources, you'll have an opportunity to review all of your investments and partnerships. Don't do anything rash (despite Uranus' promptings). This is a time to be extra careful and talk through your findings with a qualified pro.

August 17: Mercury-Mars trine
With articulate Mercury sweetly synced up with energizing Mars in your people houses, you'll know exactly what to say and how to say it—without coming off as manipulative. For your authentically social air sign, this is a wonderful outlet for your natural gifts, so use them for everyone's advantage.

August 18: Leo new moon
Been hovering on the periphery of an elite group or hoping to get one of your digital projects green-lighted by an influencer? The year's only new moon in your eleventh house of teamwork and technology could bring the perfect opportunity over the coming two weeks. But don't sit around waiting to be invited. Be proactive, and unabashed about promoting your ideas.

August 19-September 5: Mercury in Virgo
As mental Mercury glides through your imaginative twelfth house, you might not have the best discernment between what's exciting and stimulating and what's actually doable. Read between the lines and scratch beneath the surface to get more insight. And until you're 100 percent sure of something, keep digging!

August 24: Mars-Saturn square
In a rare moment of provocation, you might actually lose your cool at work and catch yourself on the verge of losing composure. But you know that no one wins in that scenario—especially not you. So breathe deeply, and if you are tempted to go off on a coworker or employee, vent to a trusted friend or professional instead.

August 25: Mercury-Uranus trine
Insight and inspiration could come through in a flash under today's brilliant mashup. Even if you can't track its source, give it a test-drive and see if it's at all plausible. And should anyone ask how you hit upon that idea, no need to reveal the source of your genius!

August 29: Mercury-Jupiter trine
Your ideas are your stock in trade, and today, as quicksilver Mercury and visionary Jupiter buddy up, you may find yourself dabbling far outside the normal parameters of your comfort zone. But don't keep your best notions to yourself. If you can contribute to a team project, no waiting for someone to ask—jump in and contribute.

August 30: Mercury-Neptune opposition
If something sent you back to the drawing board, don't be discouraged. The greatest minds have all failed—a lot—before they had their breakthrough successes. Under today's offbeat connection between left-brain Mercury and intuitive Neptune, starting from scratch could yield a surprising brainstorm.

September

SEPTEMBER: LOVE HOTSPOTS

September 1: Mercury-Pluto trine

Open up and confess your deepest feelings! Today's merger of penetrating Pluto and communicator Mercury helps you reach into those emotional recesses and reveal something you've been holding inside. Single? Follow your intuition and pay attention to "signs." They could be leading you to a soulmate connection.

September 2: Venus-Saturn opposition

Under this SOS signal from your ruler, romantic Venus, it might be up to you to let the powers-that-be at work know where your limits lie. You're hardly a slacker, but you also have a personal life. And recharging your batteries with your nearest and dearest is your most important energy source!

September 4: Venus-Mars square

Today's dust-up between the love planets could send some stressful ripples through your romantic life. Your needs might feel mutually exclusive, or one of you may be overly demanding. Make sure it isn't you, and if you have to give someone a little space for a day or so, try not to take it personally!

September 6-October 2: Venus in Leo

Lightness and levity should return to your amorous life as your ruler, affable Venus, rolls into your eleventh house of friends and group activities. Take a break if you and a love interest have been glued at the hip, or just plan some group hangs. Single? You might see a platonic pal in a new and intriguing

light. If this is a special connection, proceed with an open mind!

September 9-November 13: Mars retrograde in Aries

Lusty Mars flips into reverse in your relationship sector, which could ramp tension in your love life. An ex may come crawling out of the woodwork, or you have second thoughts on an attraction. This is a two-month transit, so give yourself plenty of time for your long-term, authentic emotions to surface. Talk to friends and maybe a therapist to get to the root of the situation. This could turn out to be a blessing in disguise.

September 12: Jupiter retrograde ends

Emotional security and optimism begins to return after a four-month backspin by enthusiastic Jupiter in your foundational fourth house. Petty arguments that conflated into major fueds should settle back down, and you can get back on the same page with a loved one. Single? Get ready to oepn your heart!

September 14: Sun-Pluto trine

Under this rare (twice-a-year) connection between the ego-driven Sun and penetrating Pluto—both in deep, dark chart sectors—you could have an epiphany about an emotional blind spot. Fun and lighthearted not-so-much, but it can help you to tap a rich vein of repressed anger or resentment. Stay at it until you feel like you've gotten clarity—and maybe even gotten over it!

September 15: Venus-Uranus square

All couples occasionally need a little time or space for themselves, and if you're feeling that strongly today, it's probably because of this edgy alignment between indie-spirited Uranus and your ruler, partnership-oriented Venus. Take whatever time or space you need, but be clear with your mate that it doesn't mean anything is wrong! Single? Focus on fun, not the end game, and you'll make the most of this liberated mashup.

September 17: Virgo new moon

The year's only new moon in your twelfth house of introspection, closure and healing could signal a turning point in a relationship. But that's not necessarily a bad thing! If you've been waiting for a sign or some cosmic wind in your sails to pull the plug, you may get it in the next two weeks. Unattached? Focus on becoming as whole and healthy as possible: When you're beaming at this high frequency, you can't help but attract someone on your wavelength!

September 28: Venus-Mars trine

Reminder: There are no hard and fast rules in relationships; it's what you and someone else mutually agree upon. Today, as the love planets align in your houses of partnership and platonic connections, you might cross a line with a pal, or decide you're comfortable being friends with benefits. For single Libras, a swipe could prove to have serious potential. Keep an open mind!

September 29: Mars-Saturn square

Mars in your partnership zone has you eager to race ahead in a new or deepening relationship, yet a caution-urging beam from restraining Saturn is giving you second thoughts. It's possible that you're getting mixed signals from a person of interest. There may not be resolution today, so stop fixating and hang out with people who don't make you wonder where you stand!

September 29: Saturn retrograde ends

Drama begone! Solemn Saturn resumes forward motion in your foundational fourth house. If you've been stressed about a relationship or not getting enough of your needs met during Saturn's five-month reversal, things should start to lighten now, leaving you feeling way more optimistic. Plans to move in or start a family resume.

SEPTEMBER: CAREER HOTSPOTS

September 2: Pisces full moon

This might be the week you observe tangible (and possibly profitable) results of your dedication to making changes in your work around service, efficiency and routines. As the year's only Pisces full moon lights up the zone associated with those areas of life, stop and reflect on how much you've accomplished and set some new milestone goals for the rest of the year to keep your motivation high!

September 3: Mercury-Saturn trine

Where normally you might just go with your gut reaction, under today's hemisphere-fusing alignment, your strength will come from trusting your instincts and then "double-sourcing" them with cold, hard facts. A little digging should give you the confirmation you need.

September 5-27: Mercury in Libra

This annual transit is your three-week hall pass to speak your mind without self-editing. Your big ideas and unique vision is exactly what's needed now, so don't hold back. Mercury in your assertive first house makes you bold and candid.

September 9-November 13: Mars retrograde in Aries

When the rash red planet flips into reverse in your sector of joint ventures and partnerships, an alliance that was gaining momentum could suddenly lose steam—or vanish into thin air. Check in with yourself: Might part of the problem be your own (seldom-seen) competitive streak? Don't try to push when nothing's happening. Give this seven weeks and, if you're still interested in pursuing, give it another shot. If not, there are plenty other opportunities waiting for you!

September 17: Mercury-Jupiter square

Watch your tone as well as the actual words you use today. With flame-fanning Jupiter agitating chatty Mercury, you might come off a little "extra" or like a know-it-all. You know the best way to get people to work is to inspire—not bully—them, so if you catch yourself in the act, stop and redirect.

September 21: Mercury-Pluto square

You never mean to be snarky or sarcastic, which is why it can catch people so off-guard that they do a double-take! Today, as shadowy Pluto throws shade at the messenger planet, pay attention to covertly negative comments. And stay mindful that someone doesn't try to ensnare you in an unwanted professional power struggle!

September 23: Mercury-Saturn square

Logic and reason will only get you so far today, as harsh taskmaster Saturn throws a resisting beam at messenger Mercury in your sign. You may think you're doing the right thing by speaking up or trying to overrule someone else's objections, but under this going-nowhere-fast clash, you might only be banging your head against a wall. Better idea: Do your own thing and maybe come back to this at the end of the week.

September 24: Mercury-Mars opposition

No matter how upset someone gets you today, resolve to hold your fire. With bellicose Mars poking communicator Mercury (in Libra) in the ribs, it'll be hard not to say something. But if this person is intent on riling you up, engaging on any level will only be a win for them. Cut them a wide berth and refuse to take the bait—or to start something yourself!

September 27-October 27: Mercury in Scorpio

This first of the mental planet's two trips to your work and finances sector will begin to give you more insight into your spending habits and blocks around money. Note that because of a retrograde from October 13 to November 3, Mercury will backflip into your sign for two weeks then return to Scorpio on November 11. Don't force anything that isn't coming. Just be observant, sit with discomfort, and know you can implement major changes once Mercury straightens out.

September 29: Mars-Saturn square

Even if you feel like you're parked on top of an active volcano, hang in there. Energizing Mars is eager to get something off the ground, yet cautious Saturn urges restraint. Jumping in before you have all the data, resources and timeline worked out could cause it to backfire. Talk yourself off the ledge, do more legwork, and then set a new deadline that's more realistic—and more likely to succeed! Take your time, Libra.

October

OCTOBER: LOVE HOTSPOTS

October 1: Aries full moon

Committed relationships steal the spotlight starting today as the year's only Aries full moon lands in your seventh house of dynamic duos. Are you happy with your tatus? Single? The next two weeks—peak manifesting time of this lunation—should be rich in opportunities to meet some intriguing new people and learn more about your inner workings. Couples can talk through any differences, officialize things or, if you've reached the end of the line, discuss how to consciously uncouple.

October 2-27: Venus in Virgo

When your ruling planet, amorous Venus, takes her annual pleasure cruise through your twelfth house of romanticism and imagination, she'll turn up the heat on your fantasy life. This is a wonderful dimension to get a little lost in, but make sure you can find the way back before Venus splashes into your sign just after your birthday season comes to a close.

October 4: Pluto retrograde ends

You've have been deeply immersed in an emotional situation ever since penetrating Pluto shifted into reverse in your foundational fourth house April 25. You might have struggled to find your footing in a key connection or undergone some deep personal transformations. Now that Pluto is in forward motion, things should settle down with your inner circle. Make sure you've integrated the lessons and are smarter/clearer/more tolerant as a result.

October 9: Mars-Pluto square

Self-awareness alert! Be mindful you're not inadvertently projecting old childhood issues onto a love interest. Today's agitating clash could bring things up on a deep emotional level before you even become aware of what's going on. Don't be afraid to talk it through—but no "dumping"!

October 10: Venus-Uranus trine

While it's not exactly easy to "expect the unexpected," that's about all you can say when unpredictable Uranus jabs vixen Venus in your most emotionally intense chart areas. Your feelings could go through the roof, or your love life might dramatically shift gears. Remember, you're actually in the driver's seat, just being taken for a wild ride!

October 18: Venus-Neptune opposition

Enjoy your daydreams and reveries, but don't for one second confuse them with cold, hard reality. In fact, if you're going through a tense time in a relationship, allowing yourself to veer off into Fantasyland might feel like a perfect escape—but not if it could cause you act in a way you know isn't in your best interests. Talk to a grounded friend before you do anything rash.

October 19: Venus-Jupiter trine

You won't be able to hold back your feelings today—so save yourself the trouble and allow yourself to gush a little. This emotionally magnifying mashup encourages you to speak from your heart without fear of censorship. Single? See how people react when you lead with your receptivity…and even vulnerability.

October 19: Mars-Jupiter square

No matter how much you'd like to be on the same page as a close connection, this edgy square makes compromise near-impossible. You're could more harm than good if "go there," so put off heavy talks for another day, when you'll both be more receptive.

October 21: Venus-Pluto trine

Keeping a stiff upper lip? There's no sense in hiding your feelings. Today's emotionally intense mashup nudges you to acknowledge an attraction or show your appreciation for your partner. Feeling stuck? Make a list of all the things you're grateful for, and stay focused on that.

October 24: Venus-Saturn trine

Under this supportive sync-up, a worthy person may let their true colors show. Don't waste this special moment; honor it by opening up, being a bit more vulnerable and letting them know you appreciate having them in your life.

October 27-November 21: Venus in Libra

Your animal magnetism reads off the charts during this three-week cycle that unleashes your charisma and appeal. You'll earn instant head-turner status when your glamorous ruler, Venus, shimmies through your sign. Enjoy this fun and flirtatious spell—but if you are attached, don't do anything to put your union at risk.

October 31: Taurus full moon

The only full moon in your intimate, erotic eighth house can deepen and intensify a new or solid relationship—and churn up buried emotions. If you can't talk to your love interest, then discuss them with a close friend or therapist so you don't explode.

OCTOBER: CAREER HOTSPOTS

October 1: Aries full moon

Seal the deal! Today's once-a-year full moon in your zone of twosomes could turn up the heat on a negotiation that's been on a low simmer. Are you ready to take the plunge into a professional partnership or team up for mutual gain? As long as the terms are favorable, it's worth a shot.

October 7: Mercury-Uranus opposition

This first of three successive Mercury-Uranus face-offs across your money axis could turn managing your cash flow into a juggling act! The next two—on October 19 and November 17—could teach you some valuable lessons. Pay attention to what might be on the docket for you to learn…so you don't wind up doing anything the hard way.

October 13-November 3: Mercury retrograde

Despite your best-laid plans, once the messenger planet flips backward in your financial sector, things could go sideways with a savings goal, or you might discover a hefty charge on your credit card statement that you somehow forgot about. You'll get a slight reprieve for two weeks when Mercury pivots back into your sign on October 27. Crunch some numbers and find the most expedient way to get out of any jams.

October 15: Sun-Pluto square

You can't always time other people's crises for after work hours, and today, you might find yourself having to put out a fire remotely. Do whatever it takes to extinguish the flames, but don't enable anyone's dramatic behavior by giving this more airtime than it deserves.

October 16: Libra new moon

The only Libra new moon of 2020 may feel like a bonus birthday present—or your very own private New Year! This is a time to wipe the slate clean and embark on fresh initiatives that are near and dear to your heart. Write out your next set of goals by hand to power them up, and then take at least one step every day toward one of them!

October 18: Sun-Saturn square

Your skin may be especially thin under today's harsh planetary alignment, but try not to take everything personally! A critical clash between demanding Saturn and the radiant Sun in your sign can teach you to focus less on where you may be coming up short and more on where you're crushing it—as well as where you can grow along the way.

October 31: Taurus full moon

This annual full moon in your house of long-term wealth can bring a long-held investment to maturity or shine a light on an opportunity to join forces with a prominent player. If you haven't been thinking along those lines, the next few months may reveal someone without your even looking!

November

November 9: Venus-Mars opposition

You might revert to some old behavior patterns when the cosmic lovebirds start chirping out of harmony. And because Venus is your ruling planet, this could hit you hard. But you don't have to succumb to old fears or anxieties. Try to trace them to their ancient source, and adamantly remind yourself that that was then, and this is now!

November 12: Jupiter-Pluto meetup

The question of "home" has been a transformational ride for you this year, thanks to three conjunctions of expansive Jupiter and alchemical Pluto in your domestic fourth house. The first two, on April 4 and June 30, may have found you deeply questioning where (and how) you live, children and families of origin. At their third and final union, all that excavation and exploration could help you finally stumble upon your truth. Ready to start perusing the real estate listings or putting your name on a baby registry?

November 13: Mars retrograde ends

The excitable (and irritable) red planet has been reverse-commuting through your partnership sector since September 9, which may have sent some shock waves through a key relationship. Now you can take the high road, forgive all non-egregious offenses, and talk through ways you use those experiences to make the union stronger than ever. Single? It's safe to get back in the dating pool after a few disconcerting months!

November 15: Venus-Pluto square

You might not feel in control of your emotions today, as cagey Pluto drags some old baggage—and maybe a few skeletons—out of the closet. You may have no choice but to face them, but you don't have to be steamrolled by them. Look for the blessing in this big reveal: Perhaps seeing this pattern so clearly means you won't be able to hide from it in the future.

November 16: Venus-Jupiter square

Take a moment to tune in to your heart before you

The AstroTwins' 2020 Horoscope

lunge into your day. Under this distorting clash from amplifying Jupiter, you may underestimate what you truly need as well as how much you actually have to give. And this could leave you in an uncomfortable position. If someone close to you can't or won't meet those needs, you might have to rethink the very foundation of this relationship.

November 19: Venus-Saturn square

Sober Saturn splashes cold water at your ruler, amorous Venus, which could force you to face up to an unpleasant truth about someone you care about. It can be hard for your giving sign to put your needs first, but if you keep getting disappointed, that's a sign that things aren't likely to change. Have a chat about your visions for your futures. If they're not even close, it may be worth pulling the plug before you get in deeper.

November 21-December 15: Venus in Scorpio

As your galactic guardian, partnership-oriented Venus, spins through your second house of security, you may feel an increased need for stability and the desire to upgrade some of your lifestyle choices. If you're inching toward settling down with someone, have "the talk" to ensure you share the same values and long-range goals. Couples might want to sit with an adviser or do a deep review of their financials. This way you can make any necessary adjustments before heading into a new (tax) year.

November 27: Venus-Uranus opposition

Money could get funny under this disruptive face-off, and when it comes to finances, Libra, love cannot conquer all. You work hard for your living, and if a partner or new love interest isn't carrying their share of the fiscal load, it's going to be up to you to say something.

NOVEMBER: CAREER HOTSPOTS

November 1: Mercury-Saturn square

This is the second time these planets square off this season, and this go-round, the messenger planet is retrograde. You may believe you've thought through every angle and can talk about something in a calm, cool, objective way, but the first critical word could cut you to the quick. If you must engage, consider putting your thoughts into a carefully constructed—and well edited—email. You'll get one more hit of this energy on November 6, when Mercury is direct and communication might be easier.

November 3: Mercury retrograde ends

Misunderstood no more! As Mercury ends a retrograde that spent its last few days in your sign, you'll finally have a chance to voice your opinions… and actually feel heard. If you've been holding back on a big idea or announcement, it's safe to start spreading the news.

November 10-December 1: Mercury in Scorpio

You'll finally be able to make up your mind about an important financial or security issue after weeks of waffling. As mental Mercury resumes forward motion in your work and money corner, clarity will come, as well as the vision and self-discipline to start taking saving and investments more seriously.

November 13: Mars retrograde ends

A wobbly business association can get its sea legs back once Mars straightens out in your partnership house. A stalled negotiation could pick up where you left off two months ago. And all that frustration you've been holding in could finally be aired—just remember to be as diplomatic as you are direct.

December

November 15: Scorpio new moon

As the year's only Scorpio new moon galvanizes your second house of money, work and security, you can recommit to a financial goal. But don't gloss over this in a superficial way. You could make a major pivot if you really pour your heart and soul into this. Where would you like to be in six months, and what steps do you need to take to get there? Plan to take a giant one in the next two weeks to jumpstart your dream.

November 23: Mercury-Neptune trine

Leave plenty of room for serendipities under today's magical mashup of mental Mercury and intuitive Neptune. Don't think in terms of "either-or," and you might just open up a whole new world of possibilities!

November 28: Neptune retrograde ends

You can restore order to the Libra court starting today as hazy Neptune concludes a five-month retrograde that may have sent a chaotic ripple through your sixth house of systems, self-care and service providers. Set some new goals around getting more organized, starting with a major decluttering mission. Motivate yourself with small rewards to stay on track, and you'll have a big head start on your New Year's resolutions!

November 30: Gemini full moon (lunar eclipse)

Under the glow of this empowering full moon in your visionary ninth house—which is also a galvanizing lunar eclipse—you can take a lofty plan and start to manifest it step by concrete step. Tie up any loose ends that don't relate to this project so you pour all your prodigious energy into it.

DECEMBER: LOVE HOTSPOTS

December 5: Venus trine Neptune

This could be a dreamily sensual and enchanting day, perfect for pampering yourself (solo or together) or getting into a healthy groove in your relationship. Being of service to your partner can boost your bond, so be generous and compassionate. If you do have to offer any criticism or negative feedback, be gentle and come from a place of kindness.

December 15, 2020-January 9, 2021: Venus in Sagittarius

When your ruler, compassionate Venus, begins her annual visit to your third house of communication, you'll get a cosmic assist in articulating what's in your heart—which can make for some spicy pillow talk. Single? Keep your eyes peeled as you spend more time in your neighborhood this winter. A charming stranger could be waiting to sweep you off your fold-over booties.

December 17, 2020-March 7, 2023: Saturn in Aquarius

As structured Saturn returns to your zone *d'amour* for the duration of his long transit, love can turn serious when you least expect it. You might consciously decide to slow the pace or take your time with the courtship process, which is not unusual for your sign anyway. Saturn can retrain you to prioritize quality over quantity. Couples may need to pencil in time for romance and affection since you could suddenly become busy. In general, this is an extended opportunity to work on dismantling blocks to love in your heart.

     The AstroTwins' 2020 Horoscope

December 19, 2020-May 13, 2021: Jupiter in Aquarius

Expansive, auspicious Jupiter returns to your passionate fifth house for the first time in 12 years, ushering in a new era of amour and glamour. Regardless of your current status, the next year should be full of opportunities for romance, connection and, for some Libras, news of a pregnancy.

December 20, 2020-January 9, 2021: Mercury in Capricorn

You love confrontation about as much as root canals, but when the cosmic communicator flits into your emotional fourth house for the next three weeks, you may actually welcome the chance to speak candidly (and compassionately) about a delicate subject. Remember to be an active and engaged listener!

December 21: Jupiter-Saturn meetup (The Great Conjunction)

Love, actually? As starry-eyed Jupiter makes its once-every-35-years union with structured Saturn, lofty possibilities could start to become real. Today these planets link up in Aquarius and your fifth house of passion and fertility. This could bring exciting baby news, deepened affection or an attractive prospect with long-term potential.

December 23: Mars-Pluto square

Sometimes the greatest breakthroughs come on the heels of what you might consider a breakdown, but hang in there! As these heavyweight planets collide, old issues could come up so starkly that you simply can't ignore them anymore. The only way to heal, as they say, is to deal. Get the support you need to soldier on, and look forward to a positive shift in an intimate relationship before the calendar turns!

December 30: Venus-Neptune square

Holiday stress could be to blame for recent mixed signals and mood swings—or it may be the biannual clash of Venus and unrealistic Neptune. But trying harder won't do much good since your attempts to have a rational discussion will likely only confuse matters more. Better to ride it out and avoid making any irrevocable decisions until this confusion passes.

DECEMBER: CAREER HOTSPOTS

December 1-20: Mercury in Sagittarius

As the eloquent messenger planet lights up your communication sector for the next several weeks, you could find the missing puzzle piece in a writing, marketing or social media initiative. Sagittarius energy helps you be more spontaneous and think outside the box, so calibrate your antenna and see what you can call in.

December 13: Mercury-Neptune square

Stay on guard for a charming manipulator attempting to butter you up and get you to do their bidding. Regardless of how much time you have or how generous you're feeling, you need to uphold your boundaries—for your sake (because who knows what legit assignment will land in your lap)—and to let them know you're on to their antics.

December 14: Sagittarius new moon (total solar eclipse)

This stimulating new moon—also a potent total solar eclipse—electrifies your communication corner and might inspire you to reach out to someone you've identified as a potential client, boss or associate. Sagittarius style is larger than life, so don't hold back on the razzle-dazzle. Let your authentic passion show through, and you'll have them at hello.

December 19, 2020-May 13, 2021: Jupiter in Aquarius

When expansive and boundless Jupiter blasts into your fifth house of creativity and fame, you could hit on a new approach to an old problem that's downright revolutionary—and that puts your name on your industry map. After a year of hosting the gaseous giant in your domestic quarters, you're more than ready to unleash your fierceness and shatter any perceived glass ceilings!

December 25: Mercury-Uranus trine

Oh right, it's Christmas! But your brain isn't working on a calendar, and when the brilliant brainstorms strike, all you can do is try your best to capture them so that when everyone is back at work, you'll have something well-thought-out enough to present to the decisionmakers. Explain your "genius situation" to your loved ones, and (hopefully) they'll understand!

December 29: Cancer full moon

The year wraps up as it began—with a full moon in Cancer and your professional tenth house (the first was on January 10). What have you been working toward all year, whether actively or on a back-burner basis? Make the last calls, put the finishing touches on the written part, and you could sail into your holidays with a major coup under your belt and a clear vision of your 2021 priorities! ✳

SCORPIO
2020

Yearly Highlights

LOVE

Flirt alert! The Scorpio coquette comes out to play, as bawdy Jupiter joins your ruler, sultry Pluto, in your communication corner. As a general rule, you prefer the depth and security of long-term relationships. But in 2020, a few sweet, ephemeral flings keep you fulfilled "in the meanwhile." Digital dating could bring a lucky swipe, or a friendship may evolve into true love. Coupled Scorpios should put more cultural activities on the shared calendar and mingle often as a pair. On November 30, the Gemini lunar eclipse brings a milestone moment for relationships.

MONEY

Put your money where your mouth is! With a planetary posse in Capricorn activating your third house of communication, it's time to start talking about your big ideas and professional goals. Casual conversation could open the doors to opportunity, and this is a year to make "network" your favorite verb. Writing, teaching, PR and digital media are all favored for Scorpios this year. Partner up for success—with a coworker or a local business owner.

WELLNESS

Deep breaths, Scorpio. The frenetic social pace of 2020 could spike your anxiety. You'll find it hard to turn off your brain at times, so adopt soothing practices. Power down digital devices at least an hour before bed, and journal to get spinning thoughts out of your head. Set up a sleep sanctuary with meditative music and an aromatherapy diffuser. Ample exercise is key to keeping stress levels at bay, especially after June 27, when energizing Mars zooms through Aries and your wellness corner for an extended six-month tour.

LEISURE

Relationships with relatives are in the spotlight all year, thanks to Saturn's do-si-do between your third house of siblings and family-oriented fourth. You could squash an ancient rivalry with your brother or start a business with your enterprising cousins. A new friend circle could grow tight enough to be dubbed your "chosen family," especially between March and July. Worldly Jupiter and stable Saturn team up in your domestic quarters starting December 19. How you spend the holidays, and who you spend them with, will be a big deal to negotiate as the year closes. ✸

SCORPIO ♏↗

2020 HOROSCOPE

2020 Power Dates

✳

SCORPIO NEW MOON
November 15 (12:07am ET)

SCORPIO FULL MOON
May 7 (6:45am ET)

SUN IN SCORPIO
October 22 – November 21

Your investigative sign loves a mystery, and there will be no shortage of riddles to solve in 2020. But this year will be different in one fundamental way: To crack any case, lead with curiosity, not suspicion. Did your eternally raised eyebrow just shoot up another millimeter? We're not surprised. But trust us Scorpio, the journey can be as blissful as the destination.

At times, this year will feel like a rollercoaster ride, kind of like the line from the cult classic Pee Wee's Big Adventure, where your Scorpio signmate Pee Wee Herman exclaims, "It's like you're unraveling a big cable-knit sweater that someone keeps knitting and knitting and knitting…" Keep pulling at those loose threads and eventually the full story will reveal its pattern. Stay engaged, even when you're frustrated. It's hard for your savvy sign to remember this, but here goes: You don't have to have it all figured out. Surrender to the unknown and let 2020 take you on a magical mystery tour!

It's certainly going to be more entertaining than *last* year! From November 2018 until early December 2019, expansive Jupiter was grinding away in

Sagittarius and your second house of work and daily routines. The perks may have included a new job and better pay. But the responsibilities of your new revenue streams also left your nose fixed to the grindstone—there was no free lunch in 2019! If your social life withered on the vine as a result, it's no surprise.

On December 2, 2019, jovial Jupiter merged lanes into Capricorn, joining stoic Saturn and your ruler, magnetic Pluto, in your convivial, mercurial third house. In 2020, these three planets are involved in a sweet choreography, gliding in close (and at some points, exact!) contact with each other all year. But since their energies are so different, figuring out which planet is leading could feel like an eternal dance-off inside your head. Should you be effusively friendly (Jupiter) or play it cool (Saturn)? Or maybe be alluringly esoteric and make them come to you (Pluto)?

Instead of fixating on this, make fun your focus in 2020. For your serious sign, this might can be downright revolutionary. Could it be that…simple? Yes, Scorpio, it can. And if you open yourself up to experimentation instead of trying to find "*the* thing," this could be the most buzzworthy year you've had in over a decade! As one of the zodiac's four fixed signs (along with Taurus, Leo and Aquarius), you pride yourself on being the expert and authority in your field. As such, you tend to focus intently on one thing at a time. Switch up your strategy this year because 2020 is all about being a dabbling dilletante instead. As you lifehack your way into this new decade, you'll gain the breadth of knowledge to match your inherent depth. A formidable combination! As you log a library of new references and experiences into your powerful memory bank, you'll be a walking, talking oracle.

Stretching your mental wingspan won't require you to travel far, since the third house rules local activity. But no matter what, your mind and your mouth will be in motion! Short-term education falls under the domain of the third house. Be the queen of the workshop scene or the emperor of online courses. The requisite training could be a Lyft ride—or a log-in—away!

Any sort of intellectual stimulation will be a major turn-on this year, and single Scorpios will bore quickly of people who can't match your brains and wit. A sapiosexual connection, however, will be a huge aphrodisiac. And while you'll be an unrepentant flirt, don't forget that you *are* a Scorpio, and you have a baseline need for stability and security.

With love planet Venus fluttering through Gemini from April 3 to August 7, you'll be in your erotic element this spring and summer. Single Scorpios could magnetize a mate who is both delectable and devoted. Surprise! An old flame could be rekindled while Venus is retrograde from May 13 to June 25. But if you sense this might turn into a dumpster fire, keep that door firmly closed.

Thankfully, there will be some grounding action going on at the bottom of your chart this year, in Aquarius and your fourth house of roots. From March 21 to July 1, stabilizing Saturn hunkers down in the Water Bearer's domain. You may feel some early rumblings of domesticity this spring and summer, but don't rush into apartment-hunting yet! Wait until Saturn returns to this realm for a longer trek from December 17, 2020, to March 7, 2023. Toward the end of the year, lucky, expansive Jupiter joins the nesting expedition, flowing through Aquarius from December 19, 2020, to December

29, 2021. Near the holidays, you could make an important decision about your living arrangements or a meaningful family matter.

The second half of 2020 could bring exciting financial developments. Beginning June 5, a series of Gemini/Sagittarius eclipses will power up your money axis for 18 months. Eclipses bring hidden possibilities to light, and there are three that touch down here this year, on June 5, November 30 and December 14. These initiatives won't just stay on the "Great ideas I'll work on someday" spreadsheet. From June 27, 2020, until January 6, 2021, motivator Mars takes an extended voyage through Aries and your industrious sixth house. The second half of the year is all about turning your ideas into tangible form!

This Mars cycle will bring lots of momentum for a wellness quest. But you'll have to fight your tendency to obsessively burrow into work. Put in measures so you don't skip meals or let exercise slip until you get the job done. Make healthy eating and movement a non-negotiable part of your daily routines. Lean into Saturn's flair for structure and schedule your work around your wellbeing—instead of the other way. A radical notion, but one that will keep fuel in your tank!

Jupiter in Capricorn: Spread your message.

December 2, 2019 – December 19, 2020

Mayor Scorpio in the house? Your low-key sign can be more of an observer than a joiner, but that changes now. As the new decade dawns, you'll feel the call to step up as social director, rallying friends for everything from cultural activities to community activism. You can thank jovial Jupiter for this people-centric surge. From December 2, 2019, until December 19, 2020, the magnanimous planet is strutting through your third house of communication, friendship and local activity. No more hiding your shrewd gaze behind dark glasses (a la fellow Scorpios Anna Wintour and Diddy) and oversized headphones cranked to full volume. Before this year is through, you could become a bona fide "people person," waving into shop windows and stopping along your commute to exchange lively bits of conversation. How refreshing!

For the past two years, your (Capricorn-ruled) third house has been activated by two "dark and stormy" planets, Pluto and Saturn. Regenerative Pluto has been parked in this zone since late 2008, which has spawned major transformations. Certain niceties have been stripped away, allowing you to reveal a more authentic side of your personality. Your daily circumstances have undergone a lot of change since then. Maybe you switched jobs and homes multiple times or had a revolving cast of friends or coworkers weave in and out of your life. Despite your tingling Spidey senses, it's been hard to tell a trusted ally from a casual friend…or frenemy! Pluto remains in Capricorn until 2024, but this year, Scorpios born from November 11 to 19 will feel your cosmic custodian's alchemical beams most intensely.

Over the past two years, you've started to create more enduring connections. Credit grounded Saturn for this. On December 19, 2017, the stabilizing planet shifted into Capricorn, steering you towards people who were capable of returning your devotion. Maybe you planted yourself in a single zip code, or created a more consistent rhythm in your daily life, which also helped. With ambitious Saturn guiding your extracurricular sector, "networking" has been one of your favorite ways to meet people since late 2017. Partying? Sure, if there was a purpose behind it, like raising money for an important cause or the chance to meet influential people.

In 2020, the ringed planet weaves in and out of the Sea Goat's sector, continuing its mission to level up your social life. Quality over quantity has always been your strategy when it comes to making friends. But over the past two years, the criteria for joining Club Scorpio has become even more exclusive. In 2020, you'll continue to mingle in elite circles, like a members-only club or professional organization. Nothing wrong with being discerning, but socializing for socializing's sake may have fallen by the wayside.

Now that Jupiter's joined the celestial squad, the mood will be so much lighter! (Can we get an amen?) While you might never reach full extrovert status, your appetite for good company and stimulating conversation could get higher than it's been in years. Make a budget for wardrobe—day into evening and "off-duty" for impromptu weekend getaways. While you're at it, invest in a chic, oversized tote for all your costume changes. During this buzzy year, an average day could mean wrapping up your last client call then zipping to 5:30 yoga before meeting a date for dinner…with a quick detour to a friend's art opening along the way.

With outspoken Jupiter in the mix, your mind and your mouth will be active. Speak up, Scorpio! By vocalizing your vision, you literally can change people's lives. Your thoughts and opinions have always run deep, but for the past decade, Pluto has kept many of them locked in the vault. Restraining Saturn didn't help much either. As Jupiter loosens your lips, you're ready to unleash in 2020—and a few sorry souls are about to get read like an entire Barnes and Noble section. But think before you live-drag anyone across social media! Sure, you could become a decorated general in the Twitter wars, banishing the trolls to Middle Earth like Gandalf the Grey. But before you get tangled in every thread, remember to self-regulate screen time so it doesn't take over your life!

> "By vocalizing your vision, you literally can change people's lives."

Speaking of which, all things mobile fall under the domain of the third house. As entrepreneurial Jupiter leaps into the ring with power players Saturn and Pluto, let your visionary side take the wheel. What daily aspects of your life could use more streamlining, and, more importantly, is there an app for that? If not, opportunity knocks! There's hardly been a better year for Scorpios to make money in the digital space. If you can help people organize, track and schedule their data, you may soon be hearing the "cha-ching!" of revenue flow into your account from every download or in-app purchase. Creating social sharing tools or groups will also be a draw for some Scorpios. How can you unite people around a common cause or interest? Start an online community or a Facebook Page. It could take on a powerful life of its own!

The third house rules your message, and Jupiter is the sign of publishing. Is there a manuscript rattling around in your head? Three times this year—on April 4, June 30 and November 12—Jupiter will meet up with transformational Pluto. As Jupiter shines its high beams into this zone of your chart, all that hidden genius that Pluto's been guarding in the vault could be illuminated. If you need to have this data copyrighted, call the lawyers, stat. Just don't keep your brilliance locked away, Scorpio. The zeitgeist is clamoring for your niche ideas!

We could write a book about all the Scorpios who have shifted the cultural landscape by creating art and media from their unique purview. Editor Jane Pratt founded the game-changing Sassy magazine. Debbie Stoller brought us the feminist magazine, *BUST,* which is one of the few of its kind that is still in print since the 1990s. Simultaneously, Stoller authored a series of needlecraft guidebooks with a punk-rock Scorpionic twist: *Stitch and Bitch* for knitting and *The Happy Hooker* for crochet. Leave it to a Scorpio to thread together seemingly disparate things—feminism and the reclaiming of traditional women's crafts—as a tool for empowerment.

Whatever your passion, "unapologetic originality" is your metric for success in 2020. And you'll have lots of local support for your mission! Stay alert. You could stumble upon a venue that's been hidden in plain sight. Maybe it's a local theater that will debut your one-Scorpio show. Or a maker's market where you sell handcrafted wares. A familiar space could also yield new possibilities. How about hosting a weekly open mic at your favorite dive bar?

Vibrant new friendships will arise in 2020, kindred spirits who might even become project partners. The key this year is to dabble and experiment, but not to lock yourself into anything binding or exclusive. Start small and grow organically. With

risk-taker Jupiter igniting this dynamic-duo zone, why not test your chemistry on a trial project and see how your styles mesh? Pro tip: This might be best done while restraining Saturn is out of the picture, between March 21 and July 1. Generally, you prefer to lock things down with an ironclad contract (signed in blood), but not this year. For a change you will be the one saying things like, "Let's just start small and see how it goes."

The key to success lies in finding people whose skills complement yours, then syncing your superpowers. For example, maybe you're an experimental DJ whose gift for mashing up rare, back-catalog beats leaves the party people spellbound. But you're also so engrossed in your process that you never think, "I should Instagram myself looping and scratching!" Team up with a savvy marketing wizard who makes sure your live performances get posted to event calendars, and that there are videos taken of you working the Midi controllers and moving the crowds! But no excuses, Scorpio. If you want to create a name for yourself in 2020, you'll have to surrender and go digital. Many among your sign are naturally tech-savvy, so there's no need to be intimidated. Get acquainted with the wonders of easy platforms such as Wix, Squarespace and Medium, to give your brilliance some visual (and shareable) appeal. You might invest in a publicist or social media pro to help build buzz.

With info-hungry Jupiter occupying these curious quarters, learning is an adventure! You could take mini-courses that build your skills or earn you a certification. But hold off on the serious degree programs. The "school of life" could be more appealing than any ivory tower. Experiment with new hobbies, especially DIY ones where you can make things by hand. Have you always wanted to learn how to play keyboards or craft your own custom-blended perfumes? Find a workshop or an online course. With your communication zone lit, this is a great year to take a writing workshop, memoir class or a webinar like Marie Forleo's The Copy Cure. When the student is ready (and Jupiter's in the third house), the perfect teacher will appear. Or, maybe you'll be the one putting together a curriculum. Funnel your wisdom into a webinar or workshop and hang your shingle!

Although Saturn probably kept you stationary for the past two years, nomadic Jupiter could give you itchy feet in 2020. With the globetrotting planet in your local action zone, you might hop between multiple cities or become officially bicoastal. Work may require frequent trips between two locations. Treat yourself to a sturdy (and stylish) carry-on suitcase that you can wheel around on these jaunts. You might also get more creative with your commute, investing in a bike or an electric scooter. One Scorpio friend is an environmentalist whose commitment to climate crisis solutions involves not driving anything that uses fossil fuels. With new models of electric cars coming to market, she might be back behind the wheel as this decade dawns.

If you're thinking of relocating, this is a great year to "try before you buy." Airbnb was basically invented for this Jupiter cycle. Jet off on as many short trips as you can, staying for a few days in an appealing city or district that you're considering calling home. Get up and go through your daily routine as if you lived there: find the coffee shop, the yoga studio, the health food store. Or hey, Scorpio, maybe give #VanLife a try so you can take your perfectly curated home on the road. Optional bonus: Invest in a great camera and document the journey.

Single Scorpios will be irrepressible flirts, and let's be honest, even if you're in a relationship, that's never stopped your seductive charms from unspooling. As long as you know where that bright line of fidelity lies, well, no, it's not cheating. In fact, allowing your inner vixen to come out and play can be a healthy aphrodisiac! By the time you're back home to your partner, you'll be turned on and ready to romp. Digital dating could bring a healthy number of options for single Scorpios in 2020. Log on to the apps, and let friends play matchmaker.

Attached? Careful that you don't get swept into an "affair by text" while your third house of mobile technology is on fire. Even if you never actually touch, sending pictures of your naughty bits or logging on to Tinder "just to see what people are posting these days" will lead down a slippery slope.

Same thing goes for providing "emotional support" to your coworker crush or your unnervingly attractive friend. (You know…the one you hooked up with once in 2014 but have never discussed the incident with since?) As life starts to imitate a rom-com this year, attention from these "will-they-won't-they" types packs some allure. For you, that's a fast track to obsession, Scorpio. Even if you're single, indulging people who are "otherwise engaged" can be a huge distraction from your own #RelationshipGoals.

Of course, maybe that's your sneaky unconscious at play. Are you avoiding true intimacy by filling your time with people who "aren't ready" and never seem to be? Like attracts like, Scorpio. Even if you swear you want something real, hidden fears may be blocking you from getting close to a partner. Work on fostering self-love and self-acceptance rather than creating these distracting smokescreens.

There is someone out there who will adore you unconditionally, even on your stormiest days. Who knows? They might be standing right next to you, but you've just been pushing them away.

Saturn-Pluto conjunction: Get transparent.
December 2019–February 2020 (exact on January 12)

How strong are the signals in the Scorpio Communication Station? Adjust your internal satellite tower on January 12, when an ultra-rare convergence of Saturn and Pluto beams into Capricorn and your third house of messaging. These potent planets have inched closer to each other since late 2017 and have been in high-frequency contact since December 2019. On January 12, they make an exact hit, at 22°46' Capricorn, which only happens every 33 to 38 years.

With your ruler, subterranean Pluto, in this zone since November 27, 2008, your inner life has been richer than ever. But most people aren't privy to that. Structured Saturn rules the material realm, where things can be measured and adjusted. This union of Pluto and Saturn will bring your esoteric thoughts, visions and ideas into tangible form.

Take inventory: How do you represent yourself to the outer world? What signals do you "transmit" when you walk into the room? Scorpios radiate power, from magnanimous sex appeal to simmering intensity that can be outright intimidating. But how authentic is this image you're projecting…really?

Forcing people to decipher your communication is just plain "extra" in 2020. Throw your fans a bone and clarify where you're coming from.

Near January 12, you may radically alter your messaging, so that people can actually see past your cloak of invisibility. But as you turn the lens on your hidden thoughts, brace for what Scorpio Brené Brown calls a "vulnerability hangover." Letting it all hang out isn't your style, especially when it comes to all you've got swirling below the surface. Even if you're the type of Scorpio who dresses like a bikini model at a lowrider exhibition (no shame in that!), your internal landscape could still remain a mystery. But near the Saturn-Pluto conjunction, you could lighten up that privacy policy and share a broader range of emotions.

It could take a few life-hacks to step into this new frontier. For example, you could cultivate a "persona" for your front-facing self, at least initially. Scorpio Kurt Vonnegut said, "You are whatever you pretend to be." Not that we're recommending that you totally fake it, Scorpio. Quite the contrary! But what if you amplified the character that represents your full-bodied expression?

Scorpio RuPaul has masterfully walked that line, sending up a message of fierce self-expression (with a side of snappy lexicon). Most people would be surprised to know that the Drag Race host spends his off-duty hours on a Wyoming ranch with his camera-shy, Australian-born husband. The two have been an item since 1994, when they met at the storied NYC nightclub Limelight. Despite Ru's media draw, their relationship remains private and tabloid-free. It's the best of both worlds for a Scorpio superstar.

If you could break out the trunk of wigs and sequined dresses (metaphorically speaking… or not), who would you "become" in 2020? For Scorpios who are still struggling to step into the spotlight, Saturn and Pluto can act as powerful runway coaches this January. Don't rush through this process or try to figure it all out in the first month of 2020. For some Scorpios, it could take all year to "rebrand" yourself in a way that hits the mark. Call in the pros: vocal coaches, graphic designers, digital media experts. When spotlight-beaming Jupiter connects with Pluto on April 4, June 30 and November 12, you'll have three golden opportunities to debut your developments.

Has a joint project been picking up steam? With power-brokers Saturn and Pluto spurring you on, January 12 could be the day where you formalize your collaboration. Is money trading hands? Spell out financial agreements to the letter, and have a lawyer put the terms into an actual contract. Pluto rules investments, so think long-term. A product or process that you co-create could fill the coffers for years to come, perhaps through royalties, licensing fees, or a future buyout.

January 12 could bring an eye-opening moment about the company you keep. Close friendships from 2019 may drift apart, or your connection to one of your peers (a sibling, coworker or BFF) could hit a challenging growth phase. Instead of fighting for things to stay the same—or going mano-a-mano over who's right—lean in to Saturn's restraint. Modern Kabbalah advises that we "restrict our reactions" in order to allow the light of higher consciousness in. In January, the best response might just be doing nothing! Breathe, punch a pillow, scream into the ether. But save that retaliatory, defensive message to your Drafts folder

(then, once you simmer down, you'll probably migrate it to the Trash).

Saturn is the ruler of our most precious resource: time. Why waste yours on people who disrupt your inner peace or drag you down with their drama? Spend your sacred hours with people who make your world feel bigger, brighter and way more exciting. New decade, new you, new crew!

Venus & Mars Retrograde: Relationship review.
Venus Retrograde: May 14 – June 25

Mars Retrograde: September 10 – November 13

A sexy spring awakening could jolt your libido out of hibernation this April 3, when sensual Venus sashays into Gemini and struts down the catwalk of your erotic eighth house until August 7. Since this is the "Scorpio house" of the zodiac wheel, you'll be in your seductive element. Meow! Normally, Venus visits a zodiac sign for three to five weeks. But due to her biennial retrograde from May 13 to June 25, 2020, she'll hover in Gemini four times longer than her usual spell. Take a deep breath, Scorpio. When Venus flips into reverse, some of that seduction could turn into intrigue, but those cat-and-mouse games may leave you dizzy.

During this six-week signal-jammer, you simply can't rely on your intuitive senses—or your tarot deck—to read what's going on with other people. Retrogrades stir up the past and Venus' pivot could bring an old flame back into the picture who actually has soulmate potential. If the connection is still strong, it could be worth exploring, but don't expect to get a clear read on the situation until after June 25. If you hear from a toxic ex, don't kid yourself about developing a "friendship." Just follow this three-step plan: ignore, delete, block!

If you want to create intimacy, you're going to have to pry open the chamber of secrets, Scorpio, and (glug) get vulnerable. The good thing about a planetary retrograde is that it can help you plunge into deeper waters. If you raced into a relationship without reviewing practical considerations (like, say, incompatible life paths or totally different financial values) you may have to tap the brakes. Or maybe you've been hiding something that's really important to you, but you're afraid to say it for fear of coming on too strong. Time for some serious soul baring. It's the only way forward between May 13 and June 25. Eventually, anyone you date or do business with will find out the truth. That's the beauty of relationships: being loved for all of who you are.

On the flip side, it might be your partner who has the deep, dark secret to share. While you don't want to interrogate like a CIA agent, don your sexiest Sherlock cap and create a safe space for real talk. If you hear something jarring, you don't have to freak out, but definitely don't sweep it under the rug. Between April 3 and August 7, figure out if your styles mesh—and if you can establish enough trust to accompany the lust!

Grab your glue gun and fire up the cold-pressed juicer. Go-getter Mars will spend the second half of 2020 in Aries, overhauling your sixth house of work and wellness from June 27 to January 6, 2021.

During this time, you'll be obsessed with routines—and you'll definitely need to have some solid ones in place by September 9, when Mars turns retrograde until November 13. Your stress levels may be directly proportional to your fitness regimen. If you aren't grounded and prepared, this two-month window might turn your neatly ordered universe inside out and upside down.

Not that this is necessarily a bad thing, Scorpio. As one of the zodiac's fixed signs, you can get stuck in a groove, taking the safe route when it's time for a risk. With swashbuckling Mars on this extended tour through fearless Aries, any shakeups that arise could be a blessing in disguise. These unexpected developments could lead to a new job or snap you out of a self-destructive pattern, forcing you to take better care of your health.

When it comes to your professional power plays, the devil will be in the details from June 27 to January 6. Make sure you can walk your talk and make good on your guarantees. Better to under-promise and overdeliver, especially during the retrograde. Exceeding expectations will impress people. You may have to develop plans with a tighter, scaled-back budget until after November 13.

The sixth house rules helpful people, and a reliable service provider may suddenly become unavailable while Mars is in reverse. Don't tell yourself that good help is hard to find (though it may be hard to trust...especially for a capable Scorpio.) Instead of picking up the slack and wearing yourself out, write up your criteria for an ideal candidate. Someone you worked with in the past may return with an updated skill set, ready to be your right hand.

Stress management is a must to remain centered through it all. Give your gym membership a workout, develop a stronger yoga practice or ping a fitness buddy to help you stay motivated. The hardest part is actually getting off the couch. Once you're in motion, the kinetic energy will build. And no need to overdo it! While Mars is retrograde, a less aggressive workout is preferable to anything that could put you at risk of overtraining and getting hurt. It's time to deal with an old injury or health issue that you've been ignoring. This may be more of a process than a quick fix, though. For example, try sessions with a chiropractor before impatiently signing up for an elective surgery, or work with a nutritionist instead of a punishing 30-day Master Cleanse. A sustainable lifestyle shift will do you more good than a month of maple syrup and cayenne pepper.

Saturn in Aquarius: Putting down roots.

March 21–July 1
December 17, 2020–March 7, 2023

Longing to plant deeper roots, Scorpio? In 2020, you begin to crave a permanent sense of "home." Serious Saturn drops into Aquarius briefly, fortifying your fourth house of family and foundations from March 21 to July 1. No, you might not be ready to commit to mortgaging that Gothic manor on the hill. (And not just because the property tax is insane!) With Saturn in the house, thoughtful and discerning choices are a must. Take your time! This three-month cycle will give you a preview of what's to come, making it a better time to shop around

thoroughly. On December 17, Saturn will roost in Aquarius for a longer phase, activating your nesting instincts through March 7, 2023.

Where does your life need more long-term planning and security? Wherever Saturn is parked, you are pushed to mature. Between March 21 and July 1, you may already be presented with scenarios that test your mettle. Are you still holding on to childhood patterns, or a dependency (emotional or financial) upon others to provide a baseline need? This is the year to give up the "binky," Scorpio, and prove to yourself how capable you truly are. By midsummer, you could feel a brand-new sense of self-confidence in an area of life that you never learned to "adult" in—no matter what your biological age.

While you might not be ready for bigger moves like house-hunting or renovating the bathroom until Saturn takes up longer-term residence in Aquarius on December 17, research while you can! Get the Pinterest board going with brass fixtures, marble-slab countertops and artisan tiles. Test the waters in a potential home location with a short-term Airbnb stay. This will be eye-opening. Who knows? You might instantly know that *this is the place*! Or, like Dorothy coming back to Kansas, your time in Oz may cultivate a greater appreciation for that "boring suburbia" or "noisy, dirty city" you wanted to flee. Maybe you just needed a little sabbatical to show you that where you started wasn't so bad after all. Or perhaps you'll move to a different part of town that's walkable, or greener, or whatever's most important to you.

This isn't going to be the easiest Saturn phase in the world, Scorpio. While in Aquarius, Saturn forms a challenging 90-degree angle (called a "square") to your Sun. Squares force us to stop procrastinating

       The AstroTwins' 2020 Horoscope

and go face the music that's been piping in through the soft speakers of our subconscious for a while. Because Saturn's job is to bring structure and form, there's no skating by on platitudes. Your Aquarius-ruled fourth house sits at the very bottom of the zodiac wheel and represents your ultimate foundation. Is yours shaky or solid? Saturn is like a cosmic building inspector who arrives to ensure that everything's up to code. And while pouring concrete and patching up cracks is hard work, you can't build on top of a shoddy construction. This year, Saturn puts on the hard hat and sends you into the trenches.

Saturn was last in Aquarius from February 6, 1991, to January 28, 1994. If you can recall back that far, you may see similar themes arise. Or, look back to the period from October 6, 2012, to September 17, 2015, when Saturn was in Scorpio. You're now at a turning point, where you can reflect on progress you've made since then. The last seven years have been all about establishing your individuality and personal identity. This next Saturn quarter, which spans another seven years, helps you find a home. You'll also find a sense of rootedness within yourself during this phase, an emotional foundation that you can carry everywhere.

If you've outgrown your current lifestyle, Saturn will slowly guide you to your next address. On a literal level, you might move into a different living situation, establish a financial nest egg or stabilize your family relationships. Maybe you've been a renter for years and want to invest in your own place. You could take out a home equity loan to add a second bath or turn your spare bedroom into temporary shelter for a relative who's fallen on hard times. That said, Scorpio, you are ultra-sensitive to all energy in your space. Scheduling a renovation

when you're studying for a licensing exam, say, could be more than just a logistic nightmare. And letting a troubled family member stay for more than a few nights can throw off your whole internal balance. Plans like these need to be carefully considered, especially between March 21 and July 1, then over the December holidays.

Female health falls under the fourth house domain, and some Scorpios might deal with reproductive or hormone-related changes (which happen to be governed by your sign). Be patient with your family planning, because restrictive Saturn could bring slowdowns around a pregnancy, IVF or adoption. The silver lining? This buys you time to make sure your life is truly set up for a new member of your household.

The fourth house is traditionally associated with women and mothers, and Saturn is the planet that governs authority figures. Between March and July, examine your relationship with your mom, a female-identified relative or a child. Scorpio parents may start becoming *bona fide* disciplinarians in 2020, even if it pains your intuitive sign to treat your kid like anything less than "a spiritual being having a human experience." Some Scorpios could become the caregiver for an aging parent or grieve a departed loved one. Growing pains around your kith and kin are possible during this Saturn in Aquarius window.

The way you "mother" yourself will also be a crucial component of your 2020 wellness plan. Time to nurture Numero Uno, especially if you've been skipping breakfast for years, relying on caffeine (or other things) to stay productive, and forgoing workouts when you're obsessively sucked into a project. That all changes March 21, at least if you want to keep running at optimal speed. Pay special attention to gut health and digestion, which can determine everything from your energy levels to your immune system to your finely-honed Scorpio intuition. Start by replacing processed foods with pesticide-free and plant-based fare, "good fats" and lean proteins. After that, you might experiment with a microbiome diet, or work in supplements like probiotics, bitters and digestive enzymes.

Regimented Saturn asks you to be more formal about scheduling self-care. You'll have to consciously carve out time while the ringed taskmaster flows through the Water Bearer's realm. The body, after all, is the "soul's address" here on Earth. Slip out for that lunchtime express yoga, and if you don't have time to cook, try a healthy meal delivery service. It could be more economical than your "hangry" Whole Foods lunch runs where you mindlessly fill your cart and overspend.

While Saturn in the fourth house can make you feel like a kid in the time-out chair, think of this as a teachable moment in your astrological history. A life of stability doesn't have to be boring, Scorpio, even for the adrenaline junkies among you. Just plan a few epic vacations and sign up for extracurriculars to counteract any cabin fever or "shut-in" feelings. Too much time between the same four walls is no good either.

Many Scorpios are masterful at decorating your spaces. Besides having a great sense of color and mood, your private sign needs to retreat to a sacred oasis. Saturn reminds you that form follows function. You might decide to take down your wall of vintage lithographs and set up a bulletin board and bookshelf for a home office. By the time Saturn heads back into Aquarius for a longer run

on December 17, you'll be ready to reclaim every random corner for a designated purpose. Most likely it will involve an empire-building effort that extends until March 2023. The holidays could be a productive time at Chateau Scorpio!

The Great Conjunction: Jupiter & Saturn unite.
December 21

In the final weeks of 2020, you'll be in your "eagle nature," Scorpio. The loyal creature, which represents the higher expression of your sign, is known for building a permanent nest and returning to it year after year. But don't start on the lowest-hanging branch. On December 19, globalist Jupiter joins stabilizer Saturn in Aquarius, tossing a wrench in the works. Have you expanded your search parameters wide enough, Scorpio? Or are you settling for what's convenient and familiar? Worldly Jupiter is not trying to hear that! Since the next three years could make you a permanent resident of one provenance, you owe it to yourself to cast the widest net and see what's *really* out there.

Jupiter hovers in Aquarius until December 29, 2021, and caravans beside Saturn for 13 months. But on December 21, the two will meet at the exact same degree in the sky (0°29' Aquarius), combining their formidable powers. This event is so rare that astrologers have a special name for it: The Great Conjunction. The last one took place on May 31, 2000, and we won't see another one for 20 years after this.

While a monumental event may not take place *exactly* on December 21, for a few weeks before and after, you may feel both the cementing influence of Saturn and the electrifying excitement of Jupiter. These planets are opposites. Saturn restrains and contracts, Jupiter liberates and expands. Together, they'll either duke it out or figure out how to combine their powers to help you with the "checks and balances" of any decisions surrounding family, financial security and domestic bliss.

With this in mind, you might want to plan ahead for the holidays. And by "plan" we *don't* mean doing the same old thing you've done every single year. While Saturn cleaves to tradition, Jupiter clamors for reinvention. Rocking around the Christmas tree (or menorah, kinara, et *al.*) could suddenly feel stultifying to dutiful Scorpio, who will be ready to shake up the status quo. On the other hand, if you haven't been home for the holidays in years, you may return with an "adult" perspective, finally making peace with your parents—and your past.

Go ahead, Scorpio, stand on ceremony. Just do it with a twist. How about meeting the family in Sydney and opening presents under palm trees instead a Douglas Fir? Or sidestep the whole, "Who's hosting?" drama and rent out a banquet room at a Filipino restaurant with tableside karaoke. Since the fourth house rules maternal figures, you might ring in the New Year doing something for the ultimate nurturer, Mother Earth. Look into "voluntourism" opportunities, like helping reforestation missions, cleaning plastic out of oceans or assisting at a coral nursery.

Since Saturn rules time and history, you could feel a bit melancholy about how quickly the years are passing. That's more reason to cherish those moments with your nearest and dearest, but also to make some new ones, guided by Jupiter's adventurousness.

One thing's for sure: As you move into 2021, you'll be reworking your formula for domestic bliss. Whether you stay put in your beloved home, invest in a *pied-a-terre*, or turn the focus to your body, remember this: Wherever you go, there you are. While it's true that your environment and the surrounding culture have influence, this rare cycle will be about fortifying your *inner* world. Developing a meditation or breathwork practice (or both) is a time-tested way of coming home to yourself, even when there's chaos swirling all around you. Let the *Eat, Pray, Love* adventures begin!

Cancer/Capricorn Eclipses: Share your big ideas.
January 10, June 21, July 5

Mic drop! As new ideas flood in this year, you won't be shy about articulating them in colorful ways. Since July 2018, a series of game-changing eclipses in Cancer and Capricorn have been striking your communication axis, helping you formulate profound theories. In 2019, four more of these eclipses unearthed fascinating data to support your vision. The research and development will continue in 2020, as three final eclipses round out this series.

Start testing your philosophies on an audience this year. While you may get a mixed response initially, stay open to feedback! Criticism is worth its weight in cryptocurrency if you can listen to it as "market research." People are inherently self-focused. They want to know, "What's in it for me?" You might have the most incredible product in the world, Scorpio, but if you can't explain how it will make people feel sexier, wealthier or happier in one sentence, you'll struggle to gain their allegiance. Refine your "value proposition." What are the benefits you're providing? Clearly spelling it out is the key to winning fans and followers. (For help with that check out the awesome book, *The Transformational Consumer*, by Scorpio Tara Nicholle-Nelson.)

On January 10, a lunar (full moon) eclipse in Cancer and your visionary ninth house delivers a breakthrough insight that helps you expand your reach. A candid conversation may be involved. Don't get your knickers in a knot if someone decides to "school" you, offering well-documented intel that shakes up some of your own findings. Thank them for enlightening you, and, if appropriate, incorporate the data into your strategy. Better yet, how about getting ahead of the curve? Gather your wise tribunal of advisers and solicit expert feedback before you dive into production mode. Since the ninth house rules higher education, this might be your cue to enroll in specialized training or travel to learn from a master teacher. The journey is the destination during a nomadic ninth house eclipse, and this one's directive is, "Explore and expand!"

Are you the student who's become the master? Near January's eclipse, map your curriculum and delivery methods. Teach the class live but have a videographer film the lessons to be used as modules for a webinar. With so many great platforms out there, like Udemy, Kajabi and iTunes U, you may be a click away from your own online school.

By the time the second Cancer eclipse rolls around—this one a solar (new moon) eclipse on June 21—you could have a course that's ready to launch. Or maybe a book to publish, a screenplay to shop around or an EP to drop at a release party. Whatever genius is percolating won't stay hidden inside of you in 2020!

If you're thinking about relocating or want to go on an epic pilgrimage, set off on June 21, as the solar eclipse activates your wanderlust. The only yellow light? Mercury will be retrograde from June 18 to July 12, also in Cancer and your ninth house. Use this supercharged new moon for investigating the voyage but wait until after July 12 to book your flight and make all the reservations. If you simply can't hold off, spring for travel insurance and read all the reviews before you settle on a hotel and shuttle service.

Eclipses pull us far beyond the familiar and help us discover new facets of ourselves—whether we were seeking it or not! But sometimes, that pull simply helps us stop overlooking the obvious. That could be the case on July 5, when the Capricorn lunar (full moon) eclipse pops up in your third house of local activity. Keep the ruby slippers handy! As this eclipse rounds out the two-year series, you could have a nostalgic longing for your own personal Kansas. After swearing off your zip code as "hipster hell" or—conversely—a "hick town," you may discover it through a fresh lens this summer, especially if you find your people. Getting involved in neighborhood goings-on is one surefire way to remember that there's no place like home. (And also to wield your Scorpionic influence on the locals!) You may be vaulted into a new role, taking a seat on city council or opening a pop-up shop.

Writing, teaching and media are focal points near July 5. Sign up for a short class or scout new hotspots instead of going to the same old haunts. With peer relationships falling under this eclipse's arc of influence, include siblings, coworkers, neighbors and friends in your plans. Or stay open to new people if you're looking to expand your social circumference. You could meet a BFF-grade kindred spirit who becomes your festival buddy and sounding board—rolled into one!

Gemini/Sagittarius Eclipses: Reveal your message.

June 5, November 30, December 14

Scorpio on top! Money, sex, power—and your approach to all three—get a major makeover in 2020. Starting June 5, a new 18-month series of eclipses lands on the Gemini/Sagittarius axis, activating the houses of your chart that rule everything from lust to trust…and trust funds. Between now and December 3, 2021, where you spend your money and who you sleep with could shift dramatically. You may have to face some limiting beliefs around financial flow and sexuality.

Old habits are hard to break, but you're being asked to do the heavy emotional lifting in order to thrive. Two of 2020's six eclipses will land in Sagittarius and your sensual-yet-sensible second house. The first, on June 5, is a lunar (full moon) eclipse. While your penchant for the finer things intensifies, this awakening moment shifts the landscape of how you earn, spend, save and invest. What you do for a living may change, or radically alter! Since Sagittarius rules your second house of professional security, this could shift your role—if not your entire position—around the office. If you've been circulating your résumé, get ready! Within a month

of June 5, a new job or revenue source may finally flow in. But don't expect this to go entirely according to plan. Eclipses always arrive with a surprise. This one will upgrade your sense of worthiness, even if it throws you a temporary curveball first. Don't stress! Just fill out the additional paperwork, apply for the licenses, and do what it takes to manifest this mission.

The June 5 lunar eclipse could also bring a job transition, a moneymaking opportunity or a changing of the guard at work. Since lunar eclipses sweep away what no longer serves us, you may suddenly and unexpectedly part ways with a client or leave a position. Or, you'll field an incredible offer that's too good to refuse. If a job is "eclipsed" out of your life, trust that something better is coming your way, even if it feels turbulent in the short-term. You may begin a radically different approach to money management, sitting down with a financial planner, buying or selling property, or investing. A legal matter, especially one related to shared property, could move toward resolution.

That said, impulsiveness isn't advised during the frenzied energy of an eclipse. If you're being rushed to sign on the dotted line, hit the brakes so you can conduct due diligence and make sure this is the right move for you. Since the second house rules self-worth, the June 5 eclipse could deliver a much-needed confidence boost. You might also change your daily habits, prioritizing your spending, time management and routines to reflect what matters most to you. If you're hoping to start a regular exercise routine or change your eating habits, your summer could get off to a salubrious start!

On November 30, the year's only eclipse in Gemini hits your eighth house of merging. As you're winding down the year, don't go into a "holidaze" or you could miss an important fiscal upswing! Before you close out Q4, the eclipse could energize a joint financial venture. Look for ways you can collaborate for mutual gain, whether through business, with neighbors or in your love life. This eclipse may prompt some Scorpios to work the barter system, or to pool your funds co-op style. Could you, for example, build someone a website in exchange for them ombre-ing your hair or feeding your cat while you're traveling? Maybe you can cut costs by sharing rides with coworkers or arranging group fitness training instead of pricey solo sessions. Get creative!

Feeling out of touch with your inner vixen? The November 30 lunar eclipse restores your siren status, which is your birthright as a Scorpio. But you're not getting hot and bothered for any slick-talking rando! The eighth house also rules your intimate emotional ties, and the shadow of this lunar eclipse could reveal someone's less-than-noble intentions…or show you how painfully you treated someone who only wanted to love you. If your suspicious mind went off the rails earlier this year, the November 30 eclipse extends a chance to clean things up, and hopefully get in good graces just in time for Cuffing Season!

The eighth house rules sex and soulmates, and this one can spark a major mind-body-spirit attraction, or the desire for a divine love where you can commune on all of these levels. But it can also bring a change in relationship status. Everything from an engagement, a breakup, a pregnancy or plans to move in together will be on the table as the year winds down.

Couples may have to sort out joint funds near November 30. Would merging your bank accounts and assets make it easier to apply for a mortgage?

Conversely, if different approaches to money management has been the source of nearly every argument, you may be happier with separate bank accounts. Or, you might decide to collaborate on a business venture, combining your superpowers for profit! With eclipses, there's no doing things halfway—and all the more with this one, which is in your eighth house of extremes. You're either in or you're out. Before 2020 is through, your most important partnerships could go through a transformation, as you finally address a neon pink elephant in the (bed)room. Bring in a trained professional if you can't figure out how to broach this topic effectively. Ready to move into a deeper realm of trust, commitment and transparency? Let these moonbeams light the way.

On December 14, a Sagittarius solar (new moon) eclipse will bring another economic boon, helping you wrap up 2020 with a positive balance sheet. This supercharged new moon confers you with clout, handing you the executive status you've been waiting for. If you have any rough edges to clean up, do so mid-December, whether that means updating the events page on your website or recommitting to being on time for appointments. Your self-worth determines your net worth! ✳

monthly hotspots

January

JANUARY: LOVE HOTSPOTS

January 3-February 16: Mars in Sagittarius

With your sizzling co-ruler, hot-to-trot Mars, muscling through your second house of self-worth and values, you're encouraged to let others know where your boundaries are—and where they aren't. The best way to earn respect is to demonstrate how much you love yourself! Confidence is sexy now, so step into your swagger. Money could become a source of tension for couples; singles might be lured by retail therapy. Think before you charge it!

January 10: Uranus retrograde ends

Old relationship issues may have been flaring up since August 11, 2019, or you might have struggled to maintain a stable connection. Get ready to exhale, though: Today, volatile Uranus corrects course in your partnership house! But as the planet of disruption, it'll continue to act as a trickster for a while, forcing you to release any outmoded beliefs or behaviors that don't serve you.

January 13-February 7: Venus in Pisces

Whether the mistletoe worked or not, you'll be stoking new love embers when amorous Venus begins her annual tour of your passionate and glamorous fifth house. You can get a head start on Valentine's Day by smiling back at intriguing strangers—or being a little kinder and "taking the initiative" more with your partner!

January 16-February 3: Mercury in Aquarius

You don't have to be tough and vulnerable all the time, Scorpio! During this tender transit, make your motto "sharing is caring," and see the subtle—and not-so-subtle—shifts in your intimate relationships.

January 26: Venus-Mars square

Where there's a will there's a way—but there could also be an epic imbroglio! When the planets *d'amour* lock horns, lovers' quarrels could erupt and things might get intense. How hard would it be, really, to just let this one thing go?

January 27: Venus-Neptune meetup

The two most quixotic planets form their annual merger in your romance sector today, making it all too convenient to hole up in your couple bubble. But easy does it with those public displays. The last thing you want to do is offend or alienate a single friend—or your future MIL! Single? This blissful fog could sweep you away—in the guise of an all-consuming attraction.

The AstroTwins' 2020 Horoscope
356

JANUARY: CAREER HOTSPOTS

January 2: Mercury-Jupiter meetup

You won't come up short in the ideas department today, as resourceful Mercury and expansive Jupiter align in your communication corner. If someone needs a little push to come on-board, throw 'em a line. You'll have an easy time connecting with people, so open your heart and share away!

January 3-February 16: Mars in Sagittarius

Activating Mars blasts into your work and finance house after a two-year hiatus, and all that pent-up energy may land you the kind of new gig or big deal you've been waiting for! Entertain all opportunities to raise your bottom line, but don't wait for the phone to ring. Get out there and do the 2020 version of pounding the pavement.

January 10: Cancer full moon (lunar eclipse)

The first of 2020's two full moons in your ninth house of travel, blue-sky dreaming and entrepreneurship (the second is on December 29) is also a potent lunar eclipse, and it can inspire you to wrap up anything that no longer blows your hair back. Set a deadline to be "so over that" and get ready to blast into your next big venture. Things could start to come together in the next few weeks!

January 10: Uranus retrograde ends

Partnerships and deal-making get back on track as erratic Uranus blows the whistle on a five-month backspin through your dynamic-duos zone. This retrograde may have muddied the waters of a few close alliances since August 2019, leaving you scratching your head and wondering WTH. But as the innovative outer planet blasts forward, you might finally team up with the perfect collaborator—who wasn't available until now.

January 12: Mercury-Saturn-Pluto meetup

Your ideas are your stock in trade, so don't be in too big a hurry to share (and thus dilute the value of) your intellectual property. Saturn lends the patience to quick-on-the-draw Mercury, but in Capricorn, even the messenger planet appreciates the value of perfect timing. And with intensifying Pluto in the mix, one of your visions could hit pay dirt—bringing a very hefty profit!

January 13: Sun-Saturn-Pluto meetup

Whether there's an actual red carpet or not, be ready to take your walk of fame today! This super-rare trio will raise your profile and the value of your personal brand's stock. This would be a perfect day to cold-call that A-list client or host a livestream on your best social media platform. Because this mashup occurs in your communication corner, you'll be able to back up that golden gift of gab with knowledge and data!

January 18: Mercury-Uranus square

Hold your tongue—yes, even when a clever manipulator who knows how to push your buttons attempts to rile you. This could be someone you think is in your camp, but if you're paying close attention, you'll be able to see through them. This is where being patient and non-reactive comes in.

January 23: Sun-Uranus square

Under this nerve-jangling biannual clash, someone's erratic behavior could push you to your limits. But rather than go ballistic on them, stay focused and centered now. Uncomfortable as this may be, trust that it's temporary. Take off the rose-

The AstroTwins' 2020 Horoscope

colored glasses and unblinkingly acknowledge, then confront, the root of any conflict.

January 24: Aquarius new moon

Your inner circle is foremost on your mind during the year's only Aquarius new moon in your foundational fourth house. While this technically occurs on a Friday, you can celebrate your love and their constant support for you all weekend long. If one of them is a coworker, invite them out for lunch! Today also kicks off the Chinese Year of the Metal Rat, a time to make shrewd business moves. And because it powers up your domestic zone, you can turn your home into a hub of productivity!

January 28: Mars-Neptune square

Beware the pitch that sounds too good to be true! Today's uneasy alignment of rash Mars and credulous Neptune could melt your normally skeptical attitude. If there's a sizable investment involved here, definitely table this for another day when you're thinking your rational best.

February

FEBRUARY: LOVE HOTSPOTS

February 3-March 4: Mercury in Pisces

Owing to a retrograde from February 16 to March 9, messenger Mercury will spend an exceptionally long time in your romance sector this winter. This is the first leg of the journey before it backflips, briefly, into Aquarius and your home zone. Action should gain momentum before then, but if it slows down (or evaporates), hang in there! There's a reason for this, and it's your sacred mission to uncover that!

February 7-March 4: Venus in Aries

Beautifying Venus blazes a trail through your fitness sector, turning your attention to self-care and getting your inside-out glow on! Couples will enjoy having a workout and healthy-eating buddy for this journey. Single? The yoga studio or indoor pool may be the perfect place to meet a sexy fellow wellness warrior.

February 16-March 9: Mercury retrograde

Love: rudely interrupted? That's one possible outcome of the reversal of effusive Mercury in your sector *d'amour*. If you blindly sped into something, this pivot can help you walk it back—or at least slow it down. But if you're blissing out with a new S.O., you might not welcome Mercury's scrambled signals. This too shall pass, so bide your time until that lovin' feeing comes flooding back!

February 23: Pisces new moon

Whether you're looking for new love, a romantic reboot or the perfect moment to take (or at least discuss) a major next step, this annual lunation in your romance sector brings it! But leave all your "needs" and "shoulds" at the door and stay open to something new and extraordinary. Make sure you're flexible enough to shift with whatever comes because, even if it's wrapped in unfamiliar packaging, it is what you want.

February 23: Venus-Jupiter square

Even happy couples hit occasional speed bumps, and today's jarring joust between the love planet and supersizer Jupiter can turn a molehill of anger or frustration into a K2-size obstacle. But rather than stew in your juices, think of what you'd want a lover to say to you in this circumstance. Then breathe through your heart, swallow your pride and approach them with genuine compassion.

February 28: Venus-Pluto square

Where are those emotions coming from? Today, when your shadowy co-ruler Pluto gets into it with the gentle love planet, you might be overcome by uncontrollable feelings of jealousy, paranoia or even rage. But just because you're experiencing this doesn't mean it's valid—and certainly not helpful. You get to decide how to act, so take some time to tune in to truer, deeper values.

FEBRUARY: CAREER HOTSPOTS

February 9: Leo full moon

The year's only full moon in your professional tenth house could bring a major success—or garner the kind of big-league recognition you deserve. It can also bring a long-running project to completion or a turning point. During the next two weeks, find the answer to the question, "So what's next?"

February 16-March 30: Mars in Capricorn

As energizing Mars burns through your third house of ideas, alliances and communication, you'll have a lot to say, but that doesn't mean you should express everything that pops into your noggin. Save your best stuff for projects that only you (and maybe one close colleague) can take to the next level. The right vision with the right collaborator at the perfect moment could yield a hefty payday!

February 21: Mars-Uranus trine

This rare and invigorating alignment might lead to a surprising—and synergistic—conversation with someone who's as innovative as you are. This phosphorescent connection might be sustainable for the long haul, but for now, be content with one modest yet groundbreaking project.

March

MARCH: LOVE HOTSPOTS

March 3: Venus-Saturn square

Make sure you know the difference between a little healthy compromise in the name of keeping the relationship wheels greased and giving in on one of your more core values. While the former is to be expected, your high-minded sign won't be happy with the latter!

March 4-16: Mercury in Aquarius

Got something you need to get off your chest? This short but activating transit of the messenger planet through your home zone could help you find the right words to express what you're feeling. Keep the focus on solutions, not on what the other person did "wrong."

March 4-April 3: Venus in Taurus

Today kicks off one of the sweetest months of your year as the love planet sweeps through sensual Taurus and your seventh house of partnerships. Keep an open mind—and heart—and you can strengthen your bond, turn up the heat on a simmering union or, if you're single, finally meet your match.

March 8: Venus-Uranus meetup

Whether you'd like to meet someone on your wavelength or hit refresh on a relationship that's stalled out, this one-day merger can bring a radical change to your relationship (or status). Envision exactly what you want—and what you need to release. If an opportunity presents itself, grab it and run with it!

     The AstroTwins' 2020 Horoscope

March 16-April 10: Mercury in Pisces

The messenger planet returns to your fifth house of passion and amour for a second visit this year (after briefly retrograding into Aquarius last month). Romantic initiatives that sparked up fast then fizzled out could heat back up again. They say patience is a virtue, Scorpio, and you're about to be rewarded for yours.

March 21-July 1: Saturn in Aquarius

Phase one of a lengthy transit, which lasts until March 7, 2023, kicks off today as steady Saturn climbs into your fourth house of home, family and emotional stability. You haven't experienced this since 1991, and now, so much wiser, you could steer your relationship with a key female through some (necessary) growing pains. During this three-year slog, you might get serious about buying or selling real estate, having children or making peace with your mother.

March 27: Venus-Jupiter trine

Is your partner your BFF? Or, if you're single, might one of your besties be soulmate material? The line blurs under today's romantic alignment of these compassionate, expansive planets in your relationship houses. Forget the old "shoulds" and forge some new ground!

March 28: Venus-Pluto trine

There will be no skimming the surface when it comes to bonding—or even flirting—under today's penetrating pairing. With love planet Venus in your partnership realm aligned with deep-diving Pluto in your communication sector, you're only interested in conversations that will touch your heart and move the needle. Single? Get out and chat up any and all interesting-looking folks in the room!

March 30-May 13: Mars in Aquarius

As lusty Mars marches through your domestic fourth house, you may be tempted to huddle in your couple bubble for the entire seven-week transit! But since the red planet can also dredge up competition, anger and repressed emotions, you actually need to come up for air occasionally. A good way to work out the kinks is with intense bursts of physical activity. Your call whether that happens at the gym or in the boudoir.

March 31: Mars-Saturn meetup

Go forward, stand still or retreat?! You're sending and receiving mixed messages today as rash Mars bangs into cautious Saturn in your emotional fourth house. You may feel hesitant to make a major move, even one you're excited about. Helpful hint: Don't try to race into a new relationship phase under this mashup. Instead, take a few days to think and talk through (in detail) what you both want. Once you align on a direction, it's full speed ahead!

MARCH: CAREER HOTSPOTS

March 9: Virgo full moon

Time to ramp those #SquadGoals! Today's lunar lift in your collaborative zone can bring a team project to completion or another major turning point. If you want to get in tighter with this group, find ways to contribute that are unique to you. Even if there's no salaried position at the moment, if you're serious about being a part of it, volunteer! It's the best way to get a foot in the door.

March 20: Mars-Jupiter meetup

Under this electrifying—and rare—alignment, your enthusiasm for a new idea will be palpable. But you may have to navigate that fine line between zeal and pushiness. One way to do that is to listen way more than you speak. And whatever you do, don't interrupt people!

March 23: Mars-Pluto meetup

You may have the most info on a group project, but that doesn't mean you have to lay all your cards on the table. Play "good cop" and let the others reveal what they know first. Wait for your perfect moment—when no one can swoop in and co-opt your ideas—and then boldly present your plan and point of view.

March 24: Aries new moon

The year's only Aries new moon is eager to blaze a trail through your sixth house of healthy living and organization. What simple hacks can make your life run more smoothly or help you to be more productive? In the two weeks following this lunar lift, embark on a major decluttering mission and streamline all your routines and systems. This is the way to work smarter, not harder!

March 30-May 13: Mars in Aquarius

Firm up those boundaries between your personal and your professional life during this empowering transit. If you've been a little too accommodating to people at work and on the home front, you could be leaking energy and not making the progress you'd like. Let close friends and family know that you can only respond to true emergencies during business hours. By the same token, make it clear to the professional powers-that-be that working 12-hour days is not what you signed on for. Then… negotiate!

April

APRIL: LOVE HOTSPOTS

April 3-August 7: Venus in Gemini

When vixen Venus starts an extended trip into your eighth house of eroticism and intimacy, encounters with your S.O. or romantic prospects will be packed with seduction. Have you been afraid to let your guard down around someone? Over the next few months, get ready to lower that mask and connect with a special person, mind, body and soul.

April 3: Mercury-Neptune meetup

Although Mercury is the rational mastermind of the zodiac, when it meets up with dreamy Neptune in your romantic sector for its annual *pas de deux*, you're easily swept up in illusions. What feels real could turn out to be a projection of your desires (or fears). Be mindful not to blur fact and fantasy in your love life.

April 4: Venus-Saturn trine

Today's commitment-minded transit gets you serious about a budding or seemingly solid relationship. With long-sighted Saturn in your foundational fourth house sweetly synced with the love planet in your permabonding zone, you need to know if this person is a reliable emotional anchor—or just there for a little short-term fun. The goal? Getting clear where you stand.

April 7: Libra full moon

The year's only Libra full moon lights up your perceptive, introspective twelfth house, sharpening your intuition. Libra rules partnership, and over the next two weeks, you'll get a strong "hit" about whether a potential person is keeper material. Couples have a beautiful opening for talking about sensitive subjects, especially if you can stay calm and let your mutual caring guide you.

April 7: Mars-Uranus square

Under this provocative clash of warrior Mars and disruptive Uranus in your relationship zones, you may be prone to angry outbursts or blurting out things better left unsaid. Even if you apologize profusely after the fact, this explosion could dent or destabilize your love life. The best way to deal with your hair-trigger temper is preemptively: by not letting it get set off in the first place.

April 22: Taurus new moon

The only Taurus new moon of 2020 sends a jolt of energizing energy through your relationship realm, helping you strengthen your union or wipe the slate clean and make a fresh start. Make sure you know exactly what you want to call in with the next person—and that you've cut any old "cords" that connect you to people you've moved past. Under this sensual lunation, couples can rekindle sparks or take a major step toward making your bond official.

April 27-May 11: Mercury in Taurus

When the messenger planet makes its annual trek through your relationship zone, you're encouraged to come right out and say what's on your mind and, more important, in your heart. You may be able to pick up on super-subtle clues, but not everyone's a mind-reader. Your guarded sign can actually find it easier—and even a huge relief—to be so candid and transparent.

April 30: Mercury-Uranus meetup

Once a year, these quick-witted and unbridled

planets align, and this time, they're convening in sensual Taurus and your partnership sector. You could start something new just like that, firm up a union that's been wobbly—or cut bait and go fish somewhere else altogether!

APRIL: CAREER HOTSPOTS

April 4: Jupiter-Pluto meetup

As candid Jupiter and secretive Pluto merge in your communication sector for the first of three rare sync-ups, you're learning when it's appropriate to be an open book and when it's better to keep things under wraps. As a Scorpio, you can be opaque with the details. While this keeps your secrets in the vault, it might also make people feel uncomfortable or suspicious. Try being a little bit more forthcoming—selectively, of course—and you'll gain their trust.

April 10-27: Mercury in Aries

When mental Mercury flits through quick-start Aries and your organized sixth house, you'll have the energy and motivation to tick some long-standing tasks off your to-do list. But rather than start with the most challenging, pick a few you know you can tackle in just a couple hours. This will help build momentum for the long haul!

April 14: Sun-Pluto square

Table any big negotiations for another day, when you'll be less emotionally invested in the outcome. Pluto can be manipulative, and you don't want anything to do with that kind of energy! But no need to be controlling or mysterious. Just pick a new date and propose it without any melodrama.

April 15: Sun-Jupiter square

No-limits Jupiter in your communication corner is at loggerheads with the expressive Sun, urging you to say less than you might initially be inclined to. Hold your tongue, limit your exposure to provocative people, and downplay anything you're offering. This way, what you ultimately deliver can only impress them!

April 21: Sun-Saturn square

Dial down the emotional pitches today and appeal instead to people's logical side. An uneasy angle between the zealous Sun and restrained Saturn could have you out of sync with your audience, and you might only get one chance to hook them.

April 22: Taurus new moon

Bring on the dynamic duos! There's only one of these new moons in your partnership sector per year, and this one boosts your confidence to approach someone about collaborating on a project near and dear to your heart. If you've got a co-pilot but you're working off different flight plans, find time over the next two weeks to get back on the same page.

April 25: Mercury square Jupiter & Pluto

Caution is required under today's restraining double square to Mercury. With the mentally astute planet trekking through your detail-minded sixth house, your mission is to find every error and correct it before the project goes out the door. Don't succumb to pressure from anyone trying to rush you or get you to cut corners. This one is worth doing right. Take the time you need!

April 25-October 4: Pluto retrograde in Capricorn

When the mighty dwarf planet (your ruler) flips into reverse for the next five and a half months, you'll need to communicate with extra care. Work slowly and carefully, and be discerning about who gets access to private intel. Password-protect important data and document instructions in writing so that anyone working with you is crystal-clear on expectations. Dodge power struggles with button-pushing colleagues by not taking their bait.

April 26: Sun-Uranus meetup

Trying to go it alone again? Why? There are so many able-bodied and quick-witted people eager to help you out. Get over any residual resistance and allow someone to pitch in on a big-deal project. Your best choice would be a complementary talent, not just a clone who duplicates your skills.

April 27-May 11: Mercury in Taurus

If you've been holding back an important piece of intel or not sharing your true opinions on a team project, these next few weeks are the perfect time to unload. People will be more receptive now, and you may actually be happy to get this out in the open.

April 28: Mercury-Saturn square

You may think you've hit on the most brilliant idea since sliced bread, but not everyone will necessarily agree with you. Today, as taskmaster Saturn throws shade at clever Mercury, you may bang up against unexpected resistance. If you can't convince them of the value of your proposal, don't persist. Go back to the drawing board and make the necessary adjustments.

       The AstroTwins' 2020 Horoscope

April 30: Mercury-Uranus meetup

A professional partnership could heat up rapidly as articulate Mercury merges with fast-acting Uranus in your dynamic-duos sector. While your instincts seldom steer you wrong, it's always worth taking the time to do the necessary background checks, including references and financials.

May

MAY: LOVE HOTSPOTS

May 3: Venus-Neptune square

This is the first of three clashes this year between the most idealistic planets in your most passionate chart sectors. While the dreamy vibes will send you straight to Cloud Nine, you could easily blur the lines between "realistic" and "obsessive" with this person. In a relationship? Dial down the need to control "where this thing is going" and relish the moment-to-moment sweetness.

May 11-September 29: Saturn retrograde

Restrained Saturn commences its annual retrograde, this year through your foundational fourth house. You could feel more guarded in a certain relationship, or old emotional patterns could resurface, forcing you to deal and heal. This pivot might delay plans to move in together, buy property or start or expand the family. The cosmic taskmaster will back into Capricorn on July 1 until December 17, but after that, action should pick up again—with a vengeance!

May 11-28: Mercury in Gemini

The expressive messenger planet spins through your intimate, seductive eighth house, ratcheting up both emotions and the compulsion to vocalize them. But really, if you're close enough to someone to share a bed, why not also unveil your fantasies and desires? While you're at it, encourage them to reveal one or two of their own. This could be a whole new ball game!

May 13-June 27: Mars in Pisces

Passionate Mars returns to your amorous, glamorous fifth house for the first time in two years, and the impatient planet is probably not keen to wait any longer to get his needs met. Let your partner know what would make you happy—or tip your crush off that you have feelings; they might be silently simmering in their juices, too! During this fiery, fertile cycle, a pregnancy could be in the cards.

May 13-June 25: Venus retrograde in Gemini

Every other year, amorous Venus flips into reverse gear, and this time around, she's performing in chatty Gemini and your house of committed relationships. While you'll have no trouble talking about issues with partners or dates, the actual interactions may become convoluted, or people's motives might be questionable. And because retrogrades rule the past, an old flame might resurface, complicating things further. Tiptoe into temptation!

May 22: Mercury-Venus meetup

When the cosmic communicator meets up with the love planet, confess a secret fantasy or reveal something that will deepen trust. This could feel a bit awkward initially, but when you're rolling in the deep with your beloved, you'll be glad you took the risk.

May 22: Gemini new moon

This new moon in your house of seduction and bonding can do wonders for your love life now, and it also opens up a six-month span during which you can change the way you "do" intimacy. New moons bring opportunities for fresh starts, so wherever you're hoping for a change—or just to mix things up—start taking steps in that direction!

MAY: CAREER HOTSPOTS

May 7: Scorpio full moon

You only get one full moon in your sign a year, and this one can act like a "404 redirect" to turn your attention to important matters you've got simmering on a backburner. Focus on your highest priorities during the next two weeks and get a handle on why you let your desires fall to the bottom on the heap. Even though you have to attend to your company's goals, there's surely a way to shuffle in some of your personal ambitions!

May 9: Mercury-Pluto trine

Don't wait for a project to go off the rails before you regroup the team and get everybody on the same page. If people are in the same office, hold a face-to-face meeting, and if they're scattered far and wide, have a video conference. You can solidify the mission and craft a winning new plan.

May 10: Mercury-Jupiter trine

Just because you've always done things a certain way doesn't mean that's still the best way. Today, as expansive Jupiter sends a signal boost to mental Mercury, be open to new procedures or software that could save you time and money in the long run. Innovation could bring a bounty!

May 11: Mercury-Mars square

Someone may seek to challenge your authority today—for seemingly no reason other than to assert their power. That's the hardest kind of person to deal with because all the logic in the world won't shift their irrational thinking. Instead of wasting energy trying to persuade them, anticipate the worst-case scenario of their machinations, and employ appropriate measures to prevent that from happening.

May 11-28: Mercury in Gemini

Put on your noise-canceling headphones, close your door or just plan to screen out all distractions for the next few weeks. Mental Mercury is making its fast-and-furious sojourn through your intensely focused eighth house. Tunnel vision will actually be your friend as you throw yourself into a major research or financial project. Refuse to give in to procrastination, and you'll have this done—brilliantly—before the end of the month!

May 12: Mercury-Saturn trine

This harmonizing sync-up of analytical Mercury in your laser-sharp eighth house and structured Saturn can help you ground your visionary ideas in practicality. But first you need to hit on those brilliant notions, so let your mind wander. Then, when you've reeled in some inspired notions, map them out and see which are actually doable.

May 14-September 12: Jupiter retrograde in Capricorn

During the next four months, you'll have plenty of opportunities to reevaluate where you might have aimed too high or overpromised what you can deliver. (Supersizer Jupiter in your communication center can do that to a person!) But now that it's shifting into its annual reversal, you should get clarity about what's realistic. You may have some "'splaining" to do, but if you're honest, humble and apologetic, people are sure to understand. And if you learn your lesson, you won't have to repeat it!

May 15: Sun-Pluto trine

Your superpower today is being a clever observer and astute listener! While others are blurting things out left and right—and not hearing what others are saying—you're picking up on every nuance, which can only benefit your cause. Just be sure to say something when asked; otherwise, your caution could be mistaken for disinterest.

May 22: Gemini new moon

If you've been mulling a move to pool resources with a solid collaborator, this annual lunation in your house of joint ventures bodes well. During the next few weeks, hash out the terms and run them by a financial and/or legal pro to make sure everything is copacetic. And when it is? Ink that deal and pop some champagne; this could be a game-changer!

May 22: Mercury-Neptune square

Focus! If you're in the home stretch of a big project, don't let yourself get distracted by a colleague's personal drama. While you don't want to turn a cold shoulder, the office is not a therapist's office. Give any immediate support, but then make it clear that you both have work to do!

May 28-August 4: Mercury in Cancer

The messenger planet embarks on an extended tour of Cancer—longer than usual because of a retrograde from June 18 to July 12. Whether moving forward or in reverse, the mental planet in your expansive ninth house will help you think way outside the box. Don't worry whether something is "realistic." Your job is to be the visionary bellwether; others will figure out how to make it operational.

June

JUNE: LOVE HOTSPOTS

June 2: Venus-Mars square

Today's clash between the cosmic lovebirds reminds you that something with lasting potential doesn't need to be rushed into. Take your time and savor the getting-to-know-you excitement. Attached? Don't take the bait if your partner tries to pull you into sweating the petty stuff! Diffuse the situation by suggesting you go do something fun. Or, reroute to the bedroom and work out your differences there.

June 23-November 28: Neptune retrograde in Pisces

When deceptive Neptune makes its annual five-month pivot—in your fifth house of romance—you could get cold feet or second thoughts about a heating-up attraction. Couples might hit a snag or get pulled into drama over a past issue. Remember: this can happen to even the happiest couples. Just stop, assess and get back in sync with each other. Returning to a nostalgic old date spot could be a sweet way to rekindle your bond.

June 27, 2020-January 6, 2021: Mars in Aries

This is an exceptionally long trek for the red-hot planet, but thanks to a retrograde from September 9 to November 13, you'll have more time and focus to take care of yourself in ways you've put off far too long. When you feel good, you're confident enough to let your sexy side out to play. Already attached? Get your S.O. involved in some of your healthy initiatives. From partner yoga to whipping up healthy dinner parties, you'll enjoy having a wellness buddy with benefits!

JUNE: CAREER HOTSPOTS

June 5: Sagittarius full moon (lunar eclipse)

The year's only full moon in expansive Sagittarius lights up your second house of work and money and helps prime the abundance pump for the rest of 2020! But it's not a magic trick. You need to get out there and pound the pavement, seek out new opportunities or simply trim your spending habits to increase your bottom line.

June 13: Mars-Neptune meetup

Your creative juices are overflowing under this rare meetup of action planet Mars and imaginative Neptune in your fifth house of inspiration and fame. Do your work but also let people see what you're producing. You might wow just the right influencer today! Bambinos on the brain? That could definitely happen right about now, as these hotter-than-hot planets line up in your fertile fifth house.

June 18-July 12: Mercury retrograde in Cancer

Oops, did you just say that? You could have nearly four weeks of these kinds of *faux pas* when the communication planet flips into reverse in your candid and outspoken ninth house. If you're not sure whether something is appropriate, run it by a tactful friend—or just assume it's not. But among close friends who will love you no matter what, your

colorful commentary may be game-changing. Just make sure you dish it out sparingly—and serve it to a warmed-up crowd.

June 21: Cancer new moon (annular solar eclipse)

The first of 2020's two Cancer new moons also happens to be a solar eclipse, and because it lands in your visionary ninth house, you'll be full of grand ideas for an exciting venture that could be a real game-changer. Whether you're aiming to launch a start-up, expand your global reach or get some advanced training, this lunar lift can give you the motivation and support you need.

June 27, 2020-January 6, 2021: Mars in Aries

Motivational Mars will spend the rest of the year parked in your sixth house of organization and systems (an extra-long visit because the red planet is retrograde from September 9 to November 13). But just because you've got months to get 'er done, don't procrastinate or take shortcuts. Should tension flare with an employee or service provider, nip any brewing bruhahas in the bud. With Mars in your zone of helpful people, a rockstar intern or assistant could help take your dreams to the next level. Put savvy systems in place to speed up efficiency.

June 30: Jupiter-Pluto meetup

The second of 2020's three rare unions of expansive Jupiter and calculating Pluto electrifies your communication house. This time, both planets are retrograde, an important review period. Take inventory of how effectively you express yourself by observing other people's reactions. Are they responding with openness or defensiveness—or something else? You might directly ask a few trusted people what works about your communication style and what doesn't. Just commit to not punishing them if their feedback is harsh, m'kay? Consider it a contribution to your greatness!

July

JULY: LOVE HOTSPOTS

July 1-December 17: Saturn retrograde enters Capricorn

Communication is the key to any lasting relationship yet, it's all too easy to take shortcuts here, especially once you're comfortable with someone. But as structured Saturn reverses through your expressive third house, you could benefit from adopting new tools that make the other person feel heard and respected. Techniques such as "mirroring" can cultivate these loving conditions, whether with a newish romantic interest or a longtime partner.

July 27: Venus-Neptune square

This third and final clash between the most idealistic planets is like a "final exam": What big lessons did you learn this summer about keeping it real? Are you now clear on the difference between an innocent crush and an unhealthy obsession? With a real partner, you should be able to say what you feel without worrying that they'll bolt. But don't worry if you're not "there" yet: Practice makes perfect!

JULY: CAREER HOTSPOTS

July 1-December 17: Saturn retrograde enters Capricorn

Six weeks into its annual retrograde, restrictive Saturn backflips out of Aquarius and your domestic zone and into Capricorn and your communication center, where it'll give you one more chance to review how you express yourself both verbally and in writing. There are plenty of valuable lessons to be gleaned. A writing or media project could gain traction. Dust off the manuscript of your novel or manifesto, and polish up social media profiles.

July 5: Capricorn full moon (lunar eclipse)

The year's only Capricorn full moon—also a potent lunar eclipse—lights up your house of self-expression. Get ready: people will hang on your every word. Make sure your message is clear, powerful and backed up with tons of well-documented data. And if you need more time for research or testimonials, take it. This lunar lift can take up to six months to unfold.

July 8: Mercury-Mars square

Saying too much could get you in hot water or push people's buttons today. Think twice before offering unsolicited coaching or being too outspoken, especially since Mercury is retrograde. Trying to make a tough decision? The more you weigh your options, the deeper you'll drive yourself into confusion. This transit will repeat on July 27 when Mercury is direct (forward). You may have a little more clarity after that.

July 12: Sun-Neptune trine

No idea is too out-there or impractical to at least give a shot. Under this mashup in your most creative and visionary realms, your outlier thinking will score a big hit today.

July 15: Sun-Pluto opposition
Believing something will "probably" work isn't good enough today, so drill down a little deeper to get the evidence you need. Optimism is a good thing, but it's no substitute for reality. Even if you have to slow down—or take a break—it's more important to get this right the first time. Do your research and line up the support of a few power players.

July 20: Cancer new moon
This is the second consecutive Cancer new moon this year, and it gives you another opportunity to plant some seeds for a major harvest you'll reap early in the new year. While it may be frustrating to wait for your seedlings to sprout, remind yourself that this is the "organic" process, and deserves the time it takes.

July 20: Sun-Saturn opposition
No matter how enthusiastic you may be about a new proposal, chances are good that someone is intent on bursting your bubble. They could be the naysayer of the office, a dyed-in-the-wool cynic or—have you considered this?—wildly jealous of your originality. Pay them no mind, except to force yourself to work a tiny bit harder at convincingly making your case.

July 30: Mercury-Jupiter opposition
It's all in the timing! You may be chomping at the bit to get something off the ground, but today's opposition between supersizer Jupiter and mental Mercury is a hint that more information is needed. Make the calls, gather the intel and ask all the important questions.

July 30: Mercury-Neptune trine
It's a day to dream big—and to think outside the box. Thanks to this creative connection between analytical Mercury and intuitive Neptune, you can outwit—and outpace—anyone vain enough to consider themselves competition.

August

AUGUST: LOVE HOTSPOTS

August 3: Aquarius full moon
The year's only Aquarius full moon brings an emotional breakthrough to your foundational fourth house—and it could be a big one! Feelings you've been trying to keep under control may erupt in ways you never saw coming. Trust that this is loosening something inside you that needs to come undone. Instead of worrying what others think, you might as well relax and just go with it, Scorpio!

August 7-September 6: Venus in Cancer
Amorous Venus takes her annual spin through your adventurous ninth house, for the next four weeks, widening your personal viewfinder. If you're in a rock-solid relationship, this is a great time for a romantic getaway—or at least to start planning one for later in the year. If you're in a shaky union, it could be tested by this liberating transit. (Too many options, so little time!) Single Scorpios may be surprisingly open-minded in your selections, able to overlook the things that previously had been deal breakers, like dating someone who lives in another time zone or even country.

August 15, 2020-January 14, 2021: Uranus retrograde in Taurus

Romantic speed bump alert! Just when you thought things were proceeding apace, curveball-throwing Uranus—which is in long-term parking in your relationship realm—shifts into reverse. You or your partner might have a change of heart; a new love interest could cool. But if the love is strong, you'll come out of this more committed than ever. In the meantime, you may decide to explore your options or just give each other a little more autonomy and space to experiment.

August 25: Venus-Jupiter opposition

Under this tense angle between supersizer Jupiter and the love planet, you might feel like you have too many options, each one as appealing as the next. Or you could have a hard time deciding exactly what you want in a relationship. Single with no one on the radar? Beware someone's too-slick pickup lines. You can't ignore your Scorpio skepticism, but do give decent prospects a fair chance!

August 27: Venus-Neptune trine

Under this toe-curling trine between vixen Venus and nebulous Neptune, you probably won't be able to resist getting lost in a fantasy. Enjoy the magic—who knows what could happen? If your relationship has been a little too earthbound and mired in practical matters, this is the perfect day to inject a little magic back into the equation.

August 30: Venus-Pluto opposition

Blurt alert! Under this once-a-year opposition of shadowy Pluto in your communication center and sensitive Venus, someone close to you might make you feel threatened and put you on the defensive. But rather than go on the attack yourself, calm down and quietly but firmly let them know you will not tolerate being spoken to that way.

AUGUST: CAREER HOTSPOTS

August 1: Mercury-Pluto opposition

It's not like your circumspect sign to just blurt out things better kept under wraps, but today's lip-loosening opposition of messenger Mercury and potent Pluto across your communication axis could have a surprising effect. While it would be an interesting exercise for you to candidly share your opinions, be careful not to cross any offensive, edgy boundaries, especially around colleagues or big-deal clients!

August 2: Sun-Uranus square

Your career, or your role in a major mission, is just taking off when, out of the blue, someone close to you seems to be undermining you. They could be envious of your success—or maybe, if it's your love interest, jealous of the time you spend away from them. While you don't want to reinforce this immature behavior, a caring conversation might alleviate their fears or doubts.

August 3: Mercury-Saturn opposition

Grand-scale ideas? Check! But before you start planning a launch party or sending out press releases, run beta tests to make sure these concepts are actually workable. Today, with quicksilver Mercury in your big-picture ninth house opposing auditor Saturn, it's crucial that you don't skim over any details or steps in the equation.

August 4: Mars-Jupiter square

Manage your anxiety today, and don't let anyone see you sweat! Even if you're nervous inside, you need to present a cool face to the powers that be, especially if you're talking about funding. While this alignment of the action planet and supersizer Jupiter fills your head with big and brilliant ideas, take extra measures to keep calm.

August 4-19: Mercury in Leo

If you've been quietly hatching a big plan for the past several weeks, it's finally safe to make your reveal. As messenger Mercury cartwheels through your career corner for the next two weeks, start a buzz on your own behalf. Let appropriate parties in on the idea, and then, when you have enough support, approach the decision makers—with all the confidence you can muster!

August 10: Mercury-Uranus square

A plot twist at work today could wind up being a blessing in disguise! When disruptive Uranus squares mental Mercury, it can throw off your rhythm or concentration at first. But instead of getting irritated, what if you considered this a happy accident and kept on digging till you found a better or more creative approach? Sometimes genius is planned, but other times, it's serendipitous!

August 13: Mars-Pluto square

You love a good challenge or lively debate, but not when the other party is so set in their ways that all you're doing is wasting your breath. You might run up against exactly this sort of person today, so be on the lookout. Engaging with them, even for a few minutes, is the opposite of a "win-win."

August 17: Mercury-Mars trine

Pace yourself, Scorpio. With action planet Mars keeping a fire lit under mental Mercury, you'll be so productive, you won't want to take a break! But don't worry about losing momentum—or any of your brilliant ideas. Giving your mind brief respites throughout the day will actually help you think even more clearly—and keep at this till it's done!

August 18: Leo new moon

Goals: rebooted! The year's only new moon in your professional tenth house can catalyze your career, but is this the path you want to stay on? You may be ready for new challenges, and this lunar lift could point the way over the coming six months. Reach out to mentors and pros in your industry. Set concrete milestones and get into action! Make a power move.

August 19-September 5: Mercury in Virgo

Team up FTW! This is your annual cycle where mental Mercury zips through your eleventh house of teamwork and technology, adding a little extra sparkle to your every idea. Don't stress about following protocol or replicating what everyone else is doing. You're the fearless ringleader whose role is to show people possibilities they haven't dared to dream of! Need to learn some new software? Take a tutorial or ask HR if someone can sit down and show you the ropes.

August 24: Mars-Saturn square

Don't waste one minute looking around trying to see how fast others are working today. As reckless Mars butts heads with slow-and-steady Saturn, focus on making your idea the best it can be. Besides, since when do you take your cue from others? Be the trailblazing force of nature that you are.

August 25: Mercury-Uranus trine

You don't have to do everything by yourself all the time, you know! Today, when communicator Mercury in your team-spirit zone gets tapped by transformational Uranus, you're reminded that many hands make light work—and similarly, many brains can solve the knottiest problem! Give yourself a break, call a mini-meeting and turn this over to the hivemind!

August 29: Mercury-Jupiter trine

Practical magic abounds under an auspicious alignment of articulate Mercury and no-limits Jupiter in your most people-centric houses. Your network truly is your net worth today, so cash in a few favors and rally the troops for some bonding, brainstorming and big-ideas-sharing. What starts as a casual get-together could finish with a few of you scheming to launch a sideline business.

August 30: Mercury-Neptune opposition

Save the big presentation or client pitch meeting for another day. Eloquent Mercury is perched in precise Virgo, but it's in direct opposition to perplexing Neptune, which could derail the most confident public speaker. You want to get it right out of the gate—since you won't get a second chance to make a good first impression. So table this for now, and in the meantime, get all those bells and whistles in perfect working order!

September

SEPTEMBER: LOVE HOTSPOTS

September 2: Venus-Saturn opposition

An impulsively begun new love affair may get walked back or at least slowed down under this speed-correcting alignment of amorous Venus and cautious Saturn. Or, if you embarked on a long-distance relationship without thinking through all the challenges, you may have second thoughts now. For couples, this mettle-testing transit could actually force you to talk about that gigantic elephant in the room—finally!

September 2: Pisces full moon

You won't need to check your weather app to know what to wear under today's emotional Pisces full moon in your passionate fifth house: It'll be your heart on your sleeve, of course! Try as you might, you won't be able to hide your feelings—and if you're attempting to, stop and seriously ask yourself what for? If this is what you want, you've got to at least give it a go. And if your affection isn't reciprocated, at least you're free to move on to someone who will appreciate and adore you.

September 4: Venus-Mars square

With the cosmic lovebirds warbling off-key, you and your love interest will probably be cranky, and one of you may be itching for a fight. But don't take the bait! Say the one thing you know will calm you both down and get you to—if nothing else—peaceably retreat to neutral corners till this testiness passes.

September 5-27: Mercury in Libra

When the mental planet downshifts into Libra and your sleepy twelfth house for a few weeks, you may prefer your own dreams and imaginings to so-called reality. It can be useful to escape stuck situations by engaging in a little creative visualization. Try journaling or meditation to tune in deeper and access powerful inner guidance.

September 9-November 13: Mars retrograde in Aries

When your assertive co-ruler, Mars, shifts into reverse in your tender sixth house, it could trigger an old wound, make you hypercritical or throw a wrench in a well-choreographed plan. It's more important than ever to manage your stress levels, so instead of reflexively bickering, channel that fiery passion into self-care.

September 6-October 2: Venus in Leo

Nothing wrong with talking about your hopes and dreams for the future—in fact, it might be a major turn-on now. These next several weeks are perfect for just that as the love planet stampedes into loyal Leo and your tenth house of long-range goals and career. If you're in a solid union, it's more than fair game to bring up your plans and get clarity around your partner's intentions. No one on the romantic radar? Think about what you could do differently to meet more eligible prospects—perhaps take industry networking events a bit more seriously?

September 15: Venus-Uranus square

You know what happens when you "assume," don't you? Today, under a disruptive clash between the love planet and rebellious Uranus, there may be more to the story. So rather than playing guessing games, come right out and ask—without putting the other person on the defensive!

September 28: Venus-Mars trine

With the love planets mashed up in the most passionate yet stabilizing sectors of your chart, making plans for the future, performing acts of service and being unquestionably there for each other are the sexiest things you can do!

SEPTEMBER: CAREER HOTSPOTS

September 1: Mercury-Pluto trine

You've got X-ray "people vision" today, as penetrating Pluto signal-boosts perceptive Mercury in your social sectors. But using this intel for mutual gain is hardly taking advantage of your (temporary) superpower. Once you understand what makes them tick, you can save everyone a lot of time by cutting to the chase and getting them working together productively.

September 3: Mercury-Saturn trine

Put some new structures in place and communicate them clearly to your team or whoever you're working with shoulder-to-shoulder. People may be looking to you to steer this ship, and under today's illuminating sync-up of clever Mercury and orderly Saturn in your interpersonal zones, you'll know precisely how to chart the most efficient course.

September 9-November 13: Mars retrograde in Aries

Driven Mars reverses through your sixth house of hard work and service, which could cause breakdowns with systems and employees. This isn't an ideal time to make a money move, but it is a perfect moment to take stock of your recent productivity levels and successes. Up your skillset by taking a course or finishing a certification.

September 12: Jupiter retrograde ends

After months of feeling unsure or stalled with an idea, outspoken Jupiter corrects course in your communication house. But no need to lunge into something that you're still fine-tuning. Tweak your message and then you should have the confidence to know that it's likely to be (more) warmly received—and appreciated—than before.

September 14: Sun-Pluto trine

Have you targeted a simpatico person that you think would be perfect to collaborate with? Your instincts seldom mislead you. Before you invest a chunk of time or money into this, test the waters with a small-scale project that will give you a good sense of your compatibility. If this person is as savvy as you think they are, they'll be totally on-board with that game plan!

September 17: Virgo new moon

Who said Scorpio doesn't play well with others? This annual new moon in your collaborative eleventh house supplies ample evidence that you can be the consummate team player—when you've had a chance to vet and approve the other members, that is! You have high standards, Scorpio, and you're not about to lower them just to be "one of the gang." But if you've found your work tribe, these next few weeks are ideal for sharing a dream project with them—and then maybe talking to big-league investors or developers.

September 17: Mercury-Jupiter square

Today's star-crossed square between chatty Mercury in your unconscious twelfth house and lip-loosener Jupiter in your communication sector could cause you to overshare or blurt out something that was meant to stay in the vault. Whoops! Even if you're just doing superficial damage control after the fact, be sure to say the right things and at least try to make an authentic apology.

September 21: Mercury-Pluto square

Go ahead: Be as skeptical as you want to be! Under a rare (twice-a-year) dust-up between manipulative Pluto and communicator Mercury, you should assume that someone is not revealing the whole truth—and quite possibly, deliberately. You could try to beat them at their own game, but that's risky. Better to call them out publicly and then let them take the heat.

September 23: Mercury-Saturn square

If something sounds a little too good to be true, it's probably not worth your time. And today, with stern Saturn wagging his finger at gullible Mercury in your hazy twelfth house, you'll want to inspect under the hood. Ask yourself: Is this really worth the risk?

September 24: Mercury-Mars opposition

So much for team spirit! With feisty Mars in competitive Aries facing off with the objective messenger planet today, it could take extra effort to get people to reach a consensus. Some will truly not be on-board with an idea while others are just being passive-aggressive to assert their will. Leave this alone for another day if you can.

September 27-October 27: Mercury in Scorpio

This is the expressive planet's first foray into your sign this year, and it's an extra-long one thanks to a retrograde from October 13 to November 3, during which it'll backflip briefly into Libra and your dreamy twelfth house. That reflective cycle is a perfect opportunity to refine your message so that when Mercury returns to Scorpio on November 10, you'll be ready to share it with a larger audience. Best part? You won't even have to raise your voice to get people's rapt attention.

September 29: Mars-Saturn square

Don't rush through a project if you're not able to maintain your super-high standards! Others may be galloping along, but you know if you go too fast, you'll lose focus or quality control. Unless you have a looming deadline, take your sweet old time.

September 29: Saturn retrograde ends

After four-plus frustrating months of spinning backward, cautious Saturn resumes forward motion in your third house of mental processes. If you've been mulling—and mulling!—a decision or how to move forward on a project, it's now time to stop thinking and to take action. Better to fail fast than stay stuck in neutral.

October

OCTOBER: LOVE HOTSPOTS

October 2-27: Venus in Virgo

When Venus swings into your outgoing eleventh house, you may actually feel optimistic about your romantic future. Singles will be eager to explore new possibilities—meeting friends of friends, checking out new dating sites—and just be happy to go out more and mingle. Couples will enjoy expanding your social circles and trying different activities that emphasize the friendship part of your bond. Time for a new shared hobby?

October 10: Venus-Uranus trine

Today's spontaneous energy could cause undeniable sparks to fly with someone you've just met. Isn't this what "chemistry" is all about? Don't think in terms of lifelong commitment. If there's a strong mutual attraction, why not follow up on it? Attached? Think of your beloved as your BFF, and make time today for long, uninterrupted conversations— letting them meander where they will!

October 16: Libra new moon

The year's only Libra new moon, which powers up your fantasy-fueled twelfth house, has "fresh start" written all over it! If you're single, you might finally go out with that avid pursuer—and possibly discover shockingly hot chemistry. In a LTR? The next two weeks are great for talking through short-term shared goals and getting some exciting plans on the books. And if you know in your heart of hearts that it's time to cut a cord, this lunar lift will give you the courage and compassion you need to let go with love.

October 18: Venus-Neptune opposition

A little drama and mystique can be fun and drive up anticipation. But there's a built-in time limit on just how much playing hard to get someone will tolerate. (Think how you'd feel if the suede ankle bootie was on the other foot!) Today's hazy opposition makes it hard to get clear answers, but it's worth meditating on why you're doing this cat-and-mouse thing in the first place.

 The AstroTwins' 2020 Horoscope

October 19: Venus-Jupiter trine

It'll be easier than you think to cross that line today between "friend" and "something else altogether"! If you're both single—and aren't putting a special relationship at risk—then it might be an exciting little side road to explore. But if one of you is eager and the other is gun-shy, don't apply (or succumb to) pressure. Attached? Pop out of your couple bubble and mingle with mutual friends, at least for a few hours.

October 21: Venus-Pluto trine

With intensifying Pluto signal-boosting the love planet, you won't be able to stay parked on the fence about a key decision. If you've been trying to establish stronger boundaries in a relationship or want to weed out the wannabes in your dating efforts, you may realize that it all starts with a firm, resolute inner commitment to your vision!

October 24: Venus-Saturn trine

Something on your mind? Today's supportive angle between structured Saturn and caring Venus in your communication houses urges you to speak your piece! No one can react to your needs or fulfill your desires if you keep them to yourself. Be direct, honest—and compassionate—and you'll get your point across perfectly.

October 27-November 21: Venus in Libra

This annual transit of the love planet through your most internal and introspective zone invites you to do what Scorpios do best: turn inward and examine your deepest emotions—on the most profound level possible. Whether you're in a complicated union, happily attached or single, you'll get the answers you seek by quieting your mind and listening to that wise voice within.

October 31: Taurus full moon

The only Taurus full moon of 2020 can bring a simmering connection to a full boil, shine a light on someone with soulmate potential or give you the courage and vision you need to "consciously uncouple." Because it's powering up your seventh house of committed relationships—and it's bringing the energy of the faithful and unfaltering Bull—you'll only have eyes for someone who can actually go the distance!

OCTOBER: CAREER HOTSPOTS

October 1: Aries full moon

You'll blast through any sense of being overwhelmed when the year's only Aries full moon sends a galvanizing jolt through your organized, hardworking sixth house. La luna reveals where to start, what to delegate (or just send to the "circular file") plus you'll have copious amounts of energy to tear through your to-do list. Need help? Ask for it—or hire it.

October 4: Pluto retrograde ends

You're free to speak with abandon now—well, as long you don't cross anyone's line in the sand. While controlling Pluto was spinning backward in your communication house for the past five months, you may have felt like you had to walk on eggshells. But now that it's back on track, you can make up for lost time with your effusive posts and #realtalk.

October 7: Mercury-Uranus opposition

This first of three face-offs between the messenger planet—in your sign—and transformative Uranus in your dynamic-duos realm could reset the terms of an important partnership or force you to reconsider a deal you're negotiating. It'll happen

again on October 19 (with Mercury retrograde) and November 17, so if you can stall until after that final hit, you'll have a lot more data and insight to make an informed decision.

October 9: Mars-Pluto square

Thinking through all your options sounds like a good thing, but when your two planetary rulers face off like this, you may wind up with an acute case of analysis paralysis (or emotional whiplash!). An intellectual or creative challenge is one thing, but reaching the point of overwhelm will only leave you feeling defeated and deflated. Stop multitasking and focus on one top-priority item till it's finished. Then pick another, rinse and repeat!

October 13-November 3: Mercury retrograde

When the messenger planet shifts into reverse, it'll bring good news and not-so-great news. On the upside, this is Mercury's final retrograde of the year, so after this, you won't have to endure any more wild mercurial curveballs until 2021. The downside? Much of this backspin is happening in your sign (until October 27), so it could muck things up in almost any area of life (not just work meetings and memos). Since you can't run away for the entire cycle, just take your time, back up everything in writing and delay any tech upgrades until the winged communicator corrects course.

October 15: Sun-Pluto square

It's not what people are saying that you need to worry about so much as what they're keeping to themselves! With manipulative Pluto throwing shade at the expressive Sun in your subterranean twelfth house, trying to figure out what's really going on is like playing high-stakes poker. This one is bluffing, that one has an ace up his sleeve... Better

to walk away from the table and pour yourself into your own work until this passes.

October 18: Sun-Saturn square

Before you go wagging a finger at someone else (always the easiest approach), stop and assess your role in this situation. If you can step back far enough, you might come to see that no one is actually to blame, and that this is simply a matter of diverging points of view. And chances are, there's merit to both of them. Drop your weapons and discuss!

October 19: Mars-Jupiter square

Newsflash: Riding hard on people isn't the best way to motivate them! Even if you're under severe deadline pressure, that's no reason to pass it on to your team members or colleagues. With Mars frothing up tension in your perfectionistic zone and clashing with supersizer Jupiter, your stress could reach dangerously high levels. Ward that off by taking a moment, whether a walk around the block or a long lunch with a friend who can talk you off the ledge.

October 31: Taurus full moon

This once-a-year lunation in your house of deals and partnerships could shine its brilliant beams on a perfect co-conspirator! If you're already "in the market," intensify your search over the next two weeks. Or just stay open to the universe delivering the ideal person. Already got a business buddy? What ingenious new project are you ready to launch before the end of the year?

The AstroTwins' 2020 Horoscope

November

NOVEMBER: LOVE HOTSPOTS

November 9: Venus-Mars opposition

Things can intensify—in any direction—under this rare (once-every-other-year) face-off between the cosmic lovebirds. And with Venus orbiting your unconscious twelfth house, you might not even have a handle on your own motivation. Are you looking for attention? Revenge? A little drama? Cut that out instantly and be more direct about your desires and needs. Whether you're single, attached or "it's complicated," you owe it to yourself (and your love interest) to treat the union with the utmost respect.

November 15: Venus-Pluto square

Listen closely to what people are telling you today and take them at their word. Even if you want another outcome, trust that penetrating Pluto in your communication corner will cut through the layers of deception and confusion and show you what's really going on. And if you don't like it, work with your date or mate to find an agreeable compromise.

November 16: Venus-Jupiter square

With seductive Venus embracing no-limits Jupiter, you could be faced with more options than you could ever think through. But your initial excitement may quickly turn to overwhelm and leave you dazed and confused. Rather than attempt to decide on a favorite, try a process of elimination, where you weed out the obvious "no thank-you's" and whittle the lot down to just a manageable few.

November 19: Venus-Saturn square

Take off the rose-colored lenses that Venus in your dreamy twelfth house has been rocking and prepare to face up to an awkward situation. With taskmaster Saturn at loggerheads with tender Venus, you could discover that the object of your affection is unhappy about something. Now that you know the real story, get proactive and work out a solution together.

November 21-December 15: Venus in Scorpio

Your sex appeal is about to shoot through the roof! As seductive Venus shimmies through your sign for the next several weeks, you'll turn heads wherever you go, and your magnetic charisma will have people hanging on your every word. It's a boon for single Scorpios, but don't abuse this cosmic gift by playing with people's affections. Attached? Tear yourself away from your adoring fans and make quality time for your beloved—you know, the one who's there for you through thick and thin.

November 27: Venus-Uranus opposition

Today's mantra bears repeating all day long: breathe! When disruptive Uranus in your partnership zone locks into an uneasy opposition with the love planet in your sign, you might not know which way is up—or out. You could feel like you need to find the exit—like, now! While that may seem like the easiest solution, it'll only ratchet up your confusion and potentially put a dent in an important relationship. You probably won't have enough clarity to talk this through today, but at the very least, aim to do no harm.

November 28: Neptune retrograde ends

You can begin to put your romantic life back in order or rebuild after five confusing months of fog-machine Neptune spinning backward in your amorous fifth house. Now that it's finally straightening out, the clouds will part, uncertainty will vanish, and you can get back to your regularly-scheduled passionate programming!

November 30: Gemini full moon (lunar eclipse)

A late-fall Monday it may be, but this could be one of the hottest, steamiest, most erotic days of your year! The annual Gemini full moon in your seductive, intimate eighth house is also a lunar eclipse, which brings efforts of the past six months to a thrilling, er, climax. If you've got a romantic partner, steal as much alone time as you can and just follow your bliss. (It won't steer you wrong!) Single? These next two weeks are peak manifesting time, so take some unprecedented (and perhaps unpremeditated) steps to meet someone worthy of your undying affection.

NOVEMBER: CAREER HOTSPOTS

November 1: Mercury-Saturn square

In this second of three squares between these formidable players—and this time with Mercury retrograde—you may not be sure whether to advance or retreat. You can't go wrong being cagily strategic, perhaps waiting to see what others do before you make your move. The final encounter, on November 6 with Mercury direct, may provide all the answers you need.

November 3: Mercury direct in Libra

Let it go, Scorpio! Communicator Mercury ends a three-week backspin and corrects course in your twelfth house of fantasy and hidden information. If you've been harboring distrust or are unsure

of someone's true intentions, Mercury's return to direct (forward) motion could help you gain clarity. Been running hot-and-cold yourself? You'll have an easier time sifting through the uncertainty, too.

November 10-December 1: Mercury in Scorpio

The cosmic communicator graces your sign for the second time this year, gilding your words with a golden glow and making it impossible for people not to sit up and take notice of what you have to say. Hopefully during the retrograde you had a chance to review and refine your message, and with the silver-tongued planet back on track, you're prepared to deliver it. Heck, by now you should be ready to shout it from the rooftops!

November 12: Jupiter-Pluto meetup

Take the microphone, Scorpio! As outspoken Jupiter and transformational Pluto make their third and final union—a rare alignment—you could have a powerful message to share. You've been crafting this idea all year, and along the way, may have learned important lessons in effective communication. Look back to April 4 and June 30, the other two Jupiter-Pluto conjunctions, for ideas of what might come together now.

November 13: Mars retrograde ends

Ready, set, goals! With the action planet (your co-ruler) sidelined in your industrious zone for the past few months, you might not have been able to gain traction on some projects. But now that it's back to full strength, you can plow right through anything resembling a roadblock and speed toward the finish line. Knowing you, all that waiting just served to pour jet fuel in your tanks, and now you'll be unstoppable!

November 15: Scorpio new moon

This glorious lunar lift in your sign is like your personal cosmic New Year. It's a moon of fresh starts, whether you're looking to change jobs—or careers—or relocate to another part of the globe. If you can dream it, Scorpio, you can do it. But be kind to yourself, please. Take a bold step over the coming two weeks to show the universe your commitment, but then give yourself until the corresponding full moon in your sign, six months from now, to have reached that lofty goal.

November 23: Mercury-Neptune trine

Far more effective than mere words today will be well-timed and targeted nonverbal communication. With intuitive Neptune in your creativity sector aligned with the messenger planet in your own perceptive sign, you're tuned in to higher dimensions. Data and logic are useful in some circumstances, but right now, work the power of authentic emotional connection.

November 30: Gemini full moon (lunar eclipse)

The year's only full moon in your house of joint ventures and investments (also an activating lunar eclipse) can inspire you to team up with someone who has some of the skills you wish you had—and who's looking for a person like you to complete them! The coming few weeks are perfect for getting a handle on your finances and how your portfolio performed this year, and to make any and all necessary adjustments to improve on that in 2021.

December

DECEMBER: LOVE HOTSPOTS

December 5: Venus trine Neptune

Ah, love! As sensual Venus (in your sign!) embraces enchanting Neptune in your passionate fifth house, feel free to conjure all the romantic holiday fantasies you can muster. These beautifying planets help you feel glamorous and desirable. You may be putting someone on a pedestal but as long as you don't hoist them too high, no harm can come of it. Enjoy the sparks and surrender to the sweetness of fantasy!

December 15, 2020-January 9, 2021: Venus in Sagittarius

Sex appeal with a side of security? Yes, please! For the next four weeks, as the planet of romance and values zips through your house of sensuality and stability, you might find that rarest of unicorns: a partner who's the whole package. Chemistry is great, but it's ephemeral, while a lover who's got what it takes on every level to make you feel safe and loved is worth hanging onto! Already together? Celebrate your joyful union with a vow renewal or some other ritual in front of witnesses.

December 17, 2020-March 7, 2023: Saturn in Aquarius

After a brief backflip into Capricorn, structured Saturn kicks off part two of its lengthy residence in your fourth house of roots and emotional foundations. You may decide it's important to unravel some old family-dynamic mysteries so you can move forward in your love life without that baggage. You might get serious about buying or selling a home, starting or expanding a family of your own, or just turning Chateau Scorpio into the Pinterest-perfect den of your dreams.

December 19, 2020-May 13, 2021: Jupiter in Aquarius

Joining Saturn in your home zone, the planet of luck, growth and enthusiasm returns to your domestic fourth house for the first time in 12 years. It's finally time to knock down those walls, expand your living quarters—or maybe downsize, but to a more upscale address—or get serious about a committed partnership. Couples will have much to discuss, with both of you envisioning so many huge next steps over the coming year!

December 21: Jupiter-Saturn meetup

Today's ultra-rare summit of expansive Jupiter and structured Saturn—two seemingly opposite forces—could help a "calculated risk" pay off in your personal life. Known as The Great Conjunction, this planetary pairing only happens every 20 years or so. Take an important step toward buying property, creating a home or growing your family. This astrological alliance may leave you feeling more emotionally rooted than you have in a long time. Enjoy the feeling of buoyant security!

December 30: Venus-Neptune square

You want a partner who enhances your life, not detracts from it. This dreamy collision of the fantasy-prone planets could spin you out into one wild daydream, but when you do come tumbling back to earth, it'll be with a new clarity around what you want in a mate, and what's a deal breaker. And you might have the gumption to give someone their walking papers!

DECEMBER: CAREER HOTSPOTS

December 1-20: Mercury in Sagittarius

Before the year draws to a close, spend some time balancing the books and making sure you've done everything you can to set you up for a prosperous 2021. For the next three weeks, cerebral Mercury will conduct a final audit in your second house of finances. This is your chance to get things in order and to incubate some fiscal goals for the new year.

December 13: Mercury-Neptune square

Even as you're poring over every line item in your 2020 budget and trying to come correct before the year draws to a close, a rash clash between mindful Mercury and impressionable Neptune in your passionate fifth house could send you running for a hit of retail therapy. And then there's the constant low-grade pressure of holiday shopping! There is a way to balance need and desire, but it requires self-discipline—and maybe tapping a "gatekeeper" friend as an accountability buddy.

December 14: Sagittarius new moon (total solar eclipse)

The year's only new moon in your money and work house is also a solar eclipse (think: fresh starts), and if you play your cards right, you can lay a solid foundation for a prosperous new year! While that's probably music to your ears, it's not a magic trick. You need to know exactly what you want and what "prosperity" even means to you. Is it just enough to scrape by? Do you need to hit a "magic number" to feel flush? This isn't greed talking, Scorpio. It's you aligning with your higher self and finding a way to monetize your natural-born talents.

December 20, 2020-January 9, 2021: Mercury in Capricorn

Forget the fact that people are packing up for the holidays and checking out for a week or more. When you're this on fire, you need to find those kindred spirits who can help you take your brilliant ideas to the next level. This is the messenger planet's annual jaunt through your expressive third house, and you'll be damned if you're going to let those creative juices go to waste. Even if you just write/sketch/video your ideas with the intention of fleshing them out in the new year, you'll be way ahead of the game when 2021 rolls around.

December 23: Mars-Pluto square

This is the third and final clash of these planetary titans—which happen to be your co-rulers—but having weathered two previous dust-ups, you should be wise and resilient enough to allow things to unfold without you trying to control every aspect of it. Could you have finally learned that incredible lesson? If so, it's well worth all the agony and frustration you had to endure.

December 25: Mercury-Uranus trine

Presumably no one is working today, but how much do you want to bet they're sneaking peeks at their social media feeds in between family moments? So if you've got something important—or clever, or just endearing—to share with your workmates, go ahead and post a dog whistle comment on one of your pages. Not everyone will understand, but those who do will love you even more as a result!

December 29: Cancer full moon

This second Cancer full moon of 2020 (the first was January 10) is like the other bookend to your calendar year, and a perfect moment to reflect on everything you accomplished over the past 12 months. Savor the deep gratitude you have for the people who helped you along your journey. As a goal-oriented cardinal sign, Cancer's energy can fill you with big ideas for 2021. And no, Scorpio, it's not too early to get started on those New Year's resolutions! ✳

Tools from The AstroTwins
for your 2020 PLANNING

Visit all year long for
new updates & additions!

www.astrostyle.com/2020tools

SAGITTARIUS
2020

Yearly Highlights

LOVE

Massive astrological activity blows through your Gemini-ruled seventh house this year, pushing you to go "all in" with a partner. On May 5, the lunar North Node arrives in Gemini for the first time since 2003, calling in a meant-to-be-mate who directs your destiny. Attached Archers could embark on a co-created mission! This year will not be without its amorous challenges. Love planet Venus spins retrograde in Gemini from May 13 to June 25, and her lusty dance partner Mars will reverse commute through Aries and your passionate fifth house from September 9 to November 13. Old wounds can erupt and exes crawl out of the woodwork. A Gemini lunar eclipse on November 30 could reveal incompatibilities, pushing coupled Centaurs to find win-wins or go your separate ways. On a bright note, this lunar lift could accelerate developments, like a holiday season engagement or pregnancy!

MONEY

Even carefree Archers will be fixated on the bottom line as your ruling planet Jupiter shares a flight path with power brokers Saturn and Pluto for most of the year. Throughout 2020, this celestial trio will meet and greet one other in Capricorn and your second house of fiscal affairs. Their combined powers—along with three final eclipses on your money axis between January and July—illuminate new ways to earn, invest and expand your empire. But be prepared to stretch, Sagittarius, because your old DIY success blueprint won't get you to the Holy Grail. Cultivate patience as you learn (and earn) by the books. This is the year to stabilize your foundation so you can fill the coffers for years to come.

WELLNESS

With your ruler, buoyant Jupiter, planted in your second house of daily habits, you'll get your glow on by embracing routine. Although your sign loves variety, in 2020, you'll appreciate the ease of preparing the same handful of healthy recipes (or at least using the same fresh ingredients in myriad ways). With your brain already addled from so many work decisions, the less you have to think about fitness, the better. Experimental Uranus flows through your wellness zone all year long. Mix some yoga in with the weightlifting and spin. Work with holistic healers, like acupuncturists and herbalists, to supplement your standard medical check-ups. You might even switch to a naturopath or functional medicine doctor who will treat the root cause instead of just the symptoms.

LEISURE

With so much emphasis on your professional life in 2020, you could inadvertently treat loved ones like bit players in your script. Reciprocate their love and attention, or they'll lose interest in The Sagittarius Show—a lonely proposition. To prevent this from happening, put some traditions in place and treat them like immovable pillars: family dinners together at least two nights a week, no phones at the table. Generous Archers may need to put up firm boundaries with demanding loved ones. Events this year continue to underscore the difference between empowering and enabling. With weighty Saturn darting in and out of Aquarius and your sector of peers, your relationship with a sibling could take on added gravitas between March and July, then again after December 17. ✳

SAGITTARIUS
2020 HOROSCOPE

2020 Power Dates

SAGITTARIUS NEW MOON
December 14 (11:16 pm ET) solar eclipse

SAGITTARIUS FULL MOON
June 5 (3:12pm ET) lunar eclipse

SUN IN SAGITTARIUS
November 21 – December 21

Ready to lock down a solid plan of action? After a year of extreme exploration, you're feeling the need to soar along a clearly defined flight path. Good news! In 2020, your focus will be as sharp as a ninja's throwing star. For this you have your galactic guardian, Jupiter, to thank—along with power brokers Pluto and Saturn, who are co-piloting the mission. Your red-spotted ruler will spend all of 2020 in Capricorn and your rooted second house. The last time these three heavy-hitters aligned was 1284-5 C.E., so yes, this is kind of a big deal.

Draft your blueprint for success and you'll keep the coffers filled for years to come.

As a Sagittarius, you have two favorite speeds: fast and faster. Cautious Capricorn, on the other hand, cruises along like a luxury car, totally capable of racing ahead, but only hitting peak acceleration when it's time for a victory lap. With the Jupiter-Saturn-Pluto trio assembled in earthy, material-minded Capricorn, you may feel a bit out of your element—even when you are knocking the ball out of the park. Winning 2020 will require the fine art of patience, which is not inherently a Sagittarius specialty. You'll have to remind yourself (over and over) that being a tortoise instead of a hare is the fastest way to the finish line. Just try not to bite your nails down to the quick while you wait for results to roll in!

For many Archers, 2019 brought its share of stops and starts, so you're already used to this "one foot on the gas, the other on the brake" routine. Saturn has been trudging through Capricorn since December 19, 2017, forcing you to work at a measured pace. Despite that, you spent a good part of 2019 barreling down the astrological Autobahn, as daredevil Jupiter raced through Sagittarius from November 8, 2018 through December 2, 2019. That once-per-decade voyage was heaven for your indie spirit. Along with an overwhelming desire for freedom, you were hellbent on breaking past a stultifying plateau. (And we're betting you did just that!)

As you greet 2020, you could have a great reason to raise a bonus champagne toast. Maybe you landed a plum new job or raised a round of venture capital. Did you get married, end a bad romance or discover a shared purpose with your S.O.? Relocate to a joy-inducing zip code that feels "so Sagittarius"? Maybe you overcame a limiting belief that was holding you back financially or emotionally. Pop that cork and send up some gratitude to the universe!

While you probably won't have a ton of dramatic updates to report in 2020, you are poised for a payoff, resulting from the strategic risks you took in 2019. The only catch? Remembering that the "discovery phase" has drawn to a close. As the new decade dawns, head to the drafting table and start running your visionary schemes through the project management filter.

You're very much at the ground floor in 2020, which means your focus should be on building a rock-solid foundation for your future empire. Visuals and branding are always part of the game, but not at the expense of other "back-end" developments. Your life may look more like a construction site than a dream home this year. But before you bring in the metaphoric cranes and wrecking balls, work like a master architect. Get crystal clear about what you want your final product to be. Holding that vision will get you through those slow-as-molasses moments that test your Sagittarius (im)patience. Then, run the numbers. What time, energy and resources will be needed to pull this off? With lucky Jupiter in your financial zone until December 19, you'll be fired up about fundraising, should you discover that pulling off your dream will be more expensive than anticipated.

And while Saturn will spend a good part of 2020 in Capricorn, from January 1 until March 21, then again from May 10 to July 1, the cosmic taskmaster also darts forward into Aquarius and your cooperative, communicative third house for a short spring stint. Then, on December 17, 2020, Saturn will officially call Aquarius its home until March 7, 2023. This is the ringed planet's first dip into the Water Bearer's well since January 1994! During this three-year cycle, you'll learn to separate the wheat from the chaff in your personal life. Relationships with siblings, neighbors, coworkers and other peers go through a renovation process. You may team up on a serious project that necessitates a formal contract. As the saying goes, people are in your life for a season, a reason or a lifetime. With enduring Saturn writing the rules of engagement, people will have to earn their loyalty points if they want to share your generous bounty!

The December 21 Winter Solstice could bring a watershed moment. That day, Saturn will make a rare (as in once every 20 years), exact meetup with Jupiter. They'll unite at 0°29' Aquarius—an event called The Great Conjunction. As 2020 draws to a close, you'll see clearly who should play a starring role in this emerging new chapter of your life. Surprise! Some people may be quiet supporters who are more traditional or conservative than the folks you tend to gravitate toward. As Saturn lumbers through Aquarius until March 7, 2023, test collaborative ventures on a project-by-project basis. Know this: With such a process-driven planet at the wheel, it might take a few missions to get your work styles aligned and your respective roles defined.

Don't hit the snooze button on 2020 yet, Sagittarius! There will be some frissons of excitement to keep your blood pumping. On June 5, a fresh, 18-month-long eclipse series erupts across the Sagittarius/Gemini axis, with two more following on November 30 and December 14. These momentous moonbeams light a fire under stalled passion projects while expediting relationship developments. The last time eclipses landed on this lunar axis was between December 21, 2010, and May 25, 2013. Flip back in your calendar to see what was happening then if you can recall. Similar themes may recur between June 5, 2020, and December 3, 2021.

Along with the eclipses, the lunar nodes, AKA the "cosmic destiny points" will also shift from the Cancer/Capricorn line to the Gemini/Sagittarius axis on May 5, 2020. The last time the nodes were in this position was between October 14, 2001, and April 14, 2003. With the South Node in Sagittarius and your first house of self-expression until January 18, 2022, your karmic gifts will be called to the fore. In many ways, you'll feel guided by a mystical force come May—which might feel like a heavier responsibility at times. And yet, Archer, there's no avoiding your "soul work." Heed the call!

Simultaneously, the moon's fateful North Node will dwell in Gemini and your seventh house of partnerships from May 5, 2020 until January 18, 2022. A soulmate (or soul friend) relationship could emerge, adding a powerful dimension into your life.

Love planet Venus also takes an extended tour through Gemini and your seventh house of partnerships from April 3 through August 7. Due to a retrograde from May 13 to June 25, Venus will hover in this sign four times longer than she does on the average year. While this may drive up some buried issues within your closest relationships, the planetary peacemaker and diplomat is here to support you. Don't just smooth over rough edges! Use the retrograde to get to the root of any recurring breakdowns. Then reconstruct your most important bonds according to a new, shared vision.

Mars will also turn retrograde from September 9 to November 13—a cycle that happens every other year. In 2020, the backspin takes place in Aries, which is the red planet's home sign. As a result, Mars will linger in the Ram's realm for six months, from June 27, 2020, until January 6, 2021. Since Aries governs your fifth house of fame, romance and creative expression, this extended transit lends a large dose of sizzle and glamour in the second half of the year. Along with that may be intense anxiety, since Mars in Aries can ratchet up stress levels. Life is not a performance, Sagittarius, it's an interactive and immersive experience. Bring your most authentic self to the "show" and watch your loyal fanbase grow.

Jupiter in Capricorn: New income streams.

December 2, 2019 – December 19, 2020

New year, new routines! Last year, while Jupiter was in your sign, you had a chance to throw the metaphoric spaghetti against the wall to see what would stick. Every day was an adventure, totally unscripted and full of discovery. Now, with your red-spotted ruler in Capricorn until December 19, you have a wall full of "noodles" to survey and figure out which ones are worth developing into a tangible product.

That also means packing up your poker chips and going for safer bets. A bit of a buzzkill, yes, but you're pretty familiar with the Sea Goat's sensible pace by now. Stern Saturn has been stationed in Capricorn since December 19, 2017, and Pluto is on a long roll through here from 2008 to 2024. Plus, you hosted take-it-slow Saturn in your sign from December 23, 2014, to December 19, 2017. Playing it safe(r) has become your M.O. It's been a long time since you truly leapt without a net, Archer, even if you danced near the edge.

Despite Saturn and Pluto's anchoring influence, your optimistic spirit will not be contained. With your ruler, elevated Jupiter, soaring through the Sea Goat's slice of the zodiac wheel until December 19, you're on a relentless tear to produce something that not only puts money in the bank, but sets you up for long-term security.

A boots-on-the-ground work ethic will be required, but how to get from Point A to Point Z? With Jupiter in your second house of daily habits until December 19, opt for a tried-and-true formula instead of going rogue. Follow the success blueprints from experts who have "been there, done that." This will quickly remove the struggle from your efforts. The challenge for you? Being patient enough to read the directions before you shift into action mode. Life really can be easier, Archer, if you surrender your stubborn insistence on doing everything from scratch.

Here's another discovery that may shock your free-flowing sign in 2020: Consistency creates freedom! As a spontaneous Sagittarius, you can't live without a generous portion of wiggle room in your life. But a scattered, "make it up as I go" schedule isn't necessarily liberating. In fact, your renegade M.O. is exhausting you. And when you're on the verge of burnout, it's impossible to connect to your intuition—or your playful spirit. Studies show that the average human is now making 38,000 decisions in a single day! This can be so taxing to the brain that psychologists have dubbed the condition "decision fatigue." With the barrage of emails and social media posts that greet you each morning, you could be ready for a nap by the time you have to choose between a gluten-free or grain-based wrap for your lunchtime sandwich.

While we'd never suggest a plug-and-play lifestyle for a mutable Sagittarius, create a routine that you love. For example, rise an hour earlier each morning to journal while you sip coffee (instead of slamming it). Listen to inspiring podcasts while you get dressed. Pick up a healthy breakfast on your way to the office, or prepare some overnight oats and keep them waiting in the fridge. Are you constantly skipping workouts and rescheduling calls? Enough of that! Devote weekly slots in the calendar for exercise and a fixed time for any recurring appointments. Begin and end your workday at set hours. Knowing when you have to be "on call" also means knowing when you're off-duty—which, by extension, makes it a heck of a lot easier to commit to fun plans, like weekend trips, evening cocktails and brunch dates.

You're a big-picture visionary, but in 2020, you'll find the "riches in the niches." If you sink your teeth into an ambitious project, you'll need to fall in love with the process. Start by setting priorities you can stick with. Then, break your mission down into small bites instead of galloping in and trying to crush the goal in record time (which has worked for you in the past, even if it nearly cost your sanity). Setting snack-sized resolutions, or "micro-tasking," prevents overwhelm and makes a monumental mission feel less overwhelming.

A novelist friend of ours finished a manuscript while Jupiter was transiting through her "lather, rinse, repeat" second house. Her technique? Committing to writing three pages per day, which she rose early to accomplish on many mornings before heading in to her IT job. With a mantra of "Writers write" spurring her on, she set aside perfectionism and banged out the text. Although a lot of it wound up on the cutting room floor, she built a solid muscle, boost her confidence—and wrote a shoppable book—by taking this step-by-step approach. The devil—and a chorus of angels—are in the details!

Since Jupiter governs long-distance connections, you may travel or relocate in connection with your work. Does your company need someone to go abroad for six months? Raise your hand, Sagittarius! Or maybe you'll play an "intrapreneurial" role within a larger company, spearheading one of their

cutting-edge new ventures to help them break into a fresh market.

If you're a business owner, keep your eye on the bottom line. Instead of developing one new product after another, think: recurring revenue streams. How about a monthly offering like a subscription box? If you have a following, an affordable membership program could keep your coffers full—and your loyal customers connected to your brand.

Have you been undervaluing yourself? Jupiter's tour through your second house of self-worth buoys your confidence. Time's up on over-functioning and giving your best to unappreciative users. Jupiter in Capricorn will reveal the value of your contributions. As a bonus, you'll care a lot less about what other people think of your choices. Now that, Sagittarius, is true freedom.

Your romantic life will benefit from this sensual and sensible Jupiter cycle. Single Sagittarians might finally stay in one place long enough to build a truly intimate connection. Stability is sexy in 2020, a year where you'll be more drawn to character than surface appearances. No, you'll never give up your wild festival weekends, but you'll also enjoy the mundane magic, like cooking dinners together and snuggling in bed. Living for the moment? No thanks! In 2020, you're looking for a slow-burning mate who can sustain your interest beyond a season.

Money may be a frequent conversation topic in relationships. Don't avoid it! Get on the same page as your partner about how much to save and how to use your discretionary funds. A few more home-cooked dinners instead of nights on the town could cover a Balinese baecation or front-row tickets to your favorite band's reunion tour.

For coupled Archers, "quality time" could become your new love language. Clear white space in your calendar to "just be" with your boo. Nesting will be blissful, with a few luxury dates sprinkled in here and there. Spoil yourselves with chef's tasting menus, theater tickets or an Airbnb weekend. All in all, this will be a lovely year for appreciating "the little things." Write your love story one page at a time instead of fixating on an end result. Each small moment you share will be a paving stone along the path to your happily-ever-after.

Saturn-Pluto conjunction: Build your new life.
December 2019–February 2020 (exact on January 12)

Old structures are crumbling away, clearing space for new systems to be implemented. This is just inevitable, Sagittarius, but it can also be a bit disorienting until you get your "land legs." On January 12, old-school Saturn will make a rare (as in every 34 years), exact connection to metamorphic Pluto in Capricorn and your second house of foundations. This is the first time these two will meet since November 1982. Although the effects of this formation will be felt from December 20, 2019, to February 5, 2020, their exact hit marks "demolition day."

Like an explosion on a construction site, events could arise that clear a space, allowing you to dig a new foundation and pour some cement. Even if you're ready to rebuild, there's something melancholy about seeing an old structure collapse.

Take a moment to memorialize what came before. You might even do a grief ritual, building an altar to commemorate what's passed (or passing) out of your life.

As you survey the rubble, you'll also realize that some your values have changed. There's no going back to the person you were last decade, no matter how nostalgic you feel about that time. Perhaps you need more comfort or less stuff in order to feel happy. You may even have to confront your own materialistic values, as your bohemian ideals give way to a need for greater security (or vice versa). Whatever it is, slow-moving Saturn has helped you get here by the sweat of your brow. There's nothing wrong with evolving, Archer, but it may herald an identity crisis early this year.

In 2020, you're poised for financial gain, but you'll want to make every dollar count in a meaningful way. Along with that will come some challenging social impacts. With shadowy Pluto in the frame, you could get some pushback from people who are jealous of your success. Users and manipulators could also crawl out of their caves, wanting a piece of your hard-earned fortune. You're a generous soul, Sagittarius, but you need to be a bit more self-protective in Q1. Remember this: You're not abandoning people by shifting into a different economic class.

By the same token, do you normally rave about your victories, wanting to share the "you can do it, too!" momentum across every social media platform? In January, use greater discretion. Keep certain gains to yourself until you've settled into these new developments—and adjusted to whatever new role you're playing. Once you hit your stride with this,

 The AstroTwins' 2020 Horoscope

you can spread the gospel of your success story to the world. No one could stop you if they tried!

Conversely, some Archers may opt out of the corporate life for a minimalist ethos. Stepping out of the rat race and living simply is not for everyone, but if you can connect this to your personal ideals, you could certainly get into it…for a while, at least. For a sign that loves to expand, discovering your definition of "enough" can bring a huge sense of relief. The Saturn-Pluto conjunction might just leave you awash with gratitude for all that you have, realizing that you've reached blissful contentment—and that you're totally good with that!

Of course, it won't be too long before your enterprising sign takes up a hobby like silversmithing or furniture restoration, and you start peddling your wares on Etsy or at weekend markets. You hate to be bored! But no matter where your metric for fulfillment lies, January will demand resourcefulness. You'll have to ensure that every penny counts. Waste not, want not, Sagittarius.

Jupiter-Pluto conjunction: Finding buried treasure.
April 4, June 30, November 12

What lies beneath, Sagittarius? Grab a shovel, because it's time to excavate! There may be burning hot lava or a vein of gold beneath your feet, and it's time to find out for sure. Three times this year, plumb-the-depths Pluto makes a rare merger with your ruler, high-exposure Jupiter. The scheduled "digs" take place on April 4, June 30 and November 12. You won't be content with

superficial explanations near these dates. You want real solutions, and you're going to drill down to find the root cause of the problem.

Brace yourself: With Jupiter shining its high beams into Pluto's shadowy underworld, you may uncover something shocking. Skeletons are often locked up in Pluto's vault, and even an open-minded Archer could be left reeling. Fortunately, both Jupiter and Pluto are parked in Capricorn and your matter-of-fact second house, allowing you to greet any discoveries with an eye toward tangible solutions. Instead of freaking out, you'll be relieved to know what you're dealing with, so you can put both long-term systems and daily life hacks in place.

If you own a home, you may need to make a budget for repairing the foundation. Something that's "hidden" in the cellar may need to be updated or renovated, like your furnace or pipes. Don't wait for a leak or damage to happen; have everything checked early in the year. You might even take out a home equity line to add on to the ground floor or finish your basement, raising your comfort level—and your property value!

A long-held limiting belief may come up for review, particularly involving finances. As a serial "under-charger," and a generous soul, you're prone to giving the metaphorical milk away for free. But the Jupiter-Pluto conjunctions can awaken you to your true value. Once you see this, your cash cow could turn into a full-scale "revenue ranch."

Pluto rules investments while Jupiter is the expansive entrepreneur. What passive income streams can you set up? (Translation: Money made in your sleep.) As the sign that rules publishing and education, you might create downloadable info products, such as online courses or instructional guides that only have to be created once. Or perhaps you'll turn a rental property into an Airbnb or become an affiliate sales rep for someone else's amazing wares.

With front-facing Jupiter playing PR agent and Pluto pulling strings behind the scenes, you have a powerful planetary tag team buoying your ambitions. Whatever you're working on, don't expect your efforts to stay hidden near these three dates. People will be curious, even eager, to learn your process. Sharing your "how I did it" story could turn into a TED-style talk that gets you hired as a paid speaker, or a YouTube series that you lock behind a paywall. Cha-ching!

During the Jupiter-Pluto meetup on June 30, both planets will be retrograde. You may decide to break away from some shady or suspicious entanglements. Review your spending habits. For example, if you bank with an institution whose investments don't align with your ethics, you may switch to a credit union. Alchemical Pluto and high-vibe Jupiter can also help you attract business opportunities with companies whose ideals are woven into their practices. Sustainable, low-impact, carbon-neutral—since this trio of Jupiter-Pluto conjunctions takes place in earthy Capricorn, environmental responsibility will play a role in your key financial decisions.

If you're an entrepreneur, be sure to vocalize your principled practices as part of your marketing. (The second house is often associated with the throat and voice.) This may be one of the key reasons people choose to work with you instead of another contractor or brand. Of course, that also means you're responsible for walking your talk—a role your truth-driven sign will gladly step into. As you

should, since there's no hiding your true practices when Jupiter and Pluto meet up!

Venus & Mars Retrograde: Relationship review.
Venus Retrograde: May 14 – June 25

Mars Retrograde: September 10 – November 13

Reunited and it feels so good? With cosmic lovebirds Venus and Mars both weathering a retrograde spell in 2020, expect some blasts from the past. People who once played key roles in your life could audition to be part of a sequel production—or you may find yourself ruminating on "the one that got away."

First to reverse-commute will be vivacious Venus, retreating through Gemini and your seventh house of committed partnerships from May 13 to June 25. Normally, Venus hovers in a zodiac sign for four weeks, but due to this retrograde, she'll extend this cycle for four months, as she electric slides through Gemini from April 3 to August 7.

How can you strike a compromise without making too many sacrifices? With the celestial sensualist stroking your twosome zone for one-third of the year, you might just learn the reason why people insist that "relationships take work." Syncing up schedules and priorities could be an angst-filled process for coupled Archers, and during the retrograde from May 13 to June 25, you may feel like two ships passing in the night.

The good news is, with Venus in clever, communicative Gemini, you can lifehack your way through these relationship rifts using simple (and digital) strategies. For example, sync your calendar with your S.O.'s to stay abreast of each other's busy lives. If it's not too much work, create a shared calendar and commit to posting appointments there. You don't need to travel to Peru for your anniversary or plan a massive vow renewal ceremony to revive your bond. (Though, we're not saying you shouldn't.) Gemini rules playful bursts of socializing and local activity. With Venus here from April through August, weekly date nights to your favorite neighborhood haunts will give you plenty to talk about. Show up for trivia at the pub, a local band's opening, barbecues. Make new friends as a pair. When you're on the road, send each other Marco Polo video messages and naughty sexts. Yes, it's an extra effort, but having the support of an amazing partner is worth it, wouldn't you say?

Iconic figures from your past may enter your world during Venus' backspin, along with some questionable characters. Single Sagittarians could reunite with an old flame between May 13 and June 25, which is sure to lend some spice to your spring-fevered fantasies. But is this the kind of heat that could leave you burned? Unless you and bae have done significant inner work (and even then), unresolved issues are likely to rear up again. Do you have the tools to greet them differently this go 'round? That could give your Act II a fighting chance. Of course, if it was merely bad timing that kept you apart, fate may finally be on your side. Give it a go, Sag. You could be making things Instagram-official by the time Venus waves Gemini farewell on August 7.

A month after Venus corrects course, her dance partner Mars begins moonwalking back through Aries and your fifth house of passionate romance and flamboyant self-expression. Look out! From September 9 to November 13, the red planet's retrograde could churn up some feisty and turbulent emotions. Mars is the warrior of the skies, and Aries is its home sign. Their combined powers could bring a double dose of passionate energy—or some world-class brawls!

Just like Venus, Mars will spend a longer-than-usual time in a single sign, checking into Aries on June 27 and remaining in this home-court advantage until January 6, 2021. Generally, the red planet hangs out in a single sign for seven weeks, but due to the midterm retrograde, this homecoming parade lasts for six whole months!

Despite any blips Mars retro may bring, its tour through Aries could herald some Hollywood highlights for Centaurs. With your fame house lit by this dashing planet for nearly half the year, you won't be shy about basking in the limelight. This could be your year to become a YouTuber, or literally appear on TV. Are you more of an "internet sensation"? Use streaming video to attract and enthrall your audience via social media. And thanks to Venus' extended tour through Gemini earlier in the year, you may be sharing the stage with a partner who can play off your wisdom and wit, like a modern-day Lucy Ricardo and Ethel Mertz.

Bring on the swagger! Your bold brand of leadership will empower others to believe in themselves. Mars in Aries fans the flames of your fire sign fierceness. You'll feel confident, unapologetic and deserving of the best! The only proviso? While Mars is retrograde from September 9 to November 13,

you'll struggle to gauge your own strength. Take a few minutes to read the room before you unleash full-frontal Sagittarius on 'em. Your audience probably needs some warming up before they can handle all of that.

Mars retrograde in Aries can make your ego a little fragile. Don't puff up to compensate for insecurity. That will only make matters worse. Instead, own up to your growing edge. (We didn't call it a "weak spot," okay?) Find yourself a metaphoric runway coach who can pump up your confidence again by teaching you some insider tricks of the trade. Hey, Sagittarius, it can be nerve-wracking to have so many eyes on you. All the same, fame is practically your birthright in the second half of 2020. Wouldn't you rather be iconic than notorious? Since we know the answer is yes (even for IDGAF Sagittarians like Nicki Minaj), fix yourself a plate of humble pie and you'll rise through the ranks with the unwavering respect and adulation of your fans.

Saturn in Capricorn & Aquarius: Monetize your message.

Saturn in Capricorn: January 1 – March 21; July 1 – December 17

Saturn in Aquarius: March 21 – July 1; December 17 – March 7, 2023

By now, you're probably seeing a theme emerge for 2020, Sagittarius: Money matters are front and center as this new decade dawns. But where the real juice comes from is identifying your beliefs, then developing your earning strategy from there. The second house is security-minded, but it's also principled. How you make your money will come under the microscope.

For the third and final year, integrity-hound Saturn weaves through Capricorn and your second house of fiscal foundations. This cycle, which began on December 19, 2017, has been pushing you to simplify, streamline and define your path. From March 21 to July 1, Saturn will dart forward into Aquarius and your cooperative, communicative third house—a preview of a three-year cycle that will resume for the long haul from December 17, 2020, to March 7, 2023.

With the ringed taskmaster weaving between your second and third houses, there couldn't be a better year to formulate your mission statement. Or maybe you already know what your soul purpose is, but you need to make it more of a daily mantra. (How about a tattoo?) In Capricorn, Saturn crystallizes your ethos. In Aquarius, the systematic planet can help you put your ideals into words.

Before you start crafting snappy soundbites, identify your driving purpose. (Simon Sinek's TED Talk "Start with Why" can be a great catalyst.) What's the deep-down reason you wake up and go to work every day—or toil after-hours on a passion project when you get home from your corporate job? What drives you to devote your waking hours to these tasks? Make it your mission to put this into words.

If you're overwhelmed, you've probably made things too complicated. Sagittarians tend to do more, more and more. As a result, you lose focus—and your audience may follow suit. Fortunately, averting "the law of diminishing returns" actually involves doing less. Learn to package your offerings in a savvier way, serving up spoon-sized bites before sending out the five-course meals. That's something the 2020 Saturn cycle will assist with! While Saturn is in Aquarius from March through July, you might even conduct a survey. Ask your colleagues, clients or customers what they value most about your offerings. The discoveries will be illuminating!

As Saturn in Aquarius pivots you toward partnership, who you link up with will matter more than ever. Align with collaborators, clients and companies who act from a principled place. You'll be drawn to ambitious folks who are on a mission, preferring no-nonsense achievers over the life-of-the-party comedians. Business guru Jim Rohm has a theory that your net worth can be calculated by averaging the income of the five people you spend the most time with. Whether or not you agree, adding a high-earning influencer (or five) to your favorites list could bring a boon to your bank account before 2023.

On a purely social basis, Saturn's move into Aquarius will lead you toward lasting friendships. Your inner circle may shrink a bit between 2020 and 2023, as you choose quality over quantity. The third house is the domain of peers, such as siblings, neighbors, coworkers and friends who are close in age. In an ideal world, you'd be besties with all of them, but things don't always pan out that way. If your daily interactions are fraught with drama, bickering and spilling of tea, draw back and put firmer boundaries in place with certain folks. You can still keep things cordial…but casual.

You're generally outspoken, Sagittarius, but after enough foot-in-mouth gaffes, you may realize the benefits of waiting before you clap back on Twitter or sound off in a team meeting. With cautious Saturn decamping to Aquarius, the wisdom of waiting will be underscored further. While you might miss throwing out a few good punchlines (or have to snicker about them privately with a couple of BFFs), being impeccable with your word will give you an air of authority when you do speak up. Not only will people lean in to hear what you have to say, but they might even pay for your sage advice.

Got an idea brewing for a podcast, book or mobile app? Saturn in Aquarius can get these dreams into development since the third house rules writing, teaching, and some forms of media. Old-school Saturn doesn't want you to change your message—just add a few more digital mediums (Aquarius' domain) so you can spread it farther. You might even take a few courses to learn the finer points of online marketing and brand strategy if you want to give your hashtags some heft.

Don't sleep on live events and IRL networking! The third house governs local activities and you could find your fanbase at a neighborhood venue. Or maybe two neighborhoods, since this Saturn cycle could inspire some Archers to embrace bi-city living. If you're stepping up to the mic or hanging your art, why not livestream the opening? You'll create more buzz for an area hangout which, in turn, will make them more amenable to supporting your endeavors. That's a team effort that cooperative Saturn in Aquarius can really get behind!

The Great Conjunction: Jupiter & Saturn unite.

December 21

Join forces for the win! On December 21, 2020, a rare (as in once every 20 years) cosmic event called The Great Conjunction arrives with the Winter Solstice. For the first time since May 28, 2000, Jupiter and Saturn will make an exact connection in the skies. This time they'll meet at 0°29' Aquarius, flooding your third house of dynamic duos and communication with their combined energy.

Have you been flirting with the idea of a collaboration? With weighty Saturn and risk-taking Jupiter aligned here, you could turn your tag-team effort into something official. But no handshake deals please, Archer! Have an attorney draft a contract and plan to negotiate before you get it all hammered out. This isn't just for longevity's sake, but also for self-protection. The deals you make near December 21 will come with added importance, and you need to make sure your rights and intellectual property are covered…yes, even if your "other half" is a sibling or dear friend. In the words of a lawyer we know, "Ambiguity breeds contempt."

An existing partnership could reach a crossroads near The Great Conjunction. Should you follow Jupiter's guidance and leap into a new, shared future? Or would it be better to slow things way down under prudent Saturn's advisement? Maybe there's a middle ground here, one that involves taking a risk, hand in hand, but making sure you have some semblance of a plan in place for this next phase of the game.

December 21, 2020 is also a day to make every word count! Bold Jupiter in Aquarius calls for big promises and sweeping resolutions, while integrity-hound Saturn demands that you back them up with action. People may be hanging on to your every word. Writers, broadcasters and media-minded Sagittarians should circle this day in neon highlighter for a launch or marketing campaign. Step up to the mic, Sagittarius, and share your message with the world.

South Node in Sagittarius: Karma is calling.

May 5, 2020 – January 18, 2022

You have a karmic purpose to fulfill, Sagittarius, and in 2020, that mission could become clear as a bell. On May 5, the lunar nodes will shift and begin their 18-month pilgrimage across the Gemini/ Sagittarius axis. These astrological "points" are your cosmic destiny line, as they represent both your natural gifts and your higher calling.

The South Node, which will be transiting through Sagittarius from May 5, 2020, until January 18, 2022, directs our collective calling, revealing the healing work that needs to be done to advance humanity. The North Node, which always moves through the opposite sign (in this case, Gemini), acts as a guide along that path. In what ways will society need to stretch in order to clear this evolutionary hurdle? The last time the nodes were in this position was between October 14, 2001, and April 14, 2003. If you're old enough to remember what was going on then, you might see some recurring themes crop up.

 The AstroTwins' 2020 Horoscope

While the South Node treks through Sagittarius for 18 months, you will feel even more like an ambassador of truth. If there's a teachable moment to be had, you'll be there with a lesson plan. But watch the preaching! It can be far more effective to model a high-vibe way of life than to pontificate about how things "should" be. The burden of proof will be upon you in 2020. Before you wag a finger and get righteous, make sure you can live up to those standards yourself!

This cosmic cycle could actually serve to make you more compassionate to people who are "different" than you. While the Sagittarius friend list looks like a U.N. delegation, you aren't always tolerant of people who hold different political views. While no one's suggesting you compromise your ideals, beginning May 5, you may get a new form of "diversity training," as the South Node in Sagittarius sends you on a marathon hike in someone else's shoes. Here's where the North Node in Gemini—and your seventh house of compromise and balance—comes into play. Gemini's gift is the ability to hold the space of a paradox. This can come across as double-talking or two-faced, but the reality is, Gemini can see both sides of every argument. While your principled sign cleaves stubbornly to your beliefs, inquisitive Gemini is a lot more open minded. Tear a page from the Twins' liner notes: Ask questions, plunge into research and survey every angle before making a final call.

By the same token, this expression holds true: He who stands for nothing falls for everything. With the South Node in your sign, you'll also be the "canary in the coal mine," chirping loudly to get people to confront an issue. United in truth? That sounds like a mantra a Sagittarius can get behind. Your gifts of passion, humor and storytelling will come in handy during this 18-month-cycle, so use them liberally. (Bring on those mic drops!)

On a personal note, the Sagittarius South Node can require a few "karmic corrections." Where have you strayed from your personal calling or abandoned your innate gifts? The demands of the modern-day world, like trying to pay your bills and support the ones you love, may be the culprit here. But if you feel hollow inside, begin refilling your tanks. Your renewed passion may come from your career… or not. It could just as easily emerge through an extracurricular engagement, a spiritual group or an amazing travel experience. Remembering who you are—in the most soulful sense of the expression—is the gift of the South Node's journey through your sign. This could be the year where you trek off for a vision quest or a silent Vipassana meditation to rediscover your independent nature.

Not that you'll be lost in a self-reflective reverie for too long. With the North Node in Gemini activating your seventh house of partnerships, a fated connection that's been brewing for years could finally evolve into a real-deal relationship. If you're partnered, you could forge ahead as a dynamic duo, co-creating something that feels like a shared destiny.

The only catch? Embracing North Node energy is like learning a foreign language. As your opposite sign on the zodiac wheel, Gemini's mercurial joie de vivre is both complementary and clashing to your innate rhythm. You may fumble and flounder before getting your bearings in these unions. When you spiral too far into the future, the Gemini North Node will teach you to "be here now."

Cancer/Capricorn Eclipses: Rolling in the deep.

January 10, June 21, July 5

Power! Intrigue! Seduction! Your charm and resourcefulness will be in demand this year as three change-making eclipses land on the Capricorn/Cancer axis. From January through July, issues around sex, money, self-worth and long-term investments will be under the microscope. Eclipses shake up whatever is stale, forcing us to update our "system software" so we can achieve optimal functioning. Their nudges are rarely gentle though; in fact, these lunations can come in like Sagittarius Miley Cyrus' wrecking ball. Fortunately, this particular eclipse series has been underway since July 2018—and served up three Cancer/Capricorn eclipses in 2019—so you're far along with integrating their lessons.

On January 10, the first full moon of the year will be a penumbral eclipse in Cancer and your eighth house of sex, intimacy and merging. This could herald a dramatic turning point in a relationship, such as an engagement, pregnancy or joint investment in something major, like property or a business venture. If a breakup's been brewing, one of you may be dashing out the door at record speed.

This eclipse falls two days prior to the Saturn-Pluto conjunction in Capricorn and your second house of income. While you hate the idea of anyone controlling your career, a stubborn insistence on doing everything independently may spell "missed opportunities," or worse, falling behind at a rapid rate. What will it take to turn your cottage industry into a noble empire? In order to grow at a competitive clip, outside funding may be needed. Since the eighth house governs investments and borrowed funds, this eclipse could prompt you to investigate new sources to help manifest your next-level dream. Whether you're selling a percentage of equity in your company or taking out a student loan so you can bring your skills up to 2020 requirements, remember that it can take money to make money.

On the flipside, if your romantic life keeps taking a backseat to your career, the January 10 eclipse could bring a sharp wakeup call. Create a better work-life balance, or the one you adore could go looking for attention elsewhere. But this isn't about finding a 25th hour in the day, Sagittarius. Instead, seek creative ways to include your boo in your life—and to become more integrated into theirs. Mutual support will leave you both feeling lighter and connected.

The June 21 new moon will be an annular solar eclipse, also known as a "ring of fire" because, as the moon covers the Sun's center, it leaves a flaming outline around it. But instead of Johnny Cash's woeful ballads, cue the sexytime playlist, since this eclipse fans the flames of a steamy summer love affair. If your mojo's been in slow-mo, it could come roaring back—or you may realize how badly you want (make that need) to get back in touch with your sensuality.

Prioritize self-care: book massages, dial back the inflammation-causing stimulants like sugar and caffeine, get your beauty rest. Then, start moving your body on a regular basis with walking, swimming, dancing or any kind of flowy movement. Connecting to your own physicality comes first, Sagittarius, but it won't be long before you're ready for some skin-on-skin contact.

The AstroTwins' 2020 Horoscope

The final eclipse in this two-year series struts in at the July 5 full moon in Capricorn. If you've been hustling toward a financial goal over the past two years, this beaming lunar eclipse could bring a well-deserved windfall. Since lunar eclipses sweep away what no longer serves us, you may leave a job or client who you've outgrown. As unexpected as this may be, trust that something better is coming your way, even if it feels turbulent in the short-term. Remember that as you release the past, you create space for something far better to flow in. Within a month of July 5, you could be fielding lucrative offers or accepting a new position that's too good to pass up!

Gemini/Sagittarius Eclipses: Reveal your message.
June 5, November 30, December 14

The balance between "mine" and "ours" will get a second reshuffling, thanks to a fresh series of eclipses falling across the Gemini/Sagittarius axis from June 5, 2020, until December 3, 2021. Three of this year's six eclipses will rumble here, making it impossible for you to ignore your burning passions—or to neglect the call for partnership. But how to negotiate these oft-dueling agendas?

If you've been putting your dreams on the back-burner to support other people, the June 5 full moon in Sagittarius could bring an abrupt end to that trend. If you don't strap on your own oxygen mask, how can you assist other passengers? Surround yourself with expert-level support and you'll have abundant resources to share with your family and community. Think of yourself as a prime "natural resource." Invest in training, sessions with a coach, healer or consultant; apply to school. This eclipse is your prompt to take concrete action to forward your life path.

No one's saying this will be easy! The first eclipse in a series is always the most intense. A wave of discontent could wash over you like a tsunami near June 5, and you'll need to do everything in your power to not let your stormy emotions follow suit. Give yourself space to process anger or frustration—but do not (we repeat *do not*) go on a blaming spree. In some ways, you "colluded" with this old dynamic of putting others' needs before your own. As of June 5, there's a new sheriff in town. During the course of this 18-month moon story, you'll be putting your people through an orientation phase. Repeatedly (and lovingly) assert your boundaries and you'll train them to interact with you differently. They may pout and whine when you say no to their demands, but if you stand your ground, they'll learn to be more self-sufficient: a true win-win.

Holiday season will feature two eclipses a couple weeks apart from each other (brace yourself!). On November 30, a Gemini lunar (full moon) eclipse activates your seventh house of partnerships. The only Gemini eclipse of 2020 could help you seal an important deal. An under-the-mistletoe engagement could be in the stars, or you may celebrate a victory with a business partner that you've been working on all year. If you've been waffling about a certain alliance, this eclipse could push you off the fence, forcing you to make a decision, one way or another. Are you in or are you out, Archer? Before the ball drops on 2021, you'll have to make a move.

The heart wants what it wants, and by December 14, yours will be beating loud and clear. The final new moon of 2020 will be a total solar eclipse in Sagittarius, providing a huge burst of courage so you can make the decision that's best for you. Forget about making halfhearted, superficial New Year's resolutions. Radar in on what you want and take concrete action to manifest it. The eclipse will give you a nice, galvanizing tailwind, so get started on December 14. An opportunity that involves leadership, status and responsibility could arrive out of the blue in the final weeks of 2020. No waffling, Sagittarius! Eclipses extend their offers for a brief window of time. If you want to capitalize on this end-of-year bonanza, you're going to have to leap! ✳

January

JANUARY: LOVE HOTSPOTS

January 3-February 16: Mars in Sagittarius

The New Year is off to a fiery start as provocative Mars blasts into your sign. This transit only comes around once every two years, so make the most of it! Capitalize on the confidence boost by getting on a new dating app and actually initiating some live hangouts. Attached? Now that the red planet has wrapped its tour of your sleepy twelfth house, you're feeling lighter, brighter, and ready for adventure. Get that "bae-cation" on the calendar!

January 10: Cancer full moon (lunar eclipse)

The first full moon of the year is also a potent lunar eclipse, illuminating your eighth house of merging, intimacy and mystery. Are you ready to take an existing bond to a deeper level? What will it take to get you there? Hold a "state of the union" to ensure you're both on the same page. You might even be ready for a lifestyle restructuring, if that supports your partnership. If you're single, resolve to be not only more open, but also a keener listener, with the people closest to you. Remember that vulnerability takes courage, and it's necessary in order to build intimacy. A second Cancer full moon will occur December 29, allowing you to revisit these themes.

January 13-February 7: Venus in Pisces

Amorous Venus flows into your sensitive, domestic fourth house, triggering your nesting instincts. You'll be sentimental and in the mood for cozy, couple-y time. Attached Archers might start making plans to rent a love nest, expand your family or purchase a home together. Single? Let your inner circle play Cupid for you. Survey your schedule and your space. If you're ready for a relationship, make sure there's room in your life and home for your future plus-one. Symbolically clearing space can create an attractive force field.

January 26: Venus-Mars square

Love and relationships require some sacrifice and compromise, but at what cost? When Venus clashes with passionate Mars, you could get swept away by strong emotions, and wonder if it's all worth it. Take a step back and look at the situation more objectively before you make any rash decisions. Your feelings are valid, but under this tense square, you may struggle to express them without losing your cool. If in doubt, wait this out.

January 27: Venus-Neptune meetup

A dreamy entwinement of Neptune and Venus sets the stage for one of the most romantic moments of the year. The catch? You have to allow yourself to be open, trusting, and vulnerable. With both planets in your emotional fourth house, you may worry about coming across as "too much" if you share from the heart. But don't mask your feelings behind humor! Authenticity is an aphrodisiac. Transcendental Neptune makes this a powerful day for manifesting the love you desire. Visualize yourself in a loving, fulfilling relationship, then ask the universe to make it so.

January 28: Mars-Neptune square

You're a sucker for flattery today, so keep your guard up. A befuddling clash between anxious Mars and elusive Neptune makes it hard to get a true read on folks. Are the charmers capable of backing up their words with actions? Even if their intentions are noble, take time to know them before plunging into the deep. It could be a long swim back to shore.

JANUARY: CAREER HOTSPOTS

January 2: Mercury-Jupiter meetup

Mental Mercury and expansive Jupiter rendezvous in your industrious second house, putting your mind on your money. If you haven't set your career resolutions in stone, sit down to determine what you want to accomplish in the coming year. Think big, as Jupiter supersizes everything and gives you the Midas touch! Once that's done, choose three small but meaningful tasks to accomplish in the next two weeks. Build momentum one day at a time!

January 3-February 16: Mars in Sagittarius

Make it rain, Sagittarius! Driven Mars buzzes into your sign for the first time in two years, pumping you up with motivation. Just in time to get your new decade initiatives underway, you'll feel a fire in your belly. The warrior planet pumps up your competitive nature. Make sure you don't go overboard! You want to win, but not at any cost.

January 10: Cancer full moon (lunar eclipse)

Show you the money! A game-changing lunar (full moon) eclipse supercharges your eighth house of assets and shared resources. Over the coming two weeks, you could cash in on an investment or someone may show up who wants to put dollars behind your dreams. From collaborations to crowdfunding, this eclipse helps you soar to new heights with support from other people. Got debt? Set a plan to repay a loan or chip away at a hefty credit card bill. Consolidating might be the answer.

January 10: Uranus retrograde ends

Streamline, systematize and set things in motion! Erratic Uranus ends its five-month backspin in your efficient sixth house, helping you get a handle on your routines again. As the tech-savvy planet resumes its forward motion, look for ways to automate your processes. Use apps to track everything from workflow to fitness and food.

January 12: Saturn-Pluto-Mercury conjunction

You've got big ideas about earning and saving, and today, when disciplined Saturn and transformational Pluto meet up in your money zone—accompanied by messenger Mercury—you could lock down a long-term plan for stability. But don't expect to follow the same old formula. You may need to tear something down in order to build it back up again. Saturn and Pluto only team up every 33-38 years, so this life-changing shift might set your mission in motion for the next few decades.

January 16-February 3: Mercury in Aquarius

When the communication planet dashes into your expressive third house, it kicks off three weeks of dynamic discussions. What starts as a casual conversation could evolve into an unexpected collaboration. Test the waters with a short-term project. Explore new venues and social activities close to home! The local scene is buzzing with possibility. This is an ideal time for writing, podcasting or any endeavor that gets your message out to the world.

January 18: Mercury-Uranus square

The only constant is change today, as fast-paced Mercury gets in a dynamic dust-up with unpredictable Uranus. Keep plans flexible and expectations reasonable. If someone cancels at the last minute or can't follow through, don't dwell on it for long. Concentrate on what you can accomplish with the resources you have.

January 23: Sun-Uranus square

Your vision may be rock-solid, but stay open to feedback. People's input might take your concept to an even higher level. Look for ways you can use technology to speed up your processes or add special effects.

January 24: Aquarius new moon

You may be up late brainstorming as the year's only new moon in your communication sector brings a flood of dazzling ideas. Enjoy the ideation phase now and watch as the well of brilliant concepts fills up! Today marks the Chinese Year of the Metal Rat, which will help you strategize the best way to bring these to life. No need to rush to production. Since new moons mark the beginning of a six-month period, you have time to let it all unfold.

January 28: Mars-Neptune square

When driven Mars clashes with starry-eyed Neptune, your intuition goes AWOL. Don't let people tug on your heartstrings or charm you with slick sales pitches. If red flags are waving, ask questions in order to resolve your concerns. Set firm boundaries and silence your phone while you're trying to get 'er done. Otherwise, family or friends could sideline your goals with emotional distractions.

February

FEBRUARY: LOVE HOTSPOTS

February 3-March 4: Mercury in Pisces

Lead with your sensitivity as messenger Mercury flits into your nurturing fourth house. You may feel more introverted during this cycle, preferring smaller gatherings and the company of your innermost circle. Entertain at home (potluck movie night, anyone?) or take a vacation with your besties.

February 7-March 4: Venus in Aries

St. Valentine makes an early arrival this year, as Venus glides into your romantic fifth house and fires up your passionate nature. Take the lead in love! Boldly ask your crush to coffee or make special V-Day reservations for you and your S.O. This glamorous cycle is also a great for a style overhaul or a mini-makeover.

February 16-March 30: Mars in Capricorn

Your drive for security intensifies as go-getter Mars motors through your second house of stability. Even the most indie-spirited Archers will want to operate with a clear plan of action. If you've been putting up with sub-par treatment, it's time to set boundaries. Does your love interest share enough of your values? Align and define. This is a good time to go a little more upscale with your dating habits. Detour away from the corner dive bar and instead meet up at a posh wine bar or the theater.

February 16-March 9: Mercury retrograde

Messages get muddled for a few weeks, as Mercury moves backward through your sensitive fourth house, briefly dipping into your third house of communication. Even if you're crystal clear with your delivery, the details could get lost in translation. Don't force it! Taking a time-out to focus on yourself may work wonders and alleviate (or totally circumvent) any tense interactions.

February 23: Venus-Jupiter square

Today's tug o' war between Venus and Jupiter presents a tough choice between steamy adventures and sweet stability. Of course, you'd love to have both, but turnabout is fair play. If you're not willing to give your partner a longer leash (or go totally off-leash), you can't expect to be able to roam without restrictions. No need to give your S.O. whiplash! Spend some solo time getting clear on what you actually want before talking it out. Single? Be clear about what you're looking for: That's exactly what you'll attract!

February 23: Pisces new moon

Your nesting instincts are activated as the annual new moon in Pisces gets cozy in your fourth house. What does your picture of domestic bliss look like? Maybe it's time to give your love interest a drawer or a key, or to talk about moving in together. Attached? Bond over a décor or renovation project.

February 28: Venus-Pluto square

A strong attraction could sweep you away…but to where? Under this murky mashup, you may be pulled into emotional quicksand with a charming but troubled soul. If red flags are waving, investigate before you go deeper. But don't let your suspicious mind run away. Snooping in your partner's texts or emails could permanently break trust.

FEBRUARY: CAREER HOTSPOTS

February 9: Leo full moon

Not that a Sag needs an excuse to broaden your horizons, but today's full moon will activate your wanderlust in a major way. Leap on any opportunity to travel, expand your knowledge base or pursue an intriguing entrepreneurial venture. If you have the funds, search for a retreat that can satisfy all three requirements, like a teacher training…in Bali!

February 16-March 30: Mars in Capricorn

Assertive Mars zooms into your second house of work and money, accelerating progress on the visionary ideas you've been cooking up since the red planet entered your sign on January 3. Structure and sound strategy are essential to victory. Pause to put a strategic plan in place, then get into production. You could have something lucrative to show for it by March 30.

February 21: Mars-Uranus trine

You might be ahead of the curve, but you're an invincible force of nature today! Your hard work speaks volumes, but how do your efforts serve other people…and moreover, change the world? As Mars and Uranus connect the dots in your career houses, you'll have people's eyes and ears, so spell out the benefits to them. Post on social media, spread the word in your community. While you're at it, spotlight someone else's meaningful mission.

March

MARCH: LOVE HOTSPOTS

March 3: Venus-Saturn square

Cautious Saturn pumps the brakes on a fast-moving romance today when it clashes with Venus in your zone of *amour*. Are there legitimate red flags that would hinder a long-term connection, or is this just fear rearing its resistant head? If you're looking for more than just a situationship, now's the moment for some real talk. Coupled? Align with your partner around schedules and budgets instead of making any unilateral decisions.

March 4-April 3: Venus in Taurus

How healthy are your relationships? Venus grapevines into her home sign of Taurus, activating your wellness zone. Quality time and clear agreements bring important relationships back into balance. The little things mean everything, so infuse more sensuality into your daily routines and activate your glow with some early spring training. Buddy workouts with your partner can elicit more "iron mans" in the boudoir. Unattached Archers could click with a CrossFit cutie!

March 8: Venus-Uranus meetup

Expect the unexpected when disruptor Uranus entwines with Venus for their annual rendezvous. With their meet-cute going down in your fitness-focused sixth house, find active ways to meet people, like joining a cycling team or going on a group hike. Shake up any stale routines if you're in a relationship. This could be as radical as trying L.A.T. status (Living Apart Together) for six months, or as simple as signing up for a weekly workshop to stimulate ideas and explore a common interest.

March 16-April 10: Mercury in Pisces

Messenger Mercury drifts into your foundational fourth house for a second trip this year, revealing emotional issues that you swept under the rug. Fortunately, whatever you "forgot" to deal with during the retrograde cycle (from February 16 to March 9) can be negotiated with compassion now—and perhaps some added layers of insight. Fair is fair: If you want others to budge, you have to give an inch yourself.

March 24: Aries new moon

Get ready for a romantic renaissance! The only Aries new moon of the year inspires single Sagittarians to circulate and coupled Archers to enjoy more passionate playtime. Raise your standards if you've been settling. (And try not to get caught on camera getting frisky under this PDA-fueled cycle!) Since Aries rules your fifth house of fertility and creativity, you could expand your family or dive into a creative project that flourishes over the next six months.

March 27: Venus-Jupiter trine

Talking about the future could be its own form of foreplay under today's passionate-but-practical starmap. If you're feeling good about a union, you may be seeking a greater sense of security. How can you combine your resources and talents to be stronger together? If you're single, cease from "pleasing" and just be you—the friendliest, most outgoing version. That's how you'll attract your authentic match.

March 28: Venus-Pluto trine

As cathartic Venus embraces hypersensitive Pluto, signal your support with more than just words. A solid connection is formed on mutual respect and consistent kindness. But to build (and cement) trust, keeping your word is a must. Little things matter, like being on time and remembering the promises you made to loved ones. If you need to clean up some oversights, humble yourself and do what's needed to get back in good graces.

MARCH: CAREER HOTSPOTS

March 4-16: Mercury in Aquarius

Your mind and mouth are moving a million miles a minute, as quick-witted Mercury sprints into your third house of communication. Dynamic discussions could lead to short-term collaborations (which later evolve into bigger things). Since this realm also rules local activity and mobile devices, you won't have to travel far to find kindred spirits. Search under geotags and hashtags and meet an Instagram friend for non-virtual drinks.

March 9: Virgo full moon

Make that professional power play, as the year's only full moon in Virgo shines in your tenth house of success. Your efforts of the past six months could bring a major victory within the next two weeks. Use this win as motivation to define your next epic goal, then outline actionable steps and zoom ahead!

March 20: Mars-Jupiter meetup

A windfall may come your way, when accelerator Mars and can-do Jupiter join forces in your work and finance zone. A moneymaking offer could land in your inbox, or you might be tapped to lead a big project. It's flattering, for sure. Plus, it sounds like a grand (and potentially lucrative) adventure. But with these impulsive planets at the wheel, get all the facts before making your decision. Whether or not it's the opportunity of a lifetime, you've got nothing to lose by conducting your due diligence.

March 21-July 1: Saturn in Aquarius

Restrictive Saturn darts out of Capricorn, releasing its three-year chokehold on your money and work sector. Budgetary limitations could finally ease up… or show signs of doing so in the near future. For the first time since early 1994, taskmaster Saturn darts into Aquarius and your communication zone (a much easier cycle), helping you speak, write and publicly present yourself with authority. But don't go on a spending spree! Saturn runs one final lap through Capricorn from July 1 to December 17, crystallizing tough but important lessons before planting you on firmer (if leaner) financial footing.

March 23: Mars-Pluto meetup

Penetrating Pluto pairs up with assertive Mars, giving you a near-clairvoyant view into your financial future. Tune in to those vibes: An investment may be worth exploring, or maybe you should set up that crowdfunding campaign. While the red planet loves to go, go, go, Pluto likes to wait and watch. Timing is everything, so keep calm and tap into your perceptive powers so you'll know when to make your move.

March 30-May 13: Mars in Aquarius

Whatever message you want to spread will catch on like wildfire as fierce Mars streaks through your third house of communication. Speak up! Tweet up! Instagram away! Writing and multimedia projects get a major boost. Working in partnership? Spell out agreements to the letter so dynamic duos don't turn into dumpster fires.

         The AstroTwins' 2020 Horoscope

March 31: Mars-Saturn meetup

As confident Mars links up with unyielding Saturn in your communication zone, you can speak with passion and authority. What's important today is being assertive and tackling conflicts proactively. You may have to defuse a dominating personality type. Killing 'em with kindness (but a firm bottom line) will win you respect from the whole office.

April

APRIL: LOVE HOTSPOTS

April 3-August 7: Venus in Gemini

Commitment on your mind? Venus takes her annual journey through your relationship house, making you long for greater certainty in love. You're one of the zodiac's futurists, but don't leap so far ahead on the romantic timeline that you skip the sweetness of the present moment! Single? Don't waste time on a short-lived spring fling. Set yourself up for summer loving by dating people who are ready to go "all in."

April 4: Venus-Saturn trine

Intellectual chemistry gives you butterflies today as serious Saturn spoons the love planet in your "sapiosexual" third house. Soulful exchanges can happen in the most mundane places! Don't wander around in a tech trance or you could miss a potential partner standing behind you in the Trader Joe's checkout line.

April 7: Libra full moon

Slide into those DMs. As the full moon in Libra logs in to your tech sector, single Archers could have more than the usual amount of luck on dating apps. If your *amour du jour* isn't "ready" yet, no need to ghost, but cushioning with other options would be wise. These experimental moonbeams could bring some edgy, frisky fun for coupled Sagittarians. Choose your safe word!

April 10-27: Mercury in Aries

You're never short on witty wordplay and arresting anecdotes, but with Mercury winging through your romantic fifth house, don't hide your attraction behind humor. Boldly make your interest known or initiate conversations about "what's next" with your S.O.

April 14: Sun-Pluto square

Separate checks, *s'il vous plait!* Money could get funny in relationships today as the Sun in your decadent fifth house gets checked by controlling Pluto. Better to just go Dutch on dates and ignore any archaic gender rules. If you're dipping into joint funds, make sure your S.O. is aligned with the purchase. Conversely, if your savings keep getting spent up, call a budgetary summit!

April 22: Taurus new moon

Make "acts of service" your love language (in accordance with author Gary Chapman's *5 Love Languages*) as the dutiful new moon in Taurus brings out your giving nature. Ask not what your plus-one can do for you. Instead, quietly lend your support. Tired of arguing over dishes and laundry? Maybe there's a better way to divvy up household duties; or, if funds allow, hire a cleaning service.

APRIL: CAREER HOTSPOTS

April 4: Jupiter-Pluto meetup

You work hard for your money, but is your moolah working hard enough for you? Today marks the first of 2020's three conjunctions between bountiful Jupiter and investment-savvy Pluto. Start investigating places where you can put your cash and watch it grow. Look into first-time homeowner loans. Build (or grow) your portfolio of stocks, bonds and mutual funds that yield compounding interest.

April 7: Libra full moon

Today's full moon in Libra beams into your teamwork and tech zone. A joint effort could culminate in a glowing milestone over the next two weeks, but this might also mark a turning point. Is there further to go with this crew, or is it time to break up the band? Don't hang on out of habit. The virtual gods are on your side, so schedule launches and post liberally. You could go viral!

April 7: Mars-Uranus square

Petty arguments could blaze into all-out dumpster fires under today's combustible Mars-Uranus clash. Check your know-it-all tendencies and don't waste time battling trolls. Avoid controversial topics with friends and family. Even the most impassioned words can wound if you strike down someone else's point of view. You've got zero impulse control when it comes to telling people what you really think. Bite your tongue before you burn a bridge.

April 10-27: Mercury in Aries

A persistent (and perplexing!) problem could yield creative solutions as innovative Mercury hands you the leadership reins. Don't wait for other people to deliver an answer. Now's the time to fix what might be standing in your way of success. The key lies in asking the right people for advice.

April 14: Sun-Pluto square

If you're spending more than you're earning, stop the flow of red ink. You might have to tighten your belt temporarily, but even as you're stemming the tide, dig deeper. Could there be some old fears around money that keep you in this perpetual state of scarcity thinking? You can stop manifesting "crises" by creating an actual savings plan. Automate those transfers! If you don't see it, you won't blow it.

April 15: Sun-Jupiter square

Not every day is going to find you whistling while you work, but are there little things you can do to keep your motivation high? Challenge yourself to hustle just a little harder or to add some bells and whistles to a presentation. Finding little ways to push yourself can make you even better at your job and bring a spirit of playfulness to your work. Even something as small as rearranging your workspace could revitalize your workflow.

April 21: Sun-Saturn square

Waiting for a decision doesn't have to halt your progress. Instead of pacing a hole in the floor, take advantage of this "bonus" time to work on something you can knock out of the park by yourself. This backburnered mission will build your confidence, and you'll be even more poised to blast ahead when you do get that green light.

April 22: Taurus new moon

As the new moon in Taurus galvanizes your orderly sixth house, you'll feel like spring cleaning everything from your desk to your work wardrobe

The AstroTwins' 2020 Horoscope

to your cluttered inbox. This lunar lift can spark a much-needed job search or inspire you to pitch a new project. Whether you're pounding the pavement or rolling up your sleeves, you'll appreciate this productivity boost.

April 25: Mercury square Jupiter and Pluto

Someone might try to bait you today, but don't even nibble at their line! With messenger Mercury butting heads with shadowy Pluto and impulsive Jupiter, you could get dragged into a raw deal. Under this tense cosmic clash, things might not be as they appear. Someone may be holding back a key piece of intel that'll be a game-changer. Rather than rush in, prepare a lengthy list of questions… and fire away!

April 25-October 4: Pluto retrograde in Capricorn

You can accumulate and save until the (cash) cows come home, but to really feel "safe" around money, you may need to examine some unconscious fears that are driving you to overspend. Starting today, as probing Pluto turns retrograde in your financial sector, you'll have more than five months to take a deep dive into those murky waters—perhaps with the guidance of a money coach or financial planner.

April 26: Sun-Uranus meetup

Is someone sabotaging the team effort? This disruptor might not even realize they're stalling progress or undoing work, but don't go another day without alerting them to the problem. You could try a proactive approach, calling a meeting to get everyone back on the same page. Establish mutual goals then brainstorm best practices for getting there You might not agree on everything, so focus on your overlapping priorities first.

April 27-May 11: Mercury in Taurus

Cerebral Mercury wings into your systematic sixth house, turning your messy mind maps into orderly Venn diagrams. Streamline your efforts and use apps to make your workflow more efficient. You can get to inbox zero…and stay there! Fitness and food trackers will keep you on target with wellness goals, so let them do the thinking for you.

April 28: Mercury-Saturn square

Even the best-laid plans can go awry, but that's not reason to give up. If your best shot didn't hit the mark, call upon Coach Saturn and seek some expert guidance. Use this temporary setback to strengthen your vision moving forward. Dust yourself off and go back to the drawing board.

April 30: Mercury-Uranus meetup

Eureka! Genius strikes under the alignment of these cosmic innovators. Question everything—especially your most engrained habits. Just because these structures are "working" doesn't mean they couldn't be vastly improved. Research apps or tools to streamline productivity; watch TED talks that get you thinking outside the box. And carve out some time for daydreaming to see what gems arise.

May

May 3: Venus-Neptune square

Don't expect to get any sort of clear read on people under today's bewildering bang-up between love planet Venus and fog-machine Neptune. Rational, reasonable thought could be in short supply as your

emotions climb into the driver's seat. This may be a joyride or an obstacle course, but check the rearview mirror to make sure you don't lose sight of what's real.

May 7: Scorpio full moon

What's holding you back from a blissed-out union? The Scorpio full moon shines a light into your twelfth house of subconscious healing, helping you unearth limiting beliefs. Let go of outdated narratives so you can write a new love story...or deepen your existing one. If you need support, this transformative lunation can light the way to an insightful professional who might help you make the shift for good!

May 11-28: Mercury in Gemini

Relationship rebalancing time! Starting today, as communication planet Mercury buzzes through your partnership house, you can restore an equal flow of give and take to your closest unions. The stage is set for open dialogues but the key to resolution lies in listening as much as you're talking.

May 13-June 27: Mars in Pisces

With make-it-happen Mars energizing your domestic zone, tackle home improvement projects or begin the hunt for your love nest. This seductive cycle can heat things up behind closed doors, but too much cozy time can make relationships feel claustrophobic. Take a night or two off!

May 13-June 25: Venus retrograde in Gemini

As Venus does an about-face in your partnership house, revisit your #RelationshipGoals. The love planet turns retrograde every 18 months, creating six weeks to review and revise as needed. How can you attract more love into your life? Or if your cup is overflowing, where can you give more *amour*? Use this contemplative six weeks to think about how you might improve your relationship or dating game to get more satisfaction.

May 22: Gemini new moon

Make it a *doppia!* The year's only Gemini new moon in your relationship realm kicks off a new chapter for mating and dating. Over the coming six months, get clearer about what you truly desire, and be transparent in how you discuss it. The sharper your parameters, the easier it'll be to manifest it! Couples should hold a "state of the union" today to align and discuss next steps.

May 22: Mercury-Venus meetup

Let's talk about love, baby! As the zodiac's fearless flirt joins forces with the gentle love planet in your committed relationship zone, you're ready to lay your cards on the table. What's been foremost on your mind? Share your desires with a new partner, or broach talks about the future with your S.O.

May 22: Mercury-Neptune square

Passive-aggressive outbursts, guilt trips and manipulation abound today as mental Mercury clashes with nebulous Neptune. Take a deep breath and try to step back from the situation for a wider perspective. If you make too many concessions now, it might be hard to recover ground later on.

May 28-August 4: Mercury in Cancer

Sweet-talking Mercury takes an extended voyage through your seductive eighth house. From sexting to pillow talk, everything's getting spicier now. To build trust, plunge into deeper dialogues and share more about your past. Rein in jealousy during the retrograde cycle from June 18 to July 12!

MAY: CAREER HOTSPOTS

May 9: Mercury-Pluto trine

Seal the deal! Your career game is skyrocketing as winsome Mercury fist-bumps intensifier Pluto. Pitches will hit the mark but don't forget your ABCs: Always Be Closing. Add a "call to action" that guides people to buy your products or sign up for your services.

May 10: Mercury-Jupiter trine

As lucky Jupiter fist-bumps logical Mercury, you can open up your thinking to include options that didn't initially feel right. Apply your incisive thinking to a wider range of possibilities. You're likely to hit on a brilliant solution that wasn't apparent before now.

May 11-September 29: Saturn retrograde

Think before you speak! Cautious Saturn turns retrograde today, first backing through your communication zone and helping you polish your delivery. When conservative Saturn rears into your second house of work and money on July 1, funds might get a little tight. But this is a perfect time to reevaluate your budget, tighten your belt and set some new financial goals. While you could experience a "reversal" with a job or client, someone from your past might also resurface out of the blue with a lucrative opportunity.

May 11: Mercury-Mars square

What's more annoying than a know-it-all? A know-it-all who also loves to argue. You might encounter one of these unpleasant types today, so brace yourself. And if they happen to be trying to sabotage you at a meeting or playing extreme devil's advocate, come prepared with all your facts and figures and be ready to fight back with a bulletproof case. This challenge can be a blessing in disguise because it pushes you to get organized and seriously level up!

May 11-28: Mercury in Gemini

Smooth-talking Mercury kicks off a two-week stint in your seventh house of deals and partnerships, helping you transform rivalries into collaborations. Under these cooperative skies, you'll see win-wins at every turn. Step right up to the negotiating table and make them an offer they can't refuse.

May 12: Mercury-Saturn trine

Teaming up with successful people is one of your favorite things, but make sure they share your values and work ethic. Under this productive pairing, you could launch a powerful collaboration. Take the necessary steps to vet prospects, then get that creative ball rolling.

May 13-June 27: Mars in Pisces

As frenetic Mars makes an awkward journey through your domestic zone, it's going to take concerted effort to keep work from bleeding into your personal time. A cottage industry business could take off quickly. If you work from home, make sure to carve out a distraction-free zone to help you manage stress—and a few places where work is off limits, like your bedroom!

May 14-September 12: Jupiter retrograde in Capricorn

When "see it, want it" Jupiter pivots into its annual four-month backspin, make sure your spending isn't outpacing your earnings. It's easy to shell out money without a thought to your budget, but eventually that's going to catch up with you. Before you make any purchases, make sure it's something you truly need (or desperately want). And even

then, do some research to guarantee you're getting the best possible price!

May 15: Sun-Pluto trine

Visualize it, then bring it into form! As a Sun-Pluto pairing heightens your powers of manifestations, invoke the Law of Attraction to draw in what you desire. But don't just think you can "ask, believe, receive" without doing your part. Meet the universe halfway by taking one bold action around your dream before bedtime.

May 22: Gemini new moon

When this annual new moon galvanizes your seventh house of partnerships, you might ink a deal or snag a game-changing contract. Events and budding alliances that occur around this lunar lift will continue to grow and develop, bringing epic gains by your birthday season.

May 28-August 4: Mercury in Cancer

Mercury begins an extra-long visit to Cancer and your eighth house of joint ventures, wealth and investments. With the hawk-like focus this transit provides, you can throw yourself into a detailed project and make major headway. Get started now so you can make traction before Mercury turns retrograde from June 18 to July 12.

June

JUNE: LOVE HOTSPOTS

June 2: Venus-Mars square

There might be trouble in paradise as Venus retrograde forms a feuding stance with her dance partner Mars. Peacekeeping efforts may be offset by someone's knee-jerk reactions, insensitivity and overblown emotions. One or both of you could be acting needy or jealous. Can you retreat to neutral corners until the storm passes?

June 13: Mars-Neptune meetup

As passionate Mars spoons enchanting Neptune, it's a boundary-melting kind of day. With these planets in your intimate fourth house, you could introduce a new love to your good friends or exchange keys with your S.O. Single? Tune in to your feelings and get crystal clear on what kind of partner you want to call in. The combo of manifestation-master Neptune and magnetic Mars makes this an "ask, believe, receive" kind of day.

June 18-July 12: Mercury retrograde in Cancer

Reading between the lines could give you eye strain as Mercury retreats through Cancer and your esoteric eighth house until July 12. Instead of investigating, look for the lesson…or just take a step back instead of getting all wrapped up in it. Someone's hot-and-cold behavior could run to confounding extremes, but with sensitivities on high, best to wait until Mercury's storm passes. An ex could reach out, but if the affair was a torrid one the first time, ignore, delete and block!

June 21: Cancer new moon (solar eclipse)

Today's Cancer new moon—the first in a back-to-back pair in 2020—is also a solar eclipse. As it fires up your seductive eighth house, it'll set the stage for a spicy connection that might even have "happily ever after" potential. Ready to deepen a commitment? Follow the urge to merge, whether it's an engagement, moving in together, or expanding your family.

June 23-November 28: Neptune retrograde in Pisces

Foggy Neptune begins its annual backspin, which might actually clear up a few befuddling situations. Have you gotten consumed by feelings or swept up in a real-life soap opera? Distance yourself from energy vampires who treat you like their on-call therapist. (And worse, ignore your thoughtful wisdom!) If you've been pondering the idea of babies, moving in together or buying a home, Neptune's reversal helps you step back and evaluate this without getting overwhelmed by emotion.

June 27, 2020-January 6, 2021: Mars in Aries

Lusty Mars storms into your passionate fifth house, heating up your primal urges for the rest of the year. Your animal instincts will be fierce, but take heed! While the red planet is retrograde from September 9 to November 13, it might be hard to distinguish predator from prey.

JUNE: CAREER HOTSPOTS

June 5: Sagittarius full moon (lunar eclipse)

The annual full moon in your sign is a potent lunar eclipse—the first in an 18-month series that galvanizes the Sagittarius/Gemini axis. Talk about a springboard! Prioritize your passions and reshuffle personal goals to the top of the list. But leave room for the X factor! Within the two to four weeks following this potent lunation, a golden opportunity could arrive out of the blue—and it might redirect your trajectory in a powerful, profitable way!

June 18-July 12: Mercury retrograde in Cancer

Lock down your data and double-check your statements. As Mercury turns retrograde in your eighth house of long-term finances, the lens zooms in on your wealth and money management. Watch out for fraudulent charges or suspicious activity on your accounts. If you're considering an investment, whether that's in property, your portfolio or a pricey possession, do all the research you can first. If possible, wait until Mercury turns direct (forward) at the end of July before making a final purchase.

June 21: Cancer new moon (annular solar eclipse)

Your eighth house of joint ventures and wealth is supercharged under today's Cancer new moon, which also happens to be a solar eclipse. How can you pool your resources for a mutually profitable partnership? And with whom? No need to rush into anything formal. New moons plant seeds that can take up to six months to bear fruit.

June 27, 2020-January 6, 2021: Mars in Aries

Creativity is spiking for the rest of the year as Mars embarks on an extended stay in your fifth house, thanks in part to a retrograde from September 9 to November 13. Your work could draw public praise and you may be called into a role of greater leadership. Don't be shy about self-promotion. The squeaky wheel gets the oil…and the gold!

June 30: Jupiter-Pluto meetup

Bountiful Jupiter teams up with astute Pluto for the second of three exact connections in 2020. With these planets pooling resources in your money zone, a riskier investment could pay off. Since both planets are retrograde today, avoid gambling. Start paying off debt and collecting what's owed to you.

July

JULY: LOVE HOTSPOTS

July 8: Mercury-Mars square

Curb your enthusiasm, even if it feels romantic to rush right in. A wave of FOMO could hit as impulsive Mars clashes with Mercury. Trouble is, both planets are retrograde, so even if you *are* reading those sensual signals accurately, you won't be able to tell where they're leading you today. You may find yourself questioning everything, including someone's loyalty, but don't go flinging accusations unless you have facts.

July 20: Cancer new moon

Bonding Time: the Sequel! Today, the second in a pair of consecutive Cancer new moons could send you rolling in the deep. With your intimate, erotic eighth house on fire, a kismet connection might draw you in. This one may be fueled by either sexual chemistry or a deep desire to actually create a life together. Explore! Coupled? This lunation favors deepening and merging, whether it's an engagement, moving in together, or expanding your family. Plans you've discussed with your S.O. since June 21 could accelerate now.

July 27: Venus-Neptune square

You might feel like you're living in "the upside-down world" today as hazy Neptune throws shade at Venus. Emotions obscure logic, and you could invest hours investigating a "situationship," only to find it was a mirage in the end. Romanticizing and daydreaming might be unavoidable, but leave a trail of breadcrumbs so you can find your way back to reality.

July 27: Mercury-Mars square

For the second time this month, the planets clash in the intimate and e of your chart. This go-round, Mercury of retrograde (though Mars is still on a reve commute). Revisiting a touchy topic could bring an opportunity for proactive growth. An argumentative approach won't work so don't go in pushing your agenda or attempting to charm people into seeing things your way. Genuinely listen to their concerns and address them one by one.

July 30: Mercury-Neptune trine

Dive deep! Your empathetic side takes the wheel under today's sentimental sync-up between communicator Mercury and compassionate Neptune. Some touching "real talk" or a sweet gesture could melt your heart and leave you misty-eyed. With Mercury in your chamber of secrets, you might feel ready to open up about your past to someone. Hey, you won't know how deeply you can trust them unless you take a chance and reveal more about your true self. Your own intuition is also dialed up, so don't be afraid to pierce the veil of pleasantries and find out what's going on below the surface.

JULY: CAREER HOTSPOTS

July 1-December 17: Saturn retrograde enters Capricorn

Saturn's retrograde continues, as the serious planet backs up from Aquarius into Capricorn and your second house of work, money and daily routines. The taskmaster was in this area of your chart for the last three years, so this final visit of the next three decades gives you one more chance to fine-tune this area of your life. While money could be

The AstroTwins' 2020 Horoscope

...will help you ...

...ar eclipse)
...l moon of 2020 ... lending its game-... ond house of work, ... windfall may arise with... ... and your luck could continue for s... apricorn is slow and steady, so you'll have the patience and persistence you need to pull off the mission.

July 12: Sun-Neptune trine

Charity begins in the home under today's compassionate trine but remember that the giving can (and should) flow in both directions. As you lend support to a relative or close friend, be receptive to the generosity from someone else in your inner circle. If you're making too many sacrifices, stop and take time to stabilize your own base.

July 15: Sun-Pluto opposition

A power struggle could break out under today's tense tug-of-war between the ego-driven Sun and domineering Pluto. Differing views on how to invest money could be the root cause, or maybe one of you wants to take a risk while the other feels more comfortable playing it safe. Good luck finding a compromise because neither wants to back down. Table the talks for a few days.

July 20: Cancer new moon

Joint ventures get a boost from today's new moon in your eighth house of long-term investments and shared finances. Since this is the second in a pair of back-to-back Cancer new moons, a financial initiative started near the June 21 solar eclipse could be ready for launch. Map out a six-month plan and tackle the first action item within two weeks!

July 20: Sun-Saturn opposition

Financial fluctuations can bring up insecurities or outdated fears. Instead of getting stuck in the old loops, be grateful that these limiting beliefs have come up so you can address them. Take a more objective look at your balance sheet. While it's important to face up to any out-of-control spending or rising debt, you don't want to limit your ability to manifest because of negativity. Instead of freaking out about what you don't have, turn your attention to creating new income streams. The universe is abundant!

July 27: Mercury-Mars square

Are people undervaluing your contributions? Today, fierce Mars brings a dynamic push to speak up for what you're worth. Don't be aggressive or confrontational though. The facts will speak for themselves, so come prepared with proof of your achievements and the results you've provided. Another possible route: Circulate a company-wide memo updating people on your progress or post a social media humblebrag.

July 30: Mercury-Jupiter opposition

Keep it real! It'll be easy to be carried away by your projections today as analytical Mercury gets blown off-course by larger-than-life Jupiter across your financial axis. Double-check your numbers and consider having an actual accountant or financial planner review them for you. Also, watch the urge to drop big bucks on an impulse buy.

July 30: Mercury-Neptune trine

Numbers don't lie, so take an unblinking look at what you owe and how much you're owed. While this can feel scary, it's also liberating. With illusory Neptune T-boning analytical Mercury, trying to figure things out in your head will only churn up anxiety. Put it on paper or in a spreadsheet and you'll know what you're dealing with. Consolidate any debt or, if people owe you money, make a list and start collecting what's due.

August

AUGUST: LOVE HOTSPOTS

August 1: Mercury-Pluto opposition

Ready to put a ring on it or otherwise make a partnership official? Awesome, but don't start making demands. Today's crackling connection between frenetic Mercury and unconscious Pluto can churn up insecurities that aren't actually rooted in reality. You may be projecting fears onto your love interest or getting jealous over something that's not actually happening. You're not crazy, you're just in need of some grounding. Spend time around people who feel safe and affirming and you'll get yourself back to center.

August 4-19: Mercury in Leo

The sky's the limit as inquisitive Mercury buzzes through your expansive ninth house. Cast a wider net when it comes to meeting people or planning dates. Your heart's desire could be waiting a few miles further from your hometown.

August 7-September 6: Venus in Cancer

Summertime gets a little sweeter as Venus moves into sensitive Cancer and your intimate eighth house. Honor your emotional needs instead of playing it cool. Practice communicating your desires before they've spiraled into an intense fury because you've repressed them for too long. If you and your S.O. have been like two ships passing in the night, pull in to port for some intimate "just the two of us" time.

August 13: Mars-Pluto square

It's a "zero chill" kind of day, as ready-to-roll Mars in your passionate fifth house collides with volatile Pluto in your eighth house of perma-bonding. Events put into motion could progress quickly, and you might get in over your head. Don't flirt with danger or waste time exploring something that has no potential to grow. Single? With secretive Pluto in the picture, make sure your "person of interest" is actually available.

August 24: Mars-Saturn square

Speed check! Are you having second thoughts about a romantic situation or is someone pressuring you to make a decision before you feel totally ready? Saturn loves to move slow, while Mars is all go-go-go. Even if you're swept away by passion or feel a burning desire to shake things up, ride the brake. A measured move would be wiser than a radical one.

August 25: Venus-Jupiter opposition

Too much work and not enough play? Invite more sensuality into your life as the love planet opposes maximizer Jupiter. Look out, though! An attraction could become a distraction if it's too all-consuming. Don't neglect your duties because you're feeling swept up.

August 27: Venus-Neptune trine

As the love planet spoons sensitive Neptune, you're craving security and may need to ask your partner for some verbal reassurance. Under this heart-melting mashup, you can fall in love with people's potential without actually knowing who they truly are. It's fine to wear the rose-colored glasses, as long as you're aware that you have them on! Nobody's perfect, but if you're thinking long-term, it's important to know if your values align.

August 30: Venus-Pluto opposition

Stay on guard for a cameo from the green-eyed monster or other intense outbursts. As Venus locks horns with intense Pluto, you might not understand what's triggering you, but chances are, it has to do with a core issue (like abandonment or feeling unlovable). Money could be a source of tension, but underneath that are some deep-seated fears around security. Take a deep breath and reflect before you lash out.

AUGUST: CAREER HOTSPOTS

August 2: Sun-Uranus square

With the Sun in your optimistic ninth house, you want to dream without limits. Trouble is, disruptor Uranus is demanding that you work from a plan. Don't resist setting up a system! This will be the backbone that supports your success. If you're getting bogged down in minutiae, do what smart managers do: delegate smaller tasks so you can move the needle on the bigger ones.

August 3: Aquarius full moon

As the full moon spotlights your cooperative, communicative third house, kindred spirits crop up everywhere, from your favorite coffeeshop to your Instagram DMs. You've seen at least one of these win-wins brewing for a while. Now's the time to lock down an official collaboration. Test the waters with a short-term project. What can you co-produce in the next 90 days?

August 3: Mercury-Saturn opposition

"Set it and forget it" can be sound advice when it comes to your savings, but it's still wise to do periodic check-ins. Saturn plays the long game, and its opposition to analytical Mercury in your house of wealth accumulation gives you an opportunity to revise your strategy. An extra set of eyes can help you glean tactics you might have overlooked, like moving funds to a higher-yielding investment.

August 4: Mars-Jupiter square

Your vision may be 20-20, but a colleague might be more opaque or unable to see the brilliance of your ideas altogether. Don't waste time trying to convince them of your merit. This short-term hurdle could prove a one-day obstacle!

August 4-19: Mercury in Leo

Don't limit your vision! This inquisitive cycle pushes you to look far and wide as you search for opportunity. Your ideal collaborators might live far away, but don't let that stop you. Connect to them via social media or by traveling to a conference and meeting there.

August 10: Mercury-Uranus square

You're famous for rocking the boat but today your renegade spirit could totally capsize the craft. With outspoken Mercury pushing the envelope in your candid ninth house, that's a real risk. Toss in a boisterous beam from erratic Uranus, and you could cross the line, especially if someone tries to micromanage or criticize you. If you're giving feedback to an employee or junior-level person, take extra care. Buffer it in a "praise sandwich" by inserting your advice between two compliments. It will disarm them and make the tough parts easier for them to swallow.

August 13: Mars-Pluto square

As brash Mars tussles with underhanded Pluto, you run the risk of coming on too strong when presenting your vision. Egos could clash and a competitor may try to elbow you out of the decision-making process. Don't fuel the hostile fires. Keep your cutting-edge concepts under wraps until this storm blows over in a few days.

August 15, 2020-January 14, 2021: Uranus retrograde in Taurus

Keep on keeping on! Perseverance will pay off over the next five months as unruly Uranus reverse commutes through your sixth house of systems, health and hustle. You'll have to work harder to stay on top of the details now. Wherever things break down, consider it a sign to set up smarter structures or bring in more qualified support.

August 17: Mercury-Mars trine

Fortune favors the bold! Communicator Mercury in your expansive ninth house is high-fiving go-getter Mars in your creative zone. Share your grand visions and be receptive to input. Even if your innovative idea doesn't pan out, you'll learn a lot just by exploring and developing it.

August 18: Leo new moon

Spread your magic far and wide! This expansive new moon inspires you to think (and travel) beyond your current "limits." Connect to far-flung followers and see what you can co-create. If you're a media-maker or a teacher, start cooking up a new project that you can launch over the coming six months.

August 19-September 5: Mercury in Virgo

As strident Mercury zips into process-driven Virgo and activates your career corner, your focus turns to the nitty-gritty. Talk is cheap, but follow-through will yield a profitable win. If you make a promise, put it on the calendar as an action item. Walking your talk is the key to cementing important relationships.

August 25: Mercury-Uranus trine

Genius-level breakthroughs are possible today as keen Mercury connects the dots to innovative Uranus. Give yourself wiggle room to test and experiment. That's how you'll know whether or not your novel ideas have proper traction to succeed. Nothing ventured, nothing gained!

August 29: Mercury-Jupiter trine

This could be one of your luckiest money days of the year as savvy Mercury and no-limits Jupiter place their bets in the most abundant, successful zones of your chart. Throw your hat in the ring for a leadership role or put in a bid for that promotion. Float one of your strategic ideas by an office VIP. Announce that you're raising your rates soon— then hold a flash sale for loyal clients and customers and rake in some bonus profits!

August 30: Mercury-Neptune opposition

The way forward may seem hazy today as shrewd Mercury in your career house gets checked by nebulous Neptune. Your heartstrings are easily tugged, and you can be swayed by strong feelings at the expense of facts. In your desire to be helpful, you could make the mistake of volunteering for something you're not qualified to handle. If that happens, back out quickly while it's still "no harm, no foul."

September

SEPTEMBER: LOVE HOTSPOTS

September 2: Venus-Saturn opposition

Slow down and schedule quality time to connect with your love interest today. Passing conversations will not be enough to feel connected, nor to resolve any of the tension this transit can ratchet up. You might find it helpful (for both of you) to repeat things back to each other. ("What I'm hearing you say is…") Instead of jumping in to respond right away, focus on hearing them out in full.

September 2: Pisces full moon

This poetic full moon in your feeling-centric and domestic zone could inspire soulful connections. You and your S.O. might be ready to move in together—or at least start talking seriously about it (after reading each other Rumi in bed). Freshen up your space with flowers or a deep clean. What do you need to make your house feel more like a home? Host a dinner party to introduce pals to your new love interest. You could start the process of finding a shared space or discuss expanding your family. If you're single, implement a few Feng Shui techniques for attracting love, like decorating in pairs and making sure there is access to climb in on both sides of the bed.

September 4: Venus-Mars square

Running hot and cold? You may feel conflicted about how to proceed with a romantic prospect. Part of you is ready to don the scuba gear and dive in, but another part isn't quite there yet. While you crave intimacy, you might not be ready to give up your equally strong need for adventure. Explore without committing to anything that feels suffocating.

September 6-October 2: Venus in Leo

A diversified dating portfolio is a Sagittarius must, so if you've been stuck on a "type" for a while, this global Venus cycle expands your horizons. You could fall for someone from a different background or who lives a few time zones away. LAT (Living Apart Together) relationships might be ideal for your independent sign. Attached? Start planning your next baecation, ASAP.

September 9-November 13: Mars retrograde in Aries

Today, passionate Mars turns retrograde in your hedonistic fifth house, insisting that you dial back the decadence. For the next two months, just say no to pricey bottle service, lazy Lyft rides and buying non-essentials on credit. You don't need to live like an ascetic. Just think long and hard before you green-light tempting purchases. And the same thing goes for potential lovers. With back-spinning Mars scrambling signals in your romance zone, check yourself before you take the plunge.

September 15: Venus-Uranus square

Your pace might not match your love interest's, and that's okay! If they're moving like a snail, you can still float like a butterfly in your own life. Just relax and give them some time and space. And if you're the one that's overwhelmed by the swift speed, don't feel like you need to rush to keep up. Set boundaries and stick to them.

September 28: Venus-Mars trine

Think locally but love globally! Today's unbounded alignment of romantic Venus and passionate Mars in the most adventurous corners of your chart has you spinning the globe in search of your next vacay. Couples may be ready to book tickets for a dream vacation (or, hint hint, honeymoon) or even a quickie getaway. Single? If you're traveling, you could connect with someone on the road or, closer to home, meet an out-of-towner in the local bookshop. Not sure how to start a conversation? Just smile and say hi.

September 29: Mars-Saturn square

Speed check! Did you bolt into something new, or is someone pressuring you to commit before you're completely ready? This planetary pairing can slow down fast-moving relationships. Even if the attraction is irresistibly magnetic, if your goals and values don't align, you're only setting yourself up for disappointment. Stop long enough to assess.

SEPTEMBER: CAREER HOTSPOTS

September 1: Mercury-Pluto trine

Your instincts are blade-sharp today, so if you sense an opportunity in the ether, investigate! With mysterious Pluto in the mix, you might not see any visible evidence yet. Don't let this stop you. Do the detective work to find out whether or not this situation is lucrative, and moreover, worth your time. Remember: Money isn't the only motivating factor. Does this situation speak to your soul? Will it help you grow?

September 3: Mercury-Saturn trine

One of your big ideas could be majorly lucrative if you stop long enough to craft an actual plan. As methodical Saturn syncs with ingenious Mercury in your success sectors, think like a project manager. Set benchmarks, crunch numbers and organize your step-by-step methodology. Turn an inspector's eye to your personal finances as well. Where could you trim spending or reallocate funds so you can start stashing for a long-lasting investment?

September 5-27: Mercury in Libra

When the communication planet moves into balanced Libra and your eleventh house of teamwork and technology, you're eager to embrace fresh perspectives and tech-savvy solutions. Disparate viewpoints could gel in fascinating ways, creating a truly innovative path to success.

September 9-November 13: Mars retrograde in Aries

Do you have Kylie Jenner dreams on a starter-kit budget? Even if you're flush with cash, you need to be smarter about how you spend it. When the go-getter planet shifts into reverse in your house of hard work and service, you might feel underappreciated or poorly compensated. While this isn't the best time to ask for a raise or make a move, it *is* a perfect opportunity to review your actions (and personal motivation) and ask if you could be doing anything different. Give yourself two months to turn around your game.

September 12: Jupiter retrograde ends

Make it rain! Auspicious Jupiter concludes a frustrating four-month retrograde in your second house of work and finances. The red-spotted giant will propel through this enriching realm until

December 19, so if you've got any aces up your sleeve, play them soon!

September 14: Sun-Pluto trine

Visualize a winning outcome and you could magnetize it in the next few days. Today's fierce and fiery energy will carry you to the finish line, providing the perseverance you need. If you're making the decisions, use your authority to support an initiative that could better your little corner of the world. What goes around comes around!

September 17: Virgo new moon

The year's only Virgo new moon supercharges your professional tenth house, motivating you to launch a new initiative. Plant the seeds for the long-term goals you want to harvest over the coming six months. You'll see major gains along the way, but don't stop until you've taken it all the way to the finish line.

September 17: Mercury-Jupiter square

Today's clash of the most communicative planets could make it hard to get through to people, especially at work. Tweak your pitch, update your information and give it your best shot! But if you're just not connecting well, pull back and wait a few days before making your case.

September 21: Mercury-Pluto square

If you see a sinking ship, grab your life vest and quietly make for the door. You might disagree with the collective decisions on how to move forward, but sometimes people aren't interested in input or advice. Save your breath for the swim back to shore!

September 23: Mercury-Saturn square

Get curious today as quick-witted Mercury faces off with cautious Saturn. What is the basis of your beliefs? Question everything, even the so-called facts taken from those you trust. Doing your own research can strengthen your decisions and help you understand the finer details. If someone asks you to go to bat for them, remember that their performance will have a bearing on your reputation. A good friend isn't always the best colleague. Declining their request is awkward, but it could save the relationship in the long run.

September 24: Mercury-Mars opposition

Team dynamics might feel tense today under an opposition of aggro Mars and mouthy Mercury. Drama could erupt and regrettable words might be exchanged in anger. Take a cool-down if need be, but don't sweep this issue under the rug. If an ego-tripping diva is making everyone walk on eggshells, map your battle plan carefully and be sure to document everything.

September 27-October 27: Mercury in Scorpio

Make like a tortoise and work slowly and steadily. Mercury makes the first of two trips to your restful twelfth house this year. (The repeat cycle is due to a retrograde from October 13 to November 3.) Instead of rushing to a resolution, let yourself simmer and steep. During this introspective cycle, you can chip away at your goals little by little each day and watch as your dreams organically shift into reality.

September 29: Mars-Saturn square

Pump the brakes! Are you feeling pressured to race ahead before you're totally ready to make a decision? As sluggish Saturn checks impulsive Mars, slow the tempo on a situation that is accelerating at a manic pace. Even if the chemistry is irresistibly magnetic, if your goals and values don't align, you're only setting yourself up for disappointment. Stop long enough to carefully assess.

September 29: Saturn retrograde ends
Your purse strings may have felt a little tight these past five months, as restrictive Saturn retrograded through your money house. As the stern planet corrects course, new ideas for increasing cash flow could hit you. You're so done with feeling like Sisyphus, rolling a rock up a hill. Lightening your load—and trimming expenses—can help you get back in the black.

October

OCTOBER: LOVE HOTSPOTS

October 1: Aries full moon
Meow! You could reflexively act on an animal attraction as the year's only full moon in your passionate fifth house turns you into a fierce jungle cat. Just be aware that under the rash energy of Aries, things could escalate quickly. If you're attached, tap into this fun-loving lunar lift to add some spice to your relationship. Under these fertile moonbeams, a pregnancy is possible, as is the birth of co-created project.

October 2-27: Venus in Virgo
The love planet glides into your future-focused tenth house, turning the tide toward commitment. If "fidelity-phobia" crops up, don't just bolt! But do use the next few weeks to see if long-term goals align. For couples, your greatest aphrodisiac might become talking about your long-term plans and a shared future.

October 10: Venus-Uranus trine
Mix a little business and pleasure today when Venus bats its lashes at experimental Uranus across your career corners. Open up a conversation about your professional goals with your S.O., trading aspirations and advice. Single? The sixth house rules service, so volunteer for a cause you care about. If you meet someone attractive in the process, you'll already have one passion in common.

October 13-November 3: Mercury retrograde
As the messenger planet retreats through your subconscious sector, tap into this cycle's powerful potential for healing and forgiveness work. Is there a grudge to release? If you've been quietly seething with resentment, find outside support from a therapist, coach, or healer to talk through those buried feelings and find resolution. Letting go means moving on, whether you choose to reconnect to the offending party or not.

October 18: Venus-Neptune opposition
Oversharing alert! Revealing the intimate details of your life could invite unsolicited feedback today. Under a clash of two sensitive planets, Venus and Neptune, you might be overly swayed by someone's (self-interested) opinion. Curb the temptations to discuss every sordid detail of your love life, and strategically excuse yourself if someone starts spouting suggestions.

October 19: Mars-Jupiter square
Even though you can see a clear path to the future, your romantic interest may struggle to get on board with your vision of love. If you're met with

The AstroTwins' 2020 Horoscope

resistance, don't keep pushing. Give 'em a few days to digest. With a little time and space they might come around and give your scheme a go!

October 19: Venus-Jupiter trine

Your eyes, mind and heart are all wide open under this expansive alignment of the love planet and optimistic Jupiter. This would be a perfect moment to start planning something big for your future—on your own or with your favorite plus-one. Business and pleasure mingle in exciting ways, like collaborating with your sweetie on a work project, or finally getting some one-on-one time in with your office crush. (Just check the company policy before you go there.)

October 21: Venus-Pluto trine

Down that cup of courage because it's time to initiate a conversation you've been putting off. Although Mercury is retrograde, its effects are offset by today's harmonious trine between loving Venus and alchemical Pluto in your communication sectors. Don't worry about delivering the perfect monologue. Lead with curiosity, sharing your point of view and finding out where your love interest stands. If you're single, stay open. Some attractions burn bright and fizzle fast, but today, stoking smoldering embers could start a blaze in an unexpected place.

October 24: Venus-Saturn trine

What's sexier than security and stability? Normally, your indie-spirited sign would be counting the ways, but under a grounding sync-up of future-oriented Saturn and amorous Venus, you're longing for greater certainty. In a relationship? Firm up your financial foundation. Find ways to save together for a shared goal, like an upcoming vacation or a down payment on a home. Single? In your search for a soulmate, be sure to investigate their fiscal fitness.

October 27-November 21: Venus in Libra

Would you care to add a "benefits package" to that friendship? During this three-week cycle, you could start seeing platonic pals in a more attractive light. Keep things breezy and fun! With the love planet logged in to your tech sector, open up the dating apps and start swiping. Prefer to meet someone IRL? Ask friends to play Cupid. Attached? Channel this expansive energy into hanging out more with your various friends and sparking up your shared social life.

OCTOBER: CAREER HOTSPOTS

October 4: Pluto retrograde ends

Metamorphic Pluto ends its five-month backspin through your second house of work and money, clearing up scarcity woes and easing the tough financial lessons it served. Big ideas that were put on the backburner are ready to go back into development. Don't worry about lost time. All the researching and ruminating you've done since April will only support your next round of rollouts.

October 7: Mercury-Uranus opposition

As expressive Mercury faces off with chaotic Uranus, one perfectly innocent comment could send everything sideways. Don't speak mindlessly today; in fact, it's best to stay out of discussions until you have all your facts in place. For the time being, just listen and observe. There will be two more Mercury-Uranus oppositions, on October 19 and November 17, which is all the more reason to play it safe.

October 9: Mars-Pluto square

As reckless Mars rumbles with ruthless Pluto, you may realize just how different your values are from someone you're working with. Question is, can you find enough common ground to make this connection viable? Don't waste time battling for supremacy! If they're micromanaging all the magic out of your cutting-edge concepts, it's never going to be a good fit. Make sure you aren't stifling other people's input today.

October 15: Sun-Pluto square

Some people will never understand (or appreciate!) your idealistic point of view. If your suggestions keep getting shot down, it could mean one of two things: A) you need to hold off on giving input until you've done more research, or B) you need to search for collaborators who better suit your style. Don't take it personally. Different strokes for different folks.

October 16: Libra new moon

Even you, the zodiac's rugged individualist, understand the value of having a rock-solid crew. And this annual new moon in your collaborative eleventh house sets the stage for a promising team effort that grows more visible and viable over the coming six months. Get a buzz started on social media, whether you're casting for new members or surveying friends and followers for feedback on your nascent ideas.

October 18: Sun-Saturn square

Not so fast! With the Sun beaming into your innovative eleventh house, you may be sitting on a goldmine. But a restraining order from Saturn in your practical second house insists that you mine a little deeper and do a cost-benefit analysis. Even if you have to go back to the drawing board temporarily it's better than presenting something that's not 100 percent up to snuff.

October 19: Mars-Jupiter square

Trouble on Team Archer could arise as aggro Mars antagonizes supersizer Jupiter. Minor issues may get blown out of proportion, and you won't have the patience to deal with things constructively. Call a time-out should things get too tense. If a narcissist is making everyone walk on eggshells, document the incidents in case you need to escalate it to someone who can properly handle matters.

October 31: Taurus full moon

Does your workspace "spark joy"? As the year's only Taurus full moon powers up your streamlined sixth house, you may be inspired to give your office area a Marie Kondo-level deep clean. Tame the chaos on your calendar, desk and inbox. Delegate tasks as needed so you have bandwidth for what's really important.

November

NOVEMBER: LOVE HOTSPOTS

November 9: Venus-Mars opposition

With these heavenly heartthrobs working at cross purposes, your emotions could be all over the map. This is not a good day to make any major or irreversible decisions about a relationship's status. Step back and examine your feelings. You can't keep pushing a nagging issue aside.

       The AstroTwins' 2020 Horoscope

November 13: Mars retrograde ends

Has your love life felt more like a *telenovela* than reality series since June 27? (Or, um, are you shaking your head and thinking, "What love life?") No matter what your complaints, they could become ancient history now that energizing Mars is resuming forward motion after a two-month retrograde that has been stirring the pot in your passionate, dramatic fifth house. The red planet will still be heating things up in this arena until January 6, so throw yourself back into the romance game. If you put a creative project on hold since the summer, unearth it now!

November 15: Scorpio new moon

Can you make amends or is it time to call it quits? The year's only Scorpio new moon lands in your house of healing and completions. If you've extended enough olive branches to assemble a small tree, you might just want to wave the white flag. Or maybe enough time has passed to allow you to release a longstanding grudge. Whatever the case, you can start mending fences or making a graceful exit now.

November 15: Venus-Pluto square

You're comfortable being an open book, but don't be such an easy read today. As shadowy Pluto bumps up against open-hearted Venus, people's intentions won't be obvious. Hold back and let them earn your trust. Beyond that, being a bit more mysterious will leave people wanting more. Willpower!

November 16: Venus-Jupiter square

You may keep getting pulled in two directions today—and feel highly confused by that! The love planet in your liberated eleventh house is clashing with free-spirited Jupiter in your security zone, making you crave stability *and* space. You want to have your chocolate ganache cake and eat it, too. It may be a tough search for someone willing to allow that double standard. Of course, if anyone can find that needle in the haystack, it's gonna be you!

November 19: Venus-Saturn square

Can freedom and stability coexist? It's a delicate balance, as Venus in your independent eleventh house locks horns with steadfast Saturn. If you're not looking for anything serious, a fun little adventure could be in store. Just don't hold out hope that someone's intentions will change. You can find a happy medium to avoid feeling smothered, but it may take a lot of trial and error…and a very loving partner!

November 21-December 15: Venus in Scorpio

Covert fantasies rise to the surface when sizzling Venus plunges into your subterranean twelfth house and activates the sultriest part of your imagination. Experimenting can be fun, and you may be drawn to edgier situations with a dash of danger. Pick your poison…and your safe word!

November 27: Venus-Uranus opposition

You're ready to jump in for the save, but what if you decided to sit this one out? You trying to "fix" the situation could actually make things worse. Let the circumstances run their course. It's best not to fan the flames right now.

November 28: Neptune retrograde ends

Clarity is on the horizon, as hazy Neptune ends its five-month retrograde through your sensitive and domestic fourth house. The lines between reality and fantasy may have been blurred, and connections might've felt unnecessarily complicated. As your intuition sharpens again, you can address anything that needs improvement with the people closest to you…without escalating the drama! If your moods and reactions have been all over the map, you'll start to feel more in control again.

November 30: Gemini full moon (lunar eclipse)

The annual Gemini full moon supercharges your partnership realm, bringing a turning point or clarity within the next two weeks. This one is a potent lunar eclipse, which could reveal something hidden, like a secret or an opportunity for growth. Strengthen your relationships by holding a "state of the union" so each of you can air your thoughts and feelings. Single Sags could meet someone who actually makes settling down sound like fun!

NOVEMBER: CAREER HOTSPOTS

November 1: Mercury-Saturn square

Curious Mercury, which is retrograde, clashes with cautious Saturn and makes you stop and rethink what you've taken as a fact. This is the second of three Mercury-Saturn squares in 2020, and this transit will repeat in a few days on November 6, when Mercury turns direct. Conduct your own research to ensure the information you've been given is accurate. Proceed with care if a colleague or friend asks for your assistance. What happens if they can't follow through? Get clear about expectations. This could preserve your relationship, and above all, your good name.

November 3: Mercury Direct in Libra

Friends, foes or frenemies? It's been hard to know where to categorize people for the last few weeks while social Mercury slipped into a befuddling retrograde. As the messenger planet powers forward, you'll know who's on Team Archer and who needs to be kicked off the island. Ready to upgrade your tech? The coast is clear to shop around for digital devices again.

November 10-December 1: Mercury in Scorpio

Messenger Mercury returns to your twelfth house for the second time this year, charging up your intuition. While the communicative planet plods through this introspective sector, dig beneath the surface for information. A meditation practice can help you stay grounded during this buzzy season, so take time each day to pull back and tune in.

November 12: Jupiter-Pluto meetup

For the third time in 2020, bountiful Jupiter gets in lockstep with shrewd Pluto in your second house of work and money. Finally! You can crystallize all the lessons you've learned about saving and earning—and making your moolah work hard for you. While you may have to cut off a few capable "dependents," you've gained a healthy respect for your finances and what it takes to create lasting security for yourself.

November 23: Mercury-Neptune trine

Connect with your colleagues on a personal level today by letting your authentic self shine through. It doesn't have to be all business all the time. In fact, sharing more about your offline life—within reason, o' candid one—can help cement a professional alliance for you. Show interest in others today, too. Strengthen rapport with colleagues by learning more about what makes them tick. While this might not be the most productive day you've had all year, the bonding will bring long-term rewards.

November 30: Gemini full moon (lunar eclipse)

The year's only Gemini full moon is also a glowing lunar eclipse, and it's charging up your seventh house of partnerships. Before the year is through, you could ink an important deal or fortify a business relationship that can turn into a profitable win-win. They say we are only as successful as those we're surrounded by. Can your collaborators match your drive and ambition? If they can't keep up, cut ties now before they bring you down.

December

DECEMBER: LOVE HOTSPOTS

December 5: Venus trine Neptune

How deep is your love? You could find out today as amorous Venus dips her bucket into Neptune's well of fantasy. Boundaries don't just blur under this alignment, they totally dissolve. Make sure you know what you're getting yourself into before you take that plunge!

December 15, 2020-January 9, 2021: Venus in Sagittarius

Your magnetism is off the charts as the love planet bursts into your sign for the rest of the year. Don your sexiest apparel and hit the holiday party circuit, whether you're solo or with your S.O. Now's a great time to tap into your creative side, so go make art for art's sake!

December 23: Mars-Pluto square

Under this tempestuous cosmic clash, be ultra-careful what you wish for. With make-it-happen Mars in your seductive fifth house throwing shade at volcanic Pluto, it'll be hard to find the brake once you hit the gas. But do you really want that situation to take off at lightning speed? If you're in a relationship, think twice before you rock the love boat. Single? Make sure your "person of interest" is actually available.

December 29: Cancer full moon

The second of two Cancer full moons beams into your intimate and mysterious eighth house. The first was earlier in the year on January 10, and now you get a replay of this seductive starmap. Pent-up desires could rise to the surface and relationships may shift into deeper territory quickly. If you do dive into a sizzling affair, don't kid yourself: Once you're in, it won't be easy to extricate yourself!

December 30: Venus-Neptune square

Help…air! As the romance planet locks into a tangled angle with hazy Neptune, someone's neediness could cramp your free-spirited vibe. How can you cultivate interdependence instead of codependence? Prioritize your own needs if you've been putting someone else first. Or if your S.O. has been waiting on you hand and foot, it's time to return the favor with an act of selfless generosity.

DECEMBER: CAREER HOTSPOTS

December 1-20: Mercury in Sagittarius

The cosmic messenger zooms into your sign, joining the Sun in your eighth house of shared resources and assets. Let the holiday party circuit double as a series of networking events. You never know who you'll meet while you're out mingling. Charm your way onto those VIP guest lists, just for good measure! With people's holiday spirits dialed up, you should meet with some receptive audiences.

December 13: Mercury-Neptune square

Stay alert! It's tempting to check out early this holiday season, but a befuddling square between analytical Mercury and dreamy Neptune might cause you to overlook a crucial responsibility. Make a list and check it thrice. You'll be more relaxed on your time off if you know every detail is handled.

December 14: Sagittarius new moon (total solar eclipse)

Start 2021 early as the new moon in Sagittarius rings in the spirit of renewal. This one is a potent solar eclipse, which could unleash a bold beginning or light the way to a path you hadn't imagined was possible. You'll be bursting with enthusiasm, but to be successful—and make this last more than a week—pace yourself and prioritize your efforts! Take the rest of 2020 to determine where you'd like to implement changes. Then, in early 2021, you can map out a six-month plan that ensures you're making sustainable progress.

December 17, 2020-March 7, 2023: Saturn in Aquarius

Your social life, especially your community interactions, will reach a turning point today, as pragmatic Saturn moves into Aquarius and your third house of local happenings until March 7, 2023. Who are the people in your neighborhood? How can you use your ability to connect to all sorts of people to make a difference for your 'hood? Over the next two years, you will be happiest in a city where you feel not only "at home," but also inspired to help create the cultural vibe. Relationships with community, friends and siblings could undergo a sea change—and for some Archers, this will come as very welcome news. Your communication style has a strong effect on these connections, so reflect not only on what you say, but how you say it—*and* everything you're not saying. Omissions can speak as loudly as words.

December 19, 2020-May 13, 2021: Jupiter in Aquarius

Even with the holidays upon you, it's time to uplevel your professional game and prepare for an expansive new chapter to begin! Your galactic guardian, auspicious Jupiter, kicks off an exciting trek through your communication house. As the red planet winds in and out of Aquarius until December 29, 2021, people will seek you out for your ideas—and your ability to package them in a savvy, persuasive way. Begin reflecting on the message you want to send out to the world. Since this realm also rules hometown happenings, you may become a big deal on the local scene.

December 20, 2020-January 9, 2021: Mercury in Capricorn

Chatty Mercury charges into your second house of work and money, boosting your earning power as 2020 winds down. Perhaps an end-of-year raise is in the cards, or a holiday bonus? The cosmic messenger will be here through the first week of January, so you can use the break to fine-tune your talking points and schedule an early 2021 review. If you're in the running for a big contract, don't sell yourself short in the bidding process. You know what you're worth, and silver-tongued Mercury can help you get it!

The AstroTwins' 2020 Horoscope

December 21: Jupiter-Saturn meetup

You're transmitting serious signals today as your ruler, big-hearted Jupiter, joins forces with masterful Saturn in your communication zone—an event astrologers call The Great Conjunction. Your words carry weight, whether you're writing, speaking or tweeting. This is a powerful day to promote yourself or get plans in motion for a writing or media project. Got something to teach? Start developing the curriculum. The expert industry is calling!

December 23: Mars-Pluto square

Ease off the gas! Frenetic Mars has kept you active and in the public eye for months. But today, low-key Pluto flashes the red light, directing you to chill—like stat! Don't worry, people won't forget you if you fly under the radar for a few days. Enjoy family time without having to turn every moment into an Instagram story. If a coworker tries to offload work on you, just say no!

December 25: Mercury-Uranus trine

Don ye now your…thinking cap? There's no telling when genius will strike, and today's brilliant mashup of savvy Mercury and inventive Uranus could bring a flood of divine downloads. When you're done exchanging gifts, pour yourself a glass of eggnog and get those big ideas recorded. Who knows? The enterprising people in your party might be down for a little brainstorming sesh.

December 29: Cancer full moon

The second of the year's Cancer full moons lands in your eighth house of wealth, joint ventures and passive income. The first was January 10, so you'll start and end the year with these themes on deck. A business partnership that launched at the previous lunation could yield lucrative gains now, just in time for the calendar to turn. If you're looking to buy or sell property, this lunar lift could move the needle on your efforts. Don your detective's chapeau: A puzzle you've been piecing together could finally make sense! ✷

Tools from The AstroTwins
for your 2020 PLANNING

Visit all year long for
new updates & additions!

www.astrostyle.com/2020tools

CAPRICORN
2020

Yearly Highlights

LOVE

People may come and go during this free-spirited year, but the one enduring relationship to focus on is the love affair with yourself. With self-authorized Jupiter in your sign, you're poised to make a massive leap into a new league! Changemaker Uranus spends its first full year in your fame and romance zone, making you frisky and experimental! Reserve swaths of time to develop your big ideas and "brand." Then, focus on quality over quantity in your encounters with the ones you *j'adore*. Don't worry, being independent doesn't mean being alone. Two Cancer eclipses on January 10 and June 21 could cement relationships. From April through August, Venus will call for support structures to keep your partnerships from fizzling out.

MONEY

Hello, influencer! The call to the throne will be impossible to ignore with a trio of heavy-hitters—Jupiter, Saturn and Pluto—all touring Capricorn! But this year, you're utterly uninterested in picking up other people's slack; in fact, you may feel weighted down by teamwork. You'd rather lead by example and let tout le monde follow in your Goliath-sized footsteps. With the moon's North Node (destiny point) moving into Gemini and your work zone for 18 months on May 5, you could discover a new path that makes your soul sing! On December 21, a rare and potent mashup of Saturn and Jupiter in your money house might reveal a fresh source of financial stability.

WELLNESS

All will not be quiet on the Capricorn home front in 2020. With enterprising Jupiter in your sign, your kitchen table could turn into the test lab for a new business venture. Frenetic Mars buzzes through Aries and your domestic zone from June 27 on. You may feel unrooted, especially during the retrograde phase from September 9 to November 13, and could make an impulsive decision around relocating or a property sale. Tension with relatives might hit a boiling point, and at times, your sacred oasis may feel like a battlefield. Don't be afraid to issue ultimatums—or eviction notices—to people who aren't willing to play by Capricorn's house rules. Boundaries!

LEISURE

Get your glow on! Robust Jupiter tours your sign until December 19, refueling your energy and flipping on your lit-from-within glow. From April 3 to August 7, enchanting Venus embarks on an extended tour through Gemini and your sixth house of wellness. Skip the punishing workouts. Both of these pleasure planets prescribe sensual self-care: regular massages and dips in natural hot springs. Avoid cosmetic procedures while Venus is retrograde from May 13 to June 25. Enlist more support! Buddy workouts with your partner and yoga dates with friends may be your favorite ways to socialize. Just make sure to warm up and stretch, since Saturn—the ruler of your skeletal system—in Capricorn calls for added measures of caution. ✳

CAPRICORN
2020 HOROSCOPE

2020 Power Dates

CAPRICORN NEW MOON
No new moons in your sign in 2020

CAPRICORN FULL MOON
July 5 (12:44am ET) lunar eclipse

SUN IN CAPRICORN
January 1–20, December 21–31

New decade, new you! If anyone has dibs on that mantra, it's you, Capricorn. In 2020, worldly Jupiter will soar through your sign, its first visit since January 5, 2009. You may already be shining like a breakout star this New Year's Day, since the red-spotted planet made landfall in your sign on December 2, 2019. Keep the momentum going! Jupiter will continue to bless you with its abundant beams until December 19, ensuring that 2020 will be a banner year for growth and expansion.

And that's hardly the full story! For the majority of the 2020, Jupiter travels astride power-broker Pluto and your ruler, masterful Saturn, as all three planets form a rare series of convergences in Capricorn. So rare, in fact, that this cosmic cluster hasn't occurred since 1285 C.E.! Thanks to this Sea Goat samba in the sky, many born under your sign will make history as the new decade dawns. Good thing you're motivated by a challenge! Instead of getting swept up in a competition with the titans of industry, make it your goal to bring forth your best self—perhaps in a public way.

Not sure where to begin? Review all of the vision boards and journal entries from 2019, while Jupiter was meditating in your "woo" twelfth house. Last year, life may have felt stalled in suspended animation. Your intuition guided you, and now, all that randomness could start to make sense. Once you zero in on the right cue or clue, the next steps will become immediately obvious. Trust your instincts! You really learned how to do that in 2019 and it's a skill to bring into this new year.

> "Thanks to the Sea Goat samba in the sky, many born under your sign will make history."

Subterranean Pluto has been helping you plumb those depths since it moved into your sign in 2008. (It remains there for four more years.) And ever since December 19, 2017, your ruler, strategic Saturn, has been touring Capricorn, fortifying that solid foundation you need to stand on if you're to operate effectively in the world.

As helpful as this planetary pairing has been, it's aroused its share of angst. Pluto has been poking at the darker corners of your psyche over the past 12 years, forcing you to explore (and hopefully make peace with) your own shadow. Have you discovered some deep-rooted fears or insecurities—or maybe a need to change your life in a fundamental way? Alchemical Pluto's mission is to help you turn that lead you've mined into gold. Continue to explore and embrace your own emotions, perhaps with the help of therapists, healers and coaches. With Pluto traversing 22°29' through 25° degrees Capricorn, Goats born between January 10 to 18 will be plunged into the deepest inner work this year.

Nevertheless, Pluto will put all Capricorns through paces in 2020. This may involve releasing a few more material-world attachments. Since 2008, changes surrounding money, marriage, career, status and family relationships (all things you hold dear) have felt like tectonic plates shifting beneath your feet. At the same time, you're undergoing an undeniable spiritual transformation. Fading away is the Capricorn people-pleaser who feels pressured to be the rock for everyone in your midst or to play every game according to society's rules. And as you release the need for outside validation, you're becoming a seriously self-authorized Sea Goat! Your unflappable power will continue to emerge and amaze in the year ahead.

On January 12, CEO Saturn and transformational Pluto will mash up at the same degree of Capricorn which could see you stepping out and stepping up, perhaps as the face of a new (green) movement! Jupiter and Pluto will dance cheek to cheek on April 4, June 30 and again on November 12. These planetary paso dobles probably won't win any Mirrorball trophies. In fact, they could be painfully awkward and here's why: Authenticity cop Jupiter is all about exposing the truth while secretive Pluto wants to guard every scrap of intel with its life. While you want to keep it real, you may feel unsure about where the TMI line is drawn. How much to share and how much to keep on the downlow?

Warning: You might not have total control over what's revealed near these three conjunctions. Make sure you can stand behind all of your choices, past and present. Are there skeletons rattling in your closet? (If you're breathing, the answer is probably "yes.") If you're worried yours may come back to haunt you, get ahead of the curve by exposing the story yourself. Better people should hear it straight from your lips than some nefarious "source" who's not on Team Cappy.

One day to highlight in neon pink is July 5, when the full moon in Capricorn arrives as a lunar eclipse—the last one in a series that began striking your sign on January 5, 2019. Eclipses reveal hidden opportunities, the kind that may be so far off of your radar that it takes some provocative (even shocking) developments to get your attention. The good news is that whatever jaw-dropping events occur in early July may bring much-desired closure—or a milestone moment that you've been waiting to celebrate for more than a year.

In 2019, a rare trio of eclipses landed in your sign, which already set these plans in motion. Look back to events that initiated near the solar (new moon) eclipses on January 5 and December 26, 2019. You may launch the next leg of this mission around July 5, 2020. Did something come to fruition within a month of the July 16, 2019, lunar (full moon) eclipse? History may repeat itself, but with an upgraded twist. Or, a missed opportunity from last July could present itself again. This time, be ready to *carpe diem!*

Radical Uranus is officially buzzing through Taurus for its first full year, activating your fifth house of romance, glamour and fierce self-expression. Can love and freedom go hand in hand? That's a worthy exploration! During this eight-year Uranus cycle (which lasts until 2026), you won't take kindly to anyone trying to tamp down your individuality. Some Capricorns may embrace their single status wholeheartedly, while others will want to balance sacred solo space against time spent with a significant other. With two Cancer eclipses firing up your relationship house, on January 10 and June 21, a partner may demand clarification and exclusivity. Those eclipses can also jailbreak Capricorns from any confining relationship agreements that have you feeling more suffocated than sexy.

Adding to this, love planets Venus and Mars will turn retrograde in 2020. While these reverse commutes can feel like setbacks at first, they are also blessed timeouts that allow you to review the way you "do" relationships. First to snooze will be peacekeeping Venus, who retreats through communicative Gemini and your sixth house of structures from May 13 to June 25. Time to negotiate new terms with your partner? You're a creature of habit, Capricorn, but a romance may hit the rocks if you're simply going through the motions. Drop the assumptions and get into dialogue about what each of you wants. Yes, you need your daily RDA of work time, exercise, relaxation and so on, but you may want to shift your schedule to accommodate the one you love.

Mars shifts into reverse from September 9 until November 13 in Aries and your fourth house of security, family, home and roots. Tension under your roof could mount, especially if you don't have enough privacy and space for yourself. A love interest could pressure you to move in together, or if you already cohabitate, you may decide to rent a studio/work space outside of the house so you can have what Virginia Woolf dubbed, "a room of one's own." A little absence can definitely make the heart grow fonder as long as you don't go AWOL on your peeps.

Capricorn season begins on December 21 along with one of the year's major cosmic events, called the Great Conjunction. This historical happening occurs approximately every 19 years, when Saturn and Jupiter make an exact alignment and combine their powers. In many ways, these two planets are total opposites. Saturn is the ringed taskmaster who moves slowly (and steadily) toward crushing every skill. Jupiter is idealistic, whimsical and broad-minded. Saturn streamlines; Jupiter expands. Together, they can deliver the perfect hybrid of traditional wisdom and daring exploration. In 2020, their meetup takes place at 0°29' Aquarius, activating your solar second house of work and money. What pot of gold will this "rainbow connection" lead you to, Capricorn? You may find it abroad or in your own backyard, but either way, you're likely to end the year with a giant leap towards prosperity!

Saturn-Pluto conjuction: Passion into profit.

December 2019–February 2020 (exact on January 12)

Ready or not, it's time to transform. On January 12, a rare conjunction between power broker Pluto and time lord Saturn, both at 22° Capricorn, could provoke a karmic evolution. These two heavy-hitters have been in deep dialogue since December 2019 and the conversation continues into early February 2020. But their exact hit on January 12 will make it impossible to ignore their impact!

If we're all on this planet for a reason, your path could become clear near January 12. Ready or not,

you may be forced to step into a role of authority and make a unilateral decision—approval ratings be damned. This could be as daunting as Daenerys Targaryen's first dragon ride on *Game of Thrones*, but if you're willing to push past that fear, there will be palpable alchemy as you embrace your power.

January 12 could also be a date of a huge metamorphosis! Like a pack of dynamite, the Saturn-Pluto conjunction can blow up your excuses and mines your buried potential. If you've been clinging to outmoded structures, transformational Pluto can force you to run from these false "shelters." It can be terrifying to give up things that are safe and predictable. But what if those comforts are holding you back from your true potential? You'll never know unless you let go. This haiku from 17th century Japanese poet and samurai, Mizuta Masahide, may sum up January's transformation: "Barn's burnt down—now I can see the moon."

Nope, Capricorn, you won't have room to hide out or play small near January 12. But like any hero's journey, this will be a test of your strength. Saturn adds a certain weightiness while Pluto can provoke rivalries with people who are jealous of your status and success. The trick is to not get distracted by the haters, because giving them even an ounce of your attention could throw you off your game, causing you to miss a crucial opportunity to get ahead.

No fanfare necessary! Instead, focus on generating results that will create the most stability for everyone involved. Should you feel overwhelmed by the projects on your plate, enlist experts who can help you map out a master plan. Dedicate time to working with a coach or consultant who can steer you back onto the Success Superhighway.

Jupiter in Capricorn: Call of the wild.

December 2, 2019–December 19, 2020

Searching for a new title of distinction? Try "global citizen" on for size! In 2020, you'll stretch and soar like a Cirque du Soleil aerialist. Gone will be your reservations about leaping without obsessively checking the net. Risk-taker Jupiter will dance through Capricorn until December 19, buoying your faith and opening your eyes to your true capabilities.

And it's anyone's guess where you'll make your dazzling dismounts! With this cosmic energy putting wind in your sails (and miles on your frequent flyer account), you could land anywhere from Cartageña to Cape Town for business, pleasure or a sweet combo platter of both. This may be the year to set up an extended apartment swap with a friend in a far-flung city or to Airbnb your place for a few months while you travel the world.

No stalling! Jupiter only visits your sign every 12 years, giving you a 13-month window to play. The last time the jovial planet was in Capricorn was from December 19, 2007, to January 5, 2009, so you might think back to what was happening in your life then. Themes could repeat themselves or you may be drawn to similar growth experiences. Novelty and adventure will lure you away from your comfort zone in 2020, making your whole universe feel bigger and brighter. Even if these new activities don't turn out to be your cup of tea, you'll be able to say, "Glad I tried that at least once."

Real talk, Capricorn: Is all this chatter about freedom tying your stomach in knots? While many signs would cheer at such a liberating proposition, hosting daredevil Jupiter can be unmooring for cautious Caps. You're not exactly comfortable with the galactic gambler's high-stakes betting style. You prefer your risks to be calculated and your spontaneity to come with a serious side of structure. Trouble is, that's not how Jupiter rolls. When a dazzling opportunity presents itself in 2020, you have to leap without a net. Capricorn Dr. Martin Luther King Jr. said it best, "Faith is taking the first step, even when you don't see the whole staircase."

You might still have a bit of planetary PTSD to shake off from 2019, when Jupiter visited Sagittarius and your twelfth house of transition, closure and healing. Your tenacious sign was forced to surrender in the face of things that were simply beyond your control. Some Capricorns experienced unexpected losses—people passing away suddenly or kids, lovers and friends having to learn tough lessons that you could not make "all better." That was definitely hard on your can-do spirit, but the worst should be in the rearview now. If you're still feeling stuck, lean in to Jupiter's wisdom-bearing guidance. Sign up for a self-development workshop—one that's a bit more radical than it is warm and fuzzy. Some hardcore wisdom could give you the perfect soundbites you need to switch on the lights and get back into action.

Here's the good news! In 2020, luck is on your side. The trick is to embrace the concept of "failing forward." In order to get to the next stage of the game, allow yourself to make a few messes and even some public mistakes. As long as you're operating from a place of true innocence, your childlike wonder will make it all forgivable. And sure, those gaffes can be embarrassing for a composed (and competitive!) Cap, but here's where your wicked sense of humor comes out of hiding. Join the ranks of luminary comedians who share your zodiac sign— Tracy Ullman, Jim Carrey, Seth Meyer, Hannah Gadsby and Julia Louis-Dreyfus— and turn those teachable moments into laughable ones. Who knows? With your knack for monetizing every experience, a side hustle doing stand-up wouldn't be totally out of the question. If nothing else, recounting the story of "the time I signed up for that twerkshop," will surely make you the star entertainer at any party.

It's also important to remember that your sign ages in reverse! Like self-professed serious child (and Capricorn) Michelle Obama, many Goats felt burdened by a sense of duty and perfectionism as kids. But with age, you really do lighten up. Dip into Jupiter's fountain of youth this year and give Benjamin Button a run for his money.

Career-wise, hosting Jupiter could peg you as an influencer. This is the year to blaze trails and flaunt your originality. Your natural leadership skills will also shine, but with this indie-spirited planet guiding your path, you won't be in the mood to manage any complex org charts. Resist the urge to run for president or committee chair. Instead, be the curator who "sets the template" with your vision and taste. Then, enlist a second-in-command who can handle the operations involved with seeing your missions through to completion.

Jupiter-Pluto conjunction: Passion into profit.
April 4, June 30, November 12

Turn your passion into profits! In 2020, enterprising Jupiter and power-broker Pluto will make three exact conjunctions (meetups). On April 4, their first tête-à-tête will draw your secret superpowers to the surface. Ready or not, Capricorn, the world will discover just how capable and talented you are. For your modest sign, this can be a double-edged sword. On the one hand, the incoming adulation is what you've been working so hard toward. Simultaneously, you might suffer a bout of "compare and despair" syndrome, obsessing over all the ways you could have improved your work before your big reveal.

Relax! The trick is to focus on making progress instead of achieving perfection. Listening to people's feedback will only make your work stronger. With Jupiter and Pluto mashing up again on June 30, while both planets are in their annual retrograde, you can go back to the drawing board to make improvements. Then, show off your upgraded model during the grand finale of this trilogy on November 12.

Financially, the Jupiter-Pluto conjunctions will put wind behind your entrepreneurial sails. If you need to raise a round of angel funding, investors might pop up at every turn. But with both planets parked in your independent first house, hold on to the majority of ownership or you could wind up feeling controlled and uninspired. If you have a clear profit plan, it might be wiser to take out a business loan or set up a crowdfunding campaign than to sell off shares of your idea to a venture capitalist. Or, just make sure you remain the controlling partner! While you're eager to get things off the ground, you don't want to spend 2021 in court, trying to wrest back the rights to your intellectual property.

On a personal note, sultry Pluto and "anything goes" Jupiter make you quite the erotic explorer! With ambassador Jupiter in the frame, you may feel a magnetic pull towards someone who breaks from your usual type. Are you traveling near April 4, June 30 or November 12? A change of scenery could be an aphrodisiac. Coupled Caps should circle these dates for a "baecation."

Caveat: During the June 30 retrograde mashup, it would be best to revisit a nostalgic locale. Single? Don't rule out a yoga-retreat romance or a crush at the corporate convention that leads to some sexytime in your business-class hotel room. Clandestine hookups may be hot, but good luck keeping them under wraps. Secretive Pluto and blabbermouth Jupiter don't make the best bedfellows and you might wind up spilling the beans yourself in a thoughtless moment.

For that reason, you might have to practice serious restraint near these days, so as not to "dip the pen in the company ink," or overstep bounds with someone who should be forever off-limits, like say, the spouse of a good friend or your next-door neighbor. Willpower, Capricorn!

> **"Pluto and anything-goes Jupiter make you quite the erotic explorer."**

Venus & Mars Retrograde: Relationship review.

Venus Retrograde: May 14 – June 25

Mars Retrograde: September 10 – November 13

In 2020, cosmic co-pilots Venus and Mars will both weather a retrograde patch—a reverse commute these planets take every other year. During these turbulent spells, you may feel like you're pushing against a strong headwind. Stay the course, Capricorn. Your tenacious sign was born to endure challenges. Getting through these retrogrades will make you—and your most important relationships—stronger!

The key? Assume nothing and treat others as innocent until proven guilty, rather than the other way around. While romance planet Venus snoozes in communicative Gemini from May 13 to June 25, don't take anything at face value. Nope, not even with the people you've loved for years.

At their core essence, humans may never change, but they are constantly evolving. Does that sound like a paradox? Welcome to Venus in Gemini—a prolonged passage that will stretch from April 3 to August 7, 2020, due to the six-week retrograde phase. Normally, Venus hovers in a sign for four weeks. This year, however, you'll have four months to work out the communication kinks. And since Gemini governs your salubrious, systematic sixth house, you could devote a good chunk of the year to improving your most important unions.

Step one is to look at the "nuts and bolts" of your shared day-to-day life. Have you been like two ships passing in the night? Use the May 13 to June 25 retrograde to sync up your schedules. Put structures in place that foster connection. The weekly date night is a no-brainer, but don't stop there. How about making other agreements like "no mobile devices at the dinner table" or "Analog Saturdays" so that you connect to each other instead of just your wi-fi network?

If you're in a relationship, use this four-month Venus circuit to get healthy—and for couples, that could be as a duo. Prepare nourishing, plant-based meals, do buddy workouts, plan activity dates like bike rides and runs in the park. Soon you'll be glowing from all those endorphins—and fired up for some Boudoir Olympics.

Taking care of your own wellbeing could be a pleasurable experience with enchanting Venus here. Preventative medicine is the key, and you could finally use those massages and acupuncture referrals that your health insurance allots. Try holistic methods like working with flower essences and oils. A caring doctor or practitioner could be a life-changing force between April and August. Look for someone who is open to questions and willing to explain everything clearly. Note: Try to avoid scheduling any medical or cosmetic procedures while Venus is retrograde from May 13 to June 25. If dates are non-negotiable, make sure you have read all the pre-treatment instructions thoroughly so that you're fully prepared.

Since the sixth house also rules your day-to-day work, dialing down professional stress could be the key to bringing sexy back. Tap into Venus' charm to cultivate partnerships with colleagues who can lift some burden off your shoulders and keep you buzzing with inspiration. Service providers fall under the domain of the sixth house. During Venus' backspin you may need to replace some slackers in the support chain, especially if you constantly edit and redo their work. At the very least, deliver an ultimatum: shape up or ship out!

Single Sea Goats will spend 2020 figuring out exactly what constitutes a healthy relationship. That label is yours to define, of course, but the retrograde may reveal ways that you unknowingly exhaust yourself by giving too much. Rather than blame the "takers," look at ways where you may be uncomfortable with (or outright blocking) yourself from receiving. As the zodiac's provider sign, you reflexively forget to ask people to contribute. Sometimes, you push away their offers! That's the downside to being so capable and self-sufficient. But just because you can do it all yourself, doesn't mean that you should. Your challenge during Venus' backspin is to sit through your own discomfort when you feel "dependent" or "out of control."

Pro tip: Don't look for the person who blows you away with credentials and swagger. The low-key ones who are consistent and stable could win your heart in 2020. And if you pace yourself through the courtship phase, you'll see whether people are trustworthy or not. After all, Capricorn, no one knows better than you that good things come to those who wait!

Activator Mars zooms through its native sign of Aries from June 27, 2020, until January 6, 2021, bringing heat and excitement to your closest connections—and a whole lotta fiery feels! Normally, Mars spends six weeks in a single sign, but 2020's retrograde from September 9 to November 13 will extend that voyage for six whole months.

Aries rules your sensitive and sentimental fourth house, which is also the domain of home, family and all manner of security, such as your nest egg. (Maybe that's why it's so hard for you to sit still on your days off.) As if hosting Jupiter didn't make you restless enough, the double dose of Mars energy makes it even harder to "settle down" in 2020.

Have your relationships become a bit too staid and predictable? You could do something radical to shake things up. But if you act rashly, you put key partnerships in jeopardy. Mars in Aries can be a selfish brew, and one YOLO move can cause years of regret. However, if you engage your love interest in the process, you'll do something game-changing in the second half of the year, like renting a shared Airbnb in a new city for six months, buying your first home (or a vacation property) or planning an epic family trip abroad.

Are you carrying too much of the load in your everyday life? Look out world! That could combust under the warrior planet's influence. Watch your temper, Capricorn, or you might permanently burn bridges with your inner circle. A better idea? Get ahead of the drama and don't wait until your fuse is that short.

When Mars hits Aries, pre-retrograde, on June 27, start divvying up household duties in an equitable way. If you're covering more of the monthly bills, make sure the others under your roof are putting in commensurate "sweat equity" with cleaning and errands. Enact a Zero Tolerance policy for slackers at Maison d'Chévre!

A home-based business could hit its stride while go-getter Mars tours Aries. But if your project creeps into every relaxation space, check yourself! That might be your cue to rent a "room of one's own" outside of your living quarters, if only to keep a clearer line between work and leisure.

Unattached Sea Goats might revel in the liberated energy that Mars in Aries brings. This independent window offers a rich opportunity to fall in love with yourself and dive in full-force to activities you back-burnered earlier in the year. Just be careful not to retreat into isolation. The moody Mars retrograde backspin could bring a bout of the blues from September 9 to November 13.

Review your savings plans—individual and joint. With make-it-happen Mars pacing through the bottom of your chart, the zone associated with personal security, you need to set clear objectives. If you don't, this impulsive cycle could cause you to burn through your earnings. Make sure you're setting aside enough for those "just in case" moments. That way, you can invest in your growth without feeling like you're teetering on the edge.

And here's the best news! If you need to plump the balance, Mars in Aries can bring tons of motivation. A home-based side hustle could fill the coffers and give you room to play Santa towards the year's end. Diversify your portfolio to include a few risky but high-yielding investments along with the stable but slower-growing ones.

Saturn in Capricorn & Aquarius: Stabilize.

Saturn in Capricorn: January 1 – March 21; July 1 – December 17

Saturn in Aquarius: March 21 – July 1; December 17 – March 7, 2023

Now for the grounding part of 2020's equation. Your ruling planet, serious Saturn, remains in Capricorn for much of the year, rounding out the final leg of its three-year tour through your sign. If you were worried that your feet wouldn't touch terra firma in 2020, relax. Saturn will keep at least a few of your toes planted in the reality zone. In some ways, Jupiter and Saturn both in your sign can leave you feeling like you've got one foot on the gas (Jupiter) and the other on the brakes (Saturn). It's going to be a wonky ride for many Sea Goats this year, so fasten your seatbelt to avoid any whiplash.

Fortunately, you've already had two full years to integrate all this Saturnian gravitas. On December 19, 2017, your ringed guardian began its extended homecoming party when it arrived on your doorstep for the first time since February 6, 1991. But odds are, you haven't sent a paper-flower-adorned float out for any parades since late 2017. Strict Saturn is the zodiac's personal trainer planet, and you've been too busy in the metaphorical gym to even notice just how strong you've become. As you wade through this final year of "astrological boot camp," you may finally see the light at the end of the tunnel.

Plus, you don't mind the hard work; in fact, you relish it! With Saturn as your celestial sentry, being pushed to your edge is what you live for. As this new decade dawns, you may be pumped up with endorphins and a little bit exhausted at the same time. Yet, as grueling as a Saturn transit may be, don't rush to close out this powerful cycle. Have you mined your full potential? Where are your weak spots, Capricorn? Instead of covering them up, stare them down. Being "coachable" is the key to getting to the finish line. If you were resistant to outside advice in 2019, change your strategy. Trying to DIY anything is like shooting yourself in the Prada loafers. This is the year to call in expert support and to work alongside masters (and on-point assistants) who can help you make your biggest leap yet.

While you love taking charge, your call to leadership of the past two years may have come with significant burdens. Heavy is the head that wears Saturn's crown, whether you're the breadwinner or the boss. But, like Capricorn Duchess Kate Middleton, you'll also keep proving yourself worthy of that royal status.

The silver lining? Saturn in Capricorn has been helping you gain expertise in ways you never dreamed possible. While Jupiter sets you up to be an influencer this year, Saturn will ensure that you earn that title based on merit. After witnessing your victory over a real-world struggle, people may have already started coming to you for advice or coaching. If you've ever thought of working in the expert industry, this could be the year to brand yourself as the pro you are. Your "How I Did It" tales could spell money in the bank. One Capricorn we know lost a significant amount of weight through a neuroscience-based nutritional program. In true Capricorn fashion, his progress wowed the company's founder and he parlayed his own savvy skills into an affiliate coaching program, which proved incredibly profitable for both of them.

Another Capricorn friend moved from the Midwest back to her coastal hometown to open her own insurance agency. Relocating was a mixed bag, since it requires a four-hour flight in order to visit her two kids, plus her first granddaughter. She's been hustling, learning the ins-and-outs of hiring, and at times, taking it on the chin. But she is buoyed by the vision of an early retirement—and the hope that this calculated move will allow her to provide for her family into her sunset years.

If you burn midnight oil in Q1, you could run a victory lap between March 21 and July 1. That's when Saturn launches out of your sign for a brief trailer through Aquarius and your second house of financial foundations. But thanks to its annual retrograde cycle, Saturn retreats into Capricorn for one last hurrah from July 1 to December 17. In Q3, your Herculean efforts will require a major push. Don't settle for "good enough" when greatness is so close at hand! (Even if you can't fully see it until the end of the year.)

Still inching your way up the ladder? Surround yourself with influential people whenever you can. The closer your proximity to prestige, the better—even if you have to make coffee runs for a CEO in order to get a statement heel in the door. Strategic name-dropping is never a bad idea, Capricorn, as long as you don't inflate your capabilities. Faking it till you make it is a no-go with Saturn in your sign. But if you legitimately PA'd on a famous photographer's shoot or did social media for a game-changing beauty brand, put it on your resume and share proudly! Your team spirit alone will make ears perk up—and that could lead to your next gig.

Does it feel like people are always underestimating you? Check your reflection. Saturn is the planet of maturity and in your first house of image, it's essential that you dress for the part you want to play, not just the one you've been cast into. Nothing wrong with rocking a youthful style when you're off-duty, but until December 17, strike the notion of "casual Friday" from your fashion lexicon. If you want people to see you as the pro you know you can be, err on the side of overdressing instead of showing up in athleisure because you tried to cram in a workout right before a client lunch. Make sleek and sophisticated pieces your professional staples—and hire a photographer to take headshots. If budget allows, begin building a wardrobe with classic designer selections that remain in your closet for years. Sticker shock aside, these numbers will pay for themselves.

Hosting Saturn in your sign might have the opposite effect for some Capricorns, making you feel older and energetically heavier than you actually appear. In truth, this may be more about your mindset than anything. There's magic to "aging gracefully," however you define it, which could mean letting your gray hairs grow out naturally to getting regular, collagen-boosting facials. Tread carefully with anything involving surgery or injections, especially if they come with unfathomable promises like turning back the clock two decades.

2020 is all about embracing your personal timeline. The goal is to be as vital as possible for the season of life that you're in. A healthy diet, restful sleep, exercise—yes, the time-tested basics—have all been proven to lengthen telomeres, the enzymes that are associated with aging, when they become shorter due to the stresses of life. Making a few lifestyle changes could be the key to your revitalization this year. One Capricorn we know relocated his thriving coaching practice to Maui and now sees clients via video chat in between leading retreats at a beachside center. Less stress can spell success.

Pay attention to your posture, too. Saturn (and Capricorn) rules the bones, skin and teeth—all things that need calcium to thrive. Having enough Vitamin D and K has been proven to help the body absorb this essential nutrient. Strength training with weights can keep bones supported with muscle mass. Dental health is linked with cardiovascular vitality. No skimping on the flossing or checkups, even if you need a pricier deep cleaning or root canal. Your longevity may depend on it.

But keep the champagne chilling on December 17, when Saturn shifts into Aquarius until March 7, 2023—not to visit your sign again until 2047! And make that a reserve bottle of bubbly, *s'il vous plaît*. When Saturn parks in Aquarius and your decadent second house, your tastes will trend towards the *bourgeoisie*.

You're no stranger to the finer things in life, as it is. But when Saturn enters socially responsible Aquarius, indulge in high-end goodies that are sustainably produced and ethically sourced. You might feel like a caricature from Portlandia at times, demanding to know the farm-raised pedigree of your chicken dinner before you take the first bite. No apologies! The way you spend and earn your hard-earned dollars will be an ethical issue for you.

You'll also need to follow protocol while Saturn rolls through Aquarius and your regimented second house. Having the rules spelled out for you again can be a relief after all the renegade energy of 2020. But it might feel like a restriction

in moments, too, especially if you realize that some of your brilliant ideas require confusing technology or expensive development costs. Don't let this take the wind out of your sails during your birthday season! Scaling down to a phased approach could be a huge relief, allowing you to think through your game plan, celebrate milestone wins and gather data and feedback before you spend more money. Resume a slower, steadier pace at the end of 2020 and trust that, as always, your tenacity will take you to the top!

The Great Conjunction: Jupiter & Saturn unite.
December 21

All year long, Jupiter and Saturn will be trading friendly fire, but their most dynamic duet will be sung on December 21, 2020. That day, these celestial luminaries will both arrive at the exact same point on the zodiac wheel, 0°29' Aquarius, heralding a rare astrological event called The Great Conjunction. This odd-couple mashup only happens every 20 years; in fact, we haven't seen one since May 31, 2000.

Jupiter amplifies everything it touches. Saturn is the lord of karma and can bring stability and success to long-term missions. Beginning December 19, 2020, they'll combine their superpowers in your second house of values and financial foundations.

It's a popular saying among the Law of Attraction crowds that "the roots create the fruits." If you've been a persistent Goat, building your platform on a sturdy structure—without sacrificing your ethics—

December could yield a well-deserved windfall. On the other hand, if you've taken shortcuts on the path to abundance, Team Jupiter-Saturn will expose fault lines and demand repair work. Get ahead of that potential pitfall early in the year! Rip out the asbestos and remove that lead paint ASAP. Yes, this damage control may require an annoying investment of time and resources. But it's better than having to pay an inflated rate for emergency repairs because you ignored the problem.

Of course, when Jupiter's winsome gifts and Saturn's expert strategizing sync up, it can be like having the best of both worlds at your behest. The key lies in balancing their opposing energies. When Saturn wags a finger at Jupiter's carefree spending style, you may feel like someone stuck a pin in your balloon. Meanwhile, Jupiter's gambling nature can give cautious Saturn heart palpitations.

Towards the end of 2020, you'll have to work hard to not go scurrying back to a lower-paying "safe" gig, especially if you're on the cusp of true fortune. That turnabout is a real risk, however, since you'll spend most of 2020 pushing yourself way outside of your comfort zone. Don't quit five minutes before the miracle, Capricorn!

That said, you may have to bring in some temporary security measures as you inch your way to the finish line. For example, maybe you keep a part-time "bridge job" so you can keep the lights on while you build your empire after hours and on weekends. Or this will be the prompt you need to set up a crowdfunding campaign or talk to your inner circle about being angel investors. Be savvy, smart and strategic, but also willing to leap into a bigger league! A well-calculated risk could bring epic rewards near December 21.

Cancer/Capricorn Eclipses: Balance "me" and "we."
January 10, June 21, July 5

Finding the middle ground between autonomy and partnership will continue to be a major theme as three of 2020's six eclipses activate the Cancer/Capricorn axis. Capricorn rules your self-authorized first house while Cancer governs your seventh house of relationships. The struggle to balance "me" and "we" continues into 2020, so brace yourself for some back-and-forth—and a few soul-stirring revelations!

You've been down this rabbit hole since July 12, 2018, when the first solar eclipse in Cancer struck and kicked off a two-year cycle. That lunation may have called in a meant-to-be partner or revealed a deep desire to change in the way you "do" relationships. In 2019, there were three eclipses in Capricorn and only one in Cancer. Last year's emphasis was more about discovering and developing new aspects of yourself that you could share with others. Since eclipses reveal what's hidden, some Capricorns could have weathered a full-on identity crisis in 2019, especially near January 5, July 16, and December 26. The Cancer eclipse on July 2, 2019, may have brought a watershed moment with a key alliance.

In 2020, you have a chance to wrap up two years of crucial lessons. Eclipses are like tough-love coaches who will not let you labor in delusion. And the Cancer-Capricorn lunations are here to help you live your best life…with your best mate by your side.

On January 10, 2020, the lunar (full moon) eclipse in Cancer could bring a joint venture to a thrilling milestone, especially if you've been hustling away at it since July 2018. Coupled Caps may decide to renew your vows, make a casual dating situation exclusive, enlist a business partner or otherwise seal a bond. A bad romance that's distracted you from your true power could be "eclipsed away," so don't cling to the past!

Need to make a fresh start with your love interest or a key business alliance? The June 21 solar (new moon) eclipse will reboot your twin engines and get your relationship revving on all cylinders again. This one is an annular solar eclipse—also known as a "ring of fire"—since the Sun's rays will shimmer around the circumference of the moon during the eclipse's maximum coverage point. There will be no tamping down the flames of attraction this June 21, or within a month of that date, which is the eclipse's arc of influence. Single and looking? A Solstice sweetie could pop up on your radar quite unexpectedly, setting the stage for long-term love. You might even get a second chance with someone who's been dancing in and out of your orbit for the past year-plus. This time, you can get it right, Capricorn, but you must be willing to devote yourself fully and go "all in."

The final eclipse in this series will be a lunar (full moon) eclipse in Capricorn on July 5. This is another day to circle for making a big reveal. All that identity work and growth you've done since January 5, 2019, is ready to be trotted out for public praise and acknowledgment. The only caveat is that Mercury will be retrograde (from June 18 to July 12) so make sure you've tested all digital assets and thoroughly edited any promotional materials that you plan to circulate.

Gemini/Sagittarius Eclipses: Health is wealth.
June 5, November 30, December 14

Give your body and soul some love! From June 5, 2020, until December 3, 2021, a new group of eclipses will galvanize the Gemini/Sagittarius axis. In 2020 three of these lunations will activate your (Gemini-ruled) sixth house of health and fitness and your (Sagittarius-controlled) twelfth house of closure, spirituality and healing.

The message of these moonbeams? Release any vitality-zapping habits and embrace a holistic approach to your wellness that nourishes both body and your soul. Perhaps you're dealing with an addictive pattern (workaholism, say) or a chronic condition, or simply need to manage stress levels. Whatever the case, these eye-opening lunations will help you get to the root of what ails you.

The series kicks off on June 5 with a lunar eclipse in Sagittarius and your twelfth house of healing. Since this is the inaugural eclipse in the series, it could come with a major wake-up call. Gone will be your bottomless refills of energy…and that's frustrating! But the message is clear, Capricorn: Implement some self-care strategies or risk a major crash. Put boundaries in place with the demanding "dependents" in your universe. You can't be anyone's Rock of Gibraltar if you're feeling as ungrounded as a tumbleweed. With this eclipse in nomadic Sagittarius, you have cosmic permission to cash in vacation days and recharge at a mountain lodge with natural hot springs, in-room spa services and a spotty (if not non-existent) wi-fi signal.

Even if you can't get away, give yourself a few solid personal days within a week of June 5. After you've caught up on your sleep and unapologetically ignored calls from needy friends and relatives, start taking inventory of all your spaces. During this 18-month eclipse series, you could go on a massive downsizing mission, selling off everything in your storage space and pruning your social media "friend" lists. Before you start ghosting, however, consider whether or not you've been upfront with the people in your life. You know how to put on a good face, Capricorn, which means they may be totally clueless that you're feeling drained or resentful. We teach people how to treat us—and admit it, there is a part of you that likes to feel needed. But from June 5 on, that desire will be dialed down bigtime. Here's a novel idea: How about cashing in on some of the favors your inner circle owes you? *Quelle* surprise! Many of those so-called users will be happy to come to your aid.

On November 30, the year's only Gemini eclipse—a lunar (full moon) eclipse—hits your sixth house of wellness, fitness and organization. As the holiday season unfurls, plan to be a "healthy hedonist." If you can't get to the gym quite as much, find your way to the dance floor. Strengthen your core while checking your email by sitting on a medicine ball instead of a standard desk chair. Pay special attention to "gut health," as the sixth house rules digestion. From a cleanse to a microbiome test to being screened for food allergies, the saying "you are what you eat" will ring especially true.

The sixth house rules work, and this eclipse could illuminate some exciting (albeit abrupt) changes around the office. You may be in line for a bigger bonus than anticipated as the year winds down, but with it could come a new set of responsibilities.

Breathe your way through the changes, which might require you to burn some midnight oil when you'd rather be sipping dirty martinis under the mistletoe. And most of all, remember that you don't have to do it all alone. This eclipse could illuminate a next-level service provider or a dream assistant who can manage all the details so you can focus where you are most effective: dealing with the big-picture strategy and leading the troops! Pets also fall under this domain, and you could find yourself (without warning) signing the adoption papers for a furry new family member.

Divine inspiration: incoming! On December 14, a total solar (new moon) eclipse lands in Sagittarius, the second to galvanize your soulful twelfth house of healing in 2020. Since this is the domain of "earth angels" and other guides, consider bringing in some expert support like a counselor, coach, shaman or masterful private teacher. The intensely spiritual and even psychic nature of this late-year eclipse could reveal prophetic dreams, *Déjà vu* moments nd buried memories. Pay attention to any strong intuitive feelings or "signs." Your subconscious will be sending major signals! If you've dealt with trauma or feel stuck around grieving a loss, you may benefit from hypnosis, EMDR (eye movement desensitization and reprocessing) or a session with a medium.

If you're a musician or artist of any kind, this eclipse gets you serious about your craft. It might even put you in the path of an agent or representative who can help bring your work to a wider audience, or a mentor who can direct your debut. Some Caps will feel the call to begin a spiritual practice. That could mean a regular yoga and meditation routine, working with crystals or even getting certified as an energetic healing practitioner. ✳

January

JANUARY: LOVE HOTSPOTS

January 3-February 16: Mars in Sagittarius

You'll have a hard time distinguishing fantasy from reality as high-octane Mars crashes into your fuzzy, introspective twelfth house. Careful not to rush to conclusions about your mate's motives and avoid making any impulsive romantic moves. The twelfth house governs healing and closure, and the red planet's direct demeanor can help you say goodbye to toxic Tinder dates and energy vampires. Or clarify your boundaries so your love interest stops (innocently) overstepping them.

January 10: Cancer full moon (lunar eclipse)

Cupid wings in on a golden chariot as the year's first full moon—also a potent lunar eclipse—powers up your relationship house. Vagueness, begone! Call a "state of the union" with anyone you're partnered with to make sure you're on the same page. Budding attractions will heat up fast for single Sea Goats, while coupled Caps could take a bold new step together. Business deals may also be cemented (and fast!) under this lunar light.

January 10: Uranus retrograde ends

Bombshell Uranus wraps a five-month retrograde that rocked your theatrical, romantic fifth house. Since the disruptive planet began its reversal on August 11, 2019, your love life has been rife with conflict and unexpected plot twists. As the provocateur turns direct, you can proactively resolve any drama—and, if you're single, have fun pursuing a new type! With your celebrity sector lit by this tech-savvy planet, you could become Internet-famous or build buzz for your brand!

January 13-February 7: Venus in Pisces

You said tomato, they said *tomahto*, but no need to call this party off. Diplomatic Venus enters your communication zone, uncrossing wires. Take turns actively listening to one another, making sure dialogues don't turn into diatribes. With Venus wired into your tech-savvy third house, single Caps could have bonus luck on the dating apps, or you could find "locally grown" love while hanging at your go-to neighborhood venues.

January 26: Venus-Mars square

People's motives will be obscured when heavenly heartthrobs Venus and Mars lock into this uncomfortable formation. Don't rush to conclusions! Even if you think someone is being passive-aggressive or neglectful, you're probably

The AstroTwins' 2020 Horoscope

not getting a true read. It goes both ways: Are you scrambling signals by being purposefully enigmatic? Check your integrity, too: There's no such thing as being "a little unfaithful."

January 27: Venus-Neptune meetup

Compassionate communication is the name of the game, as dreamboats Venus and Neptune spoon in your expressive house. Drop your guard, because under this warm-fuzzy mashup, it's safe to share your vulnerable feelings. Bond over a creative project or a shared love of music and the arts. Or use Neptune's powers of fantasy to plan an extravagant date.

JANUARY: CAREER HOTSPOTS

January 2: Mercury-Jupiter meetup

As Mercury the messenger gets an amplified boost from outspoken Jupiter, you've got the green light to be assertive. Take charge of a team meeting or present a pitch deck to a potential business associate. An eager funder might be ready to put dollars behind your dream venture, or an influential friend could help you start a buzz for a pet project. Draft an "elevator pitch" so you can share the broad strokes of your vision in 10 seconds or three bullet-points.

January 3-February 16: Mars in Sagittarius

To sleep, perchance to dream? With active Mars buzzing in your subconscious zone, you may be most productive after dark. Keep a journal on your nightstand to capture divinely inspired downloads. One of those wild hares could be highly profitable! If work gets stressful, hit the gym to sweat it out. But stick to gentle exercise since this transit makes you feel both wired and tired.

January 10: Cancer full moon (lunar eclipse)

Seal that deal! The first full moon of 2020—a potent lunar eclipse—lights up your partnership house, accelerating your urge to merge. As a can-do Capricorn, it can be hard for you to let go of control, so be sure to pair up with highly qualified people. If things aren't going well with a work associate, evaluate to see if it's time to part ways. Keep your eyes peeled for new collaborators over the next two weeks.

January 12: Mercury-Saturn-Pluto meetup

This day is one for the history books, as transformational Pluto and ambitious Saturn unite in your sign for the first time since 1518! Give an aspect of your life a "gut renovation," breaking free from a structure that no longer serves you. Or, plant your flag and announce your arrival as the new influencer on the scene. With messenger Mercury also in the mix, this is the day to shamelessly self-promote!

January 13: Sun-Saturn-Pluto meetup

Your magnetism will be palpable—and highly visible as the shimmering Capricorn Sun dials into the same confidence-boosting frequency as seductive Pluto and masterful Saturn. If you get tapped for your expertise, share it generously. Just make sure to stamp your name on your work. Strategically position yourself as a leader who's on the move…and on the rise!

January 16-February 3: Mercury in Aquarius

Set your budgetary resolutions today as meticulous Mercury zips into your second house of work and money. Map out a plan for the first quarter of 2020, trimming excess spending where you can. Don't forget the income column! Use the planet's powers of persuasion to negotiate a pay raise, woo clients or slay with a presentation at work.

January 18: Mercury-Uranus square

An antagonizing colleague could push every one of your buttons under today's tenuous Mercury-Uranus square. Don't step into the trap! Engaging will just drag this out, wasting your most productive hours. The clock is ticking, so if standing your ground doesn't get you to "yes," postpone talks for a few days. With any luck, you'll cool down and finally be able to hear what's driving their objections.

January 23: Sun-Uranus square

If progress has slowed to a crawl, a spark between the Sun and shock-jock Uranus will motivate you to restart the engine. But don't get swept into a battle of wills! Nudge the project forward slightly instead of going full-force. You can still make progress through incremental steps, so stay as neutral and non-threatening as you can. Soon, even your most resistant teammates will thank you for getting this initiative going again.

January 24: Aquarius new moon

The first new moon of the decade lands in Aquarius and launches the Chinese Year of the Metal Rat. As these industrious beams galvanize your work and financial zone, start positioning yourself for advancement. By the corresponding full moon on August 3, you may see a major uptick in your earnings. Take time to visualize your desired progress: Do you want a better job, more flexible hours, to be signing your own paychecks? Write a list and take small steps towards your goal.

January 28: Mars-Neptune square

The pressure is on to make a decision, but do you have enough empirical data to make a final choice? Don't rush to cast your vote if you still feel uncertain. Submissive Neptune conflicts with combative Mars today, adding tension to what would normally be a civil discussion. Don't get swept into a power struggle. Be polite but firm—and make a non-negotiable request for more information.

February

FEBRUARY: LOVE HOTSPOTS

February 7-March 4: Venus in Aries

Bring some decorative flair to your hibernation station as design star Venus hunkers in your domestic fourth house. Single? Make room for a special guest. During this four-week circuit, *Maison du Sea Goat* becomes a hub for intimate gatherings. Nesting is top of mind right now. Coupled Capricorns can enjoy epic cuddling and co-hosting. Single? Give the cutie-next-door a chance to woo you. The quiet ones will surprise you!

February 9: Leo full moon

Strong feelings surface as the Leo full moon lights a bonfire in your erotic and intimate eighth house. Serious sparks may ignite with someone new, so test the chemistry. An explosive interaction doesn't need to erode your standards, so don't settle for a fling if you're really searching for a life partner. Already attached? You and your mate could entwine your lives in serious ways like opening a shared bank account or shopping for engagement rings.

February 16-March 30: Mars in Capricorn

Heat index: rising! As seductive Mars shimmies into your sign, your allure and appeal rise off the charts. This transit only occurs every other year, boosting your confidence and sex appeal. The red planet can make you intense and direct, but that candor might be just what wins 'em over. Your love interest won't need to guess how you feel. Single or spoken for, you may wind up sleep-deprived from all the wild nights!

February 21: Mars-Uranus trine

You're oozing magnetism and ready for an adventure, as lusty Mars in Capricorn dances a sultry *paso doble* with experimental Uranus in your romance house. Stop worrying about "happily ever after" and try something unconventional to spice up your day. (But do choose a "safe word" if you're taking it to extremes.) If you're in a relationship, the shared adrenaline rush will be a bonding agent, and single Capricorns will have something juicy to journal about!

February 23: Venus-Jupiter square

Good luck reconciling your desire for freedom with your need for security today. Thrill-seeking Jupiter lures you toward new vistas, and the grass is looking green on the other side of Cupid's fence. Meanwhile Venus is cozied up in your domestic zone, pulling you towards the comforts of home. If you're feeling restless, you don't have to upend your romantic life. But it's definitely time to plan your next "bae-cation" or a to enjoy a night on the town.

February 28: Venus-Pluto square

Need some space? Every good relationship could benefit from a little distance, and yours is no exception. But Pluto pulls for extreme change, and its square to Venus might make you feel like throwing everything you've built out the window. Easy does it! There's no need to run for the hills if all you really need is an open window and some fresh air. Single? Someone intense could show up today who both attracts and repels you. Give yourself time to see if you can live with the paradox.

FEBRUARY: CAREER HOTSPOTS

February 3-March 4: Mercury in Pisces

Time to launch that charm offensive, o' silver-tongued Sea Goat. As messenger Mercury glides into your cooperative, communicative third house, set up meetings and get deals signed in permanent ink. A stalled solo mission will pick up steam if you bring in a project partner. Or test a new collab with a short-term project.

February 9: Leo full moon

As the Leo full moon lights up your eighth house of joint ventures and goals, something that was previously hidden may come into view. Check your accounts and investments to ensure they're on track and make any strategic adjustments that can increase your returns. Look for creative ways to share resources with others, like bartering services or purchasing equipment together that you wouldn't otherwise be able to afford.

February 16-March 9: Mercury retrograde

Mercury pivots into retrograde for the first time this year, reverse commuting through pensive Pisces, then backing through rational Aquarius on March 4. You might not do your best or most logical thinking between now and March 9. Run major decisions by the savvy sounding boards in your circle. And since Mercury's retreat through

Pisces is a bit of a double whammy, don't ignore the standard warnings to back up data in multiple places. Read (and re-read) text messages and emails closely before firing off a response.

February 16-March 30: Mars in Capricorn

Motivator Mars zooms into Capricorn for the first time in two years, clarifying your vision and supplying the determination to take that mission to the finish line. If your 2020 resolutions fell by the wayside, recommit with renewed focus. You might also pick up the ball (and run with it!) on a project that's been stalled for quite some time.

February 21: Mars-Uranus trine

Driven Mars and innovative Uranus team up, generating excitement for a genius idea. But under this distractible transit, enthusiasm could blow over just as quickly if you don't channel it in a proactive direction. While you have everyone's attention, call a brainstorming session. You could drum up solutions to overcome a previously insurmountable obstacle. People will have lots to say, but you may have to fight to get a word in with all the egos in the room.

February 23: Pisces new moon

Let your imagination meander under today's new moon in Pisces. Your logical, rational sign can benefit from the dreamy Fish's intuitive influence. Activate the non-linear side of your brain by listening to music, dancing or meditating. After you've quieted your mind, grab a capture tool and record the genius ideas that roll in. This could be the start of a profitable venture—or co-venture, since new partnerships are also highlighted under this lunar lift.

March

MARCH: LOVE HOTSPOTS

March 3: Venus-Saturn square

When Venus and your ruler Saturn come head-to-head, you could shift from certainty to cynicism about a certain partnership. Is it really them, or do your expectations need a reality check? Remember, Cap: Hoisting people onto pedestals only sets you both up for a steep fall. If you made that mistake, remind yourself that you're dealing with a mortal here!

March 4-April 3: Venus in Taurus

Get your flirt on—shamelessly—as sultry Venus sashays into your romantic, dramatic fifth house and sparks an early round of spring fever. Your wit is your best seduction tactic now, so let people see your playful side. And come out of hibernation! This glamorous transit calls for glam dress-up dates and a lavish getaway. (How do you say "vacation romance" in Swahili or Portuguese?) Couples should schedule some sexy nights in with your love interest, eschewing the usual places for buzzed-about new venues.

March 8: Venus-Uranus meetup

Sweeping changes blow through your love life as spontaneous Uranus falls into its once-per-year lockstep with amorous Venus. Feeling bored with your current relationship? If the breakup clock is ticking, you could be shockingly fine with moving on. Or maybe you just need to negotiate more autonomy and space. This cosmic combo can fuel exciting developments, too. You and your *amour* might reprise some honeymoon vibes, or talk about growing your family with a fur baby or an actual pregnancy.

March 20: Mars-Jupiter meetup

As lusty Jupiter and hot-blooded Mars rendezvous in your sign, willpower will be in short supply. *C'est la vie!* Switch up your scenery: If you're on spring break, you're well positioned for a sexy flirtation—and possible hook-up. Capricorns close to base could meet an attractive prospect while checking out a new-to-you spot in your city. And good luck keeping your desires to yourself! While today's ephemeral sparks might not light an eternal flame, the frisky adventure will be one for your memoir… and your locked diary!

March 24: Aries new moon

Raw sentiment will be hard to hold in under today's new moon in Aries, which lands in your emotionally attuned fourth house. Feelings you didn't even know you had may flow out. But since Aries energy can be aggressive, give yourself a few days to process it all before you sit down for a heart-to-heart. Domestic urges heat up under these family-focused moonbeams. Over the coming six months, you might decide to move, buy a house or try to get pregnant.

March 27: Venus-Jupiter trine

Stop waiting to be wooed! As glamorous, amorous Venus bats her lashes at generous Jupiter, you can boldly take the lead in love, knowing that your efforts will hit the right mark. The element of spontaneity works in your favor. Surprise your favorite plus-one with a pair of tickets or a weekend at an Airbnb. Single Caps could fall head over hooves for someone from a different background or upbringing.

March 28: Venus-Pluto trine

An intense attraction could surface today, catching you off guard. Though it's tempting to go all in, pace yourself and see if this person can measure up to your discerning standards. If you're attached, well, bummer. But you can treat this infatuation like a teachable moment. What qualities are you drawn to in this person and what could you do to foster them within yourself?

March 30-May 13: Mars in Aquarius

Lead with confidence! Take-charge Mars bolts through your second house of self-worth for the next few weeks. When you value yourself, other people will respect you and bring their A-game. With this lusty planet in your work sector, a colleague crush could heat up. Double-check any company policies before you make a move.

March 31: Mars-Saturn meetup

When accelerator Mars syncs up with deliberate Saturn, you might feel torn between barreling ahead at full speed and riding the brake. Indecisiveness could prevail, making it impossible to make up your mind. Avoid "analysis paralysis" by taking small steps toward what you want. A calculated risk may pay off, but do the background research so you aren't leaping without a net.

MARCH: CAREER HOTSPOTS

March 4-16: Mercury in Aquarius

Double check your balance sheet. As Mercury flits back into your second house of work and money, you may have to tweak a few numbers. While the cosmic courier is driving in reverse for the next week, keep a close eye on your spending and review all your statements with a fine-toothed comb. At work, focus on wrapping up projects that need to be finalized.

March 9: Virgo full moon

Expand, explore and break through! The full moon in Virgo taps your adventurous ninth house, pushing your traditional sign into new frontiers. Over the next two weeks, a travel or study opportunity could arise, adding a new skill (and possible passport stamp) to your arsenal. Mingling outside your usual group could connect you to collaborators who help you actualize a dream.

March 16-April 10: Mercury in Pisces

Mercury paddles into Pisces—its second lap through the Fish's waters, thanks to the February 16 to March 9 retrograde. With the messenger planet powering forward through your expressive third house, draw on your inherent eloquence. Mercury is right at home in this area of your chart, so reach out to new clients or schedule a pitch meeting to take advantage of your amplified gift of gab.

March 20: Mars-Jupiter meetup

Self-assured Mars and live-out-loud Jupiter team up in your sign, pouring you a double shot of courage. Chime in during a major meeting or start a buzz on social media for one of your latest endeavors. Today, you'll have the guts to ask HR about "growth opportunities" (including a raise) or to find out when that bigger, sunlit office might be yours. Throw some of that Capricorn caution to the wind. As the saying goes, you don't ask, you don't get.

March 21-July 1: Saturn in Aquarius

A little breathing room opens up today, as your ruler, restrictive Saturn, leaves your zodiac sign and bolts forward into Aquarius, its first visit here since 1991-94. You've hosted the taskmaster planet since December 19, 2017, which has certainly made you stronger. But the ringed guru also tested your mettle and capsized a few of your best-laid plans, forcing you to rebuild on a solid foundation. Saturn makes one more trip through Capricorn (from July 1 until December 17) before moving on for another 29 years. While Saturn's in Aquarius and your second house, you'll do more "adulting" around work and finances, but with a little belt tightening, you can build a serious nest egg.

March 23: Mars-Pluto meetup

A meetup of determined Mars and powerful Pluto in Capricorn supports you in making a clear and decisive move. You know what you want and you're feeling empowered to go after it! But don't steamroll anyone who steps into your path. Be a gracious competitor and a grateful leader and you won't wind up feeling lonely at the top.

March 30-May 13: Mars in Aquarius

You'll be a busy bee this spring, as ambitious Mars wings into Aquarius and your industrious second house. Whether you're pursuing a new income stream or charging ahead as a project lead, the red planet's influence could have you working overtime. Take breaks to avoid burnout, and whenever possible, delegate!

March 31: Mars-Saturn meetup

Should you zoom ahead or pump the brakes? It's hard to tell today, as impetuous Mars meets cautious Saturn in your financial zone. Mars makes you eager to sign on the dotted line, so you don't want to miss this opportunity! But as steady Saturn flashes a caution light, step back and survey your options. If you're about to make a major change, do your research and think through every possible outcome first.

April

APRIL: LOVE HOTSPOTS

April 3-August 7: Venus in Gemini

Radiant Venus embarks on an extended tour through Gemini, activating your sixth house of work and wellness until August 7. From your beauty routines to the food on your plate, make choices that ignite your inner glow. Opt for pleasurable workouts, not punishing ones; turn your bedroom buddy into your workout buddy. Single? You never know who'll be stretching on the adjacent Pilates mat or waiting for that post-workout smoothie.

April 4: Venus-Saturn trine

You're playing the long game today, as enchanting Venus in your intimate eighth house vibes with value-driven Saturn. Chemistry may be potent, but do your relationship goals and your ten-year plans align? Get clear on what each person wants, and if there's enough compatible overlap, start making magic together!

April 7: Mars-Uranus square

Sabotage alert! A complex clash between irascible Mars and spontaneous Uranus could leave you with one foot out the door. You're craving excitement, but don't wreck a stable relationship for a temporary thrill. You may feel a sudden and overwhelming attraction to someone who's not quite right for you. Resist! Today's turbulent transit can put you at odds with your partner. Don't fight; just keep your cool and do your best to ride it out.

April 10-27: Mercury in Aries

Drop the formalities and tell them how you really feel. Your sensitive side emerges as expressive Mercury flows into Aries and activates your sensitive fourth house. Over the next few weeks, you may divulge more personal information than usual. Take time to truly connect and be there for loved ones, even if that means skipping a few networking events.

April 22: Taurus new moon

Bring some creativity to the love game, as the new moon in sensual Taurus lights up your passionate and playful fifth house. Coupled Capricorns can revitalize their relationships with more thoughtful date planning. Dance all night to a celebrity DJ or pack a picnic and take off on a rugged day hike. Look below the surface if you're searching for a soulmate. Your date might seem like the total package, but how do they make you feel? If you've been messaging with a cutie, it's time to meet in person and test for IRL sparks.

April 27-May 11: Mercury in Taurus

Can you feel the butterflies? Flirty Mercury sashays into Taurus, unleashing its charms in your glamorous, amorous fifth house. For the next few weeks, you'll be more than just a little eager to share your loving feelings. But is it too soon? Pace yourself, warming things up with flirty texts. If you're partnered, you may feel a big "next step" brewing, like buying a house or talking babies.

The AstroTwins' 2020 Horoscope   456

Mercury gets you thinking and chatting about it, even if you're not totally ready to take action.

April 30: Mercury-Uranus meetup

You love them, you love them not. You might have to pluck some daisy petals to figure out your feelings, thanks to a fickle alignment of distracted Mercury and disruptive Uranus in your fifth house of *amour.* Whether you're turned on or repelled, the vibes will be visceral, and still…they're not a solid barometer for the long-term. Try not to make any rash moves!

APRIL: CAREER HOTSPOTS

April 3: Mercury-Neptune meetup

Messages might be muddled today when Mercury gets pulled into murky Neptune's undertow. With both planets conjoined in your communicative third house, swap the logical, left-brained work for something more imaginative. Summon your savviest friends. Bouncing ideas off these people can yield a surprising solution to a stubborn problem. Dive into tasks that allow you to lose track of time; the results of these will be especially fruitful today.

April 4: Jupiter-Pluto meetup

Hidden opportunities come to light as maximizer Jupiter beams its spotlight into powerhouse Pluto's vault. This is the first of three exact conjunctions they'll make in 2020—and in your sign, no less(!)—triggering a windfall of possibilities for expanding your influence. With both planets in your first house of leadership and self-expression, you have permission to be bold. When opportunity knocks, act swiftly and strategically!

April 7: Libra full moon

The annual full moon in Libra shines at the top of your chart, energizing your tenth house of career. This could mark the culmination of a professional goal you've been working towards for the past six months. If your path has led to a fork in the road, this lunation brings clarity around your next move—which, in partnership-based Libra, could involve collaborating with a complementary force.

April 7: Mars-Uranus square

A tense transit between impulsive Mars and erratic Uranus can push you to your breaking point. Control your outbursts, Capricorn, or you'll undermine your efforts and create friction with your team. Find an appropriate (and appropriately neutral) sounding board if you need to vent. This could be your cue to enlist expert support instead of trying to figure out solutions on your own.

April 14: Sun-Pluto square

Is someone trying to leverage your hard work for their own gain? You might have good reason to suspect that today, as power-hungry Pluto drops a cloak over the Sun's illuminating beams. Unfortunately, a direct confrontation will only yield excuses. Discreetly observe and gather intel. After that, you can determine if further action is needed to ensure that you're properly credited (and compensated) for your work!

April 15: Sun-Jupiter square

Is your work-life balance out of kilter? Today's duel between the Sun in your emotional zone and enterprising Jupiter reminds you how important it is to take breaks. If self-care has slipped, schedule it! Book a massage and reserve three slots per week for workouts. A supportive colleague may offer to take some tasks off your plate. Say yes!

April 21: Sun-Saturn square

You don't have to proselytize to make your point today; in fact, letting the "opposition" chime in could yield a powerful discussion. If you allow people to ask questions, you'll quickly connect with their concerns. Aim for a respectful exchange of ideas instead of trying to sell them on your way of doing things. Ironically, people might just get on board with your vision once their arguments have been heard!

April 25: Mercury square Jupiter & Pluto

As messenger Mercury clashes with Jupiter and Pluto, you'll encounter both big talkers and people who you just can't read. This befuddling mashup could throw off your instincts, so let your rational mind have the final say. Double check everything before running a victory lap. You might think you've scored a slam dunk, only to find out that the deal isn't quite finalized yet. For best measure, put everything in writing, and lawyer up if need be.

April 25-October 4: Pluto retrograde in Capricorn

Shadowy Pluto pivots into its annual retrograde, backing up through in your sign for the next five months. Use this depth-plumbing transit for self-reflection. What face do you show to the world? Does it accurately position you for success? Use this cycle to polish up your "branding" so people can see the most confident, capable you.

April 26: Sun-Uranus meetup

Innovative Uranus and the high-minded Sun collide in your creative fifth house, unleashing a wellspring of ingenious ideas. Keep a notebook close by to capture any lightbulb moments. Piping up in a meeting could position you as the office wunderkind; a timely Tweet might go viral. Don't hold back!

April 27-May 11: Mercury in Taurus

Unleash your imagination as clever Mercury buzzes through Taurus and fires up your fifth house of fame and creative expression. You'll have a hard time keeping the brilliant downloads to yourself, but see what happens if you drop hints and let suspense build. The response will be ten times juicier when you stage your big reveal!

April 28: Mercury-Saturn square

A mind-blowing scheme is emerging, as clever Mercury buzzes through your creativity zone. But today, you could hit a wall of resistance, due to a square from scrutinizing Saturn. Even the most well-formed plans will have to pass the ringed taskmaster's audits. If you can wait a few days for this transit to blow over, you might receive a better reaction. But this may also be a cue to polish your pitch before you trot it out again.

May

MAY: LOVE HOTSPOTS

May 3: Venus-Neptune square

You may be second-guessing the state of a certain union today, as Venus dukes it out with foggy Neptune. A romantic situation might not be playing out like a fairy tale, but is that cause to despair? Don't waste the day analyzing the blow-by-blow of what happened (or didn't happen). Distract yourself with a creative project or go out with friends. This drama could resolve by itself when you simply leave it alone.

May 10: Mercury-Jupiter trine

Your heart and mind are wide open under today's effusive Mercury-Jupiter trine. While this might make you a little gullible, better you should overshoot the mark then wonder, "What if...?" These outspoken planets make it nearly impossible to keep your desires hidden, which can be an asset in the bedroom. Meow!

May 13-June 27: Mars in Pisces

If you see something, say something! Lusty Mars paddles into Pisces and your third house of communication, spicing up your flirting game. Pillow talk could get downright poetic...and definitely naughty. Variety is the spice of seduction for the coming weeks, so plan cultural-activity dates at local venues. Road trips and weekend getaways will heat things up, too!

May 13-June 25: Venus retrograde in Gemini

The health of your relationships comes under the microscope for the next six weeks, as love planet Venus pivots retrograde. The radiant planet flips into reverse every 18 months, providing a window to fine-tune your romantic agenda and restore respectful harmony to your bonds. This year (and every eight years), Venus is retreating through Gemini, which could reveal unproductive communication patterns that need to be upgraded. Romantic themes from June 2012 may recur.

May 22: Mercury-Venus meetup

If you're feeling bogged down by daily responsibilities, try something unexpected: Carve out a little time to give back. Stepping out of your routine to focus on a cause will provide much-needed perspective. That argument over who unloaded the dishwasher last will seem petty after you've spent a couple hours cleaning up a playground or volunteering at a food bank.

May 28-August 4: Mercury in Cancer

A relationship reboot could be in order as messenger Mercury flits into your relationship house—and for an extended stay in 2020, due to an upcoming retrograde (June 18 to July 12). Want to improve the state of your affairs? Follow the communication planet—in compassionate Cancer—and speak from your heart. Couples may set up a cohabitation station or invest in a love nest.

MAY: CAREER HOTSPOTS

May 7: Scorpio full moon

Raise a toast to the Capricorn squad, as the Scorpio full moon lights up your eleventh house of teamwork and technology. After six months of hustling, you may have a shared milestone to celebrate. Tap the hive mind and see if there's a new app or service they would recommend. Ready to expand? Crowdsource for collaborators. You could meet some key players through mutual friends.

May 9: Mercury-Pluto trine

The truth will set you free under today's liberating mashup of expressive Mercury and furtive Pluto. While you might have to deliver some uncomfortable news, opening up will build trust and improve your professional relationships. If you have questions about someone's intentions, don't beat around the bush!

May 11-September 29: Saturn retrograde

Did you bite off more than you can chew? Your ruler, responsible Saturn, starts its annual retrograde, slipping back through your industrious second house until July 1, then reversing through your sign until December 17. Press pause on a project that needs to be refined; or buy yourself time by pushing back the launch date. Look past any short-term disappointment and remember that you'd rather do it right the first time. The delay could allow you to knock this out of the park bigger and better than you'd dreamed!

May 11: Mercury-Mars square

Are your majestic visions zooming way past the allocated budget? Cashflow concerns could crimp your creativity today, thanks to a balancing act between mindful Mercury in your money sector and driven Mars in your over-the-top fifth house. Find ways to go the extra mile that don't involve overspending. At work, keep your temper in check. You might upset the wrong person, which could potentially impact your job. Stay humble and choose gratitude over grandstanding.

May 11-28: Mercury in Gemini

Next stop: Spreadsheet City! Analytical Mercury logs in to Gemini and your systematic sixth house, helping you streamline your communications and workflow. Bump administrative tasks to the top of your to-do list and get organized. A few weeks from now, you may finally hit that elusive "inbox zero" or completely restructure your operations. Take time to orient collaborators to your new processes and updates.

May 12: Mercury-Saturn trine

How solid is your game plan? As strategic Mercury touches base with your ruler, structured Saturn, run your ideas through the reality filter. If you want to get a project greenlighted or attract funding, make sure your figures are accurate. They say luck happens when preparation meets opportunity, so devise a well-polished presentation before reaching out to potential collaborators or investors.

May 13-June 27: Mars in Pisces

Start a buzz and spread the word! Today, bold Mars zooms into Pisces, lighting a fire in your cooperative, communicative third house until June 27. You'll be eager to get people on board with your big plans, but careful not to deliver an overly aggressive sales pitch while combative Mars is egging you on. Connect to industry peers through social media. You could meet someone with "dynamic duo" potential, but test the waters of this partnership with a short-term project.

May 14-September 12: Jupiter retrograde in Capricorn

Make your way back to the drawing board, as broad-minded Jupiter slips into a four-month retrograde in your sign. Since the red-spotted planet blasted into Capricorn on December 2, 2019, you've been growing and expanding at an exponential rate. This annual backspin can feel like a forced slowdown, but there's a hidden blessing: Before you invest more time and money, review your progress and make any course corrections. On September 12, you can hit the gas, safely knowing that you're driving in the best direction.

May 15: Sun-Pluto trine

Buried feelings bubble to the surface under this depth-plumbing mashup, and you may feel a sudden need to discuss them. Hold on! In your fervor, you could blindside people with accusations…some that aren't altogether fair. Healing may be more of an "inside job" today; one that you process with a supportive friend or therapist before bringing up the issue with the so-called offending party.

May 20: Venus-Neptune square

Reality might not live up to your expectations under today's disenchanting Venus-Neptune square. Maybe a dream job falls through or a client whose business you fought to win starts acting like a high-maintenance headache. Fortunately, the situation may be salvageable. Where have agreements become nebulous? Set up a call or meeting to discuss where things went sideways. After that, you'll be able to negotiate better terms.

May 22: Gemini new moon

Chaos and confusion slowing down your workflow? Today, the year's only new moon in Gemini lands in your systematic sixth house, restoring order to your court. Attack your cluttered desk and inbox—and be merciless about donating and deleting what you don't need. If managing this all at once feels overwhelming, schedule 30 minutes each day for the streamlining mission. This wellness-boosting new moon calls for healthier balance. Joining a fitness studio close to the office could mean less skipped workouts.

May 22: Mercury-Neptune square

You're usually open to feedback, but today, someone's commentary could feel passive-aggressive and undermining. The critic in question might be feeling insecure or even secretly threatened by you. Dimming your lights won't help them shine, so don't feel guilty about your success. If you want to take the high road, you might "kill 'em with kindness" and offer acknowledgment of their work.

May 28-August 4: Mercury in Cancer

Let's make a deal! As savvy Mercury shifts into your seventh house of contracts and partnerships, you'll expand your reach by teaming up with other successful people. This extended visit from the social planet includes a retrograde from June 18 to July 12, which could bring an old collaborator back into the picture. If agreements are on the table, have a lawyer review them carefully to make sure you're protected. And of course, try to sign them before or after the retrograde.

June

JUNE: LOVE HOTSPOTS

June 2: Venus-Mars square

It's hard to feel the love today as antagonistic Mars throws shade at Venus in your critical sixth house. And it doesn't help that others aren't playing nice. Before you clap back, poke around and figure out what's really upsetting you. Is this really about how someone else is acting, or might your negativity be coming from a deeper well of anger? Get to the root of what's bothering you before you bring it up for discussion.

June 5: Sagittarius full moon (lunar eclipse)

Fantasies blur with reality as today's Sagittarius full moon shines into your hazy twelfth house. Since this is a potent lunar eclipse, you might also get a glimpse of your own shadow. Are you projecting qualities onto a love interest that aren't actually there…or conversely, getting a little too gloomy about a situation that doesn't warrant despair? Today isn't the best day for a reality check, but know that you're probably looking at things through a distorted lens—rose-colored or not. Since the twelfth house rules closure and healing, this eclipse may evoke a major transition, sudden closure or the courage to shut the door for good.

June 13: Mars-Neptune meetup

Who can you trust? The charmers are laying it on thick today, and you are like putty in their hands. Don't whip out your wallet or your pen, or you could wind up buying something you don't need (or even really want!) or signing off on a project that you haven't fully vetted. Avoid hard-selling tactics in your own pitches. While you might get a "yes" today, people you pressure may back out tomorrow.

June 18-July 12: Mercury retrograde in Cancer

Commit or quit? As Mercury begins its backspin through Cancer and your seventh house of relationships, you could have second thoughts about a key alliance. Issues or problems that seemed resolved might crop up again. The question is: Are you willing to do what it takes to really heal the rifts? If so, when the messenger planet resumes its direct course on July 12, you'll have a nice clean slate. An old flame could return, angling for a second chance. If it was just bad timing that kept you apart before, it may be worth another go.

June 21: Cancer new moon (annular solar eclipse)

Partnerships get a high-vibe boost from today's supercharged new moon in Cancer, which is the first in a back-to-back pair energizing your seventh house of relationships. It's also a solar eclipse, the third in a heart-opening trilogy that rocked the skies on July 12, 2018, and July 2, 2019. Dynamic duos that have been shaping up over the past two years might crystallize under these moonbeams. Already attached? You and your partner could launch an exhilarating new chapter in your shared life.

JUNE: CAREER HOTSPOTS

June 13: Mars-Neptune meetup

You don't have to sugarcoat your direct requests today, but try to deliver them with a softer touch. As bulldozer Mars meets compassionate Neptune, you'll catch more flies with locally-harvested honey. Under this mashup, you could attract a kindred spirit who is both creative and reliable. Don't let this unicorn slip away! Test your compatibility with a small project and see what emerges.

June 18-July 12: Mercury retrograde in Cancer

Try not to lose your well-honed sense of balance as Mercury turns retrograde in your opposite sign until July 12. Business relationships could hit a speed bump and communications may prove frustrating for the next few weeks. Document exchanges in email and keep a paper trail of all official agreements. If you can put off contract negotiations until mid-July, do! If not, read every line of fine print and redline liberally. A collaborator from your past might return. Explore, but don't rush into a sequel.

The AstroTwins' 2020 Horoscope   462

June 21: Cancer new moon (annular solar eclipse)

Despite Mercury's backspin, the tag team show must go on! Today, the first in a consecutive pair of Cancer new moons arrives as a solar eclipse, bringing a surge of momentum to your business partnerships. Similar solar eclipses occurred in July 2018 and 2019, setting events in motion that may develop further today. A coworker could come out of left field with an offer that's surprisingly worth considering, or you might connect to someone whose skillset complements yours perfectly. Begin exploring possibilities, but if possible, wait until the second new moon on July 20 to make any alliances official.

June 23-November 28: Neptune retrograde in Pisces

Are your actions and words in alignment? As nebulous Neptune slips into its annual five-month retrograde, periodic integrity checks will be required to stay on-point. If you're over-promising and under-delivering (or vice versa), you may be relying too heavily on gut feelings instead of harnessing legit facts. Run the numbers and spec out actual timelines before giving a thumbs up or down to a project. In other words, be a good Capricorn and follow due process!

June 27, 2020-January 6, 2021: Mars in Aries

Home is where the heat is as energizer Mars buzzes into Aries and your domestic fourth house until January 6, 2021! This is an extended voyage for Mars, due to a retrograde from September 9 to November 13. For the next six months, your kitchen table might look more like a desk, or the launchpad for a new venture. Or, you could find success working with close friends or family. But be considerate of the people under your roof! If you're overtaking the space or bringing your computer to the dinner table (or bed), it's a clear sign that you need better boundaries between work and relaxation.

June 30: Jupiter-Pluto meetup

Expansive Jupiter and alchemical Pluto meet up in your sign today, their second of three exact conjunctions in 2020. This time, both planets are retrograde, which could force you to revise the agenda you set near their first mashup on April 4. Did you overshoot the mark? Or maybe you've been a little too worried about the so-called competition, and now playing it safe is causing you to fall behind. Make the necessary course corrections and you'll be flying high by the final Jupiter-Pluto connection on November 12.

July

JULY: LOVE HOTSPOTS

July 20: Cancer new moon

Ready to turn over a new leaf in relationships? Game-changing developments emerge as the second in a consecutive pair of new moons lands in Cancer and your commitment zone. If you or your partner have been stubbornly cleaving to your way of doing things, end the standstill. Compromises emerge that feel like win-wins rather than sacrifices. A casual relationship becomes exclusive, or you may decide to formalize your bond with someone who is far too important to let slip away.

The AstroTwins' 2020 Horoscope

July 27: Venus-Neptune square

The rose-colored veil lifts under today's tense stand-off between idealistic Venus and Neptune. A certain relationship isn't exactly playing out according to the Grimm Brothers' rulebook, but this might not be "the end" to your fairy tale. Can you accept the full spectrum of this person? There's a reason wedding vows include a "for better" and a "for worse."

July 27: Mercury-Mars square

While you want to respond to every bid for your attention, a loved one's demands are exhausting you! If you don't set a clear boundary soon, this could get ugly. Before your resentment devolves into rage, have a heart to heart. Don't spend hours dissecting the problem. Instead, offer proactive solutions, like putting a date night on the calendar or picking a set time every night (or every couple nights) to talk on the phone. Structures might seem stuffy, but they'll help!

JULY: CAREER HOTSPOTS

July 1-December 17: Saturn retrograde enters Capricorn

If you're buried beneath a project that ballooned in scope, take a breath and ask for help. Your ruler, staunch Saturn, has been retrograde since May 11. Today, the seven-ringed general backs up into your sign for the remainder of its backspin (until September 29), offering relief. While you hate to pause mid-project, you may be pumping a dry well. Take a break and recharge your batteries, then, seek expert guidance: coaches, mentors, books, TED talks. If you decide to bring your idea back to square one, don't worry! Retracing your steps will lend insight on how to improve it.

July 5: Capricorn full moon (lunar eclipse)

The year's only full moon in Capricorn is also a lunar eclipse, the final in a series that began hitting your sign on January 5, 2019. A sweeping change or watershed moment could arise, or you may wrap up a major endeavor that's been growing at an accelerated pace for the past year and a half. Spend extra time finessing the details and putting on the finishing flourishes. Then, celebrate your achievements before you shift your attention to your next grand goal.

July 8: Mercury-Mars square

You may bristle when someone walks in the room under today's feisty square between Mercury retrograde and aggro Mars. There could be a reason for this: Is this person's body language signaling resistance, even disrespect? While you can't act on hunches like those in the professional world, consider whether your colleague is feeling threatened. Decide if this relationship is worth working on, and if so, try new ways of engaging, like genuinely soliciting their opinion—and really listening to what they have to say!

July 12: Sun-Neptune trine

Even tense relationships will flow with surprising ease under the simpatico vibes of today's Sun-Neptune trine. It doesn't hurt that Mercury wraps up its retrograde today, too. Make the most of this magnetic mash-up by sharing your visionary ideas. People will be receptive and might add some crucial input of their own. No need to push your agenda. Just speak from the heart and they'll feel the power of your intentions.

July 15: Sun-Pluto opposition

Is there a wolf in the Capricorn coop? The annual Sun-Pluto opposition reveals a hidden agenda. Take note…but quietly! Heed the saying to keep your friends close and your enemies closer, and sidestep any potential power struggles today. Don't get dragged into a distracting disagreement that stalls progress. Instead of trying to reason with an irrational person, retreat and focus on your own work.

July 20: Cancer new moon

Today marks a page-turning moment for partnerships, as the second in a pair of back-to-back new moons lands in Cancer and your seventh house of commitments. A connection that's been percolating since the June 21 solar eclipse could really get off the ground now. Kick off your collaboration with a small venture to see how it goes. You might be clinking glasses in celebration on December 29, under the Cancer full moon.

July 20: Sun-Saturn opposition

Don't let pride win over progress today, even if someone directly challenges you. A once-per-year smackdown between the Sun and Saturn could derail negotiations or halt a joint venture in its tracks. Fortunately, this is a fast-moving transit, so if you stay off the battlefield for a day or two, you won't risk burning bridges. That will take some willpower, so steel your resolve and don't respond to that incendiary text!

July 30: Mercury-Jupiter opposition

You're talking circles around everyone today, as excitable Jupiter locks horns with expressive Mercury. Take a breath, Cap, and give others a chance to drink in what you have to say! Or just keep things short and sweet. People might not have time to listen to your extended remix. It might be best to whet their appetites, then follow up with a longer explanation later.

July 30: Mercury-Neptune trine

What begins as casual banter could evolve into a profound discussion as social Mercury bands together with soulful Neptune. Don't veer away from meaningful topics, whether you're dialed into a conference call or taking a break at a new-to-you coffee shop. You'll discover synchronicities at every turn. Remember: There's no such thing as too many kindred spirits.

August

AUGUST: LOVE HOTSPOTS

August 7-September 6: Venus in Cancer

Good luck resisting the urge to merge as amorous Venus cruises through Cancer and your committed seventh house. If you've been casually dating, you might suddenly want to add an exclusivity clause. Diplomatic Venus can facilitate "the talk" in a way that feels downright sexy! Attached Caps may feel a wave of gratitude for your long-term loves. Single Sea Goats, your sensitive side is seductive while Venus is here, so lead with your heart!

August 18: New moon in Leo

You'll feel the allure of your purr under today's new moon in passionate Leo and your erotic eighth house. If your mojo's been in slow-mo, bring sexy back with some extra self-care. Book a massage, take a dance class, be extra affectionate with your

 The AstroTwins' 2020 Horoscope

love interest! Relationships deepen and become more exclusive under this lunar lift. You do need trust along with the lust.

August 25: Venus-Jupiter opposition

Your measured sign knows that only fools rush in, but that's a role you may be willing to play today as amorous Venus opposes Jupiter, the galactic gambler. It's fun to get swept up in the torrent of a new attraction, but only time will tell how sustainable a bond truly is. Whether single or spoken for, watch out for Jupiter's overarching influence. While it's fun to fantasize aloud, don't set people up with expectations that you have no intention of fulfilling.

August 27: Venus-Neptune trine

Boundaries dissolve under the fantasy-fueled influence of today's Venus-Neptune trine. And for your semi-guarded sign, that might actually be a good thing. Who knows how many viable candidates got unfairly screened out by your defensive snap judgments? Today, you'll see everyone in their ideal light, which could help you spot a needle in Cupid's haystack or gain a profound new appreciation for the one you *j'adore*.

August 30: Venus-Pluto opposition

A once-per-year battle between amorous Venus and penetrating Pluto could churn up your rarely seen possessive (and obsessive!) streak. An attraction may be undeniable, but make sure you aren't ceding too much power to another person. If you've been hiding your true self to gain approval, start revealing yourself more authentically. People will find out who you really are sooner or later, and relationships built on honesty are the ones that have a fighting chance.

AUGUST: CAREER HOTSPOTS

August 1: Mercury-Pluto opposition

Consensus will be hard to reach under today's Mercury-Pluto opposition, but maybe that's a good thing! Instead of jockeying for control, open your mind to new perspectives. The person who is pushing back on your plans might have some ideas worth considering. If nothing else, hearing their objections can help you formulate a stronger pitch.

August 2: Sun-Uranus square

The only way out is through! You could be sitting in the eye of the storm, dodging stressful people and trying not to trigger any emotional outbursts. Just don't freeze because you're afraid of a conflict. Letting people air their grievances may be necessary to resolve tension. Hear them out but don't feel compelled to respond. It might take you a few days to formulate an answer.

August 3: Aquarius full moon

You get out what you put in! The money moves you've been making for the past six months could come to fruition under today's full moon. You've worked hard for this, so cash in on your efforts, and be sure to treat yourself to something luxurious (big or small) as a reward. In a few days, you can set your sights on the next exciting endeavor.

August 3: Mercury-Saturn opposition

Are you already plotting your response before they've finished making their point? Check that tendency under today's argumentative Mercury-Saturn opposition. If you want peace and productivity in your associations, work on being a better listener. As it turns out, people aren't necessarily seeking your advice. They simply want to be heard. Stay present and engaged, and conversations can take a fascinating turn!

August 4: Mars-Jupiter square
Focusing on work could prove challenging today, due to friction on the home front. A relative might be encroaching on your space or making unfair demands. And the more you help out, the less appreciative they become! While you love to lend support, set some boundaries. You can't afford to let personal matters affect your livelihood.

August 4-19: Mercury in Leo
Dive into a fact-finding mission, as brainy Mercury rolls into your investigative eighth house. Since this area of your chart also rules investments and joint ventures, you could team up with people who help grow your wealth. Now that you're halfway through the year, review your personal finances and schedule a meeting with an advisor to make sure you're on track for long-term fiscal goals.

August 10: Mercury-Uranus square
A plan you thought was locked and loaded could hit a snag today. Surrender instead of trying to control things. This sudden shift could actually be a blessing in disguise. Instead of clinging to what could have been, look to the future. Now that you're freed up, what exciting new adventures might you embark on today? Go with the flow and an enchanting—but unexpected—odyssey may arise.

August 13: Mars-Pluto square
As combative Mars spars with intense Pluto, you could find yourself (and everyone around you) in an agitated state. Be mindful of your intensity. What begins as a venting session may escalate into a full-blown volcanic eruption. If you feel anger churning,

step away to cool down before you spew. And wait until you're in a clear-headed space before making any binding decisions.

August 15, 2020-January 14, 2021: Uranus retrograde in Taurus
As disruptor Uranus pivots into its annual retrograde until January 2021, you might feel temporarily off your game. That's just your cue to slow down and review your workflow. Be willing to experiment. You may discover technology that revolutionizes your entire process. If you're struggling to step into your leadership, sign up for training or work with a coach.

August 17: Mercury-Mars trine
Go with your gut! Today's flowing formation of savvy Mercury and impulsive Mars activates your intuition. You may not have all the data in front of you, but you sense that a lead is worth pursuing. Follow that thread! Remember that the decisions your colleagues make are largely emotional. Tune in to their feelings if you want to gain their trust. If you're giving feedback, remember that they've poured a lot of themselves into their projects.

August 18: Leo new moon
The fiscal floodgates open today, as the year's only new moon in Leo activates your eighth house of assets and shared finances. Put your feelers out and plant some seeds. You'll set yourself up for a six-month cycle of abundance. Every little penny adds up, so take consistent steps toward paying off debt, saving, and investing.

August 19-September 5: Mercury in Virgo
As savvy Mercury buzzes through your visionary ninth house, it's time for blue sky dreaming. Instead

of focusing on what could go wrong, open yourself up to limitless possibilities. If time and money were no object, what could you create? There's so much that could go right, so why not make it your mission to discover that? Then you can weigh the pros along with the cons.

August 24: Mars-Saturn square

Rule breaker or rule maker? With renegade Mars challenging taskmaster Saturn you could swing between extremes. One minute you want to reinvent the wheel, the next you'll feel like toeing the line. For best results, read the instruction manual thoroughly and get acquainted with the systems. After that, you can deploy some upgrades, and be confident that you've run all the safety checks and are actually making improvements…not a big old mess.

August 25: Mercury-Uranus trine

You have a few wild cards up your sleeve today as innovative Uranus and savvy Mercury combine forces and provoke your creative streak. Show your hand to the right people, and you might win an influential fan or two! Don't be afraid to color outside the lines.

August 29: Mercury-Jupiter trine

Reach across the aisle and collaborate with people who you normally wouldn't brush shoulders with. Novel approaches will arise if you set aside your resistance to seeing things from a different perspective. Your open-minded attitude could attract complementary collaborators who can elevate your ideas to profitable new heights.

August 30: Mercury-Neptune opposition

Misunderstandings could come out of left field today, as nebulous Neptune snares fast-talking Mercury in its web. Even if you express yourself with crystal clarity, people may still be too cloudy to comprehend it. Hold off on any discussions or presentations that can afford to wait.

September

SEPTEMBER: LOVE HOTSPOTS

September 2: Venus-Saturn opposition

Should you double-down on boundaries or compromise to keep the peace? Today's push-pull between withholding Saturn and people-pleasing Venus will yank you between extremes. Make sure you aren't overextending yourself for the benefit of your partner (or a date). But don't be so hardcore that the object of your affections is afraid to approach you.

September 4: Venus-Mars square

As heavenly heartthrobs Venus and Mars trade fire, you could hit a patch of turbulence. You or the object of your affections may be acting needy or possessive. Don't waste time on peacekeeping efforts. They'll only be met with resistance or insensitive outbursts. Instead of forcing a resolution, take a little space and wait for this storm to pass.

September 6-October 2: Venus in Leo

You're a highly attractive force field as vivacious Venus struts through your seductive eighth house. Reconfigure your schedule to prioritize pleasure and bonding with your partner. If you're single, this transit could help you magnetize the total package—someone who thrills your mind, body and soul. Don't waste your time if the chemistry isn't there. Coupled Caps could cement your bond in a meaningful (and ceremonial) way!

September 9-November 13: Mars retrograde in Aries

When the rowdy red planet reverses course every other year, you may feel like a storm is brewing inside you. As Mars marches back through Aries and your emotionally guarded fourth house until November 13, you'll have to fight the tendency to go into combat mode during conflicts. When you feel like putting your dukes up, count backwards from ten, and remember that your dates and mates are not your enemies!

September 15: Venus-Uranus square

With vixen Venus in your erotic eighth house, you're craving a warm body and some good loving. But an unsettling angle to temperamental Uranus could kill the mood as quickly as it heats up. Strong emotions like jealousy, hurt and rage could overtake your good senses. Detach so you can clearly think through your next move. Haste makes waste!

September 28: Venus-Mars trine

Love is in the air as the planets of *amour*, Venus and Mars, form a dazzling trine in the most affectionate sectors of your chart. Is it time to move in together, buy a ring or bring up family talks? All those options are on the table now. Single? Before you join another dating site, fill your own emotional tanks by spending more time with your nearest and dearest. The self-assurance they give you will help you attract equally confident people.

September 29: Mars-Saturn square

You're usually a beacon of self-restraint, but today's clash between your ruler, disciplined Saturn, and brash Mars could have you wanting to burn every bridge in sight. Composure will be in short supply today, but don't cross any bright lines that could damage important bonds.

SEPTEMBER: CAREER HOTSPOTS

September 1: Mercury-Pluto trine

Your instincts are razor sharp as Mercury in your candid ninth house bands together with transformative Pluto in your sign. Better still? You can deliver harsher feedback with remarkable tact and finesse. The only catch? Once people see how astute you are, they'll keep coming back for your sage advice…and that could become a drain on your time. Then again, this may be your cue to start charging as a coach or consultant!

September 2: Pisces full moon

Good news may cross your desk as the year's only full moon in Pisces blazes through your intellectual and communicative corner. A higher up could offer positive feedback on an idea or a pitch, and a joint project could progress swiftly! Speak up if you've been holding onto a brilliant proposition. Plans might take flight over the coming two weeks.

September 3: Mercury-Saturn trine

Level up! Your grandest schemes may benefit from a solid structure. Shrewd Mercury in your visionary ninth house teams up with sensible Saturn in your sign, helping you lay the groundwork. Before you get too far into development, form a group of "beta testers" to see if this has what it takes to succeed. If the first pass isn't flawless, you'll have some feedback for how to improve. Afraid of the critics? Run through every possible objection and prepare your counterpoints. When it comes time to

The AstroTwins' 2020 Horoscope

pitch, you'll be able to speak with confidence and authority.

September 5-27: Mercury in Libra

As strategic Mercury sails through your future-oriented tenth house, give your long-term goals a review. Are you on track to hit all your benchmarks? Do you have enough resources to pull this off? Now is the time to reassess and recommit, making any course corrections that are needed. Set specific milestones and rewards to keep yourself motivated!

September 9-November 13: Mars retrograde in Aries

Get your house in order! Chaotic Mars turns retrograde in your domestic zone until November 13, putting your focus on Chateau Capricorn. While this isn't the best time for doing any major renovations, it is a powerful period for deep cleaning your space, then setting it up for maximum privacy and productivity. How about a meditation corner and a great new desk? Reconnect with relatives you love, but avoid the triggering ones—Mars' backspin could make the tension especially volcanic now. Don't force togetherness when you actually need space. Instead, utilize the opportunity to foster friendships elsewhere.

September 12: Jupiter retrograde ends

You can exhale now! Jubilant Jupiter wraps up a four-month retrograde through your sign, shifting stalled personal initiatives back into fifth gear. The last four months were great for revising, researching, and re-evaluating. Now that you've had a chance to polish your project, the red planet's forward march inspires you to share it with the world. The auspicious planet is in your sign until December 19, so go forth and prosper!

September 14: Sun-Pluto trine

Outsource the minutiae and declare your space a drama-free zone. You don't have time to manage the little things today, Capricorn, as a Sun-Pluto trine puts your eye on a fast-moving ball. What will it take to move your mission into a bigger league? Devote your attention to the more expansive vision. Once you nail that, you can invite other people to play along.

September 17: Virgo new moon

The ceiling can't hold you, as the year's only new moon in Virgo vectors through your ninth house of expansion and worldly adventures. Now's the time to spread your wings and explore some novel terrain. Cross-cultural connections could evolve in game-changing ways over the coming six months. Start planning your next big trip or sign up for a workshop that leads you along an inner journey.

September 17: Mercury-Jupiter square

Did you overpromise what you're able to deliver? Don't cover it up, Capricorn. If you know that it will take more time and resources than you currently have, promptly (and humbly) negotiate a new plan of action. Assure people of your intentions to make good on this, even if you have to stretch out the timeline a little. You can't turn back the clock, but you can find a way to move forward with integrity. Best case scenario? Invite the team in to problem-solve and remedy the situation with you.

September 21: Mercury-Pluto square

An authority figure might push your buttons under today's tense transit. And thanks to mouthy Mercury getting elbowed by prickly Pluto, it's going to take serious willpower to not lose your composure. Choose your battles. Will asserting yourself start a massive power struggle? Taking one for the team could be in your best interest.

September 23: Mercury-Saturn square

A battle of wills could erupt today, as you or a key decision-maker refuse to budge on your stance. Or, you may feel disheartened by someone's apparent lack of interest, which is holding up your progress. Are you being stonewalled, or do you just need to refine your pitch? Before you assume that all is lost, try to improve the messaging in a way that will resonate with this person.

September 24: Mercury-Mars opposition

Demands from family will pull you away from your desk, but you also have deadlines to meet! To save your sanity, you'll have to delegate. Trade tasks with a colleague or see if a relative or roommate can put out that fire at home. Try not to blur the two worlds. You don't want to be taking personal calls in the middle of a meeting or answering e-mails at the dinner table.

September 27-October 27: Mercury in Scorpio

Mercury logs in to your tech-savvy eleventh house, helping you expand your virtual network. Connections heat up in real time, too. "Carpe DM" and message someone you admire on Instagram, proposing a collaboration. Or give them some love with a repost or shared link. What goes around comes around! If you need to update your gadgets, start shopping around. Just try to pick your model before Mercury turns retrograde in three weeks this October 13.

September 29: Mars-Saturn square

Drop the hardcore attitude and use a gentler touch. You risk alienating your crew if you keep coming on so strong. People aren't mind readers and expecting them to intuit your every need just isn't fair. If you want specific instructions followed, write them out in concise bullet points. Or, to avoid coming across as imperious, call a summit and design a set of agreements together. People are more likely to follow the rules when they feel a sense of ownership in creating them.

September 29: Saturn retrograde ends

Your ruler, structured Saturn, wakes up from its four-and-a-half month retrograde and powers forward in your sign. Beginning today, you'll make steady progress toward a personal goal. As you forge ahead, don't leave behind the valuable lessons you learned. If you had to go back and fine-tune a project, all the hours of seemingly endless revisions will soon be worth their weight in gold. And good news! On December 17, Saturn will officially move on from your sign after a three-year, strength-building cycle that felt like boot camp. Before then, do any last bit of training needed to bring your skills up to snuff.

October

OCTOBER: LOVE HOTSPOTS

October 1: Aries full moon

Emotions run high on the home front, as the new moon stirs the pot in your foundational fourth house. This yearly lunation can poke at an old childhood wound or even set a pattern you learned

The AstroTwins' 2020 Horoscope

from your parents into motion! Does repeating this serve your relationship? If not, now's the time to start doing things differently. Happily coupled Caps can devise home or family-related goals for the next six months, whether you're moving in together or talking family expansion.

October 2-27: Venus in Virgo

Sultry Venus shimmies into your expansive ninth house today, opening your heart and broadening your mind. Venture out of your romantic comfort zone, whether you're exploring new cultural activities with your steady plus-one or dating someone different from your usual "type." Vacation and romance go hand in hand, so follow Cupid's lead and plan a sexy getaway before October 27.

October 10: Venus-Uranus trine

Cuffing season is on and under today's deliciously naughty Venus-Uranus trine, you might experiment with a fur-lined pair. Shake off any inhibitions and let yourself play. Boldly ask a crush to meet you for coffee or 'fess up to your love about a hidden fantasy. Single? Toss out the old dating paradigms and write your own rules!

October 18: Venus-Neptune opposition

Hold a few cards closer to your vest, as a dynamic Virgo-Neptune opposition amplifies your allure. Leaving people wondering can keep them interested, as long as you don't get carried away with the cat-and-mouse games. Under this cosmic collision, miscommunications can run rampant, so aim for "mystique" not "total mystery." Can you show it instead of saying it? Try using nonverbal cues to signal your interest. The power of touch is not to be underestimated.

October 19: Venus-Jupiter trine

Today's heart-opening formation between romantic Venus and growth-agent Jupiter deepens feelings and fortifies an important bond. Don't shy away from talks about the future, whether you're picking wedding dates or musing about the first vacation you'll take together. Single? Fill your inspiration tanks by attending a live lecture, art opening or even a self-development workshop. You could meet a like-minded prospect who can match your wit and intellect.

October 19: Mars-Jupiter square

Does your inner circle respect your boundaries? If friends and family keep weighing in (unsolicited) about your love life or passing judgement about your decisions, it's time to speak up. Thank them for their concern but let them know you've got it handled. Try to keep your cool, as outspoken Jupiter is adding fuel to Mars' hair-trigger temper, which could cause you to lash out. Perhaps it's time to stop sharing so many details, which might be what's causing them to worry about you in the first place.

October 21: Venus-Pluto trine

It can be unnerving to discuss "what's next," but for your ambitious sign, it's actually more unsettling to not know where something is headed. With Venus and possessive Pluto in sync, you simply need a little reassurance about the future. And today, you can get it without coming across as anxious or jealous. That said, if you've only been out with someone a couple times, keep talks in the non-personal, big-picture realm. Stick to questions like, "Where do you see yourself five years from now?" or, "Do you want kids one day?"

October 24: Venus-Saturn trine

The twice-annual alignment between pleasure-seeking Venus and serious Saturn reminds you to hold out for the best. If you're settling for mediocrity, level up and open the vacancy for someone who makes your heart sing. Could your existing relationship use some improvement? Light candles, make a special dinner, then talk about your hopes and ideas. It's not a buzzkill to start planning for a dream home or figuring out how to save up for your end-of-year getaway.

October 27-November 21: Venus in Libra

Sensual Venus struts into your tenth house of public prestige. During this lavish cycle, you'll be especially conscious about who's by your side—and you want to be judged positively by the company you keep. But don't overlook a diamond in the rough! It's easier to help someone polish up their game than it is to make over their character and personality. Attached? You and your love interest could earn "It Couple" status or attend a few VIP events.

October 31: Taurus full moon

Chemistry is too undeniable to resist as the annual Taurus full moon lights a bonfire in your passionate fifth house. With so much heightened sensuality in the air, you could have a full stack of admirers— and it doesn't hurt that you'll be a fearless flirt. For some Capricorns, this fertile full moon might bring pregnancy news within a couple weeks. Plan ahead or protect yourself accordingly.

OCTOBER: CAREER HOTSPOTS

October 4: Pluto retrograde ends

Intensifier Pluto winds down a five-month backspin through your sign. This transit could have slowed your ambition or caused you to stray from your vision. Growth is not always linear, so don't view this forced slowdown as a waste of time. You may have grown spiritually or emotionally from overcoming roadblocks. Patience was a virtue, but in the days ahead you'll start to magnetize powerful opportunities with velocity again.

October 7: Mercury-Uranus opposition

Calling someone out could backfire today, even if the offending party deserves to be put in their place. With trickster Mercury opposing chaotic Uranus, you may come off looking like a bully. Worse, that might make people hesitant about sharing ideas with you in the future. Don't let anyone turn you into their scapegoat. The truth always emerges eventually, so just let this play out on its own.

October 9: Mars-Pluto square

Emotions intensify as fiery Mars crashes into a tense square with vindictive Pluto. While it's not healthy to bottle up your feelings, venting to the wrong people could lead to a full-blown meltdown. Make sure that "sharing concern" isn't a sly way of spilling tea…and trying to find allies to join your fight against a certain frenemy. You don't want to draw battle lines today, even if someone has pushed you to your edge. Hold off on any major moves until these strained skies clear in a couple days.

October 13-November 3: Mercury retrograde

Mercury turns retrograde in your group-oriented eleventh house today, potentially stalling progress and throwing some speed bumps into your path. This sector also rules technology, so digital devices and software could go on the fritz. Aim for clear and concise communication, even if that means daily huddles to ensure that everyone's on the same page. Whenever possible, meet face to face (if not in person, then on a Google Hangout) to avoid the misunderstandings of email and Slack.

October 15: Sun-Pluto square

If someone pulls a power move at work, don't go mano-a-mano with them. A bare-knuckled mashup between Pluto and the Sun could make for some encounters that are baffling (at best) and nefarious (at their worst). Stay out of this! You've worked too hard to have your name dragged through the mud.

October 16: Libra new moon

Prep the launch pad! The Libra new moon sends a motivating jolt through your tenth house of career ambitions, setting you up for a fresh six-month cycle of success. Get back on track with your goals. Review what you wanted to accomplish in 2020 and see what's achievable before the end of the year. If you've already ticked off every box on that list, start a new one! Get ahead on New Year's resolutions and sketch out some bold new ideas.

October 18: Sun-Saturn square

You're riding the express elevator to the top, but make sure you don't blow past important gatekeepers as you ascend. People won't take kindly to you overstepping their boundaries...even the invisible ones. Better to play politics now, even if it takes a little longer to achieve your goal. Having the middlemen in your corner is a solid strategy for long-term success. If you want to gain respect, you have to give it.

October 19: Mars-Jupiter square

Friction in your circle could throw your carefully calibrated work-life balance out of whack. You want to play peacemaker, but if you fall behind trying to save the day, you'll only wind up frustrated and resentful. And don't go opinion-polling relatives about your career goals. Without meaning to, they may undermine your confidence...just as you're poised to leap. Seek neutral counsel if you need advice, then invite your family to raise a toast with you after you've scored your victory.

October 19: Mercury-Uranus opposition

Usually if you "see something," it's good to "say something." Today is the exception to the rule, as an opposition between brusque Mercury and unpredictable Uranus causes your words to miss the mark. If someone is truly out of line, go through the proper channels to resolve it instead of taking matters into your own hands.

November

NOVEMBER: LOVE HOTSPOTS

November 9: Venus-Mars opposition

With the zodiac's love planets in opposite corners, you may feel out of sync with the one(s) you adore. Even a well-intentioned attempt to hash things out could lead to further misunderstanding. An admirer might ply you with the sweetest lines, but are they able to follow through with action? Wait and see.

November 13: Mars retrograde ends

You can restore peace and tranquility on the home front today, as pugnacious Mars ends a testy retrograde that began on September 9 and ends in your domestic quarters. If a relative or roomie has been difficult lately, you might be able to reason with them now. Leave your own anger or resentment at the door and see if you can't smooth out the kinks. These next two weeks are also great for redecorating or a major decluttering mission!

November 15: Venus-Pluto square

Politeness goes out the window today and you might witness someone's intense control issues. Who knew they had that much brewing inside of them? Now that the masks are off, look at ways you can recalibrate your relationship. If one of you is always in the driver's seat while the other is riding shotgun, find a more equitable way to share the power.

November 16: Venus-Jupiter square

Time to jump in...or go "all in"? You could feel stretched in two directions as self-possessed Jupiter in your sign locks horns with Venus. Even as you're bringing up the topic of commitment, you may be surreptitiously scoping out the emergency exits. This momentary anxiety is likely to pass, so wait for a couple days and see if the urge to bolt passes.

November 19: Venus-Saturn square

There's nothing wrong with having high expectations, but with starry-eyed Venus in your future-focused tenth house, you might have concocted some fairy tales about your current romantic situation. Realistic Saturn brings you back down to earth, helping you take a clear-eyed look at what—and who—you're dealing with. Be honest about your long-term desires, and really listen to what your love interest wants. Even if that winds up

being two different things, at least there will be no more guessing games or speculation.

November 21-December 15: Venus in Scorpio

As the love planet sashays into your eleventh house of friendship, a platonic pal could get promoted to "permanent plus-one." If you're single, start tapping the apps! This tech-savvy Venus cycle might bring the right right swipe. Mutual friends could play matchmaker, so be open to fix-ups. Attached Capricorns: Revel in the holiday cheer, power couple style.

November 27: Venus-Uranus opposition

A puzzling mashup between congenial Venus and erratic Uranus in your romance sector might have your mojo running hot and cold. Don't make promises you can't keep or string someone along because you want companionship. If you can't decide if you're into them (or not) be honest about your hesitation—and let them speak about theirs. But if you're feeling certain, this dynamic planetary lineup might inspire you to make a daring leap.

NOVEMBER: CAREER HOTSPOTS

November 1: Mercury-Saturn square

Today marks the second of three squares between mental Mercury and structured Saturn, and this time Mercury is in retrograde motion. (The first occurrence was on September 23.) After Mercury resumes its forward motion, the two will clash again on November 6. On these days, progress could be stalled by an authority figure or higher-up. Their resistance might seem unfounded, but see this as an opportunity to polish or fine-tune your creation. If you aren't communicating the benefits clearly enough, go back to the drawing board. There won't be any shortcuts, but in the end, that could be a blessing in disguise.

November 3: Mercury direct in Libra

Enough of the wild goose chases! Mercury snaps out of a confounding retrograde and powers forward through your career zone, recalibrating your professional GPS. Streamline where you've been scattered and radar in on one (or two) clear goals you want to crush while Mercury buzzes here for one week. Don't fritter this focused period away!

November 10-December 1: Mercury in Scorpio

As Mercury shifts into your collaborative eleventh house, you'll notice a marked improvement in group dynamics and the way you communicate with each other. Schedule lunch meetings, team-building activities, or a happy hour to make the most of this connective transit. Since this is the tech sector of the zodiac, shop around for new devices and make sure you're running the latest version of all your apps.

November 12: Jupiter-Pluto meetup

Dig deep into the well of inspiration, then launch! Today, subterranean Pluto and supersizer Jupiter meet up for the third and final time this year. This rare conjunction only happens every 33-38 years, so look back to what you started near April 4 (and refined near June 30 while both planets were retrograde). One of your deeply held professional passions could come to life in a headline-grabbing way! Conversely, if it's time to jailbreak from limiting circumstances, today's transit sets you free.

November 13: Mars retrograde ends

Clean house! Frenetic Mars wraps up a two-month retrograde that rippled through the most sensitive zone of your chart since September 9. If tension mounted between teammates, start passing around olive branches and making peace. Don't just clear the air; figure out where boundaries were (innocently) crossed. Knowing where everyone's limits lie can help you gracefully navigate future disagreements before they blow up again.

November 15: Scorpio new moon

Can you feel the electricity? Today's charged-up new moon in Scorpio sends high-voltage beams through your eleventh house of teamwork and technology. Whether surfing the web or socializing IRL, you could feel that instant click that says, "These are my people." This is the kind of day where you might meet your future soul squad or one of your Instagram posts goes viral. Put yourself out there and get ready for a ripple effect!

November 17: Mercury-Uranus opposition

Don't take it upon yourself to reprimand any slackers today, even if you're seething with resentment. A rebellious clash between Mercury and volatile Uranus could polarize the two of you, making you feel like the stern principal sending a bad kid to detention. If someone is truly out of line, it might be time to part ways instead of forcing togetherness. But before you do, get a second opinion. This opposition can make you prone to overreaction.

November 23: Mercury-Neptune trine

Hitting a wall? Stop plugging away at that spreadsheet. A spontaneous session with the hive mind could yield the breakthrough you're looking

476

for. As cerebral Mercury trines creative Neptune, you won't have to "lead" so much as gather brilliant people together and hold space. Then, watch the intellectual sparks fly!

November 28: Neptune retrograde ends

Get ready to spread your message to the masses, as nebulous Neptune rouses from a five-month retrograde in your communication zone. Although it might take a few days to get up to full speed, you'll have an easier time organizing (and vocalizing!) your thoughts once again. Creative projects you developed behind the scenes might be ready to share, or even shop around.

November 30: Gemini full moon (lunar eclipse)

Got some administrative duties to deal with? No more sweeping them under the rug! Under today's full moon in Gemini—a galvanizing lunar eclipse—you're ready to tie up loose ends before the year is through. Map out your end-of-year objectives and see what you can finish with a flourish before the calendar turns. With your systematic sixth house cranked up, you could revamp your workflow and even outsource a few tasks to make time for holiday celebrations. You might hire or fire a few members of Team Gemini.

December

DECEMBER: LOVE HOTSPOTS

December 5: Venus-Neptune trine

Romance without borders! As compassionate Neptune gets into a sweet sync-up with Venus, the cosmic coquette, it's anyone's guess who will sweep you into their enchanting allure. Keep an open heart and mind and have fun experimenting. Just know that you'll be rocking the rose-colored glasses for a couple days (before and after this transit) and that connections may be sweet, but ephemeral. Time will tell.

December 14: Sagittarius new moon (total solar eclipse)

The year's only new moon in your twelfth house of closure is also a potent solar eclipse, helping you release something that no longer serves you… and better still, open a vacancy for something that does! Maybe you've been clinging to a memory or refusing to cut ties to an unappreciative person. If you're struggling to let go, summon gratitude for what the situation taught you, then say goodbye and let the healing begin.

December 15, 2020-January 9, 2021: Venus in Sagittarius

Amorous Venus takes her annual sojourn through your restorative twelfth house, bringing healing and compassion to your romantic life. If it's time to close the door on a painful chapter, you can do so gracefully, then move forward. Happily coupled Capricorns will enjoy a fantasy-fueled finale to 2020. Let down your guard and explore!

December 23: Mars-Pluto square

Trigger alert! If you're not in the mood for a meltdown, don't start sharing unprocessed feelings with your partner. And don't ask the kinds of questions that could be misconstrued as jealous digging. Because combative Mars and underhanded Pluto are locked into a tense square, conflicts might erupt with the slightest provocation. Shield yourself

 The AstroTwins' 2020 Horoscope

from this energy and wait a couple days before broaching a tender topic.

December 29: Cancer full moon

The final full moon of 2020 blooms in compassionate Cancer and sends some warm-fuzzy vibes to your relationship house. A commitment could crystallize; one that's been developing since the June 21 solar eclipse or the January 10 lunar eclipse (the first of two Cancer full moons in 2020). Unattached? You could meet someone with long-term potential under the NYE confetti or while you're easing into 2021.

December 30: Venus-Neptune square

Is it real or just a daydream? A Venus-Neptune square ups the ante on romance, but it might be hard to tell if a situation has staying power or not. You don't want to ignore red flags, but it's also unclear whether these are minor concerns or actual deal breakers. While you don't want to fall in love with someone's potential, don't let fear stop you from exploring it either. Let yourself be charmed, but not swept away.

DECEMBER: CAREER HOTSPOTS

December 1-20: Mercury in Sagittarius

You've been buzzing along at warp speed, but it's time to give your mind some respite from the grind. As mental Mercury slips into your soulful twelfth house, you have no choice but to downshift. Ambitious end-of-year plans might need a more generous timeline—especially if that gives you space for evaluating them from a creative POV. This charitable social cycle is perfect for organizing holiday giving. Think about creating a group donation with colleagues and friends.

December 13: Mercury-Neptune square

You may not be at peak performance today when mental Mercury collides with foggy Neptune—but don't judge yourself! You can't be "on" 24/7, and this disorienting duet might even find you turning the house upside down to find your wallet and keys! Shift your schedule and devote today to ticking off small tasks and easy endeavors. And if you're feeling overwhelmed, let your coworkers know you could use some support.

December 17, 2020-March 7, 2023: Saturn in Aquarius

Ready to manifest some ambitious financial goals? These next two-plus years could be your most profitable yet—provided you do things in a grounded, reasonable way. Your ruler, master teacher Saturn, leaves your sign, where he's been imparting some tough lessons for the past three years. Now, he marches into Aquarius and your income sector until March 7, 2023. While you've surely grown and learned a lot about yourself, now you're eager to take all that hard-won wisdom to the bank! Saturn will insist you pay your dues, but if you do, you can look forward to real security and legit wealth.

December 19, 2020-May 13, 2021: Jupiter in Aquarius

You've been working diligently on your personal goals since December 2, 2019, as expansive Jupiter sailed into your sign and helped you clarify your mission. Starting today, the planet of abundance takes up residence in innovative Aquarius and your second house of work, finance and security. Jupiter hasn't been here since January 2009, and you're an entirely different person now. Are you ready to (re) fill your coffers? Between now and December 29,

2021, you could experience a major uptick in your earnings—and your self-confidence!

December 20, 2020-January 9, 2021: Mercury in Capricorn

Communicative Mercury ends the year in your sign, amplifying your power of persuasion. Though everyone is winding down for the holidays, you can still use this self-assured transit to plant important seeds for your career. Set up a performance review for early January. Circulate your work on social media and start a buzz. Little tweaks to your branding (or a style update) can bring a new wave of followers and fans.

December 21: Jupiter-Saturn meetup

Your money moves could yield an unexpected and sizeable bounty today, as lucky Jupiter meets up with savvy Saturn in your fiscal second house. This auspicious alignment, called The Great Conjunction, only happens every 20 years, and it brings together both your willingness to take a chance and your sensible restraint. A calculated risk could pay off! If you know it's time to raise your rates or apply for an elite new position, *carpe diem!*

December 25: Mercury-Uranus trine

Your creativity is at peak levels today, as Mercury in your sign lines up with innovative Uranus in your artistic fifth house. Share a bold and inventive idea that you've been toying with. No one will mind a little shop talk under the Christmas tree when you're brimming over with so much inspiration. While everyone's catnapping, you might feel like slipping off from the celebrations to do a little work on a passion project. No apologies!

December 29: Cancer full moon

What deals can you seal in the final days of 2020? The partnership-oriented full moon in Cancer beams through your seventh house of contracts, so don't be afraid to give a budding connection one last push. Over the next two weeks, you could land a first-rate client or finalize the paperwork for an exciting merger. Untangle yourself from flatlining alliances so you can begin 2021 with a blank slate and a fresh attitude. ✸

AQUARIUS
2020

Yearly Highlights

LOVE

With amorous Venus spending an extra-long time in Gemini and your romantic fifth house from April 3 to August 7, your heart's racing at a faster BPM. This passionate cycle includes a retrograde (from May 13 to June 25) which could bring trouble from an ex or reunite you with "the one that got away." Coupled Aquarians will want to be seen on the scene together, so bring on the dress-up dates. With the North Node moving into Gemini, along with a lunar eclipse on November 30, romantic surprises await, like meeting the love of your life, getting engaged, making babies or taking an epic leap with a partner.

MONEY

Make your mark! For the first time since 1994, masterful Saturn bolts into Aquarius from March 21 to July 1, giving you focus and ambition you haven't felt in years (if ever). While this will be boot camp at times, facing the challenge will be majorly rewarding! On December 21, enterprising Jupiter meets Saturn at the same degree of Aquarius, ensuring that you'll end this year with clarity and enthusiasm about your life path. Before then, make it your mission to clear away scarcity thinking and strategically leave a soul-sucking work situation.

WELLNESS

Healing is an inside job in 2020, as vitality-booster Jupiter joins sluggish Saturn and Pluto in Capricorn and your subconscious twelfth house. The connection between mind and body will be too obvious to ignore, especially with three eclipses striking your wellness axis in the first half of the year. Jupiter accelerates the transformational process, and as an Aquarius, you'll thrive with a mix of traditional and holistic treatments. Don't forget that the most important "medicine" is the preventative kind. Detox your diet and de-stress your life. Yin practices, like yoga, that soothe your parasympathetic nervous system will be as beneficial as high-impact cardio.

LEISURE

With your ruler, erratic Uranus, spending its first full year (of eight) in your domestic quarters, you're still defining your requirements for "home sweet home." You may bounce between multiple residences, live somewhere short-term, or have a rotating cast of roommates. Renovations and repairs could be ongoing in 2020, or a family member's unpredictable behavior could keep you up at night. Even if all's quiet on your home front, you may rebel against too much placidity. Don't shake things up just because you're bored! ✳

AQUARIUS

2020 HOROSCOPE

2020 Power Dates

AQUARIUS NEW MOON
January 24 (4:42 pm ET)

AQUARIUS FULL MOON
August 3 (11:48am ET)

SUN IN AQUARIUS
January 20 – February 18

Release the Roombas! 2020 could feel like a giant clean-up mission for Aquarians, as you inspect and transform every cluttered corner of your life. This is definitely going to be a transitional year as you straddle two worlds: the old one that you're leaving behind and the new multiverse that's slowly forming in front of your eyes.

Since December 2, 2019, accelerator Jupiter has joined taskmaster Saturn and evolutionary Pluto in Capricorn and your twelfth house of healing and transitions. Throughout the year, this heavy-hitting trio will mix and mingle with each other, triggering soulful awakenings and forcing you to surrender to the flow of "the universe's" agenda, even when you were certain you had a better plan in mind.

Not that these periodic plunges into the esoteric realm are unfamiliar. As an Aquarius, "reality" has always been a shifting concept. Plus, Saturn and Pluto have both been on a longer roll through Capricorn. The ringed taskmaster has been trudging along this path since December 19, 2017. Alchemical Pluto has been rowing through the Sea Goat's waters since November 27, 2008, a 16-year voyage that continues until 2024. On January

12, 2020, Saturn and Pluto will host an ultra-rare meetup at 22° Capricorn, a conjunction that only happens every 35 years. Together, they set your agenda for 2020: Let go so you can grow!

Now that change agent Jupiter has joined the party, there's no more time for chin-scratching and intellectualizing. Jupiter wants traction, and he wants it now! If your inner child has been on a meandering exploration—or learning "at their own pace"—Jupiter will pull them out of the metaphoric Waldorf School to do some speed learning with a superstar tutor.

> "You'll emerge stronger, savvier and more successful than you've been in years."

We're not trying to traumatize you here, Aquarius. It's just that we know you're ready to make all those shifts that you've been talking about in your moon circles, therapy sessions and online master classes. That means picking up the pace and packing up the old stuff. Yes, it will be emotional. There will be losses to grieve, bittersweet farewells, "WTF am I doing?!" moments—especially while Jupiter and Pluto team up on April 4, June 30 and November 12. But on the other side of this turbulence lies a beautiful blank canvas that's begging to be painted upon with this next chapter of your life!

You're going to have to be patient with this process though. Slow-moving Saturn makes its presence known in your sign, darting in for a quick visit from March 21 to July 1, then taking up a longer, three-year residence in Aquarius on December 17. This is Saturn's first return to Aquarius since January 28, 1994. Before astronomers had strong enough telescopes to discover your modern-day ruler, side-spinning Uranus, it was stoic Saturn who was tapped as your galactic guardian. This may explain your otherworldly ability to be totally eccentric one minute and a kickass project manager the next. Hosting Saturn in your sign can feel like cosmic boot camp. But grit your teeth and do the drills, Water Bearer. You'll emerge stronger, savvier and more successful than you've been in years.

Thankfully, you'll get solid support from jovial Jupiter. On December 19, the red-spotted planet will join Saturn in Aquarius, helping you joyfully embrace the learning curve. Highlight December 21 in orange highlighter! The Winter Solstice is also the date of The Great Conjunction, as Jupiter and Saturn meet up at 0°29' Aquarius and combine their powerful energies. This event only happens every 20 years—and the last one occurred on May 31, 2000. Where to expand and where to contract? Major insight will come by the year's end.

Yes, Aquarius, this might all sound rather formidable. But take heart! There will be plenty of uplifting transits happening in 2020. On May 5, the lunar North Node heads into Gemini and your festive, flirtatious (and fertile!) fifth house. This 18-month destiny driver will be a creative renaissance for many of you. The stage will call Aquarius performers. Bring down the house at an open mic night or go slay an audition.

Romantically, the North Node's tour of Gemini, which lasts until January 18, 2022, could bring epic developments. You might meet the love of your life, get engaged or have a baby—or achieve some

The AstroTwins' 2020 Horoscope

other self-styled milestone in the game of love. (You write those rules, Aquarius!) A new eclipse series on the Gemini/Sagittarius axis will also galvanize your relationships, beginning with the full moon on June 5. Also, amorous Venus spends an extra-long time in Gemini and your fifth house, from April 3 to August 7. Energetic Mars blazes through Aries and your social third house for nearly half the year—from June 27 until January 6, 2021, to be exact. Although both Venus and Mars will have retrograde phases in 2020, your social calendar will be booked with stimulating rendezvous, both with new people and folks from your past.

Jupiter in Capricorn: Blast through barriers.

December 2, 2019 –
December 17, 2020

No more ruminating, Aquarius. It's time to blast through any barriers standing between you and your dreams. But hang on! That's not your cue to stomp on the gas and speed off like Danica Patrick. Not quite yet. There's some unfinished business to wrap up first—and probably some potent feelings that you swept under the hand-loomed Ikat rug.

In many ways, you've been stuck in a state of suspended animation for the past two years. It's not that things haven't been happening on the surface. We saw Aquarius friends buy their first homes, step into executive positions at work, start relationships and move in with their mates. But on December 19, 2017, your co-ruler Saturn began a slow roll through Capricorn and your twelfth house of healing and completions. Evolutionary Pluto has also been in

the sign of the Sea Goat since November 27, 2008, and together, these two "karma cops" have plunged you into an exploration of your own shadow side.

To say it's been heavy would be an understatement. Pluto is private and Saturn is status-conscious, so there's a chance no one (not even your best friend) has a clue about how dark some days have been for you. You've probably put on a good face, posted goofy memes and remained head cheerleader for your squad. But inside? Woosh.

As can't-fake-it Jupiter joins the Capricorn crew this year, there's no need to hide behind smiley-face emojis. "Keep it real so you can heal," could be your mantra for 2020. This is as much an inside job as an outside one. The twelfth house rules all the stranger things that live in "the upside-down world" of your subconscious mind. No shame in that! But if you get overwhelmed, enlist a really great therapist, healer or shaman.

Maybe you're already waist-deep in this internal cleanup mission, Aquarius. But now that high-exposure Jupiter has joined the Sea Goat brigade, progress accelerates with serious velocity! Maybe you need to clean out a storage space and put your condo on the market, or to finally finish the last bit of paperwork that's required for your professional licensing…or your divorce. Roll up your sleeves and get to it!

Whatever you're pushing through, you don't have to do it alone. Planets in the twelfth house can send helpful "earth angels" your way. Don't worry that you're burdening them by accepting their offers of support. More likely you're helping them earn their wings! (Plus, you know you'll pay it forward when you get back on your feet.)

While there may be some turbulent moments, this "letting go" is a necessary rite of passage. In December, when both Jupiter and Saturn move on to your sign, you'll be starting a whole new 12-year (and 29.5-year) life cycle—and, well, you can't start fresh if your psychic space is cluttered with the past.

Saturn-Pluto conjunction: Tear down and rebuild.

December 2019–February 2020 (exact on January 12)

If you could invite Marie Kondo to come tidy up just one area of your life, Aquarius, what would it be? Hint: It's probably not "clothes, kitchen kimono, garage, miscellany," or any category the Japanese organizational expert ticks off on her Netflix show. No, Aquarius, when it comes to your 2020 KonMari mission, concentrate on "the big one." What's that thing that you've been too scared to look at? Is there something you haven't wanted to admit to anyone…most of all yourself? This could be on a larger order of magnitude, like the taxes you haven't filed in eight years, a relative's drinking problem, or differing views on children from the person you're madly in love with (glug).

On January 12, taskmaster Saturn makes a rare, exact conjunction to Pluto, the ruler of all things hidden, in your twelfth house of endings. Given that these two planets only meet up once every 35 years, this is a call to face down one of your most trenchant demons. It might take all year to exorcise this one, and that's fine! The point is to sweep away denial so you can get down to work.

One thing's for sure: Whatever bubbles to the surface in early 2020 has been buried in Pluto's underground vault for a long time. Saturn is the lord of time and karma, and it seems he has chosen January 12, 2020, as a due date for dealing. Before the problem creates any more "necessary breakdowns," fixer-upper Saturn pulls it into the light and helps you construct a plan of action—and one based on real-world solutions instead of magical thinking. Once you dive in, you'll kick yourself for putting this off for so long! With Saturn's sensible support, your actions will create traction. Before you know it, you'll have drafted a six-part plan for transforming this meltdown into a life-affirming lesson for all.

Warning: There may be tears and a few hysterical meltdowns along the way, especially while the Saturn-Pluto connection lingers on through February 5. But out of these confrontations, a deeper level of understanding and compassion could emerge. Instead of swilling from the poisonous vial of resentment, this is your cue to extend an olive branch. Forgiving (not forgetting) could be the healing salve.

For Aquarians who've been "doing the work" of inner exploration and spiritual healing for the past two years, the January 12 Saturn-Pluto merger could be so validating! As much as you love your metaphysical meanderings, you have an equally logical mind. You can be quick to doubt your (very real) gifts as a healer, intuitive or soulful guide. And it certainly hasn't helped matters much that Saturn, the planetary pragmatist, has been twitching uncomfortably in your mystical twelfth house since December 2017. But when prescient Pluto looks Saturn squarely in the eyes this January 12, you may see proof that your hunches and insights have been spot-on all along!

Since Saturn can guide your career and Pluto directs your soul calling, the January 12 conjunction could launch you out of the rat race and into more meaningful work. Or maybe you'll moonlight as a practitioner of a healing modality, slowly gaining confidence in your talents. Physicist by day, plant medicine shaman by night? Teacher-slash-animal communicator? You're such a fascinating blend of personas, Aquarius, and if anyone can hover between the 3D and the multidimensional realms, it's you!

Jupiter-Pluto conjunction: Embrace the esoteric.
April 4, June 30, November 12

If the Saturn-Pluto merger doesn't jolt you out of denial, here's what could: Until December 19, illuminating Jupiter will travel alongside plumb-the-depths Pluto in Capricorn and your twelfth house of healing. Three times in 2020—on April 4, June 30 and November 12—Jupiter will lift Pluto's covert veil as the two planets meet at the same degree of Capricorn. Time to fling open those closets and let the skeletons out!

This planetary pairing is truly a merging of opposites: Jupiter broadcasts every move while Pluto lurks around in the shadows. And in your twelfth house of buried secrets, some old "stuff" could be dredged up. Our advice? Don't just hold your breath and pray that the storm passes you by. Instead, abide by the words of Aquarius Franklin

Delano Roosevelt who said, "The only thing we have to fear is fear itself." Jupiter brings the courage to flip on the flashlight and reveal those monsters under the bed. Better still? Positive, proactive Jupiter will give you the can-do spirit you need to really deal.

You don't have to work out a solution right away, Aquarius. You just have to wave the white flag and admit that you need support—never easy for your proud, indie-spirited sign. But twelfth house issues tend to be bigger than what we can manage on our own—like grief, addictions, chronic illnesses, repressed emotions, loss and fear. Even if you're not in the throes of any such things (and we hope you aren't!), the people around you may be struggling. Warning: Figuring out how to bolster them through trying times could turn into a codependent minefield if you don't have your own network of advisers to lean on.

With lucky Jupiter—the planet of growth, faith and evolution—joining alchemical Pluto in your twelfth house, this can be a time of miracles if you're willing to be open to something greater than what you know. It doesn't matter what name you call that force, be it God, spirit, nature or serendipity. When you surrender control and admit that you don't have all the answers, it sends out an S.O.S. to the universe and opens the doors to abundant support. A flood of insight could come through a helpful friend, a perfect stranger or an amazing series of coincidences that unfolds in mind-blowing ways. Even the most skeptical Aquarius will have to admit: You can't make this stuff up!

There's a popular expression among 12-Steppers that states you're "only as sick as your secrets." If you're dealing with a health challenge, Jupiter and

Pluto in this ethereal sector will reveal naturopathic treatments and send you exploring the mind-body-soul connection. Forgiveness and recovery work can be fruitful while Jupiter is in this zone. This could be the year where you break free from the grips of a destructive addiction, be it smoking, overeating or people-pleasing. If you've been burying something out of fear or shame, find a therapist or spiritual counselor. Talking (and talking some more) is the way to free yourself from that prison. This very act could put you on a path to physical healing.

Some Aquarians could mourn a loss this year, but as the saying goes, you've got to feel it to heal it. While Pluto brings the courage to plumb the depths, wise Jupiter may help you find a new philosophical approach, one that comforts and strengthens you. A certain phase of life is coming to an end, and there's no more denying that. Buoyant Jupiter illuminates the bright side of this transition, turning your attention to exciting future possibilities…even as you see the past fading away.

Keep a journal on the nightstand! The twelfth house rules the subconscious, and yours could be especially active at night. You may have prophetic visions as you sleep, or dreams so vivid that you feel like you traveled astrally or were visited by an ancestor. Try this exercise: Before you get out of bed each morning, free-write about whatever is on your (groggy) mind. Your hand could start transcribing a message from your dreams (or "automatic writing"), even if you swore you couldn't remember them!

Trying to break a deep-rooted habit? Jupiter and Pluto transport you further into the archives of your subconscious mind. You'll be extra receptive to hypnotherapy and EMDR. You might even try a past-life regression or a shamanic soul retrieval if you want to do more karmic healing.

While you're generally the life of the party, let someone else pick up the entertainment director's baton in 2020. The real soiree is happening in your subconscious, and the merging of Jupiter and Pluto can bring some divinely-inspired creative downloads. You'll do your best work in a solitary spot where you can meditate and court the muse without interruption. If you share a busy household, consider renting studio space where you can develop your craft.

Plus, with all this twelfth house activity, you'll be an energy sponge! Spending too much time around people can drain you. Until Jupiter heads into Aquarius on December 19, you'll be sleepier and more introverted than usual. Avoid prolonged interaction with crowds and learn how to make cameos at parties, popping in for a brief appearance, then heading home without apology when you start to tire.

Jupiter rules learning, philosophy and entrepreneurship and with your mystical twelfth house lit, you may be guided towards the healing and esoteric arts. This could be the year where you enroll in acupuncture school, develop your gifts as a medium, or travel to Peru to work alongside a shaman. One Aquarius we know is a talented personal chef by day with a roster of celebrity clients. But his true passion lies in helping people heal from childhood trauma through a "re-parenting" process that involves talk therapy along with breathwork and somatic techniques. Another Aquarius—a former engineer—holds sacred medicine circles for men, healing the "wounded masculine" by providing a safe space for the guys to process and explore their emotions.

 The AstroTwins' 2020 Horoscope

The twelfth house is also the zone of mentors. Do your friends keep telling you that you'd make an amazing coach or therapist? During 2020's liberating cycle, you could join the expert industry, perhaps working with private clients or even developing your own self-help modality. As the planet that rules publishing, Jupiter's influence might guide you to write a book on the topic of healing. Or maybe, in the spirit of the twelfth house, you'll just channel it from an ancient deity. (What's the difference, really?) If literature's not your jam, maybe you'll film an eye-opening documentary or compose a collection of songs that are both uplifting (Jupiter) and heart-wrenching (Pluto). Genius!

Venus & Mars Retrograde: Relationship review.

Venus Retrograde: May 14 – June 25

Mars Retrograde: September 10 – November 13

There will be no shortage of birds and bees buzzing around the Aquarius hive this spring! (Along with some style bloggers and paparazzi, we're betting.) From April 3 to August 7, Venus struts through Gemini—and down the catwalk of your fifth house of romance, glamour and fame. During this four-month cycle, people will either want to date you or to imitate you. That's a lot of pull, Aquarius, and you're here for it!

The fifth house rules fertility, so if babies are part of your plan, you could be celebrating a pink line on that test stick before the summer is through. Already a parent? Plan to relive your childhood this summer, with a calendar full of adventures, like zipping down water slides or roasting marshmallows over an open campfire.

Aquarians on the hunt for new love will have exceptionally good fortune for much of this four-month phase. But there is a catch: From May 13 to June 25, Venus will dip into her biennial retrograde, dredging up the past. Single Water Bearers must guard against the urge to play Dial-an-Ex. Sure the sex was amazing, and maybe you haven't found anyone who could make you feel that way since. But if you're still nursing a wound, use this six-week backspin to process the pain and fully heal. You could be back on the dating scene (and crushing it) before Labor Day!

While Venus is reversing through Gemini, splurge a little on pampering. That weekly blowout and massage; the monthly facial...when you treat yourself like a million bucks, your confidence soars. If you're craving a more dramatic style update, like a pixie cut or a tattoo, put it on a Pinterest board until beauty queen Venus is back to her senses on June 25.

Attached Aquarians may find themselves revisiting old drama or even being lured into an outside attraction between May 13 and June 25. Even if nothing physical is happening, be honest with yourself: Are you sharing more personal intel and sexual fantasies with your super-sexy work BFF than you are with your partner? Maybe it seems easier to open up to them because you don't share a history—but they don't call it an "emotional affair" for nothing. This false intimacy can be exhilarating, at first. (Baring souls with no strings attached? Woohoo!) But it's like filling up on low-grade fuel. Instead, take the Venus retrograde challenge and plunge in deeper with your S.O. Have the awkward-but-honest conversations and figure out where your relationship started to grow dull. Did you get scared and stop being vulnerable? Give too much parental or caretaking energy to your partner, or start playing life coach? And while you can never replace the dopamine-fueled buzz of "new relationship energy," you might discover an equally delightful (and far more intimate) way to bond with your tried-and-true partner. Hint: It may involve doing things that the two of you have never tried before.

Get things out in the open with friends, neighbors and siblings starting June 27. Provocateur Mars shifts into Aries and your communication center for an extended tour, until January 6, 2021. During this time, you won't have to travel far to get your cultural activities fix. Action heats up on the local scene. You could discover a new "tribe" in your zip code or become the hub of a blossoming friend group. Bring on the craft nights, book clubs, potlucks and open-mics!

But from September 9 to November 13, good fences make happy neighbors, as Mars slips back into a tension-fueling retrograde. Friction could crackle in your crew during these eight-plus weeks, making you wonder if you're on the same page after all. A sibling, neighbor or coworker could become a source of stress; you might even find yourself rehashing an issue that you thought you buried years ago. There could be an undercurrent of competition; perhaps you've just gotten a wee bit too dependent on each other.

Your famously long fuse might appear to extend, but watch out, world! When you stuff down annoyances, pressure builds inside you like an active volcano—and your eruptions are never pretty, Aquarius. You're going to need to vent a lot more than usual while Mars is in reverse this fall.

That said, it's equally important that you choose the right sounding board! Otherwise, you could earn a reputation for being an untrustworthy gossip. Spilling tea to mutual friends or coworkers is a bad idea. And so is turning on the camera to live-drag a frenemy before you've privately processed your rage. Aquarius beauty blogger Tati Westbrook nearly broke the Internet in 2019 with a rebuttal rant to controversy-courting Cover Boy (Gemini) James Charles. Hours after news broke that Charles had sponsored one of Westbrook's hair vitamin competitors, the Aquarius turned on the studio lights, hit "Go Live" and began airing all of Charles' dirty laundry in a 40-minute YouTube.

The dramz may have boosted Westbrook's subscriber count by the millions—and Charles' account was temporarily #canceled by millions of fans. But as time passed, viewers were left with more questions than answers. Some believed Westbrook was just defending her brand, others accused her of queer-bashing. And given the significant age difference of the former besties (Westbrook was 37, Charles was 19 at the time) many felt the beauty blogger should have taken a high road. At the end of the day, she became embroiled in controversy—which, unlike a perfectly smudged cream shadow, is never a good look for the idealistic Aquarius.

Let this be a cautionary tale of what can happen when your high-minded sign becomes reactive. Your temper is like a lightning bolt that arrives in a flash and strikes suddenly. While your rage rarely lasts longer than a few moments, the long-term damage can be hard to repair. And sure, you may be "right," on all technical counts! But when you stoop to someone's low-vibe level, you lose credibility. While Mars is in Aries, you'll have to work hard to remind yourself of this: Revenge is a dish that's best left off the menu!

Don't swing to the other extreme if someone pisses you off, or try to hide behind jokes. Just give those charged relationships some breathing room before letting Mars' aggressive energy ruin an important bond. New and improved ways of compromising will emerge after November 13, but not without some protracted negotiating. Use Mars' backspin to examine your own sense of righteousness and to increase tolerance for people who have different life views than you do. You might need to issue a temporary peace treaty by agreeing to disagree—then close the subject until late November!

Saturn in Aquarius: Rebuild & refocus.

March 21–July 1
December 17, 2020–March 7, 2023

A three-year renovation project is underway—and you're the star of it! Your cosmic co-ruler, architect Saturn, darts into Aquarius and your first house of identity from March 21 to July 1, making you want to tear down everything that's not "up to code" and create a new life blueprint. But hold the cranes! This is just a preview of what's to come. On December 17, the seven-ringed general will drill through your sign for more than two years, until

March 7, 2023, signing all the permits you need to begin your build.

Saturn's entry into your sign marks the beginning of a new 29.5-year chapter of your life, and the planet of integrity has arrived to construct a solid foundation. Banish any thoughts of instant gratification and overnight success. Saturn helps you simplify and prioritize, but it won't let you take shortcuts. This disciplined overlord is all about hard work, paying dues and doing things right the first time. The last time Saturn visited your sign was from February 6, 1991, through January 28, 1994. If you're old enough to remember that era, you may see some recurring themes arise.

Before you can implement Saturn's reconstruction plans, there may be a teardown or two. Brace yourself: Old and outmoded aspects of your life will be demolished in order to raise the green towers and perma-cultured landscape of the Aquarius 2.0 empire. No cutting corners! Inspector Saturn will find every flaw in your architectural plan and demand that you bring it up to code. But in the long run, you'll be glad you did. You're the sign of the future, Aquarius, and anything you create should be powered by clean, renewable energy!

Did you get too ambitious and set an unrealistic timeline for developing your dreams? If so, Saturn could deliver a harsh wakeup call. And don't even think about trying to phone in favors so you can get this done faster. Authoritarian Saturn will lay down the law, forcing you to do the requisite training and due diligence. In the end, you'll be thankful for the boots-on-the-ground expertise that you gain. With Saturn in Aquarius from March 21 to July 1, how about enrolling in a summer program to get the first skill set under your belt?

We won't lie: Hosting Saturn in your sign can be challenging because it demands pristine levels of integrity and responsibility. For the idealistic Water Bearer, these tenets are already standard operating procedure. But Saturn's demand for structure? That's a horse of a different color. Although you're a legit wizard, you don't exactly love to work on anyone else's timeline. With clock-watcher Saturn in your sign, your free-flowing nature could feel stifled by all the due process, like scheduling phone calls, recording meeting notes…heck, even setting an official meeting to begin with! You may flounder in the beginning, but trust us, you'll get used to this, Aquarius—especially once you realize how much precious free time you were actually wasting by being so "spontaneous."

Saturn is the planet of maturity, and you could learn some major lessons in "adulting" between March and July. No more hiding behind that class clown persona or "charming" people with your devil-may-care rebel schtick. If you don't pull your weight, a job or relationship could hit the rocks. And be mindful of the company you keep. Trying to support your immature pals could cost you dearly, especially if you recommend them for roles they aren't emotionally ready to embrace. Your humanitarian sign loves to hook up a friend in need, but if you can't solidly stand behind their work (or relationship) ethic, don't get sucked into playing matchmaker!

Patience and persistence will be required in 2020, so please don't zone out just because you're not seeing instant results. You're more of the tortoise than the hare this year. Keep forging on, even if it's slower going. If you do the hard work, Saturn usually leaves you with a parting gift. The big payoff might not come until Saturn exits your sign on March 7, 2023. But if you stay humble, work alongside the pros and learn everything you can (and quickly learn from your mistakes!), you'll see gradual and cumulative shifts. You'll feel grounded and more certain of yourself. You'll rise to challenges with grace instead of doubting yourself. And you'll carry yourself with so much confidence that you'll naturally ascend to leadership.

Give the Aquarius "brand" a review while Saturn tours your first house of identity from March 21 to July 1. Inspect your social media profiles, your personal website, profile photos and other materials like your business cards or band merch. Are you presenting a clear and authentic message? You might get serious about building a personal platform, investing in video equipment for a YouTube channel, for example, or getting mentored by an industry veteran. Mastery falls under Saturn's domain, and if you're a ninja at a certain skill, you could be tapped to teach others your stealth moves. You can boost your status and credibility—as long as you put in the long hours and sweat equity to truly earn your title. This is not the time to "fake it 'til you make it."

Could grey be the new black for you in 2020? Saturn rules aging and the first house governs appearances. This year, the passage of time could show up on your body. (Sigh.) Should you embrace those random white strands and wrinkles or dabble in anti-aging treatments? Proceed with caution—and a light touch—if you choose the latter.

Your eternally youthful sign might find Saturn's presence a bit weighty at first, but odds are, you already have some clock-slowing practices in place like eating clean, daily meditations and cell-regenerating sweat sessions in the infrared sauna. If not, now would be the time to start implementing those. Bring on the rainbow bowls and Sun salutations! Saturn rules the teeth, skin, bone structure and knees, and these body parts may need special attention now. Chiropractic adjustments and massage therapy could also have a profound effect. Keep up to date on dental visits and don't forget to floss!

While hosting Saturn, your unicorn-bright style could take a turn for the simple and sophisticated. Saturn is a minimalist, and for the next few years, you may trade some of your neon layers for elegant neutrals and streamlined cuts. But Saturn will be in Aquarius, so odds are, you'll still retain elements of your outré style. For example, with this status-conscious planet playing image director, maybe you'll upgrade from thrift shops to designer consignment and get your vintage fix. Or, if you give yourself over to those timelessly elegant pieces that are crisp, tailored and bespoke, set yourself apart with bold statement accessories. If your wardrobe runneth over, you might adopt a less-is-more approach and give a bunch of nice stuff away. Clothing swap at Chateau Aqua, anyone?

> **"Big-thinking Jupiter and stabilizing Saturn give you the courage and credibility you need to leap."**

few weeks of 2020! On December 17, the ringed planet shifts back into your sign for more than two years. But you'll truly feel "in your lane" starting this December 19, when jovial Jupiter merges into Aquarius for the first time in over a decade and hangs out there until December 29, 2021.

But wait…there is more! On December 21, 2020—the winter solstice—Jupiter and Saturn will make an exact connection in the skies. This union, which astrologers call The Great Conjunction, is super-rare; in fact, it only happens once every 20 years. But it gets better: This time around, the potent planetary pairing will take place in your sign. Get ready! The power pack of big-thinking Jupiter and stabilizing Saturn gives you the courage and credibility you need to leap. Their meetup takes place at 0°29' Aquarius, a significant digit! In the major arcana of the Tarot, zero represents The Fool card, a daringly optimistic figure who is ready to leap into the realm of limitless possibilities. That's the energy you'll want to harness as you celebrate the holiday season of 2020!

So, Water Bearer, what lofty visions will you bring to life? The last time Jupiter blazed through Aquarius was from January 5, 2009, until January 17, 2010. Scroll back through your timelines. What expansions were happening in your life back then? Did you start a business, move to a new city, make some other unprecedented leap?

One of our Aquarius friends took the entrepreneurial plunge just as Jupiter entered Aquarius in early

The Great Conjunction: Jupiter & Saturn unite.

December 21

If Saturn's first pass through Aquarius doesn't evoke breakthrough shifts, just wait until the last

2009, purchasing the three-chair hair salon where she'd been a stylist for two years. The artsy area of town has seen a good deal of development since then, with high-rise apartments springing up and providing more walk-by traffic. Eleven years since re-opening, Salon Moxi is humming along so steadily that she's been able to reduce her schedule, seeing clients only three days per week. As Jupiter prepares to cycle through Aquarius again in 2020, our friend is busily engaged in a passionate side venture, turning her garden into an urban farm that provides fresh produce to the neighborhood and supplies flowers to local vendors.

These are the kinds of experimental moves you could find yourself making—or at least, considering—as Jupiter dashes into your sign. And with pragmatic Saturn in the picture this time (which was not the case back in 2009) think "scalability." Your vision could be more than a Jupiter-fueled whimsy. Next year, Saturn can help you attract investors for your big idea, perhaps through an Aquarius-style crowdfunding campaign. Or maybe you'll just create such a profitable revenue model that your idea funds itself. Bottom line? If you can dream it, you can monetize it starting December 21, 2020.

Uranus in Taurus: Put down roots?

May 15, 2018 – April 26, 2026

Ready to hang up those ruby slippers, Aquarius? Ever since your ruling planet, metamorphic Uranus, entered Taurus and your domestic fourth house on May 15, 2018, home and family have been in flux. If you didn't transplant your roots over the past couple years, you may have dealt with change (and turbulence) under your roof, like ongoing renovations, fluctuating roomies or a rebellious kid.

In 2018 and 2019, Uranus bobbed back and forth between Aries and Taurus. But this year, the side-spinning planet is securely in the bull's pen, where it will orbit until April 26, 2026. While the idea of "settling down" might not appeal over the next six years, you will start to feel more grounded about your lifestyle choices in 2020. If that means embracing a long-term house-sitting gig or giving #VanLife a go, so be it! Or, communal Uranus could plunk you down in a zip code that feels like the right home; a place where you can be actively involved in shaping the culture.

Even for your nomadic sign, this not the easiest cycle. Uranus is in "fall" in Taurus, one of its most challenging positions. Uranus is the planet of radical change, while routine-loving Taurus prefers familiarity. After two years, you are learning to negotiate these awkward energies. Uranus in Taurus is forming a square (a tense 90-degree angle) to your Sun until April 2026. This can provoke challenging situations that force you out of your comfort zone. Aquarians born between January 24 and February 1 will feel this most actively in 2020. But for all Water Bearers: Toto, you are not in Kansas anymore!

If you embrace this paradoxical push-pull, however, the next seven years could be full of adventure! One of our Aquarius friends bought his first house during this transit. To his surprise, it was located 50 miles outside of the metropolis where he'd lived and worked for over a decade. Turns out he loves this sleepy commuter town, and the expanded square footage doesn't hurt either. He just catches up on

   The AstroTwins' 2020 Horoscope

his favorite metaphysical podcasts on his drive into the big city. Another Aquarius we know has embraced nomadic co-living, giving up her solitary one-bedroom to live in a friend's guest house. And yet another Water Bearer worked through her deep resistance to the "parent trap," and is (happily!) welcoming her first child this year.

North Node in Gemini: Fame & fertility.

May 5, 2020 – January 18, 2022

While 2020's planetary action in your twelfth house can keep you under the radar, forget about disappearing into a meditation cave. On May 5, the lunar North Node—AKA "the cosmic destiny point"—heads into Gemini, and your fifth house of fame and fertility. This cycle, which lasts until January 18, 2022, is a golden era for Aquarius performers. Trot out your talents, show up at auditions, and if you're ready to hit the bigtime, think about getting yourself an agent who can rep you in the world. Or, embrace the independent media channels that were made for your autonomous sign. Set up the video camera and show 'em how it's done with YouTube tutorials and Instagram Lives.

Prefer to work your magic in subtler ways? The fifth house is visually focused. Even if you're not the face of the "brand," work with designers, photographers, even digital marketers. Whether you're going for streamlined minimalism or rainbow-bright maximalism, you want everything you produce to pop in 2020!

Got babies on the brain? Your hand could be rocking a cradle before 2020 is through. The North Node only lands in this "fertile crescent" of your solar chart every 19 years. No partner? No problem for some Water Bearers, who may feel confident enough that now is the time to procreate, even if that means starting the journey with a donor. As one of the zodiac's animal lovers, adopting a shelter pet as your "fur baby" could be just as fulfilling. Already have kids? Foster their artistic gifts or scout out some play-based or experiential learning that will help them evolve into the multidimensional beings you've always envisioned. Have Baby Björn, will travel!

Does that sound like way too much responsibility? The North Node's circuit through Gemini could birth a creative renaissance for you before January 18, 2022. But take note! The North Node represents the talents we develop rather than the ones we're born with. Forget DIY-ing your way through another irksome tutorial. Sign up for guitar lessons, private coaching or other hands-on training so you can learn from the pros.

Cancer/Capricorn Eclipses: Health is wealth.

January 10, June 21, July 5

That elusive "work-life balance" is well within your reach in 2020, as we round out a two-year series of eclipses on the Cancer/Capricorn axis. Since July 12, 2018, these transformational moonbeams have been shaking up your relationship to your career and calling for an inside-out transformation.

494

When you're devoted to a mission, you'll hustle tirelessly to achieve it. But over the last couple years, you've been learning how to "work smarter, not harder" by outsourcing, delegating and setting up systems that don't require you to mindlessly repeat those one-and-done tasks that could be handled in a few hours—or even automated.

Cancer rules your sixth house of health, fitness and day-to-day work. Capricorn is the guardian of your twelfth house of closure, spirituality and healing. During the January 10 lunar (full moon) eclipse in Cancer, you could end a drudgery-inducing aspect of your career. If there's no wiggle room to upgrade your job description, you may tender your resignation at a soul-sucking nine-to-five!

Stress reduction may be the key motivating factor here. Life is too short to be unhappy—and you don't want to fill your brief time on this planet with activities that deplete your vitality. If you keep pushing yourself, the July 5 lunar eclipse in Capricorn and your transitional twelfth house could bring a wake-up call from your body. Avoid a crash by taking measures early in 2020 to fix any time-sucking systems at work—or to polish up your resume and start circulating it.

And take heart! The June 21 solar eclipse in Cancer, which is the final one in this series, arrives on the Summer Solstice. The longest day of light could usher in fresh opportunities that support your vitality **and** your bank account! Consider it your gift for prioritizing self-care alongside your ambitions.

Gemini/Sagittarius Eclipses: Breakout star or MVP?

June 5, November 30, December 14

In 2020, you could flip between solo star and team player status as a new eclipse series ripples across the Gemini/Sagittarius axis. Gemini rules your fifth house of passion, celebrity and sweet romance. Sagittarius (Gemini's opposite sign) is the boss of your eleventh house of community, technology and the future. Should you flex your fierce independence or would it better to follow group consensus? You'll ping between poles throughout this cycle, which lasts until December 3, 2021.

> "You'll emerge stronger, savvier and more successful than you've been in years."

First up: A galvanizing lunar eclipse in Sagittarius that arrives with the June 5 full moon. This illuminating event shines a light on your entourage, and any of the #SquadGoals you're working toward. Since eclipses bring hidden things to light, you could discover a hidden gem in the ranks—or a bad apple. Move swiftly, Aquarius, whether you need to upgrade their responsibilities or sit 'em down for a "shape up or ship out" warning talk. You may need to confront some simmering group dynamics or distance yourself from a toxic clique. Your role in a group could shift from casual participant to hands-on change agent. Your activist spirit will also be fired up. If you see an injustice, you'll quickly jump into the organizer role and do everything in your power to make it right!

 The AstroTwins' 2020 Horoscope

November 30 supplies the next lunar (full moon) eclipse in the series, this time in Gemini and your heart-centered fifth house. Cupid could deliver sweet romantic surprises this holiday season, and some Aquarians could announce an engagement or pregnancy on Instagram. If a relationship's been rocky, however, it may hit the breaking point. Ultimately, any "surprises" that these eclipses reveal have probably been simmering for a while. Better to bring the truth out into the open so that you can deal and maybe get that sinking ship afloat once again.

By the time the December 14 solar (new moon) eclipse lands in Sagittarius, you'll be ready to restock your friends list with compatible new contacts. Since Sagittarius is the cross-cultural globalist, you might be recruiting from all around the world, or setting up a vast online community. Does a project need a cash infusion? Crowdfund it! ✳

January

JANUARY: LOVE HOTSPOTS

January 3-February 16: Mars in Sagittarius

Passionate Mars starts the year off in your social eleventh house, heating up this anything-goes sector until just past Valentine's Day. Single? You could meet someone through mutual friends or, with lusty Mars in your tech zone, strike up a sizzling affair through the apps. Coupled? Make an effort to get out and mingle as a duo, exploring cultural events or gathering with your crew. You might crave more autonomy during this time—but the person who gives you the longest leash will have the quickest path to your heart!

January 10: Uranus retrograde ends

A five-month period of emotional ambiguity (and even volatility) ends today as changemaker Uranus wraps up a retrograde that began August 11, 2019. With your ruling planet reversing through Taurus and your foundational fourth house, you've been up in the air about your living situation or family plans. On top of that, your moods have been all over the map. The silver lining? You've entertained quite a range of possibilities. Now, one of those "unlikely" ideas could turn out to be a very smart route to take!

January 13-February 7: Venus in Pisces

Romantic Venus snuggles up in your sensual, security-minded second house, making you crave the comfort of a sure thing. Ramp up the romance with a few sophisticated nights out, followed by a megadose of affection. Don't just rely on a partner or would-be companion to provide all your earthly pleasures. Book some massages, beauty treatments and whatever makes you feel like absolute divinity, inside and out.

January 26: Venus-Mars square

Venus in your practical second house wants something concrete, but it's at odds with lusty and libertine Mars in your independence sector. Don't make any fast moves in or out of a situation! Dueling desires for novelty and security are completely normal. The key: Can you get a dose of what you're craving without overturning a relationship?

January 27: Venus-Neptune meetup

Romance-aholic Venus unites with dreamy Neptune in your beautifying second house, making you crave luxe loving and a dose of decadence. Prioritize self-care, adorn yourself with a new accessory or outfit, spring for sumptuous new bedding. Anything to escape the mundane and dial up the sensuality gets a big green light!

JANUARY: CAREER HOTSPOTS

January 2: Mercury-Jupiter meetup

Read between the lines! With the two most expressive planets teamed up in your twelfth house of hidden agendas, clue into body language and subtle messages. Sometimes it's what they don't say that speaks volumes. Play a little mysterious today with your intel, rather than being an open book.

January 3-February 16: Mars in Sagittarius

The action planet fires up your eleventh house of teamwork and technology for the start of 2020. Be on the lookout for potential new partners in crime, either at industry networking events or through social media. An exciting collaboration could ignite, but make sure you're all on the same page before you rush in.

January 10: Cancer full moon (lunar eclipse)

Give those 2020 resolutions an edit! The year's first of two Cancer full moons—this one a potent lunar eclipse—lands in your sixth house of organization and wellness. Brew a matcha latte and orchestrate your plans for the coming year. Once you've mapped out where you want to go, choose a few small steps to implement. Declutter your workspace (in a big way!) and streamline your systems. While the eclipse illuminates this service-oriented sector, you could be struck by an undeniable urge to make a difference. Mentor someone from a disadvantaged community or spearhead a do-gooding initiative at work. Looking to change paths? Check out positions in a "green" or sustainable field.

January 12: Mercury-Saturn-Pluto meetup

You've been holding something in for long enough, Aquarius. As communicator Mercury, transformational Pluto and mature Saturn make an extremely rare convergence in your twelfth house of closure, your words could be powerful and healing. Your imagination is an engine that can produce epic ideas now. Discipline yourself and avoid distractions. That may require an uncomfortable but necessary conversation about boundaries with a few needy people who've appointed you their unofficial sounding board. But think how much time you'll free up to be creative! Saturn and Pluto only unite every 33 to 35 years, so whatever you discuss could be major!

January 13: Sun-Saturn-Pluto meetup

Step into heart-centered leadership today! As power-players Saturn and Pluto make their rare (once every three decades) union, the bold Sun turns it into a cosmic coming-out party. A creative, emotional or healing dimension within you is coming into the open—and ready or not, it's time to own that side of yourself. Today's stars might spawn a total rebirth of your identity. And with the high-profile Sun making you ready to sign autographs, you could gain visibility and stature.

January 16-February 3: Mercury in Aquarius

The cosmic messenger starts the year off in your sign, giving you an extra dash of charisma. Be bold and speak up! Others will marvel at your ability to say what no one else will. It's a great time to publicize your work, so take to social media and shamelessly self-promote. This is the first of Mercury's two trips to your sign; it will return in February after a brief retrograde.

January 18: Mercury-Uranus square

A tricky transit between mental Mercury and erratic Uranus could churn nervous energy into the mix. Too much stress might even lead to an emotional outburst. Don't push yourself past your limits. You're only human!

January 23: Sun-Uranus square

When the confident Sun in your sign faces off with radical Uranus in your moody fourth house, you might lash out at someone who's just trying to help. Slip on headphones and work independently if you can. If you absolutely have to meet with people who trigger you, set some boundaries and stick to them.

January 24: Aquarius new moon
Chinese Year of the Metal Rat

New Year's Eve may have already happened, but you get a fresh start today with the year's only new moon in your sign. It's also the Chinese Lunar New Year, ushering in the shrewd Metal Rat for the next 12 months. With all this activity in your sign, take some time to reflect on what *you* want for your next trip around the Sun. Are you ready to launch a side gig or take on some new initiatives at work? Or is it time to finally tell the world what you've been working on?

January 28: Mars-Neptune square

Motivated Mars in your zone of groups and technology quarrels with hazy Neptune in your financial zone, which could stir tension around money. Be careful about borrowing or loaning funds among friends and if you shop online, make sure you're on a well-secured site. Is someone taking advantage of your kindness? Asserting yourself can be uncomfortable, but pushovers finish last. Make your expectations clear and don't feel bad asking for another look at someone's projections or a comb-through of their work—especially if their job performance will reflect on you.

February

FEBRUARY: LOVE HOTSPOTS

February 7-March 4: Venus in Aries

Sync up with your loved ones when affectionate Venus glides into your communicative third house. Let them know how you feel—and don't be afraid to gush a little! If you need to bring up a touchy topic, the cosmos help you calm any discord. Holding a "state of the union" to talk about your relationship will be easier with gentle Venus here. Pour some wine, go out to coffee or drive somewhere nostalgic to take the edge off further. Single Aquarians could meet someone while casually hanging at a local hotspot or through shared friends. Get out there and mingle instead of hibernating. Don't you have a birthday to celebrate?

February 9: Leo full moon

Time to make it official? Today's full moon in decisive Leo beams into your seventh house of committed relationships. On the fence? Tap into these insightful moonbeams and you could see which way to go. If you're single, you may come across an enchanting soul with long-term potential. Keep your eyes (and heart) open!

February 16-March 30: Mars in Capricorn

Donning those rose-colored goggles again? Lusty Mars slides into your twelfth house of fantasy, illusion and hidden agendas for the next month-and-a-half, making temptation tough to resist. Watch for codependence or sketchy characters—along with your own tendency to project some idealized fantasy onto others. This area of your chart also rules letting go, so use it as an opportunity

The AstroTwins' 2020 Horoscope

to release any old grudges or resentments. If you're healing from heartbreak, do the hard but necessary recovery work. That might mean a strict no-contact policy until you've both moved on!

February 21: Mars-Uranus trine

Time out! Tempers could flare today when volatile Mars and rebellious Uranus clash. Emotions run high, a recipe for small issues getting blown out of proportion. That said, this might be exactly the air-clearing you need to resolve a lingering issue.

February 23: Venus-Jupiter square

Friends with benefits? Go slow with that arrangement, as risk-taker Jupiter conceals any drawbacks and tempts you to throw caution to the wind. If you're coupled, express your love boldly. Just make sure any over-the-top gestures don't come across as a ploy for praise. If you can't say it sincerely and from the heart, don't bother!

February 28: Venus-Pluto square

If you have needs, voice them. People aren't mind readers, so be clear and candid about what you want. Careful not to use your words to manipulate or give mixed messages in order to gain the upper hand. Someone may not be totally upfront about their agenda either. Don't take anything at face value today.

FEBRUARY: CAREER HOTSPOTS

February 3-March 4: Mercury in Pisces

Clever Mercury moves into your work and income house for an extended stay, due to an upcoming retrograde that begins in two weeks. Prepare for this impending backspin by getting a firm handle on your budget, spending and savings before February 16. Seek out an advisor if you feel unclear. Make sure all your coworkers are clear on their accountabilities before you send them into the field. Signing a client or inking a deal? Hurry and do it before Mercury retrograde starts. If you're on the fence, take time for due diligence and officialize in March.

February 9: Leo full moon

Are you in or are you out? Today's full moon in your seventh house of professional alliances helps you make a firm decision. Something you started at the corresponding new moon six months ago could come to fruition. If you're ready, take a burgeoning partnership to the next level. Or sign that major contract when it comes across your desk.

February 16-March 9: Mercury retrograde

Cashflow chaos? Analytical Mercury backspins through your second house of money and work until March 4, then rears into your sign, causing a few hiccups. Revisit your finances to see if you're on track with your goals. Check your statements to make sure there are no erroneous charges. Silver lining: Retrogrades favor a return to the past. If a project has accumulated dust, go back and see how you can spruce it up. And reach out to former clients or employers to see if they have any projects for you. A coffee catchup with an old colleague could end with a promising lead!

February 16-March 30: Mars in Capricorn

Conserve your power! Motivating Mars slides into your twelfth house of solitude, endings and closure until the end of March. Issues you thought you'd resolved could resurface for one last layer of healing. The red planet's drift through this sleepy section of your chart might make you feel invigorated one minute and exhausted the next. Create a nighttime routine to wind down before bed, because a sound night's sleep will help you manage this transit. Book a few bodywork sessions and, if possible, a relaxing escape outside city limits.

February 23: Pisces new moon

The renewing energies of the new moon in your financial zone will help you implement much-needed changes. For the last week, Mercury retrograde in this area of your chart has made it difficult to shift gears, but today's page-turning lunation gives you the spark to get work and money on track. Carve out time to craft new goals that are aligned with your priorities. Changes you embark on today may come to fruition by the corresponding full moon in six months.

March

MARCH: LOVE HOTSPOTS

March 3: Venus-Saturn square

Are you hiding parts of yourself around someone you really like? If you don't feel like you can bring your full personality to a relationship, examine whether it's insecurity—or do they just not "get" you? As Venus in your self-worth sector stares down restrictive Saturn, review your partnerships to see if they're fulfilling your needs.

March 4-April 3: Venus in Taurus

Open your heart—and your home. Affectionate Venus dives into your domestic realm, making you want to cozy up at Chateau Aquarius with someone special. Since this area of your chart rules family,

you might talk about moving in together or even broach the topic of kids. Single? Invest your energy into self-care. Skip those lavish brunches and nights on the town if you're not feeling up for it. Adopt a slow and gentle pace and watch your radiance return.

March 8: Venus-Uranus meetup

Romantic Venus and unpredictable Uranus align in your touchy-feely fourth house today. Emotions you've bottled up could spontaneously erupt. It will be hard to hold much back under these sensitive skies. At least people will know where you stand!

March 9: Virgo full moon

The year's only full moon in Virgo illuminates your eighth house of merging and seduction. If you've been on the fence about a union, clarity could arrive. Intense emotions you've been harboring can come to light. There's not much gray area happening now. You're either in or you're out!

March 23: Mars-Pluto meetup

Who knew you were feeling like that, Aquarius? As lusty Mars and alchemical Pluto unite in your twelfth house of fantasy, a few consensual power games could be mind-blowingly hot. Explore a taboo or act out a desire you've kept under wraps.

March 27: Venus-Jupiter trine

Outspoken Jupiter and loving Venus sync in the most sentimental parts of your chart. A soulful connection could reach unexpected depths. Take a chance and open up about your feelings. If you're looking for love, be vulnerable, and make it safe for others to do the same. You might meet someone and bond quickly as the "benefics" (positive, helpful planets) join forces.

 The AstroTwins' 2020 Horoscope

March 28: Venus-Pluto trine

Transformational Pluto in your hidden twelfth house could ignite a sexy secret or trigger a seismic shift. Its harmonious alignment with amorous Venus helps you connect with an open heart. Conversations might take an unexpectedly deep turn, and your perceptive demeanor could attract a like-minded partner. Follow your intuition keenly.

March 30-May 13: Mars in Aquarius

It's getting hot in here! The red planet blasts through your sign for the first time in two years, bringing passion and fire. Your charisma is off the charts, and your confident swagger draws admirers with little effort. Rekindle the flames if your current relationship has gotten a tad predictable. Solo Aquarians: be proactive and present in your daily life and you could meet someone new. Make the most of this amorous transit, because it won't happen again until 2022.

March 31: Mars-Saturn meetup

Reckless Mars and structured Saturn meet up in your sign, messing up the tempo. You might be torn between forging ahead or taking it slow. Press pause if you can, and take a moment to get to the bottom of your conflicting desires.

MARCH: CAREER HOTSPOTS

March 4-16: Mercury in Aquarius

You're especially eloquent this month as the messenger planet flits through your sign for the second time this year. Speak up in meetings and introduce yourself to power-players in your field. Take to social media to promote your latest projects and achievements. Or give people a behind-the-scenes look at the process. You have the gift of gab, so use it!

March 9: Virgo full moon

The year's only Virgo full moon lands in your fiscal eighth house and shines a light on shared resources and investments. A real estate deal or legal settlement could also come through. Is your money working hard enough for you? Meticulous Virgo helps you plan a portfolio that will carry you into the future. If you share resources with a significant other or business partner, review everything to make sure it's as equitable as possible.

March 16-April 10: Mercury in Pisces

Astute Mercury returns to Pisces and your financial zone for a second (retrograde-free) trip this year. Plans that were interrupted by the messenger planet's backspin from February 16 to March 9 are ready to be unfurled now. Remedy anything that went awry and pull in experts as needed. Mercury the scribe encourages good record-keeping. If you're trying to get a better handle on your budget, write down what you spend in a day or track it with an app. Your findings could be eye-opening.

March 20: Mars-Jupiter meetup

Assertive Mars pairs up with adventurous Jupiter, supercharging your goals and plans. Both planets are in the area of your chart that rules closure and transitions. Is it time to walk away from an unsatisfying gig? This cosmic combo emboldens you to pursue a creative or healing path. Fortune favors the brave!

March 21-July 1: Saturn in Aquarius

Your reinvention tour begins today as Saturn returns to your sign for the first time since 1993. The planet of wisdom and expertise launches a new 29-year cycle in your life. The next three years will be a time of major growth. The taskmaster planet can be a strict teacher, but whatever you're working on will serve you for the long haul.

March 23: Mars-Pluto meetup

A volatile Mars-Pluto conjunction lands in your twelfth house of hidden agendas, an alignment that only happens every two years. Manipulation could run rampant, so watch out for anyone who tries to use shady tactics to get what they want. You'll have to interrupt their agenda strategically. While aggressive Mars wants to call them out immediately, Pluto suggests more calculating tactics. You may not actually know who you're dealing with—and burning bridges wouldn't be wise.

March 24: Aries new moon

Today's Aries new moon illuminates your expressive third house, helping you launch new projects or partnerships. A brainstorming session could blossom into a big endeavor over the next six months. Write down your ideas and explore any that seem promising.

March 30-May 13: Mars in Aquarius

Energizer Mars visits your sign for the first time in two years, bringing a burst of confidence and enthusiasm. Over the next couple months, you've got license to shamelessly self-promote! Not that you'll have to; dynamic Mars will draw plenty of attention your way. Take to social media to crow about your latest undertaking. Your enthusiasm is contagious! Just keep the red planet's combative urges in check. You can tap into your confidence without devolving into cockiness. This courageous transit is perfect for launching a bold project with your stamp all over it!

March 31: Mars-Saturn meetup

But wait…not so fast! Hasty Mars, which just entered Aquarius yesterday, crashes into heedful Saturn, who's also in your sign. The effect is like having one foot on the gas and the other slamming on the brake. To avoid whiplash, slow down a little. You might be ready to sign on to a major project based on instincts alone, but unflinching Saturn demands due diligence. Take a week to set up a solid master plan before you go launching into the stratosphere.

April

APRIL: LOVE HOTSPOTS

April 3-August 7: Venus in Gemini

Love abounds as amorous Venus traipses into your passionate fifth house. Revel in a new romance and wear your heart on your sleeve. Let go of any need to control the situation and just enjoy yourself! This pleasure-filled transit is all about relishing the moment. Couples should make a dedicated effort to add more glamour and joy into your relationship.

April 4: Venus-Saturn trine

Ready for a long-term love affair? As weighty Saturn forms a fortuitous alignment to Venus in your romance sector, you want to connect with someone who matches your level of commitment. A lighthearted romance could move into serious terrain. Attached Aquarians might make a gesture of devotion, whether expressed through a meaningful gift or authentic words.

The AstroTwins' 2020 Horoscope

April 4: Jupiter-Pluto meetup

Letting go is hard to do, but as adventurous Jupiter and transformational Pluto unite in your twelfth house of healing and transitions, you see the power of forgiveness in a huge way. You could meet a soulmate or "twin flame" who sweeps into your world and completely changes your view. If you're ending a relationship, you'll find ways to "consciously uncouple" that empower you both. This rare alignment will happen again on June 30 and November 12.

April 22: Taurus new moon

Home is where your heart is as the Taurus new moon sheds light on your domestic zone. Nostalgia and bonding are the order of the day. This lunation could bring shifts to your living situation, such as a new address or a roommate. For couples, talk may turn to key exchanges, family planning or buying property.

April 25-October 4: Pluto retrograde in Capricorn

Transformational Pluto backspins through your twelfth house of healing and closure for the next five months. Pluto makes this same reversal each year, so use this time to deal with any uncomfortable emotions that arise. If you've been focusing on other people's growth and ignoring your own, start cleaning up your side of the street. Work with a professional if you need a little guidance during this transit.

April 26: Sun-Uranus meetup

Emotional power surge alert! As the ego-driven Sun and volatile Uranus conjoin in your sensitive fourth house, you could be particularly thin-skinned. Watch those knee-jerk reactions, as this combo makes you prone to taking things personally.

April 27-May 11: Mercury in Taurus

Talking about your feelings is healthy! For the next couple weeks, communicative Mercury moves through your emotional fourth house. You'll have a much easier time verbalizing your emotions. It's a great opportunity to discuss your living situation, family and any sensitive topics that need to be addressed.

APRIL: CAREER HOTSPOTS

April 3: Mercury-Neptune meetup

Retail therapy could be a temporary fix under today's tantalizing transit—and one that has lasting consequences. Every deal isn't a deal if you blow your budget. Come up with creative ways to indulge—or make sure there's a liberal return policy if you feel the urge to splurge.

April 7: Libra full moon

The Libra full moon lands in your adventurous ninth house, giving you permission to forge a new path. Your sign is naturally innovative and visionary, so use this lunation to tap into trailblazing ideas and concepts. Since this area of your chart rules travel and higher education, look for workshops or retreats in a far-flung locale. Not all learning needs to occur in the classroom. Hello, beachside leadership training!

April 7: Mars-Uranus square

When assertive Mars and rebellious Uranus butt heads, you could be tempted to lash out. If it's not constructive, keep it to yourself. Otherwise you run the risk of derailing the project and irritating your collaborators. You may be especially thin-skinned today so watch your reactions.

April 10-27: Mercury in Aries

Inquisitive Mercury in your mental third house can help you get to the bottom of a lingering issue. If you felt stymied before, it's time to view this from another angle. Too close to the problem? Ask your trusted confidantes to help you figure it out. You're almost there!

April 14: Sun-Pluto square

If a snake oil seller comes knocking, don't buy what they're peddling! Today's shadowy starmap could bring some unsavory characters into your orbit. Don't fall for their empty promises! Safeguard your resources: If someone took credit for your hard work, speak up. Hold off on posting anything that could be seen as inflammatory today. Your words can get twisted out of context.

April 15: Sun-Jupiter square

Someone could be saying all the right things, but are they actually following through? Look at their actions instead of just listening to their script. Pay attention to body language and other subtle cues that will reveal whether someone is legit, or just trying to pull one over on you.

April 21: Sun-Saturn square

With cautious Saturn straining against the confident Sun, try not to be a totally open book. You don't have to be secretive or withholding, but today, saying less is best. A trustworthy colleague could help you navigate this, so speak with them in private.

April 25: Mercury square Jupiter & Pluto

Keep your innermost thoughts to yourself, as a clash between Mercury, Jupiter and Pluto could make even the most well-intentioned words come out wrong. Same goes for social media, where innocently venting about work could be picked up by an unintended audience. Fly below the radar for now.

April 28: Mercury-Saturn square

There's a difference between hating your job and hating some of the things you have to do at your job. You might not love all of your responsibilities equally, but that's okay. With cerebral Mercury squaring structured Saturn in your sign, it can be hard to muster enthusiasm. Dig in anyway and stay open for important lessons.

April 30: Mercury-Uranus meetup

The annual meetup between intellectual Mercury and innovative Uranus delivers a flash of insight. With these two brilliant planets aligning in your emotional fourth house, tap into your intuition and emotions. You might just strike on a golden idea.

May

MAY: LOVE HOTSPOTS

May 3: Venus-Neptune square

Amorous Venus is at odds with dreamy Neptune, blurring the line between fantasy and reality. Let yourself revel in the reveries. Just leave a trail of breadcrumbs so you know how to get back. This transit will repeat again on May 20 when Venus is retrograde. If you've swept something important under the proverbial Persian rug, you'll certainly find out by then.

May 11-28: Mercury in Gemini

Chatty Mercury raises the temperatures in your romantic fifth house, setting off a sultry spring. Casual conversations can bloom into a real connection. If you're attached, charm your S.O. with gifts and meaningful expressions of affection. A few tantalizing text messages can bring playful energy back into the mix.

May 13-June 27: Mars in Pisces

Reliable romance is your jam when lusty Mars moves into your stability-minded second house. Dependable doesn't have to be boring! In fact, it dovetails nicely with trustworthiness, which is key to a good relationship. Self-assured Mars ramps up your confidence levels, which can attract a crop of respectful admirers. Since this area of your chart rules money and work, watch out for any external stressors that could impact your relationship. Sparks may fly with a coworker or someone you meet at an industry event.

May 13-June 25: Venus retrograde in Gemini

Trouble in paradise? Vixen Venus backspins through your passionate fifth house for six weeks, which could stir up drama or give you second thoughts about a budding love affair. Has a romance been racing along at warp speed? Slow down and focus on deepening your connection. A breakup or heart-healing period might be part of this cycle. If so, ramp up the self-care to keep tempestuous emotions in check. Since retrogrades bring up the past, don't be surprised if an ex reaches out. Revisit with caution but keep an open mind. The second (or third) time around could be the charm. Just don't overlook any red flags if they pop up.

May 14-September 12: Jupiter retrograde in Capricorn

Jupiter makes its annual four-month backspin, reversing through your twelfth house of healing and closure. Deal with any unresolved hurt and resentment, as this is a powerful time to do forgiveness work. Address outstanding issues or let go of what's not serving you. Try to see the bigger opportunity: Is holding a grudge really hurting anyone but you?

May 22: Mercury-Venus meetup

When expressive Mercury and romantic Venus rendezvous, you'll be able to clearly articulate how you feel. It's possible you've been keeping these emotions inside for a while. Be mindful about your delivery, omitting the blame and shame. Ask for what you need and be upfront about why it's important to you. Your partner or love interest will admire your honesty.

May 22: Gemini new moon

This year's only new moon in your amorous fifth house sets your passions ablaze. You could share a desire or cop to an attraction (finally!). Single Aquarians can set intentions for the kind of romantic partner you want to attract. Between now and the Gemini full moon in November (a potent eclipse), you've got a powerful period for turning that into reality. Feeling more frumpy than flirty? Revamp your style under these bold beams, adding glamorous statement pieces or a fresh head of highlights.

MAY: CAREER HOTSPOTS

May 7: Scorpio full moon

The year's only Scorpio full moon in your career corner supercharges your ambitions and could bring a project you've been working on to completion. What do you need to push this past the finish line? Lean in today and get 'er done. Once you've arrived, take some time to celebrate! Finishing this endeavor gives you the space to think about what's next.

May 9: Mercury-Pluto trine

Dial down distractions and tap into your intuition today. Under a cooperative mashup of mental Mercury and deep-diving Pluto, important messages can flood in. Quiet your spinning thoughts with a guided meditation and you'll gain clarity on an outstanding issue. Your dreams can also be revealing. Wind down early, turn off your phone, and let your subconscious have its say.

May 10: Mercury-Jupiter trine

You won't need to shout to be heard today. Jupiter's expansive influence may prioritize larger-than-life ideas and personalities, but authenticity will prevail. Keep your message genuine and down-to-earth, and you'll attract heart-centered collaborators who resonate with your approach.

May 11-September 29: Saturn retrograde

Did you bite off more than you can chew? Structured Saturn turns retrograde today, reverse commuting through your sign until July 1, then backing into your twelfth house of closure and transitions. If you've been moving too quickly on a new phase of your life, pause to assess and correct course.

Evaluate your commitment: How much additional time, energy and resources are you willing to pour into this? Maybe there's a more efficient and economical way to reach the same goal. Take your time during the cosmic taskmaster's tricky transit. Warning: Your self-esteem may hit a rocky period, so do things to bolster your confidence. Working one-on-one with a coach or mentor can keep you on a positive path.

May 11-28: Mercury in Gemini

Innovation is your sign's superpower, and it's highly sought after these next few weeks! Whip-smart Mercury in your impassioned fifth house fires up your creativity. Keep a notebook with you at all times (even on your nightstand) to capture any bright ideas. Make a point of speaking up more during this expressive transit.

May 11: Mercury-Mars square

Count to ten! As aggressive Mars in your sign clashes with expressive Mercury, you might feel tempted to put someone in their place. Don't take the bait or succumb to their antagonistic ways. Even if you're right, everyone loses when this gets blown out of proportion.

May 12: Mercury-Saturn trine

With clever Mercury in your creativity zone, you've got no shortage of ideas. But do any of them have staying power? Today, as Mercury forms a fortuitous angle to structured Saturn in your sign, one concept could emerge as a winner. In fact, it might even put you on the map as an expert or innovator. What would it take to make this vision a reality? Flesh out a timeline and a list of resources to see how viable it really is. If this is a proprietary idea, consider trademarking or copyrighting.

The AstroTwins' 2020 Horoscope

May 13-June 27: Mars in Pisces

Energetic Mars fires up your work and money zone, lending you drive and dynamism for the next several weeks. Pursue a plum new account or pour some of this exuberance into a project that will put your name on the map. You might decide to attack your financial goals a little more aggressively. If you find your plate piled high with more work than you know what to do with, delegate tasks and bring helpers into the fold.

May 15: Sun-Pluto trine

Trust your intuition today. With the bold Sun and persuasive Pluto in the most tuned-in sectors of your chart, your emotions are a reliable GPS. Your ability to read how people are feeling could help you understand their motives—and strike with precise timing if you need to seal a deal!

May 22: Mercury-Neptune square

Some days, it's just better to stay silent. Eloquent Mercury is at odds with nebulous Neptune, and things aren't what they seem. Your judgment might be fogged by false reports or emotionally charged circumstances. Hold off on making any decisions and get all the information you need to clear up confusion in a day or two.

May 28-August 4: Mercury in Cancer

The cosmic messenger starts a protracted journey through your analytical sixth house, lengthened by a retrograde from June 18 to July 12. Use this extended transit as an opportunity to overhaul your communications. How could you be more efficient in your workflow? Implement a new way to get closer to "inbox zero" or road-test a few hacks that reduce stress. Small shifts are the name of the game, as this area of your chart rules daily habits. You might even look at where your correspondences could use a polish. Update your e-mail signature and clean up your social media feeds! You'll have until August to chip away at these endeavors.

June

JUNE: LOVE HOTSPOTS

June 2: Venus-Mars square

Feeling on edge? Tension builds as passionate Mars clashes with romantic Venus, which is retrograde in your romance house. Before you respond, take a pause to figure out what's really bugging you. If someone pushed your buttons, your reaction might signal that you're not as grounded as you could be.

June 13: Mars-Neptune meetup

An over-the-top luxurious date night is in order as sexy Mars and enchanting Neptune unite in your sophisticated second house. Express your adoration with a special gift or tickets to a show your partner will love. Single? Activate your senses. Dress up and head to a chic rooftop bar or go hear some live music. When you're enjoying the moment to the fullest, your love light really shines.

June 27, 2020-January 6, 2021: Mars in Aries

Intensifier Mars lands in your communicative third house, making a long trek that will last for the rest of the year. This extended visit from the lusty red planet could ignite steamy conversations—and a few heated arguments. Confidently tell your S.O. or your new person of interest what turns you on (and off). Flirty banter with a stranger might turn into something more serious. But you'll require a high level of intellect and wit to stay interested. Not there? Keep it moving! Variety is the spice of life during the second half of 2020.

June 30: Jupiter-Pluto meetup

Soulmate encounter or spiritual lesson? The second of this year's three rare Jupiter-Pluto conjunctions ripples into your twelfth house of fantasy and closure. This round, both planets are retrograde, a time to deeply reflect on a key relationship—or an attachment you can't seem to release. What emotional purpose is it serving in your life? Dig deep, because the answer could be in a blind spot. Look back to the first alignment on April 4 for clues. The final Jupiter-Pluto meetup on November 12 brings the resolution you're seeking.

JUNE: CAREER HOTSPOTS

June 5: Sagittarius full moon (lunar eclipse)

Welcome to collaboration nation! The lunar (full moon) eclipse sends a jolt of energy through your teamwork and technology sector today. A group endeavor you've been working on could finally come to life. Take to social media to tell your networks about what you've accomplished.

June 13: Mars-Neptune meetup

Enterprising Mars hosts its biennial meet up with ethereal Neptune in your work and money zone, giving your dreams a dash of practical magic. What do you want to achieve by this time next year? It might be more feasible than you thought! Come up with a rough outline of how to pull it off. Creative visualization will help you see the possibilities. Then you'll need to implement new tactics—and take action on them!

June 18-July 12: Mercury retrograde in Cancer

As Mercury turns backward in your systematic sixth house, you've got three weeks to declutter, streamline and really get clear on your priorities. Back up your electronic devices and make sure all of your plans are locked and loaded. If you're giving instructions to an employee or service provider, spell things out to the most minute detail, even if that seems "extra." An ounce of prevention is worth a pound of cure! Instead of starting a big new venture, go back to any current ones to finalize outstanding issues and tie up loose ends. Manage stress by not multitasking or taking on more than you can humanly handle.

June 21: Cancer new moon (annular solar eclipse)

Get your plans in motion! Today brings the first of two back-to-back Cancer new moons, and this one is a galvanizing solar eclipse. With these bold beams in your organized, health-conscious sixth house, you're motivated to put a realistic plan behind your big ideas. Start with a slow and methodical approach, especially since Mercury is retrograde. Break this major endeavor into phases, which will make everything seem more manageable. If your job is sedentary and stress is high, make regular exercise and healthy eating a non-negotiable factor.

June 23-November 28: Neptune retrograde in Pisces

Mind your money as nebulous Neptune swims through your financial house during its annual five-month retrograde. This transit could clear up murky waters, helping you see your finances with more neutrality. Revisit your budget and make sure you're not funneling hard-earned cash into questionable investments. Aim for clarity with colleagues and collaborators as well, ensuring you're all on the same page.

June 27, 2020-January 6, 2021: Mars in Aries

Speak words to power! As make-it-happen Mars lands in your communication zone for the rest of the year, your ideas can move mountains. Writing, media and teaching are especially favored. Caveat: The red planet is here for an extended trip because it will turn retrograde from September 9 to November 13. Use that time to polish your plans instead of presenting them to the world. By the end of 2020, you could be ready to announce a big launch or team up with a kindred spirit on a totally original idea.

July

JULY: LOVE HOTSPOTS

July 1-December 17: Saturn retrograde enters Capricorn

Saturn continues its backward trajectory that began on May 11, reversing from your sign into Capricorn and your twelfth house of rest, closure and healing. You might find yourself up against a similar relationship pattern you thought you already dealt with. Saturn's longer tour through Capricorn, from December 2017 until March 2020, was an important transitional period. It wasn't easy, but it helped you release parts of your life that no longer served you. During this final lap, check your boundaries and deal with any addictive or codependent dynamics in your relationships. Saturn returns to Aquarius in December, and

won't be back in Capricorn for nearly 30 years. Now's the time to confront this head-on. Work with a therapist or in a structured program for ongoing support if need be. No shame, Aquarius—we can't see our own blind spots!

July 5: Capricorn full moon (lunar eclipse)

Change sweeps through your twelfth house of transitions and endings, as a full moon lunar eclipse sounds the call for surrender. A soulmate could appear out of the blue, or you may finally get the irrepressible urge to end a relationship that's run its course. Hard as it is, sometimes you have to say goodbye to what's not working in order to call in what you want. Free up some space! For committed couples, this is a powerful moment to release resentment and forgive—or to humble yourself and apologize.

July 27: Venus-Neptune square

The world looks so romantic through those rose-colored specs. But are you hoisting someone onto a pedestal they haven't earned? Enjoy the dreamy rush, but remember, even the most skillful lover (or would-be partner) is still a mere mortal like the rest of us. If you've been sweeping an inconvenient truth under the rug, today's cosmic clash could deliver a wakeup call.

JULY: CAREER HOTSPOTS

July 1-December 17: Saturn retrograde enters Capricorn

Head back to the drawing board when structured Saturn backs out of Aquarius and enters your twelfth house of rest and closure for a final lap. If you've been burning the candle at both ends, it's time to slow down. From now until December, you can't ignore your wellbeing in the name of productivity. Prioritize a good night's sleep. Hydrate, exercise and eat well. You might prefer staying in or sticking to intimate gatherings. All this time and space could summon the muse, so get creative when she calls!

July 8: Mercury-Mars square

Overthinking alert! With mental Mercury in your analytical sixth house, you could get caught up in minutia and lose sight of the greater mission. Today, Mercury butts heads with passionate Mars in your sign, a reminder to reconnect with that burning desire in your soul. On the other hand, if your exciting ideas are lacking a proper plan, press pause to streamline. Maybe you need to start with a simpler, scaled-down version to test the waters. This transit will repeat on July 27, when Mercury will no longer be retrograde. Think it through between now and then.

July 12: Sun-Neptune trine

Does your workspace need an upgrade? If you're feeling uninspired, add some personal touches to motivate and uplift you throughout the day. Buy fresh flowers on your way into work or a potted plant for some greenery. A lunchtime walk with sunshine and fresh air is great for energy and renewing focus. Don't underestimate the power (and necessity) of beauty to spark creativity.

July 15: Sun-Pluto opposition

Are you in over your head? Instead of missing deadlines and pushing yourself to the brink of burnout, go back to your boss, client or team to reset the expectations. Ask for help and delegate if you can. Don't allow an unconscious fear of "getting in trouble" turn you into a martyr. Just be honest and keep it simple—then deliver on your new promise

like a champion! If you're navigating an unspoken power struggle or dealing with a bully, remove yourself from their line of fire by quietly refusing to engage. When you don't feed the monster, it looks for sustenance elsewhere.

July 20: Cancer new moon

The second Cancer new moon of the year helps you organize and prioritize. Look back to what happened a month ago at the June 21 Cancer solar eclipse. Did you start a new project or make plans that got sidelined? Mercury was retrograde for the first of these two lunar events, which could have thrown an annoying curveball into the mix. Today you get another chance to implement new systems. Create a timeline and break your goals into bite-sized and actionable tasks. Where can you make a little bit of progress each day? Start there.

July 20: Sun-Saturn opposition

Reminder: Membership on Team Aquarius is a privilege, not a right. As the Sun makes its sobering annual faceoff with harsh Saturn in your hidden agendas zone, someone's loyalty could be in question. Maybe you've allowed a saboteur to slip through the cracks, or a once-reliable person has started to take advantage of your kindness. Crack the whip on the under-performers and implement new standards. Let people earn your trust and respect. Wait to divulge private information until you're sure of someone's character.

July 30: Mercury-Jupiter opposition

Is a manipulative person hovering in your midst? An offer that sounds too good to be true probably is. You might get pulled onto a big project only to find that the timeline and budget are highly unrealistic. Say something, even if you're the unpopular voice.

Better to blow the whistle now and save yourself some precious time and energy. Others might be relieved you had the courage to call it. And even if they aren't, speak up anyway.

July 30: Mercury-Neptune trine

The cosmic messenger and intuitive Neptune team up for a productive day! With Neptune's creativity and Mercury's intellectual savvy, you'll see all sides of an issue. If you're pitching or presenting a proposal, find the balance between fact and feeling. It's okay to emotionally persuade your audience, as long as you have the stats to back it up.

August

AUGUST: LOVE HOTSPOTS

August 4-19: Mercury in Leo

When mindful Mercury dips into your relationship-oriented seventh house, you'll want to connect via conversation. Sit down with your S.O. for a "state of the union." If you've been arguing, lay down your swords and make peace! Plan a date where you don't have to rush through dinner and can just catch up about your shared interests and desires. If you're single, have a casual coffee with that cutie and see how the discussion flows. Instead of rushing into serious subjects, remember that lighthearted banter can pave the way for bigger talks.

August 7-September 6: Venus in Cancer

Turn up your glow! As radiant Venus cruises into your wellness sector, self-care is your strategy for good lovin' now. A solid night's sleep, lots of hydration and a proper diet can boost your magnetism. Treat your body like a temple and others will have to follow suit. You might even inspire the object of your affections to join you for a healthy eating kick or a new workout routine. Show that you care by being of service and having each other's backs. Allow yourself to receive support—and give it generously to the ones you love.

August 15, 2020-January 14, 2021: Uranus retrograde in Taurus

Mood management alert! Irascible Uranus makes its annual five-month pivot, disrupting your fourth house of home, family and emotional foundations until January 2021. During this time your feelings could fluctuate wildly. It can be hard to find your balance. Ramp up your self-care and consider returning to an old practice (yoga, meditation) to keep yourself grounded.

August 18: Leo new moon

The year's only new moon in your commitment zone powers up your relationships. Ready to make things official with the person you're casually dating? A partner might want to talk about next steps. See how things unfold in the next two weeks. New moons can take up to six months to fully manifest. Someone you meet near this date may turn out to have long-term "keeper" potential.

August 19-September 5: Mercury in Virgo

Desires on fire! Expressive Mercury slides into your seduction sphere, spicing up your pillow talk. An air of mystery could permeate your conversations, but the intrigue is oh-so enticing! If you've been holding your cards close, experiment with being vulnerable. Sharing a bit of confidence will show you whether someone is trustworthy or not.

August 25: Venus-Jupiter opposition

Test the waters before you dive into the deep end. It's tempting to plunge, but magnifying Jupiter in your foggy twelfth house could make it hard to see the situation clearly. Can you enjoy the feeling of being swept off your feet while still keeping at least a couple toes on terra firma? It's a fine balance but staying calm will reveal if this partnership has long-term potential. If you're in a relationship, resist the urge to try to "fix" every problem in one fell swoop. Think twice before you bring up a laundry list of issues.

August 27: Venus-Neptune trine

Ask not what your partner can do for you, but how you can serve your partner! Today's compassionate connection brings you closer through loving and thoughtful gestures. Simple acts of generosity can be the glue in a relationship. Single? You may meet someone through healthy or do-gooding pursuits with a glamorous twist. RSVP "yes" to any late-summer benefit parties or host a little end-of-season cocktail fundraiser yourself.

August 30: Venus-Pluto opposition

When transformative Pluto in your intense twelfth house opposes romantic Venus, it could raise some issues that need healing. If your S.O. irritates you with an offhand comment or an irksome habit, know that something deeper is being triggered here. Pause and examine that before you lash out. This may not be about the other person at all! Control issues can flare today. Remember that micromanaging your mate never ends well.

AUGUST: CAREER HOTSPOTS

August 1: Mercury-Pluto opposition

Fact or fear? It could be hard to discern whether you're being paranoid today, as inquisitive Mercury's opposition to shady Pluto sparks your suspicions. The cosmic messenger is in your fact-finding sixth house, while Pluto is transiting your twelfth house of hidden agendas. Go ahead and play detective, but don't rush to conclusions without gathering all the intel.

August 2: Sun-Uranus square

Someone's moodiness could cause you to walk on eggshells today as the self-centered Sun clashes with rebellious Uranus. At work, careful not to let a colleague zap your energy with drama. Tension from the home front could interrupt productivity. Let loved ones know you're busy—and turn off notifications if they don't respect your boundaries.

August 3: Aquarius full moon

Today's full moon lands in your sign, encouraging you to go for the gold! Something you've been toiling away at for the last six months could come to completion in the next two weeks. Celebrate accordingly, but don't rest on your laurels. You've got more exciting schemes to come!

August 3: Mercury-Saturn opposition

With Mercury opposing authoritative Saturn, people flock to you for guidance. But you could lose hours of productivity if you play resident problem-solver. Reserve your time and energy for your own work first. Let people find the answers on their own before you jump in for the save.

August 4: Mars-Jupiter square

Heroic Mars and can-do Jupiter have you ready to tackle a big problem. But are your efforts really helping? Take a step back and let others pitch in. Sure, it might seem easier just to fix this solo—and you don't want too many cooks in the kitchen. But be willing to wave the white flag before wasting your day on an impossible mission. Careful not to take the bait if someone tries to push your buttons today. You could lose your temper and create a big mess to clean up.

August 4-19: Mercury in Leo

Ready to make this official? Negotiator Mercury graces your partnership sector, helping you broker a mutually beneficial agreement. Come to the table with the intention of crafting a win-win for all parties. That way, you'll be open to compromise, knowing that you want what's best for everyone.

August 10: Mercury-Uranus square

It will be hard to keep emotions out of your speaking today, as volatile Uranus clashes with talkative Mercury. Calm yourself before you overreact and waste hours on a senseless argument. Avoid colleagues who provoke you. It's tempting to respond, but that energy is better directed into self-care or quality time with loved ones.

August 13: Mars-Pluto square

Progress could stall on a project today, as power-hungry Mars and Pluto clash. Is someone withholding key information? Table the discussion to give them time to come forward.

August 17: Mercury-Mars trine

Team up for the win! An exciting meeting of the minds could plant the seeds for partnering on a creative project. If you've been out of sync with a colleague, make amends. Eloquent Mercury and straight-talking Mars are aligned in articulate air signs, making connection much easier. Be upfront about what hasn't been working and what you'll need to move forward. A positive outcome is closer than you think!

August 18: Leo new moon

Today's new moon in your partnership house could kick off a thriving collaboration. Someone on your contact list may turn out to be your ideal collaborator. Reach out and explore! Have you been so busy that you haven't invested in your professional relationships? Set up a few coffee dates for next month, when everyone's back from summer getaways.

August 19-September 5: Mercury in Virgo

Is your money working hard enough for you? Schedule a check-in with a financial advisor while logical Mercury visits your eighth house of shared finances and assets. See this person as a co-pilot but stay at the helm of your ship. You get to make the calls here, so retain control of your investments and decisions. That said, this person's expertise may be wildly beneficial—helping you save and invest.

August 24: Mars-Saturn square

Watch out for trouble as impetuous Mars confronts steely Saturn. If you cut corners or talk out of turn, the combination of these two temperamental planets could bring a swift backlash. Play it safe today. Take diligent notes and don't skip any details. If you sense that someone's being vague with their answers, press until you get a satisfactory response.

August 25: Mercury-Uranus trine

Your intuition is on fire today, as Mercury and Uranus align in a harmonious union. Follow your ideas and find the stats you need to back them up. Paired with your persuasive powers, you'll be unstoppable! Practice your uncanny ability to identify a client or colleague's needs, articulating what they want in a way that makes them feel heard.

August 29: Mercury-Jupiter trine

The harshest critics can be lured onto your team under today's magnetic planetary alignment. With intellectual Mercury and lucky Jupiter connecting, you can connect the dots and show people how working together will help everyone win. Be the visionary leader that you are!

August 30: Mercury-Neptune opposition

Money and shared responsibilities might seem murky when Mercury and Neptune lock into an opposition. It's okay to triple-check the numbers under this hazy transit. Does everything add up? And is it an equitable arrangement? A direct discussion can get all your collaborators on the same page.

September

SEPTEMBER: LOVE HOTSPOTS

September 2: Venus-Saturn opposition

The smallest squalls could knock you off your feet today, as rigid Saturn skirmishes with tender Venus in your finicky sixth house. Don't go near any "small" issues if you can help it. This tenuous transit might make you feel like clapping back at naysayers. Is it really worth your energy? Save your breath!

September 3: Mercury-Saturn trine

Take those gut feelings more seriously today as cosmic correspondent Mercury and serious Saturn unite in the most intuitive sections of your chart. Read people's body language and catch small inflections in tone. Subtle cues can help you pinpoint emotional nuances. Your ability to decipher the deeper meaning could be a huge benefit to your partnership.

September 4: Venus-Mars square

Splitting hairs? A clash between hotheaded Mars and sensitive Venus could cause you to jump to conclusions, criticize or judge. Take a time-out to get to the bottom of what's bugging you first. Or, de-stress with some exercise and self-care. Once you've pampered yourself, this issue may seem like more of a molehill than a mountain.

September 6-October 2: Venus in Leo

Everything's coming up roses as Venus makes her annual visit to your relationship house. And if you want that garden *d'amour* to bloom, you have to tend to the flowers. Incorporate kind gestures or gifts for your loved ones, ideally ones that align with their "love language." If you're single, set your standards high and approach every interaction with those benchmarks in mind. You might be surprised who measures up.

September 9-November 13: Mars retrograde in Aries

Return of an ex? Lusty Mars reverses course in your third house of communication, which could bring messages from an old flame. If you've always danced around a flirtation with someone, you might decide to explore it in earnest. This transit can make you argumentative or quick to combust, so watch those knee-jerk reactions.

September 12: Jupiter retrograde ends

Expansive Jupiter finally turns direct (forward) after a four-month retrograde through your bewildering twelfth house. Since this area of your chart rules endings and healing, you might have dealt with heartbreak or worked through a deep-seated emotional issue. A love interest's trust may have come into question. Now that Jupiter has corrected course, you'll feel clearer and more confident about what lies ahead. Should you forgive and try again… or cut your losses?

September 15: Venus-Uranus square

When frenetic Uranus clashes with amorous Venus, you could feel overly preoccupied with your S.O.'s actions (or inactions). Strong-arming them into a commitment or forcing your agenda won't make either of you happy, so take it slow. Single? Use Uranus's innovative influence and try the opposite of what you usually do with a new fling. If you normally wait for them to call, pick up the phone and be the first to reach out.

September 17: Virgo new moon

Today's full moon in your steamy eighth house pours on the passion! For the next two weeks, focus on fulfilling your own wants and needs, whether you're attached or single. If your partnership has hit a plateau, introduce some sexy new ideas into the mix. Novelty is an aphrodisiac!

September 28: Venus-Mars trine

Not all love affairs begin with fireworks; some start slow and heat up over time. That could be the case today, as the love planets play matchmaker in your social circle. Is a friend looking fetching? Put a little signal out to see if there's a mutal spark worth exploring. Attached? Have a heart-to-heart with your S.O. to air anything you've been holding in. No need to blame or lecture. Lead with gentleness and speak in "I" rather than "you" statements.

September 29: Saturn retrograde ends

Stern Saturn ends a five-month retrograde, powering ahead in your twelfth house of hidden agendas and closure. You're learning important lessons about trust, vulnerability and how you present yourself in the world. A chapter of your life may have ended or perhaps you had a loss to mourn. Take stock of what you've learned and what you'll carry into the next chapter.

SEPTEMBER: CAREER HOTSPOTS

September 1: Mercury-Pluto trine

Sharp-witted Mercury and discerning Pluto in your intuitive houses heighten your perception. Good luck to the person who tries to pull the wool over your eyes today! Nothing can get past you right now. Trust your instincts. In meetings and conversations, read between the lines and watch for subtle cues like body language.

September 2: Pisces full moon

The annual Pisces full moon sheds light on your second house of finances and work. A steady paycheck, benefits and stability are great, but you also love independence and the idea of being your own boss. Review how you spend your days and how fulfilled you feel. Then explore the notions of freedom and security. How can you infuse both into your days?

September 3: Mercury-Saturn trine
You could feel like you're calling all the shots before they're fired today, as razor-sharp Mercury and pensive Saturn help you tap into your intuition. Pointing out gaping holes in a proposal is usually not a way to win fans, but showing people what they missed might seriously help your team succeed.

September 5-27: Mercury in Libra
Think in broad strokes! While mental Mercury travels through your big-picture ninth house, take concrete steps toward a major goal. You're feeling adventurous and up for a risk, so stretch past your comfort zone. Just watch how much you promise. Though you may be tempted to oversell your ideas, stay humble and realistic about what you can achieve. Your mind is hungry for new info; satisfy the desire with a workshop or online course.

September 9-November 13: Mars retrograde in Aries
Argument alert! For the next two months, intense and aggressive Mars turns retrograde in your third house of communication. Conversations could get heated, especially if there are unresolved issues. With cutting Mars here, there will be opportunities to partake in snark or gossip. Combat that urge and address issues face to face. Better to nip the issue in the bud than fan the flames of drama.

September 14: Sun-Pluto trine
When the confident Sun and alchemical Pluto harmonize, your powers of persuasion are mighty. Pitching an idea? Others will lean in close to hear what you have to say. Your advice is in high demand today and people may confess some confidential intel. Be vigilant about keeping their secrets in the vault. Your own reputation depends on it.

September 17: Virgo new moon
The year's only new moon in your eighth house of investments and mergers could reveal some new paths toward financial solvency. Your sign is known for innovation, so come up with fresh ideas to increase your cash flow or grow what you already have. Schedule meetings with investors or advisors and prepare insightful questions. Take notes and listen closely. Whatever you start during today's new moon will grow over the next six months.

September 17: Mercury-Jupiter square
Keep your antenna up for exaggerations as super-sizer Jupiter clashes with mouthy Mercury in your over-the-top ninth house. People probably aren't being intentionally dishonest, just misguided or overenthusiastic. Can they back up claims with solid evidence and a real plan? Review their numbers closely to see if anything's amiss.

September 21: Mercury-Pluto square
When expressive Mercury confronts crafty Pluto, you might feel like throwing shade at a colleague or competitor. Hold your tongue! Whatever criticisms you utter reveal more about you than your target, and you wouldn't want to catch a reputation as mean-spirited or a gossip. Keep the cutting comments to yourself today, for your sake and theirs.

September 23: Mercury-Saturn square
Know-it-all alert! Outspoken Mercury tempts you to steer a conversation, if not outright dominate

it. But a balancing beam from fastidious Saturn cautions you to stay humble. Proceed slowly and carefully. If you have a lot of info to unload, stop at intervals to make sure everyone's on the same page. Accept input and feedback graciously. If you're the one listening today, ask questions—and don't worry about looking foolish. Chances are, you're not the only one who needs clarification.

September 24: Mercury-Mars opposition

If you can't say something nice, zip it. Instead of chewing someone out when you're upset, walk away. While you'll get temporary satisfaction from unloading your anger, the damage control you're stuck with later won't be worth the short-term relief.

September 27-October 27: Mercury in Scorpio

Vacation time is over! Savvy Mercury glides into your tenth house of career and long-term goals, helping you see the larger vision. Pinpoint your priorities and act decisively on them. Feeling unclear about your next professional steps? A coach or mentor can help you make a concrete plan.

September 29: Mars-Saturn square

Proceed with caution when rash Mars collides with flaw-finder Saturn. Rigorously check your work for errors and delegate to a second set of eyes. A time-saving technique might seem like a good idea now, but it could cost you down the line.

September 29: Saturn retrograde ends

Strict Saturn finally moves forward after a five-month retrograde, powering ahead in your twelfth house of hidden agendas. Shady characters from your past may have emerged, or collaborators who seemed trustworthy at first acted in undermining

ways. It hasn't been easy, but these phases of life are necessary for growth and development. Reflect on what you've learned about trust and boundaries—and keep it moving!

October

OCTOBER: LOVE HOTSPOTS

October 2-27: Venus in Virgo

Summer may be over, but your love life is just starting to sizzle. When sensual Venus visits your erotic eighth house, you'll feel magnetic and turned-on. Take it slow and draw out the seduction. For couples, dial up the intensity bit by bit to get the mojo flowing. This phase can also sweeten your emotional connection. Drop your armor and be a bit more vulnerable with each other.

October 4: Pluto retrograde ends

Metamorphosis: complete! Transformative Pluto ends its annual retrograde through your twelfth house of healing and closure. This transit, which began on April 25, may have brought back issues (or people) you thought you'd gotten over. Some of these reunions were cathartic while others felt more karmic. The intense planet's backspin was a fruitful time for deep inner work and closure.

October 10: Venus-Uranus trine

Expect the unexpected as volatile Uranus throws your love life a plot twist. Someone could reveal a secret or blurt out feelings. With the side-spinning planet making a supportive angle to romantic Venus, the news may open an exciting new chapter. An attraction might spark up out of the blue.

October 18: Venus-Neptune opposition

Foggy Neptune is at odds with amorous Venus today, turning your emotions upside-down. Neptune has a tendency to obscure reality and its confusing presence can cause you to question everything. Don't let insecurity run amok today.

October 19: Venus-Jupiter trine

Today's harmonious trine of the love planet and lucky Jupiter could bring someone into your orbit with serious soulmate status. With Venus in your eighth house of merging and intimacy, that spark you feel might blossom into something with long-term potential. Stay open!

October 21: Venus-Pluto trine

Venus in your erotic eighth house gets a major boost from transformational Pluto. This could bring a sweeping change in your relationship status or a sexy new suitor. Potent Pluto and vixen Venus can transform your already sizzling love life into a full-on blaze. Don't shy away from vulnerability, which is the bedrock of a beautiful relationship.

October 24: Venus-Saturn trine

When adoring Venus and structured Saturn meet up in your romantic and intuitive zones, work toward clarifying what you need in a relationship. You might even conclude that you don't want a major commitment right now. That's fine, too! Identifying what you really desire will help you attract it.

October 27-November 21: Venus in Libra

Your love life gets a lift when Venus leaves your mysterious eighth house and soars into your ninth house of adventure. If the last three weeks felt heavy and charged, these next three will be spontaneous and exciting. With Venus in your travel zone, a "baecation" could boost the romance.

October 31: Taurus full moon

The annual full moon in Taurus opens the floodgates to your emotional fourth house, bringing out all the feels. Your intellectual sign might rather take the rational route, but today calls for something sweeter. See what happens when you lead with your heart. Talk could turn to babies, exchanging keys or moving in together.

OCTOBER: CAREER HOTSPOTS

October 1: Aries full moon

The year's only Aries full moon lights up your sector of communication and kindred spirits, elevating your collaborative projects. If you've been waiting to launch an endeavor, take to social media and start building buzz. An email blast or video could go viral. Reach out to movers and shakers in your field and ask for help. With everyone on board, this undertaking has serious potential.

October 4: Pluto retrograde ends

Shadowy Pluto resumes forward motion today in your twelfth house of endings. You may have had trouble tying up the loose ends of a project, and this transit might have revealed someone's manipulative qualities. With Pluto powering ahead, you'll have a much easier time discerning people's true motives—and cutting loose anyone who doesn't have your back.

October 7: Mercury-Uranus opposition

Don't take it personally! With chatty Mercury at odds with temperamental Uranus, people won't think before they speak. A colleague might

The AstroTwins' 2020 Horoscope

give unsolicited feedback without taking time to understand the context. Disassociate from the fray until things cool down.

October 9: Mars-Pluto square

If you've been working toward a compromise and the other party isn't cooperating, shelve the discussion. With Pluto in your tricky twelfth house poking the cosmic messenger, people might not be forthcoming with information. Don't lower your standards for the sake of making an agreement. Just revisit the conversation when they're ready to work toward a resolution.

October 13-November 3: Mercury retrograde

Take some time to revisit your long-term goals when Mercury backflips through your career sector, then dips into your expansive ninth house. Progress could grind to a halt, or just hit a frustratingly slow pace. Instead of trying to force your agenda, pause and assess: Are you on track? And are there any changes you could implement to make this better than ever?

October 15: Sun-Pluto square

With the ebullient Sun in your visionary ninth house, you're brimming with big ideas. But a speed-check from shadowy Pluto in your subconscious zone might plant a seed of self-doubt. Don't let old fears stop you from pursuing your dreams. Unpack those limiting beliefs and remind yourself of all the evidence you have to the contrary. That said, be careful who you share with today. Not everyone can be trusted to keep these cutting-edge concepts under wraps!

October 16: Libra new moon

The annual new moon in your outspoken ninth house helps you see limitless possibilities. Don't hold back! This is an excellent moment to take a risk, especially one that involves entrepreneurship, travel or study. Choose your audience before blurting out unfiltered opinions, lest you offend a potential supporter.

October 18: Sun-Saturn square

If you caught a case of stage fright just before you were set to launch, it's time to get back on the horse. Dust yourself off and face those fears, Aquarius! Instead of giving in to the anxiety, investigate why it's cropping up, and how you can mitigate it. Even the most successful moguls feel "imposter syndrome" sometimes, but you can't let it get you down. The Sun's confidence and optimism outshine any of Saturn's lingering self-doubt.

October 19: Mars-Jupiter square

Are you trying to force an outcome? Aggressive Mars and obstinate Jupiter battle for supremacy and crank up the stubbornness! Your tenacity is a great asset when it's needed, but a heavy hand could undo your best efforts. What if you let go of expectations? A negotiation might flow more easily if you surrender your preconceived notions of how it "should" turn out.

October 19: Mercury-Uranus opposition

They said what?! When communicative Mercury opposes volatile Uranus, someone might blurt out harsh remarks. Try not to take offense under this tenuous transit, especially if you're the recipient of this negative feedback. Take what's valid, then leave the rest. Stay true to your work and remind yourself (silently) that many geniuses were misunderstood.

November

NOVEMBER: LOVE HOTSPOTS

November 9: Venus-Mars opposition

The love planets lock horns today, making communication troublesome. What starts out as a loving but honest conversation could take a wrong turn, especially if you touch a nerve. Think twice before offering an unsolicited opinion that the other party can't hear right now—even if you're just trying to help.

November 12: Jupiter-Pluto meetup

In or out? The third and final connection of truth-teller Jupiter and secretive Pluto activates your twelfth house of closure, fantasy and soulmates. Since the spring, you've been wondering how deep to go with a certain someone, perhaps dealing with issues of trust. A clandestine click may have evolved into a real connection, much to your surprise. Look back to the first two Jupiter-Pluto conjunctions on April 4 and June 30 for clues of what might come to a final resolution today.

November 13: Mars retrograde ends

Start the peace talks today! Firecracker Mars ends a two-month retrograde in your expressive third house, which made communication challenging. If arguments flared or you simply couldn't get on the same page, it's time to lay down your swords. You don't need to hold a huge intervention to get relationships back on track, but a solid heart-to-heart will make things right.

November 15: Venus-Pluto square

A clash between amorous Venus and intense Pluto might lend insight into the state of your relationship. Are you checking out instead of engaging? Perhaps you're not being fully honest about how you feel. Or maybe you're unsure whether your partner is being totally above board. Telling the truth doesn't have to be a dealbreaker—in fact, it's the foundation for true intimacy.

November 16: Venus-Jupiter square

When the love planet has a run-in with live-out-loud Jupiter, you might decide to take a relationship risk. A grand romantic gesture or a massive leap is exciting but consider all your options before you plow ahead. Is there a more subtle way of going about this? If not, say it with skywriting!

November 19: Venus-Saturn square

Poor Venus is having quite a week with so many planets throwing shade at her. Today, she comes up against Saturn, who snatches the rose-colored glasses right off her nose. Prepare for a few reality checks: Have you hoisted a love interest onto an undeserved pedestal? Notice where you might be making excuses for subpar behavior. If you've been leading people on, step back into integrity. Better to let them know you're not interested than to waste their time.

November 21-December 15: Venus in Scorpio

Real deal or bust! As Venus soars into your tenth house of long-term goals and commitments, you start craving something steady. Get clear about your bottom-line relationship requirements. Decide where you won't settle and stick to your standards. If you're coupled, plan a few exquisite date nights while Venus swans through this upscale part of your chart. Splurge on tickets to a VIP holiday party or benefit gala and go cut your best "power couple" figure together. Since the tenth house rules career, single Aquarians might meet someone through a work-related event. An attraction to someone notably older or younger may surprise you.

November 27: Venus-Uranus opposition

Unpredictable Uranus shakes up your love life when it has a stand-off with Venus in your responsible tenth house. Set aside that ten-year plan and be a little more spontaneous! Moods could run hot and cold today and emotional outbursts might take you by surprise. Don't fuel this impetuous transit by making any rash decisions. Whatever comes up today could blow over tomorrow.

November 30: Gemini full moon (lunar eclipse)

Mistletoe: check! The holiday season gets off to a flirtatious start, as the year's only full moon in Gemini lands in your passionate fifth house. Since it's a potent lunar eclipse, chemistry could ignite quickly…or a dramatic relationship may go up in flames. A spontaneous fling could "just happen" under these pleasure-centric moonbeams. Glam up and go revel in the holiday festivities—your vibrance will be wildly attractive. Eclipses bring surprises and with this one igniting your fertility zone, Aquarians of the childbearing set could have unexpected baby news to share.

NOVEMBER: CAREER HOTSPOTS

November 1: Mercury-Saturn square

Confidence gets mistaken for arrogance today when mile-a-minute Mercury quarrels with scrupulous Saturn. You might not want to slow down and explain your ideas to those who don't "get it," but be careful of alienating your audience. If people are confused, take your time and walk them through. If you're the one feeling lost, speak up. Make sure you're clear on the vision and objectives. It's okay to ask questions, and even more acceptable to review the answers multiple times to be sure you understand. With Mercury retrograde you can't be too careful. (Note: This aspect will repeat again on November 6 when Mercury corrects course.)

November 3: Mercury retrograde ends

The whole truth and nothing but! Expressive Mercury ends a retrograde that started mid-October, straightening out in your candid ninth house. You're safe to air your opinions again (reasonably) and have an honest air-clearing with colleagues. A media or educational project that got stalled will pick up speed. Bottlenecked business travel or work with a long-distance client could also move forward. Get cracking on a visionary idea for the next seven days!

November 10-December 1: Mercury in Scorpio

Goals, plans and timelines—let's do this! Mercury marches into your tenth house of career and structure, helping you prioritize. What can you realistically accomplish before the end of 2020 if you buckle down and focus? If you got sidetracked by a project over the past few weeks, take note of what you learned along the detour. Then map out your mission and stay on course.

November 13: Mars retrograde ends

Start spreading the news! Motivational Mars ends its two-month retrograde through your cerebral and communicative third house. If your train of thought was muddled—or totally off the rails—you'll soon be back on track. Clarity comes quickly now, and you can make huge strides on your ideas before the year ends. With Mars gone rogue in your communication zone, arguments may have flared. Clear up any misunderstandings so you can move forward with ease.

November 15: Scorpio new moon

With the year's only new moon in your career-driven tenth house, you're ready to craft some ambitious resolutions a few weeks early. Even if you're breaking for the holidays soon, you can still plot a few lofty goals and even take small but concrete steps. Where would you like to be professionally in the next six months? Visualize that today!

November 17: Mercury-Uranus opposition

Don your armor—and don't read the comments! Insensitive remarks fly under today's prickly transit. While your feelings can be easily hurt, try not to take things personally. If a troll comes for you, don't even dignify them with a response. Patience, cooldown tactics and maybe a good (private) cry will get you through this.

November 23: Mercury-Neptune trine

Fortune favors the receptive—and the perceptive—today. Analytical Mercury and keen Neptune harmonize in your career houses, helping you marry intuition and logic. Capture the ideas in your voice recorder app, since they'll come faster than you can write them down.

November 28: Neptune retrograde ends

Cash-positive days: incoming! Neptune ends an obscuring five-month retrograde through your work and money zone. If unplanned expenses cropped up or a source of income evaporated, you'll have more clarity soon. Adjust your projections and get back to your budget. A potential client who drifted away may resurface.

November 30: Gemini full moon (lunar eclipse)

The full moon lights up your fifth house of fame and self-expression, bringing some much-deserved attention to your work. Since this is a potent eclipse, things could move quickly and happen out of the blue. You'll come across as a natural leader today, so pitch an innovative idea or take the helm of a presentation. With la luna lighting up this celebratory sector, you'll be a hit at any holiday gathering. Performers, artists and creative types may find themselves directly under the spotlight!

December

DECEMBER: LOVE HOTSPOTS

December 5: Venus-Neptune trine

As idealistic Neptune connects with romantic Venus in your visionary ninth house, your love life gets a flood of feel-good energy. This optimistic combo inspires you to step outside your comfort zone, opening up to someone from a different type than your usual contenders. Couples: Strike the socks and sweaters from your gifting list and splurge on a gorgeous vacation for two, or some other enriching experience.

 The AstroTwins' 2020 Horoscope

December 15, 2020-January 9, 2021: Venus in Sagittarius

As Venus closes out the year in your social sector, you could find yourself smitten with someone you never thought of "that way." Before you know it, those witty texts you trade with a friend may take on a flirty tone! Single Aquarians could easily meet someone making the holiday party rounds or through any of the dating apps, since the love planet here adds a tantalizing touch to technology.

December 20, 2020-January 9, 2021: Mercury in Capricorn

Eloquent Mercury winds down the year in your imaginative twelfth house. Sharing your innermost thoughts could help you bond with your S.O. You might even decide your new love interest is trustworthy enough to be in on some deep-seated secrets. Since this zone rules healing, have a "state of the union" to see where you can support each other's growth. If a partnership has been out of balance, this starmap helps you reconnect and leave any resentment behind you.

December 30: Venus-Neptune square

Today's messy mashup of amorous Venus and illusory Neptune blurs the boundaries between reality and illusion. Are you projecting a fantasy onto someone, or is there a real connection here? If your love interest is acting cagey, don't start playing self-protective mind games or shutting down. You could swing between dueling desires for security and freedom.

DECEMBER: CAREER HOTSPOTS

December 1-20: Mercury in Sagittarius

Make the rounds, Aquarius! Messenger Mercury rolls into your teamwork and technology sector, helping you connect with inspiring collaborators in your city or online. You'll be a gregarious force of nature at the holiday parties, and an in-demand guest. Got a big goal you want to nail before the year ends? Team up with a friend or colleague. How can you support each other? A mini mastermind sesh to close out 2020 can help you make the mark.

December 13: Mercury-Neptune square

Shiny object syndrome alert! It will be hard to stick to your holiday shopping budget today as curious Mercury butts heads with impressionable Neptune. If you're scouting the interwebs for gifts, look for sites that are sustainable and have social giving programs. Trying to cut back on consumption? Organize a swap or make donations for the adults on your list.

December 14: Sagittarius new moon (total solar eclipse)

The last new moon of 2020 illuminates your social and collaborative eleventh house—made even more potent because it's a galvanizing solar eclipse. A team effort could turn into a major group undertaking. All things digital get a boost, from a viral post to a social media blast. It's a fruitful day for networking, so make the rounds of those holiday parties. Someone you meet, either in person or online, may turn out to be an important player in the coming six months. Want to throw a holiday bash? Send out the Paperless Posts and invite your most avant-garde friends—or better, co-host with one of them. Prepare to play superconnector, a role that suits you perfectly.

December 17, 2020–March 7, 2023: Saturn in Aquarius

Time to take your personal goals and dreams seriously, Aquarius! Structured Saturn settles into your sign for the next couple years, challenging you to stretch and grow. Though it may be tough at times (especially when pride and ego take a couple blows), you're creating a foundation for the next 30 years of your life. With a mission like that, it's worth doing the hard work to become your best self. Working with a coach and mentor could be integral to the process.

December 19, 2020–May 13, 2021: Jupiter in Aquarius

What a feeling! Two days after structured Saturn moved into your sign (its first visit since 1993), lucky and expansive Jupiter enters Aquarius for the first time since 2009. It's rare enough to have either of these planets in your sign, but even more unusual for them to visit together. The next year of your life will be rife with amazing changes and inspiring growth. Auspicious Jupiter is here to expand your horizons and pull you way beyond your comfort zone. Adventure awaits!

December 21: Jupiter-Saturn meetup

Power surge! The rare alignment of expansive Jupiter and structured Saturn (known as The Great Conjunction) only happens every two decades. This is especially huge for you because this time, they're meeting in Aquarius. Your Jupiter-fueled visionary ideas are backed by sensible Saturn. You could launch something personally fulfilling that can stand the test of time.

December 23: Mars-Pluto square

These two aggro and volatile planets make one last clash, igniting tensions. Is someone being evasive or shady? Trying to pin them down could be frustrating. If you can't come to an agreement before the holidays, postpone the negotiations until January. People are distracted under this strained transit, either by personal matters or by end-of-year projects. It's not worth rushing to a conclusion if neither party feels satisfied by the result. Come back to it when you're refreshed and ready for a new arrangement.

December 25: Mercury-Uranus trine

Eureka! Clever Mercury and innovative Uranus align in your intuitive sectors, giving you major insights. They're likely to come while you're engaged in self-care or bonding with loved ones (and good thing, since much of the world is off duty today). Relaxing with family or preparing a feast could be the space you need to see an issue from a new perspective. Keep your notes app open on your phone to transcribe any divine downloads.

December 29: Cancer full moon

End of year decluttering? The second Cancer full moon of the year (the first was January 10) beams into your sixth house of organization and wellbeing. Before making New Year's resolutions, clear away whatever you don't want to bring into 2021. Since this area of your chart also rules service, seek out a volunteer opportunity or a way you can make a difference for someone in need. La luna may inspire you to start your healthy habits a couple days earlier than everyone. ✳

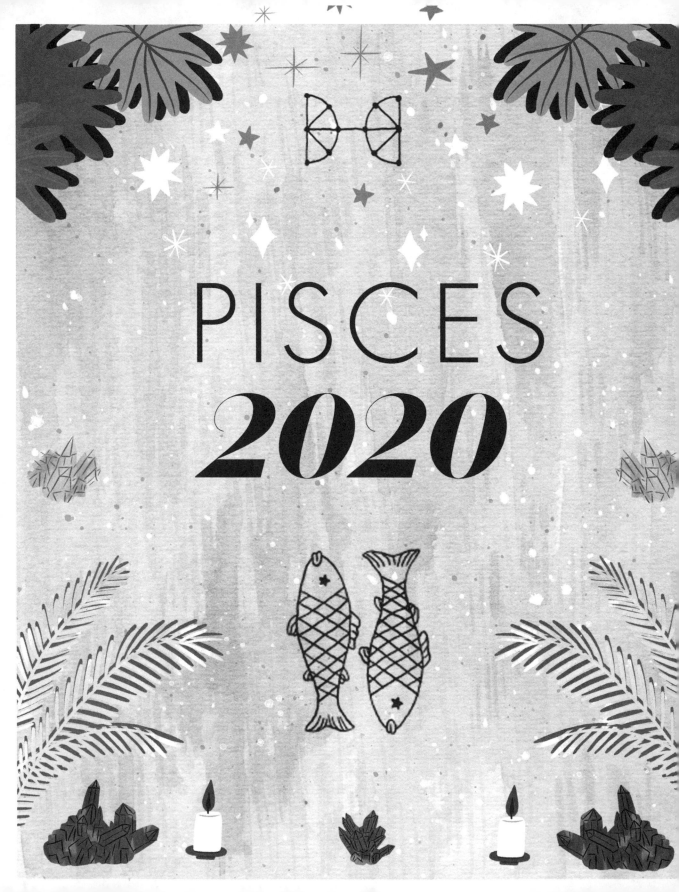

PISCES
2020

Yearly Highlights

LOVE

Tap that app! With your eleventh house of technology and community lit by three planets and an eclipse, you could find true love via a virtual connection. Or, stop resisting and let friends fix you up on blind dates. (They know you better than you think.) Coupled Pisces should mingle often as a pair. This is the year to assemble a shared friend group for dinner parties and vacations. Two Cancer eclipses, on January 10 and June 21, sizzle in your fifth house of amour. These lunar lifts bring game-changing milestones, like engagements, pregnancies or other life-changing shared experiences.

MONEY

There's strength—and fortune!—in numbers this year, as enterprising Jupiter joins power-brokers Saturn and Pluto in your teamwork zone (Capricorn). Put your money where your ideals are. Who says you can't change the world for the better and pay your bills at the same time? Digital ventures could also take flight in a profitable way. Two eclipses in your career zone, on June 5 and December 14, may launch you into the major leagues. When it comes to your cash, be careful not to burn as fast as you earn while excitable Mars blazes through your financial house from June 27 on.

WELLNESS

Group classes and team sports will keep you pumped in 2020, so dismount the treadmill and try everything from Pilates circuit to African dance. Anything holistic and metaphysical will appeal to you, and while Saturn is in your spiritual twelfth house from May 21 to July 1, you could try regular sessions with an energy worker. Pay attention to the "electricity" in your body, also known as chi or life force energy. Strengthen the current with breath-based techniques like kundalini yoga, holotropic breathwork or by seeing an acupuncturist regularly.

LEISURE

Your social circle swells to exciting proportions in 2020—and what a colorful crew you'll assemble! Thought leaders, artists and garden-variety unicorns will populate the Pisces posse this year. If family's been getting the short end of the stick, make amends when convivial Venus tours your domestic zone from April 3 to August 7. The harmonizing planet turns retrograde from May 13 to June 25, so don't wait until then to discuss shared finances or deal with issues brewing under your roof. The November 30 lunar eclipse could bring some heart-opening moments, just in time for the holidays. ✳

PISCES
2020 HOROSCOPE

2020 Power Dates

✳

PISCES NEW MOON
February 23 (10:32am ET)

PISCES FULL MOON
September 2 (1:22am ET)

SUN IN PISCES
February 18 – March 20

Come on up for air, Pisces. And while you're at it, take three deep, cleansing breaths. In 2020, you have planetary permission to exhale, and maybe slip off for a meditation retreat around the March 21 equinox. Last year, no-limits Jupiter climbed to the top of your chart, working its magic in your tenth house of success. Some Fish spent 2019 with gills to the grindstone, developing your magnum opus or creating a venture that aligned with your ideals. You may have traveled for work, hustled remotely (and independently) or, like many Pisces we know, finally screwed up the courage to leave a corporate gig to pursue your passions.

No matter what rung of the ladder you're on in 2020, it will not be lonely at the top. (Nor at the ground floor, the coworking cubicle, in coach or business class.) That's because, since December 2, 2019, Jupiter has been soaring through Capricorn and your ultra-social, egalitarian eleventh house. Until December 19, 2020, the red-spotted rabble rouser will accompany transformational Pluto and serious Saturn through this sector, lifting the heavier vibes these weighty planets have cast over your social life since December 2017. This triumphant trio hasn't teamed up in Capricorn since 1285 C.E., so yes, Pisces, 2020 is going to bring some big-deal revelations about the kinds of people you want to surround yourself with. The eleventh house is the humanitarian zone, and this planetary push could ignite your activism…just in time for a climactic U.S. Presidential election or other tide-turning global events.

Get out and mingle like it was your job this year… because it might just be, especially near January 12, when power brokers Saturn and Pluto make an exact conjunction in Capricorn for the first time since the 1500s. There's a popular equation created by business guru Jim Rohm: To find your current earning potential, average the net worth of the five people closest to you. While we're not suggesting you judge people based on their balance sheets, this can be an eye-opening exercise. You can run the same "numbers" when it comes to love: Are the five people closest to you in flourishing relationships or constantly pinging between highs and heartbreaks? You're influenced by the company you keep. Surround yourself with people who are thriving and watch your own "social capital" rise.

> "Get out and mingle like it was your job this year."

When it comes to money-making missions and creative projects, this is the year to tap the hive mind and assemble a power posse. Start casting for new collaborators as soon as January 10, when the first of two buoyant eclipses helps you magnetize your soul squad. On June 5, a new series of eclipses will ripple across your home and career axis, touching down in Gemini (your domestic fourth house) and Sagittarius (your ambitious tenth). Consider this another push from the stars to nail the "work-life balance" thing…which may require you to delegate and collaborate. Teamwork makes the dream work in 2020!

Speaking of dreams, yours could be wilder and more intuitive than ever from March 21 to July 1 as Saturn advances into Aquarius and your oracular twelfth house for the first time since 1994. During this brief spell, powerful mentors may arrive to Sherpa you along a spiritual journey. Some old hurt and baggage might rise up to be healed, but the good news is that Saturn helps you dress those wounds in something much more effective than a Band-Aid, allowing you to fully recover. Yes, you'll have your karmic work cut out for you, but this is something your deep-diving sign happens to relish. Plunge in!

This short Saturn cycle is a preview of what's to come in the last two weeks of 2020. On December 17, the ringed guru parks in Aquarius again until March 7, 2023. Two days later, optimistic Jupiter joins him there, embarking on a yearlong cycle through Aquarius. Then, fanfare: December 21, 2020, marks a monumental mashup of Jupiter and Saturn at 0°29' Aquarius—an event astrologers call The Great Conjunction—which only occurs every 20 years. Free-fall down the rabbit hole, Pisces! It's the perfect day for a vision quest, a creative jam session or whatever can bring epiphanies. Expect violet-light insights and inspired downloads unlike any you've had for years. You may also realize that it's time to set limits with people and situations that are draining your energy reserves.

Romance could take a back burner to the "one love" vibes of your friendship groups this year. But that doesn't mean Cupid's gone AWOL. Coupled Fish should find a "school" where you both feel comfortable swimming, which could literally involve signing up for a workshop series together or something more active, like crewing a sailboat or joining a summer lawn bowling league. Single Pisces could make that fortuitous right swipe on a dating app. You might even reconnect to an old flame when Jupiter meets up with seductive Pluto during a dual retrograde on June 30.

Speaking of which, both of the "love planets"—Venus and Mars—have a retrograde spell in 2020. First up is Venus, who will reverse commute through Gemini and your sensitive, domestic fourth house from May 13 to June 25. During this time, your nesting instincts go into overdrive, and you'll crave a lot more private one-on-one time with your S.O. Did you give a "nice person" the cold shoulder? Regrets could lead to recourse and a possible romance now. If you're doing any home renovations, Venus will be on an extended roll through Gemini from April 3 to August 7. Just cross out the retrograde dates…or get plans in motion before May 13! Since Venus guides our values and how we spend our cash, this cycle can get you serious about building your nest egg.

Mars is the lusty force that also drives our ambitions and will be thrusting through Aries from June 27, 2020, to January 6, 2021. The Ram rules your sensual-but-sensible second house, which is also the sector of values and income. Your tastes could fluctuate wildly—in everything from Tinder dates to job titles—while Mars emboldens you to try new things. But when the red planet flips into retrograde from September 9 to November 13, rein it in and find your center. Then, as the year draws to a close, you can stretch without snapping.

Jupiter in Capricorn: Branch out & collaborate.

December 2, 2019 – December 19, 2020

Ready to swim with a new school? Your social circles could undergo a major evolution this year as worldly, expansive Jupiter sweeps through Capricorn and your outgoing, experimental eleventh house. Review the entrance requirements to the Pisces Posse: Is it time to diversify your people portfolio? With the galactic globalist in the mix, immerse yourself in groups that broaden your horizons. Farewell, basic bores; hello, world travelers, thought leaders and disruptors!

Cutting-edge ideas can thrive during an eleventh house transit. With no-limits Jupiter here from December 2, 2019, to December 19, 2020, your legendary imagination is back at the wheel! The technology-driven eleventh house is the Silicon Valley sector of the zodiac wheel—and Jupiter's presence shifts your visionary gaze toward the future. Where do the arts, science and technology overlap with your deepest interests? This could be the year where you craft a TED talk, start an experimental dance troupe or launch a website with a social sharing feature. Le geek, c'est chic!

But even as buoyant Jupiter breaks the surface like a dolphin jumping waves, you'll still be "far from the shallow" in 2020. For much of the year, the red-spotted planet rows alongside deep-diving Pluto who's been on a slow submarine ride through Capricorn that spans from 2008 to 2024. Weighty Saturn has also dropped anchor in the Sea Goat's waters since December 19, 2017, and for the last two years this pair has brought some heaviness to your social interactions. Not that you minded terribly. Poetic, compassionate Pisces don't do "superficial." But let's be honest: Aren't you a little tired of people treating you like their on-call therapist?

Reciprocity is the name of the game in 2020. Who will be there for you this year? Having a devoted soul squad will be especially important near three key dates, when incandescent Jupiter shines its revelatory beams into Pluto's shadowy vault on April 4, June 30 and November 12. An "all hands" strategy may be required to resolve whatever rises to the surface near these days. And as the rubber meets the road, you'll see clearly who has your back and who's a fair-weather friend.

For Pisces women, spending quality time with uplifting, nurturing people will be especially important, because it helps the female brain produce the neurotransmitter oxytocin, also known as the "love hormone." Scientists have named the female stress response "tend and befriend," because when women bond supportively, oxytocin flows. Instead of producing harmful amounts of cortisol, they can relax and get through their busy lives with pleasure instead of anxiety, overwhelm and struggle. The good news? Bountiful Jupiter in this communal corner can give Pisces women a big refill of "Vitamin O."

The eleventh house turns your eye toward the future, but your nostalgic sign can get stuck in the past. While bittersweet, you may have to put some friendships on the backburner. A shared history is not enough reason to keep recycling dead-end relationships. Don't go crazy and start cutting off every innocent (but mundane) person on your friend list. Just pull back and "do you." People who are

ready to evolve will realize that if they want to keep you around, they have to keep up! Meanwhile, feel zero guilt about banishing energy vampires, critics and naysayers from your realm. With liberated Jupiter here, you need to roam without restrictions!

With folks who pass the velvet ropes into your VIP lounge, aim for the delicate intersection between intimacy and levity. Sometimes you'll want to sit around (#WineTime optional), sharing romantic battle scars and talking about the past-life regressionist who confirmed that your original residence was on Atlantis (duh!). And then there will be times—praise goddess—where you don't have to talk at all. You'll be too busy screaming yourself hoarse at an outdoor concert or chasing ninjas around an escape room. Direct the social flow of your friend group towards edifying activities. Start a book club, a progressive dinner party or a weekly live music night. Invite friends to join you on yoga retreats or to register in the self-development seminars you're taking. We hear that walking over hot coals together can be a helluva bonding experience!

Speaking of expansion, 2020 is the year to visit friends in far-flung ports. Activate your WhatsApp notifications and talk to your amiga in Barcelona about a summer apartment swap. Want to visit new places and leave them better than when you arrived? With the galactic globetrotter in this quadrant of your chart, "voluntourism" could be the perfect vacation vibe, combining worldly Jupiter's travel bug with the do-gooder instincts of the eleventh house.

The eleventh house rules all things electronic and digital, and the Internet will be your favorite sandbox to play in this year. From crowdfunding an

 The AstroTwins' 2020 Horoscope

album release to organizing charitable campaigns to selling your art on Etsy, you won't want to stray from a strong Wi-Fi signal. Jupiter rules education, so if you need to polish up your digital skills, plow through tutorials or take a class at a place like generalassemb.ly. Whether you're mastering new software or getting savvier about social media, your income could soar along with your skill set.

In love, the eleventh house vibes can keep your energy more tuned to friendships, but don't sleep on romance! With this tech-savvy sector lit, single Fish may find success by trying a few dating apps, especially ones like Meet Mindful that brings together people who want to swim in the deeper end of the pool. The Jupiter-Pluto conjunctions on April 4 and November 12 could seal the deal with someone who is both seductive and stable. During the June 30 pairing, both planets will be retrograde, and you might hear from someone who ghosted you after what seemed like a promising coffee date. Timing is everything, so if you're not too miffed, you might extend one second chance. If you're more of an analog romancer, let your crew play Cupid. In 2020, true love could emerge from the friend zone.

Coupled Pisces, this is the year to mingle as a pair. Finding common outlets for socializing will strengthen your bond, even if that means going beyond your existing circles and finding a soul squad where you both belong. You don't have to force your own friends to bond with your love interest—and by the same token, don't abandon your individual support network just because your sweetie doesn't fit in there. What suits us in love can be very different than what we need from our BFFs, and that's fine! Don't force it, just expand.

You should also seek outlets where you can be of benefit to others. This is the year to "be the change" instead of just complaining about problems or bemoaning that state of the world. No more talk—it's time to get into action by giving back. Some Pisceans could get deeply engaged in politics or activism, working the phones for a Presidential candidate. Let your idealism shine. As Pisces Anais Nin said, "Life shrinks or expands in proportion to one's courage."

Last year, Jupiter's tour through Sagittarius and your tenth house of career may have brought some time-consuming projects that kept your nose to the grindstone—but also brought some exciting change to your professional path! One Pisces friend went off the grid for two months to write copy for an app, but thanks to lucky Jupiter's influence, this enabled her to work remotely and make enough to take two months off last summer.

For other Fish, last year may have provided a jailbreak from a soul-sucking job. Your sacrificial sign tends to stick around longer than you should, often out of guilt or misplaced obligation. We know a Pisces who suffered through a draining pharmaceutical sales gig for over a decade, even though she hated it from the start. While she hit all her metrics—and even got a company-funded trip to Maui as a reward for being a top rep—the job missed the mark when it came to her values. Last year, she was laid off with a juicy severance package, and is now free to pursue her true passions, both as a talented oil painter and a hospice nurse.

If 2020 finds you at a career crossroads, think outside the box! Even if you work in a traditional field, you may find a refreshing spin you can put on it. For example, if you're a healer, as many

532

Pisces are, you might move away from treatment to preventative care, helping people help themselves through clean eating, stress reduction and natural supplements.

With entrepreneurial Jupiter turning you into a virtual vixen, this is an ideal year to launch an online business or position yourself as a social media luminary. Jupiter rules coaching and publishing, so you might consider something with an educational, empowering twist like a video course or digital downloads that rack up passive income and better people's lives. Do you have a product to peddle? Join a collective of indie business owners and creatives to get your name out there. Whether you rent a pop-up stall in a thriving artists' market or upload classes to a platform like Udemy, there's power in numbers. Bone up on SEO and email marketing—there are a ton of great resources online—to give your ideas an extra shot at being discovered.

Saturn-Pluto conjunction: Strengthen social ties.

December 2019–February 2020 (exact on January 12)

Who deserves insider status, Pisces…and who should be relocated to an anterior ring of your circle? Metamorphic shifts sweep through your social life this January, as power brokers Saturn and Pluto unite in Capricorn and your eleventh house

of teamwork and tech. The two "karma cops" have been inching closer together for more than two years. On January 12, they'll finally make an exact connection at 22°46' Capricorn, combining their formidable strengths.

Considering that this meetup only happens every 35 to 38 years (and hasn't occurred in the Sea Goat's realm since the 1500s), you should definitely brace yourself for something big… and exciting! For example, you may be invited to be part of an elite organization where you can mingle with influential people and combine resources for mutual gain. Next stop: Davos?

> "Events may occur near January 12 that force you to stand up for your ideals in a very public way."

Saturn is the ruler of time and structure, while Pluto operates on your unconscious. You might not even realize that you've been moving towards this transformation until it happens. But events may occur near January 12 that force you to stand up for your ideals in a very public way. Resistance is futile, Fish. If you find yourself shifting from curious bystander to ringleader of a cultural movement, you might as well roll with it. Since the eleventh house rules both activism and technology, you may take up this mantle in the digital realm. Social media: meet your newest social justice warrior.

Speaking of all things virtual, how troll-proof are you? With furtive Pluto and tough teacher Saturn meeting in this Internet-savvy sector, one of your first orders of business in 2020 is to update to stronger passwords. If you've been uploading proprietary material to the cloud, you might want

 The AstroTwins' 2020 Horoscope

to put it behind a firewall, and think about turning your home Wi-Fi into a VPN (virtual private network).

Since Saturn and Pluto govern wealth, give your portfolio a review. Maybe it's time to put your earnings into a socially-responsible mutual fund or buy stock in an innovative eleventh house start-up, like a renewable energies company or electric cars. A group investment could prove fruitful, whether you're pooling your savings with friends or setting up a crowdfunding campaign for one of your own ventures.

Venus & Mars Retrograde: Relationship review.

Venus Retrograde:
May 14 – June 25

Mars Retrograde:
September 10 – November 13

Starting May 13, you may feel the call to reunite with your oldest, dearest friends—especially the influential women in your world. Venus makes her biennial retrograde, pivoting back through Gemini and your family-minded fourth house until June 25. Set up that spare bedroom and invite guests, or better yet, meet for an action-packed vacation at a sentimental spot.

If you want to bury the hatchet with a frenemy or difficult relative, Venus can help, especially since she'll hover in Gemini from April 3 to August 7 and will be in direct (proactive) motion for much of the time. But when the peacekeeping planet is off her game from May 13 to June 25, you might rush to "make nice" only to find the unresolved issue rearing up ten times stronger. Start with a phone call and maybe a lunch date on neutral territory after that. Or, just give yourself a time-out if you keep hitting the same wall with your inner circle.

We teach people how to treat us, Pisces. In your moments of venting, you may have ignited their protective natures, making them worry unnecessarily about your emotional wellbeing. Be more mindful of how you present your "woe is me!" scenarios. You might bounce back like an elastic band, but you can't expect loved ones to spring back-and-forth with your moods. Feeling smothered? It may be time to shift the helicopter-style relationship with your clan.

Venus is the planet of love and romance, and this retrograde reminds you that like attracts like. To draw an emotionally-aware partner, you have to be attuned to your own inner workings. By honoring your sentient self, your existing relationships will also improve. This might be a redundant reminder for your tender-hearted sign, but it's not frivolous to feel! If you've toughened up your Fish scales so much that no one can reach your heart, try to relax and be more vulnerable this spring. That's not the same as being gullible or dropping all defenses, Pisces. Just be…accessible.

With this romantic retrograde going down in your domestic zone, you may have to negotiate some new rules if you share a home with your partner. Do you have adequate space—for relaxing in privacy and doing your creative work? If not, you could be quite the cranky member of the lair. Of course, elbowing out your S.O. or family won't work. Is it time to rent a studio for your memoir writing or band practice? If your home and workspaces just don't feel cozy enough, make a few cosmetic upgrades now. But hold off on massive renovations until Venus is back on track after June 25. Otherwise, you may spend a fortune making your bedroom look like a Moroccan love den only to wake up in six weeks to realize you prefer Midcentury minimalism. Um, oops?

You'll be money-motivated starting June 27, as action planet Mars zips into Aries for a protracted, six-month journey through your second house of income. Until January 6, 2021, make no apologies for wanting to improve your bottom line. Stability doesn't have to be an elusive goal, even for the most slippery Fish out there.

Some belt-tightening will be in order, especially once Mars backflips into a retrograde from September 9 to November 13. Your happy hour squad might be bummed to see you less frequently. But by the end of the year, you'll be laughing all the way to the bank—or maybe the auction house or real estate agency—as you flow funds towards an investment that compounds in value. (As opposed to one you can down in a few tantalizing sips.)

Start squirreling away funds as soon as possible, so you have a buffer. When Mars goes retrograde, hidden costs could pop up just as you're about to close a deal, or an offer that was so close you could taste it might suddenly hit a speedbump. Don't hit the panic button. While it's no fun to watch things stagnate and stall, reframe the situation as a golden opportunity to slow down, review your plans and make sure they're built on a solid foundation. Once Mars resumes direct motion on November 13, you might get a second chance at a gig you applied for earlier in 2020. Or a former client or colleague

could return with an offer that's (almost) too good to be true. If this is someone with an impeccable track record, you owe it to yourself to pursue!

Warning: Extra tension could brew at the office during this entire six-month cycle. Mars is the agitator, and it's likely this drama has been brewing for a while. Make a point of addressing any simmering conflicts you intuitively sense. Best to discuss it openly than to quietly hope it blows over. Your willingness to tackle these weak spots and find solutions will impress the powers that be. The only caveat? Don't bring up the issue in the heat of the moment. You want these conversations to be proactive, not destructive. For best results, use "I" language instead of the accusatory "you." For example, "I'm feeling the need for more structure in our workflow," will probably yield better results than, "You're always rescheduling our meetings!"

Saturn in Aquarius: Dive deep.

March 21–July 1
December 17, 2020–March 7, 2023

Eager to explore your inner landscape? With all the social activity of 2020, you may feel seriously shortchanged, and it's likely that you'll have to steal meditative moments when you can. Condense your two-hour journaling and yoga sessions to 30 minutes…or 15, if that's all you can spare. Without some sort of reflection practice, you just feel unmoored. Thankfully, on March 21, you can grab your headlamp and shine it inwards. Saturn, the planet of maturity, hard work and foundation building, flows into Aquarius and your healing twelfth house. This brief stint, which lasts until July 1, is a prelude to a longer Saturn in Aquarius cycle, which kicks up again on December 17 and lasts until March 7, 2023.

Saturn's dip into Aquarius provides a blessed window to enjoy your sign's solitary groove. Take your spring/summer vacation off the grid for some spiritual development or to pursue an artistic endeavor. Is it time for a silent vipassana meditation retreat or a painting workshop at a Chateau in the pastoral French countryside? Cultivate your inner landscape (and re-imagine the outer one in watercolors…or oils). From March through July, adopt a slower pace when possible. It will be hard during this busy year, but you'll need to consciously set limits and take breaks.

The twelfth house is the final portion of the zodiac wheel. It's the realm of endings and closure, and with Saturn here, you may experience some weighty transitions. As the twelfth sign of the zodiac, this zone shares similar traits to Pisces, which means you're also in your element when a planet orbits through here. Surrendering to the spiritual and esoteric vibes of the twelfth house comes naturally to you, even if the terrain is tinged with melancholy.

Have you outgrown some aspects of your life? Endings are hard, but this Saturn cycle can support you with any tough, but necessary, transitions. Has a relationship, job or lifestyle run its course? Is something that was once uplifting now draining? Tough Saturn will push you to get real about that. Like a cosmic Marie Kondo, the tidy taskmaster will demand that you part ways with anything that doesn't "spark joy."

If you've experienced a loss, this could be a period of reflection and mourning. As the saying goes, you've got to feel it to heal it—there's no skimming the surface or sweeping things under the rug between March and July. The twelfth house governs supportive people and guardian angels. Surround yourself with a wise network that can hold the space for you.

While Saturn rules boundaries, the twelfth house dissolves borders. This combination is a bit of a paradox, but this is something your dualistic sign can navigate with greater ease than most. Saturn, the ruler of all things terrestrial and tangible, ensures that these hidden parts of yourself will rise above sea level. At times, you'll have to get into those murky waters—but the plunge won't be quite as deep. As buried treasures and traumas surface, be sure to have the proper support systems in place (we can't say this too many times).

How can you set limits with people while still maintaining intimate ties? That will be your knot to unravel. Pisceans can have people-pleasing tendencies, but this Saturn cycle will teach you that compassion doesn't have to mean sacrificing your own needs or letting people walk all over you. If a few lopsided relationships fall away, so be it. Don't rush to fill up the blank spaces with new people and activities. The kindest thing you can do for yourself is to carve out time for solitude and serenity—then use that time to reflect on the kind of people you do want to bring into your universe.

Between March 21 and July 1, you can begin removing any obstacles that are preventing you from living your best life. Some of these could be buried pretty far down and stem back to early childhood. The twelfth house rules the subconscious, and in addition to "talk therapy" you might try other excavation techniques like sound healing, EMDR or hypnosis that can help you reach into those hard-to-access regions of mind and memory. With Saturn in this karmic sector, you may try a past-life regression or talk to a reputable spirit medium. But don't expect to just lie down with a crystal on each chakra while an energy worker aligns you. Saturn will ask you to participate in the process of your own inner work. It's an inside job, Pisces, but there won't be an overnight remedy. Be kind to yourself and patient with your process!

Red flags may show up as heightened anxieties or recurring patterns. For example, you get noticeably uncomfortable around a certain type of person and realize that a relative exhibited similar behaviors, and that triggers an old response. Or, you experience physical symptoms, like a persistent cough or back pain, that are clearly a mind-body-spirit connection. For clues, look to where in your life you feel helpless or wonder, "Why does this always happen to me?" Welcome to your blind spots, Pisces. We all have them, and it's time to examine yours. The silver lining? You'll emerge on the other side with rock-solid inner strength and self-awareness.

If you're struggling with any sort of addiction, this Saturn cycle can be a powerful recovery period. Your devoted efforts—guided by well-vetted professionals and practitioners—can root out blocks you didn't realize were there. Saturn is the zodiac's personal trainer planet, and this marks its first visit back to Aquarius since its 1991-94 spell. If you're old enough to remember what was happening then, you might find similar themes resurfacing.

Saturn's tour of Aquarius could be a rich creative or spiritual cycle. If you're a professional healer, this could be the year that you open a practice, earn a certification or become a recognized leader in your field. Artists may garner public acclaim after toiling away at their craft. You might seek representation by a gallery, agent or producer—someone who can add polish or put you in front of a bigger audience. Do your part by setting up a sleek website or an online portfolio, so people can understand the depth and breadth of your work. Gather testimonials and social proof to help establish credibility in a crowded industry. Your status as an "emerging talent" or "underground sensation" could make you an indie darling—one who changes people's lives with a soul-stirring message.

The twelfth house rules helpful people and Saturn governs experts. A masterful guru could take you under their wing, training you in a sacred technique. You may begin consciously seeking out coaches, consultants, shamans and other guides and signing up for every class, workshop and retreat they offer. There's good reason to invest in this kind of growth! On March 7, 2023, as Saturn enters your sign for the first time since 1994, the Pisces student might become the master!

The Great Conjunction: Jupiter & Saturn unite.
December 21

Ready for a spiritual savasana? On December 19, expansive Jupiter joins restrained Saturn in Aquarius, nestling into your twelfth house of rest, closure and healing (AKA "the Pisces house"). Throw a few more yule logs on the fire and settle down for an extended hibernation. The red-spotted planet lingers in this resting state until December 29, 2021, providing a window of rest and introspection.

Relax and release, but don't go unconscious! Jupiter's tour of Aquarius will activate your most divinely-inspired gifts. After December 19, you'll be a walking vision board, pulling genius ideas from the ether. True, these gems could come to you while you're daydreaming, or even rouse you from your sleep. Keep that inspiration notebook on your nightstand to capture the downloads.

A game-changing vision could hit you as soon as December 21, when Jupiter and Saturn host a rare, exact meetup in the skies, at 0°29' Aquarius. These heavenly heavyweights only merge once every 20 years; in fact, the last time was May 2000. Astrologers have dubbed this momentous (and somewhat mind-bending) alignment The Great Conjunction. Jupiter and Saturn are essentially opposites; one expands while the other contracts. As Jupiter hits the gas, Saturn rides the brake, but when they open up a back channel on December 21, they'll help you achieve the perfect cruising altitude. In your divinely-guided twelfth house, you could be hit with a creative breakthrough that elevates a basic plan into something truly magical. Your "rainbows and unicorns" idea might morph into tangible form, attracting backers and the resources to turn it into the Next Big Thing.

Mark your calendar and mind your mental state! The Law of Attraction will be operating with formidable strength on December 21, so whatever you're focusing on will expand. Gather your most powerful friends for a vision-boarding party. Today is also the Winter Solstice, a chance to put unwanted parts of your past to bed for good.

Since Jupiter rules higher education, its yearlong tour of Aquarius, combined with Saturn's long-range planning skills, could spur you to get certified for one of your Piscean talents. Apply for your Master's in art therapy or do the training to become a holistic doula or lighting engineer. Maybe you'll take a gap year to write your novel in a seaside cabin or teach yoga in Tulum. Or perhaps you'll rent a studio space where you can produce electronic music and start seeing clients for Tarot-based coaching, like one talented Pisces we know. Jupiter also rules publishing, and the twelfth house is associated with both poetry and film. From stanzas to screenplays, writerly Fish could be shopping (or inking!) a development deal as the calendar turns. With self-authorized Jupiter here, the script is yours to author.

What are you holding on to that no longer serves you? Where in your life is closure or forgiveness needed? Has a relationship, job or habit run its course? With eye-opening Jupiter in Aquarius, you may shed a layer or three, and this spiritual sabbatical supports your journey. You're at the end of a lengthy 12-year cycle that began back on January 5, 2009, when Jupiter started its last yearlong trek through Aquarius. Anything you launched back then could reach a transition or turning point. The Jupiter-Saturn journey that begins December 19 may yield incredible internal growth. But much like dormant seeds germinating underground, this is an astrological "winter," and you won't have a full harvest until this cycle ends on December 29, 2021.

That said, spring and summer 2021 will bring a few blooms and shoots! Next year, Jupiter will take an unusual trajectory, darting forward into Pisces from May 14 to July 29 and making you the lucky beneficiary of its charms. This bonus cycle will prep you for Jupiter's second pass into your sign in 2022, which will kick off a fresh 12-year chapter of your life. Between now and then, your assignment is to clear away anything that no longer serves you, or to tie up loose ends in preparation for this next decade-plus phase.

Cancer/Capricorn Eclipses: Curtains up!
January 10, June 21, July 5

Since July 2018, an eclipse series has been buzzing across the Capricorn/Cancer axis, helping you learn when to be the star and when it's ideal to play the best supporting actor. This year, three final eclipses will activate your fifth house of passion, creativity and fame (sparked by two Cancer eclipses on January 10 and June 21) and your eleventh house of teamwork (with a July 5 Capricorn lunar eclipse).

The first one, a Cancer lunar eclipse on January 10, puts the spotlight squarely on you, rippling through your fifth house of love, glamour and self-expression. Strong feelings may surge up, and there will be no stemming the tide once the floodgates open. A romantic relationship could get suddenly serious, perhaps with baby news or a deep conversation about carving out quality time. You might solidify your status, making things official. Or, you may pull the brake, so you can be sure you're aligned on the important stuff before zooming ahead. The casting agents or media could come looking for you, so make sure you're "camera ready" when you bundle up and step out this January. A big break might arrive at any moment—whether you're tapped by a style blogger while you're out for brunch or receive a serendipitous call from an executive recruiter.

But do expect the unexpected! At the January 10 lunar eclipse, the full moon will hold hands across the sky with the Sun, Mercury, Saturn and Pluto in Capricorn and your innovative, experimental eleventh house. If a relationship looks good on paper but falls flat in reality, this could be your cue to rewrite the script. Make it work for you, Pisces, even if that means breaking from convention. Living in separate residences, exploring non-monogamy… it's not for everyone, but some Fish might paddle in these waters. If you're solidly the one-partner type, you may need to shake things up in other ways, such as developing an independent network of friends and creative collaborators. Be the kind of culturally edified person that you'd want to date. If you're not turned on by your own life, make a change. No coasting in 2020!

June 21 is the year's only solar (new moon) eclipse from this grouping, a day when you'll wear your heart fully on your sleeve. Eclipses bring surprise twists and turns, like a new romance, a pregnancy or a bold style makeover. This lunar lift may attract a fervent fanbase and give you the courage to boldly "do you." If you're an artist, you could be pushed right onto center stage. Make like Pisces performers Rihanna and Carrie Underwood and give 'em the show of a lifetime. Budding creatives could sign with an agent or ink a contract that will put your name on the map. You might not be ready to play a stadium or sign with a major label if you're a fledgling musician, for example. But booking a gig that sets the wheels in motion and gets you established a little more? Yes, please!

The final eclipse in this series, the July 5 Capricorn lunar eclipse, may bring exciting friendships and affiliations, or an opportunity to team up around a cutting-edge cause. Adopt a collaborative approach; your combined superpowers will take everyone far. Your inner activist could have a heyday, and you might become the surprising "voice of the people," championing a cause or perhaps even running for office in some way. (Never say never!) Look back to January 5, 2019, the date of the first Capricorn solar eclipse in this series, for clues of what could develop further now.

Gemini/Sagittarius Eclipses: Taking care of business.

June 5, November 30, December 14

Prepare to rewrite your prescription for a happy and productive life. In 2020, a new series of eclipses will sweep across the Gemini/Sagittarius axis, reshuffling affairs in your domestic fourth house (ruled by Gemini) and your career sector (governed by Sagittarius). Both your personal and professional endeavors could be due for a transformation while these eclipses visit from June 5, 2020, to December 3, 2021.

Eclipses can sweep away the stale and outmoded and usher in the new. Two of them center around career, as they'll land in Sagittarius and your ambitious tenth house. A June 5 lunar eclipse and a December 14 solar eclipse could bring a new leadership opportunity or remap your priorities and goals. Ready or not, there could be a move, a home purchase or a new family member at the November 30 Gemini lunar eclipse. A job offer may come with

a relocation or you could travel in conjunction with a professional change at the holidays.

The June 5 Sagittarius lunar (full moon) eclipse may bring a major transition or professional pivot point. Since this is the premier eclipse in the series, it could announce itself with extra pomp and circumstance. Don't slip into weekend warrior mode or you might miss a crucial opportunity. In the month leading up to this eclipse (starting May 4), do everything you possibly can to position yourself as the talented upstart or the obvious "next in line" for the executive throne.

Eclipses open a short-lived window of fortune, much like the brief spell when the Earth's shadow turns the full moon blood red. Don't linger on the sidelines if your heart is singing power ballads about a particular opportunity! Being passive could mean missing the dive boat. June 5 is a day where you may have to leap without a net, saying "Yes, I'm in!" even if you aren't 100 percent certain how you'll fulfill the required duties. If you're at least 60 percent sure you're up for the task, place your chips on this bet. You could reap the rewards before the summer is through.

Sometimes lunar eclipses portend endings, and this one may push exhausting power dynamics to their limit. You don't mind a challenge, but anything too "Game of Thrones" kills your creative buzz. Near June 5, you may cut ties with a business associate or break free from a soul-crushing gig. By the same token, you could attract a serious power player who opens doors on your behalf. An existing mentor or key decision-maker may figure into events near June 5. Be strategic about nurturing key connections: Your network is your net worth, as they say.

On December 14, the solar (new moon) eclipse could bring an exciting opportunity or a major epiphany about your path. You might feel your own passion emerging from the shadows and into visibility, especially since the Sun and planetary PR agent Mercury will also be in Sagittarius. While others are kicking back for the holidays, you're just warming up. Step into your power suit and network your way into the New Year! If business can be done on a golf course, why not on the slopes? ✹

January

JANUARY: LOVE HOTSPOTS

January 3-February 16: Mars in Sagittarius

Set some ambitious love goals. With red-hot Mars blazing through your tenth house of long-term plans for six weeks, you're attracted to people on a big mission. For couples, a shared focal point could put some sizzle back into your bond.

January 10: Cancer full moon (lunar eclipse)

A Cancer lunar (full moon) eclipse in your passionate fifth house ignites sparks of romance and creativity—and since eclipses bring curveballs, these feelings could strike out of the blue. A connection that started at the Cancer new moon back in July 2018 could reach a huge turning point. Self-expression reigns supreme under this open-hearted eclipse, so tell your loved ones (or love interest) how you feel. Break out the pen and paper for a cathartic writing session or inscribe a heartfelt card to someone you've been getting close to lately. Don't be afraid to gush! The fifth house rules fertility, so Pisces of the childbearing set may find themselves with a surprise positive pregnancy test. Consider yourself notified!

January 13-February 7: Venus in Pisces

Infuse the glamorous influence of Venus into your life while the love planet visits your sign, ramping up romance right before Valentine's Day. Practice self-love with positive affirmations, treat yourself to a style update. Adorn yourself in gorgeous garments or set fresh flowers on the coffee table. It's a beautiful beginning to the year!

January 16-February 3: Mercury in Aquarius

Your naturally empathetic tendencies will be on overdrive for a few weeks, as communicator Mercury moves through your sensitive twelfth house. Loved ones could give you plenty of chances to work on your listening skills, so talk less and tune in more. Single? Open yourself up to the other fish in the sea. Vulnerability can be powerful, and it happens to be one of your sign's secret weapons. With Mercury in your dreamy twelfth house, your thoughts and conversations could roam into innovative terrain. It's also an opportune time for endings, so seek closure if there are any emotional loose ends hanging. Freeing yourself from draining situations will create space for something better.

January 26: Venus-Mars square

What's the hurry, Pisces? With the love planet (in Pisces) battling anxious Mars in your goal-driven tenth house, you could be rushing into next steps. What if you pumped the brakes to revel in the romance instead? Just be transparent and clear about your intentions and your timeline. You might not be looking for the same things, and your love interest deserves to know that.

January 27: Venus-Neptune meetup

When beautifying Venus and dreamy Neptune make their annual rendezvous in your sign, all bets are off in the boudoir! Hang the "do not disturb" sign and let yourself get carried away. No fantasy should be off-limits.

JANUARY: CAREER HOTSPOTS

January 2: Mercury-Jupiter meetup

Communicator Mercury and open-hearted Jupiter unite in your teamwork zone today. If you're moderating a discussion or arranging a deal, speak up for your beliefs. Your authenticity could win the support you need. And with a group of like-minded people championing your vision, you can't go wrong! No need to do all your campaigning IRL. Fire off a strategically-crafted post today and it could go viral.

January 3-February 16: Mars in Sagittarius

Don't wait—accelerate! For the first time in two years, motivator Mars dashes into your tenth house of long-term goals and reputation. Your career could heat up fast—along with the pressure. New projects and well-deserved accolades could be yours for the taking, but you have to show up in a big way. Call on your support systems to prevent any potential overwhelm. You don't need to go it alone!

January 10: Uranus retrograde ends

Revolutionary Uranus ends its five-month retrograde in Taurus, straightening out in your third house of communication and social activity. Have your friendships been erratic or laced with drama? Your social calendar may have seen its fair share of disruptions, and you might have questioned whether you were on the same page as your crew at moments. With the cosmic trailblazer back to normal speed, you can sort out any misunderstandings and start planning an epic winter soiree!

January 12: Mercury-Saturn-Pluto meetup

Today, Saturn and Pluto make their rare (once every 35 years!) alignment, bringing powerful alliances to light. With communicator Mercury joining the chorus, intrigue and intensity could infiltrate group dynamics. If that happens, you'll need to take the high ground. Listen to each party's opinions before coming to any conclusions. With wise and temperate Saturn in the mix, you could even invite some new voices into the fray. Is someone slyly prioritizing their own agenda? Do your best to ignore unproductive gossip and people who try to thwart your efforts for their own gain. If an informal gathering brings you face-to-face with movers and shakers, share about your work like you'd talk up a friend's accomplishments. Your track record may speak for itself, but you have an opportunity to confidently expound on it. The spotlight is yours!

January 13: Sun-Saturn-Pluto meetup

When the Sun and shadowy Pluto in your eleventh house of groups align with structured Saturn, the person pushing your buttons just might be a boss or higher up—or someone who reminds you of an old parental dynamic. Pause before you react. Egos and power plays could run amok. If you have to interact with this person, take the high road and lead with integrity. Be discerning about your online activity today, as the trolls could be circling. There's a "mute" button on your social media platforms for a reason: Instead of getting dragged into drama, build your power team. The Sun and Saturn in your eleventh house of groups could bring fresh faces into the fold or a networking event worth attending. Reach out to an influencer who might be a promising collaborator. With this transit's focus on technology, upgrade your apps and devices.

January 18: Mercury-Uranus square
A key collaborator could act fickle or flighty as communicator Mercury squares rebellious Uranus. You've been working hard to get everyone on the same page, so don't trash the project at the first sign of friction. Wait for the storm to pass.

January 23: Sun-Uranus square
Your sign is all about big dreams and even bigger ambitions. But are they achievable and attainable? Revise your reveries accordingly. Today is perfect for sitting down to sketch out a solid strategy. It could take time for your aspirations to come to fruition. Don't let a bout of impatience or self-doubt derail you.

January 24: Aquarius new moon and Chinese Lunar New Year (Year of the Metal Rat)
As the new moon moves into your twelfth house of healing, closure and the subconscious, the Chinese Lunar New Year begins. Welcome the Metal Rat, a time to be shrewd and discerning. Itemize what you can let go of in the next month—especially if you've been a "pack rat" over the past year. Then, add a column and list out what you want

to welcome in during the coming 12 months. But leave white space on your calendar instead of over-planning. You could attract some happy surprises!

January 28: Mars-Neptune square
Rushing to a conclusion is not the best course of action. When tempestuous Mars links up with manipulative Neptune, beware of people who try to coerce you into settling for less than what you want. Not ready to make a decision? It's okay to stall. If they distort the narrative or pin the blame on you, double down on those boundaries.

February

FEBRUARY: LOVE HOTSPOTS

February 7-March 4: Venus in Aries
Prioritize pleasure as the love planet enters your luxurious second house for a five-week stay. Add more beauty and an indulgence or two into your days, like fresh flowers or a set of sumptuous sheets spritzed with a favorite scent. Plan some romantic evenings for you and your S.O. Single? Try more upscale places to meet and mingle.

February 16-March 30: Mars in Capricorn
Sparks could fly with a friend (or a friend-of-friends) when the planet of desire lands in your social and free-spirited eleventh house. Keep your romantic options open, as lusty Mars visits this independent area of your chart for the next six weeks. If you're in a relationship, some breathing room could be beneficial for both parties. You might want to spend every second together but time to yourself is crucial.

February 23: Venus-Jupiter square

You may want to blow off your duties with your favorite plus-one, but responsibility is knocking! Romantic Venus clashes with adventurous Jupiter, making it hard to ignore tasks and assignments. Focus on finishing your to-do list, then make time for a concert or outing together.

February 28: Venus-Pluto square

You might experience a flurry of conflicting desires today. Pluto in your free-spirited eleventh house feels smothered by the slightest whiff of control, while Venus longs for steadfast and dependable. Perhaps you're feeling threatened by someone's autonomous moves. Take a step back and figure out why this is bothering you, instead of unleashing an intense reaction. Then figure out how to ask for what you need—calmly.

FEBRUARY: CAREER HOTSPOTS

February 3-March 4: Mercury in Pisces

The communication planet takes its first of two trips through your sign this year. Use this opportunity to promote a personal project or put yourself out there boldly. Just do it before Mercury makes a retrograde U-turn from February 16 to March 9.

February 9: Leo full moon

The Leo full moon lights up your sixth house of work, wellness and service. Systematize your workflow, implementing more efficient ways of tackling tasks. Batch assignments or see what you can outsource. Is there an app for that? Locate some tech tools to streamline your systems. Find a few helpful collaborators and review Team Pisces to see who's outlived their usefulness or might be in need of clearer instructions and training.

February 16-March 9: Mercury retrograde

Mercury turns retrograde in your sign until March 4 before dipping back into Aquarius and your twelfth house of endings. Hold off on any major tech purchases, and back up your data beforehand, storing crucial information in the cloud. Block off time to review goals and plans, making revisions as needed. If you need to tie up any loose ends, now is the time to go back and address final details. With Mercury reversing through your house of first impressions, clean up your social media accounts, updating profile photos and bios. Shy about speaking in public? If it's part of your career, consider media training.

February 16-March 30: Mars in Capricorn

For the first time in two years, your social eleventh house is set ablaze by energizer Mars. Gather a few stellar collaborators to elevate an existing project. Since this zone of your chart also rules technology, it's a dynamic time to launch. Connect with colleagues through LinkedIn and try new apps to improve workflow. Just hold off on major upgrades until Mercury goes direct on March 9.

February 21: Mars-Uranus trine

Off the fence you go! Today's ingenious mashup of driven Mars and innovative Uranus could catalyze one of your wilder ideas. With these two firecrackers at the helm, your project pitch may be greeted with some well-deserved enthusiasm.

February 23: Pisces new moon

The new moon in Pisces is the reset button you didn't know you needed. Use today's lunar reboot to freshen up any areas of your life that have become a little stuffy or stagnant. A solo venture or passion project could take flight. Whatever you start now will grow over the coming six months until the corresponding full moon. Reframe any barriers or hurdles as opportunities for growth. The Pisces new moon helps you tap into your confidence.

March

MARCH: LOVE HOTSPOTS

March 3: Venus-Saturn square

Looking for advice in all the wrong places? Your friends may have the best intentions, but their perspectives are clouded by their own bias. Only you know the intimate details of your relationships, Pisces. Trust your instincts and ignore any opinions that are out of line.

March 4-April 3: Venus in Taurus

Romantic Venus is right at home in sensual Taurus. And you'll be at the top of your game while the love planet visits your third house of communication. Fire off some flirty texts and let the witty banter flow. Single Pisces can sample from a passel of potential suitors. Coupled? Conversations will flow easily during this transit, so share your thoughts and feelings with your S.O.

March 4-16: Mercury in Aquarius

Your naturally empathetic sign will have a hard time drawing boundaries while Mercury dips back into your compassionate twelfth house—and all the more so while it's retrograde until March 9. Practice "active listening" if your mate asks for your advice, but don't get caught up trying to fix anyone's problems. Single? Let yourself daydream

about idealistic outcomes—and get nostalgic. Use Mercury's brief stay in this reflective zone to heal any resentments or limiting beliefs about love.

March 8: Venus-Uranus meetup

If you've been waiting for the right time to speak your mind, it's now. As Venus links up with uninhibited Uranus in your chatty third house, you may blurt out a shocking confession or desire. Single Pisces could meet someone online or through mutual friends unexpectedly. Stay open to someone who's not your usual type. Not interested in anything serious? Just say so! The other party will appreciate your candor.

March 9: Virgo full moon

Today's Virgo full moon in your committed relationship house could help you make a decision and stick with it. If you've been waffling over whether someone is worth investing more time and energy into, Virgo's practical, grounded energy provides clarity. Likewise, coupled Pisces might feel certain that it's time to take the next step— whether that's making things even more official or potentially parting ways.

March 21-July 1: Saturn in Aquarius

Fantasy has its place, but denial is a whole different ball of wax. Maturity planet Saturn starts the first leg of a three-year journey through Aquarius and your twelfth house of escape, its first visit here since 1991. Saturn in this closure-focused sector could herald a major chapter for healing the painful past or even a love addiction with roots in an unresolved incident. It's time to do the hard but necessary work so you can finally move forward—lighter and free!

March 27: Venus-Jupiter trine

When expansive Jupiter and sensual Venus unite in social and cerebral sectors, you crave intellectual stimulation in your love life. Couples: How can you infuse more novelty into your relationship? Single Fish could meet someone through mutual friends or on the apps, as both planets are in the most tech-savvy zones of your chart.

March 28: Venus-Pluto trine

Are you imaging things or is your friend checking you out? Love planet Venus and transformational Pluto harmonize in your interpersonal houses, infusing your talks with a sexy frisson of intrigue. Everything feels laden with innuendo. But is it? There's only one way to find out.

March 30-May 13: Mars in Aquarius

Time to end a destructive, draining dynamic? As assertive Mars swings into your twelfth house of endings and healing for the first time in two years, you'll find the courage to break an unhealthy pattern at last. Be loving but firm when resolving issues—and no beating around the bush. The red planet doesn't do subtle and passive-aggressive.

March 31: Mars-Saturn meetup

While you and your S.O. may be spending lots of time together as a twosome, today's stars make you keen to interact with others outside that couple bubble. Is it time to introduce your new love interest to your nearest and dearest? Plan a spontaneous dinner party or get the crew together for drinks. But be discerning with the invites and plus-ones. Quality company over quantity!

March 4-16: Mercury in Aquarius

Communicative Mercury dips into your twelfth house of reflection for a brief stay. Since it's in the area of your chart usually ruled by Pisces, use this period for a restful, restorative break. Clear your calendar of unnecessary obligations and declutter your workspace so you're only surrounded by things that light you up.

March 9: Virgo full moon

Ready to sign on the dotted line with a key collaborator? Today's full moon in your partnership zone could bring you to that point. If a prospect needs more information or reassurance, be sure to provide that. By showing you're committed to this joint endeavor and prepared to pull your weight, you could seal the deal under these officializing moonbeams.

March 16-April 10: Mercury in Pisces

Mercury returns for a second tour of Pisces, after a retrograde in February sent the cosmic messenger dipping back into Aquarius for a brief spell. Now that the communication planet has reestablished full power, you can press "publish" on anything you've been working on behind the scenes. Mercury is still in its "shadow" period post-retrograde, so review your pitch or presentation and amend as needed.

March 20: Mars-Jupiter meetup

Your ambition is heightened today, as spirited Mars and expansive Jupiter land in your social eleventh house. A bold move could draw influential people into your orbit. Speak up on an important issue or pitch a pioneering project. Rub elbows with other influencers at an after-work function. Nothing on the calendar? Arrange to meet your most inspiring friends to talk about your grand plans.

March 21-July 1: Saturn in Aquarius

For the first time since 1991, structured Saturn moves into Aquarius, the first phase of a transit that will last until 2023. With the ringed taskmaster in your imaginative twelfth house, this could be a powerful time to monetize your creativity or healing gifts. Limiting beliefs may arise as you level up. Confront them head-on instead of succumbing to insecurity. This zone of your chart also rules endings and closure. During the next few months, you may recognize that an area of your life is coming to a natural conclusion. Don't resist the transition.

March 23: Mars-Pluto meetup

As these two potent players unite in your networking house, you'll become keenly aware of the "who's who" of your inner circle. Don't feel guilty about wanting high-status connections, Pisces. You might also use your own clout to open doors for a deserving person—and if there's a little "you scratch my back" flavor to it, so be it. Sometimes, that's how deals are done. Got a project to put on the map? Strategically reach out to a well-connected person or an influencer in your field.

March 24: Aries new moon

Use the energy of today's new moon in your second house of income and work to define your plan. Where do you want to be in six months? As the first quarter of the year comes to a close, check in with what you want to accomplish next in 2020. Then determine what steps will get you there. Looking for new clients or a change of professional scene? This new moon fully supports you putting the word out.

March 30-May 13: Mars in Aquarius

Aggro Mars moves into your twelfth house of endings and hidden agendas. Watch your back a bit now, Pisces. Does that person acting super-friendly have your best interests in mind...or an ulterior motive? Hold off on sharing too much and observe their actions. With anxious Mars in your restful zone, you could have trouble sleeping. If your subconscious is on overdrive, journal out any thoughts or ideas before bed. Regular exercise during the day could exhaust you enough to sleep through the night. Turning on the TV or pouring a glass of wine might sound relaxing, but that pesky blue light and spike of sugar could keep you up longer! Try new, preventative tactics instead, such as winding down with an evening meditation, a hot bath or a soothing cup of tea.

March 31: Mars-Saturn meetup

Is it time to reassess who's on Team Pisces? Driven Mars is ready for a new endeavor, but structured Saturn is hesitant to move in too quick. With both of these planets in your secretive twelfth house, it might feel like someone isn't being forthcoming about their agenda. Get everyone on board with the same vision before diving in too deep.

April

APRIL: LOVE HOTSPOTS

April 3-August 7: Venus in Gemini

Turn up the tenderness! Passionate Venus visits your emotional fourth house for three weeks. You could feel extra nostalgic and sensitive now. Let down your guard a bit—your vulnerability is attractive.

Coupled? Schedule a few nights in to snuggle with your plus-one. Talks could turn to exchanging keys, babies or looking for a new home together.

April 4: Venus-Saturn trine

Are you leaning too heavily on one person for support? It's okay to vent to your trusted companion but don't take advantage of their kindness. Be aware if you start monopolizing the conversation. Or seek out a friend to chat with and give your S.O. some space. If you're single, small talk with someone new could turn deep quickly, revealing how much you have in common.

April 7: Libra full moon

Today's Libra full moon lights up your eighth house of merging, intimacy and sex. You'll feel its influence for two weeks, and it won't take much to fuel your fires! If there are sparks between you and a potential love interest, ask yourself if this union has what it takes to go the distance. It may not, but you can still enjoy that sexy frisson of chemistry. For couples, this play-for-keeps moon dance might spark an engagement, pregnancy or plans to make things a lot more permanent.

APRIL: CAREER HOTSPOTS

April 3: Mercury-Neptune meetup

Imagination and intellect find their perfect balance point today, as communication planet Mercury entwines with creative Neptune in Pisces. Mercury's rational side balances dreamy Neptune's influence, so your utopian ideas actually have a chance at becoming reality. This could be an emotional merger though, so instead of pushing for a resolution, let things run their course.

April 4: Jupiter-Pluto meetup

Who are the people you surround yourself with? A rare alignment of expansive Jupiter and power-player Pluto converges in your eleventh house of teamwork and technology, revealing the shadows as well as the lightworkers on Team Pisces. This is the first of three transformational conjunctions in 2020—a hookup that only happens every 13 years. Prepare to whittle your inner circle and move the most inspiring, ambitious people into a closer position. The next two conjunctions, on June 30 and November 12, could bring even more well-connected people into your orbit.

April 7: Libra full moon

A full moon in steady, stable Libra lands in your eighth house of shared finances, assets and joint ventures today. For the next two weeks (or longer), slow down your decision-making process to ensure you're working with the right people. Are they trustworthy? Reliable? This is also a great time to book a session with a financial advisor. Make sure your resources are working as hard as you are.

April 7: Mars-Uranus square

You could be confronted with an unsavory situation when irritable Mars faces off with unpredictable Uranus. Whether someone's intentionally annoying you or oblivious to how they're making you feel, addressing it could further exasperate you. You probably won't resolve this today. Take some time to cool down before bringing it up for discussion.

April 10-27: Mercury in Aries

Astute Mercury moves into your second house of finances, putting your mind on your money. Review your budget and savings plans to see where you might want to pivot. With info-hound Mercury sparking your curiosity, load up on inspiring

The AstroTwins' 2020 Horoscope

podcasts and books about productivity or savvy money management.

April 14: Sun-Pluto square

The Sun in your work sector clashes with secretive Pluto, so conduct due diligence and screen anyone before you share sensitive intel. Your ideas are worth safeguarding. If collaborators don't respect your contributions, or go behind your back, it's time to re-establish your boundaries.

April 15: Sun-Jupiter square

Don't quit now, Pisces! As the Sun confronts restless Jupiter, you'll feel the push you need to finalize a project. If you've been resistant to tackle this challenge, dive in—but don't just rush ahead without a plan. Plow past any self-imposed limitations and you could surprise yourself. No need to do this alone either! With effusive Jupiter amping up your eleventh house of groups, you can inspire the troops take this past the finish line.

April 21: Sun-Saturn square

Other people might be checked out or unreliable as the Sun butts heads with resistant Saturn. Pay attention to the tasks that you're able to control. If all else fails, focus on cleaning up your side of the street today. Surely there are a few projects you could tackle on your own?

April 22: Taurus new moon

The Taurus new moon in your eloquent third house turns up your powers of persuasion. Your nonverbal communication is usually sharp, so translate those inner thoughts into external exchanges. If you've been waiting to broach a topic, now's the time. Present what you've been working on and the right partners could help you elevate your endeavors.

April 25: Mercury square Jupiter & Pluto

If one of your accomplishments has turned a colleague into a green-eyed monster, don't take it personally. You may never know what triggered them, but you're not at fault. If it impacts your work, discuss it privately with a manager so they can respond appropriately. You might want to lay low until this blows over, but don't let it trick you into playing small.

April 25: Mercury-Jupiter square

Getting carried away by a supersized vision? You can thank expansive Jupiter's strained encounter with Mercury for any unexpected scope creep. It's great that you're enthusiastic but stay within the parameters of the plan.

April 25-October 4: Pluto retrograde in Capricorn

Heads up: You could encounter resistance in a collaborative environment when Pluto, the planet of power and control, turns retrograde in your eleventh house of groups for the next few months. Prep some preventative measures. Brush up on de-escalation tactics in the event of an outburst. And observe whether people's actions match their words. Is an associate feeding you false promises? Don't jump to conclusions during this transit.

April 26: Sun-Uranus meetup

Broadcast your novel ideas! The confident Sun and innovative Uranus illuminate your third house of communication today, so take center stage and stop working in the wings. Be careful not to send your visions off to any parties who might appropriate them for their own use. Put your name on the project and press "publish."

April 27-May 11: Mercury in Taurus

Someone you bump into at your local cafe could become a key connection to your next big break. Stay open to new people and ideas, as the zodiac's courier travels through your conceptual and social third house. They might come at you faster than you can caption them, so keep a notebook handy. Some won't be worth pursuing. Be discerning.

April 28: Mercury-Saturn square

Messenger Mercury quarrels with staunch Saturn, making progress feel almost impossible. You know how they say you *can* lead a horse to water but you can't make them drink? Remember that, and turn your attention to things you can actually control. Other people may not be willing to cooperate. Table any group tasks for later and fly solo.

April 30: Mercury-Uranus meetup

Is your big idea ready for prime time? Your grand schemes could gather momentum today, as intellectual Mercury links up with your creative co-ruler Uranus. Speak up in that important meeting, or reach out to someone in your field to join forces. Take it slow and see if there's a natural rapport. Even if things don't align, this person could give you new perspective on a fledgling idea.

May

MAY: LOVE HOTSPOTS

May 3: Venus-Neptune square

Just because you're feeling the love, that doesn't mean common sense will prevail. As dreamy Neptune and starstruck Venus butt heads, your overblown emotions could sway all logic. Don't ignore the red flags—but don't rush to conclusions either. If you have a nagging feeling that someone's being a little dishonest, observe but don't act for a day or two. The truth will surface.

May 11-September 29: Saturn retrograde

Reevaluate your relationships when Saturn makes its annual retrograde. Until July 1, the structured planet will backtrack through Aquarius and your twelfth house of endings, healing and the subconscious. Are you accepting less than you're worth? Determine how to establish equilibrium in your partnerships, or part ways with anyone who's ignoring your needs. From July 1 onward, Saturn will slip into Capricorn and your eleventh house of groups, giving you a sobering look at team dynamics.

May 13-June 27: Mars in Pisces

Hello, head turner! Late spring flings ignite as passionate Mars slides into your sign for a sizzling stay. When the lusty red planet makes its biennial visit to Pisces, you'll draw attention without even trying. Mars in your sign spikes your confidence and charisma (so attractive!), but it can also inflate egos and make you argumentative.

May 13-June 25: Venus retrograde in Gemini

When the planet of romance and harmony turns retrograde for six weeks in your domestic fourth house, you could be especially thin-skinned. Your moods and emotions may fluctuate, especially if you have unresolved hurt. Temper your reactions.

May 20: Venus-Neptune square

Romantic Venus meets up with dreamy Neptune in your sign, where fantasies reign. If you're swept

The AstroTwins' 2020 Horoscope

away by someone, know that you might not be seeing the full picture. Take your time and wade in slowly, even as you're enjoying the moment.

May 22: Mercury-Venus meetup

Tell 'em how you feel! You possess an uncanny ability to express yourself today, when communicator Mercury and seductive Venus align in Gemini. Have a "state of the union" with your S.O. to see where you can enhance your relationship. Or send a flirty text to someone who's caught your interest!

May 22: Gemini new moon

Today's Gemini full moon lands in your fourth house of home and family. Take time to reflect on your partnerships and their emotional health. What are you ready to let go of? And what do you want to make space for? The decisions you make now will carry you through the rest of the year. Assess your living space and see what you can do to make it more inviting and sensual.

May 28-August 4: Mercury in Cancer

Messenger Mercury flies into Cancer and your fifth house of romance for an extended journey, thanks to a retrograde that will happen June 18 to July 12. Love could be top priority for you, and it doesn't take much to sweep your idealistic sign into a daydream. With Mercury gone rogue, a budding romance may hit pause, only to resurface after Mercury goes direct (forward) in August. For couples, reconnect over shared interests, and find new ways to woo each other all over again. Ready to take the next step? Start talking about house hunting or expanding your brood.

May 7: Scorpio full moon

Have you been holding back on a big project out of fear? As the year's only Scorpio full moon lights up your ninth house of entrepreneurship and expansion, it's time for a leap of faith. If you're still hesitant to broadcast this new idea, think about all the people who need to hear it. The concept came to you because you saw a need that wasn't being met in the market. You won't know if it's viable unless you try!

May 9: Mercury-Pluto trine

Tap into the power of your network today. With potent Pluto and messenger Mercury in an auspicious alignment, a mastermind could take your ideas to a whole new level. Play superconnector and make a strategic intro of two influential friends. Test the waters to see if a savvy contact will recommend you for a coveted gig.

May 10: Mercury-Jupiter trine

Lucky Jupiter and expressive Mercury form an advantageous alignment today, giving you the green light to debut your big idea. Your confidence and verve may convince a savvy person in your field to jump on board. Conversations with kindred spirits can spark a big idea—but today is much more about "talk" than "action." Let the ideas flow but hold off on committing for a few days.

May 11-September 29: Saturn retrograde

Return to any abandoned creative endeavors when Saturn turns retrograde in your imaginative twelfth house. This area of your chart rules retreats and breaks. You could be more than ready for a respite from the grind. Remove unnecessary tasks and streamline your workflow so you can focus on recharging. Find a few easy rituals to integrate into your day. Get more sleep, cut back on indulgences, or adopt a plant to "green" your desk. Decline any engagements that don't make you smile at the idea of attending. With all this free space, the muse could be enticed to visit. On July 1, Saturn will back into Capricorn and your group sector, a time to be more mindful about the company you keep.

May 11: Mercury-Mars square

Time-out! As a group project reaches a tense impasse, resentful words could be exchanged. Intervene if you notice that people are taking out their stress on each other. Can you rearrange the workload to balance everyone's responsibilities?

May 11-28: Mercury in Gemini

The cosmic messenger powers through your fourth house of foundations and emotions. Do you feel a sense of psychological safety at work? That is, can you show up as your true self without fear of any backlash? If not, do a gut check to see if there's a past-based fear coming up or whether the climate is truly hostile. Happy at your job? Make an effort to bond with your colleagues more. Note: You're prone to taking things personally during this transit. When you're feeling sensitive, table the topic for when you're more secure.

May 12: Mercury-Saturn trine

Almost anything you need can be found within your network, Pisces. You just have to ask! Identify your strongest links and pull in collaborators to fill the gaps. Be welcoming but discerning as you screen candidates. Although you may be eager to get this project underway, you want to have the right players on board.

May 13-June 27: Mars in Pisces

Driven Mars blazes into your sign today, supercharging your already impressive productivity levels. Though Saturn's retrograde is encouraging you to slow down, you could feel a boost of energy with the red planet on your side. Use this shot in the arm as fuel to finish any lingering projects, scheduling in some well-deserved breaks.

May 14-September 12: Jupiter retrograde in Capricorn

A collaborative project that was moving full steam ahead may grind to a halt when Jupiter reverses through measured Capricorn and your group sector. During this four-month slowdown, step back and evaluate your progress. Is everyone on Team Pisces pulling their weight? Correct course as needed. If things don't come together smoothly, take a break and focus on solo endeavors instead.

May 15: Sun-Pluto trine

Ready to shake things up? The confident Sun and transformative Pluto turn you into a change-making visionary today. Connect with collaborators who are dynamic and fully committed to the cause. With more sharp thinkers on board, you'll make headway quickly.

May 22: Gemini new moon

A page-turning new moon in your domestic fourth house turns Chateau Pisces into a hub of productivity. Arrange to work remotely part of the week or cozy up your home office. Gemini is the ruler of dynamic duos, so connect with collaborators and have an emotional check-in. How can you support one another's goals this summer?

May 22: Mercury-Neptune square

Your emotive sign is always up for talking about your feelings, but communicator Mercury's clash with befuddling Neptune could scramble signals. Push any conversations back a few days, when the hazy skies have blown over.

May 28-August 4: Mercury in Cancer

Speak up! Mercury, the planet of communication and technology, starts an extra-long visit to your passionate fifth house. Post new headshots and add some dazzle to your profiles. You'll be inspired to share your talents during this creative, expressive transit. But protect your original concepts before Mercury turns retrograde from June 18 to July 12, when information can slip through the cracks or fall into the wrong hands.

June

JUNE: LOVE HOTSPOTS

June 2: Venus-Mars square

Love gone awry? As the second of 2020's three Venus-Mars clashes occurs, you're torn between a deep desire to bond and a burning urge for independence. With Venus retrograde in your emotional fourth house, all kinds of suppressed feelings could surface. Be careful it doesn't come across as anger or impatience. You could trample someone's sensitive feelings easily now.

June 13: Mars-Neptune meetup

Fantasies ignite! As lusty Mars and enchanting Neptune align in your sign, nothing your imagination can conjure (and both parties consent to trying) is off-limits.

June 18-July 12: Mercury retrograde in Cancer

Have you been overlooking a glaring issue in your love life? Mercury turns retrograde in your fifth house of romance for a few weeks, prompting a relationship review. The communication planet's backspin could bend your words in a way you didn't intend or cause a lover to send mixed signals. Tread carefully and speak clearly. You could have an unexpected encounter with an ex, as the messenger planet's transit brings back old flames. Got an apology to issue or something left unsaid? You could finally have that conversation.

June 21: Cancer new moon (annular solar eclipse)

The first of two consecutive new moons lights up your love house—and this one is also a galvanizing solar eclipse! Prepare for a fresh start in your approach to relationships. Single? You could meet someone out of the blue today, so stay alert. That cutie trying to get your attention might just have you at hello. Not sure what you're looking for? Devote some time to creatively visualizing what a swoon-worthy partner may look like.

June 27, 2020-January 6, 2021: Mars in Aries

The red planet bolsters your second house of self-worth, security, and sensuality for the rest of the year—an extended visit thanks to a retrograde this fall. This transit is all about choosing quality over quantity. Surround yourself with people who bring out the best in you. Take it slow and steady with potential partners. Since this zone of your chart rules luxury and indulgence, book opulent date nights and shower your love with tasteful gifts. Confidence and charisma are the sexiest attributes now—in you and anyone you meet!

June 5: Sagittarius full moon (lunar eclipse)

Score! All your hard work of the past six months pays off in spades as the full moon in your tenth house of career—a momentous lunar eclipse—catalyzes your grandest goals An unexpected professional transition could also arrive. If one door closes, trust that another (much bigger) portal will soon open. Eclipses sweep away what no longer serves us. A boss or client may exit, making room for an opportunity that's a better fit. Been waiting for some much-deserved kudos or a glowing performance review? That could also come today. If you don't get the feedback you hoped for, clarify expectations so you can either make the desired improvements or take your talents elsewhere.

June 13: Mars-Neptune meetup

Motivator Mars meets up with imaginative Neptune in your sign today, strengthening your manifestation muscles. Revisit your 2020 resolutions and see which ones need some attention. Your innate Piscean intuition is heightened today, so take advantage of the divine downloads to determine your next move.

June 18-July 12: Mercury retrograde in Cancer

Mayday! Mercury, planet of communication, travel and technology, turns retrograde in your expressive fifth house. For the next couple weeks, take your heart off your sleeve and keep those unfiltered thoughts to yourself. Opinions that might have branded you a "badass" or "renegade" could now just land as obnoxious—if not totally inappropriate. You may need to navigate some outsized egos. Resist the temptation to fight fire with fire!

June 21: Cancer new moon (annular solar eclipse)

A creative epiphany could strike at the first of 2020's two Cancer new moons, especially since this one is a head-turning eclipse. Major buzz, even fame, could be yours for the taking. Put your talents on display or give 'em a performance they won't forget—whether you're singing at open-mic night or pitching your idea for an industry-disrupting new app.

June 23-November 28: Neptune retrograde in Pisces

Take some time to reevaluate your aims when your ruling planet turns retrograde in your sign. Imaginative, idealistic Neptune has the best ideas and intentions, but can they become reality? For the next five months, go back to the drawing board to make sure the dream has what it needs to become a success. Map out your moves and set timelines. If a personal project or creative endeavor has been collecting dust, brush it off and dive back in.

June 27, 2020-January 6, 2021: Mars in Aries

The red planet lights up your second house of work and money for the remainder of the year, an extended visit courtesy of a retrograde from September 9 through November 13. Use this transit to break past any self-imposed boundaries and to brush up your confidence. An unplanned expense could add stress, but necessity is the mother of invention. Let Mars motivate you to lean in and solve any problems quickly and courageously. With the red planet revving up your revenue sector, work can get demanding (think: long hours and short deadlines). Be rigorous about sticking to your self-care practices to avoid burning out.

June 30: Jupiter-Pluto meetup

Don't hate, collaborate! The second of three expansive and rare meetups could bring exciting new players into your network. With both Jupiter and Pluto now retrograde, don't overlook people from your past. Mine your network for gold instead of chasing after every new person who promised you the moon. The tried-and-tested true friends could be the ones who open the doors you want. Look back to April 4 (the first meetup) for clues of what might surface now.

July

JULY: LOVE HOTSPOTS

July 8: Mercury-Mars square

Craving some breathing room? Hard as it is to bring up a need for space, suppressing your desire for freedom will only make you feel more claustrophobic. An honest conversation about your feelings could renew your attraction to your current partner. Maybe you just need a weekend to yourself—or to be less attentive to their every need. Summon the courage to speak up!

July 20: Cancer new moon

Today's Cancer new moon—the second one of 2020—is the romantic reset you didn't know you needed. You could gain clarity about how to revitalize a stale dynamic or meet someone new who lights you up. Take some time to envision what you want in a partnership. Instead of waiting around for someone to adore you, focus on self-love and self-care. Be more playful and introduce more glamour into your day. When you do meet someone worthy of a chance, you'll already feel whole and fulfilled—and they'll just be the cherry on top.

July 27: Venus-Neptune square

Everything looks better with rose-colored glasses, but your vision might not be 20/20. As Venus in your emotional fourth house tussles with hazy Neptune, it's hard to distinguish feelings from facts. Are you overlooking some important warning signs or getting mixed signals? Your own moods could be subject to change without notice.

July 30: Mercury-Neptune trine

Do your loved ones know how you feel? Communicative Mercury in your passionate fifth house forms a positive alignment to your ruler Neptune, giving you the green light to voice your emotions. Express gratitude to your S.O. and close friends during the day. Or finally tell your love interest how you feel about them. If someone on social media catches your eye, slide into their DMs and say hello. A flirty (and sweet) chat could ensue!

JULY: CAREER HOTSPOTS

July 1-December 17: Saturn retrograde enters Capricorn

It's okay to pump the brakes every once in a while. Cautious Saturn, which has been retrograde since May 11, backs into your social eleventh house for the duration of its backspin. Everything from technology to team dynamics could be tested between now and September 29. Don't let these setbacks stop you from making progress, even if it's slower going. Use this transit to make sure you have all the necessary pieces in place. By the time Saturn turns direct in late September, you'll have a solid foundation under you.

July 5: Capricorn full moon (lunar eclipse)

Today's full moon in your collaborative eleventh house is also a lunar eclipse, making it extra potent. A group project you've been working on could receive a surge of motivation or attract out-of-the-blue buzz. Since lunar eclipses can bring abrupt endings or transitions, you may suddenly part ways with a certain crew or end a toxic friendship. This is a powerful day for any digital launches. One of your ideas could unexpectedly go viral!

July 15: Sun-Pluto opposition

A certain domineering person's behavior is working your nerves, and you could have a hard time hiding it. Unfortunately, you can't control how other people act. Bow out of the conflict (no matter how tempting) and focus on what you can control: yourself.

July 20: Sun-Saturn opposition

Don't ask for opinions if you don't really care what people think. If you solicit advice that you don't take, people could feel like their input isn't appreciated—or worse, like you're just dumping on them. When you're out with your friends, connect over other topics or just keep it light. And if you're truly struggling with a daunting issue, speak to a professional instead of treating your loved ones like amateur therapists.

July 27: Mercury-Mars square

With mental Mercury in your visionary ninth house, you've got supersized ideas. But a tough beam from stressful Mars in your money zone could leave you without the proper budget or plan to execute on them. Break those grand plans into phases and you'll start to see possibilities instead of roadblocks.

July 30: Mercury-Jupiter opposition

Have long hours cut into your domestic downtime? It's possible that you've bitten off more than you can chew. Don't let pride prevent you from being honest about that. You're only one human here, Pisces! Set clear boundaries with clients or colleagues and stick to them. If you've been consumed by a big project, show appreciation to the loved ones who held down the fort while you were on duty!

August

AUGUST: LOVE HOTSPOTS

August 3: Aquarius full moon

The only Aquarius full moon of the year lights up your spiritual, otherworldly twelfth house. Your naturally strong intuition will be heightened under this transit. An optimistic, confident outlook will attract similarly sanguine types, so stay open to new connections. If you've been dating someone, their motives and values could become crystal clear. If you don't mesh, this might be the day when you make a tough but necessary decision to move on. Coupled Fish can bond over spiritual endeavors. This full moon is ready and willing to fuel some steamy fantasies, too!

August 7-September 6: Venus in Cancer

Summer sultriness heats up while passionate Venus sidles through your fifth house of romance. Integrate more sensuality and pleasure into your day, from fresh flowers to luxurious fabrics. During this glamorous transit, make bolder choices with your look (think: statement pieces, bright colors and eye-catching patterns)—and flirt with abandon!

August 25: Venus-Jupiter opposition

Temptations abound when decadent Venus in your lusty fifth house butts heads with over-the-top Jupiter. If a partnership feels stale, find ways to jump-start your connection. Flirting could feel fun for a minute, but are you breaking trust or rushing to put someone on a pedestal they haven't earned? Couples should plan a date doing something they haven't tried before. If you've gotten too liberal with your spending, have fun within your budget.

August 27: Venus-Neptune trine

You're not one to bottle up your emotions, and today is no exception. As sensual Venus syncs with dreamy Neptune, you'll catch feelings for everyone in your sight line. Focus on your loved ones during this divine and heart-expanding transit.

August 30: Mercury-Neptune opposition

Compromise is beautiful—when you're genuine about it. Today's manipulative Mercury-Neptune clash could tempt you to tell people what they want to hear. Catch yourself in the act before you do that. It will only lead to resentment down the road.

August 30: Venus-Pluto opposition

Where can you take responsibility, Pisces? It might be irritating to see how you played a part in the way a situation unfolded. But newsflash: Identifying your role can lead to powerful reflections. Instead of pointing fingers, take a deep breath and ask yourself what there is to learn here.

AUGUST: CAREER HOTSPOTS

August 1: Mercury-Pluto opposition

Someone may try to intimidate you with off-putting remarks or actions. Do your best to ignore them. Reacting may make it worse. The more attention they get, the more they'll bully. Your best move? Politely excuse yourself and step out of the situation.

August 2: Sun-Uranus square

Today's failure is tomorrow's breakthrough. A minor setback could have you doubting the merits of your work. Instead of tinkering and tweaking endlessly, reach out to your network or do some deep-diving research.

August 3: Mercury-Saturn opposition

Is the bullhorn really necessary? Your enthusiasm might be a touch over-the-top, as expressive Mercury opposes stern Saturn in your eleventh house of groups. Read the room before you make any major announcements. It's great to be passionate, but don't let emotions cloud your judgement. Since your audience might not be on the same page as you are, tailor your delivery so you don't lose them.

August 4: Mars-Jupiter square

Conflict could come to a head with a colleague when driven Mars in your work zone faces off with Jupiter in your social sector. Stay cool! The situation might provoke you to act out, but that won't get you very far. Keep an optimistic outlook and focus on creating a win for everyone.

August 4-19: Mercury in Leo

Get your systems in order! As Mercury marches into your orderly sixth house, you'll have an easier time discussing the finer points and details of everything. Since the sixth house rules organization, focus on streamlining your communications or refining your messages. Work toward inbox zero, create a calendar for your tasks, or set up new systems for greater efficiency.

August 10: Mercury-Uranus square

Flexibility is a must! Curveballs could come from all angles, and the original plan might need to be tossed out. Let go of any perfectionist tendencies to get the job done. If it's your colleagues who aren't cooperating, get curious about their resistance to see if you can address the root issue.

August 13: Mars-Pluto square

Is it really worth it? Revisit your values to see if what you're doing for money still aligns with your values. You may be asked to contribute to a questionable endeavor. Or, your associates could try to drag you into their dispute. Stay neutral at all costs.

August 15, 2020-January 14, 2021: Uranus retrograde in Taurus

Disruptive Uranus starts a lengthy backspin, interrupting the best-laid plans. Your intention to help could come off the wrong way. On the upside, this retrograde is the perfect time to reinforce your boundaries, engage in some extracurricular activities, or take on a project outside of work.

August 17: Mercury-Mars trine

Your sign's natural sensitivity can go a long way in leading others. Inspire friends and colleagues with your empathy and avoid brash criticisms or platitudes. Tell people your expectations right out of the gate, so there's no confusion. If you have a brilliant concept in mind, today's the day to vocalize it.

August 18: Leo new moon

The year's only Leo new moon illuminates the part of your chart that rules systems and organization. Is there an area of your life that could use a cleanup? Anything from your desk to your diet is fair game—and you'll see the results blossom in the coming six months as you're more focused and filled with vitality. Starting a big project? Spend a few extra hours getting the details and planning just right.

August 19-September 5: Mercury in Virgo

The communication planet moves into your seventh house of contracts and business partnerships. You might discuss a major project or connect with fellow movers and shakers. If you decide to embark on a joint venture, write down the terms so everyone is on the same page.

August 24: Mars-Saturn square

When motivated Mars clashes with severe Saturn, conversations could turn tense. If your team isn't able to agree, you might be called upon to play mediator. A negotiation may not be possible today, but you can at least help everyone keep their cool. Tension over money could erupt. Make sure the terms are equitable for all—and commensurate with the amount of work and experience everyone will contribute.

August 25: Mercury-Uranus trine

Combine your superpowers for the win! Messenger Mercury and ingenious Uranus meet up in the areas of your chart that rule communication and partnership. Instead of trying to do it all yourself, call for backup. They might have the exact skill sets you need. Look into starting a mastermind group of similarly ambitious friends so you can motivate one another (and celebrate your successes). It could be uplifting to connect with people you admire, either online or IRL. Who knows? There may be enough chemistry to compel you to join forces!

August 29: Mercury-Jupiter trine

Your big ideas can benefit from a few stellar supporters. Clever Mercury syncs up with lucky Jupiter, helping you sync to the people who can make it happen. Since the eleventh house rules technology, you could connect with someone online who helps you refine your concepts. Create a clear plan and set timelines to remain on track.

August 30: Mercury-Neptune opposition

Table any tricky topics when chatty Mercury opposes foggy Neptune. You may have perfected your pitch, but the audience's attention span is lacking. If you're the one listening, ask questions so you have all the information. Use your intuition now, as your ruler Neptune governs the subconscious. Maybe take a time-out to let it sink in.

September

SEPTEMBER: LOVE HOTSPOTS

September 2: Venus-Saturn opposition

Venus lights up your romance zone, but an opposition from serious Saturn in your detached eleventh house puts a damper on your fairytale. It's a good day to step back and look at your feelings

objectively. But don't get so distant that you lose touch with your heart.

September 4: Venus-Mars square

The last of 2020's three confrontations between Venus and Mars could pull your heart in dueling directions. The love planet in your fifth house of passion confronts Mars in your second house of priorities. Take a step back and review the situation. Are you getting so caught up in your need for security that you've forgotten to have fun? Have an honest conversation with your partner or potential S.O. to bring things back into alignment.

September 5-27: Mercury in Libra

Air it out, Pisces! Expressive Mercury in your eighth house of mystery and merging could help you open up to someone you love. Tell your romantic interest how you feel or share something vulnerable with your partner, whether that's a fantasy or an emotion you've kept inside. By doing so, you'll pave the way for greater intimacy.

September 6-October 2: Venus in Leo

Show your love through generosity and selfless acts. Sensual Venus lights up your sixth house of service, making you inclined to do kind things for those you love. You don't need a special occasion to bring flowers or a gift. Even small acts of giving will make someone feel appreciated. With beautifying Venus in your healthy living zone, ramp up the self-care—or make fitness part of the fun you have with your mate.

September 9-November 13: Mars retrograde in Aries

The red planet pivots in your second house of daily routines and priorities today. Are you slipping back into old habits? When Mars is retrograde, issues you thought you'd solved could come back up to the surface—and old flames might return. It's time to finally put the situation to rest, but you may need to find a way to clear this up that doesn't turn your world upside-down. Tempers could flare under this transit, so remain calm and excuse yourself if the discussion turns heated. It's not easy to change deeply-rooted patterns, so give yourself some grace.

September 15: Venus-Uranus square

Dash away from any dynamic that makes you feel confined or trapped. But take a minute to ask yourself how you contributed to the situation. You may need to gently reinforce your boundaries—but remember, it goes both ways. Respect other people's right to their autonomy as well.

September 17: Virgo new moon

The year's only new moon in your relationship realm gives you a chance for a fresh start. If things are a little ho-hum with your S.O., turn the page to a new chapter. Single? Jump back into the dating pool and stay open to unexpected connections.

September 28: Venus-Mars trine

Mundane daily activities get a special lift as romantic Venus meets up with energizer Mars in the more practical areas of your chart. Someone on your morning commute could catch your eye, or a casual conversation with a mutual friend might turn flirtatious. Coupled? Plan a simple date somewhere special or spend time in nature together. A fun, active day outdoors may turn up the heat when you're back inside!

SEPTEMBER: CAREER HOTSPOTS

September 1: Mercury-Pluto trine

A flicker of insight could inspire you to reach out to someone you admire—or a person whose energy is compelling. Follow that hunch! Eloquent Mercury and perceptive Pluto make a harmonious alignment in your social sectors, nudging you to connect. Send a message or make plans to meet up. Since the eleventh house rules technology, ping an influencer or share your brilliant insights in a group forum.

September 2: Pisces full moon

The year's only full moon in your sign is all about you! An endeavor you started six months ago could come to completion. Tell anyone and everyone about this huge accomplishment.

September 3: Mercury-Saturn trine

Tap your network! Outspoken Mercury and status-driven Saturn align in the collaborative areas of your chart, making today perfect for cultivating connections and supporting each other's efforts. Write a testimonial for someone's stellar services. Recommend a friend for a job or post a glowing review of your colleague's efforts on social media. When you signal-boost other people, they're just as likely to uplift you. Got a favorite brainstorming buddy? Connect for a jam session that elevates your respective projects.

September 5-27: Mercury in Libra

Put on your blinders and get to work! Mindful Mercury moves into your focused eighth house, commanding you to hunker down. You'll make major progress by tuning out distractions. The eighth house rules assets, long-term finances, and joint ventures. Schedule a meeting with a financial advisor to review your investment goals.

Conversations about joining forces could spark with Mercury in this merging-minded sector. Think long-term and strategic before getting caught in the rush of excitement.

September 9-November 13: Mars retrograde in Aries

Money acting funny? Driven Mars starts a two-month retrograde through your second house of work and income, a time to be vigilant about your finances. Set up autopayments, comb through bank statements for errors and scale back on spending to minimize monetary stress. A forgotten expense could come due. Prospecting for jobs or clients? Reach out to a former colleague, as retrogrades can bring back people from our past.

September 12: Jupiter retrograde ends

It's time to make moves! Lucky Jupiter resumes its forward motion in your networking zone, alleviating any stress in teams and collaborations. If you've been working behind the scenes, the pace of your progress could pick up. Make an effort to connect with new friends and groups. Even if you don't see yourself as a "joiner," rethink that self-image. Kindred spirits await!

September 14: Sun-Pluto trine

Strategic connections incoming! Get the word out when the expressive Sun and transformative Pluto align in your social houses. Mingle with movers and shakers in your field, both online and in person. Share what you've been working on and your networks will sit up and listen.

September 17: Virgo new moon

Compromise and collaborate! Today's new moon brings harmony to your partnerships and fresh opportunities to join forces. Of course you're fully capable of a successful solo mission, Pisces. But think of how much more you can accomplish with a righthand whiz whose skills complement yours.

September 17: Mercury-Jupiter square

Is someone on your team holding up progress? Their concerns are valid, so make time to hear what they have to say instead of being dismissive or a know-it-all. Listening to their input first, then offering some compromises will boost the team morale. Once you're all in agreement, you can forge ahead with renewed enthusiasm.

September 21: Mercury-Pluto square

Hold your tongue! When expressive Mercury clashes with destructive Pluto, even the best-intentioned words could come across the wrong way. Read the room: Are you in sync with your audience? Try listening more than speaking to establish yourself as a leader instead of a dictator.

September 23: Mercury-Saturn square

Is someone pushing you to make a decision without giving all the facts? Listen to your intuition and conduct your own fact-finding. Your colleagues may be resistant to the idea, but they'll come around when you uncover a critical piece of information.

September 24: Mercury-Mars opposition

Oversharing alert! Your heated emotions might drive you to make a decision that could be cringe-worthy down the line. If you're feeling reactive, hold off on major conclusions until this energy passes.

October

September 27-October 27: Mercury in Scorpio

The cosmic messenger zips into your ninth house of learning and growth, catapulting your visionary ideas. Step back from the nitty-gritty and attend to the big picture. Could you bring in some new perspectives through learning, reading or travel? Let yourself be more candid now, as your outspoken opinions could move the dialogue forward (provided you deliver them with tact). When Mercury turns retrograde October 13 until November 3, read the fine print before you sign anything. Make sure to back up important data and files before then, too!

September 29: Mars-Saturn square

Time out! Conversations could get fiery when tempestuous Mars faces off with stern Saturn. Your team might not be able to come to an agreement today, so schedule a recess for everyone to cool down. Step in as a referee to make sure all parties remain civil. Careful about rushing into anything that involves friends and money. Mars is like the gas and Saturn's the brake. Slamming on either one will only give you whiplash!

September 29: Saturn retrograde ends

Serious Saturn resumes its forward motion in your eleventh house of groups and technology. Teamwork may have had its fair share of hiccups over the past few months, including delayed projects and minor tech meltdowns. Continue onward with confidence—backed by a more solid plan.

OCTOBER: LOVE HOTSPOTS

October 2-27: Venus in Virgo

Sensual Venus travels into your seventh house of relationships for a few weeks, turning up the heat in your partnerships. With the planet of social graces here, coupled Pisces could host an early autumn gathering with your S.O. Single? Mutual friends might end up playing matchmaker for you and a special someone.

October 10: Venus-Uranus trine

Freedom is a turn-on! As the love planet aligns with boho-chic Uranus, seek ways to infuse your love life with independence and novelty. Have things gotten too close for comfort? As long as you're upfront with your partner, you'll get the breathing room you need. Reassure them that you'll be back (if that's your intention), then go follow your bliss. A sudden attraction may spark with a platonic pal. Could this person actually be the one you've been waiting for?

October 16: Libra new moon

Sweet seduction! The Libra new moon lands in the area of your chart that rules sex, intimacy and merging. What you start now could bear fruit at the corresponding full moon in six months. What do you want to manifest? More passion, play or a deeper partnership? If you're single, see how you can add more sensuality into your everyday life.

The AstroTwins' 2020 Horoscope

October 18: Venus-Neptune opposition

Can't make up your mind? Hazy Neptune clouds your judgement about a key relationship when it opposes cooperative Venus today. Take some time to clear your head, whether you journal, meditate or soak in a relaxing tub. Don't rush into a decision and beware of self-absorbed tendencies. You might even swing in the exact opposite direction and veer into codependence. Reframe any overly romanticized and potentially unrealistic ideas. We're all human, just doing the best we can. Give others the benefit of the doubt instead of stewing in resentment (which only hurts you).

October 19: Venus-Jupiter trine

Are you giving more than you're getting? Or are you the one who's taking a lot from your partner but not reciprocating? A harmonizing angle between the "benefics" (positive planets) Venus and Jupiter helps you right any wrongs today, restoring equilibrium. If you're single, be on the lookout for someone who can build a balanced partnership. But that doesn't mean keeping score, Pisces. Under these stars, leading with generosity is best.

October 21: Venus-Pluto trine

Someone you know could look a little more appealing under today's skies. When Venus connects with powerful Pluto in the areas of your chart that rule people and groups, a friendship could catch fire! Pluto can be intense, so it could feel like a past life connection. Don't brush it aside, but also try to glimpse what's really going on beneath the surface. Another friend or colleague could give you the advice and insight you need. Just ask! If you're attached, link up with your S.O. for an upscale evening, one befitting your supercouple status. Bonus points if your night out includes donations to a charitable cause.

October 24: Venus-Saturn trine

Romantic Venus flirts with structured Saturn, making you double down on your relationship goals. Any partnership needs work, but you can infuse fun into it, too! Instigate a standing date night and take turns with planning. Single? If no one comes to mind, ask friends to introduce you to qualified candidates, or jump back onto dating apps. Set clear intentions so you know how to spot red flags and sidestep partners who aren't looking for the same thing.

October 27-November 21: Venus in Libra

Sensual Venus slides into your sexy eighth house for the next few weeks, amping up the seductive signals. Sex and romance could reach new heights under this erotic and sizzling transit. If you're not ready to date, focus on self-care and feeling great in your own skin. Conversations with loved ones might turn toward your shared future. Is it time to join your lives in a deeper and more significant way?

OCTOBER: CAREER HOTSPOTS

October 1: Aries full moon

Ka-ching! The only Aries full moon of the year lights up your work and finance sector. A money-making venture you started as far back as six months ago (at the corresponding new moon) could come to fruition. Polish up a pitch deck and dress to impress—a big moment could be coming. If you're suddenly flush with cash, make sure you're set up to manage your funds wisely. It's an illuminating day for a budget review or to ramp up a savings plan.

October 4: Pluto retrograde ends

Power-monger Pluto finally turns forward after a long backspin that started on April 25. While the shadowy planet was retrograde in your eleventh house of groups and technology, you might have experienced issues with a collaborative endeavor or a launch. You may have seen the ugly side of people's true motives, such as greed or a hidden agenda. Now that the powerful planet is direct, teamwork should progress more smoothly. Be aware of the "who's who" in any hierarchy you encounter. Even if you idealistically believe that everything should be equal, not all organizations are run that way. You don't want to step on any toes unwittingly.

October 7: Mercury-Uranus opposition

Think it through before you blurt it out. The opposition of expressive Mercury and disruptive Uranus could make you say something you wish you could take back. If someone's antagonistic streak is working your nerves, disengage. Mute your apps (and maybe your phone) until this transit passes.

October 9: Mars-Pluto square

They want you to do *what*? A colleague could pressure you to sign onto something that doesn't align with your values. As forceful Mars faces off with manipulative Pluto, opt out of any endeavor that makes you uneasy. If your colleagues are acting combative, steer clear.

October 13-November 3: Mercury retrograde in Scorpio

You're tempted to say everything that's on your mind, as the communication planet turns retrograde in your outspoken ninth house. Best to keep it to yourself, however, since you risk being misunderstood during this murky transit. Plans to travel, publish or make a big announcement could be delayed—or maybe should be, since information and messages can get wildly scrambled now.

October 15: Sun-Pluto square

Keep your cards close as sly Pluto clashes with the conscientious Sun. Giving it all away could cause a combustion. You don't need to lie or mislead anyone. Just be careful not to share intel that you don't want getting out in the world.

October 16: Libra new moon

A new moon starts off six months of synergy in your eighth house of assets and shared resources. Bring in partners who can help you on a prime project. Seek out passive income streams so you can earn while you learn (and sleep!). Or sign on for a new collaboration that benefits everyone involved.

October 18: Sun-Saturn square

Is it time to loosen the reins or share control of them? The leadership-driven Sun in your power-tripping eighth house conflicts with serious Saturn in your collaboration zone, making it hard to create consensus. Instead of polarizing, try to forge a middle ground—or at least, agree to disagree.

October 19: Mars-Jupiter square

Having a hard time with a higher-up, or feeling mutiny among your troops? Assert your boundaries and stand your ground, rather than shutting down or stonewalling anyone. Lead with optimism and refocus everyone on mutual goals. If you can keep a cool head, this can be an opportunity to refine your negotiation skills. And remember that a tantrum is never a great look on anyone.

 The AstroTwins' 2020 Horoscope

October 19: Mercury-Uranus opposition

Avoid saying anything that might be misconstrued today, as the messenger planet quarrels with unruly Uranus. If people are provoking you, close the door or pop on your headphones for some white noise.

October 31: Taurus full moon

The year's only full moon in your expressive third house paves the way for good news. Since this area of your chart rules neighbors and social activity, you might connect with a local group. With the earthy energy of Taurus, it pays to take the slow and steady route. Stay the course and don't listen to anyone who tries to pull you down another path.

November

NOVEMBER: LOVE HOTSPOTS

November 3: Mercury retrograde ends

If the last few weeks have been roiled by romantic confusion—jealousy, mixed messages and raw feelings—you can breathe freely now that communication planet Mercury moves forward in Libra and your intimate eighth house.

November 9: Venus-Mars opposition

The blame game could be in full swing today when Venus and Mars squabble. You might feel torn between manipulating the situation to suit your needs or making a quick exit. Wait it out. Today's tempestuous skies aren't offering a great recipe for resolving issues.

November 15: Venus-Pluto square

Whiplash alert: You might passionately love someone one moment and hate them fiercely the next. A loved one's disposition might be equally unpredictable, making you feel bewildered and lost. And if that wasn't enough drama, a friend could act jealous to boot. Chances are, they're oblivious to the pain they're causing. Excuse yourself from any triggering interactions today.

November 16: Venus-Jupiter square

What's the rush? Venus in your partnership zone has you longing for more one-on-one time, but a tenuous tie to Jupiter in your future-oriented house might tempt you to dive in too quickly. If it's meant to be, it'll unfold naturally. Take it slow! If you speed up the process, you could miss out on some key components. Such as: Do you even want the same things? It's okay to have varying views on the future. But ignoring that altogether doesn't give you an opportunity to hash it out.

November 19: Venus-Saturn square

Playing amateur psychic again? Detach from those fired-up feelings today when an emotional Venus confronts stoic Saturn. Friends and lovers won't be up for your prodding questions or unsolicited probes of their psyches. Don't press for details if someone doesn't want to talk. If you've been demanding a lot of energy from your inner circle, they might need a respite. Likewise, if anyone monopolizes your attention when you don't feel like giving it, excuse yourself from sounding-board duties!

November 21-December 15: Venus in Scorpio

Passionate Venus ventures through your ninth house of travel and adventure, expanding your approach to love. Get out of town and see who you meet! And when you're in city limits, don't limit yourself to your usual "type." Open minds can attract open hearts now. Coupled? Book a trip for two, whether you pop out of town for a night or an extended vacation. (Bonus points if you do it before the holiday mayhem hits!) When planning your next date, venture far out of your comfort zone.

November 27: Venus-Uranus opposition

If you've been holding back your feelings, today's stars could make biting your tongue a little trickier. With Venus squaring volatile Uranus, your fiery opinions might fly out before you can stop them. Control the situation by choosing your words carefully. The truth may set you free, but you don't want to torch any bridges in the process.

November 30: Gemini full moon (lunar eclipse)

The annual Gemini full moon in your fourth house of home and family sends loving beams to your abode. You could feel inspired to talk about what's next with your partner: Moving in together, booking a trip, starting a family? If you're ready to attract more love into your life, research Feng Shui principles to help. Does your home have space for a new person? Clear out those old clothes and make some space in the closet. The technique of adding paired objects (two candlesticks, a bed with room for an overnight guest) is always worth a try.

NOVEMBER: CAREER HOTSPOTS

November 1: Mercury-Saturn square

Do you have the information you need to make a decision? Your colleagues could be pushing you to choose, but you're feeling resistant. There's a reason for that! Take time to do your own research.

Even if other people are in a hurry, you'll feel better knowing you practiced due diligence.

November 3: Mercury retrograde ends

If money's been funny or you've been playing catchup from an expense, take heart. Mercury, the ruler of information and communication, ends a three-week retrograde backspin. Now, it will straighten out in Libra and your eighth house of wealth, helping you think clearly about long-term finances, property and joint ventures. Been delaying a contract signing? Finish your research then decide whether to ink your name or not. You'll likely know within the next week.

November 10-December 1: Mercury in Scorpio

The cosmic messenger barrels into your outspoken ninth house, giving you the gift of gab. You might connect with people from different backgrounds or cultures, or be inspired by a fresh philosophical outlook. Now that Mercury is out of retrograde, sign any contracts that you've been sitting on.

November 12: Jupiter-Pluto meetup

Say hello to your new squad! The third and final union of expansive Jupiter and transformational Pluto lands in your collaborative eleventh house, putting together a powerhouse team. Look back to April 4 and June 30 for clues of what could finally come together now.

November 13: Mars retrograde ends

Relief is here! Aggravator Mars has been retrograde in your money and work zone for two months, making things stressful or challenging. If you clashed with a colleague or felt the looming pressure of your living costs, you'll be able to find a solution. Have you been feeling threatened by a nemesis? You two might realize that all your competition would be better suited for a killer collaboration.

November 15: Scorpio new moon

The new moon lights up your adventurous and worldly ninth house, prompting dreams of far-flung locales. New moons can take six months to come to fruition, so start planning now. Since this area of your chart also rules higher education, look into learning a unique skill or launching a new endeavor.

November 17: Mercury-Uranus opposition

Breathe before you speak! When Mercury has a run-in with unruly Uranus, you could blurt out something regrettable. If anyone aggravates you, excuse yourself before you lose your cool. Monitor your online interactions today. Does your colleague's button-pushing email really deserve a response or will you just be wasting your time?

November 23: Mercury-Neptune trine

Your naturally sharp intuition gets a boost when insightful Neptune forms a fortuitous angle to quick-witted Mercury. You could read someone like a paperback novel in an instant. But pointing fingers won't win you any fans. Find a way to offer constructive criticism without blaming or shaming.

November 28: Neptune retrograde ends

All clear! Your co-ruler, nebulous Neptune, ends a five-month backspin in your sign, which provoked uncertainty around what you're doing or where you're headed. This transit may have caused you to second-guess your work, or even your identity. Now the illusory planet turns direct (forward), restoring confidence and clarity.

December

DECEMBER: LOVE HOTSPOTS

December 5: Venus-Neptune trine

Romance reigns when sensual Venus links up with dreamy Neptune in your sign. Indulge your fantasies and desires under this tantalizing transit. You might not want to attend to the practical details of your day, but get those off your plate so you can really relax.

December 15, 2020-January 9, 2021: Venus in Sagittarius

Your sign loves spontaneity, but the love planet is ready to make plans, ending the year in your structured tenth house. You could discuss the next big step or shared goals for the coming year. Single? Since this area of your chart rules career, you might meet someone at a work-related holiday party.

December 17, 2020-March 7, 2023: Saturn in Aquarius

Structured Saturn begins a long trek through your twelfth house of fantasy, closure and addictions. You'll be learning a lot about healthy boundaries in the next couple years, and how to discern between reality and illusion. If you're stuck in a codependent dynamic or struggling to create closure with an ex, Saturn will help you do the hard but necessary work to protect your heart. Just don't build a fortress around it in the process—your vulnerability is a gift.

December 19, 2020-May 13, 2021: Jupiter in Aquarius

On the heels of restrictive Saturn entering Aquarius, expansive Jupiter joins the party, making a once-every-12-years sojourn through your mystical twelfth house. Life is but a dream for the next few months, and you'll grow through surrendering rather than attempting to seize the upper hand. Luckily, Pisces is the natural ruler of the twelfth house, so you'll be right at home with supersizer Jupiter turning up the fantasy dial to max settings!

December 20, 2020-January 9, 2021: Mercury in Capricorn

Don your event planner's chapeau! Expressive Mercury moves into your eleventh house of groups for the rest of the year. Jump into the fray, whether you're taking up a new team sport or coordinating a night out with your tried-and-true crew. You might connect with someone online, so check those DMs! For couples, hosting a holiday party together could turn up the magic.

December 21: Jupiter-Saturn meetup

Expansive Jupiter and restrictive Saturn unite every 19 years or so, an event known as The Great Conjunction. Today they align in Aquarius and your twelfth house of transitions, giving you the courage to release something that no longer serves you. Make way for a new chapter by letting the struggle go.

December 29: Cancer full moon

Wear your heart on your sleeve! Today's Cancer full moon—the second one of the year—lights up your fifth house of romance, joy and pleasure. Emotions could be heightened and come rushing to the surface before you can stem the tide. With your fertile fifth house illuminated, a pregnancy is possible for Pisces of the childbearing set.

December 30: Venus-Neptune square

Feeling foggy? Misty Neptune and amorous Venus are at odds today, making it difficult to discern what's real. Emotions and false narratives could run rampant. Resist getting wrapped up in illusions, and be careful what you promise if you're not sure you can deliver.

DECEMBER: CAREER HOTSPOTS

December 1-20: Mercury in Sagittarius

When shrewd Mercury bolts into your tenth house of career and long-term goals, you might feel like skipping the holiday parties to work on your five-year plan. Ride this ambitious wave, but don't neglect your friends and family. Attend work-related holiday parties and you might meet an influential person who can help you with your grand ideas.

December 13: Mercury-Neptune square

Have you been trying to fit a round peg in a square hole? If you're frustrated with the lack of progress on a project, ask yourself if it's time to walk away. Remember it's never a total loss if you picked up lessons or skills you can bring to your next endeavor. Giving up could make space for something better.

December 14: Sagittarius new moon (total solar eclipse)

Start your New Year's resolutions early! The year's only new moon in Sagittarius—a scene-changing total solar eclipse—ignites your tenth house of

   The AstroTwins' 2020 Horoscope

ambition and long-term goals. What do you want to manifest in the coming year? Think way bigger than you normally would. With the eclipse boosting your status and public image, all your hard work could yield major recognition.

December 19, 2020-May 13, 2021: Jupiter in Aquarius

Hopefully you took advantage of the professional opportunities and good fortune that expansive and auspicious Jupiter brought over the past year as it toured Sagittarius and your tenth house of career and public image. Now, you can welcome an outgoing new chapter as the red-spotted renegade marches through Capricorn and your eleventh house of teamwork and technology. Are you looking to get more involved with professional groups or to level up your tech skills? Adventurous Jupiter might introduce you to an inspiring new crew or even send you back to school. With the gregarious gas giant bringing growth to your teamwork sector, you'll be a networking force to be reckoned with! Travel is also highlighted: Attend conferences, festivals or thought-leader summits in far-flung locales, then have fun exploring the nearby sights.

December 20, 2020–January 9, 2021: Mercury in Capricorn

Mix and mingle! The cosmic messenger lights up your social eleventh house until the end of the year. Holiday hangouts can yield great networking, so be prepared to schmooze 'em up while you're sipping eggnog. Got a business? This is the perfect time for a last-minute flash sale. Bonus points if you donate a portion of the proceeds to charity.

December 23: Mars-Pluto square

Press pause and take in your surroundings for a minute. Are you headed in the direction you aimed for? Or are you compromising your values at someone else's behest? At the third of this year's tense Mars-Pluto clashes, check in to make sure your principles align with your paycheck. If someone on your team tries to drag you into a dispute, play Switzerland and stay neutral.

December 25: Mercury-Uranus trine

Ugly Christmas sweaters and piped-in carols? No thanks! You're thirsting for novelty as curious Mercury and innovative Uranus unite in your social houses. Your bubbly wit and unique opinions can keep things merry—or they could skirt an incendiary line. The playful but contrarian energy of these two planets tempts you to bring up charged topics. Proceed with caution, Pisces. Worried that you can't dodge the political talk? Invite friends to mix up the guest list—and increase the odds of people being on their best behavior.

December 29: Cancer full moon

Get thee to the mistletoe! The year ends with 2020's rare second Cancer full moon (the first was a lunar eclipse on January 10) blazing up your fifth house of passion and self-expression. No need to wait until New Year's Eve proper to pop the champers and party like it's 2021. Light up the celebrations tonight! ✳

2020 NUMEROLOGY

THE 4

UNIVERSAL YEAR

by Felicia Bender
THE PRACTICAL NUMEROLOGIST

2020 UNIVERSAL YEAR

Set long-range goals and take concrete action.

Whether or not you make New Year's resolutions, most of us intuitively feel a profound energy shift whenever the calendar turns. In numerology, that transition is a big deal, marking the passage into a new Universal Year—the shared atmosphere of the world for a 12-month period.

In numerology, each calendar year adds up to a single-digit number, which resonates at a unique vibration. We all feel this energy, and it's called the Universal Year.

A Universal Year means that everyone on the planet will experience the frequency of a particular number during the entire year, from January 1 until December 31.

You can think of the Universal Year as the state or country you're driving through on your yearly "road trip." The Universal Year number will set the GPS and chart our collective course.

What is "4" Energy?

In Numerology, the number 4 is the energy of long-term goal setting. It demands that we get real and formulate a plan that's practical and grounded. The 4 supports us when we put effective and updated systems into the works. Whenever a 4 shows up, hard work and hustle are required.

To support your efforts, put your ideas into concrete form. If you want to really harness this 4 Year, write a 2020 mission statement with clearly defined action items, milestones and due dates. You could support it with a vision board or a collage that you place in clear view to be a reminder. Or, color-code that 2020 spreadsheet and check in with it weekly.

How to Calculate the Universal Year:

Add the individual numbers of the current year together, like this:

$$2020 = 2 + 0 + 2 + 0 = 4$$

2020 is a 4 Universal Year

All of us will begin to feel this energy starting January 1, 2020 and the effect will end on December 31, 2020.

After 2019's creative and emotional 3 Universal Year, 2020 ushers in a new phase with a more practical focus. Develop one or two blue-sky projects into tangible form. Work on communicating effectively with clear and simple directives. The 4 has a "managerial" or formal air to it.

2020 is a year of building. It's all about making the plan, gathering new data and creating the foundation that will eventually make everything run like clockwork. This will show up in every area of life: health, finances, relationships and spirituality.

Life might feel a bit weighty as the world moves into the 4 Universal Year. We're asked to take ourselves and our enterprises seriously, and to lead with integrity. It's timely that the 2020 U.S. Presidential election coincides with the 4 Universal Year, when the importance of thorough data collection and the formulation of a long-range plan will be crucial. Which direction will we choose? What foundation are we pouring and what are we building in the collective realm?

Determination, focus and tenacity will take the front seat. It's time to get down to business!

How to Step into The Power of the 4 Universal Year

Slow down to succeed.

The energy of the 4 demands deliberate and steady action. Remember the story of the tortoise and the hare? Channel your inner tortoise and you can ride the optimal wave of the 4 Universal Year. Rushing or skipping from Point A to Point G won't work. Cutting corners will bring you nothing but grief.

Resist the temptation to take the easy route because you'll only be sent back to the starting line for a do-over.

Expect limitations and delays.

The number 4 can draw experiences that make us feel chained to limiting conditions or circumstances. In a 4 Universal Year, that can show up as a project that starts out full steam and then disintegrates mid-year, making you wonder why you put so much effort into it. Perhaps it comes into play as roadblocks in the form of consistent technical problems. Or maybe it reveals itself as people saying they'll do something and then they don't, leaving you to pinch-hit or micromanage. The great thing about knowing this is that you can be proactive. Plan to exert more effort, be patient—or both! That way, anything that goes smoothly will elicit a happy dance.

Work through family issues.

The energy of the 4 always highlights issues related to our family of origin. Even the happiest clans will have karmic issues to work through. During a 4 Universal Year, these issues bubble to the surface, whether we want them to or not. On a collective level, issues related to race, gender, equality, the economy and the environment (among other things!) emerge to be evaluated worldwide. With the tenacity of the 4, we might just make headway healing some of the divisiveness and disparity in the world.

Implement healthy habits.

The 4 is the number of health, and in a Universal Year, it supports good wellness practices. The 4 also carries a tendency for burnout and overwork. The key here is to schedule breaks with a focus on true relaxation. You might adopt the Dutch philosophy of "niksen" which literally means "do nothing"—and give yourself a few minutes each day to let your thoughts wander freely. It's believed to reduce the stress, anxiety and burnout that's taking a toll on so many people these days!

Live and let live.

Under the hard-driving 4, prepare to confront some entrenched and rigid opinions—possibly within yourself! Our already polarized world can become further divided in the dogmatic and values-driven 4 Universal Year. If you can't be flexible about your belief system (and sometimes you can't), make room to respect other people's differing ethics and lifestyles.

Don't be small-minded.

Because the 4 seeks security, people could hold tight to what we think we already know without being open to exploring other points of view. It's as though we're all being asked to give up the horse-and-buggy for the automobile, or adjust to cell phones when we've grown up using rotary phones...or to believe that the world is round when we've been told our whole lives it's flat. Change is inevitable, but the 4 Universal Year could find us clinging to the tried-and-true, even if it's outmoded, counterproductive or destructive.

The Big Picture

Focus on the practicalities and set realistic goals into motion. It won't feel breezy because there's a lot at stake right now. But 2020 offers an energetic platform to anyone who's ready to plan a successful and productive new path.

To stay positive, remember that anything worth doing is worth doing right. Commit to the long haul and hunker down. Quell any frustration or exhaustion by pacing yourself and scheduling breaks. Your mission might feel like a thankless job at moments. But if you do the grunt work that creates a firm foundation, miraculous results could unfold. They don't call it "paying dues" for nothing. Invest wisely and you could see returns by the end of the year.

FELICIA BENDER THE PRACTICAL NUMEROLOGIST

Felicia Bender, Ph.D.—The Practical Numerologist—is the author of *Redesign Your Life: Using Numerology to Create the Wildly Optimal You* and *Master Numbers 11, 22, 33: The Ultimate Guide.* She earned a doctorate in theater from the University of Missouri–Columbia. Felicia is passionate about writing, counseling, teaching, and presenting ways to use numerology, spirituality and intuition to understand ourselves and others on a deep level—to validate our life purpose and to develop tools to understand how to trust our own intuitive language. She is a contributor to elephantjournal.com, numerologist.com, and other media. Felicia's the resident numerologist for AstroStyle.com and you can find her at FeliciaBender.com.

2020 CHINESE HOROSCOPE

THE YEAR OF THE
METAL RAT

2020 YEAR OF THE METAL RAT

The resourceful Metal Rat will govern the Chinese Lunar Year from January 25, 2020, until February 11, 2021

Welcome to the rat race! 2020 is the Year of the Metal Rat, a fast-paced cycle meant for living large and doing everything with the flair of an Instagram superstar. The resourceful rodent is the first sign in the Chinese zodiac, setting a fresh 12-year cycle in motion. Expect to feel a renewed sense of excitement and possibility as soon as the New Year begins on January 25!

A Metal Rat year is meant for dreaming *and* doing. Since metal is a conductor of electricity, you'll have lots of energy at your behest to get creative plans in motion. Starting is the hardest part. Once you initiate action, you'll be a #CantStopWontStop force of nature, much like a high-voltage current pulsing through a wire.

Achievement is a huge focus during the Year of the Metal Rat, and you may find yourself juggling more activities than you realized you were humanly capable of handling. In parts of India, the rat is associated with Ganesh, the "remover of obstacles." Rats are industrious creatures who can find their way through any maze and they never forget a navigation route once they've learned it. If you need to bone up your skill set, you'll be a sharp and fast learner in 2020.

The stabilizing metal influence brings some rigidity to a Rat year, keeping you focused on your goals without wavering. Just be careful not to slip into workaholic patterns as you tirelessly obsess over whatever you're building. Watch for inflexibility, too. Sometimes, it's actually smart to take a few steps back on the game board to assess your progress before engaging in further production.

The Year of the Metal Rat can certainly attract financial abundance; just try not to burn as fast as you earn! Curatorial Rat years give us a passion for objects of "practical luxury." In 2020, we'll want everything fluffed and styled, and our tastes will run towards the *haute* end of the spectrum. If something is both useful and beautiful, it will be hard to resist!

The plot twist? Rat years can make us prone to worrying. In 2020, you may struggle to feel financially secure…even if your bank balance tells a different story. If you're going to splurge, shop around and find the best possible price. Getting a "steal" will help curb some of that unfounded buyer's remorse. Or lean in to the Rat's resourcefulness, turning trash (salvaged, vintage or gently-used pieces) into treasure with creative upcycling.

Communal rats are excellent at sharing. When it makes sense, you could pool funds for a joint purchase and co-own a decadent object with a few friends. A service like Rent the Runway, which offers subscription-based rental of designer clothing (like a high-fashion library!) was made for stylish-but-sensible Rat years.

> **"The Rat can attract financial abundance. Just try not to burn as fast as you earn!"**

Rats are associated with the Western sign of Sagittarius, which is known for its honesty and wisdom. In 2020, everyone will have advice to share, like a self-appointed Oprah on demand. The metal element blesses us with superpowers that can expedite transformation. Organize your personal "rat pack" of gurus and advisors—and find the people who need your precious pro tips. There's strength (and magic!) in numbers this year.

But…do we smell a rat? There's a tendency to present a "false positive" during this Chinese zodiac cycle instead of sharing your legit sensitivities. We all wear a social mask, but Rat years can make folks especially explosive if they hold too much in. Assemble your support squad and sounding boards

so you can vent before your emotions torch the village. Damage control helps, but there are likely to be a few blowups nonetheless. Surround yourself with people who won't ditch you for having a meltdown…even if you have some embarrassing clean-up work to do. Reading Brené Brown's work on "shame and vulnerability" can help you cope.

What goes around comes around during the Year of the Metal Rat. In the animal kingdom, rats take care of the sick and injured in their posse. Without companionship, they become lonely and depressed, another good reason to avoid isolation in 2020. Be careful not to fall prey to peer pressure though. Rats are major conformists, copying the behaviors of the rest of their "mischief" (the legit name for a rat pack…it's true!). Studies have shown that certain breeds will even eat unpalatable food if the rest of the mischief is indulging. (So, uh, maybe you *should* take a break from that friend who washes down her fast food dinners with a fifth of vodka every night?)

In love, Rat years can be sensual and romantic, although the metal element may cool off *some* of this creature's spontaneity. Be proactive about igniting that first spark, knowing that once you're in the mood, things could go from lukewarm to exothermic pretty quickly. Sharing decadent meals, enjoying high-end vacations, and stepping out in style as a couple will be pure bliss.

Jealousy may become an issue however, as Rat years make us prone to possessiveness. Don't go chewing holes in relationships because you're feeling insecure or threatened. Love is blind, but anger can be even more obfuscating. If you start to lose perspective, reach out to people who can talk you out of that sticky trap. By the same token, you will need greater amounts of reassurance in order to feel secure about love this year. Any partner who's unwilling to provide that should earn a red flag. Fortunately, the metal influence will stabilize many of our connections in 2020.

In wellness, metal is associated with the lungs and large intestines, along with the skin and nose. Those may be focus areas in 2020 when it comes to preventative medicine. Are you breathing clean air and drinking enough water? The large intestine and the skin are both elimination organs. This is a year for flushing toxins by staying hydrated, supplementing with electrolytes and breaking a sweat whenever possible. You could be sensitive to skincare and cleaning products, as the skin's pores are "conductors" themselves. Switch to chemical-free versions or wear non-porous gloves when scrubbing down.

The emotions associated with metal are grief and courage. In the Year of the Metal Rat, find the strength to let your feelings flow. It's a noble challenge! It will take bravery to harness the creative energy of 2020. But it's also a year for enjoying the best. As Remy, the epicurean rodent star of Pixar's *Ratatouille* put it, "If you are what you eat, then I only want to eat the good stuff!" ✳

What's Your Chinese Zodiac Sign?

Rat: 1924, 1936, 1948, 1960, 1972, 1984, 1996, 2008

Ox: 1925, 1937, 1949, 1961, 1973, 1985, 1997, 2009

Tiger: 1926, 1938, 1950, 1962, 1974, 1986, 1998, 2010

Rabbit: 1927, 1939, 1951, 1963, 1975, 1987, 1999, 2011

Dragon: 1928, 1940, 1952, 1964, 1976, 1988, 2000, 2012

Snake: 1929, 1941, 1953, 1965, 1977, 1989, 2001, 2013

Horse: 1930, 1942, 1954, 1966, 1978, 1990, 2002, 2014

Sheep: 1931, 1943, 1955, 1967, 1979, 1991, 2003, 2015

Monkey: 1932, 1944, 1956, 1968, 1980, 1992, 2004, 2016

Rooster: 1933, 1945, 1957, 1969, 1981, 1993, 2005, 2017

Dog: 1934, 1946, 1958, 1970, 1982, 1994, 2006, 2019

Pig: 1935, 1947, 1959, 1971, 1983, 1995, 2007, 2019

OPHIRA & TALI EDUT
THE ASTROTWINS

Dubbed the "astrologers to the stars," identical twin sisters Ophira and Tali Edut, known as the AstroTwins, are professional astrologers who reach millions worldwide through their spot-on predictions. Through their website, Astrostyle.com, Ophira and Tali help "bring the stars down to earth" with their unique, lifestyle-based approach to astrology.

They are the official astrologers for *ELLE* Magazine, Monster.com, Parade.com and MindBodyGreen.com. The AstroTwins have been featured by major media such as the *Good Morning America*, the *New York Times* and *People* and they've collaborated with major brands including Coach, Vogue, Nordstrom, Revlon, H&M, Urban Outfitters, Ted Baker and 1Hotels.

The sisters have read charts for celebrities including Beyoncé, Stevie Wonder, Emma Roberts, Karlie Kloss, Elizabeth Gilbert and Sting. They have appeared on Bravo's *The Real Housewives of New Jersey*, doing on-air readings for the cast. They have authored numerous print books, including *Love Zodiac, Shoestrology* and *Momstrology* (their #1 Amazon best-selling astrological parenting guide) and a series of self-published books, including their popular annual horoscope guides. ✳

VISIT THE ASTROTWINS AT WWW.ASTROSTYLE.COM
Follow us on social media @astrotwins